HUMAN RESOURCES MANAGEMENT

HUMAN RESOURCES MANAGEMENT

Managing Employees for Competitive Advantage

DAVID LEPAK

Rutgers University

MARY GOWAN

*Martha and Spencer Love School of
Business at Elon University*

Prentice Hall
is an imprint of

Upper Saddle River, NJ 07458

Library of Congress Cataloging-in-Publication Data

Lepak, David.
  Human resource management: managing employees for competitive advantage /
  David Lepak, Mary Gowan.
    p. cm.
  Includes bibliographical references and index.
  ISBN 978-0-13-152532-0 (alk. paper)
  1. Personnel management.   2. Supervision of employees.   I. Gowan, Mary.   II. Title.
  HF5549.L4624 2010
  658.3—dc22   2008028856

Acquisitions Editor: Jennifer M. Collins
Editorial Director: Sally Yagan
Development Editor: Stephen Deitmer
Product Development Manager: Ashley Santora
Editorial Assistant: Elizabeth Davis
Editorial Project Manager: Claudia Fernandes
Marketing Manager: Nikki Jones
Marketing Assistant: Ian Gold
Permissions Project Manager: Charles Morris
Senior Managing Editor: Judy Leale
Production Project Manager: Karalyn Holland
Senior Operations Specialist: Arnold Vila
Operations Specialist: Carol O'Rourke
Art Director: Suzanne Behnke

Interior Designer: John Christiana
Cover Designer: John Christiana
Cover Illustration/Photo: Altrendo Images/Getty Images, Inc.
Director, Image Resource Center: Melinda Patelli
Manager, Rights and Permissions: Zina Arabia
Manager, Visual Research: Beth Brenzel
Image Permission Coordinator: Angelique Sharps
Manager, Cover Visual Research & Permissions: Karen Sanatar
Photo Researcher: Kathy Ringrose
Full-Service Project Management/Typesetting: GGS Higher Education
  Resources, A Division of Premedia Global, Inc.
Printer/Binder: Courier/Kendallville
Typeface: Janson 10/12

Credits and acknowledgments borrowed from other sources and reproduced, with permission, in this textbook appear on page 471.

Microsoft® and Windows® are registered trademarks of the Microsoft Corporation in the U.S.A. and other countries. Screen shots and icons reprinted with permission from the Microsoft Corporation. This book is not sponsored or endorsed by or affiliated with the Microsoft Corporation.

Pearson Education Ltd., London
Pearson Education Singapore, Pte. Ltd
Pearson Education, Canada, Inc.
Pearson Education–Japan
Pearson Education Australia PTY, Limited

Pearson Education North Asia, Ltd., Hong Kong
Pearson Educación de Mexico, S.A. de C.V.
Pearson Education Malaysia, Pte. Ltd
Pearson Education Upper Saddle River, New Jersey

Prentice Hall
is an imprint of

Upper Saddle River, NJ 07458

10 9 8 7 6 5 4 3 2 1
ISBN-13: 978-0-13-152532-0
ISBN-10: 0-13-152532-8

To Ellen, Reilly, Addison, and Henry—D.P.L.

To Ed and Abbie—M.G.

Brief Contents

Contents

PART II Work Design and Workforce Planning *83*

chapter 4 JOB DESIGN AND JOB ANALYSIS *84*

PART III Managing Employee Competencies *147*

chapter 6 RECRUITMENT *148*

PART IV Managing Employee Attitudes and Behaviors 257

chapter 9 PERFORMANCE MANAGEMENT 258

chapter 11 INCENTIVES AND REWARDS *324*

chapter 12   EMPLOYEE BENEFITS AND SAFETY PROGRAMS   *350*

PART V Special Topics   *389*

13 chapter LABOR UNIONS AND EMPLOYEE MANAGEMENT   *390*

CREATING HIGH-PERFORMING HR SYSTEMS   *412*

Preface

FOCUS OF THE BOOK

Let's face it, where and how we work have changed. Globalization and technology have created unparalleled opportunities for workers to add to company value—and to do so literally 24/7. With these changes comes the need to understand employee management in a different way. Along with knowledge of finance, operations, marketing, and information systems, managers need to understand how to staff their areas of responsibility with the most qualified employees, and how to manage the performance of those employees using training and development, performance appraisal, and compensation techniques that fit with the goals of the organization and the larger environment within which the company operates. Supervisors today may find themselves responsible for employees in a U.S. location *and* in a location in India or Ireland; therefore, understanding the unique challenges of different work environments makes a lot of sense.

Major Themes of This Book We recognize that a number of human resources management (HRM) textbooks already exist. Consequently, we thought long and hard before undertaking the writing of yet another one. To offer a clear advantage, we knew we had to approach HRM with a fresh perspective because of the changes in how work is done in organizations. We therefore set out to craft a book that helps students understand the dynamic and exciting environment of HRM and the complex decisions that all managers must make when managing employees. We specifically focus on helping students learn about managing employees rather than managing the HR function, managing employees in context, and understanding the integration of these activities with each other and within the context of organizational demands and environmental influence to achieve a competitive advantage. Other HRM textbooks have addressed the managerial perspective, but we do so in a much more direct and different way, using three focal points:

- **Focal Point 1: Managing employees rather than managing the HR function.** Students often have difficulty separating the concept of employees as human resources from a discussion of the HR department. By incorporating a unique framework, this book places equal emphasis on the principles of employee management practices and on the application of those practices in different organizational and environmental contexts within which general managers must make daily decisions about employees that, in turn, affect firm performance. The goal is to have students understand both the theory underlying employee management practices and the reality that managing employees in different scenarios presents different challenges and requires different responses. By adopting a managerial perspective rather than an HR perspective, the book is not limited to students who want to work as HR professionals, even though its content is entirely appropriate for those students. The managerial perspective, rather than the traditional HR perspective, is likely to resonate with business majors concentrating in all areas of business.

- **Focal Point 2: Managing employees in context.** A second point of differentiation for this book is that it places the management of employees directly in the broader context of organizations and external environments. In addition to covering the fundamental principles of employee management, this book devotes substantial coverage to the role of employee management in meeting organizational pressures associated with business strategy, company characteristics, organizational culture, and employee concerns, as well as external pressures associated with globalization, technology, labor force trends, ethics, regulatory issues, and the like. The importance of context is highlighted in the overarching framework for the book and incorporated into every chapter. Each chapter discusses contextual pressures on the use of different tools for managing employees and focuses on how contextual pressures influence the effectiveness of these practices. Most current textbooks present this information only in the early chapters.

- **Focal Point 3: Integrative framework.** A third point of differentiation is this book's overarching framework, which ties together all the book material. Students learn better when they have a clear framework for understanding how different practices are used independently and interdependently to manage employees, as well as to address different internal and external environmental contingencies. This book's framework highlights the importance of three primary activities for managing employees: work design and workforce planning, management of employee competencies, and management of employee attitudes and behaviors. Moreover, the book draws on the previous two focus points and directly places priority on understanding these three critical employee management roles in the context of organizational demands and the external environment. We approach these themes from the perspective of attaining organizational objectives and striving to attain and maintain a competitive advantage. Also, to tie together the different aspects of employee management and to emphasize the types of decisions managers must make, we present a matrix outlining the topics covered for each employee management role relative to organizational demands and environmental influencers.

Our Approach This book will help current and future managers understand what practices and tools are available for managing employees, how to use them, and when to use them for different situations. Knowing that a picture is worth a thousand words, we began our work on this book by developing the integrative framework for the strategic management of employees. This framework, which is woven throughout the chapters, shows the relationships among organizational demands, environmental influences, regulatory issues, and three primary HR activities (work design and workforce planning, management of employee competencies, and management of employee attitudes and behaviors). These HR activities, when managed in concert and within the context of the HR challenges, lead to the desired employee contributions and create a competitive advantage for the organization.

THREE PRIMARY HR ACTIVITIES. In essence, the strategic management of employees requires managers to attend to three primary HR activities. First, managers must design and manage the flow of work and the design of specific jobs employees perform to ensure that employees are in a position to add value to the company. Second, managers must identify, acquire, build, and retain the critical competencies employees need to effectively perform their jobs. Third, managers must guide and motivate employees to use their abilities to contribute to company goals. By describing the activities in this manner, we help students understand the interrelationships that exist among them.

All managers need a solid understanding of the practices available for managing employees. Managers can use a wide array of practices for job design, workforce planning, recruitment, selection, training and development, performance evaluation and appraisal, compensation, and incentives and rewards. To effectively manage employees, a manager has to know how and why the various practices work as well as when to use them.

HR CHALLENGES: THE IMPORTANCE OF CONTEXT. Employee management activities do not happen in a vacuum. Rather, managers must keep in mind the context of the organization in terms of the company's strategy, characteristics, and culture. In addition, managers must consider the concerns of their workforce. Beyond organizational demands, the strategic management of HR requires managers to anticipate and take steps to meet the environmental influences associated with labor force trends, advances in technology, ethics, and globalization, as well as to ensure that companies comply with legal requirements. Having a good understanding of the options for recruiting new employees is not very useful if managers do not also have a good understanding of when the different options are likely to be effective. Knowing when to use the different practices requires that you know the context of managing employees.

Chapter Design Each chapter focuses on one or more HR activities and builds on the idea that context matters. Thus, each chapter has two parts. The first part describes the principles of the HR activity. The goal is to help students acquire the tools appropriate for each activity. For example, when we discuss performance management, we discuss aspects of measuring employee performance, tradeoffs with different performance evaluation approaches, and considerations of the process for evaluating employee performance.

We believe that our approach is what really sets our book apart. To emphasize the importance of context, in the second part of each chapter we detail how the context—the organizational demands and environmental factors—affect the choices made in applying the technical knowledge. In the second part of each chapter, we emphasize how the HR challenges—the various organizational demands and numerous environmental influences—affect decisions about which performance management approach to use and how to use it. In essence, we first explore the fundamental principles for each HR activity and then take a step back to look at how these practices can be used to meet different contextual challenges. We have found that our approach helps students put together the pieces better than simply discussing context at the beginning of the semester and then focusing on each of the major functional activities, with only minor discussion of context. In many ways, we use a decision-making approach, a "What if A? What if B?" approach. We include examples and company spotlights to highlight this information and include discussion questions, exercises, and short cases that give students a chance to apply chapter concepts.

This book also provides an edge for students interested in a career in HRM. These students will leave the course well grounded in the bigger organizational picture and be better able to make decisions about the HR tools to apply in different contexts. They will better understand the possible consequences of designing and implementing practices that support or conflict with organizational goals.

Our Audience Our approach has worked well with our students, especially those who are taking an introductory HRM course because it is required for their business degree. Often these students are focused on careers in marketing, accounting, finance, or information systems and would rather be taking courses in those areas. They do not plan to work in HR and quickly are turned off by an HR textbook because of its emphasis early on in describing HR careers and focusing on what HR departments do. Many of the current texts do acknowledge the general manager's role in HR management. Those textbooks, however, still focus more on the functional or technical aspects of HR management activities, with little to no integration within the chapters of organizational demands and the environment.

Also, we have found that even our HR majors welcome a focus on the contingencies that have to be addressed in HR activities. They know that a broader organizational perspective—understanding some of the critical decision factors—will give them an edge in their future careers. This approach is supported by professional organizations, such as the Society for Human Resource Management, that recognize the need for HR leaders to take a more strategic approach to their areas of responsibility.

Prerequisites No specific courses need to be taken before a course that utilizes this text at the graduate or undergraduate level. Many students may have little or no knowledge of the subject matter before taking a course with this text. The text provides full coverage of the major principles associated with HR.

HOW TO USE THIS BOOK: TIPS FOR SUCCESS

This text and its supplements provide an array of methods for learning about HRM. The structure of the chapters is student oriented. By providing the key principles of HRM as well as having a strong focus on the practice of HRM—HRM in use by managers—the chapters are designed to really help students bridge the gap between theory and practice. In addition, each chapter contains several tools—key terms, discussion questions, learning exercise, and case studies—that are intended to help students learn and master the material.

Key Terms Because the field of HRM includes many terms and concepts that are new to many students, key terms are listed at the end of each chapter, and the most important and unique terms are defined in the margins in the chapters. Students are advised to read the chapters before they are discussed in class and then review the key terms and concepts after the class to ensure understanding.

Review Questions The review questions are designed to review the major points and themes in each chapter. Completing the review questions requires students to reflect on the material in the chapters and demonstrate a clear understanding of the major theories, issues, and challenges associated with HRM.

Learning Exercises and Case Studies In addition to the key terms and review questions, each chapter contains several learning exercises and case studies. The learning exercises are designed to encourage students to think about how the principles of HRM might inform the use of HR practices in different situations. The case studies provide specific situations and ask the students to reflect on HRM-related problems and devise solutions to those problems. Answering the learning exercises and cases studies helps students develop a greater comprehension of the pros and cons of different practices. This allows students to go beyond simply understanding a practice to developing mastery of how and when to use the different practices in various situations.

Company Spotlights Each chapter contains several company spotlights that demonstrate the importance of the topics in the chapter, provide examples of how real companies deal with those issues, and bridge the gap between principles of HRM and the application of HR practices.

Prospera We have partnered with Prospera®, The Online People Management Tool from J. J. Keller & Associates, Inc., to provide you with interactive exercises to integrate theory and practice. As you use Prospera, you will find many additional resources on the Web site beyond what we reference. These include videos, discussion groups, and Webcasts about topics you are studying in class. You will also notice that the Web site is divided into categories that correspond closely to the primary HR activities we focus on in this book: PLAN (Workforce Design and Workforce Planning), STAFF (Managing Competencies), COMPENSATE (Managing Attitudes and Behaviors), DEVELOP (Managing Competencies), and REVIEW (managing attitudes and behaviors).

STUDENT SUPPLEMENTS

An online companion Web site is available for students who want to get additional practice with the concepts in the text. To access the Web site, visit www.pearsonhighered. com/lepak.

ACKNOWLEDGEMENTS

We have had the privilege to work with many outstanding individuals in the planning, writing, and revising of this textbook. Their contributions have been invaluable to the successful completion of this project. Specifically, we would like to thank and appreciate the following:

Kathleen Barnes, East Stroudsburg University
Jerry Bennett, Western Kentucky University
Robin Berenson, Spartanburg Community College
Chris Berger, Purdue University
Henry Bohleke, Owens Community College
Jill Bradly, California State University, Fresno
Mark Butler, San Diego State University
Macgorine Cassell, Fairmont State University
David Chown, Reinhardt College
Richard Churchman, Belmont University
Mary Connerly, Virginia Tech
David Dolfinger, Regis University
Teri Domagalski, Florida Institute of Technology

Denis Dovach, Allegheny Community College
Cathy DuBois, Kent State University
Jason Fertig, Temple University
Janice Gates, Western Illinois University
Andrea Griffin, Marquette University
John Hausknecht, Cornell University
Brad Hays, North Central State College
John Hendon, University of Arkansas
Kim Hester, Arkansas State University
William Hodson, Indiana University
Linda Isenhour, Eastern Michigan University
Avis Johnson, University of Akron
Gundars Kaupins, Boise State University
Manuel London, State University of New York, Stony Brook
Andrea Lopez, Philadelphia University
Dan Lybrook, Purdue University
Liz Malatestinic, Indiana University at Indianapolis
Stephen Margulis, Grand Valley State University
Douglas McCabe, Georgetown University
Neal P. Mero, University of Central Florida
Jitendra Mishra, Grand Valley State University
Jon Monat, California State University, Long Beach
Richard Posthuma, University of Texas El Paso
Sabrina Saladino, Texas A&M University
Susan Schanne, Eastern Michigan University
Michael Sciarini, Michigan State University
Ted Shore, California State University Long Beach
Howard Stanger, Canisius College
Ryan Stroud, Southern Connecticut State University
Tom Timmerman, Tennessee Tech University
Charles Toftoy, George Washington University
Catherine Tyler, Oakland University
Edward Ward, St. Cloud State University
Naomi Werner, University of Houston
Steve Werner, University of Houston
Laura Wolfe, Louisiana State University
Melody Wollan, Eastern Illinois University

In addition, we would like to thank several individuals from Prentice Hall for their ongoing partnership, dedication, encouragement, and support: Development Editor Amy Ray, Director of Development Steve Deitmer, Editorial Assistant Liz Davis, Acquisitions Editor Jennifer Collins, Editorial Director Sally Yagan, Senior Managing Editor Judy Leale, Project Manager Karalyn Holland, and Designer Suzanne Behnke.

Finally, we would not have been able to start, much less complete, this book without the tremendous support from our friends and families.

DAVID LEPAK

MARY GOWAN

About the Authors

David Lepak is professor of Human Resource Management and chairperson of the Human Resource Management department in the School of Management and Labor Relations at Rutgers University. He received his Ph.D. in management from Pennsylvania State University. He teaches and conducts research on a variety of HR topics, with an emphasis on strategic HR management, and has presented his research to domestic and international audiences. He is associate editor of *Academy of Management Review* and has served on the editorial boards of *Academy of Management Journal*, *Journal of Management*, *Human Resource Management*, *British Journal of Management*, and *Journal of Management Studies*. He is a member of the executive committee for the HR division of the Academy of Management.

Mary Gowan is professor of Management and dean of the Martha and Spencer Love School of Business at Elon University. She received her Ph.D. in business administration from the University of Georgia. In addition to her administrative responsibilities as a dean, she teaches and conducts research in HR management, with a focus on career management and international HR. She has published her research in academic and practitioner journals and is on the editorial review boards of the *Journal of Management* and *Human Resource Management*. She is also a member of the SHRM Foundation Board, the Alamance Country Chamber of Commerce, and the Piedmont Triad Leadership Initiative. Her consulting experience is with major corporations such as Lockheed Martin and Harris Teeter Corporation as well as with government and not-for-profit agencies.

HUMAN RESOURCES MANAGEMENT

1

MANAGING EMPLOYEES FOR COMPETITIVE ADVANTAGE

1. Discuss the potential costs and benefits associated with managing employees. *(5)*

2. Explain what it means to manage employees strategically. *(7)*

3. Identify and explain the three primary HR activities. *(8)*

4. Discuss the management practices associated with each primary HR activity. *(8)*

5. Explain the importance of HR activities alignment. *(13)*

6. Discuss how organizational demands influence the management of employees. *(14)*

7. Describe how the external environment influences the management of employees. *(16)*

8. Understand the importance of regulatory issues in establishing HR practices. *(19)*

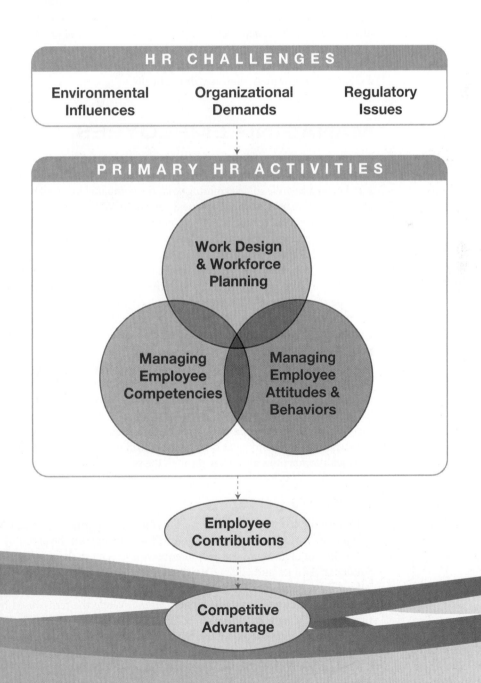

Each year *Fortune* magazine publishes its list "America's Most Admired Companies." *Fortune* invites executives, directors, and managers to rate other companies in their industry and then to choose the 10 they most admire across all industries. Panelists use eight equally weighted criteria in their rankings:

- Quality of management
- Quality of products and services
- Innovation
- Long-term investment value
- Financial soundness
- People management
- Social responsibility
- Use of corporate assets[1]

These eight criteria reflect various aspects of company operations that ultimately relate to company success. Including people management—defined as a company's ability to attract, develop, and keep talented employees—in this list of criteria acknowledges the role that employees play in the success of an organization. When a company has the right employees in place and properly develops and motivates them, the likelihood of sustaining a competitive advantage increases dramatically.

MANAGING EMPLOYEES

This book is about managing employees, the people who make organizations successful. The talent that employees bring with them when they start work or acquire after getting hired plays a key role in determining what the company does and how well it does it. Think about the company Human Genome Sciences. Its Web site indicates that the company is a "biopharmaceutical company with a pipeline of novel compounds in clinical development, including drugs to treat such diseases as hepatitis C, lupus, anthrax disease, cancer, rheumatoid arthritis and HIV/AIDS. Additional products are in clinical development by companies with which we are collaborating. Our mission is to apply great science and great medicine to bring innovative drugs to patients with unmet medical needs."[2] Now, consider the type of employees this company must have to even begin to achieve its goals. Without the right employees, the company simply could not be successful. In addition to having the right talent, the company must make sure that it motivates its employees to work as hard as possible to contribute to the company's success.

Our goal for this book is to provide you with an understanding of how to attract, develop, motivate, and retain employees and to equip you with the knowledge and skills that managers need to perform these activities. We also consider how organizations can leverage the talents of their employees in facing the challenges and opportunities the external environment presents. We focus on both what organizations need to do now to achieve their goals through employees and what organizations will need to do in the future to maintain and enhance a competitive advantage through the practices they use to manage their employees.

What's in a Name?

Before we discuss how to maximize the potential of your employees, we want to take a moment to clarify a few terms that you will see throughout the text.

Different organizations use different terms to refer to the members of their workforce. Southwest Airlines and CIGNA use the term *people*, Yahoo.com refers to its employees as *Yahoos*, Disney has its *cast*, and Wal-Mart employees are *associates*. Other companies use the terms *human resources* and *human capital*. While the terms used by companies may vary, we use the term **employees** to refer to the individuals who work for a company.

Throughout this book, we use the term **human resources practices**, often shortened to **HR practices.** When we refer to HR practices, we are not talking about the responsibilities of the human resources department of a company unless we specifically say so; rather, we are talking about the practices that a company has put in place to manage employees. We have chosen this term because it is the one most companies use to represent these activities. Also,

employees

The individuals who work for a company.

human resources practices, often HR practices

The practices that a company has put in place to manage employees.

most schools refer to the course you are taking as Human Resource Management, and most of the tools that you will have at your disposal as a manager to attract, develop, motivate, and retain employees are related to Human Resources management concepts and principles.

We use the term **line manager** or **manager** to refer to individuals who are responsible for supervising and directing the efforts of a group of employees to perform tasks that are directly related to the creation and delivery of a company's products or services. For many years, line managers had the responsibility for most, if not all, aspects of managing employees. As more employment-related laws were passed, many companies began to assign much of the responsibility for employee management to the **human resources department** (also called simply the **HR department**)—a support function within companies that serves a vital role in designing and implementing company policies for managing employees. Over time, the role of HR departments expanded to include a wide variety of tasks, including record keeping and payroll, compensation and benefits, recruitment, selection, training, performance management, and regulatory issues. Now, however, companies are increasingly recognizing that managing employees is a key organization-wide responsibility, not solely the responsibility of the HR department—and line managers are being held accountable for how effectively they attract, develop, and motivate the employees they oversee.[3] After all, managers are successful only if they are able to get the highest level of quality effort from their employees.

Of course, many companies still maintain HR departments, and the employees within HR departments serve an important role in company success. But, increasingly, managers must work with the HR department to design and implement HR practices that maximize the contributions of their employees. Smart managers understand that people matter and that without people, you cannot begin to achieve your company's goals. As we look at some of the potential costs and benefits, you will begin to understand why managing employees is the job of every manager, not just the job of the HR department.

The Costs and Benefits of Managing HR

A company's **competitive advantage** is its ability to create more economic value than its competitors. This is done by providing greater value to a customer relative to the costs of making a product or providing a service.[4] Historically, companies focused on achieving a competitive advantage by holding protected assets, having extensive financial resources, competing based on price, or benefiting from economies of scale.[5] Companies often considered employees not as a competitive advantage but simply as a cost to minimize. After all, maintaining a workforce is one of the largest fixed costs for most organizations. In addition to compensation costs, employers incur costs as a result of the time and effort needed for activities such as recruiting, hiring, training, evaluating, mentoring, coaching, and disciplining employees.

Increasingly, however, companies are recognizing that employees and how they are managed may prove to be as important to competitive success as other organizational attributes. When employees are mismanaged, they may not be able or willing to work toward organizational goals. If employees do not have the necessary skills for their jobs and are not provided the training to succeed, they may not know how to work effectively or efficiently, resulting in lower performance and greater costs to the company. How employees are managed also influences their attitudes and behaviors.[6] Employees who feel undervalued or underappreciated will not expend as much effort in performing their jobs.[7] Unhappy or unmotivated employees may be less likely to be responsive to customer needs, which can cost the company customers.[8] Mismanaging employees may lead to higher levels of employee turnover and absenteeism,[9] as well as sabotage,[10] which can have both direct and indirect costs for the organization. An employee who is not properly trained to do a hazardous job may make mistakes that lead to injury for the worker and a lawsuit for the company.

In contrast, effectively managing employees can lead to improved firm performance.[11] Studies have shown this link in industries as diverse as banking, apparel, and manufacturing.[12] When employees have the skills they need, they are able to contribute to meeting company goals. And when employees feel valued by their company, they are likely to display greater levels of commitment, loyalty, and morale.[13] Armed with the skills they need and

line manager or **manager**

The individuals who are responsible for supervising and directing the efforts of a group of employees to perform tasks that are directly related to the creation and delivery of a company's products or services.

human resources department or **HR department**

A support function within companies that serves a vital role in designing and implementing company policies for managing employees.

competitive advantage

A company's ability to create more economic value than its competitors.

greater motivation, employees may be more productive. Greater productivity may more than offset the costs associated with managing employees.

Given what we know about the outcomes of effectively managing employees, many companies increasingly view employees as more than just a cost to control. These companies know that employees are a potential source of competitive advantage and that their talents must be nurtured.[14] In fact, many companies now emphasize the value of employees to the company directly on their Web sites. For example, CIGNA, a company that provides employee benefits, states:

> Explore everything that makes CIGNA a special place to work. We offer a results-driven environment where we pay for performance. We offer competitive benefits. We have a diverse and inclusive workforce. We demand integrity and respect in all we do. Add it all up and you get somewhere great to work—CIGNA.

> We offer more than a job; we offer something essential to your career development—the opportunity to grow in a company that recognizes, respects and values individual contributions and differences.[15]

This company recognizes that when employees are managed effectively, they can be an important source of competitive advantage.

Keep in mind that there is no single best way to manage employees. Rather, each company is different and must manage employees in a way that is most appropriate, given its unique situation. The internal organizational demands and the external environment determine the context for setting HR practices. The framework we present next and reference throughout the book shows the relationship among three sets of HR challenges in an organization's internal and external environment, three primary HR activities, and the path to competitive advantage. Understanding the framework will better equip you with the skills to strategically and effectively manage employees while minimizing the costs of mismanaging them.

COMPANY *spotlight* 1.1 Southwest Airlines

Southwest Airlines has been on *Fortune*'s "America's Most Admired Companies" list numerous times and serves as an exemplar for the strategic management of human resources. There seems to be nothing particularly unique about Southwest Airlines. It uses the same airplanes (737s) available to other airlines, follows the same regulations, and uses the same airports. Yet Southwest continues to thrive while other airlines struggle. Most people agree that its success is due largely to its unique culture and how it manages its workforce. Maintaining a fun, employee-friendly, hard-working culture is critical to the company. To ensure that new hires fit in with its culture, they are hired for having the right "attitude." After all, most "skills" can be learned on the job. Because employees own 8% of the company's stock, they also try harder. While there is nothing really unique about what Southwest does, there is certainly something unique about how it does it. It continually ranks number one in terms of the fewest customer complaints, and it has been profitable for 34 consecutive years.

Southwest Airlines has a strong reputation for managing its people well

Sources: Serwer, A. Southwest Airlines: The hottest thing in the sky. *Fortune*, March 8, 2004, pp. 86–91: and Southwest Airlines. *Southwest Airlines fact sheet*, December 11, 2007, www.southwest.com/about_swa/press/factsheet.html.

FRAMEWORK FOR THE STRATEGIC MANAGEMENT OF EMPLOYEES

Have you ever tried to assemble a jigsaw puzzle? Without the picture on the box? You have all these odd-shaped little pieces of colored cardboard but no clear idea of how to start putting them together. For many managers, knowing how to hire employees, give them performance feedback, and decide on a pay raise feels much like trying to complete that puzzle without the picture. No sooner does the manager begin to feel as if she has a handle on some of these aspects of employee management than changes occur in the business environment. Maybe new technology or new laws emerge, and the manager begins to feel like the shapes of the pieces have changed.

The framework that we introduce in this chapter and use throughout the book (Exhibit 1.1) is like the guiding picture on the puzzle box. It shows the relationship between the organization's context, both external and internal, and the HR activities that the organization needs to use to manage employees to achieve its ultimate goal: competitive advantage. By understanding the relationships among these components and how the HR activities build on each other, managers can equip and position employees to maximize their contribution to company performance, which in turn

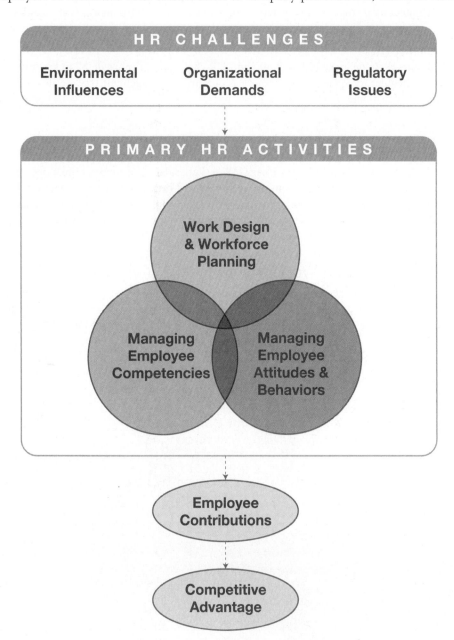

◄ **Exhibit 1.1**

Framework for the Strategic Management of Employees

creates competitive advantage. The picture of the puzzle does exist, and it helps managers put together the pieces.

Exhibit 1.1 shows that the strategic management of employees centers around three categories of HR activities, which occur within the context of three main HR challenges. The **primary HR activities** are:

1. **Work design and workforce planning.** Designing jobs and planning for the workforce needed to achieve organizational goals
2. **Managing employee competencies.** Identifying, acquiring, and developing employee talent and skills
3. **Managing employee attitudes and behaviors.** Encouraging and motivating employees to perform in appropriate ways to contribute to company goals

Managers carry out these three primary HR activities in the context of three main **HR challenges:**

1. **Organizational demands.** Internal factors, including strategy, company characteristics, organizational culture, and employee concerns
2. **Environmental influences.** External factors, including labor force trends, globalization, technology, and ethics and social responsibility
3. **Regulatory issues.** A special subgroup of environmental influences that includes federal, state, and local legislation that protects the rights of individuals and the company with regard to the employment process

We discuss these primary HR activities and HR challenges in more detail in the following section. Regulatory issues are so critical to employee management that we devote a full chapter to discussing them (Chapter 3).

primary HR activities

The strategic management of employees centers around three categories of HR activities (1) Work design and workforce planning; (2) managing employee competencies; and (3) managing employee attitudes and behaviors.

HR challenges

Challenges that managers must consider in the management of employees that relate to (1) Organizational demands; (2) environmental influences; and (3) regulatory issues.

PRIMARY HR ACTIVITIES

Exhibit 1.2 highlights the three primary HR activities. First, companies must decide how to design jobs and ensure that employees are where they need to be to meet organizational goals. Second, companies must ensure that employees have the competencies they need to perform those jobs. Third, employees must be motivated to use their competencies productively.

Work Design and Workforce Planning

Work design and workforce planning are two critical components of managing employees. Managers must design jobs in a way that ensures that employees perform tasks and responsibilities that have the most potential to add value to the company. Managers must also

Exhibit 1.2 ▶
Primary HR Activities

engage in workforce planning to make sure that the right people are in the right place in the company, at the right time, to meet company goals.

JOB DESIGN   Job design involves deciding what employees will do on a day-to-day basis as well as how jobs are interconnected. In part, job design is a function of the tasks that employees are expected to perform. However, job design also represents the choices managers make regarding how those tasks are to be carried out. There are many different ways to design jobs.

Some employees work on an assembly line, others work in self-managed teams, and still other employees work in relative isolation. Managers may design similar jobs in different ways in different companies—no one design fits all situations. Think about how the job of an accountant in an accounting firm might differ from the job of an accountant in a retail store chain, or how the job of a marketing manager might differ in a professional services firm from the job of marketing manager in a manufacturing firm. In both examples, many of the tasks will be the same, but the importance of those tasks for company success and how the jobs are performed will differ. Some questions managers need to consider for job design are:

- What tasks should you emphasize when designing a job?
- How simple or complex are these tasks?
- How many tasks can your employees perform?
- How much flexibility do you provide to your employees in terms of how and where they carry out their tasks?

The choices managers make about the tasks employees perform and how they are expected to perform those tasks have several important implications. From a company perspective, when jobs are designed to align tasks with company objectives, employees in those jobs are in a position to add value and increase company success. If managers do not consider company objectives in job design, employees may unknowingly focus on tasks and activities that are not necessarily the most important. From an employee perspective, job design influences employee satisfaction, as well as intentions to remain with the company.[16]

WORKFORCE PLANNING   The number of employees in different parts of an organization is always changing. Factors such as employee turnover and company growth challenge managers to make workforce planning decisions to maintain the necessary number of employees.

Companies must also decide how to allocate employees—through promotions, demotions, and transfers—to areas where they can contribute most significantly. Changes in strategic emphasis, a reorganization of operations, or the introduction of new products or services also influences the demand for different jobs in different parts of a company. At any point in time, some parts of a company may be facing a shortage of employee talent, while others may have a surplus.

Some companies hire full-time employees or promote current employees to address a growing demand for products or services; other companies turn to *outsourcing*—sending work to other companies—as well as the use of *contingent labor*—relying on temporary employees, independent contractors, and other forms of alternative labor—to address labor shortages.[17] In 2005, the use of contingent labor such as temporary workers and independent contractors accounted for over 9% of total employment in the United States.[18] When faced with a labor surplus, managers must often consider tactics such as downsizing, early retirement programs, and demotions or transfers to reduce the number of employees in certain parts of the company and balance supply and demand. Some of the important decisions in workforce planning are:

- How should you address a labor shortage? A labor surplus?
- When should you require current employees to work overtime versus hire additional full-time staff?
- When should you outsource work rather than hire new employees?
- What can you do to minimize the negative effects of downsizing?

While there are many options available to address labor shortages and surpluses, the challenge is to understand when different options are likely to be most effective to meet each company's unique situation.

Managing Employee Competencies

As shown in Exhibit 1.2, the second primary HR activity for managers is ensuring that employees have the necessary competencies to effectively perform their tasks. **Competencies** are the knowledge, skills, abilities, and other talents that employees possess. These competencies directly influence the types of jobs employees are able to perform. Managing competencies means recruiting and selecting the right people and training them to succeed in their jobs.

competencies

The knowledge, skills, abilities, and other talents that employees possess.

interested/
encouraging
—understanding

RECRUITMENT *Recruitment* refers to the process of generating a qualified pool of potential employees interested in working for your company or encouraging individuals within your company to pursue other positions within your company. The challenge with recruitment is having a clear understanding of the competencies needed to succeed in a job and designing a strategy for identifying individuals in the labor market who possess those competencies and who would be a good match for the organization's culture and goals. Identifying a potential CEO or an individual with rare scientific skills, for example, requires a different recruitment approach than identifying people who could fill a clerical or assembly-line job vacancy. Placing an advertisement for a job opening in the local newspaper is not likely to maximize the opportunity to identify a good CEO. Similarly, placing an advertisement in the *Wall Street Journal* is not likely to be an efficient way to identify individuals for a janitorial position. Where and how companies recruit influences the type and quality of candidates who respond to a job opening. Management has to create an employee value proposition that will attract the right individuals to apply for the open positions. A *recruitment value proposition* addresses the question: "Why would someone want to work for this company?"[19] Some key issues to address in creating a recruitment strategy are:

- For what competencies do you recruit?
- What groups do you target with your recruitment message?
- Do you recruit internally, externally, or both?
- How do you ensure that you offer an employee value proposition that will attract the right applicants?

SELECTION Whereas recruitment focuses on generating a qualified pool of candidates for job openings, *selection* focuses on choosing the best person from that pool. As with recruitment, there are a number of important questions to consider when deciding among candidates. Each job candidate brings a unique blend of knowledge, skills, and abilities. Perhaps the most critical issue to address is whether the candidate possesses the competencies that you have identified as the most important for a particular job. Some companies may emphasize past experiences while others may emphasize personality when making a selection decision. Certainly the emphasis is influenced by the nature of the job. Consider making a selection decision for a firefighter. How important is personality? How important is physical strength? How important is experience? Your answers to these questions directly influence who is hired from the pool of job candidates identified in the recruitment process.

Once a company has made a selection decision, it has made a commitment to an individual. Considering the time, money, and energy spent recruiting and selecting new employees, managers need to ensure that selection decisions are based on sound reasoning and do not violate employment laws. Some of the key issues in making selection decisions are:

- How do you generate the information you need to make an effective, and legal, hiring decision?
- Which tests are most effective for identifying employees with high potential?
- What questions should you ask candidates during an interview?
- Who makes the ultimate hiring decision?

There is no "one best way" to recruit and select employees. Each company is unique and has different needs. Yet, the choices that managers make influence the effectiveness of the staffing process and, ultimately, who is employed. The goal of recruitment and staffing is to ensure that employees have the competencies they need to contribute to the company's success or have the potential to develop those competencies.

TRAINING   Recruitment and selection focus on finding and selecting the right person for the job. *Training* ensures that new and current employees know the ins and outs of the organization and have the skills they need to succeed. Even when companies successfully hire employees who have a great deal of potential, the employees are still likely to need training, depending on the company's needs. Employees also need to learn about the company itself, its culture, and the general way it operates.

Beyond new hires, many other situations warrant training for both new and current employees. For example, all employees may need to learn how to use new technology effectively and safely, and the decision to merge with another company may require employees to learn new procedures. Beyond training for the needs of a particular job, companies also engage in training activities to develop individuals for future positions. Doing so requires foresight to identify employees who may potentially fill positions throughout the organization and then engaging in activities to provide them with the skills needed to be able to move into those positions when the vacancies emerge.

Given the time, cost, and effort required to build employee competencies, it should come as no surprise that companies place great emphasis on these processes. If companies are going to work hard to select the right people, it is important that they focus on providing employees with the specific know-how they need to be successful in their current position as well as potential positions they might assume. Some of the important decisions in training are:

- How do you know which employees need to be trained?
- How do you design an effective training program?
- Which training methods are most effective to meet your needs?
- How do you know if your training efforts have been successful?

Managing Employee Attitudes and Behaviors

Building competencies is critical, but keep in mind that it is only part of the equation. How well employees perform is a function of the effort they expend as well as their competencies. Encouraging the right employee attitudes and behaviors requires motivating workers to continually improve their performance. This forms our third group of primary HR activities. Some of the major tools that managers use to guide employee efforts on the job are compensation, incentives, performance management programs, and employee benefits, health, and wellness programs.

PERFORMANCE MANAGEMENT   Many managers may think that performance management is simply sitting down with an employee once a year to discuss her performance during that time. The manager may review an evaluation form with the employee to rate her results on certain items and then use those ratings to discuss appropriate merit raises and possible promotions. But good performance management is more complex than that. Much like with incentive systems, which we discuss next, the criteria that managers use to evaluate their employees need to represent the attitudes and behaviors managers expect of their employees. When managers clearly communicate performance criteria, employees are more likely to have a good understanding of the steps they need to take to achieve successful job performance. When these performance criteria are aligned with organizational goals, managers and employees become more confident that they are focusing their efforts on important activities.

Effective performance management involves more than just evaluating employees, however. It also focuses on providing employees with feedback (positive and negative) and on using employee development activities to improve current and future performance. The continuous improvement part of this process entails giving clear feedback regarding performance, praising good performers, and disciplining poor performers. Perhaps most importantly, effective performance management means helping employees understand how to continually improve.

There is no single best performance management system. The most appropriate system depends on the unique context of each company. Some critical issues in performance management are:

- What is the best way for you to measure employee performance?
- How should you communicate that information to employees?

- In addition to performance evaluation, how can managers give employees developmental feedback to improve their performance?
- How should you manage poorly performing employees?

COMPENSATION AND INCENTIVES A company's compensation system exerts a strong influence on the attitudes and behaviors of employees because it sends a message regarding the employees' value to the company. If employees feel that their company does not value them, they may not work as hard as possible. Instead, they may search for other employment opportunities. In contrast, if employees feel that their company compensates them at a fair level for the job they perform, they are more likely to work harder to help the organization meet its goals.[20]

In addition to compensation in the form of base pay, a rewards and incentives system shows employees how managers expect them to focus their time and energy. Some companies are more likely to reward seniority, while others may emphasize performance-based pay. Even among companies that reward their employees based on performance, the performance criteria may differ. Companies may value efficiency, creativity, knowledge sharing, and teamwork. Lincoln Electric's incentive system, for instance, is geared toward rewarding productivity, whereas 3M's incentive system places greater emphasis on creativity and new product design.[21] The incentive systems of these two companies differ, in part, because the employees add value in different ways. The size of an incentive is also an important indicator of how a firm values a particular activity or level of performance.

Some of the key questions when designing compensation and incentive systems are:

- What factors should you consider when determining the salary range for a job?
- What is the best way to determine how much employees should be paid?
- How much of that pay should be guaranteed and how much should be based on incentives?
- What types of incentives should you use to encourage the employee attitudes and behaviors the firm wants?

EMPLOYEE BENEFITS, HEALTH, AND WELLNESS The last piece of managing employees' attitudes and behaviors is managing employee benefits, health, and wellness. Some companies offer benefits in an attempt to help recruit, select, and retain employees. Think about that for a second. Would you be more willing to work for a company that had an attractive benefits program with coverage for dental care, vacation time, tuition assistance, and the like, or a company that did not offer these practices? In addition to serving as a recruitment or a retention tool, benefits practices may help ensure the health and well-being of a company's workforce. Considering the value-creating potential of employees, it is only logical that companies help ensure that employees are able to work effectively over time.

Some benefits, including some health and wellness programs, are required by law. For example, Social Security, workers' compensation, and family and medical leave are governed by regulations that most employers must comply with. Similarly, employee safety is a key concern for companies and is governed by the Occupational Safety and Health Administration (OSHA). As a manager, it is important that you understand your responsibilities to ensure that your employees work in a safe and healthy environment.

There are also a wide array of voluntary benefits programs that companies may offer, such as paid time off, health care, and retirement programs. Some critical issues when considering employee benefits, health, and wellness are:

- Which benefit programs are most appropriate for your workforce?
- What are the legal requirements regarding benefit programs?
- How can you ensure the safety of your employees?

As you can see, managing attitudes and behaviors requires careful attention to a host of issues. The challenge lies in the fact that each manager's situation is unique. This uniqueness is the result of differences in organizational strategies and in characteristics of the employees supervised. We'll discuss some of these challenges shortly, but keep in mind that instead of trying to identify a single way to manage employee attitudes and behaviors, it's important to identify the different tools managers have at their disposal to guide and motivate their employees within the unique context of their organization.

1.2 The Container Store

The recipient of *Workforce's* Optimas Award for general excellence in 2001 and included in *Fortune's* "100 Best Companies to Work For" for eight years running, the Container Store exemplifies the value of investing in employees. At the Container Store, all new employees receive over 230 hours of training in their first year and an average of 160 hours of annual training thereafter. Most employees receive a salary that is two to three times the average in the industry. Employees can participate in a 401(k) plan with matching company contributions, and both full- and part-time employees enjoy access to medical, dental, and vision plans. Moreover, to ensure that employees remain informed, the company communicates its store sales, goals, and expansion plans to its workforce regularly. Not surprisingly, the Container Store has a turnover rate of 18%, considerably lower than the 80% to 100% turnover rates in other retail estab-

lishments. And its employees spread the good word: Over 40% of all Container Store new hires come from employee referrals. Ninety-seven percent of its employees say they agree with the statement: "People care about each other here." As noted by Container Store spokesperson Audrey Keymer, "Keeping people happy, keeping them on staff, that's crucial."

Sources: Roth, D. My job at the Container Store. *Fortune*, January 10, 2000, pp. 74; Laabs, J. K. Thinking outside the box at the container store. *Workforce*, March 2001, pp. 34–38; Dobbs, K. Knowing how to keep your best and brightest. *Workforce*, April 2001, pp. 57–60; Duff, M. Top-shelf employees keep container store on track, *DSN Retailing Today*, March 8, 2004, 100 best companies to work for, 2008: 20. Container Store. CNNMoney.com, http://money.cnn.com/magazines/fortune/bestcompanies/2008/snapshots/20.html; and The Container Store. *A career at the Container Store*, www.containerstore.com/careers.

HR Activities Alignment

Each of the three HR activities described is critical, but none is effective in isolation. Work design and workforce planning, managing employee competencies, and encouraging the right employee attitudes and behaviors must align with each other to be effective.[22] When we discuss **alignment**, we are describing the extent to which the three primary HR activities are designed to achieve the goals of the organization.

Alignment can be broken down into two parts—internal and external alignment. As shown in Exhibit 1.3, to achieve **internal alignment**, you must first make sure that the specific practices used *within* each HR activity are consistent with one another as well as aligned *across* the primary HR activities.[23] If you have ever been on a sports team, you know how important

alignment

The extent to which the three primary HR activities are designed to achieve the goals of the organization.

internal alignment

The extent to which specific practices used *within* each HR activity are consistent with one another as well as aligned *across* the primary HR activities.

◄ **Exhibit 1.3**
Internal Alignment

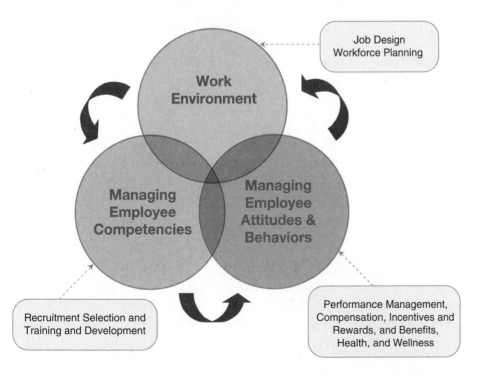

it is for all participants to have a common understanding of how to play the game, the skills required to play, and the desire to win. That is the same thing we are talking about here:

- If employees know the goals of the organization and are motivated to work toward those goals but do not possess all the competencies to do so, the results will be diminished employee performance and reduced organizational productivity.
- If employees possess the competencies they need and know the goals but lack sufficient motivation, their contributions to the company's success will be limited.
- If employees are capable and motivated but are limited in what they can do or are shorthanded due to inappropriate or poor job design and workforce planning, their ability to contribute to the organization will be limited.

external alignment

The extent to which the three primary HR activities that a company uses help them meet their organizational demands, cope with environmental factors, and comply with regulatory issues.

In addition to internal alignment, you must also achieve **external alignment** by ensuring that three primary HR activities work in concert with one another as well as with the HR challenges that companies face. We discuss these challenges next.

HR CHALLENGES

We have already discussed how managing employees in different contexts presents unique challenges. Let's take a look at these challenges in more detail. Internal factors, including company characteristics, strategic objectives, organizational culture, and employee concerns of the workforce, differ across organizations. Also, environmental factors outside the company, including competitive and regulatory forces, are constantly changing. The variety of internal and external forces affecting a company, and the challenges they pose, are briefly introduced next. In Chapter 2, we discuss internal organizational demands and environmental influences in more depth, and in Chapter 3 we focus on regulatory issues.

Challenge 1: Meeting Organizational Demands

organizational demands

The factors within a firm that affect decisions regarding how to manage employees.

strategy

The company's plan for achieving a competitive advantage over its rivals.

Organizational demands are factors within a firm that affect decisions regarding how to manage employees. We focus specifically on the demands highlighted in Exhibit 1.4: strategy, company characteristics, organizational culture, and employee concerns.

STRATEGY A company's **strategy** is its plan for achieving a competitive advantage over its rivals. Strategy drives the activities that a company performs to attract and retain customers relative to its competitors.[24] Companies realize a competitive advantage when they implement a strategy that has value for customers and that rival firms are unable to duplicate.[25]

Companies have a wide range of strategies from which to choose.[26] A company may strive to become the low-cost leader in an industry, or it may strive to sell some unique product or service that differentiates the firm from its competitors and commands a higher price. A look at the retail industry provides a good example of these differences. Wal-Mart is the low-cost leader in the retail industry and outperforms its competition by having the lowest costs in the industry. Nordstrom's strategy, on the other hand, focuses on providing

Exhibit 1.4 ▶

Organizational
Demands

a high level of customer service, under the theory that people will pay more for goods if the service is exceptional. While both companies operate successfully in the retail industry, they pursue distinctly different strategies for how they compete with their rivals.

The strategy that a company chooses influences the types of jobs that must be performed to meet its objectives and, consequently, influences its primary HR activities.[27] A company with a low-cost strategy is likely to have different expectations and objectives for its employees than a company with a strategy emphasizing customer service or creativity.[28] By shaping how employees work and add value, a company's strategy also affects the competencies employees in those jobs must possess, as well as the specific attitudes and behaviors they need to display. Consider the food service industry. The tasks that employees perform in a four-star restaurant in which service, ambiance, and excellent quality may be the focus are very different from the tasks employees perform in a local diner or a fast-food establishment in which speed and price are the focus. The strategies of these types of companies differ, resulting in differences in the required competencies, attitudes, and behaviors of employees. Strategy is a key influential factor for managers as they carry out the primary HR activities. As with all the other HR challenges, we will cover strategy in each chapter throughout this book.

COMPANY CHARACTERISTICS   Companies differ in size and stage of development. Whether a company has a handful of employees or millions, it must manage its employees. However, the challenges associated with managing employees correspond at least in part to the size of the organization. Smaller businesses often do not have the same amount and type of resources as larger companies, and they may not be in a position to provide the same level of pay, benefits, and training opportunities. Size also influences the degree of autonomy and discretion that managers may expect employees to display in their jobs. As a result, the competencies that employees need in small companies versus large ones may differ. Companies also differ in terms of their stage of development. As you might imagine, the pressures of managing employees in a young startup company are likely to differ from those in mature organizations striving to protect their market share.[29]

As we discussed earlier, the way a job is designed depends on the industry. Differences in job tasks also differ based on company size. An accountant in a small firm probably will handle all aspects of the firm's accounting, including accounts payable and accounts receivable. In a large firm, he will likely handle only one aspect of the job, perhaps accounts payable, and then the accounts of only a few vendors. Employee attitudes and behaviors can also have different consequences for companies of differing sizes. A high- or low-performing employee in a small company is likely to have a much more direct influence on the company's success than one in a company that has thousands of employees.

ORGANIZATIONAL CULTURES   Organizational culture is the set of underlying values and beliefs that employees of a company share.[30] What is particularly interesting about organizational culture is that it is unwritten, yet understood and often taken for granted. Each organization has a distinct culture that represents the beliefs of the company's founders, decisions of its top managers, types of people who work in the company, and environment in which the company operates.

Culture influences how employees do their jobs, how managers and employees interact, and the acceptable practices for executing primary HR activities. A positive culture can be a tremendous asset to an organization.[31] When a culture is positive and consistent with the organization's objectives, employees are likely to have a clear understanding of what they need to do in their jobs to contribute to the company's goals and to have a willingness to engage in those activities. Such a culture can also be a strategic asset in attracting and retaining employees. Once again, Southwest Airlines provides an excellent example for us. Southwest has a strong reputation for having a fun, friendly culture. In 2006, Southwest Airlines received 284,827 applications (from which it hired 3,363 new employees), and the company maintains one of the lowest employee turnover rates in the airline industry.[32] As you can see, culture matters.

EMPLOYEE CONCERNS   Timely address of employee issues and concerns is a critical component in a company's success. Employees may experience the stress of single parenting, caring for aging parents, or juggling schedules with an employed spouse. Successful companies are helping employees find a balance between the demands of work and their

organizational culture
The set of underlying values and beliefs that employees of a company share.

COMPANY *spotlight*   1.3 Cendant Mobility

The recipient of *Workforce*'s Optimas Award for competitive advantage in 2004, Cendant Mobility demonstrates the power of HR activities that are aligned with meeting employee needs. Cendant Mobility, a global relocation service provider, was faced with low morale and turnover hovering around 30%. To improve employee satisfaction and retention, it sought employee input and took steps to improve the work/life balance for its largely female staff by implementing flexible work hours and consolidating schedules to allow for a four-day workweek. More than 50% of the Cendant Mobility workforce participates in the Work Life program, and 30% of those employees use flexible start and end times, while 14% utilize the compressed workweek option. In addition, Cendant Mobility implemented wellness programs as well as education programs on topics such as elder care, smoking cessation, and single parenting.

As stated by Bill Maxwell, Cendant's executive vice president for global human resources and diversity and managing director of intercultural services, "What makes Cendant Mobility's work/life programs innovative is the breadth of their coverage, their cost-effectiveness to the company, the degree of acceptance they have achieved, the retention of our people, and the impact on our business results." Evidently the employees appreciated the efforts. Turnover at the company has fallen below 10%, resulting in millions of dollars in savings.

Sources: Zimmerman, E. The joy of flex. *Workforce*, March 2004, pp. 38–40; and Cendant Mobility. *Press release*, February 5, 2004. https://homepage.cartus.com/AboutCM/PressRelease.aspx?regid=1&cid=880&mid=7&sid=62/.

---

personal lives. Many companies now offer more flexibility, including flexible work schedules, family-friendly benefits, and telecommuting, to address this growing need. For example, Sun Microsystems created satellite work centers so that its employees could work from home, saving on commuting time and the associated stress.[33]

Challenge 2: Environmental Influences

environmental influences

The pressures that exist outside companies that managers must consider to strategically manage their employees.

Environmental influences are pressures that exist outside companies that managers must consider to strategically manage their employees. Exhibit 1.5 highlights that managing these influences requires tracking labor force trends, taking advantage of technological advances, addressing the globalization of industries, and meeting social and ethical obligations.

LABOR FORCE TRENDS According to the Bureau of Labor Statistics, the labor force is increasingly diverse, especially in terms of the number of women and minorities and the age of the labor force.[34] The number of women in the labor force is expected to grow by 9% between the years 2006 and 2016.[35] Similarly, while white, non-Hispanics are projected to remain the

Exhibit 1.5 ▶
Environmental
Influences

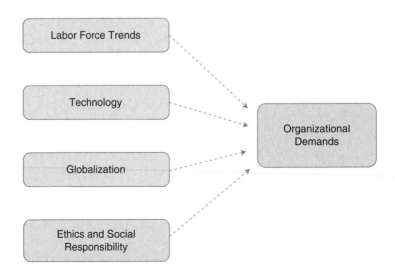

largest group in the labor force, the fastest-growing groups are Hispanics and Asians.[36] The size of the labor force in the 55-and-older age group is increasing five times as fast as the rest of the workforce.[37] For some companies, this older worker group represents a potential source of highly qualified applicants often overlooked by other employers. La Donna Burgess, of Poorman-Douglas, a leader in technology-based solutions for legal services, notes "They bring a whole wealth of knowledge and experience as well as a very strong work ethic."[38]

The changing composition of the labor force influences the primary HR activities in several ways. A diverse workforce requires that managers reevaluate how they recruit and select individuals to make sure that any potential for direct or indirect discrimination is eliminated. Further, employers need to educate employees about the value that different backgrounds and perspectives can bring to organizational performance. By directly addressing diversity issues, companies are more likely to capitalize on the many benefits associated with a diverse workforce.[39] According to Jim Sinocchi, director of diversity communications at IBM, which is widely respected for its approach to managing disabled workers, "We consider diversity strategic to our organization. . . . We don't hire people who are disabled just because it's a nice thing to do. We do it because it's the right thing to do from a business standpoint." Targeting disabled employees provides IBM with access to a larger labor pool and fresh ideas and viewpoints. Indeed, over 40% of the disabled workers at IBM hold key-skill jobs, such as software engineering, marketing, and IT architecture positions.[40]

TECHNOLOGY Technology continues to shape the nature of competition. The increasing prominence of the Internet and information technologies has considerable implications for how employees function within companies. Many employees today must possess a basic level of computer proficiency to perform their jobs. Information technologies have created new avenues for how employees interact, share information, and learn from one another.[41] Technology has also created challenges in terms of privacy issues and has increased the potential for employee misuse.

Advances in information technologies have also changed how we think about work. Not long ago, it was important to live within a reasonable distance of one's job. Today, high-speed Internet access, videoconferencing, and e-mail allow a firm's employees to live anywhere in the world.[42] As a result, companies enjoy a larger pool of potential employees, and workers experience a wider variety of potential employers.[43] JetBlue allows its reservation agents, many of whom are trying to balance work and family demands, to work from home. They may live hundreds of miles from JetBlue's headquarters, but they work and contribute to the company as if they were physically located in the headquarters.[44] Of course, managing a virtual workforce introduces new challenges regarding staffing decisions, performance evaluations, and training and development, as we will explore in later chapters.[45]

GLOBALIZATION An increasingly significant factor companies face in today's environment is the increased **globalization** of industries—the blurring of country boundaries in business activities. Many companies are actively competing on an international level, setting up production or service facilities in other countries, or establishing international joint ventures and partnerships. Companies that still operate primarily in domestic markets often find themselves competing with international companies. To some extent, all companies operate in a global arena, which creates challenges and opportunities in terms of managing employees.

Capitalizing on the global labor market requires understanding how differences in cultural values and beliefs influence working relationships among employees. When companies expand across borders, helping expatriates—employees sent to work in company facilities in another country—to work with the local labor force and thrive in a different culture is paramount.

Another challenge in globalization today is *offshoring*—sending work that was once performed domestically to companies in other countries, or opening facilities in other countries to do the work, often at a substantially lower cost.[46] Oracle has 2,000 employees in India,[47] and Levi's has closed its plants in the United States to focus operations in other countries.[48] In a 2007 survey of 500 fast-growing companies, Deloitte found that 45% are currently using offshore firms and 55% plan to use them in the next five years.[49] Making the decision to offshore jobs does have some risks. Dell, for example, stopped routing technical support calls from U.S. customers to a call center in Bangalore, India, because customers complained about the service.[50]

globalization

The blurring of country boundaries in business activities.

ETHICS AND SOCIAL RESPONSIBILITY Every company operates in a social environment based on implicit and explicit standards of ethical behavior and social responsibility. The importance of ethical behavior has gained renewed prominence in recent years as a result of the widely publicized unethical behavior of companies such as Enron and Tyco. Financial performance may be critical, but, increasingly, companies and their managers are being held accountable for ethical behavior.[51] The problem is that ethical standards are not always clear. To address these ambiguities, many companies, such as Lockheed Martin, Texas Instruments, Raytheon, and MCI, have implemented formal policies and procedures to help their employees act ethically. Lockheed employs 65 ethics officers and requires that all its employees attend ethics training each year.[52] MCI has implemented a full-scale ethics program.[53]

Beyond ethics programs, many companies are also taking steps to demonstrate enhanced levels of social responsibility. As shown in Company Spotlight 1.4, for example, Starbucks has garnered considerable attention by going above and beyond its legally required responsibilities to provide a work setting that places a strong priority on taking care of its employees.

Challenge 3: Regulatory Issues

Regulatory issues is the one challenge that has probably had the most direct influence on the management of employees. Over the past 50 years, many presidential executive orders as well as much federal, state, and local legislation have been specifically concerned with the employment process. At a basic level, legislation describes what is legally acceptable in the employment process and focuses on protecting the rights of individuals to have an equal opportunity to enjoy the benefits and privileges of employment. The challenge with regulatory issues is that the influence of legislation on employment is very broad, and the interpretation of the laws continues to evolve. Moreover, legislation is continually introduced that broadens existing statutes and creates new ones. The Americans with Disabilities Act of 1990 (ADA), for example, provides specific guidelines and provisions regarding the treatment of individuals with disabilities in employment situations.[54] This law covers management-related activities such as interviewing, selection, promotion, job design, access to training opportunities, compensation

COMPANY spotlight   1.4 Social Responsibility at Starbucks

Over the past two decades, Starbucks has become one of the most successful brands and retail stores. With more than 15,000 stores around the globe, Starbucks continues to grow at an epic pace and has shown many years of high performance. Top leaders at the company are firmly committed to the well-being of their workforce. All employees working more than 20 hours per week receive stock options and health care benefits at no small cost to the company. Starbucks also encourages its employees to get involved in the community, and it provides matching grants to not-for-profit organizations when its employees volunteer to help them—something most other companies don't do because of the costs involved. Yet the continued success of Starbucks proves that companies can be socially and financially responsible at the same time. Howard Schultz, its chairman, would argue that Starbucks is successful because it is socially responsible and shares its wealth—not the other way around.

Social responsibility is a key part of Starbucks' culture

Sources: Serwer, A. and Bonamici, K. Hot Starbucks to go. *Fortune*, January 26, 2004, pp. 60–74; Ethics in action: Getting it right. *Selections*, Fall 2002, pp. 24–28; and Starbucks Coffee. *Company fact sheet*, February 2008, www.starbucks.com/aboutus/Company_Factsheet.pdf.

and benefits, and even layoffs. The ADA is only one of the many laws and executive orders that influence the management of employees in direct and indirect ways. Other laws, such as Title VII of the Civil Rights Act of 1964, the Occupational Safety and Health Act, and the Civil Rights Act of 1992, have important implications for how companies manage their workforce.

When a company fails to comply with legal requirements, even if it simply misunderstands them, it is at risk for considerable costs. For example, Texaco settled a racial discrimination lawsuit for $175 million,[55] and Coca-Cola settled a class-action racial discrimination lawsuit for $192 million.[56] Beyond the obvious financial penalties are the potential damage to a company's reputation and diminished morale among employees.[57] Given the breadth of influence that the legal environment has on the management of employees, this is a critical area to for managers to understand. In Chapter 3, we focus on the major employment-related laws and executive orders that affect the management of employees.

THE PLAN FOR THIS BOOK

Before moving on to the remaining chapters, it is important to have a clear road map of where we are heading and why we are heading there, much like having the picture to help put the jigsaw puzzle together. The plan for this book is to explore the primary HR activities that companies design and managers implement to successfully build the competencies of their employees, to motivate them to work harder and smarter, and to design jobs and engage in workforce planning to maximize employees' abilities to use their skills and efforts effectively and ensure that the right numbers and types of people are where they need to be. Prior to discussing the HR activities, we focus on the three sets of HR challenges to help you recognize the dynamic context of organizations and to enable you to understand how to strategically manage employees. We will reference the overarching framework for this book, first introduced in Exhibit 1.1, throughout each chapter as we explore the interrelationships among the HR activities, HR challenges, and organizational goals. Exhibit 1.6 shows how the chapters fit within the framework.

The following is a brief overview of the chapters to come.

Chapters 2–3: HR Challenges

As noted previously, effectively managing employees requires that managers have a firm understanding of how the organizational, environmental, and legal challenges influence companies. In Chapters 2–3, we focus on these three sets of HR challenges.

Chapters 4–5: Work Design and Workforce Planning

In Chapters 4–5, we focus on the nature of work and allocating people throughout a company to maximize the contributions of employees to company success. In doing so, we explore the viability of alternative types of job designs to meet different organizational goals; how to use job analysis to help ensure that employees' jobs focus directly on achieving important organizational objectives; and how to balance the supply and demand for employees throughout organizations.

Chapters 6–8: Managing Employee Competencies

In Chapters 6–8, we explore different options for building and maintaining needed competencies for different jobs. We focus on how to use recruitment and selection to identify and choose the right people for the unique needs of the organization. We also focus on how to use training to translate employee potential into functional competencies.

Chapters 9–12: Managing Employee Attitudes and Behaviors

In Chapters 9–12, we focus on how to encourage and motivate employees to focus their efforts on contributing to important organizational objectives. We focus on performance management systems and emphasize how to evaluate, appraise, and develop employees to

Exhibit 1.6 ►
Chapter Overview

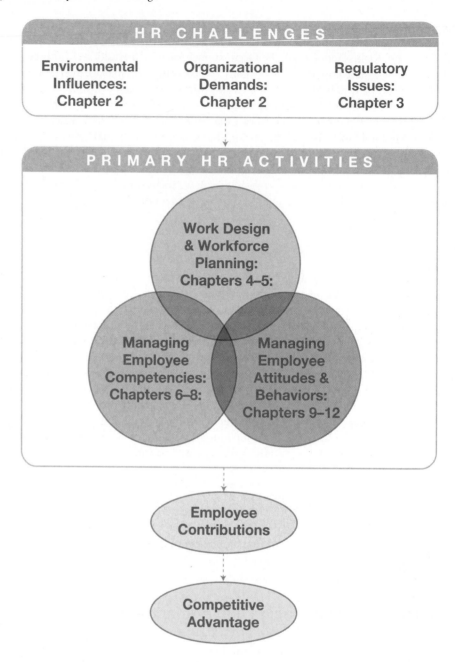

increase their contributions; how compensation systems are established and which systems are most appropriate in different circumstances; how to establish incentive and reward systems to encourage continued employee effort toward important objectives; and how to design benefits, health, and wellness programs to meet employees' needs.

Chapters 13–14: Special Topics

In Chapters 13–14, we focus on two additional topics associated with the strategic management of employees. Beyond the HR challenges, managing employees who are covered under collective bargaining agreements introduces important issues about how unions work, the unionization process, legal aspects of labor relations, negotiating collective bargaining agreements, and managing the labor agreement. We take a closer look at these issues in Chapter 13. In Chapter 14, we explore the specific issues associated with reaching alignment among the primary HR activities as well as between the primary HR activities and the HR challenges to create high-performing organizations. We also focus on how to measure the impact of alternative decisions regarding the primary HR activities to continually improve the strategic management of employees.

SUMMARY

There are many benefits associated with effectively managing employees. When employees have the necessary competencies, they can contribute to meeting company goals. When employees are motivated, they are likely to display increased levels of commitment, loyalty, and morale. And when the work environment is designed appropriately, employees are in a position to turn their abilities and motivation into greater productivity. In contrast, when employees are mismanaged, they may not be able or willing to work toward organizational goals. If employees do not have the needed skills, they may not know how to work most effectively, resulting in decreased performance and morale and greater turnover and absenteeism. And employees who feel undervalued or underappreciated are not likely to expend much effort in performing their jobs.

The strategic management of employees requires managers to attend to three primary HR activities. First, managers must design work and engage in workforce planning to ensure that employees are in a position to add value to the company. The specific HR practices that are used to manage the flow of work are job design and workforce planning. Second, managers must identify, acquire, build, and retain the critical competencies employees need to effectively perform their jobs. This is done through recruitment, selection, and training activities. Third, managers must provide employees with guidance and motivation to use their abilities to contribute to the company's goals. Performance management, compensation, incentives, and benefits, health, and wellness programs are the primary tools to influence employee attitudes and behaviors.

When companies are able to leverage the talents of their workforce, they are more likely to achieve competitive advantage. However, this is not an easy task. Managers must make sure that the tactics they use within the three primary HR activities are in alignment. The context of a company's strategy, characteristics, and organizational culture must be also kept in mind. In addition, managers must consider the concerns of their workforce. Beyond organizational demands, the strategic management of human resources requires managers to anticipate and take steps to meet the environmental influences associated with labor force trends and advances in technology. Finally, the design and implementation of the primary HR activities must be done in a manner that is in compliance with legal requirements.

KEY TERMS

alignment *p. 13*

competencies *p. 9*

competitive advantage *p. 5*

employees *4*

environmental influences *p. 16*

external alignment *p. 14*

globalization *p. 17*

HR challenges *p. 8*

human resource (HR)
    department *p. 5*

human resource (HR) practices *p. 4*

internal alignment *p. 13*

line manager (manager) *p. 5*

organizational culture *p. 15*

organizational demands *p. 14*

primary human resource (HR)
    activities *p. 7*

strategy *p. 14*

DISCUSSION QUESTIONS

1. How does managing employees contribute to achieving a competitive advantage?
2. Given the importance of employees for a company to sustain a competitive advantage, why do you think so many companies have engaged in layoffs, outsourcing, and offshoring of work to other countries?
3. What does it mean to strategically manage employees?
4. Identify and explain the three primary HR activities.
5. Which of the three primary HR activities is most challenging? Why?
6. Discuss the management practices associated with each primary HR activity.
7. Some people think that there are certain practices for managing employees that are always beneficial for companies, while others maintain that the best practices depend on the circumstances of each company. Which approach do you think is right? Why?
8. Which of the environmental influences identified in this chapter is most important for managing employees in a company pursuing innovation? What about a company with a strategy emphasizing low costs or customer service? How does a company's strategy influence the importance of different environmental influences?
9. Discuss how regulatory issues influence the management of employees.

LEARNING EXERCISE 1

Now that you have read about how companies differ and how those differences can affect employee management practices, here's a chance for you to begin applying those concepts. Lockheed Martin and Panera Bread are two very different, and very successful, companies. Lockheed Martin is an advanced technology company and a major defense contractor. Panera Bread is a fast-expanding bakery-café chain.

Lockheed Martin was formed in 1995 when two major defense contractors, Lockheed Corporation and Martin Marietta Corporation, merged. The corporation reported 2007 sales of $41.9 billion, a backlog of $76.7 billion, and cash flow from operations of $4.2 billion. Clearly, the corporation is doing well. Lockheed's vision is "To be the world's best advanced technology systems integrator."

Panera was founded in 1981 as Au Bon Pain, Inc. In 1993, the company bought St. Louis Bread Co. and in time changed the name from St. Louis Bread to Panera Bread. Because of the success of Panera, in May 1991, the company sold off all the Au Bon Pain, Inc., business units except Panera Bread and then changed the name of the company itself to Panera Bread. The rest, as they say, is history. Subsequently, Panera Bread's stock has grown 13-fold and has created over $1 billion in shareholder value. Panera Bread's mission statement is simple: "A loaf of bread in every arm."

Visit the Web sites for Lockheed Martin Corporation (www.lockheedmartin.com) and Panera Bread (www.panerabread.com). Use information provided in the "About Us" section and other parts of each company's Web site to answer the following questions.

1. Prepare a chart comparing the two companies based on the organizational demand characteristics discussed in this chapter.
2. Discuss two or three of the key environmental influences that each company would likely face. Why would there be different key environmental influences for each company?
3. Describe how the organizational demands and environmental influences identified for each company would differentially affect work flow, employee competencies, and employee attitudes and behaviors for each company.

Sources: Lockheed Martin Web site, www.lockheedmartin.com; and Panera Bread Web site, www.panerabread.com.

LEARNING EXERCISE 2

What exactly does it mean to be a manager? This may seem like an innocent question. But do you really know? Throughout this chapter, we have discussed many of the tools that managers have at their disposal for managing their employees. For this exercise, interview three managers and ask them how they spend their time. Then answer the following questions.

1. What does it mean to manage employees?
2. What aspects of each manager's job creates the most challenges?

3. Compare the responses you get from the three managers with the primary HR activities discussed in this chapter. What role do these managers play in work design and workforce planning? Managing employee competencies? Managing employees' attitudes and behaviors?

CASE STUDY # 1 — THE NEW JOB

After graduating from school, you are fortunate to receive an offer as an assistant manager of a marketing department in a company located in New York City, working for a fast-growing company that provides marketing support for companies. Your department specializes in marketing strategies for the Internet and currently consists of 10 people—you, your direct supervisor (the manager of the department), and 8 marketing associates. Your job is to help the manager lead the unit to develop long-term strategies for your unit, to maintain excellent customer service with your clients, and to strive to build future business opportunities. The marketing associates in your department work a very flexible schedule and are often offsite, working with the clients at their location to help develop marketing campaigns to improve their business presence, and performance, via the Internet.

After being on the job a short while, you realize that you really need to create another position to help make sure all the necessary work gets completed on time. Essentially, while you and your manager are focusing on the long-term inter- ests of the department and the associates are working very hard to help the clients, many of the administrative aspects of the work are falling by the wayside. For example, no one is currently tracking accounts payable from clients or handling accounts payable to your service providers. As a result, you are spending time on these tasks that are beyond your job expectations. In addition, you are spending an increasing amount of time making travel arrangements such as booking hotels and arranging transportation for your staff. After you talk with the manager of your unit, she agrees that something needs to change to allow you to devote your time to more of the strategic issues in the unit, and she permits you to create a new position to help out in your department. Your challenge now is to determine what this position will be.

DISCUSSION QUESTIONS

1. What job would you create? Why?
2. What are the employee competencies this position needs to be successful? Why?

3. What are your ideas for how you might design performance management, compensation, and incentives for this new position? Why?

4. Are there any particular challenges you would expect to encounter that would make successfully filling this position difficult? How would you overcome these challenges?

CASE STUDY # 2 — EMPLOYEES LOVE WEGMANS

In 2008, *Fortune* magazine rated Wegmans Food Market as the third-best company to work for. This should not come as a surprise since it had been a mainstay of the top 3 since 2005, the top 10 since 2003, and the top 100 since 1998. The average turnover rate for supermarkets is 47.4% (13.3% for full-time employees and 58% for part-time employees). At Wegmans, turnover is much lower. Turnover is 6% to 7% for full-time employees and 38% for part-time employees. In an industry that has not historically been known as generating intense employee satisfaction and loyalty, Wegmans has broken new ground. But what is it about this supermarket that generates employee loyalty, productivity, and commitment from its workforce?

As noted by Karen Shadders, vice president of people, "If we take care of our employees, they will take care of our customers. If employees can't take care of their families, they cannot do their jobs. The focus is on freeing up people so that they can be more productive." Shadders adds, "Our pay and benefits are at or above our competition's. It helps us attract a higher caliber of employee." Indeed, its outstanding reputation has allowed Wegmans to be very selective in its hiring processes. In 2007, the company had more than 145,000 applications but only a 6% turnover rate and hired 435 new positions.

Once employees are hired, Wegmans does a lot to enable employees to be successful both personally and professionally. On average, customer service representatives earn over $27,000 per year and receive 50 hours of training. Wegmans provides its employees with a generous work/life balance program that includes job sharing, compressed workweeks, and telecommuting. Both part-time and full-time employees can participate in medical insurance and prescription plans, 401(k) retirement savings plans, dependent care reimbursement plans, adoption assistance, and an employee assistance program. In addition, full-time employees enjoy access to dental coverage, life insurance, and personal days.

DISCUSSION QUESTIONS

1. What is it about Wegmans that helps it continually retain its status as one of the best companies to work for?

2. What role do the three primary HR activities play in achieving employee loyalty and financial success?

3. Would the Wegmans approach to managing employees work in other companies? What types of companies are most likely to benefit from a similar approach to managing their workforce?

4. Why don't other companies use the same practices as Wegmans?

Sources: 100 best companies to work for, 2008: 3. Wegmans Food Markets. CNNMoney.com, http://money.cnn.com/magazines/fortune/bestcompanies/2008/snapshots/3.html; Wegmans Web site, www.wegmans.com; Turnover in supermarkets. January 30, 2004. Workforce.com, www.workforce.com/archive/feature/23/62/39/236245.php; and Demby, E. R. Two stores refuse to join the race to the bottom. *Workforce Management*, February 2004, pp. 57–59.

HR CHALLENGES

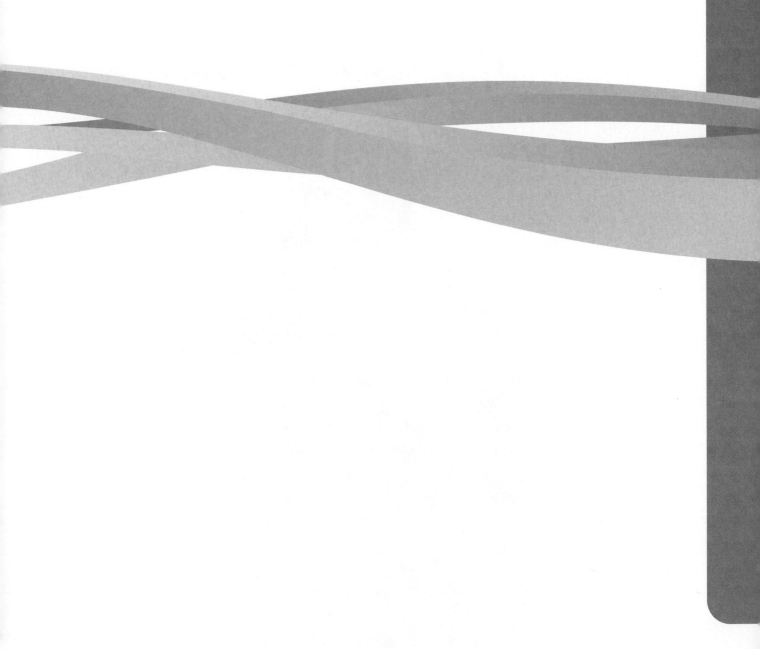

chapter

2

ORGANIZATIONAL DEMANDS AND ENVIRONMENTAL INFLUENCES

1. Describe how differences in company strategies shape the primary HR activities. *(29)*

2. Explain how company characteristics influence the way employees are managed. *(32)*

3. Discuss the role of organizational culture in effective employee management. *(33)*

4. Explain how employee concerns influence employees' interpretation and response to different HR activities. *(34)*

5. Discuss the impact of labor force trends on how companies manage employees. *(38)*

6. Identify how advances in technology affect employee management. *(41)*

7. Explain the challenges of managing employees in a global context. *(41)*

8. Understand how ethics and social responsibility influence managerial decisions. *(44)*

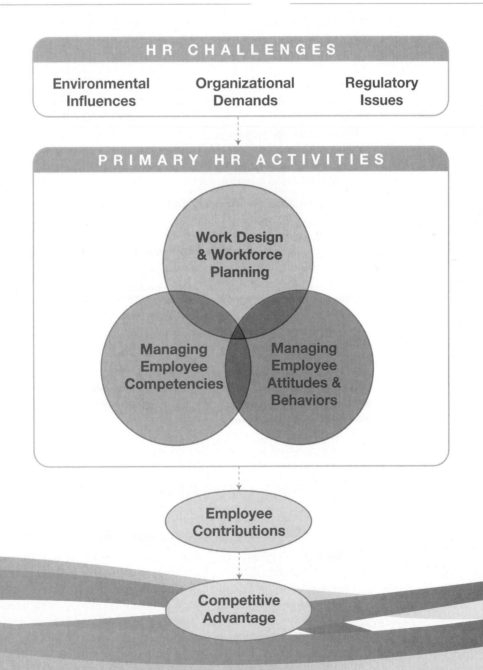

THE IMPORTANCE OF CONTEXT

Have you ever heard the phrase *the right tool for the job*? It is a simple but meaningful phrase. After all, would you ever consider mowing a lawn with a pair of scissors? Would you ever dig a hole with a screwdriver? Would you ever try to saw a piece of wood with a hammer? Sure, the hammer might work—it could break the wood in half, but you would end up with two damaged pieces of wood, neither of which would be likely to be effective.

Managing employees strategically is a lot like looking for the right tool for the job. When we think about tools, we usually think about things in a garage—a hammer, saw, or screwdriver. But a tool is anything that gets a particular job done. The different practices used to carry out the primary HR activities are managers' tools. These practices may actually be knowledge, skills, or abilities, but they are nonetheless tools that you use to accomplish organizational goals through employee management.

In Chapter 1, we defined *HR system alignment* as the design of the primary HR activities to reinforce one another to build the needed competencies, motivate the right attitudes and behaviors, and manage the allocation of work to make sure the right people are doing the right things when they need to be done. In addition to alignment among the HR practices (internal alignment), companies must also achieve external alignment—making sure the HR activities are set up to help companies confront the HR challenges of meeting organizational demands, navigating environmental influences, and complying with regulatory issues. To be an effective manager, you have to understand which HR tools, or practices, are available, how to use them, and which ones are the most appropriate in different circumstances. In short, you have to know which HR tool is right for the job. This knowledge requires an understanding of how different HR challenges affect organizations and your management options. We provide you with three axioms as a foundation for this understanding:

1. **No two companies are the same.**   Each company's strategy, characteristics, culture, and employee needs are unique. Companies may face similar environmental influences and regulatory issues, but the impact of these influences is different for each company.
2. **There is no one best way to manage employees.**   What is effective in one company may not be effective, and may even be damaging, in another company. As a manager, you need to understand how and when to use the different HR practices.
3. **Using the wrong practice, or using the right practice poorly, can cause more harm than good.**   Sometimes people may pick the wrong practice for the job because they don't know enough about the different tools at their disposal. Other times, managers may use a practice that is appropriate for a particular scenario but they may implement it poorly.

In this chapter, we have two objectives, as highlighted in Exhibit 2.1. First, we will provide an in-depth look at the types of organizational demands that exist within companies. Second, we will examine the environmental influences that exist outside companies that affect employee management. Later in the book, as you build your knowledge of HR activities, we will tie specific HR practices—such as recruitment, training, and performance management—back to these organizational demands and environmental influences.

MEETING ORGANIZATIONAL DEMANDS

Organizational demands are factors inherent within a company that influence how employees are managed. There are four key challenges associated with organizational demands:

1. **Strategy.**   Employees contribute to the achievement of strategic goals and, ultimately, company success. Differences in company strategies influence the specific competencies and behaviors that managers require of employees.
2. **Company characteristics.**   Each company has unique characteristics that affect what it asks of employees and its options for how it manages employees.
3. **Organizational culture.**   Companies have distinct cultures that influence what work is done, as well as how it is done, within companies.
4. **Employee concerns.**   Managers are most likely to be effective if they take into account the concerns of their employees.

Exhibit 2.2 depicts these challenges.

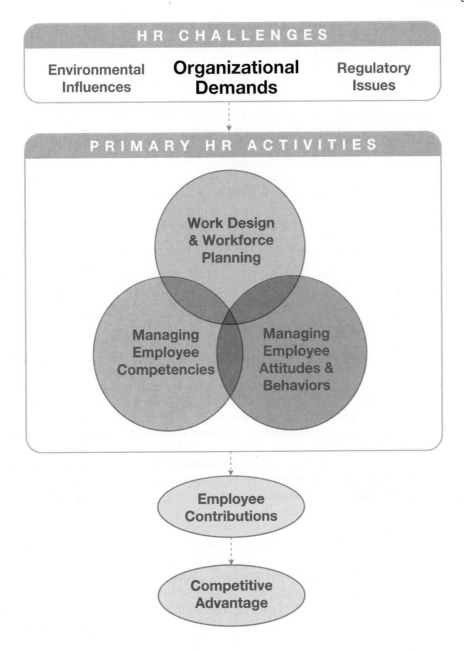

◄ Exhibit 2.1
Framework for
the Strategic
Management of
Employees

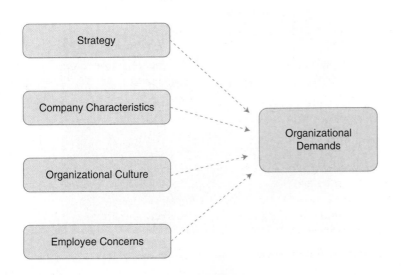

◄ Exhibit 2.2
Organizational
Demands

Strategy

A company's strategy is its plan for achieving a competitive advantage over its rivals. At a basic level, you can think about business strategy as positioning, meaning the decisions companies make about how they attract and retain customers relative to their competitors.[1] There are two broad types of strategies that companies can choose.

cost leadership strategy

A strategy that focuses on outperforming competing firms within an industry by maintaining the ability to offer the lowest costs for products or services.

A **cost leadership strategy** focuses on outperforming competing firms within an industry by maintaining the ability to offer the lowest costs for products or services.[2] For companies that concentrate on cost leadership, issues related to efficiencies and cost reductions dominate management decisions. Because costs are the underlying focus, facilities need to run smoothly and at maximum capacity, and the company must minimize overhead and extraneous costs associated with administration, service, advertising, and research. Companies with a cost leadership strategy may serve one or many different industry segments but typically focus on products that are capable of reaping the benefits of high volume or economies of scale. To be successful, however, a company must be *the* cost leader in its market because the benefits of this strategy result from consistently achieving higher profits, relative to costs, than competitors. In other words, there can be only one cost leader in an industry. While more than one company may focus on providing low costs to consumers as a potential source of competitive advantage, only one company is able to be the lowest-cost leader. For example, Wal-Mart retains its cost leadership position by maintaining the most efficient operations in the retail industry. As a result, Wal-Mart is able to offer lower prices for its products than competing firms while remaining profitable. Indeed, many smaller and midsize stores are facing financial difficulties trying to compete directly with Wal-Mart stores in their area because of the significantly lower prices at Wal-Mart.[3]

differentiation strategy

A strategy that emphasizes achieving competitive advantage over competing firms by providing something unique for which customers are willing to pay.

A **differentiation strategy** emphasizes achieving competitive advantage over competing firms by providing something unique for which customers are willing to pay.[4] Unlike with a cost leadership strategy, many companies within an industry may succeed with differentiation strategies, particularly when they each provide something unique to their customers. In fact, there are an unlimited number of potential sources of differentiation from rivals. For example, companies may focus on unique product features, location, innovation, reputation, status, customer service, or quality as a source of competitive advantage. Consider the automobile industry. There are a large number of different types of cars that claim to offer something unique. Some cars are best known for being rugged, sporty, safe, or luxurious. By focusing on attributes that different customer groups value, multiple companies can succeed within the same industry. For example, companies competing in the minivan segment target different customer groups from companies competing in the luxury automobile segment. And within each segment, different cars offer different attributes in an attempt to reach consumers. The key success factor for a differentiation strategy is providing something that competing firms do not provide that their customers value. By doing so, companies are able to either reduce the importance of price in the customer's decision-making

Wal-Mart is well known for its lower prices.

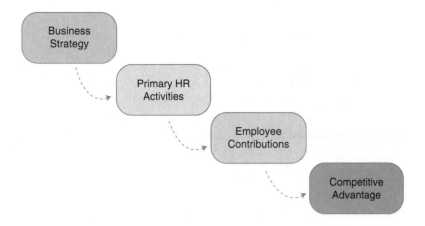

Strategy and HR
Activities

process or command a price premium for their products that exceeds the cost of providing the differentiation.

As shown in Exhibit 2.3, while strategy sets the overall objectives for a company, it also sets the parameters for the needed employee contributions or how people add value within a company. Different strategies require different employee contributions to create a competitive advantage. A company focused on low cost, for example, requires employees to be highly productive and efficient. A company with a differentiation strategy focused on innovation likely requires employees to be creative and generate many new potential products or services. As strategy influences how employees add value toward competitive advantage, it affects the types of jobs employees perform, the specific competencies employees need, and the attitudes and behaviors employees must display on the job to help reach company goals. In short, strategy affects all three of the primary HR activities.[5] Let's now look more closely at some of the basic differences in the primary HR activities for different strategies.

LOW-COST STRATEGY AND MANAGING EMPLOYEES   Given their focus on efficiencies and cost reduction, companies with a cost leadership strategy tend to design jobs in a way that maximizes predictable employee outcomes. Consider an assembly line. The jobs on an assembly line are designed to maximize employee productivity while minimizing errors and deviations from the expected output. In this type of work environment, employees are expected to perform jobs that are narrow in focus, with an emphasis on standardized and repetitive actions. When jobs are narrowly structured and well defined, the competencies employees need to perform these tasks are generally relatively simple, and the required behaviors are likely to be fairly well understood. As a result, managing employees in a cost leadership strategy often focuses on ensuring acceptable job performance by hiring individuals with the basic skills needed for these jobs, training employees to efficiently carry out their responsibilities, making sure employees clearly understand the specific expectations of their jobs, paying employees based on the jobs they perform and how efficiently they perform them, and evaluating employees based on adherence to established job expectations.

DIFFERENTIATION STRATEGY AND MANAGING EMPLOYEES   A differentiation strategy requires employees to perform jobs geared toward a particular objective, such as creativity or customer service. Employees need to possess specific skills related to the source of differentiation and need to engage in behaviors that help set the company apart from its competition. For example, a company with a differentiation strategy focused on innovation would not likely succeed if employees were required to perform narrow tasks and rigidly defined jobs. Instead, in companies such as Google and Microsoft, innovation often requires cooperation, creativity, and knowledge sharing among employees, which call for broad job responsibilities. To foster creativity, managers may recruit employees who bring new skills or new perspectives to the company. Rather than focus on efficient job performance, managers may adopt a long-term HR orientation for employee growth to help employees develop new skills that might prove valuable in the future. Similarly, pay decisions are more likely to focus on individual potential, unique experiences, team accomplishments, and long-term results than on volume and efficiency.

As you can see, by influencing the types of jobs employees perform, strategy shapes the competencies, attitudes, and behaviors required of employees. While the specific HR practices that are most appropriate vary across different strategies, effectively managing employees requires managers to align the primary HR activities with strategic objectives to maximize employee contributions. Studies have found improved organizational performance in companies with better alignment than their peers.[6]

Company Characteristics

No two companies are the same. Companies differ in size and stage of development, and these differences directly affect how firms manage employees. Company characteristics represent the second organizational demand in our framework.

COMPANY SIZE When we talk about managing employees, most of us think about working for a large company with an established reputation and clientele and a long history. Yet, did you know that the following?

- Small businesses have generated between 60% and 80% of net new jobs over the past decade.
- Small businesses hire 40% of high-tech workers (scientists, engineers, and computer workers).
- Small businesses represent over 99% of all employers.
- Small businesses employ roughly 50% of all private-sector employees.
- More than 600,000 startup businesses are created each year.[7]

The reality is that small businesses comprise a major portion of the U.S. economy. Whether a company has only a handful of employees, such as a local diner or landscape firm, or is a giant such as Microsoft or General Motors, employees have to be managed. However, the challenges of effectively managing employees differ for companies of different sizes.

Larger companies typically have more resources to hire staff dedicated to supporting the management of employees than do smaller companies, which often lack formal HR departments to provide similar support.[8] Of course, this does not eliminate the need to attend to people issues in smaller companies; rather, line managers or company owners must perform HR practices in addition to their other activities.[9] Also, smaller businesses often do not have the resources to provide the same level of pay, benefits, and training opportunities to employees as larger companies. For example, fewer than 50% of all employees in companies with fewer than 500 employees are included in pension plans or employer-paid health insurance.[10] One recent study found that some of the most pressing issues for small business owners were the availability of quality workers and the ability to provide competitive wages, benefits, and training.[11]

Although small companies often do not have the same type or level of resources enjoyed by larger companies, the importance of effectively managing employees may be magnified in smaller companies. With a smaller staff, managers may expect employees to display greater autonomy and discretion.[12] As a result, the types of knowledge, skills, and abilities that employees may need in small versus large companies, even for the same job, differ. Moreover, in contrast to large operations, in a small company, the performance of each employee is likely to have a larger, more direct impact on company success. After all, a single employee in a company of 100 employees has a greater influence on the bottom line than a single employee in a company with more than 10,000 employees. For these reasons, effective employee management is of heightened importance in smaller companies.

STAGE OF DEVELOPMENT As shown in Exhibit 2.4, companies differ in terms of their stage of development. As you might imagine, the pressures of managing employees in a young, startup company are different from those in a mature organization striving to protect its established market share and competitive position.[13] The objectives and needs of companies at different stages of development introduce new and distinct challenges for effectively managing employees.[14] While young companies tend to focus on growth and survival, mature companies may be more concerned with customer retention and perhaps extending their operations into new markets for future opportunities.[15] In addition, mature companies often have more resources and support staff, as well as established policies and procedures, for handling employee-related issues. Young companies face pressures

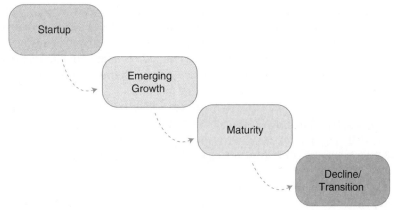

Sources: Kimberly, J. R., & Miles, R. H. *The organizational life cycle*. San Francisco: Jossey-Bass, 1980.; Quinn, J. B., & Cameron, K. Organizational life cycle and shifting criteria of effectiveness: Some preliminary evidence. *Management Science* 29:33–51, 1983; and Drazin, R., & Kazanjin, R. K. A Reanalysis of Miller and Friesen's life cycle data. *Strategic Management Journal* 11:319–325, 1990.

◄ **Exhibit 2.4**
Organizational Life Cycle

to identify and hire people who can help the company grow. Given the limited resources that small companies typically have for pay and other benefits, it is sometimes very difficult for small firms to attract top-notch employees.

As companies mature, the pressures regarding the management of employees evolve as well. Companies such as Apple and Microsoft, regarded as highly informal and entrepreneurial in their early years, have had to adopt more formalized approaches to managing their employees as they have become more established. Increased size and success often bring more bureaucracy in how things are done. Managers in more mature companies must pay particular attention to how employees do their jobs to ensure that they comply with established procedures and routines. As you can see, a company's stage of development affects company goals, the role of employees in meeting those goals, and the most appropriate way to manage employees.

Organizational Culture

Have you ever noticed how different companies seem to have unique personalities? If you have worked for several different companies, you have probably noticed that each company has its own way of doing things. Differences in how companies operate and how employees act signal what is called *organizational culture*.

As defined in Chapter 1, *organizational culture* is the set of the basic assumptions, values, and beliefs of a company's members.[16] In some ways, it is useful to think about a culture as the informal or unwritten side of organizations; these values and beliefs are not necessarily spelled out but are of great importance. In fact, the observable elements of a company's culture—how employees talk to one another, how employees interact with customers, the practices used to manage employees—represent the values that organizational members share.

There is no predetermined list of types of cultures that companies choose from. Each company has its own distinct culture. Some cultures may be more bureaucratic in nature than others, valuing rules, formalization, and hierarchy as the appropriate ways of doing business. Other cultures may be more entrepreneurial in nature than others, emphasizing creativity, knowledge exchange, and innovation. Similarly, some companies may have a culture that values competition among employees, while others may be more team oriented, valuing cooperation and support for one another. And while there is no right or wrong culture nor is there a limited set of cultures, the nature of a company's culture exerts a significant influence on how employees behave on the job.

Compare most banking and financial institutions and their traditionally white-collar bureaucratic cultures, which value formality, with high-technology companies, such as Google or Yahoo!, which value employee flexibility, autonomy, and employee growth. Company Spotlight 2.1 provides a window into the organizational culture at Google. How do you think its culture would fit in a company that values formality, procedures, and tradition?

While employees might not be able to clearly articulate the exact culture of their company, most employees understand that within their company there are certain ways of doing things, making decisions, and interacting with each other as well as with customers. Some employees may describe their company as fun; others might describe their company as being like a family; others might refer to it as a tightly run ship. All are describing some aspect of their company's culture.

It is important to acknowledge that culture is shaped by a number of factors. For example, the values and beliefs of a company's founder, as well as important decisions that the founder makes in the early stages of a company, shape subsequent values and beliefs of organizational members. The history of a company also has a strong influence. Consider Southwest Airlines. In its early years, it faced a long, drawn-out legal battle with existing airlines simply for the right to enter the industry and fly its planes. This early event significantly affected the future actions of the company and helped define an "us" versus "them" feeling that solidified the culture among its employees.[17]

Similarly, the actions of top managers and the HR practices used to manage employees send messages to employees that signal the values and behaviors that are most appropriate. What companies look for in new employees and the specific attitudes and behaviors that are rewarded provide cues to employees about what is important. In addition, supervisors, mentors, and co-workers continuously reinforce an organizational culture when socializing with employees who are new to the company. Because of the evolution of cultures and the continued reinforcement of the underlying values through history, stories, and socialization, cultures tend to be fairly rigid once established. In fact, even as people come and go, the culture tends to persist, which is why trying to change an organization's culture is so difficult.[18]

Organizational culture influences employee management in several ways. First, the culture of a company affects managerial decisions about which specific practices to use with regard to work design and workforce planning, building of competencies, and management of attitudes and behaviors. In many ways, employee management practices are mechanisms to transfer cultural values into expectations of how employees should carry out their everyday tasks and activities.[19] For example, a company with a competitive culture might be more likely to reward people for individual sales rather than for being good team members.

Second, the culture of a company also influences the effectiveness of different HR practices. The same HR practices may be acceptable or unacceptable to either employees or managers across different companies, depending on the cultural values of the organization. Even if a practice itself is a good idea, it might not necessarily fit with the underlying cultural values of a company. For example, employee participation and empowerment might be more accepted by employees, managers, or both in a company with an informal culture than in a company with a formal culture that values hierarchy and status. When HR practices are consistent with organizational culture, they are likely to be more effective.

Third, the strength of the culture further influences the effectiveness of employee management practices.[20] Strong cultures provide clear, consistent signals to employees regarding how they should behave and what is or is not acceptable. In contrast, weak cultures are ambiguous and lack a clear, coherent message.[21] When a culture is strong and consistent with organizational objectives, employees are likely to have a clear understanding of what they need to do in their jobs to contribute to company goals and a willingness to undertake the efforts to meet those goals. It is possible, however, that a strong culture might conflict with company goals. This is most likely to happen when companies make strategic changes without considering the cultural values of the company. Culture conflict may also occur in the case of mergers and acquisitions. In fact, one of the reasons mergers and acquisitions fail is lack of attention to blending cultures from different companies.[22]

Employee Concerns

Up to this point, we have focused on aspects of companies—their strategies, characteristics, and cultures. There is one additional component of organizational demands that is critical to consider for effectively managing employees—the employees themselves. After all, this book is about managing people, and without consideration of their needs and concerns, companies are unlikely to be successful in getting employees to work toward company goals.

COMPANY spotlight 2.1 Google

Ranked as The Best Company to Work For by *Fortune* in 2008, ranked eighth in America's Most Admired Companies by *Fortune* in 2007, and recipient of *Workforce's* Optimas Award for general excellence in 2003, Google places high priority on maintaining its innovative culture. At Google, formality and convention are not the corporate values. According to Dr. Eric Schmidt, chairman of the executive committee and chief executive officer, "What we really talk about is how we can attract and develop this creative culture.... Innovation comes from invention, which you cannot schedule." So how does Google do it?

To create a culture for creativity, Google hires the best and brightest employees and provides them with an environment to generate creative insights. Rather than work in traditional offices, many people work in high-density clusters with three to four people sharing spaces with couches to enable the exchange of information. And to keep employees happy and relaxed while working long hours, employees have access to a workout room with weights and rowing machine, locker rooms, washers and dryers, assorted video games, Foosball, a baby grand piano, a pool table, and Ping Pong, as well as roller hockey twice a week in the parking lot. Google also provides onsite dental care, massage, and a physician two days a week. To top it all off, breakfast, lunch, and dinner are free.

Evidently, all these efforts are making a difference. In 2007, Google received more than 760,000 applications—more than 2,000 a day! Given this pool to draw from, it's no surprise that Google has successfully hired some of the most talented engineers and Ph.D.s around the globe to help push the company's innovative ideas and has managed to keep employees happy and focused; turnover is virtually nonexistent. Susan Wojcicki, director of product management, notes, "It's about

Google's culture helps make it a very attractive place to work.

creativity, enabling people to be creative about their jobs.... It's not a culture about standardization."

Sources: 100 best companies to work for 2008. *Fortune online,* http://money.cnn.com/magazines/fortune/bestcompanies/2008/full_list/; America's most admired companies, 2007. *Fortune* online, http://money.cnn.com/magazines/fortune/mostadmired/2007/index. html.; Raphael, T. At Google, the proof is in the people. *Workforce,* March 2003, pp. 50–51; Withers, P. Retention strategies that respond to worker values. *Workforce,* July 2001, pp. 37–41; Elgin, B. Google: Why the world's hottest tech company will struggle to keep its edge. *BusinessWeek,* May 3, 2004, www.businessweek.com/magazine/content/04_18/b3881001_mz001.htm?chan=search; Google. *Life at Google.* www.google.com/jobs/balance.html; and Google. *The Google Culture.* www.google.com/corporate/culture.html.

To understand how employees view and react to different HR practices, think about how employees view their relationship with their company. In many ways, this is an exchange: Companies use pay, benefits, and training as incentives for employees to perform their jobs in exchange for the employees' commitment to the organization. There are two ways employees evaluate this exchange. First, there is a rational component: Do employees perform the work they are expected to perform, and do they receive what they are promised? Second, there is a perceptual component of this exchange. The term **psychological contract** means the *perceived* obligations that employees believe they owe their company and that their company owes them.[23]

The perceptions of these obligations are certainly influenced by the rational side of employment. But they are also based on interpretations that might not be explicitly stated. For instance, did employees receive the raise that they believe they earned? Choices managers make regarding job design,[24] pay systems,[25] job security,[26] and performance appraisal systems[27] send strong messages to employees about their company's intentions toward

psychological contract

The *perceived* obligations that employees believe they owe their company and that their company owes them.

them. Employees' perceptions of these signals influence the extent to which they feel a need to reciprocate through certain attitudes and behaviors. When employees perceive that their company values them, they often feel obligated to provide the organization with something of equal or greater value in return.[28] This favorable perception leads to greater loyalty, commitment, and effort among employees toward the company.

The importance of a psychological contract is that it governs how employees evaluate company decisions regarding how they are managed, and, as a result, it governs how they act on the job. When we view the management of employees from the employees' perspective, two concerns emerge. First, employees expect that their company will help them balance work and life obligations. Second, employees constantly evaluate the extent to which their company holds up its end of the bargain and fulfills what they believe the company owes them for their hard work and dedication. A leading aspect of this assessment is whether an employee thinks the company behaves in a fair and just manner.

work/life balance

The balance between the demands of work and the demands of employees' personal lives.

WORK/LIFE BALANCE   As noted in Chapter 1, an issue that is gaining increased attention from many companies is a need to help employees with **work/life balance**—the balance between the demands of work and the demands of employees' personal lives. Consider that 60% of mothers in the U.S. workforce today have children under the age of three, compared to fewer than 35% in the 1970s.[29] Moreover, approximately 57% of households today are dual-career households.[30] But work/life balance isn't about only caring for children. The U.S. population is getting older and, as a result, many employees today need to care for their elders. Many are caring for both older family members and children. Some are working as single parents; others as part of dual-career couples. Yet another work/life issue for some employees is dealing with traffic or long commutes.

In response to these issues, many progressive companies are taking steps to help employees achieve work/life balance by providing them with more flexibility to attend to their personal or family needs. One increasingly common approach is to provide employees with flexible schedules. According to the U.S. Bureau of Labor Statistics, in 2004 about 27 million full-time employees had flexible work schedules that allowed them to vary the time they began or ended the workday.[31] Beyond flexible scheduling, some companies help parents meet their child-care demands. For example, Abbott Laboratories built a $10 million state-of-the-art child-care center for its employees, and Procter & Gamble operates an onsite center around the clock to accommodate night-shift workers who can't leave their children at home alone.[32] Rather than build its own center, Texas Instruments invested its money in improving the quality of existing centers and worked with local community colleges to help with the chronic shortage of day-care workers.[33] Other companies have turned toward family-friendly benefits and telecommuting to increase the ability of their employees to balance their work and personal lives.

distributive justice

The fairness of what individuals receive from companies in return for their efforts.

While establishing work/life balance programs clearly involves considerable costs and effort, companies are finding that family-friendly practices help current employees remain effective contributors toward company goals and also provide an additional point of attraction for many potential job applicants. At companies such as Goldman Sachs, Macy's, and Towers Perrin, work/life benefits serve as a recruitment tool to attract and retain female and minority employees who might be unable to work if they didn't have the flexibility to balance work and family needs.[34]

Onsite day-care facilities are one way to help employees achieve work/life balance.

JUSTICE   Whereas work/life balance programs strive to meet the personal needs of employees, issues of justice focus primarily on the expectations of employees about how they should be treated while at work. Understandably, employees expect to be treated fairly. The challenge is that, unlike with legal issues that also govern how companies manage employees, there are no clear-cut standards regarding fairness. Fairness is in the eye of the beholder—what is fair for one person may not be perceived as fair by another. Managers and employees may disagree regarding the extent to which the company has met its obligations to the employee.[35] But even while individuals differ in how they view fairness, there are three primary aspects of their relationship with their companies that employees tend to monitor: distributive, procedural, and interactional justice.

Distributive justice is the fairness of what individuals receive from companies in return for their efforts.[36] Ideally, this is a balanced exchange, with employees receiving compensation or

Procedural fairness has been shown to be related to six criteria:

1. **Consistency.**   Managers should ensure that allocative procedures are consistent across people and over time.

2. **Bias suppression.**   Managers need to prevent personal self-interest and blind allegiance to narrow preconceptions.

3. **Accuracy.**   Decisions must be based on good information and informed opinion.

4. **Correctability.**   Managers must be open to opportunities to modify or reverse decisions based on inaccurate information.

5. **Representativeness.**   The allocation process must represent the concerns of all important subgroups and individuals.

6. **Ethicality.**   The allocation process must be compatible with prevailing moral and ethical standards.

Source: Rousseau, D. M. *Psychological contracts in organizations: Understanding written and unwritten agreements.* Thousand Oaks, CA: Sage Publications, 1995, p. 128.

other benefits that they view as being of equal value for the time and effort that they put into their jobs. **Procedural justice** focuses on whether the processes that are used to make decisions, allocate rewards, or resolve disputes or that otherwise affect employees are viewed as fair.[37] As shown in Exhibit 2.5, a number of factors influence employee perceptions about whether the procedures used are fair. For example, employees are more likely to accept evaluations or decisions regarding their pay raises when they believe that the methods used to make those decisions are consistently applied to all employees and are based on valid or accurate data.

Interactional justice represents how employees feel they are treated by their managers and supervisors in everyday interactions. Do managers treat employees politely and respectfully? The underlying principle of interactional justice is that *how* managers treat their employees is something that is as important to employees as the actual decisions regarding their treatment.

Perceptions of justice are particularly noteworthy because they influence the extent to which an employee believes that the company has met its obligations within the psychological contract.[38] When employees perceive that their company has not met its obligations, they are likely to display lower trust and commitment toward the company and are more likely to leave the company.[39] According to Denise Rousseau, a leading expert on psychological contracts, employees may engage in several actions in response to perceived violations of psychological contracts:

- **Voice.**   Actions an employee might take to correct a situation that he or she views as unfair
- **Silence.**   A form of non-response and a willingness to live with the circumstances, even if they are viewed as unfair
- **Neglect.**   Failure to completely fulfill one's duties
- **Exit.**   Departure from the company
- **Destruction.**   Counterproductive behaviors that damage the company, such as vandalism, theft, and aggression[40]

A number of factors influence the specific course of action that an employee chooses. For example, the history of the relationship between the employee and the company as well as the degree of trust that an employee has toward the company may encourage the employee to exercise his or her voice before exiting or acting destructively. The presence of other job alternatives for an employee may encourage the person to leave sooner rather than later in response to unfair treatment. The presence of a formal grievance procedure may encourage an employee to try to remedy the situation before choosing another action.

procedural justice

Perceptions of whether the processes that are used to make decisions, allocate rewards, or resolve disputes or that otherwise affect employees are viewed as fair.

interactional justice

How employees feel they are treated by their managers and supervisors in everyday interactions.

It is important for managers to maintain open lines of communication with employees to monitor their attitudes about justice in their jobs. In larger companies, this is often difficult to do on an informal level. Many companies now conduct attitude surveys of their employees on a regular basis to monitor their overall perceptions. This provides useful information to management, and it also reassures employees that the company cares about their views and opinions. In addition, some companies perform exit interviews with employees who have voluntarily terminated their employment to better understand why they are leaving and what changes might improve the environment for current employees.[41]

ENVIRONMENTAL INFLUENCES

Whereas organizational demands are factors that exist within the boundaries of a company, environmental influences are pressures that exist outside a company. And while there are certainly many different influences, our framework focuses on four, as shown in Exhibit 2.6: labor force trends, technology, globalization, and ethical and social obligations.

Labor Force Trends

The labor force means the individuals who are available for work. According to the U.S. Bureau of Labor Statistics, the future labor force will be markedly different from the labor force of the past. Companies will have to consider several notable trends in the labor force in the coming years. Specifically, the composition of the workforce is becoming older and more diverse.[42]

THE AGING WORKFORCE   The years immediately following World War II, namely 1946 to 1964, witnessed a boom in births in the United States compared to other years. In the year 2014, this group of people, often called "the baby boomers," will be over 50 years old. Companies are now realizing the need to start planning for the graying of the workforce. As shown in Exhibit 2.7, the percentage of individuals in the 55-and-older age group is expected to grow five times as fast as the rest of the workforce, and the percentage of people in the 65-and-older age group is expected to increase more than 10 times as fast as the total labor force.[43] In contrast, the growth rate of individuals in younger age groups is markedly smaller and is expected to decrease by 7% by 2016.[44] The aging of the labor force is not limited to the United States. In fact, the United States ranked 32nd on a list of countries with high proportions of people age 65 and older. Italy ranked the highest, with 18.1% of its population 65 or older, followed by Greece, Sweden, Japan, and Spain.[45]

An aging workforce brings with it a number of challenges and opportunities for companies. For example, there are likely to be increased challenges with workforce planning. As the baby boomers approach retirement, companies are facing a situation in which a considerable number of their employees may leave the workforce. With the slower growth of younger workers to replace them, many companies are increasingly competing for a limited supply of workers to replace individuals who retire. Some companies have already started

Exhibit 2.6 ▶

Environmental
Influences

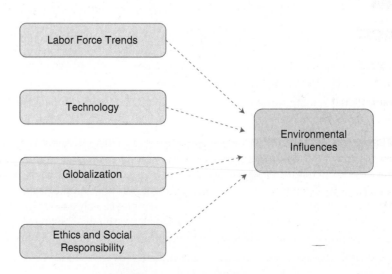

**Percent of labor force by age group, 2006
and projected 2016**

Percent of labor force

Source: U.S. Department of Labor, Bureau of Labor Statistics. *Tomorrow's jobs. Occupation Outlook Handbook*, December 18, 2007, www.bls.gov/oco/oco2003.htm.

capitalizing on the aging workforce by explicitly recruiting and retaining older individuals beyond their retirement years. As highlighted in Company Spotlight 2.2, Baptist Health South Florida has taken a number of innovative steps to help older employees remain in the workforce. Similarly, in 2008, the AARP (formerly the American Association of Retired Persons) announced that it had established relations with companies such as Scripps

COMPANY spotlight   2.2 Baptist Health South Florida

Faced with severe labor shortages, companies in the health care industry are struggling to identify workers to meet their needs. Baptist Health South Florida, a health care provider with 10,000 employees, has taken a nontraditional approach to this pending crisis: It keeps its current employees well into their older years.

Baptist has taken steps to make it more attractive for workers to remain in the workforce. For example, it has worked with new pension laws to allow employees who want to tap into their retirement savings to do so while working reduced hours. Baptist also uses a bridgement-of-service policy that allows workers who leave the company and return within 5 years to resume their seniority and benefits. And any employee with 15 or more years of service cannot be demoted, fired, or be given a pay cut without a review by a

three-person committee that includes Baptist's president. Beyond making jobs attractive, Baptist is also striving to make jobs more feasible for older workers. Two of Baptist's recruiters spend roughly one-fourth of their time helping older workers find jobs within the company that are less physically demanding. Baptist recently installed spring lifts in its laundry containers to make it easier for housekeepers to bend down to pick up their loads. In addition, Baptist has a pilot project with "minimal lift" equipment to help nurses move heavier patients. With a good percentage of Baptist's employees over age 50, and the number to climb in the coming years, it seems Baptist is well positioned to cope with the looming labor shortage.

Source: Mullich, J. New ideas draw older workers. *Workforce*, March 2004, pp. 44–46.

Health, Bright Horizons Family Solutions, Home Instead Senior Care, and Synergy, as well as the Internal Revenue Service and the Peace Corps, that are looking to hire people over 50. As noted by Deborah Russell, director of workforce issues for AARP in Washington, "They recognize the fact that mature workers bring good experience and skills to the workplace."[46] Of course, with an older workforce, companies may face other HR management issues as well, such as the increasing costs of health care and other benefits and the need to retrain older workers to ensure that their skills are compatible with company needs.

DEMOGRAPHIC DIVERSITY   In addition to the population aging, certain demographic groups are expected to grow more rapidly than others. For example, the number of women in the labor force is expected to grow by 9% between the years 2006 and 2016.[47] Women are expected to make up 47% of the U.S. labor force in 2016. This stands in contrast to the 1950s, when the share of the workforce for women was less than 40%.

Similarly, while white, non-Hispanics are projected to remain the largest group, the fastest-growing groups in the labor force are Hispanics and Asians.[48] Between 1990 and 2000, the foreign-born population in the United States increased by 57%, with 52% of the foreign-born population from Latin America, 26% from Asia, and 16% from Europe. As shown in Exhibit 2.8, Los Angeles and Miami are two examples of cities whose populations are composed of more than 40% foreign-born citizens.[49]

Trends in migration, coupled with differences in birth rates across demographic groups, will continue to shape the racial composition of the workforce. The *Bureau of Labor Statistics* projects that by 2015, the U.S. labor force will include 21 million black, 11 million Asian, and 24 million Hispanic individuals. It also indicates that by the year 2050, Hispanics will make up 24% of the U.S. labor force, blacks 14%, and Asians 11%.[50]

These changing labor force demographics have implications for managing employees. For example, how companies manage the diversity in their workforce affects their ability to attract future employees as well as their overall reputation. Companies must take steps to manage diversity to help employees learn the value that different backgrounds and perspectives offer in terms of organizational performance. By directly addressing diversity issues, companies are more likely to be in a position to capitalize on the benefits associated with a diverse workforce.[51]

The growing presence of a diverse workforce also requires that managers continue to pay attention to issues of discrimination and eliminate any potential biases that might harm one or several demographic groups. As we will discuss in Chapter 3, an array of federal, state, and local regulations, as well as presidential executive orders, govern the decisions that

Exhibit 2.8 ▶

U.S. Cities with 100,000 or More Foreign-Born Population

	Total Population	Foreign-Born Population	Percent of Total Population
Miami, FL	362,470	215,739	59.5%
Los Angeles, CA	3,694,820	1,512,720	40.9%
San Francisco, CA	776,733	285,541	36.8%
San Jose, CA	894,943	329,757	36.8%
New York, NY	8,008,2787	2,871,032	35.9%
Houston, TX	1,953,631	516,105	26.4%
San Diego, CA	1,223,400	314,227	24.4%
Chicago, IL	2,896,016	628,903	21.7%
Phoenix, AZ	1,321,045	257,325	19.5%
San Antonio, TX	1,114,646	133,675	11.7%
Philadelphia, PA	1,517,550	137,205	9.0%

Source: Bergman, M. Foreign-born a majority in six U.S. cities; Growth fastest in south, Census Bureau reports. *U.S. Census Bureau News*, December 17, 2003, www.census.gov/Press-Release/www/releases/archives/census_2000/001623.html.

companies make regarding the management of employees, especially to ensure that practices are not discriminatory.

Technology

Technology continues to shape the nature of competition and how companies conduct business. There was a time when customers actually had to go to a store and talk with a salesperson to purchase a product. Today, many people do much of their shopping online. Companies such as eBay and Amazon.com are convenient, online sources for virtually any product imaginable. And most companies now have their own sophisticated Web sites that allow a customer to shop from the convenience of his or her home or office. Since the mid-1990s, the Internet has changed how businesses function.

The prominence of the Internet and information technologies also has considerable implications for how employees function within companies. An increased reliance on the Internet as a medium for meeting customer needs influences the types of competencies that employees must possess. In today's environment, most employees need a certain level of computer proficiency, as many people work with a computer at some point during the workday. Even manufacturing jobs, traditionally viewed as manual labor, are becoming more high tech, with advances in computer-aided procedures and robotics.

In many companies, information technologies have also created new avenues for how employees interact, share information, and learn from one another.[52] For example, it is possible to have group meetings online or through videoconferences that do not require employees to physically meet in a central location. Indeed, advances in information technologies have expanded how we think about work. Not long ago, employees had to live within a reasonable distance of a company. In today's digital environment, many employees can **telecommute**—work away from the traditional office setting. With high-speed Internet access, videoconferencing, and e-mail, it is conceivable that employees can live anywhere in the world.[53] And because employees can work from home or from a satellite location, they do not have to waste time commuting to and from a particular location. By providing employees with more flexibility in terms of when and where they work, telecommuting helps employees manage the work/life balance.

telecommute

Work away from the traditional office setting with the use of technology.

As technology enables employees to work anywhere, it also expands the pool of potential employees for companies. Individuals who require flexibility to stay at home and care for children or aging parents might not be able to commit to a traditional 9-to-5 workday with a commute. With the option to work offsite and with flexible hours, this portion of the labor force becomes accessible to some companies. In addition, it is conceivable that companies may expand their workforces to include people around the globe without having to establish formal offices.[54]

Of course, there are downsides to telecommuting. Indeed, one recent study found that with an increase in telecommuting, non-telecommuting co-workers had fewer emotional ties to their co-workers, felt less obligated to the organization, and found the workplace less enjoyable. One explanation for this reaction is that non-telecommuters are faced with greater workload and less flexibility as they have fewer co-workers available to share work.[55] Another study indicated that up to 75% of non-telecommuting employees have concerns about their telecommuting colleagues.[56] Nevertheless, advances in technology have thrust telecommuting into the daily language of companies, and employers and employees alike are exploring whether it is a good option for their circumstances.

Globalization

Many companies are actively competing on an international level through exporting products and services, sending work to foreign companies, setting up production or service facilities in other countries, or establishing international joint ventures and partnerships with foreign firms. Even when companies focus primarily on their domestic market, they are increasingly finding themselves competing with international companies for a share of that market.

The push toward globalization is further influenced by the trade agreements among countries. The North American Free Trade Agreement (NAFTA) is a pact among Canada, the United States, and Mexico that calls for the gradual removal of tariffs and other trade barriers on most goods produced and sold in North America. Since its implementation on January 1, 1994, NAFTA has had a considerable impact on business in North America. For example, total trade among NAFTA partners increased from $302 billion to $652 billion from 1993 to 2003.[57]

Similarly, the European Union (EU), a union of 27 independent states based on the European Communities, was founded to enhance political, economic, and social cooperation. Formerly known as European Community (EC) or European Economic Community (EEC), a major goal of the EU is to establish a single market unifying the EU members through defining common commercial policy, reducing economic differences among its richer and poorer members, and stabilizing the currencies of its members.[58] The Asia Pacific Economic Cooperation (APEC), with membership from 21 countries, has worked to reduce tariffs and other trade barriers throughout the Asia-Pacific region.

These agreements are serving as catalysts for globalization. The growth in globalization has implications for how companies compete, where they establish operations, and the location of their labor force. It also brings new challenges for managing employees.

INTERNATIONAL STRATEGIES While globalization exerts a considerable impact on just about every industry, companies differ in the extent to which they compete on a global level. Bartlett and Ghoshal, leading experts on international strategy, provide a useful framework that views international strategies in terms of their focus on local responsiveness and global efficiency.[59]

A **domestic strategy** focuses primarily on serving the market within a particular country. In contrast, when firms follow an **international strategy**, they expand the markets in which they compete to include multiple countries. An international strategy is an extension of a domestic strategy that focuses on penetrating markets in other countries through exports or moving some operations into other countries. When following a **multinational strategy**, companies take an international strategy a step further and establish autonomous or independent business units in multiple countries. One of the major objectives of a multinational strategy is that it provides business units in other countries with the authority to meet the unique local needs of their country (local responsiveness).[60]

While a multinational strategy strives to be responsive to local preferences, a **global strategy** strives to achieve global efficiency. When following a global strategy, companies are not aligned with a particular country, nor do they target the unique tastes and preferences of individual countries. Rather, a global strategy focuses on aligning business units across countries to realize gains in efficiency and scope. It does this by focusing on standardizing products that are valued across multiple markets. Finally, companies that follow a **transnational strategy** strive to achieve the benefits of both a global strategy and a multinational strategy. This is done through a combination of extensive efforts to foster a shared vision and coordination across business units while maintaining a commitment to provide each unit with the ability to tailor products to meet the needs of the local country. For example, automobile manufacturers such as Ford try to increase efficiencies in the production process through plants across the globe while enabling variation in the specific attributes of the cars that are sold in different markets.

The importance of international strategies has gained increased attention recently with greater reliance on offshoring by U.S. companies. **Offshoring** is the practice of sending work that was once performed domestically to companies in other countries or opening facilities in other countries to do the work, often at a substantially lower cost.[61] Companies such as AOL, Dell, and General Motors have turned to other countries such as China and India as sources of labor to supplement their full-time employees in the United States. The prevalence of offshoring and the supporting benefits associated with access to skilled labor for lower costs influence how investors view a company. Some venture capitalists now expect a company to have an offshoring strategy before they will fund new business ventures for the company. Of course, offshoring has limitations, which we will discuss throughout the chapters.

GLOBAL FACTORS The success of different international strategies depends, in large part, on the management of employees. As companies become more global in focus, they have to make important decisions regarding the locations of their international operations. These decisions are certainly affected by factors such as proximity to the target market and access to resources, but it is also critical to consider how differences across countries influence

---

domestic strategy

A strategy that focuses primarily on serving the market within a particular country.

international strategy

A strategy used by companies to expand the markets in which they compete to include multiple countries.

multinational strategy

A strategy used when companies establish autonomous or independent business units in multiple countries.

global strategy

A strategy whereby a company strives to achieve global efficiency.

transnational strategy

A strategy whereby a company strives to achieve the benefits of both a global strategy and a multinational strategy.

offshoring

The practice of sending work that was once performed domestically to companies in other countries or opening facilities in other countries to do the work.

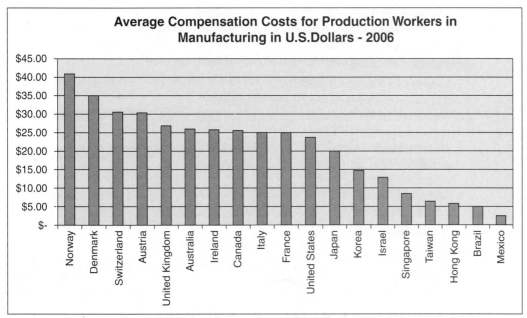

◄ Exhibit 2.9

Average
Compensation
Costs for
Production
Workers in
Manufacturing,
in U.S. Dollars,
2006

Source: U.S. Department of Labor, Bureau of Labor Statistics, *International comparisons of hourly compensation costs in manufacturing, 2006*, www.bls.gov/news.release/ichcc.nr0.htm.

the management of human resources and the effectiveness of different HR practices. There are two major factors that are particularly important in an international context: economic considerations and cultural differences.

Economic Considerations.   We noted earlier that labor costs are a vital factor when companies consider alternative locations for international facilities. As you might imagine, average wages for employees, even for performing the same types of jobs, vary dramatically across countries. For example, Exhibit 2.9 shows that the average wages in manufacturing jobs for countries such as Mexico, Brazil, Taiwan, and Hong Kong are less than 25% of the wages for the same jobs in higher-wage countries such as Norway, Denmark, Switzerland, and Austria.

In addition to labor costs, an important consideration is the availability of qualified labor. Countries differ in the types of skills that their workforces have as well as the level or supply of workers with those skills. For example, during the late 1990s, many of the dot-com companies faced a severe labor shortage in the United States for people with the appropriate computer skills. As a result, some companies were forced to pay high wages and provide excessive benefits to lure employees from competing firms. Other companies looked to the global labor market to fill positions with individuals from other countries as a solution.

A country's unemployment level influences the availability of skills and workers. Higher levels of unemployment create a larger supply of workers with certain skills. In contrast, lower levels of unemployment force companies to work much harder to identify and hire qualified employees. Relatively high unemployment in countries such as India and Ireland make them attractive locations for companies looking to expand internationally because they provide a relatively high number of skilled, available workers.

When considering establishing operations in foreign countries, countries with low levels of skills or facing a shortage of workers with certain skills are less attractive locations for international operations, while countries with high levels of skilled workers are more attractive. For example, countries such as Mexico, Brazil, and Taiwan have a large supply of workers with desired skills who command relatively low wages compared to U.S. companies. This is one reason many companies have established *maquiladoras* (U.S.-owned manufacturing plants located in Mexico): They provide labor for much lower costs than in the United States. Other countries are more attractive for companies that need higher-skilled workers. One reason that companies increasingly offshore facets of their operations to India is the availability of relatively highly skilled workers who command lower labor costs.

Cultural Differences.   In addition to differences in skill levels and economic conditions, companies must also consider cultural differences when managing employees internationally. Geert Hofstede, a leading scholar on cross-cultural differences, identified five major cultural dimensions on which cultures tend to differ:[62]

1. **Individualism–collectivism.** The degree to which people in a country prefer to act as individuals rather than as members of groups

2. **Power distance.** The degree of inequality among people that a population of a country considers normal

3. **Uncertainty avoidance.** The degree to which people in a country prefer structured situations with clear rules about how one should behave over unstructured situations that are more ambiguous

4. **Masculinity–femininity.** The degree to which a society stresses values that have traditionally been viewed as masculine (assertiveness, performance, success, and competition) over values that have traditionally been viewed as feminine (quality of life, personal relationships, service, care for the weak, and solidarity)

5. **Long-term versus short-term orientation.** The degree to which the population of a country focuses on future-oriented values such as saving and persistence versus more short-term values such as respect for the past, tradition, and fulfilling social obligations

IMPLICATIONS OF GLOBAL FACTORS ON MANAGING EMPLOYEES In addition to assessments of locations for international operations, globalization also creates unique challenges for managing employees on international assignments. First, cultural differences affect what HR practices and management decisions employees deem acceptable. For example, employees in a *collectivistic* culture may be less receptive to placing a strong emphasis on individual performance in reward systems and performance management systems than those in a more *individualistic* culture. Similarly, individuals from a *high power distance* culture may accept a work environment that emphasizes multiple layers of hierarchy and strong status distinctions between managers and employees more easily than those from a *low power distance* culture.

Second, cultural differences also influence which HR activities managers and supervisors view as appropriate for how they manage employees. Asking managers in a *high power distance* culture to encourage employee participation and decision making might be viewed as contrary to their strong values for maintaining status differences. Similarly, companies might encounter resistance when asking managers to reward individual achievement in *collectivistic* cultures that value the community more than the individual.

The importance of effectively managing international assignments cannot be emphasized enough. Companies that fail to develop international work experience among their managers may not be able to achieve their long-term strategic goals in a global context. Lack of international management experience may be a factor in less-favorable productivity of operations located in foreign countries and in lost opportunities for creating or penetrating markets. It may also cause difficulties building and maintaining relationships with stakeholders in the country in which the operations are located.[63] Not surprisingly, international work experience is often one of the major requirements for promotion to higher-level managerial positions.[64] CEOs with more international experience are often more highly recruited than those who lack that experience.[65]

Ethics and Social Responsibility

Organizations are increasingly expected to cope with HR challenges in an ethical way, which leads to the fourth environmental challenge in our framework: ethics and social responsibility. Ethics and social responsibility have always been important to companies. Questions of child-labor abuse in sweatshops received considerable attention for years in the retail industry. More recently, public awareness regarding financially unethical behavior in companies has gained prominence as a result of the widely publicized problems at Enron and Tyco. In 2006, several top managers at Hewlett-Packard, including the chief ethics officer, were accused of using spyware, seeking phone records, physical surveillance, and photography to identify a member of the board believed to be discussing information about confidential company operations with a reporter.[66]

But what exactly is ethical behavior? How much responsibility do companies have toward the environment? Toward other countries? Toward minority groups? According to *Business Ethics* magazine, it is useful for companies and managers to think about ethical behavior with regard to eight stakeholder groups:[67]

1. Shareholders
2. Community
3. Governance
4. Diversity
5. Employees
6. Environment
7. Human Rights
8. Product

Each of these stakeholder groups is affected by the actions of companies, and each has a vested interest in evaluating how companies are performing to meet their needs. How ethically companies behave toward these groups has several implications for company success. Would you shop at a company that offered a great product for a low price? What if that company was able to achieve exceptionally low costs by using child labor in another country? What if that company achieved its low costs by dumping chemical waste in a local stream?

Ethical actions and socially responsible behavior can help foster a positive reputation that spurs additional consumer support. Procter & Gamble, Avon, Intel, Starbucks Coffee, Motorola, and Nike are a few companies that have had the honor of being identified as some of the 100 best corporate citizens by *Business Ethics* magazine.[68] Though it happened about 25 years ago, perhaps the most famous example of corporate ethical behavior is by Johnson & Johnson. In 1982, Johnson & Johnson received tremendous public praise when it pulled more than 31 million bottles of Tylenol off store shelves when it was discovered that someone had tampered with several bottles and replaced the Tylenol with cyanide pills. This was no small task, and it resulted in an immediate loss of over $100 million. After its handling of this incident, however, Johnson & Johnson benefited from increased consumer confidence that the company truly places its customers first. It is not just reputation that is affected. Research shows that companies rated among the 100 best corporate citizens financially outperform their business counterparts.[69]

COMPANY spotlight   2.3 Company Spotlight: Gap Inc.

When you shop at the Gap, Old Navy, or Banana Republic, you probably don't spend too much time thinking about a retail store as being socially responsible. But the reality is that as one of the leading apparel retailers in the world, and having contracts with factories in about 50 countries, Gap Inc. is well aware of the potential problems and the potential for abuse of workers in the garment industry. In an effort to help improve working conditions, Gap Inc. has more than 90 employees whose sole job is to conduct visits to factories around the world to monitor the treatment of workers. In 2003, they made over 8,000 visits to 3,000 factories. And these visits are actually effective: More than 130 approvals for factories were revoked because of compliance issues related to their Code of Vendor Conduct. Gap Inc. was granted membership in the U.K.-based Ethical Trading Initiative (ETI). ETI works to identify and promote good practice in the implementation of corporate codes governing supply-chain labor conditions, primarily in the food and clothing sectors. In 2006, Gap Inc. ceased business with 23 factories due to code violations. These efforts culminated in a ranking by *Business Ethics* as one of the top 100 corporate citizens.

Unfortunately, later in 2007, reports surfaced regarding the unethical behavior of one of the subcontractors for the Gap. The subcontractor was accused of using child labor in India under inhumane conditions. As noted by Gap President Marka Hansen, "It's deeply, deeply disturbing to all of us." The subcontractor was fired, and the Gap did not sell the clothes made in the sweatshop. Despite the prompt response and commitment by the Gap to maintain ethical standards, this case reminds us that being ethical around the globe requires consistent monitoring of all facets of operations. If can happen to a company with a long tradition of ethical standards, it can happen in any other company.

Sources: The Gap Web site, www. gapinc. com; Survey: Sweating for fashion. *The Economist*, March 6, 2004, p. 14; 100 best corporate citizens 2007. *Business Ethics*. www.business-ethics.com/files/100Best-CorporateCitizens_2007.pdf; Gap: Report of kids' sweatshop "deeply disturbing." *CNN.com*, October 29, 2007. http://edition.cnn.com/2007/WORLD/asiapcf/10/29/gap.labor/; and McDougall, D. Child sweatshop shame threatens Gap's ethical image. *The Observer*, October 28, 2007, www.guardian.co.uk/business/2007/oct/28/ethicalbusiness. india.

Given the importance of ethics, how can you encourage your company to act ethically? Perhaps the best place to start is by recognizing that ethical decisions are made by people. Employee behavior, from the entry-level new hire up to the CEO of a corporation, defines the ethical nature of companies. After all, companies don't behave, the people within them do. Unfortunately, a 2003 business ethics survey administered by the Society for Human Resources Management found that over half of the respondents indicated that they felt pressure to act unethically in their jobs.[70] The top five causes of this pressure, according to the survey, are shown in Exhibit 2.10. When asked what types of unethical behavior were most prevalent, the respondents reported misrepresenting hours of work; lying to supervisors; management lying to employees, customers, vendors, or the public; misusing the organization's assets; and lying on reports or falsifying records.[71]

Considering that a company's ethical behavior rests on employee decisions and actions, it is important that employees understand how to act ethically. There are several steps that companies can take to encourage ethical behavior in employees:

- Appoint an "ethics officer"
- Constantly monitor the aspects of the company's culture that concern its value system, including ethics
- Provide ethics training
- Perform background checks on incoming employees
- Devote time at regular staff meetings to talking about responsibilities[72]

Once accused of abusing child labor around the globe, today Nike has about 80 corporate responsibility and compliance managers working with locations around the world who focus solely on ensuring that their vendors and suppliers comply with the Nike code of conduct.[73] (See Nike's code of conduct in Exhibit 2.11.) Similarly, as described in Company Spotlight 2.3, Gap Inc. employs 90 people whose job is to ensure that the company's foreign labor has satisfactory working conditions. The Society for Human Resource Management 2003 ethics survey also indicated that 79% of U.S. companies have written codes of ethics.[74] Beyond asking employees to behave ethically, some companies take steps to *show* employees how to behave ethically. For instance, Lockheed Martin requires all employees to attend ethics training each year,[75] and MCI has implemented a full-scale ethics program.

Financial performance has long been a measurement tool for company success. However, the ethics and social responsibility that companies display are increasingly playing

Exhibit 2.10 ▶

Pressure Points for
Unethical Behavior

Following the boss's directives (49%)

Meeting overly aggressive business/financial objectives (48%)

Helping the organization to survive (40%)

Meeting scheduling pressures (35%)

Wanting to be a team player (27%)

Sources: How to help reinvigorate your organization's ethics program. *HR Focus*, June 2003, p. 80; and Schramm, J. A return to ethics? *HRMagazine*, 48:144, July 2003.

▶ Exhibit 2.11   Nike Code of Conduct

---

1. **Forced Labor.**   The contractor does not use forced labor in any form—prison, indentured, bonded or otherwise.

2. **Child Labor.**   The contractor does not employ any person below the age of 18 to produce footwear. The contractor does not employ any person below the age of 16 to produce apparel, accessories or equipment. If at the time Nike production begins, the contractor employs people of the legal working age who are at least 15, that employment may continue, but the contractor will not hire any person going forward who is younger than the Nike or legal age limit, whichever is higher. To further ensure these age standards are complied with, the contractor does not use any form of homework for Nike production.

3. **Compensation.**   The contractor provides each employee at least the minimum wage, or the prevailing industry wage, whichever is higher; provides each employee a clear, written accounting for every pay period; and does not deduct from employee pay for disciplinary infractions.

4. **Benefits.**   The contractor provides each employee all legally mandated benefits.

5. **Hours of Work/Overtime.**   The contractor complies with legally mandated work hours; uses overtime only when each employee is fully compensated according to local law; informs each employee at the time of hiring if mandatory overtime is a condition of employment; and on a regularly scheduled basis provides one day off in seven, and requires no more than 60 hours of work per week on a regularly scheduled basis, or complies with local limits if they are lower.

6. **Environment, Safety and Health (ES&H).**   From suppliers to factories to distributors and to retailers, Nike considers every member of our supply chain as partners in our business. As such, we've worked with our Asian partners to achieve specific environmental, health and safety goals, beginning with a program called MESH (Management of Environment, Safety and Health).

7. **Documentation and Inspection.**   The contractor maintains on file all documentation needed to demonstrate compliance with this Code of Conduct and required laws; agrees to make these documents available for Nike or its designated monitor; and agrees to submit to inspections with or without prior notice.

Source: Nike. *2007 Nike, Inc. Code of conduct*, http://nikeresponsibility.com/tools/Nike_Code_of_Conduct.pdf.

---

a role in how people evaluate organizations. Companies need to not only set ethical standards for employees but also take steps to show employees how to carry out ethical actions in their jobs. After all, if employees don't adhere to ethical standards, social responsibility and ethics may become simply an exercise in public relations.[76]

SUMMARY

To be an effective manager, you have to understand which HR practices are available. But it is equally important to understand which HR practices are most appropriate for different circumstances. In short, you have to understand how employees add value and how the HR challenges affect your options for managing employees. In this chapter, we have explored the organizational demands that exist within companies as well as the environmental influences that exist outside companies that impact how to manage employees.

Organizational demands are factors within the boundaries of a company that impact what you need to do to manage employees. One of the key challenges facing managers is to understand how employees contribute to realizing strategic priorities and, ultimately, company success. Different strategies require employees to perform in different ways, and employees in different companies add value in unique ways. Moreover,

each company is unique in how it is set up to carry out its operations. Companies vary in terms of size, stage of development, and transformation process. These differences affect what resources are available to manage employees as well as the types of tasks and responsibilities employees are expected to perform. Beyond strategy and company characteristics, each company also has a unique culture that influences how employees interact with each other and with customers based on differences in values and beliefs. Finally, managers are not likely to be very effective if they do not take into account the concerns of the individuals they are managing—their employees.

While organizational demands focus on factors that exist within the boundaries of a company, environmental influences are pressures that exist outside companies. Changes in the labor force are occurring, and the workforce is becoming older and more demographically diverse.

Technological advances have provided companies with new options for when and where employees work as well as how employees are managed and controlled. Globalization continues to introduce new challenges regarding where companies establish facilities as well as how to manage cultural differences. In addition, companies are increasingly being expected to cope with these challenges and opportunities in an ethical way.

Successful companies are able to navigate these HR challenges by understanding how to use the primary HR activities to cope with the challenges and take advantage of the opportunities that the changing competitive landscape presents.

KEY TERMS

cost leadership strategy *p. 29*

differentiation strategy *p. 30*

distributive justice *p. 36*

domestic strategy *p. 42*

global strategy *p. 42*

interactional justice *p. 37*

international strategy *p. 42*

multinational strategy *p. 42*

offshoring *p. 42*

procedural justice *p. 36*

psychological contract *p. 35*

telecommute *p. 41*

transnational strategy *p. 42*

work/life balance *p. 36*

DISCUSSION QUESTIONS

1. List as many different types of differentiation strategies that you can imagine a company pursuing. What implications do these different strategies have for employee management?

2. What are some of the unique HR challenges associated with managing employees in small companies versus large companies?

3. As a manager, what can you do to help instill new values and beliefs among your employees?

4. How much responsibility do companies have to help employees balance their work and personal lives? What options are available to help achieve work/life balance? Which options are best?

5. What are the benefits and challenges of having a diverse workforce? How can you help employees embrace diversity?

6. What types of managerial challenges would you expect to encounter if your employees were to telecommute to work? How would you address those issues?

7. Companies are increasing their global operations and staffing their international operations. What are some of the challenges that a company would face when going global? What could you do as a manager to help people working internationally deal with these challenges?

8. How have advances in technology affected how companies manage their employees?

9. As a manager, what can you do to encourage your employees to act in an ethical and socially responsible manner?

LEARNING EXERCISE 1

Given the well-documented scandals in corporate America involving unethical behavior, many companies are increasingly encouraging their employees to act ethically. For this exercise, choose four different companies. Research their approaches to ethics and their codes of ethical conduct by visiting their company Web sites and reading about them in the popular business press. Then answer the following questions.

1. Which company's approach to ethics impresses you the most? Why? Which is least impressive? Why?

2. If you were to write a code of ethical conduct for your employees, what would it say? In your opinion, what are the key components of a good code of ethical conduct?

3. What are some ways that you would make sure employees comply with your code of ethical conduct?

LEARNING EXERCISE 2

In light of the trends highlighted in this chapter, there is a good chance that you will work in a small company—or even create one! It is therefore important to think about some of the issues that you might encounter in managing employees in a small or entrepreneurial firm.

1. What challenges would you expect to encounter as a manager in a small company that are different from those you might encounter in a larger, more established company?

2. How would these challenges influence how you manage your employees?

3. If you were to create a new company, or at least be part of the founding team, how you manage employees would set the tone for the culture of the company as it grows. Would this influence your decisions about how to manage your employees? How?

CASE STUDY # 1 — SUSTAINING SUCCESS AT ST. STEVENS COMMUNITY COLLEGE

Emma Barnes is a senior administrator at St. Stevens Community College (SSCC), and she has recently been asked to assess the sustainability of SSCC's strategic mission and to develop a long-term plan for SSCC to overcome any pending challenges and capitalize on any potential opportunities. Established in 1965, SSCC is a midsized community college serving the local population that partners with students to maximize their college experience. SSCC's competitive advantage is to be a high-quality educational option for diverse students at an affordable price and to serve a valuable role in the community. It provides small classes, cutting-edge classrooms, and great resources to enable students to get the most out of their educational experience. Based on all assessments, SSCC has been successful. In just over 40 years, it has grown to more than 12,000 students and enjoys financial profits with enough funds to reinvest in maintaining the administrative infrastructure of the college, enhancing the technology in the classrooms, and bolstering the quality of the athletic facilities.

Despite the college's success, Emma is worried that it may be experiencing the calm before the storm. There are several reasons for her concerns. First, many of the faculty are approaching retirement age, and hiring faculty replacements is difficult because newly minted Ph.D.s have many options for employment. Moreover, new hires are demanding salaries that are above what SSCC is typically able to afford. The quality of the faculty is a key attraction for students, and Emma worries that SSCC may not be able to maintain the

level of education without planning now for the future. In addition, there has been a growing increase in the number of students who have decided to pursue distance education rather than attend community college, with the goal to attend a four-year university after the completion of an associate's degree online. Finally, the composition of the student population continues to become increasingly diverse in terms of gender, race, national origin, and age. While everyone at SSCC agrees that it is a great asset, Emma wonders what implications the increased diversity of the student body might have for how SSCC moves forward.

While everything seems to be fine, Emma is determined to develop a plan to ensure that SSCC is able to take advantage of its opportunities and minimize its constraints. The problem is, she doesn't have a clear answer for how do so.

DISCUSSION QUESTIONS

1. What is your assessment of the organizational and environmental challenges facing SSCC?

2. Which of these HR challenges would you view as most important and least important for Emma to consider as she develops a plan for the future?

3. Given your assessments of these challenges, what recommendations would you make to move forward in a way that ensures that SSCC is able to sustain its strategy of high-quality education at affordable prices?

CASE STUDY # 2 — GLOBALIZATION AT LEVI STRAUSS

Blue jeans are a legendary component of American culture. They were created in the United States in 1873, when Levi Strauss patented the riveted denim jeans that proved so successful among customers that they launched an entire industry. Yet, the one company that has perhaps been most synonymous with blue jeans—Levi Strauss—doesn't actually make its blue jeans in the United States.

In the late 1990s and early part of this decade, Levi Strauss undertook a substantial shift in the location of its manufacturing operations. In 1997, Levi Strauss closed 11 plants and laid off 7,400 employees to cut excess production. In 1999, Levi's announced a large-scale layoff of almost 6,000 jobs and the closing of more factories in Georgia, North Carolina, Virginia, Texas, Tennessee, and Arkansas in an effort to move production to foreign facilities. Over time, the layoffs and the closing continued. Once a mainstay of U.S. manufacturing, plants in areas such as San Antonio, San Francisco, El Paso, and Brownsville, were closed, and by 2004, Levi Strauss had shut its domestic operations and moved production facilities to foreign countries such as Mexico and China. Costs were a major factor for this decision. What might cost $6.67 to make in the United States costs about $3.00 in Mexico and $1.50 in China. While Levi Strauss was reluctant to move these jobs, it faced a competitive market operating with lower costs and lower prices.

DISCUSSION QUESTIONS

1. How did the four environmental factors discussed in this chapter influence Levi's decision to move its manufacturing outside the United States?

2. How would you evaluate this decision from a business perspective? What about from an ethical perspective?

3. Assume that you are an employee working for Levi Strauss and are assigned to the management team in one of the manufacturing facilities in Mexico. What differences would you anticipate in terms of how you manage your Mexican employees versus how you manage employees located in the United States?

Sources: Kaufman, L. Levi is closing 11 factories; 7,600 jobs cut. *New York Times online*, February 23, 1999, http://query.nytimes.com/gst/fullpage.html?res=9405E6DC103DF930A15751C0A96F958260; Kaufman, L. Levi Strauss to close 6 U.S. plants and lay off 3,300. *New York Times online*, April 9, 2002, http://query.nytimes.com/gst/fullpage.html?res=9F06E6DB133DF93AA35757C0A9649C8B63; and Thiruvengadam, M. Apparel industry no longer a good fit in El Paso. *San Antonio (Texas) Express-News*, October 15, 2005, http://www.citizenstrade.org/pdf/sanantonioexpress_apparelindustryoutofelpaso_10152005.pdf.

chapter

3

REGULATORY
ISSUES

1. Understand why equal employment legislation exists. *(52)*

2. Describe basic equal employment opportunity (EEO) concepts. *(53)*

3. Explain the background and basic principles of the main EEO and related laws. *(60)*

4. Discuss the EEO responsibilities of multinational employers. *(72)*

5. Explain the process for filing discrimination charges. *(72)*

6. Identify the components of an affirmative action plan. *(73)*

7. Describe non-EEO legislation related to fair treatment of employees. *(75)*

8. Discuss fair employment practice laws. *(77)*

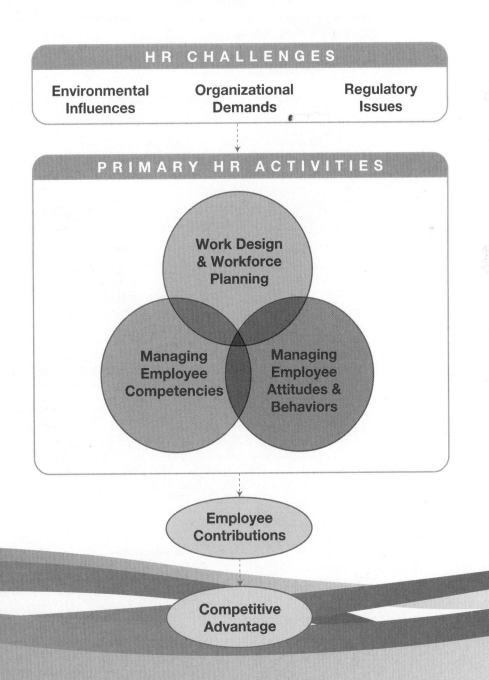

EQUAL EMPLOYMENT OPPORTUNITY AND OTHER WORKPLACE LAWS

What do you want out of a job? A paycheck (the bigger the better!)? Or maybe you want an opportunity to be challenged, to show what you know and can do? Perhaps you desire success and recognition in your profession? Regardless of your main motivation for working, we expect that you would like to be treated fairly and with respect in the workplace. You want an equal chance to get interesting and challenging jobs, promotions, and, ultimately, the bigger paychecks that come with all those opportunities. The employees you will manage will want similar outcomes.

In Chapter 2 we described how two sets of HR challenges, organizational demands and environmental influences, affect employee management. This chapter is about a third HR challenge, highlighted in Exhibit 3.1: regulatory issues. We devote a full chapter to this topic because of its extensive impact on employee management practices. Employment regulations come from laws that are passed by Congress, state legislatures, and local governing bodies. They also originate from executive orders (EOs), which are enacted by the president of the United States for the purpose of managing the operations of the federal government, including the operations of federal contractors. Employment regulations focus on fair

Exhibit 3.1 ▶

Framework for the Strategic Management of Employees

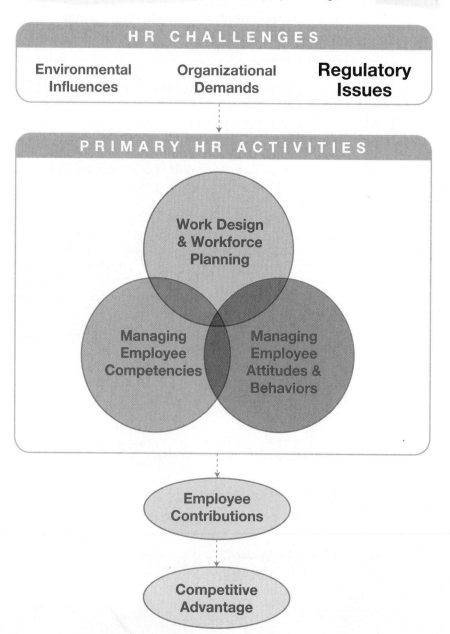

treatment of individuals in the workplace by requiring employers to concentrate on the qualifications of the individuals rather than their gender, nationality, or other characteristics not related to their ability to perform the job. These regulations influence employee contributions to organizational performance by guiding managers in the design of work and in the management of employee competencies, attitudes, and behaviors. How an organization manages its workforce relative to regulations is a vital factor in whether the organization can gain and maintain a competitive advantage.

In this chapter we focus primarily on regulations in the form of **equal employment opportunity (EEO)** laws and other regulations related to fair treatment of employees. We cover additional regulations later, in the chapters for which they are most relevant. For instance, in Chapter 10 we talk about the Fair Labor Standards Act (FLSA), which emphasizes what employers can and cannot do with regard to paying employees for work done. We introduce issues related to diversity management in this chapter and then expand on it throughout the text.

equal employment opportunity (EEO)

The term used to describe laws, regulations, and processes related to fair treatment of employees.

INTRODUCTION TO EQUAL EMPLOYMENT OPPORTUNITY

EEO laws and executive orders are intended to eliminate discrimination in the workplace. **Discrimination** means treating people differently, which in and of itself is not a bad thing. Discrimination is problematic when people are not treated fairly because of characteristics they possess that have nothing to do with their ability to perform a particular job. EEO laws exist on the federal, state, and local levels and are created following the same basic model as other laws.[1] Exhibit 3.2 provides a simple overview of the process leading to the passage of an EEO law and what happens following passage of the law.

The two main regulatory agencies that oversee compliance with the equal employment regulations are the **Equal Employment Opportunity Commission (EEOC)** and the **Office of Federal Contract Compliance Programs (OFCCP)**. The EEOC is responsible for developing guidelines and overseeing compliance with most of the antidiscrimination laws, while the OFCCP is responsible for the same activities relative to executive orders.

Noncompliance with antidiscrimination laws and EOs can lead to negative consequences, including fines to the company and charges of discrimination that result in costly, time-consuming legal battles. Merrill Lynch & Company discovered the cost of noncompliance when a court-ordered panel found that the firm had a pattern of gender discrimination. The plaintiff in this particular case, a former stockbroker at Merrill Lynch in San Antonio, Texas, successfully showed that she had been the victim of repeated sexual harassment and

discrimination

Treating people differently in employment situations because of characteristics, such as race, color, and gender, that have nothing to do with their ability to perform a particular job.

Equal Employment Opportunity Commission (EEOC)

Agency responsible for enforcing compliance with antidiscrimination laws such as the Civil Rights Act of 1964, the Age Discrimination in Employment Act, and the Americans with Disabilities Act.

Office of Federal Contract Compliance Programs (OFCCP)

Agency responsible for developing guidelines and overseeing compliance with antidiscrimination laws relative to executive orders.

◄ **Exhibit 3.2**

Development and Implementation of EEO Laws

Societal or economic problem exists and/or a group lobbies Congress to address a problem

↓

Congress passes a law to address the problem

↓

Congress designates an existing enforcement agency to oversee compliance with the law or establishes an agency expressly for that purpose

↓

The agency develops and communicates guidelines and regulations for compliance

↓

Employers follow the guidelines and regulations, often relying on legal precedent

↓

Courts hear cases involving violations of the laws or issues of interpretation had been discriminated against with regard to promotions and pay raises. The panel awarded her $2.2 million.[2] However, the award was only part of the more than $100 million Merrill Lynch had to pay for 912 claims filed as part of a class-action lawsuit by females because of the gender discrimination that had occurred for many years at the company. In addition to the monetary cost, the company lost much productive work time while fighting the lawsuit, which started in 1997 and wasn't resolved until seven years later.[3]

Before we discuss the EEO laws, we introduce some of the concepts you need to know to understand the laws. These concepts include protected classifications, bona fide occupational qualification, business necessity, and discriminatory practices such as disparate treatment, disparate impact, harassment, and retaliation.

Protected Classifications

The primary objective of antidiscrimination legislation and EOs is to ensure that individuals are given equal opportunity in the workplace. Each law or executive order identifies one or more demographic characteristics that a company generally cannot use to make employment decisions. For instance, an employer cannot refuse to hire Asians or Mormons simply because they are Asian or Mormon. Doing so would violate EEO laws, which specifically forbid using the characteristics of race (Asian) or religion (Mormon) as the basis for employment decisions. The demographic characteristics that cannot be used for employment decisions are known as **protected classifications**, or protected classes. The main protected classes are:

protected classification, or protected class

Demographic characteristics that cannot be used for employment decisions.

- Race
- Sex
- Religion
- Color
- National origin
- Age
- Disability
- Veteran status

As you read through this chapter, you will see that some laws specify which group within a protected classification is protected while others do not. For example, when you read about the Age Discrimination in Employment Act (ADEA), you will see that it specifies that individuals age 40 and older are the protected class. In contrast, when you read about Title VII of the Civil Rights Act of 1964, you will see that it indicates that sex is one of five protected classes. It does not state that female is the only sex protected from discrimination. People sometimes believe that is the case because traditionally females are more likely to be the victims of discrimination in the workplace than males.

Bona Fide Occupational Qualification (BFOQ) and Business Necessity

Are there times when sex or nationality or another protected classification *can* be used to make an employment decision? That's a good question. Let's take a look at when that can happen by way of an example.

A modeling agency has a client that designs clothes exclusively for women. The modeling agency decides to hire only women to model the clothes. The employer in this example would claim that gender (the term we will use interchangeably with *sex* and the more common term used now) is a **bona fide occupational qualification (BFOQ)**. A BFOQ exists when a protected classification can legally be used to make an employment decision. The modeling agency could argue that it can give preference in hiring to one gender, female, over the other gender, male, because of **business necessity**. Claiming that a protected classification is a business necessity means that the employment practice has some relationship to legitimate business goals and that it is essential to the company's survival. In our example, the clothing designer focused on women's clothing and needs to sell the clothes to buyers looking for women's clothing to stay in business. Gender, therefore, would be an acceptable BFOQ in this case.

bona fide occupational qualification (BFOQ)

A protected classification that can legally be used to make an employment decision.

business necessity

An employment practice that has some relationship to legitimate business goals and is essential to the company's survival.

COMPANY *spotlight*   3.1 Integration of the Zoo Crew

The Equal Employment Opportunity Commission (EEOC), the enforcement agency for most EEO laws, resolved a sex bias lawsuit against the Phoenix Suns Limited Partnership and Sports Magic Team, Inc., an Orlando-based sports entertainment firm. The organizations agreed to pay over $100,000 to females who had charged the firms with sex bias for restricting them from positions on the Zoo Crew. The Zoo Crew provides entertainment during Phoenix Suns basketball games, assists with promotions at half-time, and performs related activities. Apparently, the Phoenix Suns and Sports Magic Team, Inc., had adopted a new selection policy that restricted positions on the Zoo Crew to only "males with athletic ability." This decision was curious because women had successfully performed as part of the Zoo Crew in the past.

The Phoenix Suns and Sports Magic had gone as far as posting job announcements and placing newspaper advertisements indicating specifically that they wanted male employees only. That wasn't a smart move. When the EEOC investigated, the two organizations could not provide sound justification that being male was actually a BFOQ for the job. They could not show that all or substantially all women could not perform some aspect of the job and that aspect was essential to the business. In fact, one of the plaintiffs had successfully worked as a Zoo Crew member in the past but wasn't rehired because of the new selection criterion— gender. In addition to paying the plaintiffs over $100,000 and apologizing in a letter to the former Zoo Crew member who had not been rehired, the Phoenix Suns agreed to strengthen its policies prohibiting sex discrimination. It also agreed to train employees to prevent future discrimination.[7] After the lawsuit, the Zoo Crew included female members.

Source: Adapted from U.S. Equal Employment Opportunity Commission. *EEOC resolves sex discrimination lawsuit against NBA's Phoenix Suns and Sports Magic for $104,500*, October 9, 2003, www.eeoc.gov/press/10-9-03b.html.

The general guideline accepted by the EEOC and the courts to determine the appropriateness of a protected class as a BFOQ came from a landmark 1971 case, *Diaz v. Pan American World Airways.*[4] Celio Diaz wanted to be a domestic flight cabin attendant for Pan American World Airways (Pan Am). He didn't get the job because he was the wrong gender. He subsequently filed a charge of gender discrimination. Pan Am argued that females are more nurturing, give more courteous personal service, and generally make flights more pleasurable for passengers than males would. Remember that in the late 1960s and early 1970s, most air travelers would have been business*men.*

The 5th Circuit Court of Appeals pointed out, however, that gender can be a selection criterion only if gender affects business operations. Business convenience is not a reason for using gender as a BFOQ. Consequently, an employer who uses gender as a BFOQ needs to show that "all or substantially all members of that sex cannot reasonably perform some aspect of that job, and that aspect is necessary."[5] By the way, at the time of the case, Pan Am already had 283 male stewards (which are now called flight attendants) on its foreign flights, providing further evidence that gender was not an appropriate BFOQ![6]

In summary, an employer can sometimes make a case that gender, religion, national origin, and age are BFOQs. The likelihood of successfully doing so, however, is usually very low. An employer can never use race or skin color as a BFOQ. Company Spotlight 3.1 describes a gender discrimination case in which gender could not be shown to be a BFOQ.

Discriminatory Practices

The EEOC describes four practices that it considers to be discriminatory:[8] disparate treatment, disparate impact, harassment, and retaliation. Let's take a look at what each of these involves.

DISPARATE TREATMENT Most people think of discrimination as being obvious and intentional in nature, occurring when a protected classification is used as the basis for an employment decision. Not hiring a qualified woman simply because she is a female would be obvious and intentional discrimination. Under this definition, if someone is turned down for an employment opportunity and can show that it was because of a particular

Target Corporation agreed to pay $510,000 to four African Americans, revise its document-retention policies, train supervisors on employment discrimination and record keeping, and provide reports on its hiring practices as part of a consent decree ending a lawsuit against Target brought by the EEOC. Target was accused of violating Title VII of the Civil Rights Act of 1964 in some of its Milwaukee and Madison, Wisconsin, stores. The court found sufficient evidence that Target had denied assistant store manager jobs to the four plaintiffs because of their race, thus engaging in disparate treatment of the plaintiffs. In making the case, evidence was provided that Target may have identified the race of the applicants as African American based on their names or the accents heard during telephone conversations. Also at question in the case was whether employment applications had been inappropriately destroyed.

Source: Adapted from U.S. Equal Employment Opportunity Commission. *Target Corp. to pay $510,000 for race discrimination*, December 10, 2007, www.eeoc.gov/press/12-10-07a.html.

disparate treatment

Treating individuals differently in employment situations *because of* their membership in a protected class.

prima facie case

Establishing the basis for a case of discrimination.

McDonnell Douglas test

A four-step test, named after the *McDonnell Douglas Corp. v. Greene* 1973 U.S. Supreme Court case, used to make a case of disparate treatment.

mixed motive

A legitimate reason for an employment decision exists, but the decision was also motivated by an illegitimate reason.

disparate impact, or adverse impact

Discrimination that occurs when an employment practice results in members of a protected class being treated less favorably than members of a non-protected class even though the discrimination was not intentional.

attribute that is protected by law—religion, sex, race, or whatever protected class is at issue—that individual has the right to file charges against the employer. When this type of discrimination occurs, it is known as **disparate treatment**. In disparate treatment cases, an individual is treated differently *because of* the characteristic that defines the protected class. Disparate treatment also means that the company *intentionally* discriminated against a person or persons because of the characteristic, and a BFOQ for that characteristic does not exist. Company Spotlight 3.2 describes a case of disparate treatment discrimination.

An employee who believes that he or she has been the victim of disparate treatment must make a **prima facie case**, or preliminary case, using the **McDonnell Douglas test**, named after the *McDonnell Douglas Corp. v. Greene*[9] 1973 U.S. Supreme court case that identified a four-step test. To make a case of disparate treatment, the plaintiff must show all of the following:

1. That he or she is a member of a protected class.
2. That he or she applied for the job (or other employment opportunity, such as being eligible for a raise or promotion) and was qualified.
3. That he or she was rejected.
4. That someone else got the job, or the employer continued to seek applications from individuals with the plaintiff's qualifications.

Once the plaintiff has made a *prima facie* case, the burden of proof shifts to the employer to provide a legitimate, job-related reason for the decision.[10] For instance, an employer might show that the person selected had more relevant experience or performed better on selection measures.

The courts have been clear that even though an employer may have had a job-related reason for a decision, if protected class membership played any part in the outcome, discrimination has occurred. In other words, a **mixed motive** has affected the outcome: A legitimate reason for an employment decision exists, but the decision was also motivated by an illegitimate reason (such as membership in a protected class).

DISPARATE IMPACT Disparate *treatment* refers to intentionally unfair and illegal treatment of a particular individual. But discrimination may also take a more subtle and usually unintentional form, known as **disparate impact**, or adverse impact. Disparate impact occurs when a company uses an employment practice that unintentionally discriminates against members of a protected class. For example, a job requirement at a home improvement store might state that all employees must be 6 feet tall to perform a job that requires regularly reaching up to obtain items from high shelves. This job requirement might not be intended to discriminate against anyone. It may, however, lead to discrimination against several protected classifications, such as females and members of some minority groups. The average height for women in the United States is 5'4"; the average height for men is 5'9".[11] Although it would not be intentional discrimination, the height requirement would yield an unequal outcome for women because fewer women than men would be tall enough to be hired.

A useful way to think about the difference between disparate treatment and disparate impact is that disparate treatment focuses on the *treatment* of a particular person or group of persons within a particular protected class and explicitly considers the *motivation* for the company's actions. Disparate impact, on the other hand, focuses on the *consequences* of the employment practices.

The court case that identified disparate impact as discrimination was *Griggs v. Duke Power Company*,[12] decided in 1971. At Duke Power's generating plant, black employees challenged the employer's selection requirements. Specifically, to be hired for or to be transferred to other jobs at the plant, applicants had to possess a high school diploma and pass two professionally prepared aptitude tests—selection requirements not designed to measure ability to learn a particular job. Also, prior to the passage of major civil rights legislation in 1964, the company had a history of discriminating on the basis of race, even to the extent of restricting black employees to the lowest-level jobs within one department and paying them less than the lowest-paying job in the other four operating departments.

In reviewing the case, the U.S. Supreme Court held that the company had not intended to discriminate; however, the selection criteria resulted in discrimination. The relevance of the criteria was suspect because there were employees doing just fine in the jobs in question who did not have high school diplomas and who had not taken the tests. Also, blacks in the area were less likely than whites to have a high school diploma and would be less likely to pass the tests because of their lack of education. Because the employer could not show that having a high school diploma and passing the tests were necessary to be able to perform the jobs, discrimination had occurred even though that was not the company's intent.[13]

The issue in disparate impact is whether the employer can show that there is a valid, job-related reason for using the selection criterion that discriminates. In establishing selection criteria or deciding who gets raises or promotions or training, managers need to think through the possible outcomes of their choices. Unintentionality is not an acceptable defense in a disparate impact case. Most importantly, using non-job-related criteria for making such decisions ultimately affects the success of the organization as it rewards the wrong behaviors and attitudes. We will discuss these issues further later but first want to elaborate on how a plaintiff can make a case that disparate impact has occurred.

First, the plaintiff must demonstrate that the outcome of the employment practice was less favorable for his or her protected class than for the majority. The **four-fifths rule** is a guideline generally accepted by the courts and the EEOC for making such a *prima facie* case of disparate impact. To see how it works, let's consider an example.

Assume that your company is expanding and needs to hire multiple people for the same job. You place an advertisement in the local newspaper, and 800 people apply for the 95 openings. Some applicants are white (non-Hispanic), and some are Hispanic. A selection criterion used in the hiring process requires passing a test written in English, even though English was not listed in the advertisement as a job requirement. After your company completes its hiring process and fills the 95 openings, several Hispanic applicants express concern that they were not selected for the job even though they were qualified. To determine whether there is disparate impact as these individuals believe, you will need to know the number of job applicants from each group and the number hired from each group. The breakdown looks like this:

four-fifths rule

A guideline generally accepted by the courts and the EEOC for making a *prima facie* case of disparate impact by showing that an employment practice results in members of a protected class being treated less favorably by an employment practice than members of a non-protected class.

Applicants	Number Hired	Selection Rate
Hispanic = 300	20	20 / 300 = 7%
Whites (non-Hispanic) = 500	75	75 / 500 = 15%

When you have this information, you need to determine whether 7%, the selection rate for the Hispanics, is equal to at least four-fifths, or 80%, of the 15% selection rate for the majority group. In this case, when you divide the selection rate for Hispanics by the selection rate for whites, you find the following:

Selection rate for Hispanics (7%) / Selection rate for whites (15%) = 47%, which is less than 80% (or four-fifths)

Because 47% is below the four-fifths threshold, evidence of disparate impact exists.

Exhibit 3.3 ▶
Acceptable Defenses in
Disparate Impact Cases

- Provide evidence that the practice is *job related*
- Demonstrate that the practice is a *business necessity*
- Show that the decision is a result of a *bona fide seniority system*

A cautionary note is in order here. As a manager, you should not try to "hire by the numbers." What we mean is that a manager should not simply calculate how many minority group members need to be hired and hire that many to be in compliance based on the four-fifths rule. Doing so defeats the purpose of hiring based on job-related qualifications. Remember, your goal as a manager is to ensure that you have the best-qualified employees so that your company can achieve its goals. Hiring by the numbers is not the way to accomplish that goal. In later chapters, you will learn about developing job-related selection criteria so that you will know how to hire the best talent.

Once the plaintiffs, in our example the Hispanic applicants, make a *prima facie* case of disparate impact for the particular practice that is discriminatory, the employer can use one of several defenses for the practice, as shown in Exhibit 3.3. First, companies may provide evidence that the practice in question is *job related*. Companies can do this by demonstrating that the employment practice is connected to a measure of job performance or that it in some other way is directly related to ability to perform the job. For instance, requiring a CPA license for a job of auditor in a public accounting firm would be job related, even if it meant that certain protected classes would be less likely to be hired for the job.

A second possible defense is that the practice is a *business necessity*. A strenuous physical-ability test as a job requirement for a firefighter might have disparate impact for women, but it is a business necessity for fire departments. Firefighters must be physically fit and capable of lifting heavy loads such as fire hoses and people. A fire department can readily show that passing the test is a strong predictor of firefighter safety on the job.

The existence of a *bona fide seniority system* is a third defense that companies can offer. Seniority systems give employees rights based on length of time with the company. Rights can include opportunities for better working hours, for instance. A bona fide seniority system is one that is officially sanctioned by the organization. To successfully use this defense, the employer must show that the seniority system has been in effect for some time and was not created to keep certain protected classifications from being eligible for the job in question.

Harassment

harassment

Subjecting employees to unwanted and unwelcome treatment because of their race, color, religion, sex, national origin, age, or disability.

hostile work environment

A situation that exists whenever an employee is the subject of unwelcome harassment because of his or her membership in a protected class and that harassment is severe and abusive.

Most people have heard about sexual harassment in the workplace, but you need to remember that **harassment** occurs when employees are subjected to unwanted and unwelcome treatment because of their race, color, religion, sex, national origin, age, or disability.[14] Harassment can include, but is not limited to, offensive jokes, unwelcome comments related to a person's protected class, graffiti targeting the protected class, and physical threats. Because of the harassment, employees experience a hostile work environment. A **hostile work environment** exists whenever an employee is the subject of unwelcome harassment because of his or her membership in a protected class and that harassment is severe and abusive.

Such was the case for seven employees at Barber Dodge and Fairfield Toyota in Solano County, California. The employees alleged that they were victims of name-calling; other employees called them names such as "terrorist" and "thief" because of their Afghan national origin, Muslim faith, and dark skin. In settling this case, the dealerships agreed to pay $550,000 to the seven former employees, although the dealerships denied the charges.[15]

Later in this chapter, we provide more details about the different types of harassment that can occur in the workplace. Exhibit 3.4 outlines what a company should do and what a manager should do to reduce the likelihood of harassment. As you review the two lists, you will note that there is a great deal of overlap between them. The overlap occurs because a manager is an agent for a company and therefore has responsibility for implementing the company guidelines.

Company's responsibility:

1. Develop and regularly communicate an anti-harassment policy to all employees, providing examples of the kinds of behaviors that constitute sexual and other types of harassment

2. Provide training to managers to ensure that they understand the anti-harassment policy and know their responsibility for enforcing the policy

3. Establish a process for reporting incidents of harassment that doesn't involve reporting to the direct supervisor*

4. Ensure that all reports of harassment, no matter how minor they seem, are investigated immediately and that those reporting the incidents are treated with respect

5. Take prompt action against harassers, ensuring that the disciplinary action is appropriate, given the nature of the offense

6. Follow up with the victim of harassment to ensure that the harassment has stopped and that the victim is not experiencing retaliation for having reported the harassment

*This step is important in case the direct supervisor is the harasser or has not addressed the harassment. Often, someone in the human resources department or the affirmative action office can serve in this role. In a smaller firm, employees may be directed to go to a manager other than their own.

Manager's responsibility:

1. Recognize that, as a manager, you are responsible for creating a harassment-free environment for your employees

2. Make sure you understand what constitutes harassment and what your role is when a problem occurs

3. Ensure that employees who report to you receive training and understand the anti-harassment policy and that they know their responsibility for abiding by the policy

4. Report any incidents of harassment immediately

5. Make sure that incidents are investigated and that individuals making the reports are not further harassed

6. Participate in any follow-up actions requested

7. Always maintain confidentiality about situations that occur

◄ **Exhibit 3.4**
Guidelines for
Reducing Harassment
in the Workplace

Retaliation

Many of the laws that prohibit discrimination have non-retaliation requirements. **Retaliation** occurs when an employer takes an adverse action against an employee who has filed a discrimination complaint. Retaliation is often a punishment, or a threat of punishment, because an employee exercises the rights provided under the antidiscrimination laws. Retaliation can take many forms, including but not limited to the following:

- Denying a promotion to the employee, who is otherwise qualified
- Demoting the employee
- Suspending the employee for a period of time
- Writing a negative evaluation of the employee
- Threatening the employee if the complaint is not withdrawn[16]

When a manager takes any of these actions, he or she is discriminating against the employee.

Now that we have defined many of the terms associated with equal employment opportunity and regulatory issues, let's explore the laws themselves.

retaliation

Punishment that occurs when an employer takes an adverse action against an employee who has filed a discrimination complaint.

EQUAL EMPLOYMENT LEGISLATION

By now you should have a good understanding of the basic concepts underlying EEO laws and the types of problems that can occur in the workplace. These problems have led to the creation of laws and executive orders to protect employees from discrimination. As you study them, remember that even though you may be thinking about them from the perspective of a manager, they provide protection for you as an employee as well. Exhibit 3.5 outlines the main equal employment opportunity laws that we discuss in this chapter.

▶ **Exhibit 3.5** Equal Employment Opportunity Laws and Executive Orders

Regulation	Provisions	Covered Employers
Equal Pay Act of 1963 (EPA)	Prohibits discrimination in pay on the basis of gender for individuals performing jobs with the same skill, effort, responsibility, and working conditions unless there is a factor other than gender used to determine the pay difference.	All employers with 1 or more employees, including the federal government.
Title VII of the Civil Rights Act of 1964	Prohibits employment discrimination on the basis of race, color, religion, sex, or national origin; established the EEOC as an enforcement agency.	Employers with 15 or more employees, including all private employers, state and local governments, federal government, and education institutions, private and public employment agencies, labor organizations, and joint labor management committees controlling apprenticeship and training programs.
Executive Order 11246	Similar to Title VII; prohibits employment discrimination on basis of race, color, religion, sex, or national origin by federal contractors; requires affirmative action plans for federal contractors.	Federal contractors with contracts greater than $10,000 must not discriminate; federal contractors with 50 or more employees and contracts over $50,000 must have affirmative action plans.
Age Discrimination in Employment Act of 1967 (ADEA)	Prohibits employment discrimination of individuals aged 40 or older.	All employers with 20 or more employees, including employment agencies and labor organizations, federal, state and local governments, and school districts.
Pregnancy Discrimination Act of 1978 (PDA)	Specifies that women who are pregnant or who are affected by pregnancy-related conditions are to be treated the same as other applicants or employees with similar limitations or abilities.	Same as Title VII of the Civil Rights Act of 1964.
Americans with Disabilities Act of 1990 (ADA)	Prohibits discrimination in employment practices against qualified individuals with disabilities who can perform the job with or without reasonable accommodation.	Same as Title VII of the Civil Rights Act of 1964.
Civil Rights Act of 1991	Clarifies defense in disparate impact cases, provides for monetary damages in cases of intentional discrimination, and eliminates race norming.	Same as Title VII of the Civil Rights Act of 1964.

Equal Pay Act of 1963 (EPA)

Most people today agree that marital status, gender, and other non-job-related factors should not influence how much a person gets paid. However, prior to 1963, employers frequently considered gender and marital status when making such decisions. It was not uncommon for employers to pay males more than females, particularly if the males were married. Newspaper advertisements often had separate listings for male and female jobs, and companies routinely reserved their higher-paying jobs for males. The assumption was that males were the primary breadwinners for their families and needed to make the most money. Even when males and females performed the same jobs, males generally received higher pay. In 1963, Congress made it clear to employers that such pay differences were no longer acceptable when it passed the Equal Pay Act (EPA) as an amendment to the Fair Labor Standards Act (FLSA). The FLSA of 1938 had established general guidelines for employee pay, but the EPA specified that gender could not be a factor in paying employees. We will discuss the FLSA in detail in the Chapter 10; we include the EPA here because it is an antidiscrimination law.

Today, if a male and a female in the same company are performing jobs that require *substantially* equal skill, effort, and responsibility and that have similar working conditions, the law requires the employer to pay them equally. Pay differences for employees in the same job are allowed if they are based on merit, seniority, quality or quantity of production, or another non-gender-related factor, such as night shifts versus day shifts.[17]

The EPA was passed more than 40 years ago, yet, in many situations, women are still not being paid equally with men. In 2007, a study by the American Association of University Women Educational Foundation found that females were earning only 80% of what males were earning 1 year after college and that 10 years later, females were earning only 69% of what males were earning. Even after taking into account factors such as occupation, hours worked, and parenthood, 25% of the pay gap was still unexplained, suggesting that sex differences may be affecting the outcome.[18] Several arguments have been offered to explain this continuing gap, including women's later entry into the workplace compared to men's, women taking time out to have and raise children, gender differences in negotiation skills at time of hire, percentage of women in traditionally female jobs, and ongoing gender discrimination.

Title VII of the Civil Rights Act of 1964 (CRA 64)

Imagine this scenario: You get on the bus to go to work and are told that you have to move to the back, even though there are plenty of seats up front. You get to work and are thirsty. When you go to the water fountain, you find that there are two fountains and that one has a sign above it that says "Whites only." Later, you try to talk to your boss about a promotion, and he tells you that "your kind" aren't eligible for promotions. Blacks in the United States, and to an extent Hispanics, had just these experiences before the passage of the Civil Rights Act of 1964. Across the nation, but particularly in the South, blacks were considered second-class citizens. They were not allowed to vote, were denied entry to many public places, and had separate seating areas in public places. These events were commonplace even though the Civil Rights Acts of 1866 and 1871, plus the 13th and 14th Amendments to the U.S. Constitution had attempted to provide equal rights to all persons.

Not surprisingly, blacks were extremely disadvantaged economically. Education was segregated, with black schools traditionally lower in quality than white schools. Think about what it would be like to not have an education and to have a job in a segregated workplace that offers only low-level, low-paying jobs. These conditions help you begin to understand why blacks had little money and few opportunities to improve their quality of life during that time in history. Many U.S. citizens at the time believed that these conditions, in turn, affected the entire nation negatively. Low income led to reduced buying power, which led to reduced production, which led to fewer jobs. A segregated society led to the need for duplicate facilities, such as schools and other public services, as well as duplicate facilities in the workplace, such as cafeterias and restrooms. Money that could have been used in more productive ways, such as for increased wages, was used to keep blacks segregated.[19]

The civil rights movement of the 1960s brought to light the need for reform. As the world watched, peaceful demonstrations led by Martin Luther King and others to call attention to

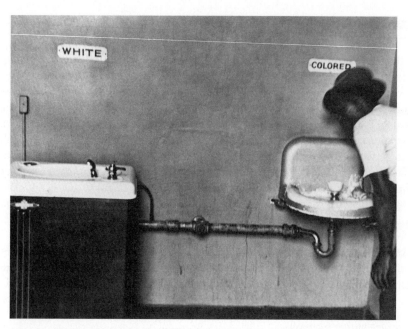

Before the passage of the Civil Rights Act of 1964, segregated water fountains were common.

discrimination and its outcomes turned violent. Demonstrators were beaten and abused in other ways by the police. Seeing the abuse galvanized the nation, forcing it to confront the issue of discrimination.[20] Finally, to address the societal and economic need for change, Congress passed the Civil Rights Act of 1964. With the passage of the Act, Congress explicitly stated that the time had come to abolish discrimination in employment and other areas.

Title VII is the part of the Civil Rights Act that specifically addresses employment discrimination. Title VII prohibits employers from discriminating against any individual on the basis of that individual's race, color, religion, sex, or national origin. Employers with 15 or more employees, including state and local governments, employment agencies, labor unions, and the federal government, have to abide by this law. Also, the law covers U.S. citizens and legal residents of the United States who are working for U.S. companies in other countries.

Title VII states that it is against the law for an employer to discriminate with regard to:

- Selection
- Termination
- Compensation
- Terms and privileges of employment
- Promotion or transfer of employees
- Work assignments
- Any other activity related to employment

Thus, as a manager, you need to make sure that you are aware of the antidiscrimination laws and that you treat all your employees fairly in conducting these activities. The law applies to employment agencies and labor unions, as well as to private employers. It does permit the use of religion, sex, and national origin as BFOQs, but only when necessary for the normal operation of the business.[21]

In 1972, Congress amended the Civil Rights Act by passing the Equal Employment Opportunity Act. The amendment broadened coverage of the Civil Rights Act to state and local governments, as well as to public and private educational institutions. The Act also gave the EEOC the right to sue employers to enforce the provisions of Title VII.

As part of the Civil Rights Act, Congress created the EEOC to provide oversight of Title VII for all covered entities, except the federal government. The Office of Special Counsel and Merit Systems Protection Board oversee discrimination issues related to federal employees. The OFCCP oversees compliance by federal government contractors.

The EEOC has developed and continues to develop regulations and guidelines to help employers and employees interpret Congress's intent in the Civil Rights Act. It provides a

Web site (www.eeoc.gov) and numerous other resources to answer questions managers have about equal employment opportunity. A section of the Web site provides answers to many questions about compliance requirements for small businesses (www.eeoc.gov/employers/smallbusinesses.html).

The EEOC is involved in interpreting the meaning of the term *discrimination*, determining how individuals can prove that discrimination has occurred, identifying what remedies are available in the law, and addressing how to reconcile seniority rights of current employees with the rights of victims of discrimination.[22] Title VII's influence on the management of employees and HR activities is best understood by closely examining each of the protected classifications covered in the act. Exhibit 3.6 provides an example of each of the types of discrimination that we discuss that are covered under Title VII.

RACE AND COLOR DISCRIMINATION   Much progress has been made in reducing racial discrimination in the workplace since the passage of Title VII. However, in 2008, the EEOC reported that the number of racial harassment charge filings had more than doubled from 3,075 in 1991 to 7,000 in 2007. During that time, the EEOC received 27,238 charges of race-based discrimination and resolved 25,992 cases (cases carry over from one year to the next) with monetary benefits of $61.4 million for plaintiffs. This last figure does not include monetary benefits obtained through litigation.[23] Under certain conditions, plaintiffs can file charges in court and may receive additional monetary benefits.

Employers violate Title VII when they use race itself or race-related characteristics and conditions to make employment decisions, tolerate the harassment of employees because of their race or color, segregate or classify employees based on race or color, or collect pre-employment information about race in such a way that it is available to those making the hiring decisions.[24]

The following are examples of race and color discrimination by employers in violation of Title VII[25]:

- **Using race or race-related characteristics and conditions to make employment decisions.**   A "no-beard" policy may discriminate against African American men because they are predisposed to a medical condition that makes shaving difficult. Selecting only light-skinned employees because they best fit the preferred company image is discrimination on the basis of skin color.
- **Tolerating the harassment of employees because of their race or color.**   Permitting racial slurs and racist graffiti creates a hostile working environment. Making derogatory remarks about an employee's skin color and then firing the employee for complaining to management is a violation of Title VII.
- **Segregating or classifying employees based on race or color.**   Assigning racial groups to work only in areas where the customer base is predominantly of the same racial group is discriminatory. Assigning employees of a certain racial group exclusively to work in certain jobs in the company is also discriminatory.
- **Collecting pre-employment information about race in such a way that it is available to those making the hiring decisions.**[26]   Asking for information that would identify race as part of the pre-employment process is not permissible. Coding applications or resumes so that the interviewer knows the race of applicants is another example of illegally classifying employees (similar to what is described at Target in Company Spotlight 3.2).

Type of Discrimination	Common Example
Race and color	Not hiring dark-skinned applicants because they don't fit the company image.
Religious	Refusing to allow a practicing Muslim to take off work for a religious holiday
Gender	Not providing the same benefits for female employees as for male employees
National origin	Giving preferential treatment in employee decisions to individuals born in the United States

◀ Exhibit 3.6

Examples of Discriminatory Practices under the Civil Rights Act of 1964

RELIGIOUS DISCRIMINATION   Religious discrimination has gradually been on the rise. In 1992, there were 1,388 religious discrimination complaints filed with the EEOC, with 1,297 resolutions and reasonable cause found in 4.2%, or 55, of those cases. Reasonable cause exists when the EEOC believes there is enough evidence that discrimination has occurred to make a case. In 2006, the number of charges rose to 2,541, with 2,387 resolutions (some cases carried over from the previous year) and reasonable cause found in 5.7%, or 136, of the cases. These numbers indicate that incidents of religious discrimination either are occurring more often or are being reported more often than in the past. This rise is undoubtedly related to the increase in the proportion of people in various religions represented in the workplace in recent years.[27]

Religious discrimination occurs in a variety of forms. An employer might refuse to hire an applicant because of his particular religion, in which case disparate treatment occurs. Or an employer might have a policy that requires Sunday work. Such a policy could have disparate impact on an employee whose religion does not permit working on Sundays. In the former case, the employer is blatantly discriminating in violation of Title VII. In the latter case, the employer is not intentionally discriminating, but that is the result of the policy. The employer would either have to accommodate an employee by permitting him or her to work on a day other than Sunday or prove that adjusting the schedule would impose an undue hardship on the company. **Undue hardship** can take the form of diminished job efficiency, higher-than-usual administrative costs, impaired safety in the workplace, need for co-workers to perform hazardous or burdensome portions of the employee's work, or violation of a law or regulation.[28]

Employees may also experience *religious harassment*, which occurs when employees are subjected to a hostile work environment because of their religious affiliation. Since the terrorist attacks on the United States on September 11, 2001, members of some religious groups, such as Muslims, have experienced direct discrimination and harassment in the workplace. Company Spotlight 3.3 describes just such a case of religious discrimination.

Another important issue for companies is the extent to which employees can express religious beliefs at work. According to the EEOC, "employers must permit employees to engage in religious expression if employees are permitted to engage in other personal expression at work, unless the religious expression would impose an undue hardship on the employer."[29] If an employer allows employees to keep personal books on their desks to read during breaks, the employer would have to allow an employee to keep a Bible or a copy of the Koran on his desk to read during breaks.

Religious organizations are permitted to use religion as a BFOQ for certain positions. If a professor at a church-affiliated university is teaching a course based on religious principles, the university may specify that the person hired must be a member of the university's religion. It would be hard to make a case, however, that the custodial staff or clerical staff at the same university had to be members of that particular religion.

undue hardship

Situation that exists when accommodating an employee would put the employer at a disadvantage financially, or would otherwise make it difficult for the employer to remain in business and competitive.

COMPANY spotlight   3.3 Alamo Car Rental Fires Young Muslim Woman

Before 9/11, Alamo Car Rental had permitted a young Somali customer sales representative, Bilan Nur, to wear a headscarf during the Muslim holy month of Ramadan. In December 2001, Alamo fired Ms. Nur after refusing to permit her to continue to cover her head, even when she offered to wear an approved Alamo-logo scarf. Wearing a headscarf did not violate company dress policy, but Nur was fired eight days before Ramadan began and told that she was ineligible for rehire. When the Phoenix EEOC district office brought the case before Judge Roslyn Silver, she decided the case was so clear-cut that it did not require a jury to reach a resolution; the jury was only asked to decide how much monetary damage should be awarded. The case resulted in Alamo having to pay $21,640 in back pay, $16,000 in compensatory damages, and $250,000 in punitive damages to Nur.

Sources: Adapted from U.S. Equal Employment Opportunity Commission. *Phoenix jury awards $287,640 to fired Muslim woman in EEOC religious discrimination lawsuit*, June 4, 2007, www.eeoc.gov/press/6-4-07.html.

GENDER DISCRIMINATION   The EPA, which you read about earlier, specifically prohibits employers from discriminating on the basis of gender in terms of pay. Title VII makes it unlawful for an employer to discriminate on the basis of gender in *any* employment situation or opportunity. For example, an employer cannot refuse to hire a female for fear that she will get married, have children, and decide to quit her job. We now review some of the ways in which employers have engaged in gender-based discrimination. These include gender as the basis for an employment decision, gender-plus discrimination, and sexual harassment.

First, employers engage in gender discrimination when they use the person's gender as the basis for an employment decision. This form is the most straightforward and obvious way that gender discrimination occurs. Let's say you have an opening for a sales associate at your car dealership. You may think that men are the best employees in this job because you believe they know more about cars than women (which may or may not be a true stereotype). As a result of your stereotype, you won't even consider a woman for that job. You have just discriminated on the basis of gender.

The second form of gender discrimination occurs when an employee would have been treated differently if it had not been for that employee's gender. This is known as *gender-plus discrimination.* An employer who refuses to hire women with preschool-age children but hires males with preschool-age children is guilty of gender-plus discrimination. In this instance, the women would have been hired "but for" their gender. Personality, as the next case shows, and appearance can also be factors in gender-plus discrimination.

In the 1982 *Price Waterhouse v. Hopkins*[30] case, Hopkins, an associate, brought a lawsuit against Price Waterhouse when she was denied a partnership. Apparently some of the firm's partners didn't like her use of profanity and thought she was too macho and too aggressive, even though she had an exemplary record. She had, in fact, played a critical role in securing a multi-million-dollar contract for the company with the Department of State. She had also been lauded as "an outstanding professional," and clients found her to be capable, yet she did upset some co-workers and partners with her aggressive manner. After the firm refused to make Hopkins a partner despite her qualifications, Hopkins filed a sex discrimination lawsuit against the firm, charging that she would have been treated differently had she been a male. In the end, the court found that gender-based discrimination had occurred: A male behaving as she had likely would have been made a partner in the company, but the firm considered these same behaviors unfeminine. "But for" her gender, Hopkins would have been promoted to partner.[31]

The third form of gender discrimination is sexual harassment. You already know that under Title VII, any form of gender discrimination is illegal. In 1986, the Supreme Court ruled on a gender discrimination case, *Meritor Savings Bank v. Vinson*, which clarified that creating a hostile environment for someone because of her gender was also prohibited under Title VII and was sexual harassment. Sexual harassment is a form of gender-based discrimination because the harassment is directed at members of one gender but not the other. Females are directing the behavior at males but not at other females; males are harassing females but not other males. Keep in mind that sexual harassment can also involve two members of the same gender. This type of sexual harassment occurs, for instance, when a gay male makes sexual overtures or otherwise sexually harasses another male. The gay male would not be treating a female the same way.

According to EEOC guidelines for preventing sexual harassment, sexual harassment includes, but is not limited to, the following:

Unwelcome sexual advances, requests for sexual favors, and other verbal and physical conduct of a sexual nature when:

1. submission to such conduct is made either explicitly or implicitly a term or condition of an individual's employment,
2. submission to or rejection of such conduct by an individual is used as the basis for employment decisions affecting such individual, or
3. such conduct has the purpose or effect of unreasonably interfering with an individual's work performance or creating an intimidating, hostile, or offensive working environment.[32]

quid pro quo harassment

A type of harassment that is made explicitly or implicitly a condition of employment.

In its guidelines, the EEOC has identified two types of sexual harassment. The most straightforward type is called quid pro quo harassment. Quid pro quo means "something for something." When this type of harassment occurs, submission to sexual conduct is made explicitly or implicitly a condition of employment. For example, a manager might agree to give an employee a raise or a promotion in exchange for her going on a date with him; no date, no raise. The manager's request constitutes quid pro quo harassment.

The other form of sexual harassment is referred to as *hostile work environment sexual harassment*. We defined hostile work environment in an earlier discussion of harassment. Hostile work environment sexual harassment is quite controversial in some instances and more straightforward in others. The challenge arises because what may not appear to be a hostile work environment to one person may appear to be so to another person. Some people are offended by jokes with sexual overtones while others are not. Because some employees might be offended, the jokes do not belong in the workplace.

Managers have an obligation to take corrective action once they are informed of a potential sexual harassment situation. According to the EEOC, a company may be guilty of harassment if the company knew, or should have known, about the harassment. A manager who ignores a complaint is allowing a climate to exist that is offensive to an employee in the work unit.

If the employee pursues action through the EEOC or through the courts, the question becomes whether there is a pattern of such behavior in the firm's workplace and whether a *reasonable person* would find the behaviors offensive. In sexual harassment cases in which the victim of the harassment complains to management and nothing is done, or management should have known about the problem even if the victim did not speak up, the victim will have a better chance of winning the case. Therefore, it is important for managers to act quickly and decisively when any suggestion of sexual harassment occurs. Managers are agents of the company and put the company at risk if they are the harassers, or if they fail to take complaints seriously when their employees tell them about possible sexual harassment incidents.[33] Organizations spend a lot of time and money fighting sexual harassment charges when those charges frequently could have been avoided with proper training of managers and an established process for dealing with sexual harassment in the workplace.

In sexual harassment cases, the EEOC and courts generally respond more favorably to employers who have clearly communicated to employees that behavior of a sexual nature is not welcome in the workplace and who have taken immediate and decisive action to investigate and resolve any reports of sexual harassment. Also, employers can improve their chances of defending a case brought against them by showing that the plaintiff did not take advantage of corrective and preventive opportunities offered by the employer.[34] If the company can prove that the incident was never reported even though the company had a clearly defined complaint process and the employee should have been aware of the process, the company will have a better chance of defending its lack of responsiveness. Company Spotlight 3.4 provides an example of a situation in which the damages awarded the plaintiff were large in part because the company did not respond to the concerns of the employee. The EEOC has clearly articulated basic guidelines for employers to follow to reduce the incidence of sexual harassment in the workplace. These guidelines are the same as those outlined in Exhibit 3.4 for reducing the likelihood of any type of harassment in the workplace.

NATIONAL ORIGIN DISCRIMINATION   Discrimination on the basis of national origin can take the form of harassment, disparate treatment, or disparate impact, and it results from:

- Treating an individual differently from others in employment situations because of his or her ancestry, ethnicity, or accent, or because he or she is married to or associates with someone of a particular nationality
- Assuming that a person is of a particular national origin because of physical, linguistic, or cultural traits associated with an ethnic group[35]

After September 11, 2001 (9/11), many individuals of Arab ancestry experienced discrimination in the workplace. One such case involved the Plaza Hotel and Fairmont

3.4 Retaliation by Madison Square Garden Against an Employee

In what has been described as a landmark sexual harassment case, Anucha Browne Sanders was awarded $11.6 million in punitive damages by a jury. Browne Sanders was a team executive for the New York Knicks at Madison Square Garden when she was fired for complaining about being sexually harassed. She claimed that Isiah Thomas, the team's general manager, repeatedly subjected her to unwelcome advances from the time he was hired until she was fired. In the lawsuit, she alleged that Thomas verbally harassed her and made her uncomfortable with physical advances and invitations to leave the office with him for trysts. Apparently, the Knicks did nothing when she reported his behavior and, instead, fired her. This case is a landmark case in part because the verdict awarded to her was for $2 million more than she had requested.

Sources: Based on Anucha Browne Sanders responds to verdict. *ABC News* online, October 3, 2007, http://abcnews.go.com/GMA/story?id=3682294&page=1.

Hotel and Resorts, Inc. The EEOC lawsuit in this case alleged that after 9/11, Muslim, South Asian, and Arab employees were called "terrorist," "Taliban," and "dumb Muslim." Such names were written down instead of the employees' actual names when they were given their room keys for the day's work. In addition, they were cursed at and accused of being responsible for the events of 9/11. According to the EEOC, the employer knew about, or should have known about, the harassment.[36] The EEOC reached a $525,000 settlement agreement with the company on behalf of the 12 affected employees, and the company agreed to train managers and employees about diversity to prevent future hostile environment situations.[37]

The EEOC has identified ways in which language requirements used by employers can lead to discrimination. Exhibit 3.7 provides examples of how language cannot be used as the basis for employment decisions.

Civil Rights Act of 1991 (CRA 91)

The outcome of a number of Supreme Court cases in the late 1980s led Congress to revisit the issue of civil rights in the workplace and amend the Civil Rights Act of 1964. The Civil Rights Act of 1991 (CRA 91) was needed to "strengthen and improve federal civil rights laws, to provide for damages in cases of intentional employment discrimination, to clarify provisions regarding disparate impact actions, and for other purposes."[38]

The provisions of CRA 91 strengthened employee rights in several ways. The following is a summary:[39]

- **It clarifies the burden of proof in disparate impact cases.** After the plaintiff shows that a particular employment practice has disparate impact, the burden of proof is on the employer to show that the practice is job related and that the practice is consistent with business necessity.

- *Accent discrimination:* Making an employment decision based on an applicant or employee's accent when the accent does not interfere with job performance.

- *English fluency:* Requiring fluency in English when such is not required for effective job performance.

- *English-only rules:* Having a rule that employees may speak English only when it is not essential for the safe or efficient operation of the business.

Sources: Adapted from U.S. Equal Employment Opportunity Commission. *National origin discrimination*, March 4, 2008, www.eeoc.gov/origin/index.html.

◄ **Exhibit 3.7**
National Origin Discrimination Resulting from Language Requirements

- **It addresses rights of U.S. employees working abroad.** CRA 91 specifies that U.S. citizens working outside the country for U.S. employers are to receive the same equal employment protections as employees working within the United States under Title VII of CRA 64.
- **It prohibits race norming.** Companies cannot use lower cutoff scores or otherwise adjust the outcome of employment-related tests based on race, religion, gender, or national origin to give minority groups an advantage.
- **It eliminates the use of the mixed-motive defense in disparate treatment cases.** CRA 91 makes explicit that employers cannot defend their discriminatory actions in disparate treatment cases by arguing that the outcome would have been the same because of some additional reason even if the protected class had not been a consideration.
- **It allows jury trials and damage awards.** CRA 91 provides plaintiffs with the option for a jury to decide discrimination cases and permits punitive and compensatory damage awards in disparate treatment cases. (Punitive awards are paid to address the harm caused by discrimination done with malice and reckless indifference to legal rights. Compensatory damages under CRA 91 are not to compensate for back pay and related costs but rather to compensate for emotional damage and other anguish caused by the discrimination. Punitive and compensatory damages under CRA 91 are not to exceed $300,000.)

Age Discrimination in Employment Act of 1967 (ADEA)

Many of you reading this book might think that 40 is a really old age. Others of you know that is definitely not true! (Maybe 90 is old, but some of us aren't so sure about that anymore.) You may remember that when we first defined protected classification at the start of the chapter, we mentioned the Age Discrimination in Employment Act of 1967 (ADEA) as one of the few EEO laws that specifies which group the law protects. The ADEA makes it illegal for an employer to discriminate against any individual age 40 or older because of that individual's age when making employment decisions. These decisions include activities such as promotions, layoffs, and pay raises.

The ADEA resulted from employment practices in which employers preferred younger workers over older workers and even terminated older workers to avoid having to pay retirement benefits to them. The act applies to employers with 20 or more employees and includes state and local governments, employment agencies, labor organizations, and the federal government. The ADEA applies to apprenticeship programs, job notices and advertisements, pre-employment inquiries, and benefits, as well as most other employment practices. Years of service cannot be used by employers as a proxy for age when making employment decisions.

Age discrimination can occur even if both individuals are in the protected class.[40] For example, if an employee who is age 50 is denied a promotion, and the promotion goes to someone who is 42, discrimination may have occurred even though both individuals are over 40. The older employee would use the four-step McDonnell Douglas test to make a *prima facie* case of disparate treatment, which the company would then need to defend by establishing a nondiscriminatory reason for the decision.

Courts have tended to uphold early retirement incentives and waivers offered by employers as long as the employees were not coerced into signing the agreements, the agreements were presented in a way that the employees could understand, and the employees were given enough time to make a decision. In addition, the courts have supported the use of BFOQs based on age when a company can demonstrate that age affects performance in a job and could create a risk to public safety or adversely affect company efficiency. The law also has a provision for compulsory retirement of high-ranking executives who are guaranteed by their employer a certain level of retirement income.

The ADEA was amended in 1990 by the Older Workers Benefit Protection Act (OWBPA), which specifically prohibits employers from denying benefits to older workers. The OWBPA does allow employers in limited circumstances to use age as the basis for reducing benefits, as long as the cost of those benefits is still equal to the cost of providing the benefits for younger workers.[41]

Not surprisingly, age discrimination charges have risen in recent years as the number of older employees in the workforce has increased and as more employers use downsizing as a business strategy. Yet many organizations are finding that older workers make excellent employees and are actively recruiting them for the skills and knowledge they can bring to the job. One such organization is the home-improvement retailer Home Depot. In 2004, Home Depot partnered with the AARP (formerly the American Association of Retired Persons) to recruit older applicants to fill some of the 35,000 new positions the company anticipated having that year. This alliance between AARP and Home Depot was successful and led to the creation of the AARP National Employer Team, a group of 30 employers who are friendly to older workers. Companies on the team include MetLife, Inc., the Principal Financial Group, Inc., and Borders Group, Inc.[42]

Americans with Disabilities Act of 1990 (ADA)

Legislation to provide equal employment opportunity for individuals with disabilities dates back to the Vocational Rehabilitation Act of 1973. The ADA applies to companies with federal contracts over $10,000 and is administered by the OFCCP. As noted earlier, the OFCCP is part of the Department of Labor's Employment Standards Administration and is specifically tasked with administering regulations for federal contractors. Companies covered by this act are required to affirmatively seek and hire qualified individuals with disabilities. Court cases that occurred as a result of this act have provided guidance for implementation and interpretation of the ADA, which applies to all employers with 15 or more employees.[43]

Approximately 12% of males between the ages of 16 and 64, and the same percentage of females in that age bracket, have disabilities.[44] In 1990, Congress passed the Americans with Disabilities Act (ADA) to provide greater opportunities for access in general and employment in particular for these individuals. The ADA specifically prohibits employers from using a disability as the basis for discriminating against qualified individuals in making employment decisions. *Qualified* is a key word in interpreting the ADA—and in other employment laws as well.

Keep in mind that none of the laws we have discussed, including the ADA, requires an employer to hire someone who is not qualified—that is, someone who does not have the knowledge, skills, and abilities or other characteristics required to perform a job. The ADA, however, further defines *qualified* in terms of individuals with disabilities: "a qualified employee or applicant with a *disability* is an individual who, with or without *reasonable accommodation*, can perform the *essential functions* of the job."[45] Definitions of these terms are in order.

Home Depot understands the value of employing older workers.

disability

A physical or mental impairment that substantially limits one or more major life activities.

essential functions

Job tasks, duties, and responsibilities that must be done by the person in a particular job.

reasonable accommodation

Making modifications in how the work is done or in the work environment so that someone who is qualified for the job and who has a disability can perform the job.

According to the ADA, a **disability** is a physical or mental impairment that substantially limits one or more major life activity. Individuals who have a record of such impairment or who are regarded as having such impairment are also covered.[46] Major life activities include breathing, walking, eating, and similar activities that are associated with being able to live and care for oneself.

Essential functions are the job tasks, duties, and responsibilities that must be done by a person in a job. *Must* is another important word in the context of the ADA. If there is someone else who can perform the function instead of the person in the particular position, or if someone else can assist in performing the function, then it probably is not an essential function for that specific position. If, however, the job exists to perform that function, or if there is no one to assist with doing it, then the function is considered essential. In that case, the question becomes whether the person with the disability can perform the function with or without *reasonable accommodation*.

The EEOC defines **reasonable accommodation** as making modifications in how the work is done or in the work environment so that someone who is qualified for the job and who has a disability can perform the job. For example, a reasonable accommodation might include restructuring a job, modifying a work schedule, acquiring or modifying equipment, or making existing facilities easily accessible and usable for someone with a disability.[47] Most accommodations cost less than $500. Only 18% of accommodations cost over $1,000. Some people may wonder if employing individuals with disabilities raises the costs of benefits or creates workplace safety issues for a company. Research has shown that the levels of benefits offered by employers and the incidence rates of occupational illnesses and injuries in the workplace have been unaffected since the ADA went into effect.[48] Exhibit 3.8 provides examples of reasonable accommodations.

Reasonable accommodation is not required if providing the accommodation will create an *undue hardship* for the employer. In other words, an employer with limited financial resources would not be required to spend a large sum of money to make a reasonable accommodation. The EEOC notes that undue hardship is determined by the difficulty and expense of the accommodation relative to the size, financial resources, structure, and nature of a company's operations.[49]

We cover employment selection issues in greater detail in Chapter 7 but need to highlight a few issues related to employee selection and the ADA. Specifically, the ADA prohibits employers from asking job applicants whether they have a disability and from asking about details of a disability. As a manager, you may ask a candidate if he or she can perform the essential functions of the job, and, in fact, that should be a question you ask *all* applicants. In addition, if there is a job-related reason to require the applicant to take a medical examination, you may do so, but only after you have made the job offer, and only if you require all entering employees in similar jobs to have medical exams. Tests for illegal drug use are

Exhibit 3.8 ▶
Examples of Reasonable Accommodations

- Providing amplified stethoscopes for use by hearing-impaired physicians, nurses, and other medical staff members in a medical clinic

- Changing the design of store displays so that a sales associate in a wheelchair can have access to do his job

- Reallocating a non-essential task, such as occasionally taking boxes to a storage room, for an employee with a back problem to another employee and replacing it with a different responsibility

- Allowing an employee to work from home if doing so will not create an undue hardship on the employer

- Training managers to communicate assignments in writing rather than orally for someone whose disability limits concentration but who can otherwise perform the essential functions of the job

Sources: Adapted from U.S. Equal Employment Opportunity Commission. *The Americans with Disabilities Act: A primer for small businesses*, February 4, 2004, www.eeoc.gov/ada/ adahandbook.html.

not considered medical examinations under the ADA and can be administered per the employer's policy. Applicants and employees who use illegal drugs and alcoholics are not protected under the ADA.[50] Recovering drug addicts and recovering alcoholics or drug addicts and alcoholics currently in a treatment program are covered by the ADA.

Companies need to keep all medical information separate from other personnel records to ensure that the information remains confidential and is seen only by individuals who have an absolute need to see it. A supervisor working to make a reasonable accommodation or an emergency medical technician who is called in to treat an individual for a workplace injury would need to see the information.

While Congress may have tried to be clear regarding the terms and conditions of compliance with the ADA, court decisions have created some ambiguity in interpretation. For example, are individuals covered if they have medical or corrective devices that compensate for their disability? And does a disability automatically mean you are covered by the act if you can't do a particular job but can do other jobs? The first question was addressed in the case of *Sutton v. United Air Lines, Inc.*,[51] described in Company Spotlight 3.5.

The second question was answered in part by the *Toyota v. Williams*[52] case. The plaintiff in this case had carpal tunnel syndrome, a condition affecting the wrist and hand caused by repetitive motion. This problem limited her ability to perform her job on one of Toyota's manufacturing assembly lines. She filed suit, charging her employer with failure to provide reasonable accommodation for her. The Supreme Court ruled that her impairment did not limit one or more major life activities; therefore, the ADA did not apply.[53]

Pregnancy Discrimination Act of 1978 (PDA)

In 1978, Congress passed the Pregnancy Discrimination Act (PDA) as an amendment to Title VII. The purpose of this act is to prohibit employers from discriminating against women because of pregnancy, childbirth, or a related medical condition. That means that an employer cannot refuse to hire a woman because she is pregnant. Nor can an employer fire a woman because of her pregnancy. Also, an employer must treat pregnancy the same way it would handle any other medically related condition or temporary disability of an employee. If an employer modified work tasks for an employee with a broken leg (a temporary disability), the employer would have to make similar temporary modifications for a pregnant employee, if needed. In addition, the PDA spells out employer requirements regarding benefits. Companies' health insurance plans cannot exclude pregnancy. Employers are required to provide the same health coverage to spouses of male employees as they do to spouses of female employees. Companies have to provide the same benefits and privileges to pregnant employees, regardless of marital status, that they would provide to other employees who are temporarily disabled.[54]

COMPANY *spotlight*   3.5 Is Correctable Vision a Disability?

Twin sisters applied to become pilots for United Air Lines. Both sisters were severely myopic. Their uncorrected visual acuity was 20/200 or worse. Their corrected vision allowed them to function as do people without their impairment. They applied for jobs as commercial airline pilots with United Air Lines but were turned down because their uncorrected vision did not meet the airline's minimum standard of uncorrected visual acuity of 20/100 or better, even though their corrected vision did meet the standard. Because the vision was correctable, they were not considered disabled, which meant they were not covered by the ADA. They argued that United

perceived them as being disabled because of their uncorrected vision. The Supreme Court ruled that correctable impairments do not qualify as disabilities under the ADA. The twin sisters simply did not meet one of United's job requirements for global airline pilots.

Sources: Adapted from Dunn, R. C. Determining the intended beneficiaries of the ADA in the aftermath of Sutton: Limiting the application of the disabling corrections corollary. *William and Mary Law Review*, Volume 43, February 2002; and Legal Information Institute. *Sutton v. United Air Lines, Inc.* (97-1943) 527 U.S. 471 (1999), www.law.cornell.edu/supct/html/97-1943.ZS.html.

EEO RESPONSIBILITIES OF MULTINATIONAL EMPLOYERS

It is likely that you will work for a multinational corporation for some part of your career. Managers need to consider several questions regarding multinational corporations and employee law:

1. Do the U.S. EEO laws apply to employees of U.S. companies in other countries?
2. What are the responsibilities of U.S. companies operating abroad relative to the laws of those countries?
3. Do non-U.S. companies operating in the United States have to follow the U.S. equal employment laws?

Employees of U.S. companies who are working for those companies in other countries are covered by Title VII, the ADA, and the ADEA. You may remember that we noted this coverage as one of the provisions of the Civil Rights Act of 1991. U.S. employers are not required to abide by these laws, however, if doing so would result in the company violating a law of the country in which the workforce is located. This situation provides employers with a *foreign law defense*. For example, if a country has a mandatory retirement age law, the U.S. employer has to honor that law. Yet, the EEOC does caution that a U.S. employer is not permitted to transfer an employee to another country to keep the company from having to treat the employee in accordance with the U.S. EEO laws. For example, an employer cannot purposefully send an employee to a country that has a mandatory retirement age law so that the employee has to retire.[55]

Companies headquartered in other countries but doing business in the United States are also bound by the U.S. EEO laws. The only way a company from another country can give preference to employees from its own country for jobs in the United States is when there is a binding international agreement or treaty to that effect. If such an agreement or treaty exists, the company is not bound by the EEO laws in that situation. Likewise, U.S. employers operating abroad have a responsibility to know the employment laws of the countries in which they are working and to ensure that they do not violate those laws when managing the local country employees.

Let's turn now to the steps an employee would take if he believes his employer is in violation of an employment law.

FILING PROCESS FOR DISCRIMINATION CHARGES

An individual who believes he or she has been discriminated against in violation of an EEO law can file a charge of discrimination by contacting the nearest EEOC office. The EEOC Web site (www.eeoc.gov) provides contact information for all the district, field, area, and local offices. Individuals can also contact their state Fair Employment Practices Agency. These offices work closely with the EEOC and vice versa. The charge should be filed within 180 days from occurrence of the alleged violation. The time to file can be extended to 300 days under limited circumstances.

Once a charge is filed, the EEOC will review the charge and decide if it warrants investigation. If deemed appropriate, the EEOC will begin an investigation, seeking to collect as much factual information as possible about the allegation. At any point in the process, the EEOC can seek to settle with the employer.

If settlement efforts are not successful, and if the investigation indicates that discrimination occurred, the EEOC will try to work with the employer for conciliation. Compared to litigation, conciliation is a voluntary, less formal, and less costly process used to resolve a discrimination charge. The EEOC may also select the case for its more formal Mediation Program, which is a voluntary program that uses a neutral third party as a mediator and is available at no cost to the employer or employee. Like conciliation, mediation is a good way to avoid a costly, lengthy litigation process.[56] In fact, the EEOC is increasingly encouraging employers to use these techniques, known as **alternative dispute resolution (ADR)**, to resolve

alternative dispute resolution (ADR)

A process for resolving disputes among employees and employers using a mediator or an arbitrator.

discrimination complaints. ADR provides a process for resolving disputes among employees and employers using a mediator or an arbitrator, and it generally leads to a more productive outcome than taking a case to court.[57] If settlement, conciliation, or mediation efforts are not successful, the agency will decide whether to take the case to court. In the event that the EEOC decides not to sue the employer on the individual's behalf, the individual has 90 days to file a lawsuit on his or her own.[58]

EXECUTIVE ORDERS AND AFFIRMATIVE ACTION

Recall from earlier in the chapter that executive orders are enacted by the president of the United States for the purpose of managing the operations of the federal government, including the operations of federal contractors. The executive orders we discuss here are those that directly influence how an employer manages human resources. These executive orders require employers to do more than not discriminate. They require employers to make concerted efforts to bring underrepresented groups into the workplace and to help them advance once hired. Compliance with antidiscrimination executive orders is under the jurisdiction of the OFCCP.

Executive Order 11246 (EO 11246)

Executive Order 11246 (EO 11246) was signed into law in 1965 to prohibit discrimination based on race, color, religion, sex, or national origin. You may be wondering how this EO differs from Title VII. Good question. In many ways, it doesn't, except that it applies specifically to federal contractors and subcontractors, most of which also have to abide by Title VII regulations. The big difference is that EO 11246 specifically requires federal contractors and subcontractors to put into place *affirmative action* programs, which we will describe shortly. Under EO 11246, federal contractors are required to do all of the following:

- Ensure that the job application process and subsequent employment experience are not based on race, color, religion, sex, or national origin
- Conspicuously post notices from the OFCCP, describing the provisions of the nondiscrimination clause in EO 11246
- Provide notices to labor unions or other groups with whom the employer has a collective bargaining agreement
- State on all job advertisements that the company is an EEO, affirmative action employer

The federal government can withhold payment to contractors that fail to comply with this EO.

The affirmative action requirement of EO 11246 is very important. The following sections describe what is meant by *affirmative action* and what employers do as affirmative action employers, whether because they are required to or out of goodwill.

Affirmative Action

Affirmative action employers actively seek to identify, hire, and promote qualified members of underrepresented groups—that is, to do more than simply not discriminate. Affirmative action programs exist for one of three reasons. You have already learned about the first reason, which is to comply with EO 11246. Second, any employer can decide to engage in affirmative action, even if it is not required to do so by law. Many managers understand the contributions that a diverse workforce can make to company success, and they actively seek to recruit, hire, and promote individuals from many different racial and ethnic groups. This type of affirmative action program exists out of the goodwill of the employer, the belief that affirmative action is the right thing to do, and the belief that it can help the company prosper in the long run. After all, if your customer base is diverse, doesn't it make sense for your workforce to be diverse?

affirmative action

The process of actively seeking to identify, hire, and promote qualified members of underrepresented groups.

Affirmative action has helped increase the diversity of the workforce.

Third, companies may have affirmative action programs resulting from a court-ordered consent decree. These decrees result from a court finding that an employer is guilty of discriminating against protected groups in its employee management practices. In such cases, the court will identify what the employer needs to correct and how long the company will be under the decree.

Affirmative action plans under EO 11246 are periodically reviewed by the OFCCP and require the company to engage in three activities:[59]

1. **Conduct a utilization and availability analysis.**   This analysis is a profile of a company's current workforce relative to the pool of qualified workers in the relevant labor market. Companies must first identify the demographic profile of current employees in certain job groupings (for example, managerial, secretarial, technical). Second, companies must identify the percentage of individuals in the *relevant labor market*—the appropriate comparison group of skilled employees—who are in each job grouping. Third, companies must then compare these two demographic profiles. For example, the company will have to determine what percentage of administrative assistants already in the company are female and what percentage of individuals in the workforce that may work as administrative assistants are female. If a company's percentage for a demographic category is considerably lower than the percentage of that demographic category available in the labor market, that protected group is said to be underutilized for that job.
2. **Identify goals and timetables.**   The next step is to establish goals and timetables to address underutilization. It is important to understand that goals are not the same as quotas. Quotas involve hiring to have a certain number of employees from a protected classification and are often met by hiring unqualified applicants or applicants who are less qualified than others, just to make the numbers. The OFCCP explicitly bans quotas.
3. **Develop and implement an action plan.**   The last step in an affirmative action program is to develop and implement an action plan to accomplish the goals established in step 2 to eliminate underutilization in the company's workforce. Companies may use a number of tactics to provide greater opportunities to underutilized groups. Companies can modify where they advertise open positions to target certain demographic groups. Also, they can train current employees to increase the potential for promotions into job categories that are underutilized.

The OFCCP reports many successes as a result of affirmative action programs required of federal contractors, including more females moving into management positions in *Fortune* 1000 companies, employment of people with disabilities, and minority groups entering positions in companies that might not otherwise have been as accessible to them.[60]

There is a downside to affirmative action, however. Employees hired under affirmative action plans may be perceived as less qualified than other workers. As a result of this perception, they may end up not receiving equal treatment in the workplace.

By now you know that affirmative action leads to greater diversity in the workplace. Throughout this book we will talk about the importance of diversity. As you read this information, keep in mind that researchers and managers are not always convinced of the benefits of diversity. Some argue that it improves the quality of group performance and creativity and can lead to a greater variety of perspectives. Others point out the negative outcomes, such as less group integration and lower organizational attachment.[61] Another problem associated with affirmative action is **reverse discrimination**. This type of discrimination occurs when members of a protected group are given preference in employment decisions, resulting in discrimination of non-protected groups. However, if two parties—one minority and one not—are equally qualified and the company is an affirmative action employer, hiring the minority is okay.

reverse discrimination

A type of discrimination where members of a protected group are given preference in employment decisions, resulting in discrimination of nonprotected groups.

RELATED EMPLOYMENT LEGISLATION

We will discuss other laws and executive orders in later chapters, where we can show their direct effects on HR activities in more depth. We briefly discuss a few more laws here, including the Immigration Reform and Control Act of 1986, Family and Medical Leave Act of 1993, 2008, Vietnam Era Veteran's Readjustment Act of 1974, Uniformed Services Employment and Reemployment Act of 1994, state and local government fair employment practice laws, and the doctrine of employment-at-will.

Immigration Reform and Control Act of 1986 (IRCA)

In 1986, Congress passed the Immigration Reform and Control Act (IRCA) in an attempt to control unauthorized immigration to the United States. The law also has antidiscrimination provisions. Specifically, employers with 4 or more employees are prohibited from using national origin or citizenship as a basis for their employment decisions. This portion of the law provides protection against national origin discrimination to a group not covered by Title VII—employees in firms with 4 to 14 employees.

Employers are responsible for verifying that all employees they hire have the legal right to work in the United States. Companies confirm this by having employees complete INS Form I-9, "Employment Eligibility Verification," and by collecting the specified documentation that verifies the workers' identities. To prevent discrimination on the basis of citizenship, employers are encouraged to wait until after a job offer has been made to request that Form I-9 be completed.[62]

The Immigration and Naturalization Service (INS) enforces the IRCA. Employers who hire workers who are not eligible to work in the United States can be fined from $250 to $10,000 for each unauthorized employee. A persistent pattern of violating this law can result in up to a six-month prison sentence for the business owner.[63]

In recent years, the enforcement of this law has garnered greater attention as more focus has been placed on national security issues and as efforts have been made to more closely guard U.S. borders since 9/11. In 2007, a new Form I-9 went into effect, changing the list of documents that someone could use to verify employment eligibility. Employers who fail to ensure that I-9s are completed and/or who do not retain the documents can face penalties of $110 to $1,100 for each employee for whom the form or data on the form is missing.[64] In fact, U.S. Immigration and Customs Enforcement (ICE) has been aggressive in targeting employers believed to be employing unauthorized workers.[65] Exhibit 3.9 provides some steps for companies to follow to reduce their risk of violating the IRCA.

Family and Medical Leave Act of 1993, 2008 (FMLA)

What would you do if you had to choose between taking care of a sick child and going to work? In 1993, Congress passed the Family and Medical Leave Act (FMLA) to provide job protection for employees in just such situations. The FMLA requires employers with 50 or

Exhibit 3.9 ▶

Steps to Reduce the Risk of
Violating the IRCA

1. Be thoroughly familiar with and follow I-9 requirements.

2. Ensure that Form I-9 is completed within three days of hiring a new employee.

3. Reverify I-9s for employees before the expiration date of their work eligibility.

4. Have a plan for handling questionable I-9 documents.

5. Develop an action plan for covering work in the event that employees turn out to be in violation of immigration laws.

Sources: Adapted from Smith, A. Expert: Audit to ensure I-9 compliance. *SHRM Online*, October 31, 2007, www.shrm.org/hrnews_published/articles/CMS_023526.asp.

more employees in a 75-mile radius to grant up to 12 weeks of unpaid leave to an employee who needs to take time away from work because of his or her own illness; to care for a sick member of his or her immediate family (such as a child, spouse, father, or mother) but not including his spouse's immediate family; and for the birth, adoption, or foster care of his or her child. Employees must have worked for the employer for at least 12 months and for 1,250 hours during the 12 months preceding the beginning of the leave.

In 2008, the FMLA was amended to allow leave for family members of soldiers who are on or about to go on active duty for any qualifying exigency. Also added as part of the amendment was the provision for caregiver leave for wounded service members. This provision extends leave eligibility to spouse, son, daughter, or next of kin for up to 26 weeks of unpaid leave.[66]

The FMLA requires prior approval for leave to count as FMLA leave. Under the FMLA, the employer can permit or even require its employees to designate vacation or sick leave time as FMLA leave so that they receive pay during at least a portion of the 12 weeks. In addition, the leave may be taken intermittently throughout a 12-month period. Except in the case of key employees, the law requires that the employer provide the same or an equivalent job for the employee when he or she returns from FMLA leave. *Equivalent* refers to both pay and duties. Key employees are those whose absence could lead to substantial and grievous economic loss to the company.[67]

Vietnam Era Veteran's Readjustment Act of 1974

The Vietnam Era Veteran's Readjustment Act of 1974 provides employment protection for Vietnam era veterans, special disabled veterans, and other veterans who served on active duty during a war or recognized military campaign. Employers with federal contracts or subcontracts of $25,000 or more are required to give equal opportunity and affirmative action to this group of protected class individuals. Affirmative action under this act includes listing all job openings with the local state employment service, with the exception of top management and executive positions, positions of less than three days' duration, and positions to be filled internally.[68]

Uniformed Services Employment and Reemployment Act of 1994

The Uniformed Services Employment and Reemployment Act of 1994 was passed after the Gulf War of 1990–1991. The purpose of this act is to ensure that noncareer military personnel can keep their civilian employment and benefits when volunteering for duty or being involuntarily called to duty. Noncareer military include individuals in the reserve units of any branch of the uniformed services (for example, Army, Air Force) as well as members of the National Guard. In addition, the act is designed to ensure that these individuals can seek employment without being discriminated against and to encourage others to join the uniformed services noncareer programs.[69] With some exceptions, the total length of time a covered individual can be absent from work and retain his or her employment rights is five years.[70]

The war in Iraq has led to greater use of the provisions of this act as large numbers of reservists have been called away from their regular employment. Most employers are required to abide by this act, even if they have only one employee. Any individual who has served in the uniformed services has rights if that individual seeks employment after serving or was employed and took a leave of absence to perform the service. These rights affect initial employment, re-employment after serving, employment retention, promotion, and other benefits.[71] Employers are not required to pay regular wages to employees on military leave, although one study found that about 60% of employers said they intended to provide full pay to active-duty employees, minus their service pay. Other companies have leave policies that provide additional pay to make up for the difference between the civilian pay and the military pay of an employee.[72]

FAIR EMPLOYMENT PRACTICES

Many state and local governments or municipalities have employee management regulations known as **fair employment practice laws**. These laws are often more stringent than the federal government's regulations. When these regulations exist, the more stringent regulations are to be followed. If the state laws are less stringent, then the federal regulations must be followed. Differences between state and local laws and federal laws can exist in all aspects of the employer–employee relationship, from minimum wage to protected classifications. For instance, in New York, California, and Illinois, protected classifications include sexual orientation, marital status, and genetic predisposition to diseases, none of which are protected classifications at the federal level.[73] Managers need to be sure that they are familiar with and abide by the laws of the states in which they work. Information about the regulations for each state is readily available online from each state's labor department.

fair employment practice laws
State and local government employee management regulations.

EMPLOYMENT-AT-WILL AND WRONGFUL DISCHARGE

What happens when an employee receives consistently negative evaluations because of poor work performance, and her company wants to terminate her? **Employment-at-will** provisions give employers the right to terminate (or hire or transfer) employees at any time, unless it's illegal to do so. Firing someone because of his or her membership in a protected class would be illegal. Firing someone because he or she is not performing the job or has violated company policy would be allowable.

Essentially, under the employment-at-will practice there is no contractual obligation to which either an employee or the employer must adhere. Either party can terminate the relationship at any time, for any legal reason. Wrongful discharge and terminating an employee for illegal reasons or for reasons that the courts have found to be inappropriate for discharge are known as exceptions to the employment-at-will doctrine. These exceptions include:

employment-at-will
Hiring provisions based on state laws that allow employers to terminate (or hire or transfer) employees at any time and that allow employees to quit at any time.

- **Public policy exception.** An employee can sue if he or she was fired for a reason that violates public policy—that is, if his or her company acted in bad faith, malice, or retaliation.[74] Serving on jury duty, refusing to violate one's code of professional ethics, and refusing to commit a white-collar crime at the company's urging are examples.
- **Implied employment contract.** An implied contract is one that is inferred (orally, written, or otherwise) by the conduct of the parties involved.[75] Telling employees they will not be fired as long as they do their jobs is an example. Policies printed in corporate employment manuals can constitute implied contracts, too.
- **Implied covenant of good faith and fair dealing.** Employers have an implied contractual obligation to act in good faith toward their employees and vice versa. If an employee has been promised a bonus and then is fired so that the company does not have to pay that bonus, the company will not have acted in good faith and fair dealing.[76]

REGULATORY ISSUES AND COMPETITIVE ADVANTAGE

We have spent a lot of time discussing employment legislation, especially equal employment legislation. As we close this chapter, it is important to make one additional point. A company must not get so caught up in regulatory issues that it loses sight of its purpose as a business. Some companies make hiring decisions to meet quotas and fail to terminate employees who are not contributing to organizational goals out of fear of getting sued. This yields dysfunctional employees and resentment from other employees who have to work with them. The result is lost productive time and often more, rather than fewer, charges of discrimination, including reverse discrimination. Managers face a delicate balance, as imposing controls to reduce harassment and discrimination can overly restrict employee behavior and lead to low morale and lower productivity.[77]

Successful organizations know the value of finding the most qualified applicants, treating them fairly once hired, and treating them fairly and with respect if they have to be terminated. These companies make hiring and other employment decisions with a focus on finding and keeping the most qualified employees rather than on the basis of one of the protected classifications or solely to be legally compliant. As we will show throughout each of the following chapters, this focus, combined with efforts to treat all employees fairly, not only helps organizations stay legally compliant but also carves the path to their competitive advantage.

SUMMARY

Equal employment opportunity laws exist to prevent employers from discriminating in employment practices. Specifically, EEO laws prohibit discrimination on the basis of race, color, religion, gender, national origin, age, and disability, and they seek to ensure that individuals are treated fairly in the workplace.

Disparate treatment occurs when employers use one of the protected classifications to make employment decisions. Employers can defend a charge of disparate treatment by providing evidence that the employment decision was based on a reason not related to the protected classification. Disparate impact occurs when a neutral employment practice leads to an unfavorable outcome for a protected classification. Disparate impact charges can be defended by showing the job relatedness of the practice, business necessity, or the presence of a seniority system or BFOQ.

The main EEO laws include the Equal Pay Act, Title VII of the Civil Rights Act of 1964, the Age Discrimination in Employment Act, the Americans with Disabilities Act, and the Pregnancy Discrimination Act. Each of these laws identifies protected classifications, and the EEOC oversees employer compliance with the practices. In addition, the Civil Rights Act of 1991 provides guidance on discrimination issues.

EEO laws prohibit harassment in the workplace on the basis of race, color, religion, national origin, and gender. While national origin and religious harassment is becoming more of a problem in the workplace, sexual harassment continues to be of particular concern. The EEOC has issued guidance on what an employer should do to discourage sexual harassment in the workplace.

The ADA is one of the most recent EEO laws. The ADA requires that employers look at whether an individual with a disability is qualified to perform the essential functions of the job, with or without reasonable accommodation. Most reasonable accommodations cost less than $1,000.

The EEOC has developed guidelines for multinational companies to assist them in knowing to what extent they are bound by EEO laws. The guidelines cover U.S. employers with U.S. employees in other countries, employers from other countries operating in the United States, and responsibilities of U.S. companies with regard to the laws of the countries in which they are operating.

In addition to EEO laws, a number of executive orders prohibit discrimination by federal contractors and subcontractors and also require that these employers engage in affirmative action activities. Affirmative action means the employer goes beyond not discriminating by actively seeking to increase the representation of minority groups in the organization.

Other related employment laws that affect employee rights include the Immigration Reform and Control Act, Family and Medical Leave Act, Rehabilitation Act, Vietnam Era Veteran's Readjustment Act, Uniformed Services Employment and Reemployment Act, state fair employment practice laws, and the employment-at-will doctrine.

KEY TERMS

affirmative action p. 73

alternative dispute resolution (ADR) p. 72

bona fide occupational qualification (BFOQ) p. 54

business necessity p. 54

disability p. 70

discrimination p. 53

disparate impact p. 56

disparate treatment *p. 55*
employment-at-will *p. 77*
equal employment opportunity
  (EEO) *p. 52*
Equal Employment Opportunity
  Commission (EEOC) *p. 53*
essential functions *p. 70*
fair employment practice laws *p. 77*

four-fifths rule *p. 57*
harassment *p. 58*
hostile work environment *p. 58*
McDonnell Douglas test *p. 55*
mixed motive *p. 56*
Office of Federal Contract
  Compliance Programs
  (OFCCP) *p. 53*

prima facie case *p. 55*
protected classification *p. 54*
quid pro quo harassment *p. 66*
reasonable accommodation *p. 70*
retaliation *p. 58*
reverse discrimination *p. 75*
undue hardship *p. 64*

DISCUSSION QUESTIONS

1. Why do equal employment opportunity (EEO) laws exist? What can employers do to prevent the need for new laws?

2. One of your employees has just complained that the new promotion system leads to the advancement of fewer Hispanics compared to other groups. Which type of discrimination appears to be occurring? What would the employee have to do to make a *prima facie* case of this type of discrimination? What would the company need to show to defend against that charge?

3. Prepare a brief summary of Title VII of the Civil Rights Act of 1964, the Americans with Disabilities Act, and the Uniformed Services Employment and Reemployment Act. For each law, name at least two examples of what employers need to do to comply with the law.

4. A number of employees have complained to you that they have been sexually harassed in the workplace, citing unwelcome comments by co-workers and the posting of sexually explicit material in the break room. As their manager, how would you handle their complaints?

5. An employee with a hearing impairment has applied for a promotion. The job requires that the employee supervise 10 employees in a call center that responds to technical questions from customers. Discuss how you, as the manager, should handle the application for this promotion.

6. You are working for a Japanese company in the United States. Do you have any rights under U.S. EEO laws? If so, which laws apply, and what are your rights?

7. Executive orders that prohibit employment discrimination apply specifically to federal contractors and subcontractors and require affirmative action programs for some of these employers. Why would these executive orders exist? What is their role in reducing workplace discrimination? Do you believe that the U.S. president has the right to require employers to have affirmative action programs? Why or why not?

8. Discuss the difference between affirmative action and quota systems. Why do you think employers often confuse these concepts?

LEARNING EXERCISE 1

One of your employees, Suzanna, a dark-skinned Anglo-American (non-Hispanic) has come to you, complaining about racially oriented comments made to her by another worker. She says that the comments have been made three times in the last month and that she is "sick and tired" of this kind of treatment. Describe how you would handle this situation.

1. What information would you need from the employee?
2. If your company does not have a policy prohibiting racial harassment, how would you handle the situation?

Would the absence of a policy affect how you deal with the situation?

3. What should be included in an anti-harassment policy?
4. Discuss with your classmates why you think one employee would harass another employee in the workplace and why racial harassment charges are on the increase in the United States.

LEARNING EXERCISE 2

Just as you are leaving the office on a Friday afternoon, looking forward to a relaxing weekend with your family, you find out about a situation involving several of your employees. Evidently, a regional manager has told the company recruiter that he is not to hire or refer for hiring any female applicants for sales jobs in the company. When the recruiter complained to other managers about this request, he became the victim of retaliatory harassment and was forced to resign. So much for your relaxing weekend.

1. What should/must you do?
2. What law, if any, has been violated?

3. If a law has been violated, is there evidence of disparate treatment, disparate impact, both, or neither? Make a case for your answer.
4. Is it possible that gender is a BFOQ in this situation? Justify your answer.
5. How should you handle this situation?
6. Discuss with your classmates the likelihood of this type of situation occurring. Justify your opinions. Pay attention to possible differences in opinion among the males and females in your group.

CASE STUDY # 1 — A CASE OF AGE AND GENDER DISCRIMINATION?

Forklifts and Drills LLC is a major supplier of equipment for the oil field industry headquartered in Dallas, Texas, and doing business in Oklahoma, Texas, Alaska, the Middle East, and Russia. Following a decline in sales and market share, the company hired a new CEO, a 42-year-old male. He planned to turn the company around in 16 months. He immediately hired a VP for Marketing (male and age 41) to investigate the reason for the decline in sales. The CEO suggested to him that he might want to look at the gender and age mix of the sales force of the company because he suspected that might be the problem. After all, everybody knows that women don't belong anywhere near an oil field, especially in the Middle East, and younger employees work harder because they have more energy and are more motivated. The results of the investigation revealed that the decrease in sales was due to an "inferior sales team." The average age of the sales force was 52, and 20% were female. The new CEO then instructed the VP for marketing to replace the older members of the sales force with younger hires, and to get rid of those women while he was at it.

Over the next 12 months, 75 employees lost their jobs. Most of these individuals were over age 40 and had received excellent performance reviews in the past. All of the women were replaced. The "official" reason given for the terminations was "inability to adapt to change." Most of the new employees who were hired to replace them were in their 20s, and all were male. The company directed the employment agency used to find these replacements to look for qualified individuals under the age of 34.

DISCUSSION QUESTIONS

1. Visit the EEOC web site (www.eeoc.gov) and read what it says about age and gender discrimination. Prepare a short summary of the information. Based on the information provided in this chapter and your research on the ADEA and the Civil Rights Act of 1964, has discrimination occurred in this example? If so, what type (e.g., disparate treatment, disparate impact, both)?

2. What would the company have to do to prove that their decisions were not discriminatory? Will it be easier to provide that defense on the basis of gender, age, or neither? Justify your response.

3. What would you have done if you had been the VP of Marketing in this situation?

4. Using the U.S. Census Web site (www.census.gov, search for "age data"), find information on the age of the U.S. workforce. What inferences can you draw about this information? Why might an aging workforce lead to an increase in discrimination charges against employers?

5. What might be some reasons that having females and older employees in this company on the sales force could be good for business?

Sources: Based on Luwa, E., & Kleiner, B. H. What employers need to do to ensure compliance with EEOC and FEHC requirements. *Equal Opportunities International* 20:5–7, 2001.

CASE STUDY # 2 — ARE AFFIRMATIVE ACTION PLAN GOALS EVIDENCE OF DISCRIMINATION?

Xerox Corporation's Balanced Workforce Initiative (BWF) involved the publication of specific affirmative action goals for each job and each salary grade level within the company. This plan was started in the 1990s in an effort to ensure proportional representation of all racial and gender groups throughout the company. The BWFs were based on government labor force data and established annually. Part of the annual performance evaluation for managers was how well they met the desired racial and gender compositions for their locations. In one instance, reports compiled for the Houston office indicated that black employees were overrepresented and white employees were underrepresented. To correct this imbalance, over a period of five years, steps were taken to reduce the percentage of black employees in the office.

Six black employees filed suit against Xerox, stating that they were denied promotion opportunities even though they were qualified for the jobs into which they wanted to be promoted. They also indicated that they felt the BWF adversely affected their opportunity for advancement.

DISCUSSION QUESTIONS

1. Based on the evidence presented, has discrimination occurred? If so, which type of discrimination (i.e., disparate treatment, disparate impact, both)? If you aren't sure, what questions would you want to have answered to make your determination?

2. Which party (plaintiffs or defendant) has the burden of proof in this case? What defense could Xerox offer if the plaintiffs make a case of discrimination? Discuss how successful you think the company will be at defending its actions.

3. Could Xerox have achieved the same goals in a less discriminatory manner? If so, how? If not, why not?

Sources: Based on *Frank v. Xerox Corp.*, 5th Cir., No. 02-20416, September 30, 2003; and Kaylin, A. *Affirmative action plan goals: Evidence of discrimination?* Southfield, MI:: American Society of Employers, 2004.

PROSPERA EXERCISES

The Case of Visions Optical

For the past two years, Drs. Alex and Lourdes Luthen have been concerned about how to continue to grow their business, Visions Optical. High employee turnover and a changing economic picture have caused them to realize that they need a different business model than the one they currently have if they want to remain competitive. Their business has grown from 5 employees in one optical store 10 years ago to 250 employees spread across 18 locations in the southern part of Ohio. The couple bought their first office from a retiring ophthalmologist. Soon after they bought the practice, they adopted as their mission "to provide state-of-the art optical solutions for individuals who have discerning tastes and who appreciate high-quality eyewear." A booming economy led to more disposable income and fast growth of their business. Customers bought multiple pairs of fashion eyewear and colored contacts because they could afford to do so. Now, however, the economy is not doing as well. The Luthens understand that a high level of customer service and quality products are essential to attract and retain customers. Repeat business has become crucial for business success. The right people are needed to provide that high level of service, and the Luthens therefore need to identify and reduce the causes of turnover.

Employees at Visions Optical include optometrists, ophthalmologists, dispensing opticians, and different types of support staff, ranging from accountants to receptionists. The current turnover rate of 50% is costing the company a lot of money. Taking time to train a new employee leads to lost productivity and, frequently, lost customers who get frustrated by the lower level of service they receive from employees in training.

You have been a manager for the Luthens for three years, moving quickly from a store manager position to the position of vice president for operations for all Visions Optical stores. Your job is to oversee everything from purchasing to human resources management. You have recently hired a human resources director, but you know that to reverse the turnover problem, you must be intimately involved in the design of the new human resources management practices that you and others have identified as essential.

The first step you need to take is to develop a mission statement, strategy, and objectives for human resources management at Visions Optical that support the overall organizational mission (provided above).

1. Using the code provided to you by your instructor, log on to the Prospera Web site, at www.prospera.com/education. Spend some time moving around the site, becoming familiar with the resources available to you.
2. Complete the following activities for Visions Optical by going to the "PLAN" area of the Web site. (You will likely have to make some assumptions; just be sure to let your professor know what they are when you turn in your work. Also, the online program allows you to edit most of the items.)

   - Create a mission statement for human resources management at Visions Optical. You can find information on how to do this in the "Define Your HR Mission Statement" feature. You will need to provide a rationale for what you select, and the mission statement will drive other choices you make throughout the online case activities at the end of each section.
   - Use the "Define your HR Strategy" feature to support the achievement of your mission.

J.J.Keller's
PROSPERA®
The Online People Management Tool

WORK DESIGN AND WORKFORCE PLANNING

JOB DESIGN
AND
JOB ANALYSIS

1. Explain the importance of job design. *(86)*

2. Describe how managers use efficiency and motivational approaches to design jobs. *(88)*

3. Explain the trade-offs between the efficiency and motivational job design approaches. *(90)*

4. Understand the importance of job descriptions and job specifications. *(94)*

5. Discuss the advantages and disadvantages of different sources of data for job analysis. *(96)*

6. Understand how organizational demands influence job design. *(100)*

7. Discuss how environmental challenges affect job design. *(104)*

8. Explain the importance of job design and job analysis for legal compliance. *(108)*

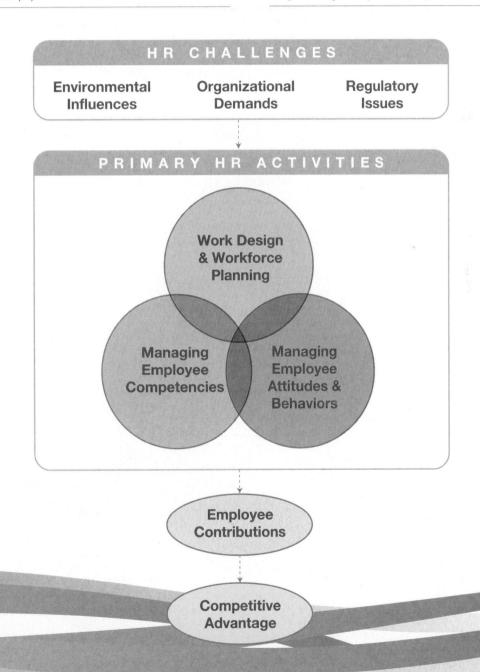

HR CHALLENGES

| Environmental Influences | Organizational Demands | Regulatory Issues |

PRIMARY HR ACTIVITIES

Work Design & Workforce Planning

Managing Employee Competencies

Managing Employee Attitudes & Behaviors

Employee Contributions

Competitive Advantage

THE IMPORTANCE OF JOB DESIGN AND JOB ANALYSIS

Have you ever wondered why jobs are set up the way they are? Compare the job of a cook in a fast-food restaurant to that of a chef in a fine restaurant. The cook typically follows a predetermined process to assemble the product that the customer has ordered in a timely manner. The chef has much more latitude in how to prepare the food as well as what to include with the meal and performs a wider array of tasks than the cook. Why are these jobs so different? Both jobs focus on preparing food to satisfy the customer. Both jobs use similar equipment to cook the food. Yet the duties each job requires differ, as do the knowledge, skills, and abilities (KSAs) each cook must possess to perform the job successfully.

Differences in the tasks and responsibilities for different jobs, or even for similar jobs in different companies, do not occur by chance. Managers consciously make decisions about how they design jobs to improve company performance. Looking at the framework for the strategic management of employees in Exhibit 4.1, you can see that a critical goal of managing *the primary HR activities* is to maximize the employee contributions that yield competitive advantage. **Job design** involves determining the tasks and responsibilities that employees in a particular job are expected to perform as well as how they need to interact with their co-workers to

job design

Determining the tasks and responsibilities that employees in a particular job are expected to perform as well as how they need to interact with their coworkers to realize those contributions.

Exhibit 4.1 ▶

Framework for the Strategic Management of Employees

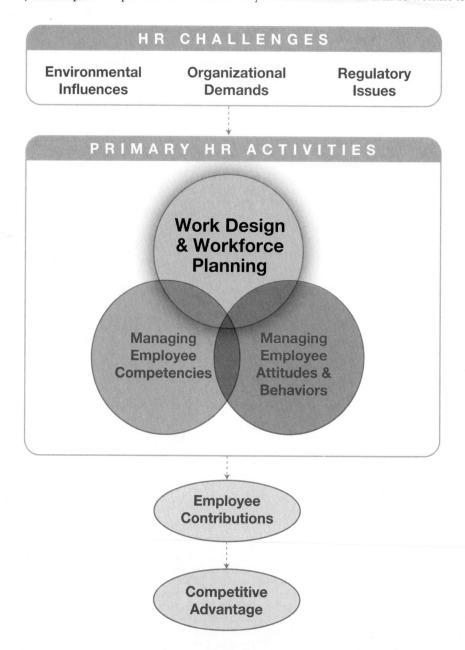

realize those contributions. Job design is a key component of effectively managing employees because it is one of the major ways to translate company goals into the specific actions that employees perform in their jobs. When done effectively, job design helps employees focus on the tasks and responsibilities that optimize their potential contributions for competitive advantage. Some of the key issues managers must consider are:

- What tasks should you emphasize when designing a job?
- How simple or complex are these tasks?
- How many tasks can your employees perform?
- How much flexibility do you provide to your employees in terms of how and where they carry out their tasks?

In addition to deciding how to design jobs, managers must understand the competencies that a person needs to have to be successful in performing the job. This secondary aspect of job design is called job analysis. **Job analysis** is the process of systematically identifying the tasks, duties, and responsibilities expected to be performed in a single job as well as the competencies—the knowledge, skills, and abilities (KSAs)—employees must possess to be successful in the job. Two important outcomes of job analysis are the creation of job descriptions and the identification of job specifications. *Job descriptions* are written summaries of the specific tasks, responsibilities, and working conditions of a job and include a list of the job specifications. *Job specifications* are the specific competencies required by a jobholder to be able to perform a job successfully.

Job descriptions and job specifications serve as valuable tools for the other employee management activities managers must perform. For example, by clearly articulating the abilities employees need to be successful in their jobs, job descriptions serve a critical role in managing competencies. After all, without a clear understanding of the necessary competencies to perform those tasks successfully, how does a company know what to look for when recruiting employees or which job candidate to hire? Similarly, as you may recall from our discussion of the legal environment in Chapter 3, hiring decisions must be based on job-related criteria. How do you know if the hiring standards you use are legally defensible? And how can companies make effective training decisions without knowing which competencies are actually needed to succeed in a current job or a future job? Later in the book, we explore how job descriptions and job specifications are valuable tools for *managing employee competencies*, especially when recruiting and hiring employees.

Job design and job analysis also serve a critical role in *managing employee attitudes and behaviors*. As we will discuss in Chapter 9, an effective performance management system is grounded, in part, on evaluating how well employees perform all aspects of their jobs and providing developmental feedback to improve their job performance. Similarly, compensation decisions are directly influenced by job design. If you have work experience, you'll quickly recognize that salary decisions are typically based on the relative worth of a job performed within a company. Establishing pay levels that are fair and equitable requires a good understanding of a job's tasks and responsibilities, as well as how the value of that job to company success compares with the value of other jobs within the company.

Exhibit 4.2 shows the relationships among job design, job analysis, and job descriptions and specifications. In this chapter, we examine the principles of job design and

job analysis

The process of systematically identifying the tasks, duties, and responsibilities expected to be performed in a single job as well as the competencies—the knowledge, skills, and abilities (KSAs)—employees must possess to be successful in the job.

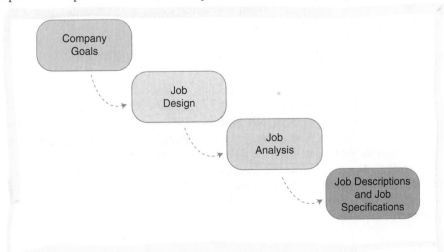

◄ **Exhibit 4.2**
The relationships among job design, job analysis, and job descriptions and specifications

explore alternative approaches to designing jobs to increase employee efficiency and motivation. Our discussion focuses first on job design based on the logic that to perform a job analysis, there must be a job in existence, or at least the idea of a particular set of tasks and responsibilities to be performed. We then discuss the process of job analysis and wrap up with examination of how the HR challenges—organizational demands, environmental influences, and the legal environment—influence job design in practice within companies. The appendix to this chapter provides more detailed information regarding the specific approaches to job analysis.

JOB DESIGN

The ultimate goal of job design is to enhance company performance. There are two considerations in this perspective. First, managers have to understand the role that different jobs play in attaining competitive advantage for the organization. Each job is unique and adds value in different ways. What specific tasks and responsibilities, if performed as expected, will maximize the value added of each job? For example, within a single company, some jobs add value because their tasks contribute to efficient operations. Other jobs add value because their tasks create innovative products or services, maintain customer satisfaction, or contribute to another important aspect of organizational functioning. If customer service is a high priority for the company, what specific tasks, behaviors, and responsibilities lead to exceptional customer service? The challenge for managers is to understand *what* tasks and responsibilities need to be performed in each job to maximize the company's success.

Second, managers must make decisions about *how* employees will perform their jobs. These decisions shape the nature and extent of employees' contributions toward company objectives. Most jobs may be performed in many different ways. For example, in a manufacturing company, employees may work on an assembly line performing a limited set of tasks throughout the day, without interacting with co-workers unless a problem is detected. In another manufacturing firm, employees may perform a broad set of tasks working in self-managed teams and have a high level of interaction among their co-workers. Similarly, for computer programming, some companies may design jobs so that employees work in relative isolation in cubicles, solving complicated problems. Alternatively, some companies may design the job environment to encourage a high level of interaction among programmers. The ultimate choice about which job design approach to implement should be based on how a job adds value within a company. Overall, we can think about how employee jobs are designed as being oriented toward achieving organizational goals through one of two ways: employee efficiency or employee motivation.

Efficiency Approaches to Job Design

Not surprisingly, efficiency has been the dominant model for job design for much of the past 100 years. With the rise of big business fueled by developments of the industrial revolution in the late 1800s, companies began to employ large numbers of workers in a single location to take advantage of the technological breakthroughs in manufacturing. But with these large workforces, companies faced a growing demand for coordination across employees in the work they performed, as well as increased difficulties in staffing and training employees. Scientific management, pioneered by Frederick Taylor in 1911, emerged as a dominant perspective that examined how work should be structured to maximize worker efficiency.[1]

One of the primary contributions of scientific management was the standardization of production processes. This standardization included how employees performed their work, how employees' workdays were structured, when and how often employees took breaks from their work, and how much responsibility employees were allowed on the job. One of the most famous job designs, the assembly line, was based on the principles of scientific management. As highlighted in Company Spotlight 4.1, Henry Ford and his assembly-line production of the Model T revolutionized the automobile production process through the use of scientific management principles. These principles are still in use in many automobile plants today.

COMPANY spotlight   4.1 Henry Ford and the Model T

Just how important can job design be for a company's success? In the early days of the automobile industry, most cars were hand-built by craftspeople. Building cars was art as much as science. The components were not standardized, and the workers had to finesse them into place. Realizing the inefficiencies of this approach, Henry Ford implemented a mass-production assembly line in his automobile plant, with each employee performing a single task throughout the day. As each task was completed, a mechanized assembly line moved the product along to the next worker. The result? Production soared because of the labor efficiencies of the process. The purchase price of the cars dropped as well. In 1912, Ford sold roughly 89,000 cars for $600 each. In 1916, Ford sold 585,388 cars for $350 each. Given this type of growth, it is evident that how jobs are designed can dramatically affect a company's bottom line.

The assembly line transformed how many employees work.

Sources: Krebs, M. The starting line. *Automotive News*, 77:16, 2003; Putting America on wheels. *Economist.com*, December 23, 1999, www.economist.com/business/displaystory.cfm?story_id=347288; and Harrington, A. The big ideas. *Fortune* 140:98–103, November 22, 1999.

The critical outcome of scientific management and efficiency-oriented approaches to job design is a detailed analysis of the specific tasks and worker actions to identify the ideal method or procedure for carrying out each task.[2] One common method for this type of analysis is **time and motion studies**—a systematic evaluation of the most basic elements of the tasks that comprise a job. Each job is broken down into its basic parts so that industrial engineers or managers can design jobs in a way that minimizes excessive movements or wasted time and that maximizes the time employees spend working on core job tasks.[3] Consider the assembly line again. Rather than require employees to search for necessary parts to assemble a product, the process is designed so that employees remain relatively stationary, and a mechanized line brings the product to the employee. As you can imagine, this substantially increases the efficiency of the process. Another effect of this type of design is that it alters the specific tasks and responsibilities of employees through job specialization and job simplification.

Job specialization is the process of breaking down jobs into their simple core elements. By focusing on the core elements of a job, a company is able to limit the variety of tasks employees perform and increase the efficiency with which they perform them. When repetition is built into a job, employees are able to master a specific task and perform it with increasing efficiency, which maximizes company productivity. Recall our earlier discussion of fast-food restaurants. When a company reduces the variety of tasks in each job, the individuals performing those jobs are able to carry out their tasks efficiently, quickly, and with minimal mistakes. And because speed is one of the key sources of competitive advantage for a fast-food restaurant, an efficiency approach to job design enables employees to maximize their contributions toward that competitive advantage.

Another technique in the efficiency approach is **job simplification**, which involves removing decision-making authority from the employee and placing it with a supervisor. By removing the discretionary components of jobs, companies are able to lower the necessary competencies required of employees. One benefit is that this opens up a wider pool of job candidates, and jobs can be staffed faster. Job simplification also reduces the amount of time that employees might spend thinking instead of doing their jobs. Employee training can be more focused and, as a result, more cost-effective.

time and motion studies

A systematic evaluation of the most basic elements of the tasks that comprise a job.

job specialization

The process of breaking down jobs into their simple core elements.

job simplification

Removing decision-making authority from the employee and placing it with a supervisor.

Of course, a common result of job simplification, high repetition, and job specialization is that jobs are narrow in focus, without much, if any, discretion afforded employees. These jobs could be performed efficiently, but they often lack complexity and variety, which can lead to boredom, fatigue, and diminished job satisfaction. An interesting note about Ford's production plants in the early 1900s is that while productivity increased with the implementation of scientific management principles, turnover did as well.[4] However, because of job simplification, more people were able to perform the tasks, and training requirements were reduced. These results allowed companies such as Ford to quickly fill their frequent vacancies. This is a pattern that still exists today in many industries.

Motivational Approaches to Job Design

Motivational approaches to job design maximize an employee's drive to work as hard as possible. A useful way to think about the difference between efficiency and motivational approaches to job design is that an efficiency approach focuses on maximizes employee productivity by simplifying jobs so that employees make fewer mistakes and maintain a high level of performance according to preset job procedures.[5] In contrast, a motivational approach focuses on making jobs more interesting, challenging, and complex to encourage employees to want to work as effectively and efficiently as they can.

The most famous motivational approach to job design is the *job characteristics model*, shown in Exhibit 4.3. The **job characteristics model** identifies five job dimensions and three psychological states of employees that affect employees' internal motivation and satisfaction, as well as absenteeism, turnover, and productivity.[6] The three **psychological states** are (1) experienced meaningfulness of the work, (2) experienced responsibility for outcomes of the work, and (3) knowledge of the actual results of work activities. The five core job dimensions are:

1. **Skill variety** – The degree to which a job includes different tasks and activities that challenge an employee's skills and abilities
2. **Task identity** – The degree to which the job involves completing a whole identifiable piece of work
3. **Task significance** – The degree to which the job has a substantial and perceivable effect on the lives of others
4. **Autonomy** – The degree to which the job permits substantial freedom and discretion to the individual in scheduling the work and in determining the procedures to perform the work
5. **Feedback** – The degree to which performing the job requirements results in the individual receiving direct and clear information about the effectiveness of his performance

job characteristics model

A motivational model of job design based on five job dimensions and three psychological states of employees that affect employees' internal motivation and satisfaction, as well as their absenteeism, turnover, and productivity.

psychological states

In the job characteristics model employees may experience three psychological states relating to (1) experienced meaningfulness of the work, (2) experienced responsibility for outcomes of the work, and (3) knowledge of the actual results of work activities.

Exhibit 4.3 ▶

The Job Characteristics Model

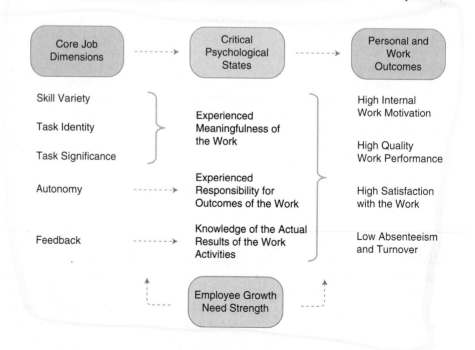

The greater the existence of these five job dimensions, the more motivation employees should feel in their jobs. As shown in Exhibit 4.3, the first three job dimensions influence whether they feel that the work they perform is meaningful and valued. The more skill variety, task identity, or task significance within a job, the more experienced meaningfulness an employee is likely to feel. The fourth job dimension shows that jobs that grant employees autonomy allow them to take ownership and responsibility for the outcome of their work. People with high levels of autonomy know that they are personally responsible for success and failure. The fifth job dimension emphasizes that when employees receive feedback, they understand how well they are performing and the direct results of their work.[7] This allows employees to know whether their work performance is satisfactory.

Viewed together, when these job dimensions are low, employees tend to be less satisfied with their jobs and less motivated to work hard. They tend to have lower-quality performance and higher turnover and absenteeism.[8] In contrast, employees in jobs that are designed to support the three psychological states have higher internal motivation to perform well.[9]

How well this model works depends, in part, on the individual employee. Some employees have a higher need for growth in their jobs than others. **Growth need strength** is the extent to which individuals feel a need to learn and be challenged, a need to develop their skills beyond where they currently are, and a strong need for accomplishment. Employees with high growth need tend to respond more strongly to the presence of the three psychological states than employees with low growth need. One implication of this discussion of growth need strength is that it highlights the importance of considering the fit between individuals and job requirements when making staffing decisions (as we will discuss in Chapters 6 and 7).

Understanding how employees react to the absence or presence of the psychological states and core job dimensions helps managers decide which tactic to use to improve employee motivation and satisfaction. As shown in Exhibit 4.4, three primary methods for improving employee motivation and satisfaction through job design are to change the tasks that employees perform, provide employees with more responsibilities or authority regarding the performance of their jobs, and restructure the work environment to include teams.

CHANGING JOB TASKS   Managers may modify the variety of tasks that employees perform to make jobs less boring and more satisfying through job enlargement and job rotation. **Job enlargement** is the assignment of additional tasks to employees. This involves increasing the volume or variety of tasks that are of a similar level of difficulty

growth need strength

The extent to which individuals feel a need to learn and be challenged, a need to develop their skills beyond where they currently are, and a strong need for accomplishment.

job enlargement

The assignment of additional tasks to employees of a similar level of difficulty and responsibility.

▶ Exhibit 4.4   Methods to Improve Employee Motivation and Satisfaction Through Job Design

Change job tasks

Job enlargement — Assign additional tasks of a similar level of difficulty and responsibility to employees.

Job rotation — Move workers from one job to another within an organization.

Increase responsibility

Job enrichment — Increase the level of responsibility and control regarding tasks performed in a job.

Participation — Permit employees to participate in decisions that may affect them in their jobs.

Voice — Provide employees with access to formal channels within their company to express concerns about their work situation.

Create employee teams

Create small groupings of individuals who work collaboratively toward a common goal and who share responsibilities for their outcomes.

job rotation

Moving workers from one job to another job within the organization to provide exposure to different aspects of the company's operations.

job enrichment

Increases in the level of responsibility or control employees have in performing the tasks of a job.

empowerment

Providing employees with higher level tasks, responsibility, and decision making in the performance of their job.

and responsibility. One of the primary benefits of job enlargement is that increasing the number of different tasks employees perform causes skill variety to increase as well. Greater task and skill variety are effective in countering boredom and fatigue.[10]

Job rotation means moving workers from one job to another job within the organization to provide exposure to different aspects of the company's operations. Unlike job enlargement, job rotation does not change the tasks of a particular job. Rather, it changes the tasks that individual employees perform by moving them to different jobs in a systematic manner. One of the major benefits of job rotation is that it can break up the monotony of performing relatively simple jobs while still enabling efficiency in the performance of each specific task. Another benefit is that companies can use job rotation as a training tool to ensure that employees are able to perform a number of tasks and have a broader overview of the company.[11] A manager in training, for instance, may work for several weeks or months within the marketing department, rotate to a term within the production department, and then move into the design department.

INCREASING RESPONSIBILITY AND PARTICIPATION   While job enlargement and job rotation focus on changing the breadth of tasks that employees perform, **job enrichment** increases the level of responsibility or control employees have in performing the tasks of a job. In some ways, it is useful to think of job enrichment as an opposite approach to the job simplification that we discussed earlier in this chapter. As job simplification removes most of the cerebral or higher-level aspects of work and allocates them to managers and supervisors, job enrichment, also called *empowerment* or *delegation*, entrusts higher-level tasks and responsibility to employees. **Empowerment** builds on the job characteristics model dimension of autonomy but takes it a step further by permitting employees to have not only input in how they carry out their tasks but also authority to modify the job itself.[12] When delegated authority and responsibility, employees often realize heightened job satisfaction and task performance.[13] There are a number of ways to accomplish job enrichment, including the following:[14]

- Provide employees with discretion to set schedules, decide work methods, check quality, and help less experienced employees.
- Provide employees with greater amounts of authority.
- Allow employees freedom to decide when to start and stop work, when to break, and how to prioritize their work.
- Encourage employees to solve problems as they encounter them.
- Provide employees with knowledge and control over budgets.

Of course, companies have to be careful when empowering employees through job enrichment. While it can be an effective means to increase employee motivation and to transfer authority to levels in an organization where decisions are implemented by employees,[15] job enrichment must be accompanied by ability and accountability. Both the employee and the company suffer when employees are asked to take responsibility for tasks that they do not have the competencies to perform effectively. And empowering employees without also holding them accountable for their decisions may result in haphazard decision making.

As an alternative to transferring decision-making authority to employees, managers can also improve employee satisfaction by increasing employee participation in decision-making processes. **Participation** is the extent to which employees are permitted to contribute to decisions that may affect them in their jobs. In contrast with job enrichment, participation does not necessarily transfer responsibility or discretion to employees. It does achieve a similar benefit, however, by allowing employees to take part in decisions that affect their jobs. A specific form of participation, called **voice**, gives employees access to channels within their company to complain or express concerns about their work situation. Whether the channels for employee participation are formal or informal, the more employees are able to have a say in aspects of their work that impact them, the more satisfied they are likely to be in their jobs. Company Spotlight 4.2 shows how Boeing effectively uses job enrichment and participation to motivate its employees and maintain a competitive advantage in its industry.

participation

The extent to which employees are permitted to contribute to decisions that may affect them in their jobs.

voice

A specific form of participation that gives employees access to channels within their company to complain or express concerns about their work situation.

COMPANY *spotlight*   4.2 Empowerment and Participation at Boeing: Making Employees' Ideas Fly

More than likely, you have flown on a Boeing airplane. Boeing is the world's leader in producing aircraft. Of course, building airplanes is not all that Boeing does. It is also a world leader in integrated defense systems and related activities. A core value at Boeing is "People working together." When you think about it, how could a company such as this one stay in business without people working together?

Innovation has always been at the heart of what Boeing is about, dating back to 100 years ago, when William Boeing founded the company. Today, Boeing has a program called the Chairman's Innovative Initiative that allows employees to work on new ideas and take them to market. Employees with innovative ideas complete an application, and, when applications are accepted, the Boeing Ventures Team works with the employees to move their ideas forward.

Another example of how Boeing encourages participation comes from the Commercial Airplanes business unit. Every Thursday, the leadership team for this business unit meets with its employees. This meeting isn't just to make reports. Instead, employees discuss world events, Boeing's markets and customers, competition, partners, and opportunities. These meetings started in 1998, and since that time, the business unit has had continued financial improvement.

Boeing understands that the knowledge and experience its employees bring to the job every day are critical to the company's remaining a leader in its industry.

Boeing doesn't just assume that these and other employee involvement activities matter. It regularly conducts employee surveys to find out how employees feel about the involvement efforts. Results of these surveys suggest that employees who feel they can share ideas and be involved in decisions within their work group are more productive and have a better attitude about being at work than employees who don't feel this way. Boeing's actions show that employee involvement pays off not only in what employees do and how they feel about doing it but also in financial returns to the company.

Sources: Adapted from Boeing. *Employment : Culture:* http://www. boeing.com/employment/culture/index.html#peop; Boeing. *What we do: Commercial airplanes*, http://www.boeing.com/employment/ whatWeDo/commercialAirplanes.html; and Marcellino, E.. Boeing, Tunnel Vision: T-38 modification team has its eye on efficiency. *Boeing Frontiers*, August 2004.http://www.boeing.com/news/frontiers/ archive/2004/august/i_ids3.html and Employee Survey Trends Rise: Team participation cultivates positive attitude, *Boeing Frontiers*, September 2003. http://www.boeing.com/news/frontiers/archive/ 2003/september/i_nan1.html.

EMPLOYEE TEAMS   A third method of increasing employee satisfaction and motivation is the use of teams—small groupings of individuals who work collaboratively toward a common goal and who share responsibility for their outcomes. There are several basic types of teams: work teams, parallel teams, and project teams.[16] *Work teams* are typically well defined, stable, and have full-time members working under the direction of a supervisor to produce some good or service. *Parallel teams* pull people from different areas of a company to address a particular problem or issue. Parallel teams include quality circles and problem-solving teams. One distinction of parallel teams is that members retain their formal positions in their own departments while working on the team; these teams exist in parallel to the existing organizational structure. *Project teams* are unique because they typically exist for a limited time under the guidance of a project leader. Often, project team members disband once they accomplish a particular objective, such as the design of a new process or product.

Teams offer a number of benefits to managers. By integrating individuals with diverse experiences and talents, teams allow members to examine issues from multiple perspectives, which would not be possible with individual employees working in isolation. And when teams are composed of members with complementary abilities, they may be able to achieve performance levels that exceed the potential of individuals working alone.[17] Team-based job designs also have the potential to improve employee interaction and social support for team members. When team members are cross-trained, multiple people can perform team tasks, which increases task variety and reduces boredom and fatigue among employees.[18]

In addition to these benefits, research has shown that a higher level of self-management in any of these types of teams leads to greater motivation, job satisfaction, and effort among team

self-managed team

Type of team in which team members, rather than a supervisor of the team, work collaboratively to make team decisions, including hiring, planning, and scheduling decisions.

members.[19] In a **self-managed team**, the team members, rather than a supervisor of the team, work collaboratively to make team decisions, including hiring, planning, and scheduling decisions.[20] One of the major reasons that self-managed teams are effective is that they are based on the principle of empowerment that we described earlier. Decision making rests with the team members, who, after all, are responsible and accountable for carrying out the team's tasks. By giving authority to a team, a company may be able to cut bureaucracy in decision making and improve the effectiveness of the team.[21] Of course, there are potential downsides to team-based structures. Teams require high levels of interaction among team members, and their success depends directly on the willingness of team members to share their knowledge and ideas. If there is a low degree of trust or insufficient face-to-face interaction, teams may not be able to meet their objectives.[22]

Which Approach to Use? Balancing Efficiency and Motivational Approaches

Focusing on efficiency is certainly an important component of organizational effectiveness. After all, inefficient workers are less productive and contribute to higher company costs than efficient workers. However, when taken to the extreme, a focus on efficiency can lead to jobs that employees may view as boring and unfulfilling.[23] Similarly, focusing on employee motivation alone in job design neglects the potential benefits of efficiency that might be realized through task simplification and specialization.[24] Managers need to balance the tension between motivational and efficiency approaches cautiously, as each approach has fundamental trade-offs and distinct outcomes.[25] In addition, these two approaches are negatively related; emphasizing one diminishes the odds of realizing the other.[26]

The job design choices that managers make should be driven by the strategic objectives of the company. Recall the framework in Exhibit 4.1. How jobs are designed dictates how employees add value to the company. When managers design jobs in a way that aligns the tasks and activities that employees perform with the primary objectives of the company, employees are in a position to contribute to their company's success. In contrast, when this alignment is weak or missing, employees may focus on tasks and activities that are not necessarily the most important for company success.

JOB DESCRIPTIONS AND JOB SPECIFICATIONS

job description

A written summary of the specific tasks, responsibilities, and working conditions of a job.

job specification

Description of the competencies—the knowledge, skills, abilities, or other talents—that a jobholder must have in order to perform the job successfully.

Before managers can effectively manage employees' competencies and attitudes and behaviors, they need to have a clear understanding of job tasks and job specifications. A **job description** is a written summary of the specific tasks, responsibilities, and working conditions of a job. **Job specifications** are the competencies—the knowledge, skills, abilities, or other talents—that a jobholder must have in order to perform the job successfully. Job descriptions and job specifications are technically separate, but most companies include job specifications as part of the job description, as the example in Exhibit 4.5 illustrates. While there is no standard format, most job descriptions provide the following information:

- *Job title.* The first portion of a job description usually states the title of the job and the specific level, if any, of the job in a particular job grouping. For example, some job groupings have multiple levels, such as materials handler I, materials handler II, and materials hander III.
- *Job identification section.* The job identification section specifies important administrative aspects of the job, such as the department in which the job is located, who conducted the job analysis, when the job was last analyzed, the wage category of the job, and the job code, if the company uses a job classification system.
- *Essential duties and responsibilities section.* The essential duties and responsibilities section is a summary of the key tasks, worker behaviors, and responsibilities of the job. These statements, called *task statements*, typically appear in order of importance or in order of the time each task requires. Some companies distinguish the essential duties from marginal duties and responsibilities in this section for legal purposes.

- *Job specification section.* The final portion of the job description is the job specification. This section documents all the qualifications that a job candidate must possess in order to successfully perform the job—for example, educational level, work experience, or specific abilities, such as mathematical, language, or computer skills. A key point is that job specifications are *requirements* for job success, not *desirable* attributes that go beyond what is required. For example, a doctoral degree is not likely to be a true requirement for job success in many entry-level positions. Some companies identify desirable or preferred qualifications as well, as shown in Exhibit 4.5.

A clear job description with job specifications is critical for effectively managing employee competencies and behaviors. Managers often use the task statements in the job

▶ **Exhibit 4.5** Sample Job Description for an Accounting Assistant

Job Title:	
	Accounting Assistant

Job Identification Section:

Department:	Accounting
Reports to:	Director, Accounting
Position Number:	05-0246
Wage Category:	Non-Exempt
Salary Grade:	04
Analyst:	Ellen Kassman
Date Analyzed:	April 8, 2008

Summary:
The accounting assistant works under the direction of the accounting director and provides professional accounting, financial analysis, and budgeting support for assigned accounts.

Essential Duties and Responsibilities:

- Maintain financial planning and administration of the accounting office.
- Prepare a variety of financial documents, analyses, and reports, including year-end reports, for internal and external purposes within established deadlines.
- Reconcile administrative and overseas bank accounts, manage accounts payable and receivable, and perform financial planning.
- Analyze and reconcile financial data of internal records with the department's systems.
- Implement billing policies.
- Act as a liaison with other departmental units.
- Perform other duties as assigned by director of accounting.

Job Specifications:

- A bachelor's degree, preferably in accounting, finance, or related field, or an equivalent combination of education or related experience that demonstrates knowledge and understanding of general accounting principles and practices required.
- Two years of experience in a financial or accounting function required.
- Experience with computers and common word-processing, spreadsheet, and database applications required.
- Excellent communication and organizational skills required.
- A basic understanding of global finance and market forces on exchange rates desired.

Exhibit 4.6 ▶

Checklist for Writing a
Job Description

_____ **1.** Provide job-identifying information, such as title, assigned location, and classification.

_____ **2.** Prepare a brief summary of the job.

_____ **3.** Write task statements, making sure to include the following in each:

    a. What is done (action verb)

    b. To whom or what (object)

    c. For what purpose

    d. Using what resources, tools, or equipment

_____ **4.** Identify the job requirements:

    a. Knowledge

    b. Skills

    c. Abilities

    d. Minimum work experience and education

_____ **5.** Describe the work context:

    a. Schedule

    b. Physical requirements

    c. Environmental conditions

_____ **6.** Have job incumbents and supervisors review the description accuracy

description as the performance standards that employees in a particular job are expected to meet. As we will discuss in Chapters 6 and 7, the job specification section is particularly critical for recruiting and selecting employees to ensure that staffing decisions are relevant, effective, and nondiscriminatory. Exhibit 4.6 provides a checklist to keep in mind when writing a job description. And as discussed in Chapter 3, job relatedness is a key criterion for complying with regulatory issues.

Given the importance of job descriptions and specifications, both for company success and legal compliance, it is critical that these documents accurately represent each job. The accuracy in identifying the tasks and qualifications of a job relies on collecting and analyzing information about each job—a process called job analysis.

JOB ANALYSIS

Job analysis is the systematic study of the tasks, duties, and responsibilities that are expected to be performed in a single job. The primary goal of job analysis is to attain a clear understanding of what is expected to be performed in each job (job descriptions) and the specific competencies that are necessary for successful performance of the job (job specifications). Often, trained professionals from the HR department perform job analysis, but managers participate in a variety of ways. Managers typically provide information during the process and, most importantly, verify the accuracy of the final job description.

Job Information

To gather the necessary job information, _job analysts_ (trained professionals who specialize in analyzing jobs) and managers typically rely on one of several methods: observations, diaries, interviews, questionnaires, and generic information available through O*NET, an online database of jobs.

OBSERVATIONS AND DIARIES   Observations are one source of information about the tasks performed in a job. In this approach, a manager or a job analyst observes and documents all the activities performed by current jobholders while they work. One of the primary advantages of this approach is that it is based on actual work behavior rather than on someone's memory about what a job involves. In addition, the neutral perspective of the job analyst helps reduce bias or inflation in identifying the tasks that jobholders may claim to perform. However, it is sometimes difficult to capture all aspects of a job through observation or to observe all tasks for jobs that are not standardized or simplified. The job of a consultant or a supervisor, for example, may be difficult to accurately analyze using observation because of its many diverse tasks. In addition, observation may miss tasks that are performed infrequently and may not fully capture tasks that require considerable judgment.

A variation of the observation approach is to ask employees to keep **diaries**, or logs of the tasks and activities that they perform throughout the course of a day, week, or month. In this approach, employees, rather than a job analyst, observe their own actions on the job and document them in a diary. One advantage of this data-gathering method is that it relies on the source of information that knows the job the best—the employees. However, employees might log only the tasks that they tend to emphasize and might not document other tasks that they should also be performing. In addition, employees may perceive keeping a diary as frustrating and time-consuming. It is critical to seek input about the process from various employees and managers when using diaries or logs.

INTERVIEWS   Another method of gathering data about a job is conducting interviews. In this method, a job analyst conducts structured interviews with jobholders and supervisors, using a series of job-related questions to identify the tasks and responsibilities of a job. The advantage of this approach is that it can uncover or clarify work tasks that are not directly observable. For example, gathering data on managerial positions through observation may not provide information on the cognitive components of the job that command a good part of the manager's time. The interview approach allows a job analyst to discuss such aspects of a job with the jobholder. Exhibit 4.7 provides a checklist for conducting a job analysis interview.

diary

Log of the tasks and activities that employees perform throughout the course of a day, week, or month.

The process used to collect job information during a job analysis interview will influence the quality of the information obtained. Some pointers to enhance the outcome of a job analysis interview follow:

_____ 1. Make an appointment in advance with the job incumbent or supervisor to be interviewed, and make the interviewee aware of the purpose of the appointment.

_____ 2. Engage in casual conversation, including making introductions, when you arrive to help put the interviewee at ease.

_____ 3. Answer any questions the interviewee may have about the job analysis process and outcomes.

_____ 4. Use a predetermined set of interview questions to make sure the information obtained is the information needed for the purpose of the job analysis. This also ensures that both the interviewer and interviewee stay focused on the task at hand.

_____ 5. Guide the interview assertively, if necessary, to stay on task and ensure that needed information is collected during the allotted time.

_____ 6. Allow the interviewee to return to a question if the answer is not immediately clear in his mind, but be sure to return to the question.

_____ 7. Before ending the interview, summarize the major points of the information you have gathered and allow the interviewee to make any corrections needed.

◄ **Exhibit 4.7**

Checklist for Conducting a Job Analysis Interview

The interview approach can, however, be time-consuming for the analysts and the interviewees. In addition, this approach depends on the ability of jobholders and managers to accurately convey all the tasks and responsibilities for a position. Employees and managers may believe there is a benefit to exaggerating or inflating the types of tasks performed on a job—a situation that is especially likely to occur if the results are linked with compensation decisions.[27]

QUESTIONNAIRES   Questionnaires provide yet another method of gathering information about job tasks and responsibilities. Whereas the interview and observation methods are time-consuming, questionnaires can be used with a large number of individuals at the same time. In addition, using the same questionnaire for all positions provides standard types of data across jobs. As we will discuss in Chapter 10, one of the benefits of having similar data is to help establish equity or fairness in how much people are paid based on the relative value of their jobs. However, the questionnaire approach requires considerable up-front work to ensure that the questions capture all dimensions of the jobs surveyed. Another limitation of questionnaires is that, unlike interviews, they don't offer an opportunity for immediate follow-up questions that may provide additional insights into jobs. Also, they assume that the individuals completing the questionnaire accurately understand all the questions asked and can clearly communicate the answers in writing

OCCUPATIONAL INFORMATION NETWORK (O*NET)   A final method of collecting information about jobs is by using the **Occupational Information Network (O*NET)**, located online at www.online.onetcenter.org. The O*NET database, created by the U.S. Department of Labor, is a comprehensive source of information for more than 800 occupations. For each job, O*NET provides a summary rating of the tasks and work-related behaviors performed in the jobs. In addition to task-oriented information, O*NET also provides data on the job specifications of each job—the knowledge, skills, abilities, and experience levels required to perform the job.

One of the primary advantages of O*NET is that it offers managers an online resource to help with the job analysis process. It is especially helpful to managers who do not have a full HR department or job analysts to assist them, as in many small businesses. Rather than completing the entire job analysis process themselves, managers can build on O*Net job descriptions that have been generated for similar positions across a large number of companies. This is especially an advantage for managers who may be creating a job description for a job that doesn't exist yet within their company. The job description on O*NET can be a starting point to understand the types of tasks a person in a particular position might perform as well as the specific knowledge, skills, and abilities to look for when hiring to fill the new position. Finally, accessing O*NET Online does not require substantial capital investments—it is free. The appendix to this chapter contains more details about O*NET and a sample job entry from its database. Exhibit 4.8 provides a summary of each of the five data-collection methods we have covered, along with recommendations for when each is most appropriate to use.

Job Analysis Techniques

Several techniques may be used to analyze job information, classified as either standardized or customized approaches. We briefly describe the differences between the two approaches here, and then we provide a detailed look at each of the specific job analysis techniques in the appendix to this chapter.

First, job analysis techniques differ in terms of whether they focus on a standardized approach to categorizing jobs or a customized approach to studying the unique dimensions of a particular job within a company. Second, they differ in terms of whether they focus on identifying the tasks performed in each job, the needed competencies (knowledge, skills, and abilities) required to successfully perform each job, or both. Exhibit 4.9 provides a summary of the primary job analysis techniques.

Sometimes a company needs to perform job analyses on many different jobs.[28] For example, if a company creates a new unit with a variety of positions (secretarial, technical, professional) or if it wants to establish the relative worth of a variety of jobs for

Occupational Information Network (O*NET)

An online database created by the U.S. Department of Labor that serves as a comprehensive source of information for more than 800 occupations.

▶ Exhibit 4.8 Methods for Collecting Job Information

Method	Source	Process	Applicable Jobs
Observation	Job analyst	Physical observation or videotaping of employees performing the job. Notes made or videotape analyzed to determine main tasks performed.	Jobs with repetitive tasks performed over a short cycle, such as an assembly-line position.
Diary/log	Employee	Records activities at specified intervals for a specific time period. Information analyzed to identify patterns suggestive of typical types of work performed.	Most jobs. May be disruptive to use in retail, manufacturing, and construction.
Interview	Job analyst/ employee	Face-to-face question-and-answer session to identify tasks, duties, responsibilities, competencies, and working conditions.	Most jobs, especially managerial and professional level. Time-consuming and costly.
Questionnaire	Employee	Written survey instrument administered in group setting or individually. Can be done electronically. Ensures standardized information collected.	All jobs. Literacy of participants can affect quality of information collected.
O*NET	Occupational Information Network	Online database www.online. onetcenter.org) of more than 800 occupations that includes information on tasks, work-related behaviors, and job specifications needed to perform the job.	All jobs. Customization of jobs to specific company circumstances may be limited.

compensation purposes, it would benefit from using a standardized approach so that all jobs are analyzed based on similar standards or criteria. A standardized job analysis approach uses a single instrument—typically a questionnaire or O*NET—to collect similar data that may be used to evaluate multiple jobs within a company or across many companies. This approach identifies underlying job dimensions that apply to a variety of different jobs and that allow comparisons of dissimilar jobs in meaningful ways.

The two most common standardized approaches used by companies for analyzing job data are the Functional Job Analysis (FJA) and the Position Analysis Questionnaire (PAQ). The FJA is based on the notion that it is possible to systematically compare jobs that are dissimilar in the tasks they perform by focusing on job dimensions that apply to all jobs.[29] The *functional* part of its name represents functional categories, which are broad categories of work-related activities that are applicable to all jobs and focus on three distinct work domains related to data, people, and things. The PAQ is a standardized survey that

▶ Exhibit 4.9 Approaches to Analyzing Job Information

Standardized approaches	Functional Job Analysis (FJA)	Focuses on the level of three broad categories of work-related tasks in each job, related to *data, people*, and *things*.
	Position Analysis Questionnaire (PAQ)	Focuses on work-related behaviors that employees must display to successfully perform a job, related to *information input, mental processes, work output, relationships with other persons, job context, other characteristics*.
Customized approaches	Critical incidents	Focuses on obtaining specific, behaviorally focused descriptions of work behaviors that distinguish exceptionally good performance in a particular job from exceptionally poor performance.
	Task inventory	Focuses on identifying the specific tasks that are necessary to successfully perform a job.
	Job element	Focuses on identifying the employee competencies (knowledge, skills, and abilities) that are necessary to successfully perform a job.

measures a number of different employee work-related *behaviors* necessary to perform a wide variety of tasks in different jobs. The appendix to this chapter provides more explanation of these standardized approaches.

Sometimes managers need to conduct a more customized analysis of jobs within their company. Whether it is for a newly created position or a unique position that is simply not captured through standardized approaches, customized techniques allow managers to develop a job description and job specifications that represent the unique attributes of a job. The three primary approaches for customized job analyses are the critical incidents approach, the task inventory approach, and the job elements approach. The *critical incidents approach* focuses on obtaining specific, behaviorally focused descriptions of work activities that distinguish exceptionally good performance in a particular job from exceptionally poor performance. The *task inventory approach* focuses on collecting information to identify the tasks that are necessary to successfully perform a job. Finally, the *job element approach* focuses solely on analyzing the employee competencies that are necessary for successful job performance rather than the tasks to be performed in a job. When adopting a customized approach, observations, diaries, and interviews may be preferred as data collection techniques to allow the collection of unique information about specific jobs and specifications. The appendix to this chapter provides more details about these customized approaches.

JOB DESIGN IN PRACTICE: MEETING ORGANIZATIONAL DEMANDS

We have covered a lot of material regarding job design and job analysis within companies. With this background in place, we now turn to the decisions managers have to make in designing jobs to meet HR challenges, as outlined in Exhibit 4.10. We'll start with organizational demands.

▶ **Exhibit 4.10** Job Design in Practice

Context	**Work Design and Workforce Planning** **Chapter 4, "Job Design and Job Analysis"**
Organizational Demands	
Strategy drives . . .	• Job design approach adopted • Breadth of tasks, duties, and responsibilities performed
Company characteristics determine . . .	• Formalization of jobs • Breadth and depth of tasks
Culture establishes . . .	• Managerial choices of job design tactics • Employee acceptance of job design decisions
Employee concerns include . . .	• Perception of fairness of job duties • Need for flexible work arrangements
Environmental Demands	
Labor force influences . . .	• Skill availability to perform tasks • Job design decisions for the aging labor force
Technology affects . . .	• Telecommuting • Virtual teams
Globalization impacts . . .	• Need to address cross-cultural issues • Relevant labor market
Ethics/social responsibility shapes . . .	• Concerns about types of tasks required • Attitudes toward physical conditions of job design
Regulations *guide* . . .	• Importance of identifying essential and non-essential job duties • Job design and employee safety

Strategy and Job Design

In Chapter 2, we discussed different types of business strategies. We noted that companies compete based on having the lowest costs in their industry or having some form of differentiation, such as customer service, high quality, or an image for which customers are willing to pay a premium. The type of strategy that a company pursues has two direct implications for job design: how jobs are structured and what tasks, duties, and responsibilities employees need to perform.

JOB DESIGN APPROACH ADOPTED   Recall our earlier comparison of jobs in a fast-food restaurant to jobs in an upscale restaurant. While the types of jobs may be similar, how the jobs are designed differs considerably, given the different strategies of these companies. Fast-food establishments compete based on costs and efficiency. One of the primary ways their employees contribute to the company's strategy is to perform narrow jobs efficiently and quickly. This job design allows the company to serve its customers affordable meals quickly. In contrast, most upscale restaurants are not focused on speed or cost. Instead, they focus on the quality of the food, the ambiance, and the experience of being waited on for an evening. For these restaurants, a strategy of differentiation through customer service and high quality, rather than low costs, is the primary source of competitive advantage. Given this focus, jobs are designed to give employees, such as the wait staff and the chef, much greater latitude to modify how they perform their tasks to meet the unique needs of each customer.

Although the example about restaurant jobs is simplistic, the same logic applies for most positions in the workforce, such as accountants, marketing analysts, and consultants. The focus of a company's strategy drives how managers structure these jobs to be performed. In companies in which employees contribute through creativity and innovation, managers might base their job designs on teamwork to facilitate knowledge sharing and knowledge creation. In companies that compete based on costs, managers may structure jobs to maximize efficiencies through the principles of scientific management discussed earlier (job simplification, job standardization, and repetition). A useful way to think about the relationship between strategy and job design is to think about what customers are paying for and how the job contributes toward meeting customer expectations.

BREADTH OF TASKS, DUTIES, AND RESPONSIBILITIES PERFORMED   Jobs should be designed in a way that maximizes the potential contributions of employees toward implementing a company's competitive strategy. Given their focus on efficiencies and cost reduction, companies pursuing a cost strategy tend to design jobs in a way that maximizes predictable employee outcomes. In contrast, a differentiation strategy requires employees to perform jobs geared toward some particular objective, such as creativity or customer service.[30] Of course, one direct implication of designing jobs to achieve different strategic objectives is that how jobs are designed directly affects the scope or breadth of the tasks, duties, and responsibilities employees need to perform to be successful in their jobs. When jobs are designed to maximize efficiency through job simplification and standardization, one outcome is that the range of tasks, duties, and responsibilities performed by an employee are often limited. By focusing on performing few tasks more frequently, this job design approach strives to encourage maximum levels of productivity and efficiency among employees. In contrast, greater levels of autonomy and empowerment, for example, often involve a wider array of tasks for employees to perform on a regular basis.

Company Characteristics and Job Design

Company characteristics, such as size and stage of development, influence job design in terms of the level of formalization or standardization of jobs as well as the breadth and depth of tasks performed by the jobholder.

FORMALIZATION OF JOBS   Smaller organizations may be forced to adopt a more fluid, open-ended approach to the design of jobs. Researchers have demonstrated that larger organizations are associated with greater formalization and bureaucratization.[31] As companies grow, they tend to develop more rules and regulations regarding how business is carried out on a day-to-day basis. In addition, greater bureaucracy is often associated with greater levels of specialization in jobs that employees perform. One extension is that smaller companies may be more able and willing to be more flexible in how and when employees perform their jobs. For example, the *2005 National Study of Employers* indicated that smaller companies offer employees more opportunities for workplace flexibility through flextime, returning to work gradually after childbirth or adoption, and taking time off for education or training to improve skills or phasing in to retirement.[32] A similar study by the Small Enterprise Research Team at the Open University indicated that more than 90% of small businesses in England offer flexible working options.[33]

BREADTH AND DEPTH OF TASKS   Company size and stage of development influence the breadth and depth of tasks employees are expected to perform. Given limited resources, smaller companies often need employees to perform multiple tasks that may or may not be within their job descriptions.[34] As a result, the types of knowledge, skills, and abilities that employees need in small versus large companies, even for the same job, can differ. Entrepreneurial companies or companies in an early stage of development may face growth opportunities that outpace their ability to fully staff all the necessary jobs. As a result, like smaller companies, younger companies may need employees to perform a wider array of tasks than an established company might require in the same job.

Culture and Job Design

In Chapter 2, we described how organizational culture—the basic assumptions, values, and beliefs of organizational members[35]—provides unwritten cues to employees about what attitudes and behaviors a company values. Because culture informs employees about the types of actions that are and are not appropriate, culture also influences managerial choices of job design tactics and employee acceptance of job designs.

MANAGERIAL CHOICES OF JOB DESIGN TACTICS   Earlier in this chapter, we discussed a host of tactics that managers can use to increase employee efficiency (job specialization, job simplification, and repetition) and motivation (job enlargement, job enrichment, job rotation, and teams). One consideration when choosing a job design tactic is whether it is consistent with the company's culture. In a company that has a very formal, hierarchical culture, managers may be reluctant to use empowerment and participation methods for lower-level employees. They may be more comfortable with a traditional, top-down approach for conducting business. In contrast, managers and employees in a company that has an egalitarian culture may have difficulty executing and accepting rigid or narrow job designs. Do you think officers in the military would adopt the same job design approach for soldiers as an entrepreneurial company would for programmers or a pharmaceutical company would for its R&D scientists?

EMPLOYEE ACCEPTANCE OF JOB DESIGN DECISIONS   Equally as important as to whether managers are comfortable implementing various job design tactics is whether employees will accept these decisions. At its root, organizational culture is a shared perception of how things are as well as how they should be within companies. Conflict between how jobs are designed and the cultural values shared by employees can result in unhappy and potentially unproductive employees. For example, employees who are content with and expect explicit instruction for how they are to spend their time at work may resist job design changes that increase their autonomy and decision making because the changes are inconsistent with their cultural expectations. Similarly, employees who are used to and expect a very friendly and open culture, might not easily accept an increase in rules and regulations they must follow to perform their jobs. The key point is that while managers have many job design tactics at their disposal, they need to choose tactics based on the unique cultural values within their company.

Employee Concerns and Job Design

Naturally, a critical organizational demand to consider when designing jobs is the effect of job design on employees. After all, employees are the ones who are directly affected by job design considerations. Two issues that are particularly important for employees are their perceptions of fairness in the job duties they perform and their needs for flexible work arrangements.

PERCEPTION OF FAIRNESS OF JOB DUTIES Beyond the tasks employees of a company perform, each employee also has a role in the company. Roles are the expectations that companies and co-workers have regarding how employees are to allocate their time in the performance of their jobs. While the tasks may be straightforward in a job, employee roles may not be as clearly defined, resulting in employee stress. For example, some employees may experience **role overload**, too many expectations or demands placed on employees in the course of performing their jobs. Many times, this occurs because employees perceive that their job demands exceed their abilities.[36] Alternatively, some employees may experience **role underload** from having too few expectations or demands placed on them. **Role ambiguity** is uncertainty that employees may experience about the daily tasks expected of them and how to perform them.[37] Finally, **role conflict** is tension caused by incompatible or contradictory demands on a person. Role conflict often stems from the simultaneous occurrence of two or more stressors (demands) such that focusing on one demand makes meeting another demand more difficult.[38] One particularly common form of role conflict that we discuss next is conflicting expectations between work and personal life.

NEED FOR FLEXIBLE WORK ARRANGEMENTS Balancing the conflicting demands of work and family or other personal obligations is difficult for many employees. Demands for travel or overtime, for example, may conflict with personal demands to spend time with family. To help employees achieve this balance, many companies offer flexibility through several alternative work arrangements: flextime, compressed workweeks, and job sharing.

With a **flextime** work arrangement, employees may choose the starting and ending time of their workday as long as they work the appropriate number of hours per day or week. Often, flextime requires employees to be at work during a predetermined set of core hours in which all employees must be at work. According to the Bureau of Labor Statistics, in 2004, about 27 million full-time employees had flexible work schedules that allowed them to vary the time they began or ended their workday.[39] At pharmaceutical company Eli Lilly, more than 5,500 employees—about 25% of the company's U.S. workforce—work some version of a flexible schedule.[40]

While flextime provides employees with choices regarding the hours that they work each day, a **compressed workweek** provides employees with the option to reduce the number of days that they work within a week. The most typical form of a compressed workweek is the 4/10, also called the 4/40. In this approach, employees work 4 days in a week instead of 5 days but work for 10 hours per day rather than the typical 8 hours per day. Another version of a compressed workweek is the 9/80 in which employees work 80 hours in a two-week period in 9 days instead of 10 days. Among the benefits of compressed workweeks are reductions in the number of shifts worked, in travel time and commuting costs, and in sick time, overtime, and personal leave time.[41] For an employee, working a compressed schedule offers the benefit of more time for leisure activities and personal or family matters.[42] However, compressed workweeks can have potential negative consequences, such as fatigue, reduced work quality, and staffing challenges to ensure that the necessary number of people are at work each day.[43]

A third form of flexible work arrangement is job sharing,[44] which consists of having two employees work part time to complete the tasks of a single job. In this scheme, the two

role overload

Too many expectations or demands placed on employees in the course of performing their jobs.

role underload

Too few expectations or demands placed on employees in the course of performing their jobs.

role ambiguity

The uncertainty that employees may experience about the daily tasks expected of them and how to perform them.

role conflict

Tension caused by incompatible or contradictory demands on a person.

flextime

Work arrangement whereby employees may choose the starting and ending time of their workday as long as they work the appropriate number of hours per day or week.

compressed workweek

The option to reduce the number of days employees work within a week.

Many employees struggle to balance work and family demands..

COMPANY *spotlight* 4.3 A Lesson in Work/Life Balance at Pearson Education

With headquarters in Upper Saddle River, New Jersey, Pearson Education, the world's leading educational publisher, has been chosen as one of the 100 best companies for working mothers by *Working Mother* magazine for *seven* years in a row. How did the company achieve this distinction? In large part, Pearson Education did it by providing mechanisms for women to balance their personal lives with their work obligations. For example, Pearson Education allows employees to telecommute from one to five days per week. It provides flextime, compressed summer workweeks, emergency backup child care, financial assistance for prospective adoptive parents, and paid leave to care for a seriously ill family member or new child—a benefit rarely still seen among most American companies. Do all these tactics for work/life balance really make a difference? They certainly do. Pearson Education has an enviable reputation for the advancement of women. While many companies contemplate whether to implement work/life balance programs, Pearson Education serves as a testament to the potential benefits of these programs for both employees and companies.

Sources: Pearson Education. *Flexibility, diversity, help put New Jersey–based Pearson Education on Working Mother's Top 100 list for seventh straight year*, www.pearsoned.com/pr_2006/092506.htm; and 2006 100 best companies, *WorkingMother.com*, www.workingmother.com/web?service=direct/1/ViewTopListingPage/dlinkDetails&sp=76&sp=77.

jobholders work out how to split the work and responsibilities and establish ways to coordinate with one another to complete the job tasks. Jobs may be split in any way, but a common arrangement is for both employees to work 2.5 days each week. The pay and benefits are split among the two employees, so the company does not incur any additional costs compared to the job being performed by just one person.[45] The prevalence of job sharing in organizations varies. One study noted that 46% of employers offered job sharing for some employees, while 13% allow it for most, if not all, of their employees. Moreover, job sharing was more likely to be allowed in smaller companies than in larger ones.[46]

Establishing flexible work arrangements clearly requires costs and effort. Companies that implement these programs, however, often find that the programs help employees remain effective contributors toward company goals and provide an additional point of attraction for many potential job applicants. Indeed, practices such as job sharing may be particularly effective for attracting and retaining workers who might otherwise opt out of the labor force to raise families.[47] Research has even found a positive relationship between company initiatives that facilitate work/family balance and shareholder returns.[48] Company Spotlight 4.3 illustrates how Pearson Education has successfully incorporated work/life balance solutions into its design of work arrangements.

JOB DESIGN IN PRACTICE: ENVIRONMENTAL INFLUENCES

Factors in the external environment influence job design within companies. Labor force trends, technology, globalization, and ethical considerations each exert unique pressures on companies and must be considered when designing jobs.

Labor Force Trends and Job Design

Job design should be based on the strategic objectives of a company. But another part of making job design decisions is looking at the labor force. This means considering the competencies of the people in the labor force who may fill a job and the changing demographic composition of the labor force—particularly the aging labor force.

SKILL AVAILABILITY TO PERFORM TASKS If a job is designed so that only a select few individuals are able to perform the job, a company is likely to experience considerable difficulty filling the job. In this regard, the skills that are available in the labor market may

At CVS older employees are a key resource with a strong work ethic and attention to detail.

influence what job designs are feasible. Think about industries such as health care that face labor shortages in the coming years. As the supply of qualified individuals decreases, companies may need to modify their design of jobs to reduce the necessary qualifications to perform jobs successfully. For example, a company may restructure a single job into two separate jobs, each with a narrow range of tasks to perform. By doing so, the company can increase the number of viable candidates to perform the tasks. In contrast, when there is a labor surplus in a particular industry, occupation, or region, companies may be able to implement more of the job design dimensions that foster employee motivation and satisfaction. While these techniques often raise the necessary skills to perform a job, a labor surplus is likely to make it easier for companies to find qualified people to fill the jobs.

JOB DESIGN DECISIONS FOR THE AGING LABOR FORCE   The aging workforce presents a particularly important demographic trend that influences how companies design jobs. At CVS, a national drugstore chain, workers over the age of 50 represent more than 15% of the workforce. This is a deliberate approach at CVS. The company credits older employees with having a strong work ethic and attention to detail that is valued in many facets of CVS stores.[49] While some companies recruit older workers by choice, others do so out of necessity. For example, faced with a shortage of qualified nurses, St. Mary's Medical Center, in Huntington, West Virginia, has drawn on its own retirees and older alumni of a local nursing school to fill vacancies. One approach the medical center used to help these older employees readjust to working was to assign them to less physically demanding tasks.[50] Baptist Health South Florida has followed a similar approach by allowing older employees to change jobs internally to positions with less physical demands and less heavy lifting.[51] Another job design modification that companies may use to help older employees succeed in their jobs is flexible scheduling and part-time shifts. For example, at Brethren Village, a continuing-care retirement community in Lancaster, Pennsylvania, employees may take extended time off—for instance, to spend time in Florida during the winter months.[52]

Technology and Job Design

One of the most prominent environmental factors that has influenced job design in recent years is technology. Its presence has been felt in two ways—the emergence and rapid growth of telecommuting and the increased use of virtual teams.

TELECOMMUTING   In 2001, the U.S. workforce had an estimated 28 million telecommuters—employees who use technology such as the Internet, videoconferencing, and e-mail to connect to their jobs from remote locations.[53] By 2004, that number had jumped to 44.4 million.[54] Telecommuting offers many benefits to companies and employees. Perhaps the most important benefit is that it provides flexibility in the hours and location of work. Because employees can work from home or from a satellite location, they do not have to spend time commuting to and from a particular site. This arrangement also benefits individuals who might not be able to commit to a traditional 9-to-5 workday

telecommuter

An employee who uses technology such as the Internet, videoconferencing, and e-mail to connect to his or her job from remote locations.

with a commute because, for example, they are caring for their children or aging parents. By providing flexibility in when and where work may be performed, telecommuting can help employees achieve better work/life balance.

Of course, there are potential drawbacks to telecommuting or working remotely. Establishing telecommuting policies requires technology. The costs of providing employees with computers, Internet access, fax machines, and the like may be prohibitive for some companies. Smaller companies do not have the same resources that larger firms have, and they may struggle to provide these options to their employees. It is also possible that relying too much on telecommuting may erode the environment at work. If everyone is working offsite, who is at work? One possible outcome may be a disengaged work culture in which people no longer feel the need to attend to the social side of work, even though that is an important part of organizational functioning, communication, and knowledge exchange. In addition, not all jobs are well suited for telecommuting. Jobs with major requirements for customer interaction may require employees to be at work simply so they can work with their clients. For example, working in retail sales often involves helping customers one-on-one to select merchandise to meet their needs—a task that is obviously difficult to do via telecommuting.

Despite the potential drawbacks of telecommuting, many companies realize that, when done effectively, telecommuting can have a positive effect on employees and help them contribute to company success. AT&T's telework program, for example, has been estimated to have saved the company $30 million in real estate costs and been associated with enhanced productivity and reduced turnover among employees.[55] Of course, managing a workforce that is not at work introduces new challenges, which we will revisit later in this book, regarding issues such as staffing decisions (chapter 7), training and development (Chapter 8), and performance evaluations (Chapter 9).[56]

VIRTUAL TEAMS Advances in information technology have provided companies with the ability to use virtual teams. The Internet, videoconferencing, and specialized software allow dispersed individuals to collaborate electronically as virtual teams that work together even when they cannot physically be in the same location.[57] Eastman Kodak, Hewlett-Packard, General Electric, and Sun Microsystems are just a few of the companies that rely on virtual teams to work on important business objectives.[58]

The trend toward virtual teams is understandable, given the growth in telecommuting and the fact that virtual teams do not require face-to-face interaction. Virtual teams are able to respond quickly to pressing issues, problems, and opportunities. An additional organizational benefit of virtual teams is that their use dramatically expands who can be part of a team. Virtual team members may be located anywhere in the world—a benefit that is particularly helpful for companies operating on a global scale. Virtual teams require the appropriate technology to communicate quickly and effectively with other team members, however, and employees must be trained on how to use the technology.[59] Some of the practices that have been identified for effectively leading virtual teams are:[60]

- Establish and maintain trust through the use of communication technology
- Ensure that distributed diversity is understood and appreciated
- Manage the virtual work/life cycle (meetings)
- Monitor team progress using technology
- Enhance the visibility of virtual members within the team and outside the team in the organization
- Enable individual members of the virtual team to benefit from the team

Globalization and Job Design

While technology has provided a medium for companies to pursue virtual teams, increasing globalization has provided a strong incentive for them to do so. As companies continue to expand into the global marketplace, they increasingly have employees located in multiple countries and continents who have to somehow work together to meet customer needs. Virtual teams help accomplish this coordination, and continual improvements in information technology have enabled companies to be more prepared for long-distance working relationships that help meet the needs of globalization.

NEED TO ADDRESS CROSS-CULTURAL ISSUES As companies continue to build their presence in other countries or employ people from other countries in a single location, they are likely to face challenges that stem from cultural differences. As noted in Chapter 2, different regions of the world have different norms, standards, and expectations that influence the way business is conducted. Diverse workplaces that have individuals from distinct cultural backgrounds may realize that assumptions about job design in the United States may not be consistent with expectations of individuals from other countries. Individuals may differ in their comfort with formality, preference to work in teams or individually, perception of the importance of meeting deadlines and being on time, or view of how much work constitutes a workday. In short, different cultures have different job design styles, experiences, needs, and expectations. Employees in a collectivistic culture, for example, may be more willing to devote time and energy toward a work team's success compared to employees from a more individualistic culture. Similarly, different cultures vary in terms of their expectations of how much of their life revolves around work, and some of these values may be reflected by different laws. British employees, for example, have a statutory right to seek flexible work arrangements,[61] and this right might not be legally mandated in other countries.

RELEVANT LABOR MARKET Globalization magnifies the importance of the labor force trends that are unique to each country. The average education level of the workforce, the occupational background, and the supply of workers with different skill sets establish the parameters for the amount of autonomy, discretion, and variety companies can feasibly build into different jobs. Companies must be attuned to the composition of the relevant labor force trends when assessing what approaches to job design are most likely to be successful in different scenarios. For example, in developed countries with a ready supply of skilled labor, companies experience more success implementing more motivational tactics such as empowerment and job enlargement compared to countries in which the workforce tends to possess significantly lower skill levels.

Ethics and Job Design

When we talk about how jobs are designed, we need to consider ethical issues. One issue that is of particular importance is the impact of job design decisions on the level of stress employees experience. In general, a certain amount of stress is good; it helps employees stay excited and focused on the task at hand. Too much stress, however, may lead to employee dissatisfaction, illness, absenteeism, turnover, and reduced productivity.[62] Job-related stress can stem from many sources, but two of the most common sources are the types of tasks performed in a job and the physical demands of the job.

CONCERNS ABOUT TYPES OF TASKS REQUIRED Jobs vary in the extent to which the tasks that are expected to be performed inherently cause a high level of stress for employees. For example, it is easy to imagine that the job of a soldier during wartime is very stressful. The jobs of air-traffic controllers, police officers, firefighters, and stockbrokers all require the performance of tasks that are stressful, albeit for different reasons. For air-traffic controllers, a single mistake could result in compromised safety for air passengers. Police officers and firefighters often face uncertain situations that put their personal safety, as well as the safety of others, at risk. Stockbrokers work at a frantic pace every day. In addition, many jobs that require dealing with the public can be very stressful. A survey of 25,000 British workers across 26 jobs found that those experiencing the most stress were paramedics. Teachers and social workers had the next most stressful jobs.[63]

In a review of studies on occupational stress, the National Institute for Occupational Safety and Health (NIOSH) reported that 40% of employees claim that their jobs are extremely stressful.[64] Several of the key factors associated with stress on the job are directly related to job design—heavy workload, infrequent breaks, long work hours/shifts, routine tasks with little meaning, little sense of control, uncertain expectations, too many responsibilities, too many tasks, lack of participation, and poor social support. As you can imagine, prolonged exposure to any of these types of job features would likely lead to increased stress for employees, which can have an associated impact on employee health, well-being, and safety. In an attempt to address these concerns, NIOSH has developed some based tactics to help organizations prevent stress on the job. These are highlighted in Exhibit 4.11.

Exhibit 4.11 ▶

How to Change an
Organization to
Prevent Job Stress

- Ensure that the workload is in line with workers' capabilities and resources.
- Design jobs to provide meaning, stimulation, and opportunities for workers to use their skills.
- Clearly define workers' roles and responsibilities.
- Give workers opportunities to participate in decisions and actions that affect their jobs.
- Improve communications to reduce uncertainty about career development and future employment prospects.
- Provide opportunities for social interaction among workers.
- Establish work schedules that are compatible with demands and responsibilities outside the job.

Sources: Sauter, S. L., Murphy, L. R., & Hurell, J. J., Jr. Prevention of work-related psychological disorders. *American Psychologist* 45:1146–1159, 1990; and National Institute for Occupational Safety and Health. *Stress . . . at work*, www.cdc.gov/niosh/stresswk.html.

ATTITUDES TOWARD PHYSICAL CONDITIONS OF JOB DESIGN   An additional key factor associated with stress on the job relates to the physical conditions of a job. Some jobs have physical conditions that may lead to heightened levels of employee stress. A job may, for example, require performing tasks in unpleasant conditions, such as working in extremely hot or cold temperatures, working without privacy, or working with extensive noise. Some jobs require employees to perform strenuous labor that is physically demanding on the human body. Construction workers and firefighters, for example, perform jobs that require an extensive amount of physical exertion. But physical stress is not limited to extreme jobs. Manufacturing and office workers, for example, face physical stress that, if neglected over time, can lead to repetitive motion problems such as carpal tunnel syndrome.

In response, many companies are increasingly considering the **ergonomics** of how jobs are designed. According to the International Ergonomics Association (IEA), ergonomists contribute to the design and evaluation of tasks, jobs, products, environments, and systems in order to make them compatible with the needs, abilities, and limitations of people.[65] Topics such as posture, repetitive movements, musculoskeletal disorders, workplace layout, safety, and health are the primary focus of physical ergonomics. You may have used, or even own, an ergonomic keyboard that minimizes the physical stress of working on a computer. This is an example of ergonomics. Ergonomists examine how individuals interact with machines, tools, and equipment in an attempt to minimize the physical demands of a particular job that may lead to high levels of stress, fatigue, and possibly injury.[66] In fact, in a recent survey by Microsoft Hardware, 50% of the respondents indicated that being provided the tools needed to perform their jobs efficiently was the best way their employers could show that they wanted employees to succeed. Respondents also indicated that they felt their productivity was linked to workstation design.[67]

In addition to modifying the process of work, managers may also use job rotation to help minimize physical stress. By allowing employees to alternate between tasks that require high and low physical exertion, job rotation may help to diminish the physical demands on employees.[68] And as we will discuss in Chapter 8, managers may use training and development to help employees learn to cope with stressful situations on the job.

ergonomics

The science of understanding the capabilities of humans in terms of their work requirements.

JOB DESIGN IN PRACTICE: REGULATORY ISSUES

In Chapter 3, we emphasized that managerial decisions must be based on job-related reasons to comply with equal employment laws and regulations. But how do you know if a reason is job related? Sound job design and job analysis play key roles in this compliance. In this section, we look at two laws that have important implications for job design decisions: the Americans with Disabilities Act (ADA) and the Occupational Safety and Health Act of 1970.

Importance of Identifying Essential and Non-essential Job Duties

As discussed in Chapter 3, the Americans with Disabilities Act (ADA) specifically prohibits employers from using a disability as the basis for discriminating against qualified individuals in making employment decisions. This law specifies that all individuals, including disabled individuals, are qualified for a job if they can perform the essential functions of a job with or without reasonable accommodation. Essential functions are the job tasks, duties, and responsibilities required of a person in the job.[69]

Recall from our discussion of job descriptions that essential functions differ from marginal functions, which may also be performed in a job but are marginal or non-essential for the primary reasons the job exists. Determining whether a specific task, duty, or responsibility is an essential function or a marginal function of a job is achieved through the job analysis process. Without conducting job analysis, companies must rely on subjective assessments of what tasks are truly essential for employees. And basing decisions on subjective assessments puts a company at risk for claims of bias or discrimination. As a result, companies increasingly turn to job analysis techniques to ensure that job descriptions are correct and to document essential and non-essential tasks for their positions.

While job analysis provides insights into the essential tasks of a job, job design helps to address the issue of reasonable accommodation. Recall that a reasonable accommodation is a modification to how work is done or to the work environment so that someone who is qualified for a job and who has a disability can perform the job. According to the U.S. Equal Employment Opportunity Commission, there are three general categories of reasonable accommodations: (1) changes to a job application process to permit people with disabilities to be considered for jobs; (2) changes to enable people with disabilities to perform the essential functions of a job; and (3) changes to give people with disabilities equal access to the benefits and privileges of employment.[70] Job design considerations play a direct role in facilitating these forms of reasonable accommodation. For example, a reasonable accommodation might include modifying a work schedule, allowing employees to share a job, modifying equipment, or making existing facilities easily accessible and usable for someone who has a disability. The reality is that most accommodations that organizations make involve modifications to how jobs are designed and do not involve substantial costs.

Job Design and Employee Safety

In Chapter 12, we explore in depth the Occupational Safety and Health Act of 1970, which is overseen by the U.S. Department of Labor. The Occupational Safety and Health Administration (OSHA) is the primary agency for overseeing employee safety and health on the job. But it is important to note that employee safety has an important influence on the design of jobs. On its Web site (www.osha.gov/oshinfo/mission.html), OSHA states that its mission is to assure the safety and health of America's workers by setting and enforcing standards; providing training, outreach, and education; establishing partnerships; and encouraging continual improvement in workplace safety and health.[71]

OSHA's basic premise is that companies must provide employees with an environment that does not pose recognized hazards to their safety or health. OSHA guides job design in areas such as exposure to hazardous chemicals or biological agents, regulations for machine operators, requirements about protective equipment, and standards for working surfaces and environments. In the beginning of this chapter, we explored the trade-offs between pursuing efficiency and motivational approaches to how jobs are designed. Whichever job design approach you choose, you cannot compromise the safety and well-being of your employees to achieve those goals. Besides being an ethical obligation, designing jobs to be OSHA compliant is a legal requirement.

SUMMARY

The ultimate goal of job design is to enhance company performance. Managers achieve this goal by using job design to determine the specific tasks and responsibilities that employees should perform to maximize their individual contributions to company success. Managers must also decide how employees will perform the specific tasks and responsibilities in each job.

There are two dominant approaches to job design that influence how tasks and responsibilities are performed. First, managers may enhance the efficiency with which employees perform their jobs, using job specification, job simplification, and repetition. Second, managers may strive to maximize employee satisfaction and motivation to work hard toward company goals. This is accomplished through job design techniques that change the tasks that employees perform, provide employees with more responsibilities and authority regarding the performance of their jobs, or use team-based work arrangements. Because it is difficult to simultaneously maximize efficiency and motivation, managers must make trade-offs in which approach they emphasize—decisions driven by how employees add value within their company.

Before companies can take action based on job design to make decisions regarding managing competencies and managing the attitudes and behaviors of employees, they need to have a clear understanding of the job descriptions and job specifications. A job description is a written summary of the specific tasks, responsibilities, and working conditions of a job. Job specifications outline the competencies—the knowledge, skills, abilities, or other talents—that a jobholder needs in order to successfully perform the job. Job descriptions serve as a valuable tool for communicating to employees the essential tasks of their job, and they help managers make important decisions related to recruiting, hiring, evaluating, and paying employees.

Job analysis is the systematic analysis of the tasks that are expected to be performed within the scope of a single job. The primary goal of job analysis is to attain a clear understanding of both the tasks, duties, and responsibilities expected to be performed for each job (job descriptions) and the specific competencies that are necessary for successful performance of the job (job specifications). There are several primary sources for collecting job information: observations, diaries, interviews, questionnaires, and generic information available through O*NET. Managers may use a standardized or a customized approach to job analysis, depending on several factors.

Decisions regarding job design are influenced by the three HR challenges—organizational demands, environmental influences, and legal compliance. Strategy, company characteristics, and culture guide which job design approach is likely to be most effective to achieve company goals and to reinforce cultural values. They also influence which job design options are feasible, given organizational resources. Employee concerns about work/life balance also play a role in managers' job design decisions.

Environmental influences—labor force trends, globalizations, technology, and ethics—affect job design in several ways. They influence the feasibility of using different approaches to job design, the viability and need for telecommuting and virtual teams, and the level of stress employees experience on the job. Many companies use tactics such as ergonomics and job rotation to help employees cope with physical and psychological job stress. Finally, the legal environment has a strong influence on job design and job analysis, requiring that managers have a clear understanding of what tasks and responsibilities are essential for job success. Managers must also ensure that jobs are designed with consideration of the safety and well-being of employees.

KEY TERMS

compressed workweek *p. 103*

critical incident *p. 116*

diary *p. 97*

Dictionary of Occupational Titles (DOT) *p. 113*

empowerment *p. 92*

ergonomics *p. 108*

flextime *p. 103*

growth need strength *p. 91*

job analysis *p. 87*

job characteristics model *p. 90*

job description *p. 94*

job design *p. 86*

job enlargement *p. 91*

job enrichment *p. 92*

job rotation *p. 92*

job simplification *p. 89*

job specialization *p. 89*

job specification *p. 94*

Occupational Information Network (O*NET) *p. 98*

participation *p. 92*

psychological states *p. 90*

role ambiguity *p. 103*

role conflict *p. 103*

role overload *p. 103*

role underload *p. 103*

self-managed team *p. 94*

telecommuter *p. 105*

time and motion studies *p. 89*

voice *p. 92*

DISCUSSION QUESTIONS

1. What is the difference between job design and job analysis? Why is it important for a manager to understand both concepts?

2. Discuss why manufacturing firms have traditionally focused more on efficiency in job design than on motivation.

3. Call centers often experience costly, high turnover. These centers, which handle everything from computer help desk functions to processing of mortgage applications, have been described as white-collar factories. Large numbers of employees work in cubicles, responding to phone calls all day, often from upset customers. Often they have quotas for the volume and types of calls they handle each day. Is it more important to design these jobs to increase efficiency or motivation? As a manager, how might you make such a change?

4. Which of the environmental considerations do you think will have the greatest impact on how companies design jobs in the next 5 to 10 years? Why? What types of implications do you think this environmental consideration will have?

5. The choice you make in how you analyze jobs has a direct impact on the results of your analysis. Compare and contrast the different job analysis approaches and explain when you would use each one.

6. Identify three job design issues that would be affected by extensive use of virtual teams. How would you manage these issues?

7. An employee who is your firm's only accountant tells you that due to an illness, he will be able to come to work only half-days from now on. As his manager, how could you redesign the job to retain this valuable employee?

LEARNING EXERCISE 1

Research the relationship between job design and a topic related to either employee stress or work/life balance. Using information from this text, from class lecture, and from your research, prepare a one-page summary of best practices that companies have used to manage stress or work/life issues.

1. How does job design affect either employee stress or work/life balance?

2. Are certain job design approaches better than others for addressing employees' stress or work/life balance? Why?

3. What organizational or environmental factors might prevent managers from implementing the job design options you noted in your response to question 2?

LEARNING EXERCISE 2

Obtain a job description and job specifications. Critique the content of the job description and specifications.

1. Does the job description appear to be complete?

2. Do all relevant competencies (KSAs) appear to be included?

3. Is any information missing? Be specific in listing areas for improvement.

LEARNING EXERCISE 3

Decide on a job you think you would like to have when you graduate. Develop a structured job analysis questionnaire for that job. Arrange to interview someone who is currently employed in the type of job you selected.

Use the information that you collect to prepare a job description following the job description checklist in Exhibit 4.6. Be sure to include tasks, duties, responsibilities, job specifications, and working conditions.

CASE STUDY # 1 — HOME-SOURCING AT ALPINE ACCESS

The Alpine Access Web site says:

Alpine Access is the premier provider of customer service solutions using home-based employees. Alpine Access' clients are organizations that value their customers and are passionate about their brand. Our Alpine Customer Experience (ACE™) solutions mean access to quality employees, compelling operational efficiency and economic success.

Located in Golden Colorado, Alpine Access has positioned itself in the call center industry as a company that provides exceptional talent that is available for other organizations.

The company's key point of differentiation is that rather than shipping its jobs overseas to international call centers, its employees work from home.

One of the primary benefits of this home-sourcing arrangement is that it removes the costs of "bricks and mortar" associated with housing a full-scale call center operation at the company facilities. This obviously helps keep costs down. In addition, this approach allows the company to have a virtual presence throughout the United States. Its employees are scattered across the United States, and all they really need to do their job is some basic technology. As noted by employee Martha Libby, one of the 7,500 distributed home-based agents, "I have a computer with high-speed Internet access and a hard phone line. That's pretty much it."

With clients such as ExpressJet, J. Crew, the Internal Revenue Service, 1-800-Flowers, and Office Depot, it certainly seems that Alpine Access is on a path to success. And the employees have responded well to their arrangement. As noted by former CEO Garth Howard, "The employees, with traffic and gas, there are a lot of things that challenge them in getting to work. . . . A lot of people can work from home and be very productive. They commute in bunny slippers instead of traffic. Who wouldn't want to do that?"

DISCUSSION QUESTIONS

1. What types of jobs are best suited for home-sourcing arrangements?

2. As a manager, what challenges would you anticipate for designing jobs for individuals who work offsite in their own homes?

3. What are the greatest risks associated with this job design approach? As a manager, what would you do to overcome those risks?

4. Would you want to work in a home-sourcing arrangement? As an employee, what challenge and opportunities would doing so present?

Sources: Armour, S. Cost-effective "homesourcing" trends grow. *USA Today*, online March 15, 2006, http://www.usatoday.com/money/workplace/2006-03-12-homesourcing-grows_x.htm Mello, J. P., Jr. "Home-sourcing" vs. offshoring: It's not all about price; allowing people to work at home "leads to a virtuous cycle of productivity". *CFO.com*, January 26, 2005, www.cfo.com/article.cfm/3597944; and Alpine Access Web site, www.alpineaccess.com.

CASE STUDY # 2 — RETHINKING JOBS AT ELLERS TECHNICAL SUPPORT PROFESSIONALS (ETSP)

Ellers Technical Support Professionals (ETSP) is a young company that was started five years ago by William "Bill" Ellers. Bill created the company to serve a relatively small but growing need among companies in the Washington, DC, area, including nearby Reston, Virginia, and Columbia, Maryland. ETSP provides technical support as well as administrative oversight for the computing needs of a variety of small to midsize public organizations. Approximately 60% of ETSP's business is supportive in nature. When clients experience computer problems or require the development of new computer programs, Bill's staff provides these services on an as-needed basis. The remaining 40% of ETSP's business involves serving as an outsourcing partner for clients to completely oversee the administrative aspects of their computer-related activities. In these relationships, Bill's staff members are responsible for the design, implementation, and maintenance of all computer systems.

Because the ETSP client base is not-for-profit organizations, clients are typically unable to pay high costs for computer support. As a result, ETSP's primary source of competitive advantage is the delivery of these services at an acceptable level of quality for low costs. To achieve this objective, ETSP focuses on cost containment throughout its company. For example, to increase efficiency, programmers typically perform a fairly narrow array of programming activities across the client organizations. Each programmer is an expert in a particular technological domain, and each works independently on relatively standardized problems.

While the potential for high growth at ETSP is strong, Bill has not been able to devote as much attention to generating new business as he would like. Instead, he has been spending a good amount of his time dealing with relatively high turnover among his programmers. ETSP currently employs 20 programmers but is averaging about 50% turnover per year. While there is a wide supply of entry-level programmers in the labor market, the process of recruiting, hiring, and training each programmer requires a fair amount of cost, time, and effort.

In an attempt to reduce the turnover problem, Bill decided to meet with the current employees to ask what changes he can make to improve employee retention so that he can focus on growing the business. After an extensive discussion, the employees suggested that Bill consider redesigning the jobs. Now Bill has to decide what to do.

DISCUSSION QUESTIONS

1. What job design options might help Bill reduce turnover among the employees?

2. What are the advantages and disadvantages of these options?

3. What job design changes would you recommend that would allow ETSP to focus on low costs and quality service for public organizations?

APPENDIX
Standardized and Customized Approaches to Job Analysis

STANDARDIZED APPROACHES TO JOB ANALYSIS

As noted earlier in this chapter, a standardized job analysis approach uses a single instrument to evaluate multiple jobs within a single company or across many companies. This type of standardized approach requires identifying underlying job dimensions that are applicable to a variety of jobs, allowing for comparisons of dissimilar jobs in meaningful ways. The two most common standardized approaches that companies use are Functional Job Analysis (FJA) and the Position Analysis Questionnaire (PAQ).

Functional Job Analysis (FJA)

FJA was designed in an attempt to create a single job analysis instrument that might be used to evaluate a wide array of dissimilar jobs. As described in this chapter, the FJA is based on the notion that it is possible to systematically compare jobs that are dissimilar in the tasks they perform by focusing on several job dimensions or functional categories of job tasks rather than on actual tasks.[72] Functional categories are broad categories of work-related activities that are applicable to all jobs and that focus on three distinct work domains relate to *data*, *people*, and *things*. According to this approach, all jobs comprise these three job dimensions and vary in the functional levels or levels of difficulty associated with these dimensions.

Procedurally, an FJA requires that a job analyst study each job to evaluate the difficulty level for each of these three dimensions and the percentage of the time the job incumbent would be expected to perform at a particular difficulty level for each dimension. For example, when evaluating jobs along the people dimension, jobs may range from simply taking instructions to supervising others to mentoring subordinates. Similarly, when evaluating jobs along the things dimension, jobs may range from handling to setting up. The more difficulty associated with each job on a dimension, the lower the score. Each job is given a numeric score that facilitates comparisons across jobs and that serves as the basis for subsequent HR activities such as establishing job groupings for compensation decisions.

A popular form of the FJA approach is the **Dictionary of Occupational Titles (DOT)** created by the Employment and Training Administration and published by the U.S. Department of Labor.[73] First published in 1939, with approximately 17,500 concise job definitions, the DOT is based on data that were collected by occupational job analysts. The DOT has been updated regularly since then and contains a large number of job definitions that are organized alphabetically, by title, with a coding arrangement for occupational classification. Exhibit A4.1 shows the functional levels for the three job dimensions in the Department of Labor's approach to classifying jobs.

The DOT was eventually replaced by the Occupational Information Network (O*NET). The O*NET system can be accessed online or through a variety of public- and private-sector career and labor market information systems.[74] Under the sponsorship of the Department of Labor's Employment and Training Administration (ETA), O*NET data collection activities are conducted by the National Center for O*NET Development, located in Raleigh, North Carolina. Data are collected directly from incumbent workers in targeted occupations at businesses statistically selected from a random sample. These workers complete standardized questionnaires that are analyzed and incorporated into the O*NET database periodically. The new occupational information is made available through the O*NET Online application and in the downloadable O*NET database files.[75] The O*NET database is a comprehensive source of information for more than 950 jobs. Exhibit A4.2 provides a sample excerpt from the O*NET Web site (http://online.onetcenter.org) for the job of an accountant.

As mentioned earlier in this chapter, one of the primary advantages of O*NET is that it serves as an online resource to help managers with the job analysis process. Managers can look to O*NET as a starting point for job descriptions and an understanding of the specific knowledge, skills, and abilities to seek when filling a position, especially for jobs that might not have existed in the company previously.

▶ **Exhibit A4.1** The Department of Labor Version of FJA

Data	People	Things
0 Synthesizing	0 Mentoring	0 Setting Up
1 Coordinating	1 Negotiating	1 Precision Working
2 Analyzing	2 Instructing	2 Operating–Controlling
3 Compiling	3 Supervising	3 Driving–Operating
4 Computing	4 Diverting	4 Manipulating
5 Copying	5 Persuading	5 Tending
6 Comparing	6 Speaking–Signaling	6 Feeding–Offbearing
	7 Serving	7 Handling
	8 Taking Instructions–Helping	

Exhibit A4.2 ►

Excerpt from
O*NET for the Job
of an Accountant

Analyze financial information and prepare financial reports to determine or maintain record of assets, liabilities, profit and loss, tax liability, or other financial activities within an organization.

Sample of reported job titles: Accountant, Staff Accountant, CPA (Certified Public Accountant), General Accountant, Accounting Manager, Business Analyst, Certified Public Accountant, Cost Accountant

Tasks

- Prepare, examine, and analyze accounting records, financial statements, and other financial reports to assess accuracy, completeness, and conformance to reporting and procedural standards.

- Compute taxes owed and prepare tax returns, ensuring compliance with payment, reporting and other tax requirements.

- Analyze business operations, trends, costs, revenues, financial commitments, and obligations, to project future revenues and expenses or to provide advice.

- Report to management regarding the finances of establishment.

- Establish tables of accounts, and assign entries to proper accounts.

- Develop, maintain, and analyze budgets, preparing periodic reports that compare budgeted costs to actual costs.

- Develop, implement, modify, and document record keeping and accounting systems, making use of current computer technology.

- Prepare forms and manuals for accounting and bookkeeping personnel, and direct their work activities.

- Survey operations to ascertain accounting needs and to recommend, develop, and maintain solutions to business and financial problems.

- Work as Internal Revenue Service agents.

Knowledge

- *Mathematics*—Knowledge of arithmetic, algebra, geometry, calculus, statistics, and their applications.

- *Economics and accounting*—Knowledge of economic and accounting principles and practices, the financial markets, banking and the analysis and reporting of financial data.

- *Customer and personal service*—Knowledge of principles and processes for providing customer and personal services. This includes customer needs assessment, meeting quality standards for services, and evaluation of customer satisfaction.

- *English language*—Knowledge of the structure and content of the English language including the meaning and spelling of words, rules of composition, and grammar.

- *Computers and electronics*—Knowledge of circuit boards, processors, chips, electronic equipment, and computer hardware and software, including applications and programming.

- *Law and government*—Knowledge of laws, legal codes, court procedures, precedents, government regulations, executive orders, agency rules, and the democratic political process.

- *Clerical*—Knowledge of administrative and clerical procedures and systems such as word processing, managing files and records, stenography and transcription, designing forms, and other office procedures and terminology.

- *Personnel and human resources*—Knowledge of principles and procedures for personnel recruitment, selection, training, compensation and benefits, labor relations and negotiation, and personnel information systems.

Work Activities

- *Interacting with computers*—Using computers and computer systems (including hardware and software) to program, write software, set up functions, enter data, or process information.

- *Analyzing data or information*—Identifying the underlying principles, reasons, or facts of information by breaking down information or data into separate parts.

- *Processing information*—Compiling, coding, categorizing, calculating, tabulating, auditing, or verifying information or data.

- *Getting information*—Observing, receiving, and otherwise obtaining information from all relevant sources.

- *Documenting/recording information*—Entering, transcribing, recording, storing, or maintaining information in written or electronic/magnetic form.

- *Establishing and maintaining interpersonal relationships*—Developing constructive and cooperative working relationships with others, and maintaining them over time.

- *Organizing, planning, and prioritizing work*—Developing specific goals and plans to prioritize, organize, and accomplish your work.

- *Communicating with supervisors, peers, or subordinates*—Providing information to supervisors, co-workers, and subordinates by telephone, in written form, e-mail, or in person.

- *Making decisions and solving problems*—Analyzing information and evaluating results to choose the best solution and solve problems.

- *Interpreting the meaning of information for others*—Translating or explaining what information means and how it can be used.

◄ **Exhibit A4.2**
Continued

Position Analysis Questionnaire (PAQ)

The second common standardized job analysis technique is the Position Analysis Questionnaire (PAQ), which is a 194-item survey that measures a number of different employee work-related behaviors necessary to perform a variety of tasks in different jobs. Of these survey items, 187 relate to worker behaviors that employees must display to successfully perform the required tasks of a job (e.g., estimating sales or analyzing information).[76] The remaining items focus on documenting the type of compensation employees receive in their jobs. These 187 survey items are designed to measure the extent to which six broad job domains are representative of a particular job:

1. **Information input**—Where and how do employees get the information they need to perform the job?

2. **Mental processes**—What reasoning, decision-making, planning, and information-processing activities do employees perform in the job?

3. **Work output**—What physical activities are required to perform the job, and what tools are used?

4. **Relationships with other persons**—What relationships with other people are required to perform the job?

5. **Job context**—What are the physical and social aspects of the work environment in which the job is performed?

6. **Other characteristics**—What activities, conditions, or characteristics, other than the previous five, are relevant to the job?

The underlying logic of this approach is that while the specific tasks performed across jobs may differ, there are certain *work behaviors* common in the performance of most jobs. Procedurally, this approach follows a simple format. First, a job analyst assesses the extent to which different job elements are involved in a job. This is usually done through observation of the job and interviews with current job holders and job supervisors. Then, the job analyst rates the applicable job elements in terms of their importance to the job, the amount of time spent on the tasks, their extent of use, their possibility of occurrence, and any other special codes.[77] Finally, these ratings are sent to PAQ corporate headquarters, where they are scored and a report is generated regarding the job's scores on each of the dimensions.

Because the PAQ is widely used for job analysis across many companies, results that are submitted to the PAQ headquarters may be used to identify comparisons between similar jobs in different companies. In addition to identifying the specific job behaviors that are performed in a job, the PAQ approach may be extended to provide insights into the job specifications or knowledge, skills, and abilities (KSAs) required to successfully perform the job (see www.paq.com). For example, research has shown that the PAQ is related to the General Aptitude Test Battery (GATB), a standardized ability test. This facilitates a link between dimension scores on the PAQ and estimates of the KSAs needed to perform a job.[78]

Of course, as with all other standardized techniques, the PAQ has trade-offs. The disadvantages of the PAQ are that it is fairly complex, sophisticated, time-consuming, and potentially quite costly. And, due to the complexity of the evaluation process, it is recommended that the PAQ be administered by trained analysts. In addition, the PAQ is believed to be more suited for blue-collar jobs than for professional, managerial, and some technical jobs.[79] Due to these limitations, the PAQ approach is not the most appropriate for analyzing every situation. The PAQ method does, however, provide an excellent method for classifying different jobs into a coherent structure that is useful for other HR activities, such as administering pay and benefits programs. And, because the work behaviors may be linked to necessary job specifications, the PAQ may prove useful for staffing and training purposes as well.

CUSTOMIZED APPROACHES TO JOB ANALYSIS

While standardized approaches focus on job dimensions that are represented in most jobs, customized techniques allow managers to develop a job description and job specifications that reflect the unique attributes of a particular job. We will look at three approaches for customized job analysis: the critical incidents approach, the task inventory approach, and the job element approach.

Critical Incidents Approach

The critical incidents approach obtains specific, behaviorally focused descriptions of work activities. Critical incidents are specific behaviors that distinguish exceptionally good performance in a particular job from exceptionally poor performance in the same job. For example, the critical incidents approach may be used to develop indicators of good or poor performance for the professor teaching this course in terms of how he or she responds to student questions. An example of exceptionally good performance for this job dimension might be "When students have questions about course material, the professor listens carefully and takes the necessary time to completely answer the questions." In this same context, an example of poor performance on the same job

dimension might be "When students have questions about course material, the professor dismisses the questions as disrupting the flow of the class and continues to present new material to the class."

The process of conducting a critical incidents analysis is fairly straightforward. First, individuals familiar with a job, such as supervisors, employees, or subject-matter experts, identify the major dimensions of the job. Next, they specify behaviors that, when displayed on the job, lead to high or low performance on those dimensions. These behaviors (critical incidents) are then reviewed by all knowledgeable individuals to ensure that all relevant job dimensions are captured and that all critical incidents for those dimensions are identified.

The primary benefit of the critical incidents approach is that it focuses specifically on job behaviors that are critical for job success. Managers can use these behaviors as the foundation for other HR activities, such as training programs and performance evaluations. To be effective, however, the critical incidents that are identified should be specific and should focus on behaviors that are observable in the performance of a job. In addition, critical incidents must be detailed enough so that different individuals viewing the critical incidents will be able to understand the specific behaviors that drive successful or unsuccessful job performance.[80]

Task Inventory Approach

Whereas the critical incidents approach focuses on specific behaviors that drive job success, task inventories focus on the tasks that are necessary for job success. The task inventory method of collecting information generally involves asking current jobholders or their supervisors to evaluate the extent to which different tasks are performed.[81] After tasks are identified, they are rated in terms of their importance for job success, the amount of time devoted to each task, the difficulty of the task, and the time needed to learn how to perform the task.

Although typically focused on the tasks required to execute a job, task inventories may be extended to also identify the job specifications (competencies) necessary to perform the job successfully.[82] For example, after the tasks performed in a job are identified, subject-matter experts, supervisors, and jobholders may then identify the specific KSAs needed to perform each specific job task. After compiling the data, the result of this process is a specific listing of the job specifications necessary to complete each of the tasks in the job.

Job Element Approach

The third customized approach to job analysis is the job element approach. This approach is distinct because it focuses *solely* on analyzing the employee competencies that are necessary for successful job performance rather than focus on the tasks to be performed in a job. With this approach, people who are familiar with a job evaluate the specific skills necessary to perform the essential tasks. The essence of this approach is that it focuses on job elements—specific worker requirements that are necessary to perform a job. Job elements can be cognitive abilities, such as reading blueprints or understanding statistics, psychomotor elements, such as driving a car or operating machinery, or work habits, such as willingness to work long hours. For example, some specific job elements for a firefighter might be good physical stamina and the ability to work well under pressure.[83]

After the job elements are identified by job analysts or subject-matter experts, they are collected and evaluated along four dimensions:

- **Barely acceptable**—The number of barely acceptable employees who have this element
- **Superior**—The degree of how useful an element is for distinguishing superior workers from average workers
- **Trouble likely if not considered**—The probability of trouble occurring in the performance of a job if employees do not have this element

- **Practical**—The extent to which job applicants are likely to possess this element.[84]

Each element is then rated 0 (element has minimal value), 1 (element has some value), or 2 (element has high value). Rating the usefulness of each element for each dimension provides additional information regarding which predictors are particularly important. For example, using our firefighter example, ability to work under high pressure would likely score high for the superior, trouble likely if not considered, and practical dimensions. But this job element would likely score low for the barely acceptable dimension. In other words, in this example, the ability to work under high pressure is a trait that not all people possess, but it is an important distinguishing factor for high performers, an important element for job success, and a practical tool for evaluating job applicants.

chapter

5

WORKFORCE PLANNING

1. Explain why workforce planning is an important activity of managers. *(120)*

2. Describe the internal and external factors that affect labor supply and demand. *(122)*

3. Discuss the tactics managers use to remedy labor shortages and labor surpluses. *(128)*

4. Discuss the advantages and disadvantages of various workforce planning tactics. *(130)*

5. Describe how a firm's organizational demands affect its workforce planning decisions. *(132)*

6. Explain the impact environmental factors have on a firm's workforce planning decisions. *(135)*

7. Discuss the legal aspects of the workforce planning tactics companies use. *(140)*

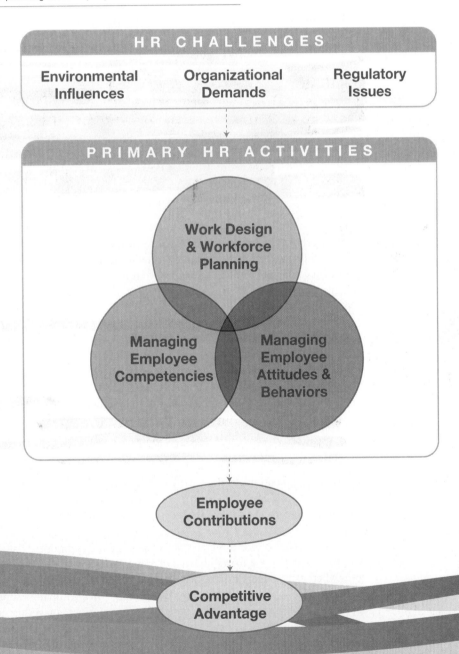

THE IMPORTANCE OF WORKFORCE PLANNING

During the twentieth century, Ford and General Motors (GM) were two of the most successful companies in the automobile industry. At one point, GM garnered almost 51% of the global automotive market share.[1] Ford's introduction of assembly-line technologies reduced the company's production costs to a point where nearly every American family could afford to own an automobile (or multiple automobiles).[2] Today, however, these two companies are facing tough times. In 2006, for example, both companies experienced escalating fixed costs, negative profits, and diminished consumer demand for their products.[3] Both companies are now closing plants and laying off employees.[4] Ford, for instance, announced that it would cut up to 30,000 jobs by the year 2012 to match its workforce capacity with the demand for its products.[5] In 2008, GM announced that it would extend a buyout option for its 78,000 employees and special incentives for its 40,800 workers who are eligible for retirement to retire sooner rather than later.[6]

Major decisions such as these are most often made by a firm's top managers. However, managers at all levels provide input into how the plans will be implemented. Decisions have to be made about which parts of the organization to close and/or which employees will be let go in units that remain open. In smaller companies, managers have even more direct input into the workforce planning decisions and implementation process. Even in companies where the HR department is able to provide assistance in workforce planning decisions, managers should play an active role in the process. After all, managers are ultimately responsible for the success of the groups of individuals they supervise. Thus, the quality of a firm's workforce planning decisions directly affects the performance of a manager's staff.

If, as a manager, you do not have the right number of employees with the right skill sets, you will find your unit unable to take advantage of potential business opportunities. Alternatively, operating in excess of your staffing requirements or employing people who are not adding a sufficient amount of value to the activities they do is an inefficient use of your firm's financial capital. A surplus of employees translates into bloated payroll levels, benefits, and other employee-related expenses. The greater your labor costs, the lower your profitability is likely to be.

Finally, the effectiveness of the people you manage is likely to be directly affected by the quality of your workforce planning decisions. As we will discuss later in this chapter, if your staff members operate short-handed for any length of time or lack the skills they need, they are likely to feel overworked and experience burnout. This, in turn, can lead to higher turnover and diminished performance on their part.[7]

In Chapter 4, we discussed job design. Remember that job design does the following:

- Focuses on decisions about how jobs should be structured
- Ensures that job-related tasks and activities are performed in a way that has the most potential to add value to the company and its customers

The best-designed jobs in the world add no value if people are not in a position to perform them, however. As Exhibit 5.1 shows, work design and workforce planning require managers to pay equal attention to how jobs are designed and to workforce planning.

In the remainder of this chapter, we examine the components of workforce planning. We first discuss how a firm's internal demand for labor relative to its internal supply dictates whether managers experience labor shortages or surpluses among their workforces. We then explore how external factors put pressure on a company's supply and demand for labor. Third, we discuss the different tactics that you, as a manager, can use to remedy labor shortages and surpluses. Finally, we wrap up the chapter with examination of workforce planning in the context of coping with organizational demands, environmental considerations, and regulatory issues.

◀ **Exhibit 5.1**
Framework for the
Strategic Management
of Employees

HR CHALLENGES

| Environmental Influences | Organizational Demands | Regulatory Issues |

PRIMARY HR ACTIVITIES

Work Design & Workforce Planning

Managing Employee Competencies

Managing Employee Attitudes & Behaviors

Employee Contributions

Competitive Advantage

WORKFORCE PLANNING

Exhibit 5.2 provides a visual framework for **workforce planning**—the process of making sure that individuals with the right skills are where they need to be, at the right time, to meet a firm's current and future needs. In many ways, workforce planning is an ongoing balancing act. Companies must balance the demand for labor with the available supply of labor. A firm's **labor demand** refers to the number and types of employees the company needs to meet its current and future strategic objectives. The **labor supply** refers to the availability of current or potential employees to perform a company's jobs. In other words, managers have to look at both the labor supply and the labor demand within their companies (internal considerations), and they also need to anticipate and plan for factors outside their companies (external considerations).

Understanding the supply and demand for labor is only half of the equation, though. Managers must also take action to address labor shortages and surpluses. A **labor shortage** exists when the demand for labor exceeds the available supply of it (demand > supply). In

workforce planning

The process of ensuring that individuals with the right skills are where they need to be, at the right time, to meet a firm's current and future needs.

labor demand

The number and types of employees the company needs to meet its current and future strategic objectives.

labor supply

The availability of current or potential employees to perform a company's jobs.

labor shortage

The situation when demand for labor exceeds the available supply of it.

Exhibit 5.2 ▶

The Framework for
Workforce Planning

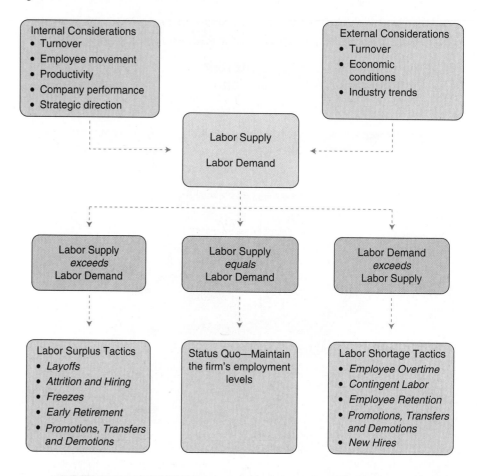

labor surplus

The situation when supply of labor is
greater than the demand for it.

contrast, a **labor surplus** exists when the supply of labor is greater than the demand for it (supply > demand). Overtime, outsourcing, and offshoring are examples of tactics a manager can use to cope with a labor shortage. Tactics such as layoffs and early retirement programs can be used to cope with a labor surplus. Knowing which tactic to use requires that you have some insight into your company's actual labor supply and demand.

FORECASTING LABOR SUPPLY AND LABOR DEMAND

A variety of factors affect the relative supply and demand for labor in companies. As noted previously, managers must examine both the internal and external environmental factors that exert pressure on the labor supply relative to its demand. We next discuss these two types of factors.

Internal Factors

The number of employees in different parts of an organization is always changing due to a variety of factors. Employee turnover is one factor. The productivity of the firm's employees, the company's performance, and changes in the firm's strategic direction also affect the demand for different jobs in different parts of a company. Companies must also allocate employees via promotions, transfers, and demotions to areas in the firm where these people can make the biggest contributions. At any point in time, some parts of a company may be facing shortages of employee talent, whereas others may have surpluses. Let's now discuss these internal factors in more detail.

TURNOVER   Managers consider the internal labor force, or a company's current employees, when it comes to meeting their current and long-term workforce needs. However, the internal labor force is not static but changes over time. Employee **turnover**, which directly affects a firm's labor demand, includes the voluntary and involuntary termination of employees within

turnover

The voluntary and involuntary termination of
employees within an organization.

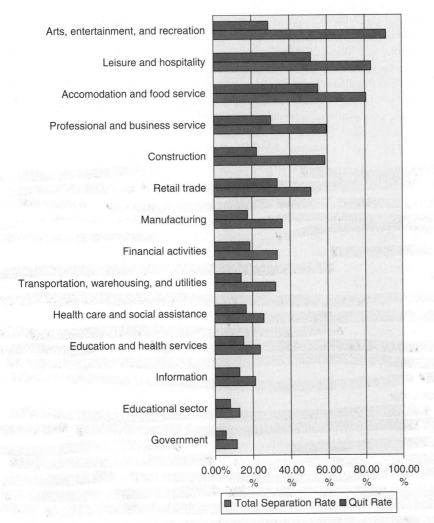

◄ **Exhibit 5.3**

Separation Rate
and Quit Rate by
Selected Industries

Sources: U.S. Bureau of Labor Statistics. *Table 8: Quits levels (1) and rates (2) by industry and region, not seasonally adjusted,* www.bls.gov/news.release/jolts.t08.htm; and U.S. Bureau of Labor Statistics. *Table 7: Total separations levels (1) and rates (2) by industry and region, not seasonally adjusted,* www.bls.gov/news.release/jolts.t07.htm.

an organization. The primary difference between the two types is whether the turnover is initiated by the company (involuntary turnover) or by the employee (voluntary turnover).[8] As shown in Exhibit 5.3, industries vary in their total rate of separation (voluntary and involuntary turnover) as well as their voluntary turnover. Some industries, such as the arts, entertainment, and recreation, struggle to cope with a separation rate over 90%, while the educational sector and the government experience a separation rate of less than 15%.

Turnover has a significant impact on companies. The most obvious impact occurs when a company loses a talented employee. Another problem occurs when an employee's former co-workers—those who remain with the firm—must pick up the slack to make sure the work still gets done. Even when a replacement employee is eventually hired, his or her co-workers are still likely to experience stress until the newly hired person gets fully up to speed.

In addition, there are both costs and time demands associated with filling open positions. For example, at WFS Financial, Inc., a large automobile financing company, a turnover rate approaching 33% was costing the company approximately $5 million per year.[9] Similarly, facing a 213% turnover in 2003 (compared to an industry average of just over 125%), managers at Steak n Shake realized that profitability, employee morale, and customer service at its restaurants were suffering from the constant crew turnover. Steak n Shake estimated that it could save up to $4 million per year if it could reduce its turnover. The company subsequently took steps to do so.[10]

Managing turnover involves time demands for managers. Imagine working in a company with 1,000 employees. If your company has a turnover rate of 10%, this means that you are losing 100 people each year. To remain competitive, you have to make sure that those 100 jobs get filled and their associated tasks and responsibilities are completed. If your company is losing 20 people per month, or 240 per year, maintaining sufficient staffing levels will be that much more difficult. For example, when employees leave, there are fewer individuals who are able to move to other positions in the company. Although this might improve the promotional prospects of the employees who remain with the firm, it diminishes the potential internal labor supply available for higher-level openings. This concern is related to the second component of the internal workforce framework, the actual and potential movement of employees throughout companies.

EMPLOYEE MOVEMENTS Even without turnover, the profile of a company's workforce changes over time as employees move into different jobs. Companies use promotions, transfers, and demotions to move employees from one job to another. **Promotions** involve moving employees to higher level positions, which often are associated with increased levels of responsibility and authority. Employees can also **transfer** to other jobs with similar levels of responsibility. (Most transfers within a company are viewed as lateral moves.) Employees can also be **demoted,** or moved to lower-level positions within their companies. Of course, moving people throughout an organization should not be done haphazardly. Managers can use several tools to help track employee movements: replacement charts, succession planning, and transition matrices. Next, we discuss each.

Companies use **replacement charts** to identify potential replacement employees for positions that could open up within their organizations. Essentially, a replacement chart shows the employees who could potentially be moved from one job to another if vacancies occur. With such a system in place, a company is ready to make personnel changes on short notice.

Succession planning is similar to using replacement charts but focuses on identifying employees who might be viable successors for top managerial positions—that is, for key jobs that could become vacant. As the name implies, succession planning involves identifying who is next in line for higher-level jobs. It also requires the company to fill in information about any skill a potential successor needs to develop. A well-defined succession process is important for a variety of reasons. First, the existence of a plan is more likely to lead to appropriate development of employees for advancement opportunities. Second, a succession plan ensures that someone who has the right experience is ready at all times to step into a critical but vacant higher-level job. When Gordon Teter, chairman and CEO of Wendy's, died unexpectedly in 1999, no successor was in place to take over his role. As a result, Dave Thomas, the company's founder, had to assume some of Teter's roles until a new chairman and CEO could be named.[11]

Once identified, successors undergo development activities and experiences to prepare them for jobs they could potentially fill. Depending on the position and the length of time it would take a potential successor to get up to speed, companies sometimes realize that they need to begin recruiting immediately to fill positions that may not become vacant for months or even years. However, without engaging in succession planning, firms might not be aware of this. In addition to helping companies identify their long-term workforce planning needs, the process of identifying replacement employees for positions can also reveal that a firm could potentially face a shortage of employees to fill its lower-level jobs if its upper-level jobs became vacant and workers were promoted to them.

A third tool that managers can use to understand the internal movement trends of their workforces is a **transition matrix**. A transition matrix provides a model for tracking the movement of employees throughout an organization, rather than for a single job, over a certain period of time. Exhibit 5.4 shows an example of a transition matrix for a hypothetical company for a one-year time period.

The data in the completed matrix in Exhibit 5.4 provide a wealth of useful information. For example, we can see that the turnover rate is highest among managers (40%) and lowest among employees (20%). Knowing the average turnover rate of different groups of employees provides some insight about the number of employees a company needs to hire for each position.

A transition matrix also highlights the movement of employees throughout the organization, which, as we have explained, further affects a firm's internal demand and supply

---

promotion

An employee's move to a higher-level position, which often is associated with increased levels of responsibility and authority.

transfer

An employee's move to another job with a similar level of responsibility.

demotion

An employee's move to a lower-level position within the company.

replacement chart

A tool used to identify potential replacement employees for positions that could open up within their organizations.

succession planning

A method that focuses on identifying employees who might be viable successors for top managerial positions.

transition matrix

A model for tracking the movement of employees throughout an organization over a certain period of time.

2008	2009				
	Vice President	Manager	Supervisor	Employees	Exit the Company
3 Vice Presidents	2 (67%)				1 (33%)
10 Managers	2 (20%)	3 (30%)	1 (10%)		4 (40%)
20 Supervisors		2 (10%)	12 (60%)		6 (30%)
200 Employees			10 (5%)	150 (75%)	40 (20%)
Anticipated Labor Supply	4	5	23	150	50 (out of 233)

◀ **Exhibit 5.4**

An Example of a Transition Matrix

of labor. Each row in the transition matrix shows where the employees at the beginning of the year ended up a year later. For example in Exhibit 5.4, we can see that 2 managers were promoted to vice president, 3 managers remained in their managerial positions, 1 manager was demoted to a supervisor, and 4 managers left the organization. After completing the data for all the positions, the columns in the table highlight the anticipated labor shortage or surplus of internal labor for each position. Looking at the column for managers, we can see that the internal labor supply of managers was 5—the 3 managers who remained in their positions and the 2 supervisors who were promoted to manager positions. Given the starting number of 10 managers in 2008, this suggests that there will be a labor shortage of 5 managers for 2009. In contrast, the data show that there will be a labor surplus of supervisors. In 2009, there will be 23 supervisors compared to 20 supervisors in 2008.

One of the primary benefits of a transition matrix is that it provides data to help prepare for workforce demands in the future. Hiring now for anticipated labor shortages, for example, can help a firm avoid the unnecessary stress and costs associated with its current employees having to work overtime. To truly understand your firm's internal labor supply and demand, however, you also have to have a firm grasp of the productivity of your workforce—that is, how well employees will be able to meet the anticipated growth or decline in the demand for your products and/or services. We discuss this aspect next.

EMPLOYEE PRODUCTIVITY Productivity refers to the level of a firm's output (products or services) relative to the inputs (employees, equipment, materials, and so forth) used to produce the output.[12] A **productivity ratio** reflects the *number* of employees (labor demand) needed to achieve a certain output level (level of sales, production, and so forth). You can figure out these ratios by collecting data on your firm's output levels versus number of employees in prior years. Sales data and amount of products produced in previous years are examples of the types of output data firms use to calculate their productivity ratios.

Exhibit 5.5 shows a hypothetical productivity ratio for a manufacturing plant for assembly-line employees. In this case, you can see that the productivity ratio for 2002 was 40 (5,000 units/125 employees). Once the ratio is calculated for each of the previous years, an average productivity ratio is established. In this case, the average is 42.86 units per employee. To use this information as a forecasting tool, managers simply need to project the output they anticipate their firms will produce in future years. For example, in Exhibit 5.5, the estimated productivity output is 7250 units. If you divide 7250 by the productivity ratio (42.86), you get a forecasted labor demand of 170 employees. Based on this information, the company will need to hire 10 more assembly-line employees to maintain its current level of productivity.

One of the benefits of understanding the productivity ratio is that it allows you to plan for different potential scenarios that reflect the growth or decline in the demand for your products. For example, if your company anticipates the demand for its products to increase by 10%, it can simply adjust the output level and calculate a revised labor demand figure. The same process can be used to forecast your labor demand if you are experiencing a decline in the demand for your products. Moreover, the calculations can be performed in a

productivity

The level of a firm's output (products or services) relative to the inputs (employees, equipment, materials, and so forth) used to produce the output.

productivity ratio

The number of employees (labor demand) needed to achieve a certain output level (level of sales, production, and so forth).

Exhibit 5.5 ▶

Calculating
Productivity Ratios

Year	Productivity Output (units per month)	Number of Employees	Productivity Ratio (output/ employees)
2002	5000	125	40
2003	5500	125	44
2004	6000	135	44.44
2005	6000	140	42.85
2006	6250	150	41.67
2007	6500	150	43.33
2008	7000	160	43.75
2009*	7250	X = 170 employees needed	Average Ratio = 42.86
2010*	7500	X = 175 employees needed	Average Ratio = 42.86

* Estimates

variety of industries. For example, depending on the type of businesses they are in, companies can use sales figures, phone volumes, Internet volumes, or customer interactions. In other words, as long as there is some quantifiable output measure, managers can calculate their productivity ratios and the associated number of employees they will need.

Of course, companies can intervene in ways that directly impact their productivity ratios. As we discuss about in Chapters 6 through 8, more extensive recruitment, better selection decisions, or even more comprehensive or effective training can change a firm's productivity ratio. With a more talented workforce, for example, a firm could anticipate its level of productivity per employee to increase.

COMPANY PERFORMANCE   As our discussion of Ford and GM at the beginning of this chapter highlighted, the overall performance of a company influences its labor supply and demand. Facing diminishing customer demand, Ford and GM realized that their demand for labor was not at the same level as it had once been. In fact, they were facing a labor surplus. This is a common problem among companies that are performing poorly; they simply do not need or cannot afford the same number of workers as they did previously.[13] In contrast, when companies excel in terms of their performance, they often realize that their demand for labor is outpacing their current supply. Moreover, all other things being equal, better-performing companies are more likely to have the financial resources to employ a greater number of employees as well as pay for top-notch employees.

STRATEGIC DIRECTION   One limitation to solely tracking the actual or potential movement of employees through your firm via replacement charts, succession planning, and transition matrices is that this approach is often based on maintaining the status quo.[14] Productivity ratios are also limited to some extent because they assume that a firm's current processes and procedures will remain intact for the foreseeable future. However, companies evolve. They take steps to improve their performance by continually making decisions about whether they should strive for growth, maintain the status quo, retrench, or refocus their operations.[15]

Of course, all these changes directly affect whether a company will experience a shortage or surplus of labor. Companies that are planning to expand their operations to facilitate growth are likely to try to increase their productivity in an attempt to capture more market share. As a result, they are likely to face labor shortages. In contrast, companies that are planning on reducing the scope of their operations are likely to try to curtail their output levels. These companies are more likely to experience labor surpluses.

Companies also engage in mergers and acquisitions that affect their supply and demand for labor and the tactics they use to balance the two. For example, when two companies merge, their goal is to achieve greater efficiencies or leverage some corporate know-how across units to realize a competitive advantage. One of the major implications of a merger or an acquisition relates to the overlapping skill sets the employees of the two companies are likely to have. When two companies become one, there are likely to be some redundancies across positions. For example, both companies are likely to employ workers doing similar activities, such as accounting, marketing, production, grounds maintenance, mail service, and management activities. When the companies merge, they are forced to deal with these redundancies. Oftentimes they do so by laying off employees.

External Factors

To some extent, managers can control internal labor factors. However, managers also have to evaluate factors in the external environment over which they have less control. These factors relate to the local labor market, economic conditions, and industry trends that impact the supply and demand for goods and services.

LOCAL LABOR MARKET   People in the local labor market represent a potential external labor supply for firms. One of the major drivers of the size and composition of the local labor market available to a firm is its location. As we will discuss further in Chapter 6, local labor markets vary dramatically in terms of the number and types of individuals within them available for work. A company located in New York City will have access to a much larger pool of potential workers than a company located in rural South Dakota, for example. Similarly, in certain geographic areas, employees will lack the types of skills an employer needs. In this case, the availability of the local labor supply might not be sufficient to meet a company's labor demand. In contrast, college towns generally have a relatively large supply of highly educated people available to do a variety of types of work. Clearly, the relative size and composition of a local labor market, with individuals with different skills sets, directly affects the labor pool's potential to adequately serve as a viable source of labor for companies.

ECONOMIC CONDITIONS   The general health of the economy—particularly the unemployment rate—has a big impact on the availability of workers. As the unemployment rate rises, firms find it easier to hire qualified individuals in the external labor market. In contrast, when the unemployment rate drops, hiring qualified individuals becomes more difficult. Companies competing on a global basis face a particular challenge with unemployment. For example, in February 2005, the unemployment rate in the United States was around 5.6%. At the same time, the unemployment rate in Germany was significantly higher, at 12.6%.[16] As you can imagine, with a greater supply of available labor, companies in Germany would likely have an easier time finding employees.

Beyond unemployment figures, the general health of the economy also affects a firm's workforce planning. When the economy is stagnant, or in a recession, the demand for many products drops. In contrast, during periods of high economic growth, the demand for many products increases. The level of consumer demand—whether it is growing or declining—directly affects the amount of labor companies demand to meet their customers' needs. The demand for information technology (IT) workers during the Y2K boom is a good example. Contrary to what people feared would happen, few computers experienced problems following the new year in 2000. As a result, the demand for IT workers in many segments of the economy fell dramatically.

INDUSTRY TRENDS   Many industries experience predictable purchasing patterns that fluctuate over time and directly influence when they experience labor shortages or surpluses. Retail establishments are a prime example of this. Although retailers such as Toys 'R' Us, Radio Shack, and The Limited operate their stores on a year-round basis, their sales follow a predictable pattern: Their highest sales occur in the weeks and days leading up to Christmas. As a result, these firms demand a greater amount of labor during this time of the year. Understanding cyclical patterns such as these helps managers ensure that they don't have too many employees during the slow times and that they have enough employees during busy times.

Many companies are also suppliers to other companies. In other words, they don't sell to individual consumers but to firms. To some extent, the labor demand of supplying firms such as these is a function of the success of their customers. Consider the computer

The iPod has changed the music industry and how customers enjoy music.

industry. Computer manufacturers such as Dell, HP, Gateway, and Toshiba rely on suppliers for many of the components that make up the computers they sell, including the computers' monitors, storage devices, processing chips, and so forth. Consequently, the amount of labor these suppliers demand is directly influenced by the relative success—or failure—of the computer manufacturers that purchase their products. If a company is a direct supplier of monitors for Dell, for example, it can estimate its demand for labor based on the computers Dell anticipates selling. So, for instance, if Dell expects to sell 5% more computers in the coming year than it sold this past year, the supplier can expect to be asked to provide 5% more monitors as well.

Although an economy's leading indicators—indicators such as its unemployment rate, inflation rate, and so forth—are often fairly predictable, sometimes labor demand patterns are subject to industry shocks. Shocks are dramatic changes in the nature of the products or services offered in the economy or dramatic changes in how companies compete. Do you own an iPod, produced by Apple Computer Corporation? You perhaps do. Depending on the type of iPod, you can store up to 40,000 songs on a single device.[17] That's a lot of songs—many more than a CD or cassette tape can hold.

Now, take a second to think about how the introduction of the iPod and other MP3 players affected labor supply and demand. It is more straightforward than you might think. Prior to the sudden popularity of the MP3 player in the consumer market, consumers generally had to rely on portable CD or cassette players, such as the Sony Walkman. But as the demand for digital music grew, the producers of CDs and CD and cassette players watched the demand for their products drop. Many of these firms surely realized that the number of employees they had on staff was too high. In contrast, companies that produced MP3 players surely realized that they would have a labor shortage on their hands. As you can see, the actions of other companies and how they affect consumers' preferences for products or services directly affects the labor demanded by other companies.

TACTICS FIRMS USE TO BALANCE THEIR SUPPLY AND DEMAND FOR LABOR

Based on our discussion to this point in the chapter, it should be evident that the supply and demand for employees within companies is constantly shifting. Effectively managing the workforce involves anticipating where employees will be needed (or not) within the firm and balancing their demand with their available supply. Once you have a good idea about where labor surpluses and shortages exist within a company, the next step is to take action to balance those pressures.

Labor Shortage Tactics

When faced with a labor shortage, most people initially think about recruiting new employees. Although this is certainly a viable option, other tactics can be used to address labor shortages, too. Some of the typical methods are using overtime and contingent labor; increasing employee retention rates; strategically using employee promotions, transfers, and demotions; and hiring new employees.

EMPLOYEE OVERTIME One of the quickest ways to handle a labor shortage is through the use of overtime. Overtime refers to employees working additional hours beyond their standard schedules. Most full-time employees work a 40-hour workweek. To address a labor shortage, managers may require their employees to work additional hours to meet a company's needs. Retailers often ask their current employees to work extra hours around the holidays, for example.

Although federal and state laws regulate how much overtime employees are allowed work (an aspect we will discuss in Chapter 10), using overtime is a viable way for a company to cope with a labor shortage quickly. The tactic is very useful when a labor shortage is expected to be of short duration. As the length of the anticipated labor shortage increases, however, paying overtime might prove too costly. (Hourly employees are generally paid

1.5 times their hourly wage for working overtime.[18]) Another potential downside is that when employees work too many overtime hours, they can become dissatisfied and/or experience burnout. Eventually, overtime can lead to increased employee turnover, creating further labor shortages.

OUTSOURCING AND CONTINGENT LABOR   In addition to overtime, a second tactic you can use to remedy a labor shortage is to arrange for external, or outsourced, workers to produce your goods and sources. Outsourcing is the practice of sending work to other companies. Companies often outsource activities such as the maintenance for their grounds, food service for their cafeterias or vending machines, and payroll management. Moreover, because external service providers often focus on a single service and provide their services to many different companies, they are often able to do them more efficiently. Wheeling-Pitt, a large steel manufacturer, is a case in point: The firm saved $170,000 in transportation costs simply by outsourcing the oversight of its trucking of steel coils to Pittsburgh Logistics Systems Inc.[19] Besides saving money, outsourcing allows companies to focus on the activities they do best— the ones that give them a competitive advantage. Instead of having to deal with transportation issues, for example, Wheeling-Pitt can focus on developing better steel products.

In addition to outsourcing, companies also hire contingent labor to remedy labor shortages.[20] Contingent labor refers to employees hired on a temporary or contractual basis as opposed to a permanent basis. In 2005, there were 10.3 million independent contractors, 1.2 temporary help agency workers, and 2.5 million on-call employees in the U.S. workforce.[21] Like outsourcing, hiring contingent labor can also help a firm save money and hone its strategic focus. Contingent labor also provides companies with both numerical and functional flexibility. Numerical flexibility refers to the number of employees working for a company. Using contingent workers gives companies the flexibility to adjust their number of employees relatively quickly. This can be a major benefit for companies that face predictable variations in the demand for their services. As Company Spotlight 5.1 shows, H&R Block relies extensively on contingent workers to cope with the surging demand for its tax preparation services prior to April 15 every year.

Functional flexibility refers to the types of skills employees possess. Because companies can readily adjust which contingent workers they use, they can quickly modify the composition of the knowledge, skills, and abilities of their workforces. As a result, the companies don't have to have to make long-term investments to develop or hire workers for particular skills that are needed for only a short period of time. At the same time, however, relying too heavily on contingent labor can prevent companies from investing in the employee competencies they need for their long-term success.[22]

outsourcing

The practice of sending work to other companies.

contingent labor

Employees hired on a temporary or contractual basis as opposed to a permanent basis.

numerical flexibility

A form of organizational flexibility related to the ease of adjusting the number of individuals working for a company.

functional flexibility

A form of flexibility related to the ease of adjusting the types of skills a workforce possesses.

COMPANY *spotlight*   5.1 Handling Tax Season at H&R Block

What do you do if a considerable portion of your yearly business happens in only three or four months of the year? That is precisely the scenario that occurs at H&R Block, the world's largest tax services provider. The answer? You need to understand trends in the consumer demand for your services and take advantage of a large seasonal workforce, as H&R Block does.

Although H&R Block has a large full-time workforce, during the busy tax season (January through April), the size of its workforce swells with contingent, or seasonal, workers. In St. Louis, for example, H&R Block has 95 offices in seven districts throughout the metropolitan area. During the year, each district is staffed by fewer than 10 people. As the tax season emerges, however, roughly 1,450 workers are hired. Nationwide, H&R Block hires approximately 80,000 tax professionals to work from January until the end of April. The result: H&R Block is able to continually adjust the size of its labor force as it needs to.

Sources: Kerth, S. H&R Block, Jackson Hewitt staff up local tax offices: Firms bring in 95% of revenue from January to April. *St. Louis Business Journal*, January 14, 2005, www.bizjournals.com/stlouis/stories/2005/01/17/focus2.html; Wright, S. A. Seasonal hiring helps put some people back to work. *The Seattle Times*, March 17, 2004, http://seattletimes.nwsource.com/html/businesstechnology/2001880755_jobless17.html; and DeZube, D. *Seasonal tax-preparation jobs*. http://finance.monster.com/articles/taxprep/.

EMPLOYEE RETENTION   As noted previously, turnover is a significant cause of labor shortages. Wal-Mart has an annual turnover rate of roughly 50% among its 1.3 million employees; more than 600,000 Wal-Mart associates leave every year and need to be replaced. Once the replacements are found, they also need to be trained, which takes additional time and money.[23] One way to address this problem is to focus on employee retention. At a basic level, reducing turnover lowers a firm's recruitment and selection costs, reduces its need to train new employees, and helps ensure that productive employees remain with the company. It is not surprising that companies such as Southwest Airlines, Lincoln Electric, and Wegmans, which have lower turnover rates than other firms in their industries, also lead their industries in terms of employee productivity and corporate performance.

Knowing that you will be able to retain a steady number of your employees will also improve your workforce forecasting, at least on the internal supply side of the equation. Employee satisfaction is a key predictor of turnover, and in the remaining chapters of the book, we will look at how to improve it.[24]

EMPLOYEE PROMOTIONS, TRANSFERS, AND DEMOTIONS   Rather than rely on your current employees to work longer hours, as a manager, you might opt to move employees from one area of a company into another area that has a labor shortage. This can be a very effective way to deal with a labor shortage, especially because it can be done quickly. Because companies are already familiar with their current employees, managers are also likely to be better informed about the potential of these employees to succeed in their new jobs. Of course, one of the disadvantages of relying on employee transitions is that you're simply shifting the labor shortage from one area of your company to another. Every employee who is promoted, transferred, or demoted to another job leaves behind a vacant job with tasks, duties, and responsibilities that someone else must take on.

NEW HIRES   The final tactic for addressing a labor shortage is to recruit and hire new, full-time employees. While overtime and employee transitions focus on addressing labor shortages with current employees, hiring new employees increases the size of your workforce. One of the primary benefits of full-time hires is that this approach provides a more permanent solution to a labor shortage instead of a temporary one. At the same time, however, hiring new employees involves making a long-term commitment to their employment. As a manager, it is important that you understand whether your labor shortage is permanent or temporary before hiring new full-time employees. If the shortage is temporary, hiring new employees could, of course, result in a labor surplus down the road.

There is no single best solution for how to deal with a labor shortage or surplus. Each of the tactics discussed here has advantages and disadvantages that must be considered, such as how long you expect a shortage or surplus to last. As we have indicated, using overtime and contingent labor can remedy a shortage very quickly. In contrast, improving employee retention to remedy a shortage takes more time to accomplish, as does hiring new employees and getting them up to speed.

Labor Surplus Tactics

As noted earlier, employing surplus labor is likely to be financially prohibitive for many companies, particularly when the surpluses are anticipated to be permanent or last for a long time. Layoffs, attrition, hiring freezes, early retirement programs, and movement of employees (either temporarily or permanently) to other work areas are some of the common tactics managers use to address labor surpluses. Let's now examine each of these tactics.

LAYOFFS   A layoff involves quickly reducing the number of workers you employ. As shown in Exhibit 5.6, in 2007, there were more than 15,000 mass layoffs in the United States, affecting more than 1.5 million workers. And these trends are not limited to the United States. In 2005, the Dutch phone company DKN announced plans to eliminate 8,000 jobs over a five-year period in response to a sharp drop in annual profits.[25] In an ongoing effort to cut costs, British Airways reduced its headcount by 13,000 employees between 2001 and 2005.[26]

The primary advantage of layoffs is that a company can use them to relatively quickly adjust the size and composition of its workforce. When carried out effectively, a layoff can

Year	Layoff Events	Initial Claimants for Unemployment Insurance
1996	14,111	1,437,628
1997	14,960	1,542,543
1998	15,904	1,771,069
1999	14,909	1,572,399
2000	15,738	1,835,592
2001	21,467	2,514,862
2002	20,277	2,245,051
2003	18,963	1,888,926
2004	15,980	1,607,158
2005	16,466	1,795,341
2006	13,998	1,484,391
2007	15,493	1,598,875

Each action (layoff event) involved at least 50 persons from a single establishment.

Source: Bureau of Labor Statistics. *Table B. Number of mass layoff events and initial claimants for unemployment insurance, 1996–2007*, February 27, 2008, http://stats.bls.gov/news.release/mmls.nr0.htm.

be an isolated event that results in a good balance between an organization's needs and the capabilities of its employees. However, layoffs are associated with several disadvantages. Companies sometimes focus solely on short-term cost-containment efforts when making layoff decisions rather than their long-strategic objectives. When this happens, they often lose employees who are critical to their future success. In other words, although layoffs lower a company's immediate expenses, they don't always generate future business improvements or operational efficiencies.[27] Announcing a layoff can also produce feelings of job insecurity on the part of a firm's employees. This, in turn, can lead to higher turnover and lower employee commitment and loyalty.[28] A firm that engages in layoffs is likely to have a harder time attracting new employees in the future than one that does not engage in layoffs.

ATTRITION AND HIRING FREEZES   Two tactics that companies may turn to for coping with a labor surplus focus primarily on delaying the hiring of new employees. Attrition refers to a decision to not fill vacant positions that emerge as a result of turnover or other employee movements in a company. Hiring freezes put a temporary ban on the hiring of new employees for a specified period of time. One of the advantages of using attrition and hiring freezes to "right-size" the workforce is that they create lower levels of stress among employees than layoffs do. The downside of attrition and hiring freezes, however, is that the employees who are not laid off often find themselves performing extra duties to make up for staffing shortages.[29] Furthermore, it can take a long time to reach a firm's desired employment levels once a freeze or an attrition period is over.

EARLY RETIREMENT   Early retirement programs are an additional tactic companies turn to address their labor surpluses. The goal of these programs is to provide employees with a financial incentive to retire early, thereby lowering the number of a firm's employees and the company's labor costs. In 2006, for example, GM said that employees who had 30 years of service could have $35,000 and full pensions if they retired.[30] Although there are certainly costs associated with early retirement programs, companies can use them to trim the size of their workforces without having to resort to layoffs. However, if an early retirement program is too enticing, it can result in a greater exodus of employees than a company planned for. For example, in 2003, Verizon Communications initiated an early retirement program in an attempt to trim about 12,000 workers from its payroll. More than 21,000 employees accepted the offer, leaving Verizon with a labor shortage.[31]

attrition

Not filling vacant positions that emerge as a result of turnover or other employee movements in a company.

hiring freeze

A temporary ban on the hiring of new employees for a specified period of time.

EMPLOYEE PROMOTIONS, TRANSFERS, AND DEMOTIONS A final tactic for addressing labor surpluses is to use employee promotions, transfers, and demotions. Just as these practices can remedy labor shortages, they can also remedy labor surpluses. For example, rather than reduce the size of a group of employees through layoffs or early retirements, a company might move some employees to other areas in the firm that are facing labor shortages. This way, employees don't lose their jobs, and the company doesn't have to bear any layoff-related costs. The major disadvantage of this tactic is that there may be no area of the company that's experiencing a labor shortage. Even if there is, the employees in the surplus labor areas might not have the needed skills to succeed in the new jobs.

WORKFORCE PLANNING IN PRACTICE: ORGANIZATIONAL DEMANDS

Different companies are likely to use different workforce planning tactics. As shown in Exhibit 5.7, the tactics firms use by companies are likely to vary as they cope with different organizational demands, environmental influences, and regulatory issues. We start with organizational demands.

Strategy and Workforce Planning

A firm's strategy affects its workforce planning in several ways. First, it affects how quickly the company is likely to need to respond to labor shortages or surpluses. Second, it affects how critical different skill sets are in the organization, which, in turn, determines the workforce planning tactics managers are likely to use.

▶ **Exhibit 5.7** Workforce Planning in Practice

Context	**Work Design and Workforce Planning** **Chapter 5, "Workforce Planning"**
Organizational Demands	
Strategy drives . . .	• Required speed to deal with shortages and surpluses • Criticality of employee groups
Company characteristics determine . . .	• The relative impact of labor shortages and surpluses • Who carries out workforce planning
Culture establishes . . .	• Likelihood of firms using different tactics • Employee reactions to workforce planning tactics
Employee concerns include . . .	• Employee stress and work/life balance issues • Perceptions of procedural and distributive justice
Environmental Demands	
Labor force influences . . .	• Availability of internal and external workers • Which tactics to use
Technology affects . . .	• The number of employees needed • The types of workers needed • The quality of workforce planning forecasts
Globalization impacts . . .	• Where the workers are • Which workforce planning tactics to use
Ethics/social responsibility shapes . . .	• Community reactions to workforce planning tactics • How companies help employees cope
Regulations *guide* . . .	• Requirements for mass layoffs and plant closings • Determining who is an employee versus an independent contractor

REQUIRED SPEED TO DEAL WITH SHORTAGES AND SURPLUSES As noted in Chapter 2, some companies focus on low costs as a key source of their competitiveness. Others attempt to differentiate themselves from their competitors in terms of the quality, types of products, and/or services they offer. In other words, they try to offer products, services, or features for which customers are willing to pay a premium. Different business strategies such as these affect how quickly firms must cope with labor shortages and surpluses. Companies focused on keeping their costs low will view a labor surplus as particularly problematic. These companies are likely to reduce a surplus by using tactics that can be carried out quickly (e.g., via layoffs). In contrast, firms that pursue a differentiation strategy might have a bit more cushion to absorb the costs of a labor surplus. These firms are likely to be more willing to rely on labor reduction tactics such as early retirements and attrition—tactics that are slower but less stressful for employees.

CRITICALITY OF EMPLOYEE GROUPS A firm's strategy affects which of its employees are most critical to its success. Firms focused on differentiation strategies such as product leadership and innovation, for example, are likely to more heavily depend on R&D skills. Firms competing on customer service are likely to be particularly dependent on their sales and customer relations staff. In contrast, cost leadership firms are likely to depend on employees with efficiency-related competencies, such as operation management skills. This factor, in turn, affects the workforce planning tactics managers of different firms are likely to use. The greater potential strategic impact certain positions in a firm have, the more reluctant a company will be to outsource, offshore, or turn to contingent workers to fill them.[32] Instead, the firm will tend to hire and retain permanent employees for these positions to keep them staffed.

Company Characteristics and Workforce Planning

As noted in Chapter 2, every company is unique in many ways. These differences place pressures on the relative labor demand and supply as well as the tactics they use to cope with surpluses and shortages. In particular, a company's size and stage of development will affect the relative impact of labor shortages and surpluses as well as who will carry out the company's workforce planning activities.

THE RELATIVE IMPACT OF LABOR SHORTAGES AND SURPLUSES In particularly small companies, the relative impact of labor shortages or surpluses is likely to be greater than in larger companies. Imagine that you are a manager in a company that employs 20 people, and you are short 5 employees. Trying to cover the tasks and responsibilities of 5 people in a firm such as this will be more difficult than covering the tasks formerly performed by 5 people in a company that has 50,000 employees. One of the reasons is that smaller companies, or companies that are in much earlier stages of development, usually have considerably less labor slack—excess labor capacity. Because they generally have leaner workforces, the internal labor supply available for covering these tasks or for filling new or vacant positions in these companies may be limited. In contrast, larger companies have more employees, so their managers have more options to transfer, promote, or demote people to fill positions internally.

Now suppose that your company of 20 employees loses a client and needs only 15 employees: The labor costs of employing 20 versus 15 people might prove impossible. As you can see, the pressure to quickly deal with a labor shortage or surplus will make certain workforce tactics less feasible than others. If labor shortages must be addressed quickly, relying on new hires may take too long compared to relying on overtime or using contingent workers. Similarly, attrition or hiring freezes might not be fast enough to adjust the labor costs to be sustainable. Rather, a quicker response, such as a layoff, may be needed in a smaller company facing a surplus.

WHO CARRIES OUT WORKFORCE PLANNING Your responsibility for carrying out workforce planning activities will vary depending on the size and stage of development of your company. Larger companies are likely to have greater resources, support staff, and perhaps a formal HR department to devote to these activities.[33] Companies such as this are also likely be in a better position to invest in technology that helps them track labor force trends and the labor supply throughout their organizations.[34] In smaller companies, however, workforce planning activities often fall directly on the managers responsible for supervising the employees who need to be hired. As a manager in a firm such as this, you will have to keep track of the movement of people throughout your unit, the availability of replacement employees to fill open positions, and the viability of using outsourcing or contingent labor, if it's needed.

A similar pattern is likely to exist in younger, startup companies than in more established organizations. Companies in the early stages of development are often understaffed, particularly in terms of support staff. As a result, managers in these companies often find that they have to wear many hats and perform a wide array of activities, including making sure they are able to tap both internal and external sources of talent. As companies grow and become more mature, they are in a better position to add more support activities, including formal HR processes, to accomplish these tasks.

Corporate Culture and Workforce Planning

A company's corporate culture affects the different tactics firms use to deal with labor shortages and surpluses as well as how their employees will react to those tactics.

LIKELIHOOD OF FIRMS USING DIFFERENT TACTICS As discussed earlier, the various tactics for dealing with labor shortages or surpluses vary in terms of how fast they address the problem as well as the degree of stress and overload that employees feel during the process. Some companies have cultural values that prevent them from fully pursuing a particular course of action. Companies that are very paternalistic or extremely loyal to their employees might be hesitant to implement layoffs, even if doing so makes sense.[35] Pella, S.C. Johnson, Lincoln Electric, and Southwest Airlines are examples of companies that have longstanding traditions of fighting for the job security of their employees. For example, when serving as the CEO of Southwest Airlines, James F. Parker stated, "We are willing to suffer some damage, even to our stock price, to protect the jobs of our people,"[36] In contrast, some companies are driven by highly competitive, or cutthroat, cultures. In firms with cutthroat cultures, managers may be more willing to take drastic measures to remedy labor surpluses and shortages—even if those measures create a lot of stress for employees.

EMPLOYEE REACTIONS TO WORKFORCE PLANNING TACTICS Any discrepancy between the corporate culture of a firm and the workforce tactics its managers use is likely to result in a negative reaction by the company's employees. For example, if your company has a culture of attending to the long-term well-being of its employees and rewarding their loyalty, a decision to swiftly lay off a large number of them is likely to be poorly received. Similarly, using contingent labor, outsourcing, or offshoring to deal with a labor shortage might run counter to a corporate culture that puts a priority on the long-term job security of employees. In contrast, using tactics that are consistent with your cultural values is more likely to strengthen those values and increase the bond between employees and the company.

While there are a variety of workforce planning tactics you may use to balance labor supply and demand, it is important that you consider how well the tactic you choose fits with the cultural values in your company. If the choice you make is inconsistent with the company's cultural values, your choice may lead to lower employee morale and commitment and possibility to greater turnover.

Employee Concerns and Workforce Planning

The final organizational demand, employee concerns, is particularly important to consider when we discuss workforce planning. After all, discussions about labor shortages and surpluses, and the tactics that you use to deal with them, directly affect your employees. As a manager, you need to understand that your choices affect not only the level of stress employees experience but also their perceptions of justice and fairness.

EMPLOYEE STRESS AND WORK/LIFE BALANCE ISSUES When the term *workforce planning* is brought up, many people automatically think about layoffs. Although they can quickly "fix" a labor surplus, layoffs create a considerable amount of stress and turmoil not only for the people who lose their jobs but for their families and the communities in which they live. Even employees who "survive" a layoff are likely to experience a great deal of stress.[37] While layoffs are certainly logically linked to employee stress, other labor surplus tactics may also create stress for employees. Any time companies engage in activities that actively or passively try to reduce the number of employees, other employees are affected due to having valued co-workers removed, having to perform additional tasks to make up for the missing employees, and simply being exposed to a change in the work environment.

Workforce planning tactics that are geared toward dealing with labor shortages may also create stress for employees, albeit for different reasons. When experiencing a labor shortage, current employees may have to work harder, or work extra hours, to make sure the additional tasks and responsibilities are performed. If prolonged overtime is used to deal with the labor shortage, employees may experience heightened stress, fatigue, or even injuries from trying to do more than they should do in their jobs.[38] Stress can also result from employee promotions, transfers, or demotions. For example, transferring an employee from one unit to another puts the employee in a new work environment with new colleagues and new tasks and responsibilities to perform. This is likely to create stress for the employee until the person achieves a certain level of proficiency and feels comfortable in the job. Beyond how employees cope with stress on the job, workforce planning tactics may also affect how able employees are to achieve a desirable work/life balance. Working overtime forces employees to spend less time at home or enjoying other personal activities. Similarly, attrition and hiring freezes may require employees to work harder and perhaps longer hours to perform the tasks their former co-workers used to do.

PERCEPTIONS OF PROCEDURAL AND DISTRIBUTIVE JUSTICE The extent to which employees understand and accept the workforce planning tactics managers use is influenced by their perceptions of procedural and distributive justice. As noted in Chapter 2, procedural justice refers to whether employees view the processes used to make a decision as being fair. Distributional justice refers to whether employees believe the actual decision that was made is fair. When you make workforce planning decisions, it is important that your employees understand the rationale behind the decisions. For example, a company facing a major performance problem for several years might be in a better position to present a layoff announcement to employees than a company that has been profitable for many years. When employees believe that your decisions were made fairly, the survivors of a layoff are likely to be less negative.[39] They will also be more willing to regroup and help work toward the company's goals.[40] In contrast, employees who disagree with the decisions or tactics used are less likely to be committed to helping the company move forward.

Even if employees agree with a course of action, they may disagree with how the practice is carried out. For example, identifying which employees are to be targeted for layoffs is typically based on individual performance, seniority, or some combination of the two. With an emphasis on seniority, one approach is to lay off people based on their organizational tenure. With LIFO (last in, first out), those with a shorter tenure with a company are let go first. In other organizations, performance ratings may be used, rather than simply seniority, to target the lower-performing individuals to lay off first. Obviously, how employees view a company's decisions regarding who is targeted for layoffs, transfers, demotions, promotions, overtime, and the like will be a function of what they believe the criteria should be, not necessarily the criteria actually used by the company. An employee with many years on the job might believe seniority should be the primary criterion for layoff and promotion decisions. In contrast, an employee with only a few years on the job might believe performance should be the primary criterion. Employees hold justice perceptions, and the best way for a manager to maintain positive justice perspectives is to keep open lines of communication with employees to maximize their involvement and acceptance of the tactics chosen.

WORKFORCE PLANNING IN PRACTICE: ENVIRONMENTAL INFLUENCES

As you might guess, the external environment—in particular, labor force trends, technology, globalization, and ethical considerations—acutely affects the workforce decisions managers make. Next we look at each of these factors.

Labor Force Trends and Workforce Planning

Earlier in this chapter, we referred to the external labor force as an essential part of the workforce planning process. In addition to considering your current employees, as a manager you have to consider the individuals in the labor market outside your company who are available for work. But the external labor force is not static—it continues to evolve. Effective workforce planning requires you to stay on top of emerging labor force trends that are likely to affect your company both in the near term and the long term. Two trends—occupational trends and demographic trends—have a huge impact on the supply of and demand for employees as well as the workforce planning tactics managers will be able to be effectively use.

AVAILABILITY OF INTERNAL AND EXTERNAL WORKERS As discussed in Chapter 2, the United States is facing an aging workforce due to the boom of individuals in the workforce born between 1946 and 1964—the baby boomers. As this group of individuals gets older, companies are beginning to realize that they have to start planning for "the graying of the workforce."[41] Mass numbers of these people are entering their retirement years. Because there are fewer younger workers to replace them, many companies are increasingly competing with other companies for the limited supply of workers.[42] Company Spotlight 5.2 shows how Volkswagen of America is coping with this problem.

Occupational trends also have a big impact on the availability of internal and external workers. In our discussion of job design in Chapter 4, we emphasized the importance of clearly understanding the competencies that individuals must possess to successfully do certain jobs. If certain occupations experience a decrease in the number of individuals who enter that occupation, over time, this will significantly reduce the level of external labor supply for that job. The nursing industry, for example, is projected to experience this problem. The number of people entering the nursing field is not on pace to meet the demand.[43] In fact, hospitals are expected to realize a labor shortage of over 500,000 nurses by 2020.[44] To compound the problem, hospitals cannot simply hire people and train them on the job to become nurses because nursing professionals require very specific qualifications and training.

In contrast, if certain occupations experience growth, companies will have a larger external labor supply to draw from. The growing number of jobs in the U.S. service sector is an example. Many of these jobs are very standardized and have few requirements pertaining to the particular occupational backgrounds or training workers must have. Companies with jobs such as these are likely have a much greater external labor supply available to them.

The key point here is that, as a manager, you need to be aware of the emerging demographic and occupational trends that are affecting and will affect your supply of workers. A good source to consult for labor force trends is the Bureau of Labor Statistics of the U.S. Department of Labor (www.bls.gov).

WHICH TACTICS TO USE Labor force trends affect the tactics managers can feasibly use to address labor shortages. For example, if there is a shortage of workers in the labor force, companies might have to draw on the abilities of their current employees to cope with the labor crunch. Tactics such as overtime and employee transitions will likely be more feasible in such a case. Some companies have taken more active steps toward retaining their employees to prepare for pending labor shortages. For example, Home Depot, CVS, and Wal-Mart are coping with the aging of their workforces by modifying the nature of jobs to accommodate older employees and encourage them to keep their jobs beyond the typical retirement age.[45] Other organizations are working actively to recruit older employees. For example, after the terrorist attacks on the World Trade Center September 11, 2001, the FBI hired retired agents to work as intelligence analysts and evidence examiners.[46] Of course, companies sometimes have to retrain older workers to ensure that their skills are comparable to those of younger employees. The increasing costs of the health care benefits provided to older employees can also be an issue for some companies.[47] Despite these issues, many companies are realizing that the older workforce represents a talented, and available, labor force to staff their organizations.

Technology and Workforce Planning

Technological changes affect the numbers and types of workers firms need, as well as the quality of managers' workforce planning forecasts. We discuss these two aspects next.

COMPANY spotlight   5.2 Older Workers at Volkswagen

Facing the aging of its workforce, Volkswagen of America, Inc., has taken a number of steps toward becoming an "age-friendly" employer. The company provides employees with a flexible spending account for dependent care that covers elder care, wellness/health fairs and screenings, financial assistance for fitness expenses, counseling for work/family issues, financial and retirement planning, and flexible schedules. These actions have not gone unnoticed; AARP has ranked Volkswagen of America, Inc., as one of the best employers for older workers. AARP chooses winners based on employee development opportunities, health benefits for employees and retirees, the average age of the employer's workforce, and the alternative work arrangements and retirement benefits the employer provides.

"We are honored to have been recognized by AARP," says Mike Beamish, the executive director of human resources for Volkswagen of America. "Nearly one-quarter of Volkswagen's U.S. workforce is over the age of 50. We value the comprehensive experience and industry knowledge that benefits our staff, company and customers."

Sources: Mullich, J. They don't retire them, they hire them. *Workforce Management*, December 2003, pp. 49–54; AARP. *Best employers for workers over 50*, www.aarp.org/money/careers/employerresourcecenter/bestemployers; Volkswagen of America. Volkswagen of America, Inc. named a "Best Employer for Workers over 50" by AARP for the third consecutive year, September 2, 2005, http://media.vw.com/article_display. cfm?article_id=9678; and Christiansen, K., & Catsouphes, M. Accommodating older workers' needs for flexible work options. *Ivey Business Journal*, July/August 2005, pp. 1–4.

THE NUMBER OF EMPLOYEES NEEDED   When you think about the use of technology in organizations, perhaps you think about **automation**—using machines to perform tasks that could otherwise be performed by people. Automated kiosks, for example, are all around us. When you use an ATM (automated teller machine) to withdraw money from your banking account, the machine is performing tasks that a person once had to do. The self-checkout machines at Home Depot and Wal-Mart are another example. Technological changes such as these can create a situation in which companies simply have more employees than they need to remain competitive.

Similarly, companies often implement technological improvements or engage in process redesigns that improve their productivity ratios. Improving your manufacturing technology will generally allow your employees to be more productive. If fewer employees are needed to sustain a certain level of productivity, managers can end up with a surplus of labor. Understanding how these types of company interventions affect the level of productivity among employees helps improve the accuracy of basing labor demand forecasts on productivity levels.

THE TYPES OF WORKERS NEEDED   Technological changes are not solely used to replace employees; they can also be used to complement or change how employees do their jobs, thereby affecting the types of workers firms need. Depending on the nature of the technology in place, technological upgrades and automation may also lead to an increase or a decrease in the level of skills needed to perform tasks or the need for fundamentally different skill sets.[48] The increasing popularity of the Internet is a good example: As customers increasingly rely on the Internet for shopping, what impact does this have on the labor demand for salespeople in stores? If customers who would have previously gone to a store to purchase an item choose to do so via the Internet, there is a chance that the demand for salespeople to work in the store will diminish. Over time, this will result in a labor surplus of salespeople. At the same time, however, the need for people to design, support, and manage Internet sites has increased. The net effect is a change in the types of skills companies need to service their customers. The introduction of sophisticated computer technologies has also required workers to have a heightened level of knowledge to do their jobs,[49] including greater technical, conceptual, analytical, and problem-solving skills.[50] For example, did you know that today's railroad employees check the safety of railcar wheels using infrared technology and acoustical listening devices while the trains are moving? Clearly, this requires the employees to have different skills than they did in the past, when they visually inspected the wheels. It is critical that

automation

Using machines to perform tasks that could otherwise be performed by people.

Technology can affect the number and type of employees firms need.

you, as a manager, consider how technological changes such as the ones described here can affect your workforce plans.[51]

THE QUALITY OF WORKFORCE PLANNING FORECASTS   Technology has clearly had an impact on the demand for labor throughout organizations. It is also helping managers better predict their future workforce needs and talent gaps.[52] Recall our discussion of replacement charts and succession planning, which can be used to track a firm's internal workforce. In a very small company, it might be easy to map out all the viable positions and people able to move into them. However, as companies grow in size and employ more people with different qualifications, this task is likely to become overwhelming. Using technology, however, companies of all sizes can track the skill sets of their employees and identify potential matches for jobs that become vacant. When a client for IBM needed a consultant with a particular clinical background, IBM's Workforce Management Initiative, a technological database that contains more than 33,000 resumes, immediately targeted a single person who perfectly fit the needs of the client.[53] That type of responsiveness certainly helps keep customers happy.

The potential to identify and track future replacements also greatly increases the accuracy and the effectiveness of succession planning in organizations.[54] When coupled with projections of labor force trends, the firm's strategic direction, or long-term productivity prospects, having a sound information system that facilitates skill inventories and tracking allows managers to know that the right individuals are where they need to be within the organization. And the more accurate a firm's forecasts, the less likely that the company will need to resort to tactics to manage labor shortages or surpluses.

Globalization and Workforce Planning

The continued presence of globalization affects workforce planning in several ways. First, it highlights the importance of understanding that labor force trends vary across countries as well as within countries. Second, the option of employing a global workforce has fueled the trend toward offshoring.[55] Infosys Technologies Ltd. and Tata Consultancy Services Ltd., two prominent offshoring companies in India, both have experienced tremendous growth in recent years as the offshoring movement has gained steam.[56]

WHERE THE WORKERS ARE   As noted previously, the aging workforce is particularly problematic for developed countries such as Japan, Italy, and the United States. And despite the growing trend to send work to India, India is actually experiencing a labor shortage for professionals such as project managers, manufacturing professionals, retail managers, sales clerks, and pilots.[57] Countries vary in the quality of their human capital as well as the relative supply of labor. For example, according to the International Labour Organization, 61% of the global population of working age (roughly 3 billion people) was employed in 2007, and the number of unemployed people was 189.9 million people. By region, the Middle East and North Africa have the highest unemployment rates (11.9% and 10.8%), followed by Latin America and the Caribbean, central and southeastern Europe (non-EU) and the Commonwealth of Independent States (CIS) (8.5% each). East Asia and South Asia had the lowest unemployment, at less than 6%.[58] Given differences in the demographics and supply of global labor forces, companies are often forced to engage in different tactics for parts of their business in different global locations to respond to the unique labor force trends.

Workers are becoming increasingly aware of their global opportunities. Some individuals, for example, have sought out opportunities in countries experiencing high global demand for their labor, such as in India and China.[59] According to the National Association of Software and Service Companies (NASSCOM), in 2005, roughly 30,000 workers in IT and outsourcing companies in India were from other countries.[60] Companies such as Microsoft, Intel, and Cisco Systems are increasing their investments in their overseas operations. Consequently, it's not surprising that some individuals are relocating from the United States to countries with the best prospects for job growth.[61]

WHICH WORKFORCE PLANNING TACTICS TO USE   As a result of offshoring, countries around the world are being evaluated as potential locations for establishing offshore operations Although the United States has witnessed an increasing trend toward the offshoring of its manufacturing jobs, more recently it has witnessed the offshoring of professional and white-collar jobs, too. For example, many IT jobs, call centers positions, and back-office operations are being offshored to India, eastern Europe, and the Philippines.[62] By viewing the external workforce at a global level, rather than at a local or domestic level, companies have a significantly larger labor pool to choose from.

Countries vary dramatically with regard to their labor costs, and this has, of course, fueled the offshoring trend. For some firms, the availability of a large labor supply in another country, coupled with potentially lower labor costs in those nations, is a very attractive option. Given these considerations, it should not be surprising that U.S. companies such as American Standard have set up operations in countries such as Bulgaria, where wages are a fraction of what they are in the United States.[63] Even the wages in countries in close proximity to one another range widely, as Exhibit 5.8 shows for the countries in central Europe.

Although offshoring may present challenges in terms of distance, it also presents an opportunity for operating a firm "'24/7"—operating without any downtime, that is. A partner of a U.S. firm in India, for example, may conceivably start its workday just as the employees in the United States are completing their workday. By taking advantage of this situation, companies have been able to decrease the time it takes to create products or services while dramatically increasing their firms' labor pools. Given the continual pressures firms are under to bring out new products faster than their competitors and at lower costs, it is logical that companies such as General Electric, Citigroup, and American Express continue to expand their offshoring operations.[64]

There are, nonetheless, risks associated with adopting a global workforce planning approach. Companies must balance their cost savings with achieving the strategic objectives they are trying to achieve, such as improved product quality and operational performance, greater market access, better customer service, and so on.[65] It is imperative that you be able to ensure that offshoring your business processes and activities will not compromise the quality of your operations. Saving costs at the expense of other performance outcomes is unlikely to be a sustainable strategy over time.[66]

Ethics and Workforce Planning

In addition to their business implications, workforce planning decisions can also be viewed from an ethical perspective. To be sure, these decisions affect the viability of a company's operations. However, as indicated earlier, workforce planning decisions also affect individuals, their families, and the communities in which companies operate. As a result, one of the challenges you must consider when making workforce planning decisions relates to how these activities are viewed from an ethical perspective.

COMMUNITY REACTIONS TO WORKFORCE PLANNING TACTICS Layoffs, contingent labor, outsourcing, and offshoring are certainly viable workforce planning options for firms. However, they are not without controversy. Many people believe that not only does offshoring take jobs away from domestic employees, but companies use it as a way to exploit low-cost labor and avoid complying with domestic labor laws and regulations that

Country	Factory Worker	Engineer	Accountant	Middle Manager
Poland	$3.07	$4.32	$4.03	$6.69
Czech Republic	$2.81	$5.38	$4.10	$6.81
Hungary	$1.96	$5.09	$4.62	$7.44
Slovakia	$2.21	$4.15	$3.37	$5.48
Romania	$1.41	$2.58	$1.23	$3.23
Bulgaria	$0.73	$1.43	$0.83	$2.80
Germany	$18.80	$38.90	$26.40	$40.40

◀ **Exhibit 5.8**
Labor Costs in Central Europe

Source: Ewing, J., & Edmondson, G. The rise of central Europe. *BusinessWeek*, December 12, 2005, pp. 50–56.

PRACTICE

are designed to protect employees.[67] As highlighted in Chapter 2, Nike is a company that experienced backlash due to rumors of poor working conditions and the use of child labor among its international suppliers. In response, Nike has done an admirable job turning around that image by instituting a rigorous process for identifying and managing its international supplier network.

Decisions related to workforce planning are often about emotionally charged topics. These decisions directly affect whether people are able to keep their jobs, how hard they have to work, and whether they enjoy the benefits of full-time employment. In many cases, these issues have social, political, and competitive implications. Managers would be well advised to be fully informed about how the relevant stakeholders of their organization are going to view the workforce planning decisions they make. The ethical vantage points of different groups will influence how they react to workforce planning actions. Communities with high unemployment rates, for example, are likely to be particularly sensitive to a firm's decisions to outsource or offshore jobs.

HOW COMPANIES HELP EMPLOYEES COPE   In light of the impact that the different workforce planning tactics have on individuals, many companies take steps to help their employees cope with these changes. Some companies provide employees with extra breaks to help them cope with the extra tasks they have to do during a labor shortage, for example. Similarly, managers can make sure the employees transitioning to new jobs are properly trained. Many companies that resort to layoffs establish **outplacement assistance programs** to help employees who are being let go find new jobs. Outplacement services often help individuals cope with the reality of losing a job, prepare individuals to transition to a new career opportunity quickly and successfully, and provide a sounding board or a channel for emotional support during the transition. Sometimes managers or individuals within the company provide this counseling, but oftentimes it is better left to outside service providers who are specifically trained to provide the counseling and support individuals need.

outplacement assistance program

A program to help employees who are being let go find new jobs.

WORKFORCE PLANNING IN PRACTICE: REGULATORY ISSUES

Ethical considerations revolve around many of the workforce planning decisions companies make. However, there are also several legal requirements that are important to consider for workforce planning. Two specific issues that have garnered considerable attention in recent years relate to the legal requirements associated with mass layoffs and plant closings and properly classifying workers as either employees or independent contractors. We discuss these issues next.

Requirements for Mass Layoffs and Plant Closings

The **Worker Adjustment and Retraining Notification (WARN) Act**, passed in 1989, mandates the amount of notice workers, their families, and their communities must receive prior to a mass layoff. The act covers the following companies:

Worker Adjustment and Retraining Notification (WARN) Act

An act passed in 1989 that mandates the amount of notice workers, their families, and their communities must receive prior to a mass layoff.

- Companies with 100 or more employees, not counting part-time employees
- Companies with 100 or more employees, including part-time employees who in the aggregate work at least 4,000 hours per week

A company that meets one of these qualifications is required to provide 60 calendar days' notice in advance of a plant closing or mass layoff.[68] According to the act, a plant closing is a situation in which a single employment site (or one or more facilities or units within a site) will be shut down, with loss of employment for 50 or more employees during a 30-day period. A mass layoff, in contrast, does not result from a plant closing but is an employment loss during a 30-day period of 500 or more employees, or 50 to 499 employees if those targeted for the layoff make up at least one-third of the company's workforce.[69] The intention of this act is to provide workers and their families with a transition period during which to adjust to an impending layoff in order to obtain other employment or begin training to become competitive for new jobs.[70]

Determining Who Is an Employee Versus an Independent Contractor

As shown in Exhibit 5.9, determining whether an individual should be considered an employee or an **independent contractor** is based on three primary considerations: behavioral control, financial control, and the relationship of the parties. *Behavioral control* focuses on the extent to which there is a right by the company to direct or control how the individual performs the work. *Financial control* considers the extent to which the individual has control over the business side of the work and the degree of investment the person makes in the work—that is, whether the person is reimbursed for his or her business expenses and has the opportunity to realize a profit or loss on the work. The *relationship of the parties* examines how the company and the individual perceive their work relationship and considers two factors: the presence or absence of employee benefits and the terminology of any existing written contract.

In general, the key distinction between an employee and an independent contractor revolves around the issue of control. If you can control the details of what and how an individual performs services for you, the individual is most likely an employee. In contrast, independent contractors typically maintain control over the means and methods of their services. You may control the result of their work but not the details regarding how that work is completed. The notion of control spans many aspects of employment.

To help people understand whether an individual is an employee, the Internal Revenue Service has issued Publication 1779, part of which is reprinted in Exhibit 5.9.[71] If you would like personal help determining the status of a worker, you can file Form SS-8 (see www. irs. gov/ formspubs/ index. html) with the IRS.

As a manager, you are responsible for withholding income taxes, withholding and paying Social Security and Medicare taxes, and paying unemployment taxes on the wages paid to your employees. You are not responsible for withholding or paying taxes for independent contractors. Beyond these costs, managers are not likely to provide independent contractors with other employment benefits, such as retirement benefits, access to incentive systems and stock option plans, or medical insurance. Given these cost savings, the appeal of hiring independent contractors is understandable. However, an important caveat is worth noting: Misclassifying employees as independent contractors is not without costs. Some of the potential costs a firm can be forced to pay for misclassifying employees are back payroll taxes, overtime pay, retirement or other employment benefits such as incentive pay, and medical coverage for injuries an employee incurred during the contractual arrangement.[72] Microsoft learned that the costs of misclassifying employees can be substantial, as Company Spotlight 5.3 explains. Nevertheless, one study indicated that approximate 38% of the employers examined by the IRS had misclassified employees as independent contractors.[73]

independent contractor

External worker who performs work for an organization but maintains substantial control over the means and methods of their services

COMPANY *spotlight*   5.3 Microsoft's Lesson Learned

During the 1989–1990 tax year, the IRS audited Microsoft and found that the company had misclassified as independent contractors thousands of software testers working alongside its full-time employees between 1987 and 1990. The IRS determined that despite these employees' classification as independent contractors, Microsoft exercised a substantial amount of control over the services they provided. Microsoft complied with the IRS's decision and paid the employment taxes it owed and the wages the workers would have made had they been properly classified as employees. However, several of the misclassified employees filed a lawsuit to gain access to the benefit plans they were denied due to their misclassification.

In 1996, the courts ruled that the individuals were eligible to participate in Microsoft's stock purchase and "Savings Plan Plus" programs. After several failed attempts to reverse this decision, Microsoft agreed to settle the lawsuit for $97 million.

Sources: Mister, W. G., Rose, D. M., Rowe, B. J., & Widener, S. K. The contingent workforce. *Internal Auditor*, April 2003, pp. 42–47; Flynn, G. Temp staffing carries legal risk. *Workforce*, September 1999, pp. 56–62; Bernstein, A. Now temp workers are a full-time headache. *BusinessWeek*, May 31, 1999, p. 46. Foust, D. The ground war at FedEx. *BusinessWeek*, November 28, 2005, pp. 42–43; and Bishop, T. Former Microsoft temps still waiting to be paid. *Seattle Post Intelligence Reporter*, May 3, 2004 http://seattlepi.nwsource.com/business/171664_msfttemps03.html.

▶ **Exhibit 5.9** Employee or Independent Contractor: Which Are You?

The courts consider many factors in determining whether a worker is an independent contractor or an employee. These factors fall into three main categories: behavioral control, financial control, and relationship of the parties.

1. **Behavioral Control**—A worker is an employee when the business has the right to direct and control the worker. For example:

   Instructions—If you receive extensive instructions on how work is to be done, this suggests that you are an employee. Instructions cover a wide range of topics, such as:

   - How, when, or where to do the work
   - What tools or equipment to use
   - What assistants to hire to help with the work
   - Where to purchase supplies and services

   If you receive less extensive instruction about what should be done but not how it should be done, you may be an independent contractor.

   Training—If the business provides you with training about required procedures and methods, this indicates that the business wants the work done in a certain way and suggests that you may be an employee.

2. **Financial Control**—Is there a right to direct or control the business part of the work? For example:

   Significant investment—If you have a significant investment in your work, you may be an independent contractor. However, a significant investment is not necessary to be an independent contractor.

   Expenses—If you are not reimbursed for some or all business expenses, then you may be an independent contract.

   Opportunity for profit or loss—If you can realize a profit or incur a loss, this suggests that you are in business for yourself and that you may be an independent contract.

3. **Relationship of the Parties**—These facts illustrate how the business and the worker perceive their relationship. For example:

   Employee benefits—If you receive benefits, such as insurance, pension, or paid leave, this is an indication that you may be an employee. If you do not receive benefits, however, you may be either an employee or an independent contract.

   Written contracts—A written contract may show what both you and the business intend. This may be very significant if it is difficult, if not impossible, to determine status based on other facts.

Sources: Internal Revenue Service. *Independent contractor or employee . . . Which are you?* www.irs.gov/pub/irs-pdf/p1779.pdf; and Internal Revenue Service. *Employment taxes: Form 937*, November 1994. www.unclefed.com/IRS-Forms/1996/P937.PDF.

SUMMARY

Companies engage in workforce planning to ensure that employees with the right skills are where they need to be, at the right time, to meet their firms' current and future needs. The key challenge with workforce planning is that the composition of a company's workforce is constantly changing. Employee turnover; the movement of employees via promotions, transfers, and demotions to other parts of the organization; the level of employee productivity; company performance; changes in strategic direction; economic conditions; and industry trends all affect the relative supply and demand for labor within companies.

A labor shortage is a situation in which a firm's demand for employees exceeds its supply. There are a variety of tactics that managers may use to address a labor shortage. Managers can ask their employees to work overtime, hire contingent workers, try to reduce employee turnover, move current employees, or hire new full-time employees. A labor surplus is a situation in which a firm's demand for employees is less than the supply of employees it currently has. To address a labor surplus, managers can implement layoffs, rely on attrition and hiring freezes, implement early retirement programs, or move employees to other parts of the company.

The specific choices that managers make regarding workforce planning decisions are influenced by the three HR challenges. Organizational demands (strategy, company characteristics, culture, and employee concerns) influence how quickly a labor shortage or surplus must be addressed, which tactics are most likely to be used, which employees are likely to be affected, who is involved in the workforce planning process, and how the firm's workforce planning decisions will affect employees.

Environmental influences—labor force trends, globalization, technology, and ethics and social responsibility—also affect the workforce planning process. Labor force trends affect the availability of internal and external workers available to firms as well as the tactics managers can effectively use to address a shortage or a surplus. Technology affects the number of employees firms need, the types of skills they must possess, and the quality of firms' workforce planning forecasts. Globalization has provided companies with the opportunity to view the workforce from a worldwide perspective rather than a purely domestic perspective. This is affecting where work is performed and where the workers are locating. From an ethical perspective, managers must be aware of how their communities will react to their workforce planning tactics as well as how they can help employees cope with their workforce planning decisions. Finally, the legal environment requires that managers provide fair notice to workers, their families, and the community in the case of plant closings and mass layoffs. Managers are also legally responsible for correctly classifying individuals as independent contractors or employees.

KEY TERMS

attrition *p. 131*

automation *p. 137*

contingent labor *p. 129*

demotion *p. 124*

functional flexibilit *p. 129*

hiring freeze *p. 131*

independent contractor *p. 141*

labor demand *p. 121*

labor shortage *p. 121*

labor supply *p. 121*

labor surplus *p. 122*

numerical flexibility *p. 129*

outplacement assistance program *p. 140*

outsourcing *p. 129*

productivity *p. 125*

productivity ratio *p. 125*

promotion *p. 124*

replacement chart *p. 124*

succession planning *p. 124*

transfer *p. 124*

transition matrix *p. 124*

turnover *p. 122*

Worker Adjustment and Retraining Notification (WARN) Act *p. 140*

workforce planning *p. 121*

DISCUSSION QUESTIONS

1. Which is more important for workforce planning—labor supply or labor demand?
2. Explain the primary factors that affect labor supply and labor demand. Which factors are most important to consider?
3. As a manager, what workforce planning tactics should you use to address a labor shortage?
4. What workforce planning tactics should you use to address a labor surplus? Why do you think many companies immediately implement a layoff when faced with a labor surplus?
5. How do the four organizational demands affect managers' workforce planning decisions?
6. Explain the impact environmental factors have on managers' workforce planning decisions. Which environmental influences do you think will have the greatest impact on workforce planning in the next five years?
7. How, as a manager, can you use technology as a tool to address a labor shortage?
8. What ethical and legal considerations must you consider when making workforce planning decisions?

LEARNING EXERCISE 1

As a manager, you have a number of tactics to choose from to cope with a labor shortage or surplus. Relying on overtime; hiring contingent labor; focusing on employee retention; using promotions, transfers, and demotions; and hiring new full-time employees are tactics you can use to remedy a labor shortage. When faced with a labor surplus, you might consider implementing layoffs, focusing on attrition and hiring freezes, developing early retirement programs, or using promotions, transfers, and demotions to move employees to other areas of the company.

1. What are the advantages of each of these tactics?
2. What are the disadvantages of each of these tactics?
3. Considering the advantages and disadvantages of each tactic, develop a strategy for when each of the tactics should be used and should not be used. Which organizational demands and environmental considerations are particularly important in your strategy?

LEARNING EXERCISE 2

Many companies experience conflicting pressures when they consider offshoring work to other countries. On the one hand, a company knows it will be able to save on costs as well as access a wider labor pool to meet the company's needs. And with a much larger labor pool to choose from, the company is potentially able to work with the best employees, or employees with the lowest labor costs, around the globe. This can result in greater operational efficiencies, help improve the bottom-line performance of a firm, and satisfy company shareholders.

At the same time, however, firms know that offshoring is taking jobs away from domestic workers and providing them to foreigners. This, in turn, can have negative trickle-down effect on the families and communities of people who used to hold these jobs. Moreover, according to the International Labor Organization, approximately 487 million workers around the world—or 16.4% of all workers—still don't earn enough to lift themselves and their families above the US$1 per person per day poverty line while 1.3 billion workers—43.5%—still live below the US$2 per day threshold.

Considering that one of the benefits of offshoring is that a company can use it to pay lower wages, critics have expressed concerns over the abuse of international workers. Given these concerns, is the practice of offshoring unethical?

1. What are the greatest risks associated with offshoring? What are the greatest benefits?
2. What criteria would you use to decide whether to offshore work to a company in another country?
3. What types of jobs are best suited for offshoring? Be specific in your rationale.
4. How do you reconcile the financial and operational benefits companies realize from offshoring with the perspective that offshoring is damaging to the country and potentially exploitive of international labor?

Sources: International Labour Organization. Press Release. *ILO projects global economic turbulence could generate five million more unemployed in 2008*, January 23, 2008, www.ilo.org/global/About_the_ILO/Media_and_public_information/Press_releases/lang--en/WCMS_ 090085/index.htm.

CASE STUDY # 1 — PLANNING FOR THE FUTURE
AT EAST COAST BANK

Paula Mason is one of three new assistant regional managers of East Coast Bank (ECB). Her position was recently created to provide administrative support and advice for the regional manager in charge of the southwest region, Ian Swartz. In their first meeting as a team, Paula and the two other assistant regional managers met with Ian to discuss areas throughout their branches that might be addressed to lower costs and raise profitability. Each of the assistant managers was given different aspects to emphasize, and Paula was asked to focus on ways to reduce labor costs and/or increase labor productivity among employees throughout the eight branches. In part, this was a response to feedback from the branches regarding an increase in recruitment and training expenses as well as a decrease in employee morale.

Paula's first course of action was to evaluate some direct and indirect labor costs related to turnover and retention as well as areas of bloated labor (labor surpluses) through the southwest region. Based on her analysis, Paula arrived at the some basic points of information for the branches. First, ECB is organized into several broad regions throughout New Jersey, Pennsylvania, and Delaware. Each region comprises 8 to 12 bank branches. Each branch consists of 4 primary positions: branch managers, assistant managers, loan officers, and tellers/customer service agents. On average, each bank has 1 branch manager, 3 assistant managers, 4 loan officers, and 15 tellers/customer service agents.

Beyond the average staffing levels, Paula was also able to get some information regarding the movement of employees throughout and out of the organization. As shown in the following transition matrix, ECB averages 26% turnover, with turnover among the tellers/customer service agents slightly higher, at 33%, and turnover at the assistant manager level the lowest, at 17%.

Transition Matrix for Southwest Region

2008	2009				
	Branch Managers	**Assistant Managers**	**Loan Officers**	**Tellers/Customer Service Agents**	**Exit the Company**
8 Branch Managers	6 (75%)				2 (25%)
24 Assistant Managers	2 (8%)	16 (67%)	1 (4%)	1 (4%)	4 (17%)
36 Loan Officers		2 (6%)	26 (72%)		8 (22%)
120 Tellers/Customer Service Agents		14 (12%)	2 (2%)	64 (53%)	40 (33%)
Anticipated Labor Supply	8	32	29	65	26% (54 out of 204)

DISCUSSION QUESTIONS

1. Based on the transition matrix for ECB, which positions are experiencing a labor surplus or a labor shortage?

2. What tactics would you use to address the labor shortages? Why?

3. What tactics would you use to address the labor surpluses? Why?

4. When you look at the overall pattern of employee movement, do you see any areas that are of particular concern?

5. What plan would you recommend for the future to prevent ECB from having excess surpluses and shortages?

CASE STUDY # 2 — THE TURNAROUND AT FORD

For the past several years, Ford has been going through difficult times. The company's share of the automobile market continues to shrink, and its cost structure has contributed to financial losses. In 2006, Ford lost $12.6 billion. In 2007, Ford did better, posting losses of only $2.7 billion. At the same time, however, Ford's market share continues to dwindle. In 2007, its share was 14.8%—down from 26% in the 1990s. In an effort to match its production with the demand for its products, as well as address concerns with its high labor costs, Ford has decided that smaller is better—and necessary—to achieve long-term success in the automobile industry.

One of the primary ways for Ford to achieve this goal is to take further steps to reduce the size of its workforce. As of 2008, Ford employed about 54,000 U.S. union workers. It had about 23,900 salaried workers in North America and about 12,000 U.S. workers eligible for retirement, or about 22% of its hourly workforce. Ford has announced a new round of buyouts and early retirement packages to all of its 54,000 U.S. hourly workers in an effort to cut costs and replace those leaving with lower-paid workers. Ford is offering eight different packages for employees. Some of the features of these plans are:

- Workers who are eligible for retirement will get a $50,000 offer, higher than the $35,000 in the previous round of buyouts.
- Skilled-trade workers, such as maintenance workers, will get an additional $20,000, bringing the total potential payout for such a worker to $70,000.

Other packages will follow the basic pattern of buyouts Ford offered in late 2006:

- Younger workers could leave for a $100,000 lump-sum payment and receive health care benefits, for a limited time.
- Older workers could get $140,000 and receive pension benefits if they retired immediately, but they would forfeit future health care benefits.

The automaker's goal in offering the companywide buyouts is to cut as many as 11,000 hourly jobs and as many as 2,000 salaried positions. One of Ford's goals with these buyouts is to replace many workers with new employees who will earn a lower wage under the terms of its recently negotiated labor agreement. New hires will earn a little more than $14 per hour, about half of what current union workers earn. The number of these so-called second-tier wage workers is capped at 20% of Ford's workforce under terms of a new pact with the UAW (formerly the United Auto Workers union). Ford President and Chief Executive Alan Mulally said the automaker will also trim salaried staff, mostly through attrition but possibly also through layoffs, as it tries to adjust to the slumping U.S. market.

DISCUSSION QUESTIONS

1. What factors have contributed to the large-scale labor surplus at Ford?

2. Ford has decided to pursue employee buyouts and attrition in an attempt to shrink its workforce to match its productivity demands. Why do you think Ford is using these two tactics? Do you think these are the best options for Ford to achieve its goals?

3. What are the downsides of these two approaches? Are there any other approaches you might recommend to address its labor surplus?

Sources: Spector, M. Ford looks to trim up to 13,000 more jobs: buyouts could pave the way for lower-paid replacements; packages get more generous. *Wall Street Journal*, January 24, 2008, p. B1; Associated Press. *Ford offering buyouts to all hourly workers. Automaker lost $2.8 billion last year, sees grim sales outlook for 2008*, January 24, 2008, www. msnbc. msn. com/ id/ 22819848/; and Maynard, M. Ford chief sees small as virtue and necessity. *New York Times*, January 26, 2007.

Part II
PROSPERA EXERCISES

By now you know that workforce planning is important. One important result of a good workforce development plan is alignment between the activities of the human resources in the company and the strategic goals of the company.

Recall that the overall mission of Visions Optical is to "provide state-of-the-art optical solutions for individuals who have discerning tastes and who appreciate high-quality eyewear." Achieving this mission requires that all employees be focused on the same outcome. One way to increase the chances of this happening is to identify, as part of the work design and workforce planning process, competencies that all, or almost all, employees should possess. You also know that good job descriptions help to ensure that employees know what is expected of them in doing their jobs.

Section I: Identifying and Defining Competencies Required

Go to the "PLAN" area of the Prospera Web site (www.prospera.com). Using either the "Creating a Workforce Plan" feature (interactive) or the "Competency Library" (not interactive), identify critical competencies that will be needed to support the strategic goals of Visions Optical. (Unless your instructor provides data, skip the sections that address employee records and demographics if you use the interactive tool.) Choose competencies that are key success indicators for the company in achieving its mission and goals. Prepare a report for your instructor that includes the company mission statement, strategic goals that you identify, competencies required, and a justification for inclusion of each competency.

Section II: Creating Job Descriptions

Job analysis is the process of identifying the tasks, duties, and responsibilities that must be done in a particular job, as well as the competencies, skills, and knowledge required for that job. The information from a job analysis is used to prepare a job description. Existing job description information provides a good starting point for developing a new job description. That information can then be verified with individuals performing the job, supervisors, and other personnel familiar with the job requirements.

1. In the "STAFF" area of the Prospera Web site, find the section "Recruiting Tools," which includes the "Build Job Descriptions" interactive feature. Use this feature to develop job descriptions for the following jobs at Visions Optical: dispensing optician, receptionist, and one other job you choose that would exist at Visions Optical (either for headquarters or in one of the stores).

   The *Occupational Outlook Handbook* published by the Bureau of Labor Statistics (www.bls.gov) is an excellent reference. You can consult it as well as other resources to find information for completing the job descriptions. Be sure to include the competencies that you identified in Section I in the competencies lists for these jobs.

2. Prepare a rationale for the decisions that you made in Sections I and II, keeping in mind the company's mission statement and the HR mission statement and strategy that you identified at the end of Part One of this book. Answer this question: What role can an effective recruiting and selection process play in addressing the problems at Visions Optical?

J. J. Keller's
PROSPERA®
The Online People Management Tool

Part III

MANAGING EMPLOYEE COMPETENCIES

chapter 6

RECRUITMENT

1. Define *recruitment* and explain its importance for gaining a competitive advantage. *(150)*

2. Describe the components of a successful recruitment strategy. *(152)*

3. Identify multiple sources for recruiting employees and discuss their advantages and disadvantages. *(152)*

4. Prepare a recruitment advertisement. *(155)*

5. Discuss the role recruiters play in the recruitment process. *(164)*

6. Explain several ways to evaluate recruitment success. *(165, 179)*

7. Distinguish between effective recruiting strategies based on organizational demands. *(165)*

8. Understand the impact environmental factors have on a firm's recruiting strategy and the outcomes the organization achieves as a result. *(169)*

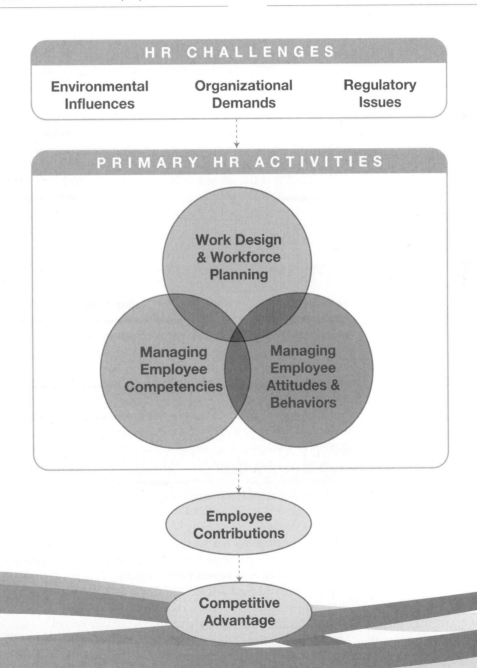

HR CHALLENGES

| Environmental Influences | Organizational Demands | Regulatory Issues |

PRIMARY HR ACTIVITIES

Work Design & Workforce Planning

Managing Employee Competencies

Managing Employee Attitudes & Behaviors

Employee Contributions

Competitive Advantage

What are your employment prospects if you are in the market to change jobs? Are there a lot of jobs available with not many applicants in your field of interest, or are there more applicants than jobs? For professions in which there are more jobs than applicants, you are likely to see companies spending a lot of money to recruit. Companies looking for applicants in professions with many applicants are less likely to be investing heavily in recruitment activities. In this chapter, we introduce the concept of employee recruitment and address questions such as these, introduced in Chapter 1:

- For what competencies do you recruit?
- What groups do you target with your recruitment message?
- Do you recruit internally, externally, or both?
- How do you ensure that you offer an employee value proposition that will attract the right applicants?

In this chapter, we also describe what your role as a manager will be in the recruitment process. We start the discussion by describing the general process of recruitment and what research has shown about best practices for recruitment. We follow that with a discussion of how organizational and environmental demands, including legal issues, affect the decisions managers have to make when they are recruiting employees.

If you haven't already, you may soon find yourself caught up in the whirlwind of the recruitment process as you look for a job. So grab a cup of coffee and settle in to learn more about the process you will experience. Remember, what you are learning now will give you an edge as a manager (and even an edge as a recruit!). Managers who are the most successful at recruitment understand its importance and how to do it well. Successful recruitment makes the rest of the job of managing employees much easier. When recruitment is done well, you identify and hire employees with the competencies needed by the firm. And, as shown in Exhibit 1, employee competencies are a key factor in determining organizational success.

THE PURPOSE OF RECRUITMENT

recruitment

The process of identifying potential employees, communicating job and organizational attributes to them, and convincing them to apply for available jobs.

The term **recruitment** refers to the activities companies engage in to identify potential employees, communicate job and organizational attributes to them, and convince qualified individuals to apply for existing openings in the company.[1] When we discussed the Americans with Disabilities Act in Chapter 3, you learned the importance of understanding what it means for an employee to be *qualified* to do a job. Recall that when an individual is *qualified*, he or she has the knowledge, skills, and abilities (KSAs)—the competencies, in other words—to do the job and help the firm achieve its organizational goals.

Recruitment is a process that occurs over a period of time, beginning with the identification of the job openings a manager needs to fill. These openings occur for a number of reasons, as you learned in Chapter 5 when we discussed workforce planning. Job vacancies occur, for instance, when employees leave the company, are promoted, or accept different positions internally. Companies also create new jobs to cope with growth, new corporate strategies, and reengineering of the workplace.

The importance of recruitment is considerable. Think for a minute about what would happen if you had an employee quit, and it took several months to find a replacement. If the work that the employee did was critical to your organization's success (and it should be; otherwise, why did you need the employee in the first place?), then someone is going to have to do the work until you can hire a new employee. As a manager, you may have to pitch in and help—or even do most of the work if you are in a small company. We will discuss more about how company size affects recruitment later in this chapter. Overall, if managers cannot attract employees, they have to find alternative ways of getting work done, or they have to change the nature of the work that is done. They may have to raise the salary of the job to attract applicants, which results in additional and often unexpected costs for the company.

The importance of aligning a firm's recruitment to its organizational goals cannot be overstated.[2] When a company and its managers recruit well, the rest of the firm's employee management activities will require less time and effort, and time and effort saved equals money saved.

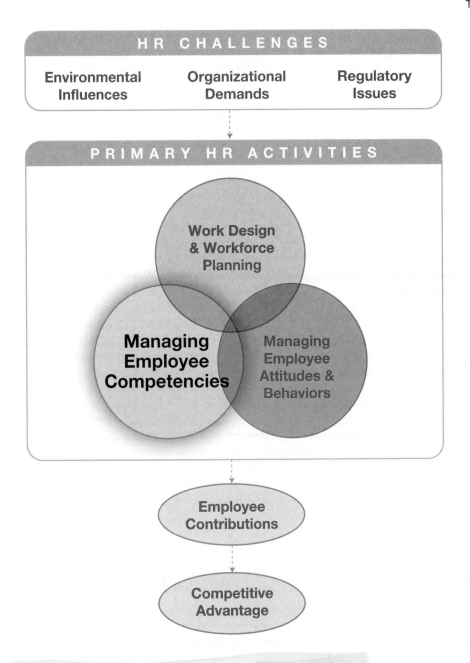

◄ **Exhibit 6.1**
Framework for the
Strategic Management
of Employees

THE RECRUITMENT PROCESS

A successful recruiting process results from understanding why you are recruiting employees and the type of employees you need.[3] Too often, managers have an opening and immediately pull together a recruitment advertisement to send off to the local newspaper or to post on the Internet. They do this without giving much thought to what they are doing or why they are doing it. "Have an opening, fill it," seems to be the mentality.

To be sure, managers are often under pressure to fill job vacancies as quickly as possible. They generally do not want to overwork other employees who are performing necessary tasks, and they do not want to let critical work slow down or be left undone, so they want to get the recruiting completed. These same managers would never consider spending a large sum of the organization's money for new equipment without careful planning, however. Shouldn't they spend just as much time and effort planning for employee recruitment as they do for purchasing the right equipment? Actually, recruitment probably deserves more time and attention. After all, employees hired today will be the employees making decisions tomorrow about how the company will spend its money! Of course, many managers *do* understand that spending some time developing a recruiting strategy will save their firms time and money later.[4]

The first step in a successful recruitment plan is to decide on the objective for the recruiting process.[5] Is the objective to generate a few applicants and make a quick hiring decision? Or is the objective to recruit a large number of applicants and hope some are qualified to fill the openings? Knowing the best sources for recruitment and carefully crafting a recruitment message is part of a solid plan. The recruiter, the person who talks with potential applicants, also plays a key role in the outcome of the process.

In Chapter 4, you learned how to conduct a job analysis and how to write a job description. The job description includes a job specifications section, which is a detailed account of the specific competencies employees must possess to succeed in the job. Whether you prepare a job description yourself or use one prepared by someone else, having a good grasp of a position's job duties and requirements is essential.[6] Even if you, the manager, have someone else prepare the ad copy, you have to give the preparer the information to include. This information, coupled with your knowledge of the firm's goals and values, lays the foundation for the recruitment plan. In other words, before you can really look for ways to generate interest in job vacancies and identify high-potential individuals, you have to know what specific knowledge, skills, and/or abilities are needed to succeed in the job.

When you understand the required competencies, how do you recruit employees who have them? If you are a manager in a small business, you might be involved in each step of the process, even to the extent of performing all of your firm's recruitment activities. In a larger organization, you are likely to work closely with a company recruiter. In either case, your role as a manager is critical to successful employee recruitment. You are the one who best knows what type of employee will fit with the job and with the organization. Therefore, you need to be able to make strategic decisions during each step in the process. One of these strategic decisions relates to where you look to find employees.

A successful organization recognizes that it is important to recruit both internally (within the organization) and externally (outside the organization). As you read the following sections, think about an organization with which you are familiar and how that organization would likely go about recruiting employees. Think, too, about the advantages and disadvantages of using the various approaches described. Knowing these advantages and disadvantages strengthens your ability to make informed decisions when you are recruiting employees.

INTERNAL RECRUITMENT

Many organizations recognize that the best place to find employees for job openings is within the organization itself. Cintas, the largest uniform supplier in North America knows that it makes good business sense to retain current employees by giving them an opportunity for new challenges and promotions.[7] Also, employees who have greater opportunities within their organization are more satisfied than employees with fewer opportunities.[8]

Internal Recruitment Methods

internal recruiting

The process of seeking job applicants within the company.

Now let's take a look at some of the ways companies and managers inform employees about current job openings. As a manager, you need to be familiar with these methods so that you can decide how to approach your **internal recruiting**. Even if you have a staffing department, you need to ensure that the appropriate methods are used to identify the best applicants for you; your role in recruitment should not be a passive one.

Perhaps the simplest, but not always the most effective, way internal applicants are recruited is through word of mouth. A manager has a job opening and talks to other managers or employees to find out who in the company might be a good person to fill the vacancy. However, more formal techniques will ensure that managers are identifying the most qualified candidates. Formal techniques also ensure that employees have an equal opportunity to find out about openings and apply for them.

job posting

The most frequently used technique for notifying current employees about job openings within the company.

A **job posting** system is the most frequently used technique to notify current employees about job openings. Such a system can be as informal as posting a note on the cafeteria bulletin board or as formal as having job announcements listed in the company newsletter and

1. Make sure the site's navigation is intuitive.

2. Have prominent links from other company Web pages frequently used by employees, such as the e-mail login page.

3. Ensure that employees who reply to postings receive acknowledgements.

4. Emphasize to employees that the intranet is for their use.

5. Use the intranet to encourage employees to engage in career development.

6. Encourage competition among managers for internal talent.

Source: Based on Frase-Blunt, M. Intranet fuels internal mobility. *Employment Management Today*, Spring 2004, www.shrm.org/ema/EMT/articles/2004/spring04cover.asp.

◄ **Exhibit 6.2**
"Netiquette" for
Advertising Jobs on a
Company Intranet

posted on the company intranet. The goal of job posting is straightforward—to get word of a job opening out to as many employees as possible within the company. A company intranet, an internal Web site for employees, allows a company to access a wide internal applicant pool. When using an intranet for job postings, managers need to make sure that it is just as easy for employees to find jobs within the company as it is to find jobs at other companies. Exhibit 6.2 contains pointers for ensuring that job postings on an intranet are user friendly.[9] Company Spotlight 6.1 gives an example of how an internal job posting system can make a significant difference in a company.

Companies that use a human resource information system (HRIS) have an added way to identify internal candidates for job openings. These companies create an **employee inventory,** or a searchable database, that can be used to identify employees who meet certain job requirements. After a job is posted, employees who match the criteria may be automatically notified about it. Inventories provide managers with targeted information regarding which employees might be good candidates for an opening so that these employees can be approached and encouraged to apply for the job. If a company needs an electrical engineer with three to five years of experience in Asia, for example, a search of the employee inventory produces a list of employees within the company who meet those job requirements. In addition to talking to employees interested in the job, the manager with the opening can review their recent performance appraisals and talk to their supervisors rather than having to solely rely on references for such information. The hiring manager is then in a much better position to determine how well a particular employee will perform in the new job. After all, past performance is generally the best predictor of future performance.

Many companies have embraced the idea of having an employee inventory as part of their HRIS. The companies have found, however, that there is one critical challenge related to using such a system. For the inventory to be effective, the information must be kept up to date. That sounds like it shouldn't be a problem, but often it is. Some companies request their employees to enter the data themselves through an intranet portal; other companies maintain the data through the company's human resources department. If employees fail to enter the data, or if the HR department doesn't get the information for updates, the usefulness of the inventory is limited.

employee inventory

A searchable database used to identify employees who meet specified job requirements.

"Help Wanted" advertisements can take many forms.

PRINCIPLES

COMPANY *spotlight*   6.1 Deloitte's Internal Recruiting Success Story

Deloitte is a multinational financial services firm. In 2001, Deloitte faced a "workforce adjustment" that included downsizing. The firm decided to deal with the problem by using its intranet to redeploy its internal talent around the world. The endeavor was so successful that the company ultimately launched Deloitte Career Connections to provide a way for employees to find out about other job and career opportunities internally. This program is intranet based and provides all Deloitte employees with one-on-one career coaching and development information as well as job and career opportunity information. The intranet program provides career-management tools, self-assessments, a resume builder, and information on seeking jobs. The first weekend the program was up and running, 2,000 employees logged on, created accounts, and searched the company's internal job openings.

Since the program launched, Deloitte has documented 140 "retention successes." Rather than leave Deloitte for other companies, these employees have found what they were looking for at Deloitte. The success equals about a $14 million return on the company's investment. The satisfaction experienced by employees who have greater control over their career destinies is just as important as the financial return to the company.

Source: Based on Frase-Blunt, M. Intranet fuels internal mobility. *Employment Management Today*, Spring 2004, www.shrm.org/ema/EMT/articles/2004/spring04cover.asp.

Advantages and Disadvantages of Internal Recruitment

Organizations realize that there are tangible and intangible advantages to recruiting internally. Internal recruitment can be more cost-effective than running ads or engaging in external recruiting. Existing employees are already familiar with the company's operations, which cuts down on the time and money it takes to train them. In addition, current employees like being given opportunities for advancement. Employees want to know that their employer recognizes their value to the company. In turn, these employees are more likely to be committed to the company, more loyal, and more productive. Also, as we have mentioned, the firm's hiring managers have access to applicants' performance appraisals and can talk to the employees' supervisors. Last, a benefit of internal recruitment is that hiring managers often have less to worry about regarding whether the individual fits the company's culture.

Sometimes companies need new ideas or want to change their corporate culture, or they need to increase the diversity of their workforce. These companies know that the best way to reduce "inbreeding" and to increase diversity is to bring in new employees rather than promote current employees who are already entrenched in the company's way of doing things, especially when there is little diversity in terms of demographic and/or personality attributes, in the existing workforce. Bringing in "new blood," or new employees, does not come without a cost, however. Managers need to be aware that employees who apply for openings and aren't selected for them may become disgruntled, be less productive, or leave the company. Of course, promoting or transferring an employee internally creates a new vacancy elsewhere in the organization. Consequently, even when companies recruit internally, they need to look externally to build their workforces at some point. In the next section, we examine the options for external recruitment.

EXTERNAL RECRUITMENT

An organization that cannot fill jobs internally, or that has decided "new blood" is needed, can choose from a wide range of sources for recruiting job applicants from outside the organization. When we think about **external recruiting**, we often think about advertisements, job fairs, and the Internet. Choosing an external recruitment source is often dictated by several factors, including the nature and location of the job.

A sign observed on the back of a pickup truck traveling down the Washington, DC, Beltway read: "Plumbers and Foremen Wanted." The message included a telephone number.

external recruiting

The process of seeking job applicants from outside the organization using activities such as advertisements, job fairs, and the Internet.

Clearly, someone believed that this advertisement would attract workers. What were the underlying assumptions in this approach? First, someone had assumed that the truck would be driven and/or parked in locations frequented by plumbers and foremen or plumber and foremen "wannabes." The second assumption was that those individuals would be the kind of employees needed by the company; that is, they would have the required competencies and fit the company's culture.

In general, two factors have the greatest impact on where recruiting should take place. The first factor is the skill level of the job. The higher the skill level, the harder it may be to find qualified candidates. This second factor is related to the first: The harder it is to find qualified candidates, the broader the geographic area in which you must search. If you are recruiting a vice president of operations for a multinational company and you either don't have someone internally who is qualified or you want some fresh ideas and perspectives, the search will likely need to be far and wide. In contrast, recruiting for a plumber position would not likely require a large national recruitment campaign. An advertisement in a local paper or a sign on a truck would be sufficient. The two factors together—skill level of the job and geographic location—are used to identify the **relevant labor market** for the recruitment campaign. Therefore, the relevant labor market is the location in which one can reasonably expect to find a sufficient supply of qualified applicants. Going back to the advertisement for plumbers, we see that the relevant labor market was presumed to be the area in which that truck was being driven—the metro DC area.

Let's take a more detailed look at external recruitment methods. In some organizations, a manager will have assistance for developing and implementing an external recruitment strategy. In other organizations, the manager will have to do all this alone.

Advertising

The newspaper has long been the most popular place to advertise jobs, and Sunday has traditionally been the most popular day of the week to run these ads because more people read the paper on Sunday than during the week. Newspapers still are a viable option for advertising, but the advent of the Internet has dramatically changed where people go to look for jobs. Employers now use the Internet as much as or more than they use newspapers to post jobs.

Employers have typically advertised in their local newspapers and sometimes in regional, state, or national papers if the job required high competency levels, was unique, or required skills that were in high demand. The *Wall Street Journal* and *USA Today* are two popular, broadly distributed newspapers in which firms often advertise high-level finance and corporate jobs. The downside to newspaper advertising is the expense. In 2008, the cost of advertising a job in the *Washington Post* print edition ranged from $30 to almost $50 per line for the Sunday paper. Compare those one-time costs to the $395 charge for a job ad to run for 30 days online with unlimited text for the job description and tracking information about the number of times the ad is viewed. You can quickly see that one reason employers have transitioned to online ads is cost. In fact, the more jobs you post online, the lower the charge per ad on many job boards.[10]

Many of the largest U.S. newspapers sell only online help-wanted ads and some, such as the *Washington Post*, have even developed online job posting services that compete well with the major Internet job boards. CareerBuilder.com, another popular online job board, was developed through a partnership between Microsoft and three large newspaper publishing firms—Gannett, Tribune, and McClatchy.[11]

Log on to most company Web sites, and you will find a "Careers" or "Job Opportunities" link. The use of company Web sites to recruit applicants has increased steadily in recent years. However, many job seekers find them too complicated to be useful, and job seekers have even turned down jobs because of poorly designed Web sites, most likely seeing them as a signal of the culture of the company.[12] Therefore, the design and content of these sites matters. People form more favorable perceptions of a company when its recruitment Web site contains information about career paths within the firm and detailed job descriptions.[13] In this regard, recruitment Web sites have the potential to be a far greater tool than other types of advertisements for disseminating job and organization information because of their capability to allow individuals to access large amounts of information in an easy and convenient

relevant labor market

The location in which one can reasonably expect to find a sufficient supply of qualified applicants.

Many companies include a Careers page on their web site.

manner 24/7 and from around the world. Exhibit 6.3 lists the Web sites of a sample of companies that have done a good job of setting up their online recruitment advertisements.

Another plus for using your company's Web site to advertise externally is the cost: The cost of adding a recruitment advertisement is negligible. Another plus is that people

Exhibit 6.3 ▶

Outstanding Employer
Web Sites

www.statefarm.com

- Detailed information about career paths, sample interview questions, list of recruiting events, and an "Ask the Recruiter" link
- Lots of information about benefits, work/life balance, compensation, and diversity

www.anheuser-busch.com

- "Careers" link prominently displayed on the home page
- Sends job seekers a consistent and engaging message with information about the company's job opportunities, branding message, and diversity efforts

www.lyondell.com

- Searchable jobs section
- Copy that tells potential applicants what the employer expects and what it has to offer them as an employer, including its work atmosphere, vision, values, and benefits

www.abbott.com

- Much information about job disciplines
- Focuses on college students, with attention-getting discussions, such as the type of internship opportunities the company offers

Source: Based on Martinez, M. Improve your web postings. *HRMagazine*, April 2004, www.shrm.org/ema/library_published/nonIC/1CMS_006204.asp.

interested in working for the company can review all the available openings, domestic and international, on one Web site. Compared to print advertisements, company Web sites provide a more cost-effective method to reach a wider array of potential employees, both internally and externally.

In addition to using their own company Web sites, companies may also use online job posting bulletin boards at colleges and universities as well as sites such as CareerBuilder.com, Monster.com, and HotJobs.com. They can also use CareerOneStop.org, a U.S. Department of Labor–sponsored Web site. These publicly available online sites help employers get job information out to large groups of potential applicants in a timely manner. Take a look at the costs of posting a job on Monster.com, and you will see that it is a relatively inexpensive way to reach millions of job seekers. Employers can also use the sites to recruit qualified applicants by reviewing the resumes posted there. There is usually some reasonable cost associated with reviewing resumes.[14]

There are other specialized recruitment job sites as well. The American Institute of Certified Public Accountants (AICPA), for example, provides specialized recruitment and career-management services targeted at professionals in the accounting field. Professionals can post confidential resumes online, view current job listings, and complete job applications on the site. Employers can post job listings, review the resumes of job seekers, and have background checks conducted on candidates who interest them. Some of the services are fee based. The AICPA resource is just one example of the specialized recruitment services available online.

A company should not, however, just advertise online. Although many people use the Internet for their job searches, not everyone has Internet access. Moreover, recruiting for certain jobs on the Internet might be less effective than recruiting through other sources. The Internet makes it easy for individuals—qualified or not—to apply for jobs which means there are more applications to sift through and document. Also, recall our discussion from Chapter 3 about what it means to be an affirmative action employer. To ensure that you reach the most diverse audience possible with your recruitment message, you should use multiple sources for advertising. One last note about posting jobs online: Make sure the listings are kept up-to-date. Outdated listings signal to potential applicants that the company is not really invested in its human resources.[15]

Educational Institutions

Along with newspaper advertisements, one of the oldest forms of employee recruitment has been sending recruiters, or at least job opening announcements, to college campuses. Organizations like to attract potential employees right out of college. Why do you think that would be the case? If you answered that these companies want younger workers, you are only partially right, and don't forget that age should not be a basis for recruiting employees. Some companies prefer new college graduates because they have less work experience and can be trained more easily to fit in with the company's culture. It is much easier to train someone to do things your way when you don't first have to "untrain" them because they have already learned to do things a certain way in another company.

When the economy is doing well, companies are more willing to spend money to send recruiters to college campuses. Recruiters are often looking for applicants for multiple jobs. The goal of a recruiter is to identify individuals who are most likely to fit in with his or her firm's corporate culture and who have the KSAs to do the job. The college degree serves as a baseline indicator that the applicant meets minimum requirements and can learn as needed to perform many jobs.

The typical college recruiting seasons run from September through November and from February through April. Many companies work to develop ongoing relationships with their preferred recruiting schools to ensure that the short recruiting periods are used most effectively. In addition to participating in campus interviewing sessions and career fairs, IBM sponsors leadership development workshops on campuses. The purpose of these workshops is partly to position IBM in the eyes of students as a company that values leadership.[16] The recruiters of different companies often speak to student professional organizations, are involved with alumni groups, provide students with internships, and

internship

An employment situation in which students work during the summer or academic year in a job related to their chosen vocation to test out a vocation and to give the employer a chance to determine if the student is a good future employee.

connect with faculty. All these activities are geared toward networking. Networking can help a company recruit the best and brightest talent.

Internships are a particularly good way for employers to connect with students who could become future employees. They help get prospective employees onsite to consider a company's career opportunities. They also give an employer more time to evaluate prospective employees for future opportunities. Productive internships provide students not only with structured work activities but also with social events, training programs, and mentoring opportunities.[17] Hiring interns provides companies with a means to build a positive reputation with students as well as a means to get prospective employees onsite to encourage them to consider their long-term careers with the company.

Employment Agencies and Employee Search Firms

A company might decide to seek outside assistance to find job applicants for a variety of reasons. The company might have a small HR department with limited time to conduct recruitment activities, for example. Or, to make the process more efficient and productive, the firm might decide that a search firm specializing in a particular profession will be able to access more qualified applicants and do the initial screening of applicants. Several types of employment agencies and search firms exist: public agencies, private agencies, and executive search firms.

public employment agency

A not-for-profit job placement agency affiliated with a local or state government.

Public employment agencies are not-for-profit agencies affiliated with the U.S. Department of Labor's Training and Employment Services. They are located in cities and counties throughout the country. In addition to processing unemployment claims, public agencies assist job seekers by providing career guidance, testing, training, and placement activities. They assist employers by giving them access to a large pool of skilled and unskilled workers. A nationwide database, at CareerOneStop.org, matches employers with potential employees. The best part for many employers and job seekers is that the services of these agencies are free. Federal contractors are required by law to post many of their jobs with such government-run agencies.[18]

private employment agency

A business that provides job search assistance for a fee, and often to select professions only.

Private employment agencies provide job search assistance for a fee, and often to select professions only. The fees can be paid by companies listing jobs and/or by individuals using the agency's services to find jobs. **Contingency recruiting agencies** are paid by the company at the conclusion of a successful search. The recruiter conducts the initial recruiting, screening, and interviewing and sets up the interview with the company. The agency is paid a flat fee or a percentage, usually 20% to 30% of the hire's first-year salary, after the hire has worked 30 days. Often a 90-day to one-year guarantee is given for the placement.[19]

contingency recruiting agency

A type of employment agency used by employers with payment made as a flat fee or percentage of the new hire's first-year salary and only paid if the search is successful.

Retained agencies are often used for recruiting high-level positions, such as CEOs and vice presidents. The main difference between this type of agency and a contingency agency is who pays the fee. In a retained agency, the employer pays a retainer for the agency to conduct the job search rather than paying at completion of the search. Typically, one-third of the fee is paid upfront (whether or not there is a successful hire), one-third is paid 30 days after the search is done, and the rest is paid at the time of hire.[20] Retained agencies are often referred to as **executive search firms**, or **headhunters**. In working with these firms, it is important to ensure that they adhere to a code of ethics such as that developed by the Association of Executive Search Consultants (AESC). These firms deal with sensitive company information and sensitive information about candidates who may not want their current employers to know they are considering other opportunities.[21]

retained agency (also executive search firm or headhunter)

An employment firm used for recruiting high-level positions, such as CEOs and vice presidents, with the firm paid a retainer for the work it does.

A third type of recruiting agency has developed in recent years. These agencies, known as **on-demand recruiting services**, charge based on the time they spend recruiting rather than per hire. The services of these organizations can be purchased weekly or monthly, and they are often a cost-effective alternative to contingency or retained agencies. Access to an on-demand recruiting service is particularly useful when a firm expands rapidly and needs a large number of new employees quickly. Such was the case for the biotech manufacturer Centocor when the U.S. Food and Drug Administration gave approval for expanding production of one of its drugs. Centocor didn't want to hire more recruiters to find and screen hundreds of applicants for manufacturing and scientific jobs, and the company did not have the budget to outsource the work to a traditional recruiting agency. Doing so would

on-demand recruiting services

A type of recruiting agency that charges based on the time spent recruiting rather than paying an amount per hire.

have cost 20% to 30% of the annual salary for each new hire. What the company needed was a temporary solution. Centocor turned to an on-demand recruiting service agency and has been pleased with the result.[22]

Professional Associations

Most professions have one or more organizations or associations that individuals in the profession can join; some even have student chapters. These organizations provide a variety of services to members, such as access to resources about the profession, opportunities to network with others in the same field, information about job openings, and access to specialized research. A placement service is often a feature at annual meetings, providing an opportunity for members to interview for jobs. The jobs may also be listed on the association's Web site, as is done with the AICPA .

Temporary Employees

Hiring temp workers is often a great method for recruiting permanent employees. Often, temporary positions are truly temporary in nature. However, many temp positions are considered **temp to hire**, meaning the employee comes in for a short period of time but may become a permanent employee. One of the primary benefits of this approach to recruiting is that a company gets a good idea of the capabilities of temporary workers after having the opportunity to observe how well they perform in the actual jobs they would be doing. In addition, temporary employees have the opportunity to evaluate the company and determine whether they want to work there.

temp to hire

A person who is employed to work for the company for a short period of time but who may become a permanent employee.

Employee Referrals

Many companies rely on employee referrals to identify potential job candidates. SRI International, an independent, not-for-profit research institute that provides services to government and industry clients, is an example of a company that has an employee referral program. At SRI, current employees can complete an online employee referral form and receive a bonus if their referral is hired. A $1,000 bonus is paid when the referred employee has worked 90 consecutive days for SRI.[23] A delayed bonus, such as this one, is an increasingly common part of referral plans. By delaying the bonus, the firm can be sure it is paying the bonus only when the employee referred turns out to be a good hire.

Research has shown that recruiting programs such as the one at SRI are among the most effective. Moreover, employees hired as a result of referrals tend to have lower turnover and experience greater job satisfaction than employees recruited through more formal approaches.[24] One of the primary reasons for their success is that employees tend to refer people they already know and whom they think will fit in with the company and be able to do the job. Referral programs also have the benefit of tapping people who might not be formally looking for a job but who are friends or acquaintances with a current employee who has encouraged them to explore the opportunity.

Sourcing Applicants

Over the past 10 years, companies have begun to use skilled researchers to identify, attract, and screen potential applicants who are not actively on the market. This process of finding passive job candidates is known as **sourcing**. It was first used in the United States during the late 1990s due to a shortage of skilled labor at the time.[25] Social networking sites such as LinkedIn.com provide an excellent resource for sourcing passive candidates.[26] Often the recruiters in charge of sourcing applicants are very good at identifying people who appear to be good matches with a job and a company, even when the individuals aren't looking for jobs. These recruiters know how to acquire and use Web search tools such as **resume spidering**, a process of tracking down passive job applicants by searching the Web for resumes on private Web pages, professional association sites, university and college alumni sites, and company Web sites.[27]

sourcing

The process of identifying, attracting, and screening potential applicants who are not actively in the market for a new job.

resume spidering

A process of identifying passive job applicants by searching the Web for resumes on private Web pages, professional association sites, university and college alumni sites, and company Web sites.

Re-recruiting

In a tight labor market, firms may decide to try to entice former employees to return to their companies. These employees may have left for better opportunities or may have been downsized in a company restructuring. They are already knowledgeable about the firm's business, so they are able to get up to speed easily and quickly.

Advantages and Disadvantages of External Recruitment

External recruitment is generally more costly than internal recruitment. There are media fees to pay to get an ad printed or posted, and there are agency fees to pay if an employment agency is used. Consequently, it is important to understand what may make the benefits outweigh the financial costs.

One clear advantage of external recruitment is the opportunity for a company to bring in employees who have a fresh perspective. Whether they are new college grads or employees with work experience at other companies, "outsiders" can help the company see new ways of doing business. In addition, recruiting externally allows companies to target specific competencies that their current employees might not possess. If a company is implementing new technologies or changing its strategic priorities, it might have to look outside for people with the skills it needs. To be successful, however, managers must understand which external recruitment source is optimal for filling a particular position. Managers should be cautious when recruiting externally. Bringing in outsiders can upset internal applicants who didn't get the job, resulting in lowered morale and productivity on their part. Exhibit 6.4 summarizes the advantages and disadvantages of internal and external recruiting. The appendix to this chapter discusses how to measure the effectiveness of both internal and external recruiting methods.

MAXIMIZING RECRUITMENT EFFECTIVENESS

A number of factors influence the effectiveness of a firm's recruiting efforts. These factors include the message conveyed in the recruitment advertisement, the personality and knowledge of the recruiter, and the willingness of the company to continually evaluate its recruiting activities. We will now give you some guidance on how these and related activities should be managed. As you study this information, keep in mind what recruiting is all

Exhibit 6.4 ▶

Advantages and Disadvantages of Internal and External Recruiting

Internal Recruiting		External Recruiting	
Advantages	**Disadvantages**	**Advantages**	**Disadvantages**
More cost-effective	Creates a new vacancy	Brings new ideas into the company	More expensive than internal recruiting
Existing employees know company operations and culture	Employees too entrenched in current operations and culture to make needed changes	Employees who will help change the culture can be recruited	New hires have to learn company operations and culture
Advancement opportunities motivate employees	Employees not selected may become problematic and/or leave	Can bring in needed skills	Lack of performance data
Performance data are available about applicants	Existing employees may not have needed skills	Opportunity to change diversity profile of the firm	Existing employees not selected may be resentful

about: identifying and attracting individuals who have the competencies needed for an organization's success. Also, consider what your role as a manager would be in each activity.

Preparing Recruitment Advertisements

The quality of a recruitment advertisement has a major impact on the success of a firm's recruitment efforts. Effective recruitment advertisements are no different from effective advertisements for products or services. Successful product ads first attract the attention of the consumer and then compel them to buy it. Likewise, successful recruitment ads attract potential applicants and then compel them to actually apply for the job advertised. Even if a company is using the services of an employment agency, it is still up to the company and, generally, the hiring manager to identify the information that needs to be included in communications designed to attract potential applicants.

Developing a Recruitment Value Proposition

In the late 1990s, employers were having a hard time attracting employees. As a result, they started paying more attention to how marketers persuaded customers to buy goods and services. These employers subsequently adopted and applied marketing concepts such as *creating a value proposition* and *branding*.[28] Recruiters frequently speak of creating a value proposition for recruiting employees, especially for recruiting top talent. A marketing value proposition demonstrates to potential consumers the reasons they should purchase one product or service rather than another. In the same way, a **recruitment value proposition** helps potential applicants differentiate what one company offers to its employees versus what other companies offer.

recruitment value proposition

A marketing concept used in recruitment to design the advertising message in such a way that potential applicants can differentiate what one company offers to its employees versus what other companies offer.

According to J. W. Marriott, Jr., the CEO of the Marriott hotel chain, people looking for jobs are just as conscious of value as consumers shopping for products or services.[29] Marriott and other companies that offer successful value propositions have designed both their jobs and corporate cultures to attract the talent they need now and in the future.[30] These companies focus on aligning all their HR management activities with their recruitment activities. They know what sets them apart, and they communicate this message throughout the recruitment process. Communicating their corporate cultures is just as important as communicating their job openings.[31]

The recruitment value proposition conveyed to potential employees includes information about a job's duties and associated working environment, total rewards offered by the firm, and the company's corporate image. In fact, the information found in most recruitment ads can be grouped into these three categories.[32] The nature of the information presented makes the difference: Unlike traditional recruitment communications, a value proposition lets prospective employees know what they will experience when working for the company. The experience can include everything from the level of compensation and type of leadership development opportunities the position affords to the nature of the work environment. The critical component is to know what your target audience is looking for and to let the potential employees know what the company can offer relative to that.

Marriott Hotels creates a value proposition to attract employees like this one.

employer branding

The development of a long-term strategy to manage how a firm's stakeholders—including its current and future employees—perceive the company.

The value proposition is different for each company. It helps a potential applicant understand what day-to-day life in the firm would be like.[33] A well-designed value proposition and accompanying brand can help a potential applicant decide whether there is likely to be a good person–organization fit. Those who perceive a better fit are more likely to want to work for the organization.[34] Therefore, as a manager, you need to carefully consider what you are communicating to prospective employees throughout the recruitment process, both in printed form and in person. If your advertisements imply certain values, but your actions and words or those of other employees during the interview process convey something else, you have a very real problem to address.

Once a company has specified its value proposition, it can then turn its attention to developing a brand to embody that proposition and help the company become an employer of choice.[35] **Employer branding** involves developing a long-term strategy to manage how a firm's stakeholders—including its current and future employees—perceive the company. Like product branding, employer branding is about creating a connection—in this case between the potential applicant (either external or internal) and the employer—rather than the customer and the product. Capgemini is a consulting, technology, and outsourcing firm that adopted an employer branding strategy. The firm realized that by doing so, it could differentiate itself in the marketplace. It also realized that the branding strategy would be difficult for other companies to copy. Capgemini understands that how it treats its employees affects how they treat customers. Consequently, the firm can't have a different branding strategy for one group than for another because one is tied to the other. Now, Capgemini has created an employer branding award to recognize the branding strategy efforts of other companies.[36]

Writing a Recruitment Message

A recruitment advertisement should be written to convey both the value proposition and brand, as well as other basic job and company-related information. Recruitment advertisements that provide visual cues and specific information about the job and the company, along with personally relevant information, will generate more applicants.[37] Company Spotlight 6.2 provides an example of what we are talking about here. Individuals are more attracted to jobs for which they have more information, especially when that information is specific about job or company attributes such as benefits, location, culture, and job requirements.[38] The information reduces the amount of uncertainty job seekers have about a particular job opportunity. When writing an advertisement, it is useful to think in terms of why a highly talented person would want to work at the company.[39] Providing little information in the advertisement tends to reflect poorly on a company and signals to potential applicants that the company does not value its employees highly enough to create a persuasive, informative ad designed to attract good workers.[40]

Exhibit 6.5 provides some tips on writing successful print ads. At the very least, it is important to include a brief description of the job and its minimum requirements, as well as how to apply for the job and any deadlines for applying. Most of the research about successful recruitment ads has focused on newspapers and similar media, such as trade journals. Unfortunately, because of the costs involved, ads placed in print publications such as these are often limited to the bare essentials.

Charges for print advertisements are typically by the line so these ads are often kept short to keep costs down. Print ads also are by their nature non-interactive and presented in a linear manner (one fact following another in some logical order) and individuals are passively exposed to the information in them. Online advertisements, on the other hand, are relatively inexpensive as we have already noted. Using the Internet helps companies provide a wider and more immediate scope of communication between themselves and prospective job applicants. In Web-based media, individuals must actively find the information, which gives them more discretion in deciding what is of interest. If an advertisement is posted on a company's Web site, various links to other pages of content can be included. Many companies even include links to streaming video of current employees talking about working for the company. Regardless of the format, the ads must focus on the target audience's needs and communicate the information in an easily understood and accessible manner. Sometimes straightforward is still the best route.

COMPANY *spotlight*
6.2 Carroll's Foods of Virginia: High on the Hog

Not many companies choose to use a hog in their recruitment ads. But that's just what Carroll's Foods of Virginia does, and with great success. Carroll's Foods is a 550-employee swine production company. The company decided it wanted to add some life to its newspaper ads for recruiting employees to better reflect the culture of the company. The firm's efforts were rewarded with a Creative Excellence Award. More importantly, the efforts were rewarded with a lot of interest in the advertised jobs.

In an ad for truck drivers, the company featured a pig standing atop a big-rig truck with the words "High on the Hog" written below. The ad for inventory clerks showed a pig working at a computer; "Pigs in Cyberspace" was the theme. The ad for financial analysts included a cartoon pig talking on the telephone and the slogan "Never a Boar." The pig theme caught on so well that it also was used in other recruiting materials at Carroll's Foods, including billboards and college recruiting materials.

Carroll's Foods is located between Virginia Beach and Richmond, Virginia, so the advertisements are typically published in the local paper of each of these cities. The response to the ads has been positive, and people are even willing to drive a little further to work than they normally would. Applicants are attracted by the upbeat, fun culture conveyed by the ads. Of course, the ads emphasize more than just the culture. They include information about the jobs, too.

Creating each pig ad cost Carroll's Foods between $75 and $100. Even adding in the cost of typesetting and publication, the ads were still relatively inexpensive. Including the company logo and the pig illustrations made the ads stand out from other ads and proved to be a winning combination.

Source: Based on Martinez, M. N. Winning ways to recruit. *HRMagazine*, June 2000, www.findarticles.com/p/articles/mi_m3495/is_6_45/ai_63324382.

Content

- Job title
- Brief description of the duties
- Minimum education, experience, and skill levels required
- Special criteria, such as extensive travel or relocation
- Brief overview of the company
- Benefits provided
- EEO/affirmative action disclosure

Writing

- Start with an attention-getter, such as "Looking for a great place to work?"
- Use proper grammar and punctuation
- Minimize the use of abbreviations and acronyms
- Keep it focused
- Avoid discriminatory language (e.g., "young and energetic employee sought")

Applying

- How to apply
- Where to apply (include your company's logo, if possible)
- Deadline for applying

Source: Adapted in part from Business Owner's Toolkit. *Information to include in job ads*, www.toolkit.cch.com/text/P05_0673.asp; and Business Owner's Toolkit. *Writing a job advertisement*, www.toolkit.cch.com/text/P05_0670.asp.

◄ **Exhibit 6.5**
Minimum Requirements for a Job Ad

Companies that are incorporating videos into their recruitment campaigns need to remember that the requirements for a successful recruitment video are the same as for other recruitment messages. They need to be geared to the target audience, reflect the culture of the organization, and be of high quality. The content and quality, just as with other recruitment techniques, will be perceived as a reflection of the company and will affect the willingness of potential applicants to pursue job opportunities.

Recruiters

The recruitment information conveyed by a recruiter has a considerable impact on the effectiveness of a firm's recruitment efforts. Generally, there are two categories of recruiters. One category comprises professional recruiters. These are the people whose job it is to find applicants to fill open positions in companies. They can be company employees or work for employment agencies. The second category comprises the managers who are involved in identifying and attracting potential employees. As we have explained, if you are working in a small company, you may have responsibility for the entire recruitment process. A larger company is likely to have a staffing department with full-time recruiters. Your role in the larger company will be to ensure that the recruiters have the information they need to assist you in filling open positions and to solicit their input on applicants of interest.

The recruiter can make a difference in whether potential applicants continue to be interested in the company.[41] Research has consistently shown that how the recruiter is perceived and the ability of the recruiter to convey information about the job and the company affects the willingness of individuals to apply for jobs.[42] The warmer the personality of the recruiter and the more the recruiter knows and conveys about the job and the company, the better.

Whether a company uses professional recruiters or has managers do the recruiting, these individuals should be trained to convey the company's value proposition and brand in an effective manner. They should be trained on EEO issues so that they do not discriminate in the recruitment process either intentionally or unintentionally. The training should also address issues such as false representation. Telling a recruit that the job will provide certain benefits that it does not and telling a recruit that the firm's financial position is better than it is are examples of possible false misrepresentation that can lead to the company being sued.[43] We will discuss more about legal issues such as these later in the chapter.

Realistic Job Previews

As with any other marketing effort, in recruiting, a decision has to be made about what and how much information to give to job applicants. Research suggests that a balanced recruitment message will have the best long-term results for the company. A balanced message provides positive information about the job and company as well as information that is likely to be less favorable to some potential applicants. Such a message is referred to as a **realistic job preview.** One outcome of providing a realistic job preview is that individuals will screen themselves out of the application process when they realize that some aspects of the job or aspects of the company are not attractive to them. This outcome seems even more likely to occur when that information is presented by an interviewer rather than in written form.[44] However, applicants who accept jobs with the company after being provided with a realistic job preview are more likely to have accurate expectations and are more likely to stay with the company longer.[45]

Saint Francis Medical Center, a nonprofit hospital located in Nebraska, has found that realistic job previews not only decrease turnover but often convince applicants that Saint Francis is where they want to work. As part of the medical center's realistic job previews, applicants spend time shadowing someone doing the job in which they are interested.[46] Surgical Programs at Children's Hospital Boston has also found that job shadowing is an effective recruitment tool. After a highly successful pilot program, the entire facility adopted the model. The organization now uses it to attract other health care providers as well as nurses.[47]

Recruitment Follow-up

All too often, people apply for jobs and wait a long time to hear back from companies or never hear from them at all. It is important to remember that the recruitment process is concerned with generating interest in the company. Maintaining communication with

realistic job preview
Providing individuals with a balanced overview of a prospective job to encourage applicants who are not a good fit to screen themselves out of the hiring process and to ensure that applicants who are hired understand what the job will involve.

prospective employees is an effective way to signal to them that you and your company value them. You may not have a job for an applicant now, but he may be just the right person for a future job or may become a customer in the future.

At a minimum, a recruiter or manager should prepare and send a standardized but personalized letter to each applicant to let him or her know the status of the application, even if it is a rejection. A well-done rejection letter can actually leave a favorable impression of the company with the applicant. Later, the applicant will be more likely to consider the company as an employer and/or will speak more positively of the company to others. In other words, it's important to always leave the applicant with a good impression of the company. You never know when you are going to need this person to come to work for you.

Recruitment Effectiveness

The appendix to this chapter discusses a number of metrics that companies use to evaluate recruitment effectiveness. **Yield ratios, cost-per-hire, time-to-fill,** and managers' feedback are all techniques designed to measure the success of a recruitment program. Paying attention to these metrics helps a company determine the most effective recruitment methods to use in terms of costs and quality of applicants. The appendix also includes a discussion of benchmarking as a way to evaluate how well a company is doing with regard to its recruitment.

RECRUITMENT IN PRACTICE: ORGANIZATIONAL DEMANDS

Let's now take a look at the organizational, environmental, and regulatory factors that affect the decisions managers make about how to recruit and where to recruit employees. The topics we cover are outlined in Exhibit 6.6. As you will see, recruitment can play a key

Yield ratios

A metric that shows the effectiveness of different recruiting sources by computing the ratio of number selected to number applied.

Cost-per-hire

The sum of all recruiting costs, including such items as advertising, travel, search-firm fees, and background checks, divided by the number of new hires.

Time-to-fill

A measure of the length of time it takes from the time a job opening is announced until someone begins to work in the job.

◀ **Exhibit 6.6**
Recruitment in Practice

Context	Employee Competencies Chapter 6, "Recruitment"
Organizational Demands	
Strategy drives . . .	• Content of recruitment message • Choice of recruitment methods
Company characteristics determine . . .	• Use of internal vs. external recruiting • Who does recruitment
Culture establishes . . .	• Recruitment value proposition • Balance of internal vs. external recruiting
Employee concerns include . . .	• Appraisal of recruitment message • Perception of fairness of process
Environmental Demands	
Labor force influences . . .	• Who is targeted for recruitment • How much recruitment is needed
Technology affects . . .	• How recruitment is managed • Skills recruited
Globalization impacts . . .	• How recruiting is done • Where recruiting is done
Ethics/social responsibility shapes . . .	• Response to value proposition • Truth-in-hiring • Target of recruitment
Regulations *guide* . . .	• Content of recruitment message • Recruiter words and actions • Recordkeeping

role in how well a company attains and maintains a competitive advantage. Without the right people in the right place doing the right things, a firm cannot be successful.

All companies need to recruit employees, but organizational demands and environmental influences differ. These differences affect the decisions managers make about recruiting employees. Even so, do remember what you have learned in the first part of this chapter about the importance of a clearly defined description of the job requirements. Regardless of the organizational demands and environmental influences, recruiting cannot be effective unless a manager first has a solid understanding of what the person hired will be doing and how the job fits into the overall goals of the company. A manager is likely to make decisions based on incomplete and/or non-relevant criteria, resulting in less-than-optimal outcomes without such information.

Strategy and Recruitment

To illustrate how the strategy of a firm affects recruitment, we focus on two aspects of the recruitment process—the content of the recruitment message and the recruitment methods selected. We will once again focus on low-cost versus differentiation strategies. Keep in mind that there are other strategies firms pursue, but these two are particularly important to consider during the recruitment process and serve to illustrate why strategy matters.

CONTENT OF A RECRUITMENT MESSAGE   A central goal of a recruitment message is to attract applicants who will be the best fit with the job and the organization. The information conveyed to prospective applicants should address the advantages of working for the organization, such as relocation allowances and other special perquisites, as well as the nature of the competencies sought. The recruitment message needs to tell a positive "story" about why employees would want to work for the company. Remember that the goal for the company is to stand out during the recruitment process in order to attract top talent; recruitment is marketing, after all. At a minimum, the specific content of the recruitment message should reflect the types of people and competencies needed to ensure that the firm achieves and retains a competitive advantage in the marketplace for its products and services.

Let's look at two examples that help to illustrate how differentiation of a firm affects its recruitment message. A hotel focused on customer service will want to ensure that customers will return and will tell other customers to use that hotel. If you were a manager in this hotel, what would you want to focus on in the recruitment message? You would probably want to convey something to the effect that prospective employees should be customer service oriented and have the ability to take initiative—two characteristics critical to providing hotel customers with a high level of service during their stay.

As another example, consider a biotech firm focused on innovation. How might the recruitment message you craft for this firm differ from the hotel recruitment message? Perhaps you would tell future employees about the firm's focus on adventure, change, learning, and discovery. You might also highlight major advances the company is known for in its field. The target audience for this firm will be very different from the target audience for the hotel, and the recruiting messages will reflect these differences.

Now let's take a look at the recruitment message for a firm that uses a cost leadership strategy. This strategy suggests focusing on outperforming competing firms by offering the lowest costs for products or services.[48] Issues related to efficiencies and cost reductions dominate. As discussed in Chapter 4, in these work environments, employees are typically expected to perform jobs that are narrow in focus and that involve standardized and repetitive actions. Think about how the recruitment message for K-Mart, a discount store, would differ from the recruitment message for Tiffany & Co., a high-end jewelry store. Both companies are in the retail industry, but the similarities both begin and end there. K-Mart wants people who are willing to work at a minimal rate of pay, keep merchandise stocked efficiently on its shelves, and check out customers. Tiffany & Co. wants people who can provide a luxury shopping experience for its customers. These differences affect the recruitment message. K-Mart has a low-cost strategy. Tiffany & Co. has a differentiation strategy that focuses on the customer experience.

CHOICE OF RECRUITMENT METHODS   Strategy affects which recruitment methods a company is most likely to use. The recruitment methods emphasized by companies pursuing a low-cost strategy are likely to emphasize low-cost approaches. Word-of-mouth (employee referrals) is a low-cost method for identifying potential employees, for example. Current employees talking about how much they like working at the company and/or emphasizing the benefits offered them doesn't cost a lot and can add to a firm's value proposition as an employer.

Companies pursuing differentiation, in contrast, may have to be more focused in how they reach the targeted audience. Depending on the source of differentiation, they have to use the method that attracts individuals with the specific competencies required to achieve company goals. Trade publications and Web sources are two methods managers can use to target individuals with particular backgrounds or occupational skills. And, because employees often associate with people with similar backgrounds and interests, employee referrals actually may prove to be an effective approach to identifying people with special skill sets.

Company Characteristics and Recruitment

The size of a company and its stage of development affect the extent to which internal recruiting is used, where recruiting is done, and who manages the process. Larger companies generally have more resources and a greater need for more formal processes than smaller firms. Older, more established firms are also more likely to have formalized recruitment processes. The size and stage of a company's development affect the extent to which internal recruiting is used versus external recruiting and who does the recruiting.

USE OF INTERNAL VERSUS EXTERNAL RECRUITING Unlike small businesses, large companies have a ready supply of labor from which to recruit new employees. As discussed in Chapter 5, larger companies are more likely to have **succession planning** activities in place and other tools, such as **replacement charts,** to identify employees who can move into vacant positions within the company. They are also more likely to have employee inventories and formal job posting systems that provide information about and for current employees relative to job openings. Small businesses do many of the same things, but they do so in a more informal manner. The owner of a small business might promote a current employee into a higher-level position because she knows the employee is capable of performing the new responsibilities. At other times, smaller organizations might lack employees with the needed competencies, leaving the manager no choice but to recruit externally.

WHO MANAGES RECRUITMENT A manager working in a large, established multinational company will have different recruiting responsibilities than a manager working in a small, or even medium-sized, business. The large multinational will have a formal recruiting staff responsible for creating advertisements, selecting recruitment methods, and managing the process. As indicated previously, as a manager, you will need to provide the recruiters with a job description and suggest methods for recruitment. You may even be asked to make a recruiting trip to a college to talk to prospective applicants. In fact, a lot of organizations are sending their employees to their alma maters to recruit students for internships and permanent positions.

In a smaller enterprise, you may be the recruiter. You would have to write the recruiting message, decide which methods to use, and manage the entire process. Unlike in a larger organization, you will not have a formal recruiting department to handle the details for you. More than likely, you will advertise in only a few places, and only locally, for most job openings. The local newspaper and a company Web site may be the recruiting media you use most frequently. Your recruiting responsibilities in a startup company will be similar to those in a smaller business. As the company grows, more formalized processes and specific staff will be needed to assist with recruitment. If the company stays small, you may remain responsible for many of the recruiting activities.

Culture and Recruitment

Early in this book, we began talking about the need for alignment between how a firm manages its HR activities and its corporate culture. You should consider your firm's organizational culture in terms of all your recruiting activities, including the value proposition you offer and the balance you strike between recruiting candidates internally versus externally.

succession planning

The process of planning for the future leadership of the company by identifying and developing employees to fill higher level jobs within the company as they become available.

replacement chart

A method of tracking information about employees who can move into higher level positions within the company in the future.

RECRUITMENT VALUE PROPOSITION A company should focus on communicating information about the specific job available, the reputation of the company, how the company positions itself in the marketplace, and the compensation and benefits that go along with the job and with working at that company. How the company presents this information will signal a lot about its organizational culture to prospective applicants. A company that emphasizes compensation and benefits in its recruitment message suggests to applicants that the culture values employees and rewards them accordingly. A company that emphasizes growth and opportunity in its recruitment message may be signaling that financial rewards are not as great but that its cultural values provide more intrinsic rewards. Or a company could emphasize both a job's financial rewards and opportunities for growth, signaling through the recruitment process that employees are highly valued and that the firm aims to be an employer of choice.

In addition, the people chosen to do the recruiting will communicate a lot about the company's value proposition. If a firm's recruitment activities are handled primarily by the company's staffing department, applicants are likely to perceive that a formal culture exists. If more employees are involved at various levels, the applicant is more likely to get a realistic view of the organization and believe that the firm's culture is more open. As a manager, your involvement in the recruiting process and what you do as you interact with prospective applicants will signal a lot about the culture of your company, whether you intend it to or not.

BALANCE OF INTERNAL VERSUS EXTERNAL RECRUITING In many companies, every effort is made to fill a position internally before recruiting externally. Employees are groomed to move up in the organization. In other organizations, finding the best person for the job is most important, regardless of whether that person is internal or external. In still other organizations, key positions are almost always filled externally because these companies are seeking change.

As we have already noted, there are pros and cons to each type of recruitment strategy. A company should carefully consider the balance between its external and internal recruitment and decide how that balance affects the culture of the organization. If there is too much focus on internal recruitment, the company might become insular and lose its competitive edge. If there is too much external recruitment, employees will feel less valued and seek opportunities outside the firm. Thus, as a recruiting manager, it is important for you to understand your company's objectives and policies about internal recruitment and seek to ensure that you help maintain the appropriate balance.

Employee Concerns and Recruitment

From an employee perspective, two issues are important during the recruitment process: how the employee/applicant appraises, or views, the recruitment message and the fairness exhibited during the process.

APPRAISAL OF RECRUITMENT MESSAGE When you look for a job, what attracts you most? The compensation or the benefits? The location? The culture of the company? We have already spent some time discussing the type of information that needs to be included in a recruitment message. Now, we want to turn to the importance of considering how prospective employees are likely to view that message. Certainly not everyone is looking for the same things when seeking a new job. Some applicants will focus most on a company's culture. They may be interested in the development of their careers or opportunities to create innovative new products or services. Or they may be drawn to a company that values the work/life balance of its employees. Other applicants may focus on the tasks of the job itself. They want to know what they will be doing to see if that fits with their interests and competencies. Still other applicants will focus on the job's benefits and compensation level. Of course, there are applicants who pay attention to all three of these issues. By emphasizing one aspect more than another, the company is sending a message about what it values most or what it believes the employees it wants to recruit will be looking for in a company. Applicants are likely to evaluate different aspects of the recruitment message to discern whether they are interested in the job and whether they are a good fit with the company.

PERCEPTION OF FAIRNESS OF THE PROCESS   As a manager, you want to make sure that information in print and in other media as well as direct recruiter communications represents the job fairly and accurately. Overselling a job will have short- and long-term consequences for the company. Word travels quickly about an employer that is found to be less than honest in its recruitment activities—especially in small, local labor markets and highly specialized labor markets. If you engage in such practices, fewer applicants will respond to your firm's future recruitment efforts. In addition, as a manager, you will be put in the position of having to deal with unhappy new employees who feel they were misled in the recruitment process. In contrast, a credible employer will attract a large applicant pool and employees who feel they were fairly treated.

As noted earlier, realistic job previews are one way to try to increase perceptions of fairness. Describing both the positive and negative aspects of a job will reduce the size of your applicant pool. However, applicants who accept jobs with the company after being given a realistic job preview are more likely to view the recruitment process as fair and stay with the company longer.[49]

RECRUITMENT IN PRACTICE: ENVIRONMENTAL INFLUENCES

Along with organizational demands, companies must account for environmental influences when conducting a recruitment campaign. The labor force, technology, globalization, and ethical and corporate social responsibility issues all affect what employers do to recruit employees.

The Labor Force and Recruitment

By now you should be well aware that a critical element of a successful recruitment plan is directing your message to the right audience. The nature of the targeted labor force also affects how much recruiting you will have to do to yield the number of employees required to achieve the company's goals. Let's now look at both of these aspects.

TARGET OF RECRUITMENT   Obviously, when companies are recruiting, they target employees who have the competencies they need. In addition, most companies, even those not required to have affirmative action programs, understand the importance of targeting a diverse applicant pool. The changing demographics of the labor force in many parts of the world—not just the United States—mean that companies have to be open to diversity to recruit the most qualified workers.

Employers limit their ability to attract needed workers when they either intentionally or unintentionally target their recruitment messages to a young or non-diverse population. Older workers, minorities, and individuals with disabilities are often highly qualified potential employees. Days Inn, Avon, and Cisco Systems are companies that have recognized the value of these employees by actively recruiting them. As a manager, you have a particular responsibility to oversee the recruitment process to ensure that it is managed in a nondiscriminatory manner. Let's take a look at some of the groups you might target with your recruitment efforts.

We have already noted that baby boomers currently represent the largest segment of the workforce. This generation is now reaching retirement age at the same time as there are fewer new entrants into the workforce.[50] And this is not limited to the workforce in the United States. Other countries around the world, such as Canada and Japan, have to address similar issues. To cope with this trend, companies need to take a proactive stance and develop recruiting plans targeted at these older workers.[51] Many older workers actually need to and want to work, and they also need to know that their contributions are valued.

In Chapter 3 we talked about the AARP and Home Depot partnership to employ older workers. Home Depot is in the minority, however. The Society for Human Resource Management's Older Worker Survey found that only 41% of companies target older workers with their recruitment efforts. Companies that target these people recognize their strong work ethic, willingness to work nontraditional hours, reliability, and invaluable

Older workers play an important role in the success of Home Depot.

experience.[52] Days Inn has found that recruiting older workers is a win–win strategy. Older workers do well in both sales and service responsibilities.[53] Universal Studios targets older workers, especially for seasonal work around the Christmas holidays. Universal advertises in retirement communities in Florida and even provides buses to transport the workers to their jobs. Recruiting minorities is a plus for the reputation of businesses, too. Exhibit 6.7 shows a list of the companies included in *Fortune*'s 2008 ranking of the "100 Best Companies to Work For" that have the largest percentages of minority employees.

For many years, Avon Company, a global leader in the beauty-products market, was selected as one of *Fortune*'s "50 Best Places for Minorities." The company has also been recognized as a best company to work for by *Working Mother* magazine, *Latina Style Magazine*, and *Hispanic Magazine*. These honors result in part from the company's efforts to recruit more minorities to its workforce in the past 10 years.[54] Many other companies actively recruit minorities also. After all, if the company's customer base is going to be diverse, shouldn't the employee base be the same? Read more about Avon's efforts in Company Spotlight 6.3.

Companies have begun to realize that individuals with disabilities make up a large segment of the workforce and are excellent candidates for many job openings. For example, Cisco Systems, a computer networking company, regularly recruits disabled individuals. Doing so makes good business sense and also increases the diversity of its workforce. The company even teaches its recruiters how to work with disabled individuals. Microsoft and IBM also actively recruit workers who have disabilities.[55] All is not rosy, however, for disabled workers. In 1999, when the United States was experiencing the lowest unemployment in 29 years, many disabled persons were not able to find work, even though they were highly skilled and educated.[56] While the opportunities have increased somewhat, there is

Exhibit 6.7 ▶

Companies with the Largest Percentages of Minority Employees from *Fortune*'s 2008 "100 Best Companies to Work For" List

Company	# Employees	% Minority
1. Baptist Health South Florida	9,838	72%
2. Four Seasons Hotels	12,851	66%
3. Methodist Hospital System	10,481	66%
4. Marriott International	123,203	61%
5. Station Casinos	14,920	52%
6. Qualcomm	10,095	51%
7. Erickson Retirement Communities	10,248	47%
8. Scripps Health	11,223	47%
9. Navy Federal Credit Union	6,069	47%
10. Stew Leonard's	2,282	46%
11. Whole Foods Market	41,385	46%

Source: 100 best companies to work for, 2008. *Fortune*, http://money.cnn.com/magazines/fortune/bestcompanies/2008/.

COMPANY spotlight   6.3 Diversity Matters at Avon

Avon bills itself as the "Company for Women." Yet for many years, the company's top managerial positions were mostly filled by men, and its marketing was geared toward one subset of women: white Anglo-Americans. That has changed. Avon now has more women in top managerial positions than any other *Fortune* 500 company—more than 86%. About half of the company's directors on the Board are female.

Avon prides itself on embracing diversity and being an affirmative action leader. The company recognizes that it makes good business sense to seek top talent of any race, color, or ethnicity, especially if it wants to sell products to its now very diverse clientele.

The company has internal networks for its employees that include a parents' network, a black professional association, a Hispanic network, an Asian network, and a gay and lesbian network. These associations provide a voice, or way, for these groups to discuss with Avon's top managers critical workplace and marketplace issues for these groups. This strong focus on diversity plays a big part in Avon's recruitment efforts and enables the company to attract top talent with whom the company shares its values.

Source: Based on Avon. *Workplace diversity at Avon*, www.avoncompany.com/responsibility/diversity.html.

still much work that needs to be done to identify and provide opportunities for this segment of the population.

HOW MUCH RECRUITMENT IS NEEDED   In 1999, the unemployment rate in the United States was only 4.3%.[57] Companies had to recruit extensively to attract potential employees. They did so by, among other things, setting up career fairs in city parks where potential employees congregated on Sunday afternoons and offering extra employee benefits, such as concierge services, to attract applicants. Keep in mind that the labor market is seldom tight for all jobs in all locations. Nor does a tight labor market mean that all qualified workers obtain employment. Thus, as a manager, you may find yourself having to heavily recruit for some jobs at the same time that you a have large number of applications for other jobs. The overall unemployment rate and nature of the relevant labor market in terms of skills and location will determine how much recruiting has to occur. How you define your target group also influences what you do. In general, the broader the targeted recruitment pool, the less recruitment effort needed.

Technology and Recruitment

We noted earlier in the chapter that technology has heavily influenced employee recruiting. Technology also influences how companies manage the recruiting process and the types of skills for which they recruit. The choices you make about how to use technology in the recruiting process can make your job as a manager both easier and more difficult. The use of technology can make your job easier by automating many of the processes, such as resume collection, and more difficult because you are likely to have more resumes to review! Company Spotlight 6.4 provides an example of just how important technology can be for attracting employees.

HOW RECRUITMENT IS MANAGED   Online job posting and sourcing of passive applicants are two recruiting approaches we have discussed that didn't exist prior to 1991, the year the Internet became readily available. Technology affects recruiting in other ways as well. Companies with an *enterprise resource planning (ERP)* system, a system that integrates information from different functional areas across a company, can use the Web recruitment function included with that program. Another option is to purchase a *recruitment application package* from a software vendor. These programs are often tailored to a particular industry or target businesses by size. Such a program can link to companies' human resource management systems (HRMS) or stand alone. The third option involves contracting with an *application service provider (ASP)*, a company that hosts software on its own Web site so your company doesn't have to do so. The decision about which route to take should be driven by

PRACTICE

COMPANY spotlight   6.4 Online Recruiting at Borgata Hotel Casino & Spa

In the five months prior to the opening of the Borgata Hotel Casino & Spa in Atlantic City, New Jersey, the company had to hire 5,000 employees. Imagine having to review that many applications and resumes! Remember that 5,000 is the actual number hired.

The Borgata used two portals, or gateways, to the Internet to accomplish the task. One portal was designed to help Borgata's management team recruit employees. The other was used to let the public know about the company and the available jobs.

The team charged with recruiting employees set up a trailer with 30 kiosks outside their temporary office in the Atlantic City Convention Center. Potential employees used the kiosks to review job information, apply online, and schedule recruiter appointments. Atlantic City's public library was brought into the recruiting process. The library agreed to use the Borgata's recruiting Web site as its home page on its network. Potential applicants could go into any of the city's libraries and apply online for a job at the Borgata. In addition, a group of recruiters took laptops into the streets of Atlantic City to bring applications to the public in a program called "Laptops and Lemonade." Ultimately, more than 70,000 applicants were screened for the 5,000 jobs.

The efficiency and effectiveness of the recruiting process helped the Borgata live up to its "Work Someplace Different" recruitment slogan.

Source: Adapted from Roberts, B. HR technology. *HRMagazine*, August 2004, www.shrm.org/hrmagazine/articles/0804/ 0804hrtech.asp; Borgata Hotel, Casino & Spa Web site, www. theborgata.com; and Schadler, J. Creative recruiting helps hotels attract the best employees. *Hotel & Motel Magazine*, November 1, 2004, pp. 20, 21.

the strategy and the resources of the organization. For instance, a company with a low-cost strategy may choose to go with an ASP to avoid investing heavily in computer hardware and having to recruit software and personnel to manage their upkeep.

Some of the software available for posting jobs and collecting applications online can track and screen applications and resumes, reducing the time-consuming resume-review process. Previously, managers and recruiters had to personally review each resume and application to determine who should be considered for job opportunities. Now, resumes and applications can be entered online or scanned into resume tracking programs. The programs use search criteria to determine whether applicants have the key KSAs the job and organization require.

Online recruiting on company Web sites has given employers a unique opportunity to aim their recruitment efforts at a more diverse workforce. Visuals can be used to communicate the company's focus on diversity. For instance, the career section for many companies' Web sites includes a number of photographs representing employees. Generally, these pictures show a diverse group in terms of race, ethnicity, color, gender, and age. It is not uncommon for a site to include a picture of someone in a wheelchair to show the company's commitment to employing individuals with disabilities. Research has shown that this approach works.[58]

Beyond enhancing a firm's diversity efforts, technology has provided managers with many new tools for managing their recruitment efforts. Earlier in the chapter, we mentioned LinkedIn.com as a good source for passive recruiting. Intermedia Inc., an e-mail Web hosting company, uses social networks such as LinkedIn to find qualified job applicants. Intermedia believes that these networks provide a higher-quality pool of applicants than job sites such as Monster.com. Job seekers can easily post their resumes to many companies via job sites. In LinkedIn, the posting is much more selective because of the design of the sites, which requires an invitation to join.[59] Care must be exercised, however, to ensure that a reliance on social networks for recruiting does not eliminate older workers. Older workers may be less likely to be "linked in."

SKILLS RECRUITED Technology has changed the skills required for many jobs as well as changed where employees work. Most people use some computer technology on the job. But the nature and extent of that use varies considerably. Manufacturing plants, for example, increasingly rely on computers to help workers design and manufacture products and control the quality of their production. As a result, the individuals recruited to work in these plants are likely to need computer skills they would not have needed in years past. As a result, managers must ensure that the recruitment message accurately portrays the level and type of technological skills the firm needs.

Also, many jobs that require computer skills do not have to be performed in a specific location. As a result, the recruitment pool can be expanded. For example, recall that in Chapter 1 we discussed the fact that JetBlue reservationists work from their homes.[60] Many stay-at-home moms and dads, who often are highly computer literate, find jobs such as these very attractive. They are good potential targets to recruit for jobs where location doesn't matter but computer skills do.

Globalization and Recruitment

Globalization affects employee recruitment in a number of ways. First, multinational companies have to consider the impact of national origin norms and values as well as country laws when recruiting globally. A single recruitment message will not work in multiple countries. Second, technology enables companies to recruit a larger target group. This gives a company the opportunity to select employees from a larger labor pool; however, it also allows lots of other companies to vie for the same group of skilled employees. Let's now look closer at how globalization affects how and where recruitment is done.

HOW RECRUITING IS DONE   Recruiting on a global scale complicates the recruiting process because people from different parts of the world have different values and needs.[61] Thus, the recruiting message may have to be crafted in multiple ways in order to be viable for different target audiences. China provides a good example. Recruiting methods in China are similar to those in the United States. (The methods include advertising in newspapers, making campus visits, employing search firms, and so forth.) It is the value proposition that must be tailored differently to attract workers. Seldom is housing a job benefit in the United States. However, in China, where there is often a shortage of qualified workers for professional jobs and also a shortage of housing, companies that include housing as part of the value proposition have an advantage over companies that do not, especially when recruiting for senior positions where such a perk is expected.[62]

To try to increase the effectiveness of the recruiting process, some multinational companies hire individuals as recruiters from the country where employees are needed. Other companies use a search firm that specializes in identifying talent globally or in a particular country. Qualifind is one such search firm. This company has six offices in Mexico and two offices on the U.S./Mexico border. Honeywell Aerospace turned to Qualifind when it built a new *maquiladora* in Mexicali, a town in northern Baja. A *maquiladora* is a factory that imports equipment and materials and turns them into finished products to ship back across the border. Qualifind helped Honeywell Aerospace identify the 300 engineers it needed for the new plant, and it received approximately 25% of the first year's salary for each employee placed.[63]

Differences also exist across borders in terms of preferred recruitment methods. In some countries, newspapers would be effective; in other countries, word-of-mouth may be the best recruitment method. Managers need to remember that the Internet is still not available in every part of the world. Consequently, relying solely on Web postings might not yield sufficient numbers of employees needed in some locales, especially in less developed countries. In fact, utilizing only that method might cause a company to miss out on identifying some highly qualified workers.

WHERE RECRUITING IS DONE   As we have explained, the Internet certainly has broadened the ability of firms to find the employees they need anywhere in the world and vice versa. Now, if you need an employee in Bangkok, you can post the job on any number of international job sites and on your own corporate Web site, and you are likely to receive applications from all over the world. A number of restaurant firms, for instance, use the Web to attract the best job candidates from around the globe.[64]

In cases where the work can actually be done virtually, you can advertise in India for employees to work on a project with employees in two or three or more other countries. Technology, thus, opens up the labor market for many jobs. There is a caveat to all this good news about having access to workers all over the globe: More and more employers are looking for employees in the same world labor pool, a pool that at times is geographically dispersed but not very large.[65]

Ethics, Corporate Social Responsibility, and Recruitment

Companies have a great opportunity during the recruiting process to showcase their ethical practices and social consciousness. The value propositions they offer, truth-in-hiring, and the groups they target send signals not only to potential employees but to the world at large.

VALUE PROPOSITION OFFERED   Recall that one aspect of a value proposition is a firm's corporate image. *Fortune* magazine publishes a list of the 100 best companies to work for each year. The list includes companies such as Google, Genentech, Wegmans, and Starbucks.[66] The work/life balance firms offer their employees and the degree of corporate social responsibility they exhibit are among the factors *Fortune* evaluates. Being included on a list like this one enhances the reputation of a company and its ability to recruit employees.[67]

TRUTH-IN-HIRING   What message is being sent by the recruitment tactics you use? For instance, is it okay to exaggerate claims about what the job candidate will get if he or she accepts the job? A judge in Texas ruled in favor of two diving students who were able to successfully argue that they had been recruited under false pretenses. The divers were enticed to work for a Texas offshore oil company by being told they would get "plenty of diving work" and "get in the water immediately." Instead, the two were given land jobs. The judge ordered the payment of damages to them because there was enough evidence to indicate that the promises made were not true.[68] The number of lawsuits over lack of truth-in-hiring is increasing. This increase results primarily from two issues: (1) efforts of employers to aggressively attract employees in a tight labor market and (2) employees who are terminated and now seek recourse against their former employers. Often these truth-in-hiring lawsuits, which are *tort claims*, occur when a job candidate has been lured away from an existing, high-paying job by promises of great opportunities at the new firm that fail to come through. These lawsuits can be expensive because courts may award compensatory and punitive damages.[69] Exhibit 6.8 provides information on how to reduce the probability of a truth-in-hiring lawsuit.

TARGETS OF RECRUITMENT   Organizations that are ethical and socially responsible approach recruiting differently than companies that are less concerned about these issues. Ethical and socially responsible companies convey their beliefs in the value propositions they offer, and they go a step further by actively recruiting employees who can live by the company's code of ethics. By focusing on finding the right people during the recruiting

Exhibit 6.8 ▶

Ways to Reduce
the Probability of a
Truth-in-Hiring
Lawsuit

1. Don't exaggerate information about the company or job.

2. Be honest and give the candidate a realistic job preview.

3. Include disclaimer language in the job offer letter to make it clear that conditions addressed in the letter represent only the company expectations.

4. Make sure the job offer letter includes a statement that the offer is contingent upon a clean background check.

5. Include employment-at-will language in the offer letter.

6. Spell out any contingencies in the offer letter.

7. Specify compensation and benefits information on a pay-period basis rather than on an annual basis to avoid implying that the job is guaranteed for a year, and do not state amounts anticipated for commissions or variable pay.

Source: Based on Hansen, F. Avoiding truth-in-hiring lawsuits. *Workforce Management* online, http://www.workforce.com/archive/feature/25/26/34/index.php.December 2007.

process, a company will have fewer violations of the code. In fact, a company code of ethics should be shared with applicants during the recruitment process and should include a statement about the values that are important to the company and the behaviors it expects of its employees.[70]

In addition, companies that choose to "poach" employees from other companies need to think carefully about what they are doing and how they are doing it. Poaching occurs when there is a labor shortage for a particular type of worker. In Singapore, for instance, a shortage of qualified executives and employees in the private banking industry resulted in increased employee poaching in the industry.[71] Companies that engage in this common practice must realize that the employees they recruit in this way are just as likely to go with the next good offer that comes along as they are to stay.

RECRUITMENT IN PRACTICE: REGULATORY ISSUES

A number of regulatory issues affect what can and cannot be done during the recruitment process. We will start with an example. A business owner decides that he wants a cute college student to work in his store as a sales associate. After all, someone who is attractive and female might just bring in more customers. Doesn't he have the right to hire whomever he wants? Well, not exactly. He cannot target his recruitment activities in such a way that he discriminates or gives the appearance that he would discriminate against anyone on the basis of their race, color, religion, sex, national origin, age, or disability unless he can show that the criterion is essential for the performance of the job—even if it is discriminatory. In this example, the owner would have a hard time showing that males and older workers cannot be effective as sales associates. Let's take a look at issues related to recruitment content, words and actions, and recordkeeping that can become problematic if not properly managed.

Content of a Recruitment Message

When writing a recruitment message, it is very important to think about what is said beyond how the job is described. A seemingly innocent comment such as "Young, energetic workers sought for part-time opportunity" immediately tells older workers that they are not wanted. As we have explained, limiting entry-level positions to recent college graduates can be problematic and has the potential to lead to charges of age discrimination as well. If your organization comes under an affirmative action plan (discussed in Chapter 3), you are required to indicate on ads that the company is an equal employment opportunity company.

Always keep in mind that all your recruitment activities have to be nondiscriminatory. To foster affirmative action, part of a company's recruiting strategy has to be a desire to reach as many qualified applicants in underrepresented groups as possible. Recruiting managers often do this by advertising open positions at historically black and historically Hispanic universities and women's colleges. They also make sure that they advertise in newspapers as well as on the Internet, and they list job openings with public employment agencies.

Recruiters' Words and Actions

Employment recruiters need to understand the importance of not discriminating unintentionally. Often, as a manager, you will be filling the role of recruiter. Even seemingly innocent comments to an applicant or to someone else about an applicant can be construed as discriminatory. Statements such as "We are really looking for an American," asking women if they intend to have children, and making offensive comments can be perceived as discriminatory. The first example suggests that ethnicity discrimination is occurring. The second example seems innocuous enough—like you are just making conversation. However, it might be construed that you believe that having children will disrupt a woman's work and career. Finally, making offensive remarks, such as telling an off-color joke or making suggestive comments, not only sends a very negative message about your company's work culture but also suggests that you might engage in discriminatory behaviors.

Recordkeeping

A final concern we need to discuss regarding regulatory issues and the recruiting process is the need for careful recordkeeping. Employers need to retain resumes and applications as required by local, state, and federal laws. For instance, the ADA and Title VII require resumes and applications be kept for at least one year. Other laws have similar provisions. And, if a company is required to be an affirmative action employer, it must document its recruitment activities to demonstrate that it has actually targeted underrepresented groups with its recruitment efforts. We will elaborate more on the recordkeeping requirement in Chapter 7, as we talk about the definition of a job applicant.

SUMMARY

Employee recruitment is a process that involves identifying and attracting potential applicants for available jobs within the organization. In essence, recruitment involves marketing the organization and the open jobs such that prospective employees want to work for the company. Creating a value proposition that communicates the vision and values of the company helps differentiate it from its competitors and allows it to attract a larger pool of qualified applicants.

Before a company begins the recruitment process, it must develop a recruitment strategy. The first step in developing the strategy involves reviewing the goals and objectives of the organization and understanding how its jobs help it achieve those goals and objectives. A well-prepared job description provides managers and recruiters the information they need for the next step—deciding where and how to recruit.

The company may decide to recruit internally and use a job posting process and/or employee inventories to identify potential applicants. Some companies have well-defined succession plans and executive development programs, which can be used to identify potential applicants for open positions. Internal recruiting programs such as these give the company a way to communicate how much it values its current employees. Internal recruiting is also cost-effective because the employees are already familiar with many aspects of the organization; advertising jobs internally is also relatively inexpensive, especially compared with the high costs associated with some external recruitment activities.

Sometimes organizations want to hire people with new ideas. Firms can do so by using a variety of external recruitment sources, including advertising in newspapers and on the Internet, recruiting at colleges and other educational institutions, and engaging placement agencies to handle the recruitment activity. Along with fresh ideas, employees recruited externally bring with them the knowledge and experience they have gained from their previous jobs. They will have to be trained and oriented to the company culture, however. Also, current employees may be unhappy when external applicants are hired to fill the openings for which they applied.

A recruitment message must be informative and communicate information about both the job and the company. A recruitment message is like any other marketing message: It must attract the attention of those to whom it is targeted so that they will want to take action.

Recruiters play a key role in the success of the recruitment process. Ensuring that recruiters are warm, personable, and knowledgeable about the company and the openings it has will increase the likelihood that potential applicants will follow through and apply with the company. A realistic job preview can help balance an applicant's positive and negative impressions of the job and the company. Realistic job previews have been found to lead to higher satisfaction and better met expectations on the part of applicants who continue onward in the recruitment process.

An organization's demands, including its strategy, culture, and financial resources, all affect what the firm does and how it does it during the recruitment process. Environmental influences such as technology, globalization, and the labor market also need to be considered when a company is designing a recruitment strategy. Host country nationals and global search firms are used in addition to the Internet for global recruiting, but it is important to remember that applicants in developing countries often do not have access to the Internet, so firms recruiting there have to use other strategies.

A firm should ensure that its recruitment advertisements and other recruitment activities communicate to potential applicants that the company values diversity and supports equal employment opportunity.

KEY TERMS

contingency recruiting agency p. 158

cost-per-hire p. 165

employee inventory p. 153

employer branding p. 162

executive search firm p. 158

external recruiting p. 154

headhunter p. 158

internal recruiting p. 152

internship p. 158

DISCUSSION QUESTIONS

1. Jackson Electric installs electrical systems in residential and commercial buildings. The company was started by three brothers four years ago and now has 12 employees. The owners want to expand the company and eventually have locations in several cities around the state. Discuss the role recruitment will play in this growth strategy. What recommendations would you make to the owners about developing a recruitment strategy?

2. Describe the role job analysis plays relative to recruitment.

3. Identify several ways organizations can reduce the negative impact on current employees of adopting an external recruiting strategy.

4. Find a copy of a Sunday newspaper and review the advertisement for a job of interest to you. Critique the ad based on the criteria discussed in this chapter.

5. Discuss the role a recruiter plays in terms of communicating a company's recruitment value proposition.

6. Your company has just undergone a great deal of growth. You have been assigned to chair a task force to identify lessons learned during the recruitment process to staff for this growth. What metrics would you recommend to use and why?

7. A small real estate company on the coast of North Carolina and a large financial institution in Charlotte, North Carolina, are both looking for employees. Describe the organizational demands of each type of company and how they would affect the recruiting decisions of each.

8. The demographics in the neighborhood around the bank you manage have changed greatly in the past five years. Instead of a primarily Caucasian and African-American population, there are now large numbers of Hispanics and Asians. How are these demographic changes likely to affect your recruiting message and why?

LEARNING EXERCISE 1

Choose two companies in different industries that have career information posted on their Web sites. Spend time reviewing the information provided about the careers at these companies and then prepare a critical evaluation of the type of information included. Consider the following questions as you prepare your review of the two companies.

1. How much detail is provided? Do the companies simply list their available openings, or do they provide an overview of what it is like to work at the company? What information is not included that you wish was included?

2. What are the processes for applying for jobs at the two companies?

3. Did you leave the Web sites feeling like you had a good understanding of what it would be like to work for the companies?

4. What do the sites do particularly well? What could they do better? How easy were the sites to navigate?

5. If you were interested in working in these two industries, how likely would you be to apply for jobs with these companies, given your experience with their career Web sites?

6. As a manager, what recommendations would you make to improve the quality of the sites and why?

LEARNING EXERCISE 2

Find a job description for a job of interest to you or write a job description for a job that you have had in the past or have now and prepare a recruitment message and a recruitment plan.

1. Write the advertisement.

2. Where would you place the ad and why?

3. What aspect of the ad do you think is most important? Discuss your decision.

4. Show the advertisement to at least two other people and ask them to give you feedback to improve the ad. Describe their comments and ideas and whether you agree with them.

5. If you were a manager preparing to recruit for this position, what information other than the job description would you use to decide what to include in the ad?

CASE STUDY # 1 — THE RECRUITING GAME AT L'ORÉAL

What does playing games have to do with getting a job at L'Oréal? Everything. Gropu L'Oréal has designed a number of different games for the purpose of recruiting marketing students. The company believes that this approach to recruiting gives it an edge in fast-growing and emerging markets. Students play the games online. A computer tracks students' decisions and awards points to them as they work to increase the market value of a simulated company. Winners of local contests travel to Paris to participate in the finals competition. Winners receive job offers from L'Oréal executives who have seen how they perform under pressure. Participants come from all over the world, from countries as diverse as Indonesia and Brazil.

The games are e-Strat, a business simulation; Brandstorm, a game for turning ideas into products; and Ingenius, an industrial strategy game. The most popular of the three games is e-Strat. In this simulation, students make decisions about retail strategy and spending on R&D. The games attract more than 50,000 students per year, and the company has provided scholarships and endowed chairs to about 200 universities worldwide. Undoubtedly, the biggest winner in the competition is L'Oréal because of the publicity the games provide to the company and the opportunity to hire top marketing students worldwide.

DISCUSSION QUESTIONS

1. Visit L'Oréal's Web site (www.loreal.com) and review the information about each of the games.

2. Critique the use of these games as a recruiting strategy. What are the advantages and disadvantages? Are there any ethical problems with this approach? Any EEO issues? Besides the opportunity to get a job with the company, why do you think the games have worldwide appeal?

3. Discuss whether you would participate in an activity such as this approach in order to get a job with a company.

Sources: Adapted from Matlack, C. Case study: For L'Oréal, recruiting is all a big game. *BusinessWeek*, January 17, 2008; and L'Oréal Web site, www.loreal.com.

CASE STUDY # 2 — ENRON: A NOT SO HAPPY ENDING TO A GOOD RECRUITING PLAN

Enron Corporation was launched in 1985, with the merger of Houston Natural Gas and InterNorth, a Nebraska company. In 1990, Enron—which was just a natural gas transportation company at the time—started a new division to trade natural gas. The company went from being a "stodgy" gas pipeline company to being a "world-class" company overnight. Enron soon became a $55 billion empire, trading gas, electricity, minerals, water, paper, and broadband capacity.

A critical part of Enron's success was the company's employee value proposition (EVP). The EVP focused on Enron as a dealmaker and was designed to attract the top talent the company needed to continue to move it forward. The EVP provided employees with the opportunity to do something "big" and to change how business was done in other industries. Jobs were restructured to give employees a lot of elbow room and headroom. Traditional gas pipeline employees were not the employees needed for this new, never-before-tried venture.

Internal job movements at Enron were an important part of the EVP. Managers were strongly encouraged to allow employees to move within the company. The goal was to not hold anyone back. When the Global Broadband unit was launched, 100 top performers from around the company were brought together in Houston. By the end of the day, 50 had been recruited for the new project. Overall, the recruiting strategy focusing on internal recruitment paid off. The business continued to grow and attract entrepreneurial employees.

The company that thought it had no way to go but up came crashing down in 2001, when it was charged with illegal activities. By 2004, Enron's corporate officers faced numerous charges of wrongdoing, and the company was a shell of its former self. Managers were charged with manufacturing profits, hiding debt, and bullying Wall Street to buy into its questionable accounting and investment practices. An extensive amount of downsizing had occurred, and many employees had lost all of their retirement savings after Enron's stock collapsed. Faced with bankruptcy and a sullied reputation, the company struggled to continue but finally made the decision to cease to exist once all litigation concludes.

At one time, Enron's recruiting efforts were described as a model for other employers. Enron portrayed itself as an exciting company with lots of growth opportunity—a firm in which employees experienced a great deal of autonomy and responsibility.

DISCUSSION QUESTIONS

1. Enron did a lot of things right from a recruiting standpoint. Discuss its recruiting strategy and why it worked.

2. Do you think that Enron's overall recruitment EVP and strategy played any role in the problems that resulted at Enron? If so, what and how?

3. Discuss why it's important to create a recruiting message that's attractive but that doesn't "oversell" the company.

4. Assume that in a few years Enron decides to reconstitute itself in some form. Develop a recruiting strategy that the company could use to attract employees.

Sources: Based on Michaels, E., Handfield-Jones, H., & Axelrod, B. *The war for talent.* Boston: Harvard Business School Press, 2001; Swartz, M., & Watkins, S. *Power failure: The inside story of the collapse of Enron.* New York: Doubleday, 2003; and Enron Web site, www.enron.com.

APPENDIX
Metrics Used to Evaluate an Organization's Recruiting Effectiveness

Companies frequently engage in activities without stopping to evaluate what is working and why or how the activities can be improved. Recruitment is one such activity. Companies often continue to advertise jobs in the same publications year after year, without evaluating the usefulness of doing so. Recruiters are tasked with identifying and attracting one of the most precious resources the company will ever have. Yet often recruiters are held accountable for the number of employees they bring in to the organization—not the quality of those employees.

Exhibit A6.1 provides examples of some of the metrics used to measure a firm's recruitment success. We will take a look at the metrics that companies typically track, including yield ratios, cost-per-hire, time-to-fill, and managers' feedback.

YIELD RATIOS

We have already talked about some of the costs associated with various recruiting sources. Because these costs are so varied, evaluating the outcomes of each in terms of new hires

- **Cost-per-hire:** Total recruiting costs—advertising, travel, office rent, equipment, staff salaries, search-firm fees, background checks and more—divided by the number of new hires. This metric gauges a firm's recruiting expenses but does not measure the quality of the firm's hires.

- **Staffing efficiency ratio (recruiting efficiency index):** The firm's total recruiting costs divided by the total starting compensation of its new hires. This metric is more precise than cost-per-hire because it accounts for the different pay levels of new employees. It costs more to hire executives than to hire line workers, for example, and there are variations between industries and regions. The metric does not measure quality of the firm's hires.

- **Time-to-fill (time-to-acceptance):** The average number of days from the day a manager requests a job be filled to the day a candidate accepts an offer. This yardstick measures how quickly jobs are filled but does not include other considerations, such as the type of position, the state of the labor market, and the hiring manager's schedule.

- **Time-to-start:** The average number of days from the day a job is requisitioned to the day a new employee starts the job. Some staffing experts prefer this metric to time-to-fill because most hiring managers care more about when new employees start working than when they accept offers.

- **Hiring manager satisfaction:** The hiring manager's satisfaction with the performance of the firm's recruiters and his or her new employees. Managers can be asked to complete a survey that uses a ratings scale to measure a recruiter's timeliness of contacts, sourcing, quality of referred candidates, scheduling, and other factors. A new employee's performance can be assessed three, six, or more months after the person starts the job.

- **Turnover:** The number of employees who leave a firm divided by the firm's total number of employees. This metric, which is a rough indicator of the quality of a firm's hires, can be gauged for each recruiter. Some employers measure the flip side of turnover. In other words, they measure employee retention.

◄ **Exhibit A6.1**
Commonly Used Recruiting Metrics

Source: Adapted form Hirschman, C. Incentives for recruiters? *HRMagazine*, November 2003, www.shrm.org/hrmagazine/articles/1103/1103hirschman_metrics.asp.

made per source and retention per source provides valuable information to the company. Just because a recruitment source is cheap or expensive doesn't mean that it is effective. **Yield ratios** provide a metric of the effectiveness of different recruitment sources. A yield ratio measures the outcome from using a specific recruiting source compared to the number of applicants generated by the source. An example of how yield ratios are computed is shown in Exhibit A6.2.

Based on the yield ratios shown in the last line of Exhibit A6.2, the online job posting was the better source of applicants who met the requirements to be interviewed. Yield ratios should be calculated at each step of the hiring process and over time to evaluate which recruiting source leads to the hiring of employees who are retained longer and perform better in the organization. Yield ratios tell that story.

COST-PER-HIRE

Calculating the **cost-per-hire** involves first identifying all the factors that affect a firm's cost-per-hire. Exhibit A6.3 shows examples of some of the costs related to just the recruitment part of hiring a new employee. Both direct and indirect costs have to be considered. By comparing the costs of different sources and then comparing that information to the yield ratios for the sources, you can make an informed decision about where the firm should best spend its limited recruiting dollars.

TIME-TO-FILL RATE

The **time-to-fill rate** is a measure of the length of time it takes from the time a job opening is announced until someone begins work in the job. A few years ago, DuPont's global staffing department had an average time-to-fill rate of 90 days. The department decided that was too long and reduced the time to 60 days. To reduce the rate, the staffing employees had to first sit down and look at what they were doing and what could be done differently. They came up with a process whereby they first talk with the hiring manager about who will be involved in the hiring and selection process, designing a strategy for that particular job, and determining who will do what. They also include a time for the interviewers to provide their reactions to the candidates and the process. By determining the weak points in the process, they were able to develop a more effective and efficient recruiting plan that supported DuPont's goals.[72] The importance of time-to-fill rate for recruitment is considerable in many cases. Taking a long time to fill a position can result in increased stress and diminished productivity for employees who have to make up for the staff shortage.

MANAGER FEEDBACK

A firm's cost-per-hire and time-to-fill rate are important. However, they tell only part of the story; they don't measure the quality of the people the firm hires. To obtain this information, you need to gather ongoing feedback from the people who manage and work with the new hires.[73] If outdated job descriptions are being used in the hiring process, applicants might be hired quickly and at a low cost but then not succeed on the job. As a manager, you should work with your recruiting staff so they can decide what to continue to do or what to do differently. If you function as the recruiting staff, it is just as important to try to gauge the quality of your firm's new employees hired and what you can do to improve on that quality, if need be.

Exhibit A6.2 ▶
Yield Ratios for the Job of Systems Engineer

Job Title: Systems Engineer		
Recruitment Sources:		**Online at Company**
	Trade Journal	**Web Site**
Resumes Received	150	255
Applicants Selected for Interviews	35	69
Yield Ratio	35/150 = 23%	89/255 = 35%

Exhibit A6.3 ▶
Components of Recruitment Costs

The following are examples of the types of costs that must be considered when computing cost-per-hire:

- Advertising costs (printing materials, posting, etc.)
- Agency fees (if applicable)
- Employee referral bonuses
- Recruiters' salaries
- Recruiters' assistants' salaries
- Cost of operations not included in above (overhead)
- Travel for recruiters and/or applicants

BENCHMARKING BEST PRACTICES

Companies use benchmarking as another way to evaluate their recruitment practices. Benchmarking involves identifying the strategies used by other organizations in your industry that are similar in size and location. Why do you think that benchmarking recruitment practices are necessary to achieve a competitive advantage? It is important to know what your competition is doing so you can match and exceed it. In a tight labor market, companies that benchmark against their competitors are more likely to be able to hire an ample number of qualified employees because they are leaders in their industry. Often industry or professional associations publish their best practices.

Of course, benchmarking should be done with caution because each company has its own unique organizational demands and environmental influences. As a result, not every company will engage in the same recruitment activities, nor should they.

7

SELECTION

1. Describe how employee selection affects the performance of firms. *(184)*

2. Discuss the meaning and importance of person–job fit. *(186)*

3. Identify the standards managers must adhere to for an employee selection process to be effective. *(187)*

4. Explain the various types of employee selection methods managers can use. *(190)*

5. Understand how managers make final employee selection decisions. *(192)*

6. Understand how organizational demands affect the employee selection process. *(204)*

7. Incorporate environmental demand factors into the employee selection process. *(209)*

8. Ensure that a firm's employee selection process is legally compliant. *(213)*

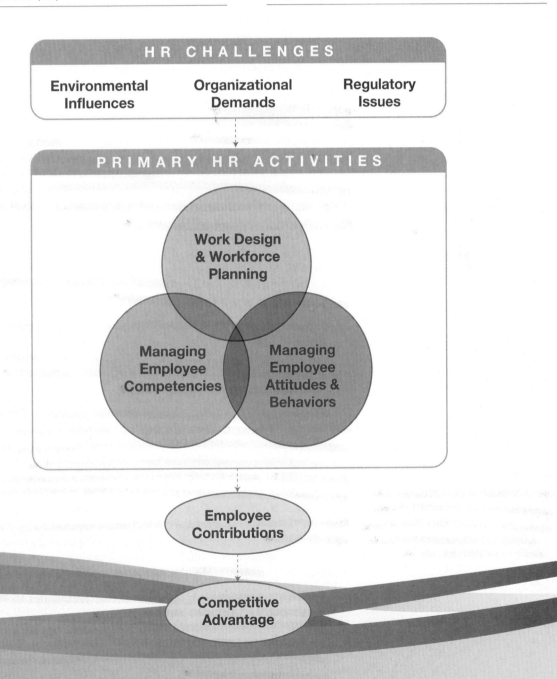

HR CHALLENGES

Environmental Influences **Organizational Demands** **Regulatory Issues**

PRIMARY HR ACTIVITIES

Work Design & Workforce Planning

Managing Employee Competencies

Managing Employee Attitudes & Behaviors

Employee Contributions

Competitive Advantage

EMPLOYEE SELECTION AND THE PERFORMANCE OF FIRMS

If you have ever had a job, think about the process your manager used to hire you. Did you have to fill out an application? Take a test? Answer questions in an interview? Do you know how the company decided that you were the right person for the job?

If you are a manager in any type of organization—public, private, for-profit or non-profit, you will play a role in selecting people for jobs. Many companies have HR departments to assist with this process, but the ultimate responsibility for selection rests with you, the hiring manager. In fact, in most companies, managers conduct the final interviews and make the final hiring decisions. Managers are the ones who work with the employees on a daily basis, so they have a vested interest in making sure they hire the right ones.

By now you know that job design dictates the tasks, duties, and responsibilities of a job, which then become the focus of the recruitment process. In this chapter we look at the next step: selection. We discuss the relationship between a firm's selection process and its performance, emphasize the importance of person–job fit, identify the standards for an effective selection process, and describe the methods used to assess applicant fit. We wrap up our discussion by describing how HR challenges affect the decisions you, as a manager, will make when you're setting up a selection process and hiring employees.

Selection Defined

Remember that the *competencies* referred to in Exhibit 7.1 are the knowledge, skills, abilities—or KSAs—and other talents employees need to perform their jobs effectively and efficiently.

In Chapter 6 we focused on the recruitment component of managing competencies and emphasized the need to generate the best pool of qualified applicants for the organization. Once you have that pool, you need to decide which applicants to keep for further consideration, and, ultimately, which ones to hire. This process is not always easy. For starters, some companies receive thousands of applications per month. Southwest Airlines, for example, receives about 180 job applications from potential employees each day, and that number was even higher when the company was featured in a reality TV series in 2004.[1]

As mentioned in Chapter 1, during the selection process, managers need to consider a number of key questions, such as the following:

- How do you generate the information you need to make an effective, and legal, hiring decision?
- Which tests are most effective for identifying employees with high potential?
- What questions should you ask candidates during an interview?
- Who makes the ultimate hiring decision?

selection

The systematic process of deciding which applicants to hire.

prediction

Making a determination about how likely it is that candidates selected will be successful in the job based on their current ability to do the job or the potential that they will be able to learn the job and do it well.

Selection is the systematic process of deciding which applicants to hire. The primary decisions are: (1) which applicants should be hired as new employees? (2) which employees should be promoted to higher-level jobs? and (3) which employees should be moved to other jobs within the company that don't involve a promotion? At a basic level, selection is about **prediction**. When a manager selects an applicant for a job, she is predicting that the applicant either can already do the job or will be able to learn the job and will do it well. People think about selection most often in terms of hiring new employees, but managers also have the option to move current employees into vacant positions—a process called *internal selection*. As we discussed in Chapter 5, companies may use promotions, transfers, or demotions to move individuals to different areas within a company. The following activities are typically part of the selection process for both new hires and internal transitions:

1. Review applications and resumes to determine which applicants best match the requirements of the job and the organization.
2. Identify and implement appropriate methods to assess the degree of fit among the job requirements, the qualifications of the applicants, and the organizational culture.
3. Make a final decision about which applicant is the most qualified for the particular job and should be offered the job.

We will discuss these concepts throughout the rest of this chapter.

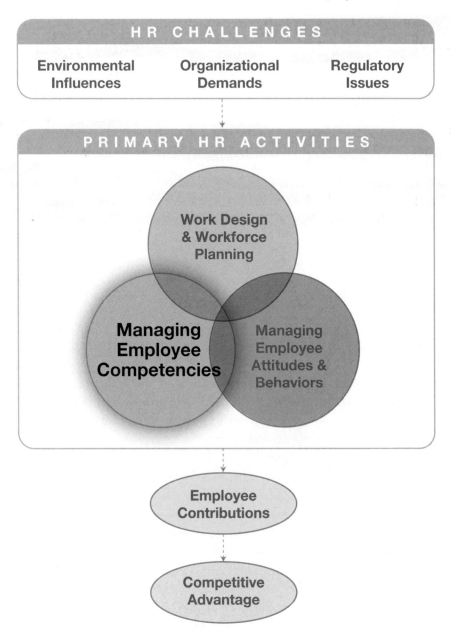

How Employee Selection Processes Affect the Performance of Firms

Employees who are not a good fit with the jobs for which they are hired and the organizations that hire them tend to leave their firms. The cost to replace such a worker can equal an employee's annual salary plus benefits and perhaps more, depending on the industry in which the employee works.[2] But these costs are just one reason managers need to make good hiring decisions.

A second, and potentially more damaging, situation can occur when bad selection decisions don't end with turnover. If employees are not qualified to do their jobs, a company is likely to make more mistakes, experience higher production costs, and experience lower employee morale. Ultimately, the company might lose customers and money. Conversely, if a company selects the right employees, it is more likely to gain customers, have happier employees, and make more money. In short, a company realizes many benefits by hiring the right person for a job and incurs many costs by hiring the wrong person.

PERSON–JOB FIT

person–job fit

The extent to which there is a good match between the characteristics of the potential employee, such as knowledge, skills, values, and the requirements of the job.

In terms of the selection process, you need to understand why **person–job fit** is crucial. Have you ever had to do something that was really difficult? Or something that just wasn't interesting? Would you want to do those tasks every day for 40 plus hours per week? Each of us has different abilities and interests, and it is unlikely that all potential employees would enjoy the tasks required for all jobs or possess the abilities to succeed in all jobs. Employees who believe there is a good match between their own KSAs and interests and the requirements of their jobs are going to be more satisfied with their positions.[3] And, as you know and research has shown, satisfied employees tend to be more productive.[4] A strong person–job fit maximizes the benefits for both employees and the organizations for which they work. In contrast, companies can expect to face higher turnover and absenteeism, along with lower employee morale and productivity, when there is a poor person–job fit.

Company Spotlight 7.1 describes a unique situation in which person–job fit is especially critical. Most employment situations aren't quite as dramatic as working in Antarctica. Nonetheless, making good selection decisions is important, regardless of the location or type of job.

COMPANY spotlight 7.1 Raytheon Polar Services Co.: Hiring for "The Ice"

Winter arrives in Antarctica in February and lasts through August. During an Antarctic winter, it's dark outside 24 hours per day, and temperatures range from 40°F to 100°F below zero. In fact, the mean annual temperature at the South Pole is −56°F. Once winter sets in, people on the continent employed by Raytheon Polar Services Co. (RPSC) know they won't be going anywhere until August, when weather conditions are good enough for planes to once again land. RPSC exists specifically to meet the needs of the National Science Foundation (NSF) Office of Polar Programs. The main function of RPSC is to provide support to the U.S. Antarctic Program.

Given the harsh conditions in Antarctica, you might think that it would be difficult for RSCP to find employees willing to move there. In reality, it's not: A lot of people are attracted to the challenges associated with living on the continent; doctors apply for janitorial jobs, and lawyers apply for kitchen jobs just to experience it. However, many of these people find out that they can't handle the challenges and quickly want to leave.

RPSC's employee selection process is extremely stringent. It has to be to increase the likelihood that the people the company hires can actually endure the harsh conditions. Applicants have to be U.S. citizens or permanent residents with valid passports. They must also pass stringent dental and medical examinations. Also, early on in the hiring process, applicants are sent an extensive printed guide that serves as a realistic job preview (RJP). The publication spells out very clearly that working in Antarctica is no picnic. The guide emphasizes that employees at RPSC's four locations, or stations, are hired to support science, maintain the

stations, and ensure the well-being of the personnel assigned there. Employees are expected to work long hours six to seven days per week and as hard as necessary to get the job done. Family members are not allowed to visit during any part of the employment period.

A candidate who is willing to "winter over" on "The Ice" has to pass a background check, followed by a psychological assessment that includes the Minnesota Multiphasic Personality Inventory (MMPI-II) and the 16PF Questionnaire. A personal interview and drug and alcohol screenings are also part of the selection process. Individuals who want to work at RPSC's South Pole Station undergo additional assessments before they're hired. They also take a team-building course in the mountains near Denver, Colorado, before being sent to the South Pole.

Despite the harsh conditions in Antarctica and RPSC's intensive employee selection process, the rehire rate of employees who complete a season on the continent and then sign up for another is around 60%. That percentage suggests that the selection process RPSC uses is quite effective. The right people are chosen, and the experience "hooks" them. Think you have what it takes to work in Antarctica? Check out http://rpsc.raytheon.com and click on "Employment" for information on how to apply for a job.

Sources: Based on Pomeroy, A. HR on "The Ice." *HR Magazine* 49:96–103, June 2004; U.S. Antarctic Program Web site, www.usap.gov; and Raytheon. *Polar services,* www.rayjobs.com/index.cfm?NavID=21&ANTARCTICA_JOBS

The 2007–2008 South Pole Traverse team at Amundsen-Scott South Pole Station.

STANDARDS FOR AN EFFECTIVE SELECTION PROCESS

A number of standards must be met for the selection process to accomplish its goals. At a minimum, all steps need to be *reliable, valid,* and *unbiased.* On the surface, these standards might seem easy to understand and follow. In fact, they are quite complex. Selection is about measuring the degree to which each applicant possesses the competencies required to do a job. The precision of the measurement at each step will largely determine the success of the process.

The measurements would be relatively easy if we had something equivalent to a tape measure to gauge the competencies of one applicant versus another. Unfortunately, there is no instrument that measures all of a job applicant's traits and skills with complete accuracy. There are, however, tools that can help a manager predict the future job success of candidates. Before deciding which predictor to use, you have to first understand how consistent the method of prediction is, meaning the *reliability* of the method and how well it serves as a predictor of job success, which refers to the *validity* of the method. The effectiveness of any selection tool is a function of reliability and validity.

Reliability

Reliability is how well a selection measure yields consistent results over time or across raters. The key word here is *consistent.* We all want a reliable car to drive; just ask anyone who has had to call a tow truck on a rainy day. We want to be able to count on the car performing the same way each time we use it. We need reliable selection measures just like we need reliable transportation.

Several types of reliability are important for selection. First, selection procedures need to be reliable *over time.* If an applicant takes a test today and then retakes it a week from now, we expect the scores to be similar. This correlation between the scores means there is *test–retest reliability.* If the applicant studied the subject matter between the two test administrations, or if the applicant remembered how he or she responded the first time and responded the same way the second time, the test scores will not be reliable. They won't give you a picture of the true capabilities of the person. Exhibit 7.2 shows the results of a test–retest conducted to determine the reliability of a particular selection measure. A high correlation (indicated by the *r* value) between two test administrations indicates that the test is reliable.

Second, selection procedures need to be reliable *across raters.* If three people interview an applicant for a job and are using the same questions and the same scoring mechanism, they should evaluate the interviewee in a similar manner. If they do so, we would have *high inter-rater reliability.* Discrepancies among interviewer scores occur when interviewers have different expectations about how the questions should be answered or what the questions mean.

As a manager, you need to know a test's reliability before choosing it if you are purchasing a test. If you are developing your own test (and keep in mind that even the interviews you conduct with candidates are a type of selection "test"), you need to make sure the test is reliable. The appendix to this chapter provides additional information about the reliability and validity of different selection methods.

reliability

The extent to which a selection measure yields consistent results over time or across raters.

Exhibit 7.2 ▶

Test–Retest Reliability

Applicant	Test Score	Retest Score
James	70	75
Carlos	95	96
Juanita	83	86
Maria	75	78
Caitlin	77	75
Mehdi	90	92
Jun	88	86
Aaron	91	91
Camille	86	83
Dexter	70	73
Brandon	98	96
	$r = .97$	

Validity

validity

The extent to which a selection method measures what it is supposed to measure and how well it does so.

Reliability alone does not ensure that a selection method is going to predict success on the job. Selection methods must also be valid. **Validity** is the extent to which a selection method measures what it is supposed to measure and how well it does so.[5] A personality test should measure personality. An accounting test should measure accounting knowledge and skill. When we talk about validity, we are really focusing on how much evidence there is to support the conclusions that are made based on the scores of the selection measures.[6] Simply stated, we are investigating the job-relatedness of the selection measure.

As an example, a company might have developed a selection test for customer service skills that gives consistent results over time. However, if the test doesn't correlate with any other established measures of customer service skills, such as the performance of good customer service representatives, it will be reliable, but it won't be valid. Why, then, would the company want to use the test to select its employees? As you might imagine, consistently measuring the wrong KSAs instead of those actually needed to do a job would not result in good hiring decisions. Exhibit 7.3 summarizes the criteria for a selection method to be considered both reliable and valid. Selection is an art rather than a science, though. Consequently, we have to recognize that there will always be less than perfect measures in the selection process. However, that does not change the need to be as precise as possible.

Exhibit 7.3 ▶

What Makes a
Good Test?

An employment test is considered "good" if the following can be said about it:

- The test measures what it claims to measure consistently or reliably. This means that if a person were to take the test again, the person would get a similar test score.

- The test measures what it claims to measure. For example, a test of mental ability should, in fact, measure a person's mental ability and not another characteristic.

- The test is job relevant. In other words, the test measures one or more characteristics that a person needs to be able to do the job.

- By using the test, more effective employment decisions can be made about individuals. For example, an arithmetic test should help you select qualified workers for a job that requires knowledge of math.

The degree to which a test has these qualities is indicated by two technical properties: *reliability* and *validity*.

Source: U.S. Department of Labor. *Testing and assessment: An employer's guide to good practices.* Washington, DC: U.S. Department of Labor, Employment and Training Administration, 2000, p. 3–2.

Unbiased

In addition to being reliable and valid, selection measures also need to be unbiased. Unfortunately, bias often creeps in and compromises the fairness of the selection process. *Bias* occurs when one's personal views are allowed to affect the outcome of the decision-making process rather than the decision being based on the results of the selection measures. Measurement bias can occur, also, but that discussion is beyond the scope of this book.

Consider the following situation: A company decides to use a written test, a work sample, and an interview to find the best candidate for a position. A particular candidate performs poorly on the written test and work sample, but the interviewer really likes the applicant and wants to hire him, despite his poor test scores. In this case, bias has entered into the process: some factor other than the actual outcome of the selection process has affected the decision. We next discuss four common types of bias: (1) the influence of personal characteristics, (2) the contrast effect, (3) the halo/devil's horns effect, and (4) impression management.

CANDIDATES' PERSONAL CHARACTERISTICS   A person's attractiveness, age, and gender are examples of personal characteristics that can affect employee selection decisions due to the preferences of interviewers, stereotypes, and poorly designed selection processes. As we discussed in Chapter 3, disparate treatment results when a selection decision is based on a personal characteristic that is also a protected classification, such as age. Disparate impact occurs if the personal characteristic used to select employees leads to a lower percentage of a protected class being hired because they are less likely to have that characteristic.

CONTRAST EFFECT   The contrast effect happens when an evaluation of one or more job applicants is artificially inflated or deflated compared to another job applicant. For example, suppose a manager has four candidates to interview for a job opening, and the first candidate is really impressive. Despite the fact that the candidate doesn't meet the test for previous work experience, one of the main requirements of the job, she rates very highly on all the other requirements. If the manager judges the remaining candidates based on the first candidate, causing the others to appear less than stellar by comparison, the contrast effect has occurred. The contrast effect could also occur if the first candidate did poorly, causing the other candidates to appear more qualified than they really are.

> **contrast effect**
>
> Bias that results when an evaluation of one or more job applicants is artificially inflated or deflated compared to the evaluation of another person.

HALO/DEVIL'S HORNS EFFECT   A halo effect or devil's horns effect occurs when a positive or negative characteristic of a job candidate affects the evaluation of the candidate's other attributes. Based on the job description, you decide that applicants for a sales position need to be able to (1) make sales presentations, (2) work as part of a sales team, and (3) maintain accurate, detailed records of sales calls. Using interview questions and role playing, you assess the ability of the applicants to meet each criterion based on a scale of 1 to 5 (5 = excellent). Candidate A really wows you with his sales presentation, and you score him 5 on this criterion. He doesn't do as well on the other two criteria, but you rate him high anyway, choosing to ignore the negative results because of his dynamic presentation. By overlooking possible problems because the applicant is so strong in one area of interest, you are demonstrating the halo effect. Likewise, the devil's horns effect would occur if Candidate A performed really well on the other two parts of the assessment, but you rated him low on all three parts because of his poor sales presentation.

> **halo effect (also halo error)**
>
> The bias that occurs when a positive characteristic of a person affects the evaluation of the person's other attributes.

> **devil's horns effect**
>
> The bias that occurs when a negative characteristic of a job candidate affects the evaluation of the candidate's other attributes.

IMPRESSION MANAGEMENT   The final type of bias that we will discuss is impression management, which occurs when a job applicant engages in actions to present himself or herself in a positive light to the interviewer. Self-promotion, ingratiation, and opinion conformity are typical types of behaviors.[7] If an applicant who is good at impression management thinks the employer is looking for someone who is industrious and hard working, he will try to portray himself as industrious and hard-working during the selection process even if he is not.[8] By *impressing* those doing the hiring, the applicant is likely to get the job, regardless of whether he is really qualified.

> **impression management**
>
> The actions, such as ingratiation, self-promotion, and opinion conformity, used by applicants to present themselves in a positive light to the interviewer with the idea of biasing the outcome of the interview in their favor.

initial screening

The preliminary review of the information provided by job applicants and the collection of additional information to decide which applicants should be given more serious consideration for the job.

final screening

The in-depth look at the applicants who have made it through the initial screening prior to hiring by using techniques such as reviewing references, performing background checks, and conducting additional interviews.

SELECTION METHODS: INITIAL SCREENING

Just what are the selection tools that can help a manager identify the most qualified applicant for a job? Selection methods can be grouped into two categories: initial screening methods and final screening methods. Initial screening involves reviewing the information provided by job applicants and collecting additional preliminary information to decide which applicants are worthy of more serious consideration for the job. Final screening involves taking a more in-depth look at the applicants who make it through the initial screening prior to hiring them, including reviewing references and conducting background checks. In addition to the information we discuss, the U.S. Department of Labor's Employment and Training Administration posts a free online guide, *Testing and Assessment: An Employer's Guide to Good Practices* (www.onetcenter.org/dl_files/empTestAsse.pdf), to help managers and HR professionals with their selection practices.

There are several selection methods managers can use for initial screening to narrow the pool of job applicants to a manageable number of qualified candidates. Recall from Chapter 6 that a company that does a good job of recruiting will have an applicant pool that includes a number of highly qualified applicants. The applicant pool is still likely to have some less qualified applicants as well, though. Many people are not very good at self-selection and apply for jobs for which they are not qualified. Testing and interviewing everyone who applies for a job is simply not cost-effective or practical for an employer; therefore, managers use methods such as collecting and reviewing *applications* and *resumes* and administering *screening interviews* to make the first cut in the applicant pool. As you read about these methods, think about how you would ensure that each is reliable and valid and how you would keep biases from affecting the outcome.

Applications and Resumes

If you have ever applied for a job, you probably completed an application or submitted a resume (or both), which gave the employer a first impression of you. Applications and resumes serve similar—but different—purposes.

Applications are standardized forms employers use to collect job-related information about applicants. The information is reviewed and used to determine which applicants meet the minimum job requirements and should remain in the selection process. Typically, application forms inquire about a person's eligibility to work in the United States, the person's education, current and previous work experience, skills, hours available to work, and references. Exhibit 7.4 provides guidelines managers can use to prepare application questions.

Some companies weight application questions and score the responses to arrive at an overall score. By using weightings, managers are able to highlight which questions are more important than others in the selection decision. Having a score for each applicant makes it easier to compare applicants to determine who is most qualified for the job. This type of application is referred to as a *weighted application blank (WAB)*. A WAB helps ensure that the review of the application is objective, and it provides a more objective way to initially compare applicants' qualifications.[9]

A job applicant usually provides a *resume* to prospective employers, regardless of the level of the job. A *resume* is an overview of the applicant's qualifications and typically includes contact information and information on education, previous work experience, and special skills and interests. Resumes are usually shorter for less experienced individuals than for people who have a lot of experience. However, even more experienced workers are encouraged to limit their resumes to one to two pages because recruiters have only limited amounts of time to review resumes.

A resume used in lieu of an application is still considered an application for EEO purposes. If an applicant provides personal information, such as age or marital status, that information should not be used in the selection process.[10] Exhibit 7.5 provides some tips for screening resumes. Note the focus on looking for job-related information. Also, it is important not to read more into the document than what is actually there.

- Keep all questions job related.

- Ask questions about the relevant past work experience, skills and abilities, education obtained, and goals and interests of applicants.

- Don't ask personal questions or any other questions that could imply that personal characteristics unrelated to the job will be used to make the employment decision.

Examples of questions not to ask:

1. Are you married/do you plan to marry?

2. Do you have any children/do you plan to have children?

3. How old are you/what year did you graduate from high school?

4. What is your religious affiliation?

5. Do you have a mental or physical disability?

6. How many sick days did you take last year?

7. Have you had any workers' compensation injuries?

Examples of questions you can ask:

1. This job requires travel 50% of the time. Can you fulfill this requirement?

2. This job requires lifting 35 pounds. Can you lift this much weight?

3. Do you have the legal right to work in the United States?

4. Do you have transportation available to come to work at the required times?

5. Can you meet this job's attendance requirements?

6. Did you have any problems in your last job/why did you leave your last job?

◄ **Exhibit 7.4**
Guidelines for
Application Questions

- Focus on identifying job-relevant training and/or experience. Degrees earned, previous jobs held, and recent experience provide some information about how well the applicant matches the job requirements.

- Visualize the applicant working in the job. Consider whether you can picture the person actually working in the job, based on the information provided.

- Assume nothing. Read only what is written, without conferring attributes on to the applicant. For example, being president of a student organization while in college doesn't automatically mean an applicant has leadership skill.

- Be aware of red flags. View vague information with caution.

- Disregard discriminatory information. Information such as number of children and marital status is sometimes included on a resume and is hard to ignore but can't be used in the decision-making process.

- Be open. The color of paper applicants choose to use for their resumes should not automatically disqualify them, for example.

◄ **Exhibit 7.5**
Tips for Screening
Resumes

Source: Adapted from Klinvex, K. C., O'Connell, M. S., & Klinvex, C. P. *Hiring great people*. New York: McGraw-Hill, 1999.

Employee interviews are used for initial and final screening.

Screening Interviews

Reviewing applications and resumes narrows down the list of applicants worthy of further consideration. A screening interview can then be used to gauge an applicant's fit and interest in the position. A typical *screening interview* consists of the manager or someone from HR calling the applicant and conducting a short telephone interview. The goal is to confirm that the person is still looking for a job and is interested in the position, as well as to verify the information the person has already provided to the firm. The screening interview also provides a clue about the person's oral communication skills, which can be useful information if those skills are essential for successful job performance.

SELECTION METHODS: FINAL SCREENING

A firm's final screening activities narrow down the number of job candidates to the number of employees the company actually needs. Many selection methods are available for this purpose, including various types of employment tests, interviews, and assessment centers. Reference and background checks are also used for screening. These methods are sometimes used for initial screening, but managers most often use them later in the selection process because they can be quite time-consuming and costly. It is better to reduce the applicant pool before using them.

Employment Tests

Employment tests generally can be categorized as *ability tests*, *achievement/competency tests*, or *personality inventories*. We describe these in the following sections.

ABILITY TESTS   Ability tests, sometimes called *aptitude tests*, measure basic talents, or abilities, of individuals.[11] In the context of staffing, they provide information about an individual's potential to perform the job. For example, Barclays Capital, an investment-banking unit of Barclays PLC, gives aptitude tests to graduate and undergraduate students in place of using first-round interviews to narrow the applicant pool. Students who are successful on these tests receive interviews, and the top performers receive $1,500 prizes. Barclays believes this process is more fair and objective than using an initial interview.[12] Cognitive ability and physical ability tests are common types of ability tests.

cognitive ability test

A test designed to measure general intelligence or level of specific aptitudes, such as numeric fluency and general reasoning.

Cognitive ability tests measure general intelligence or level of specific aptitudes, such as numeric fluency, general reasoning, verbal comprehension, mechanical reasoning, logical evaluation, and memory span. These tests are the best predictors of job performance across all types of jobs, and they are also among the lowest-cost selection methods. Their predictive value increases as the complexity of the job increases.[13] Education is often used as a replacement for cognitive ability tests to screen job applicants. Research has shown that an educational level equal to at least one year of college is related to higher cognitive ability levels among applicants.[14]

There is, however, a caveat related to using employment tests and cognitive ability tests, in particular: Minorities typically score lower than nonminorities, often because the terminology and concepts used on the tests are more familiar to nonminorities than to minorities.[15] Consequently, extreme caution must be exercised to ensure that tests are not used in a way that results in adverse impact. Using multiple selection methods can help offset the potential discrimination that would result from using these types of tests alone.[16]

Physical ability tests focus on physical attributes of job candidates, such as a candidate's endurance, strength, or general fitness. Firefighters need to be able to carry people out of burning buildings and firefighting equipment into buildings. A UPS driver needs to be able to lift a certain amount of weight to deliver boxes. Employers can administer a physical ability test to candidates in the course of the selection process prior to making a job offer, but only if there is a clear, job-related reason. Clearly, a fire department and a company such as UPS would have such job-related reasons. Keep in mind that the average female will perform differently from the average male on many physical ability tests, so beware of the potential for disparate impact.[17] (Again, think "job related.")

ACHIEVEMENT/COMPETENCY TESTS

Achievement tests, or competency tests, measure an applicant's current knowledge or skill level in relation to the job requirements.[18] Rather than focus on a candidate's potential, these tests examine the extent to which a job candidate can actually perform the job tasks. Someone without previous work experience or training related to the job requirements would not do well on these assessments.[19]

One of the best ways to determine whether someone can perform a job is to have the person actually perform some or all aspects of the job. Job applicants view this selection method quite favorably.[20] A **work sample** may be practical for some jobs but not for most. Having a candidate for a word processing job prepare documents using the software that will be used on the job is relatively inexpensive and straightforward. Work samples for lots of other jobs would have to be much more complex and would be expensive to develop and use. Consequently, work samples are used more often for skilled craft jobs such as carpenter,[21] computer programmer, food service worker, and so forth, rather than for professional jobs such as manager, attorney, and doctor.

Knowledge tests measure the extent to which an applicant has mastered the subject matter required to do the job. Does an accountant applicant have knowledge of accounting practices? Does a human resource applicant have knowledge of human resource practices? Licensure exams are examples of knowledge tests. These tests have high validity,[22] especially if they are tailored to the specific job rather than an "off-the-shelf" version.[23] Applicants generally perceive these tests positively.

PERSONALITY INVENTORIES

If you are hiring someone for a job that requires selling, you probably want someone who is assertive and maybe even extroverted. During the selection process you will need a way to assess whether applicants have these traits. When used as part of the selection process, *personality inventories* can identify the extent to which an applicant possesses certain characteristics, such as assertiveness, self-confidence, conscientiousness, motivation, and interpersonal attributes. These inventories are appropriate to use as long as there is a job-related reason. If a job requires working as part of a team, then it is appropriate—and, in fact, necessary—to predict how well the candidate will fit into a team setting. However, care must be given to define exactly what is meant by the term *fit*. The job analysis should help you to define this and then choose the appropriate personality inventory. Some job analysis techniques (discussed in Chapter 4), such as the Position Analysis Questionnaire (PAQ), actually identify appropriate worker personality dimensions; others, such as the task approach, provide information about required tasks that are useful for inferring that candidates have the appropriate personality dimensions.[24]

Of all the ways to measure personality in the context of selection, the one that has garnered the most attention is the Big Five approach. This approach suggests that all personality traits can be grouped under one of five dimensions: extroversion, agreeableness, conscientiousness, emotional stability, and openness to experience. These dimensions are defined in Exhibit 7.6. Of these dimensions, conscientiousness has been shown to be the most valid across all occupational groups. Emotional stability and extraversion are valid across some occupational groups, but not all.[25] For instance, in a study of the Big Five

physical ability test

A selection test that focuses on physical attributes of job candidates, such as a candidate's endurance, strength, or general fitness.

achievement test or competency test

A test to measure an applicant's current knowledge or skill level in relation to the job requirements.

work sample

A test in which the person actually performs some or all aspects of the job.

Exhibit 7.6 ▶

Examples of
Characteristics
Representative of
the Big Five
Personality Traits

- *Neuroticism*—lack of emotional stability evidenced by excessive or inappropriate anger, anxiousness, paranoia, or depression

- *Extraversion*—outgoing personality, positive, and sociable, active

- *Conscientiousness*—self-control, achievement oriented, dependable, orderly

- *Openness to experience*—philosophical and intellectual, unconventional, cooperative, and likable

- *Agreeableness*—cooperative, good-natured, gentle, and cheerful

Source: Adapted from Judge, T. A., Higgins, C. A., Thoresen, C. J., & Barrick, M. R. The Big Five personality traits, general mental ability, and career success across the life span. *Personnel Psychology* 52:621–652, 1999.

and sales performance, the researchers found that conscientiousness and openness predicted sales performance, but agreeableness had a negative relationship to sales performance, and extraversion and neuroticism were not related to sales performance.[26]

Two concerns have surfaced with the use of personality inventories (also referred to as *personality tests*). First, like physical impairments, mental impairments are covered under the ADA. A personality inventory that could lead to the identification of a mental impairment or disorder is considered a medical examination and is subject to ADA guidelines.[27] Remember that the ADA specifically prohibits the use of medical examinations until after a job offer has been made.

Personality tests that are designed to identify deviant and other extreme behaviors are inappropriate for all but a few types of jobs. These tests are appropriate for law enforcement jobs because hiring a deviant person for a law-enforcement position could be especially problematic. Another example of the appropriate use of personality inventories is provided by the case of Overnight Transportation of Atlanta, a motor freight company. This company reduced on-the-job delinquency behaviors such as drunkenness, fighting, and damage to vehicles by 50% to 100% by using the Hogan Personality Inventory. Savings were over $1 million each year; a single trucking accident can cost $100,000.[28]

The second concern relates to privacy rights. When the wording of questions on inventories lacks *face validity*—that is, it doesn't "appear" to measure job-related attributes—applicants perceive the tests to be an invasion of their privacy, regardless of how valid the inventories have been shown to be.[29] Overall, personality tests can be an important part of a selection process if the personality traits they evaluate are job related and if the tests are used in conjunction with other selection methods.

WHEN TO USE EMPLOYMENT TESTS   Even though most human resources professionals advocate identifying or developing job-related selection tests, we realize that not all organizations can afford to use such tests, at least not for every job. Here are five situations in which the cost of *not* testing is greater than the cost of using the tests—as long as they are reliable and valid. In short, you should use tests when:[30]

1. Your organization's current selection process does not result in the quality employees desired.
2. Turnover or absenteeism in your organization is high.
3. The current selection methods your firm uses do not meet professional and legal standards.
4. Productivity in your organization is low.
5. Errors made by your employees could have serious safety, health, or financial consequences.

Interviews

Interviews are the most frequently used selection method. Following our coverage of the main types of selection interviews, we discuss some of the most significant research regarding the use of interviews. Keep in mind that each type of interview can be used by individual interviewers or by a panel. Companies sometimes use **panel interviews**—several people interviewing the applicant at the same time—as a way to increase the reliability of the interview process.

UNSTRUCTURED INTERVIEWS A large percentage of selection interviews are unstructured interviews. The interviewer, often the hiring manager, will have a general idea of what a successful applicant should know and be able to do and will ask the candidate job-related questions, but without a defined format and without asking the same questions of all applicants. Some managers claim that they are good at judging character and that they need just a few minutes with an applicant in an interview to make a good decision. The reality is that many managers are not as good as they think they are at selecting employees. A more structured process will lead to a better hiring decision and will be more defensible should an applicant file a charge of discrimination because of the selection process.

STRUCTURED INTERVIEWS Starbucks provides its hiring managers with interview guidelines to ensure that each manager is equipped to select the best employees for jobs at Starbucks. These guidelines include a list of behaviors characteristic of the ideal candidate. These behaviors, in conjunction with job analysis information, help managers identify questions that will determine whether an applicant has the desired core job skills.[31] All applicants are then asked the same questions. This process, which is called a **structured interview**, ensures greater job-relatedness and also provides a more accurate means for comparing responses across applicants because the same type of information is collected from all interviewees. We will discuss two types of structured interviews—situational and behavioral. Properly designed situational and behavioral interviews, which include a rating scale, lead to better selection decisions.

Companies such as J. P. Morgan and General Electric use **situational interviews**. In this type of interview, an interviewer poses hypothetical situations to the interviewee and gauges the person's responses relative to how the individual would be expected to respond in a similar situation on the job. Situational interviews have been shown to be accurate in predicting performance as much as 54% of the time.[32] This type of interview has proven valid in numerous research studies.[33]

A situational interview for a trader on Wall Street might go something like this: What would you do if a client asked you to provide confidential information to her? The applicant would then describe how he would typically handle this situation. His answer would be compared to the rating scale and a score determined for the interview. The problem with situational interviews is that applicants may tell you what they think you want to hear rather than what they would actually do. Behavioral interviews provide a way to address this issue.

The premise of the **behavioral interview** is that past behavior is the best predictor of future behavior. Rather than simply asking a candidate how she *would* handle a situation, the interviewer asks the candidate how she *has* handled the situation in the past. For example, "Tell me about a time when you had to deal with an intoxicated passenger" would be a good question to ask an applicant for a flight attendant position. If the applicant has limited work experience, the interviewer could instead ask, "Tell me about a time when you had to deal with an extremely obnoxious person. Describe what led up to the event, your involvement in the situation, and how the incident was resolved." Follow-up questions further help the interviewer learn how an applicant has actually behaved in situations as opposed to how the applicant thinks he or she would behave in them.

Exhibit 7.7 provides an example of a rating scale for a behavioral interview that is designed to evaluate candidates applying for a marketing analyst position. The behaviors that represent high and low scores to each question are determined by doing a critical incident job analysis. Each interview question can be weighted relative to its importance to the job. The rating for each response is then multiplied by the weight of its associated question, and the results are summed to give an overall score for the applicant. This approach, which has proven to be very effective, ensures that the interview process is reliable and valid.[34]

Much of the research of the interviewing process has focused on interviewer and applicant characteristics and how they affect the outcomes of the interview process. Research has shown that pre-interview information can affect the outcome of an interview, nonverbal behaviors of applicants can affect interview outcomes, individuals good at self-promotion are

panel interview

A type of interview process in which several people interview an applicant at the same time.

unstructured interview

A general interview in which the interviewer has an idea of what a successful applicant should know and be able to do and uses that information to ask the candidate job-related questions but without a defined format and without asking the same questions of all applicants.

structured interview

An interview process that uses a set of predetermined questions related to the job and usually includes a scoring system to track and compare applicant responses.

situational interview

A type of interview in which applicants are asked to respond to a series of hypothetical situations to determine how they would respond in a similar situation on the job.

behavioral interview

An interview process based on the premise that past behavior is the best predictor of future behavior, therefore, having job candidates respond to questions about how they have handled job-related types of situations in the past will be the best predictor of their success at the job for which they are interviewing.

P R I N C I P L E S

Exhibit 7.7 ▶

An Example of a
Rating Scale for a
Behavioral Interview
for a Marketing
Analyst Position

Dimension: Preparing reports to meet client deadlines; using information gathered from primary and secondary sources.

Describe a time when you had a deadline to meet but realized you would not be able to meet it. What were the circumstances that led up to your realization? How did you handle the situation? What was the outcome? What would you do differently next time?

Rating Scale: Compare the applicant's answer to the following anchors. The score for the applicant is the number with the most similar response.

5—Describes situation in detail, including specifics about the incident itself, and about how it was resolved. Answer indicates applicant has a strong ability to prioritize projects and that the applicant is willing to admit when things don't go as smoothly as planned. Applicant has a clear plan for how to avoid the same situation again.

4—Describes situation in detail, including specifics about the incident, and its resolution. Answer indicates that applicant is willing to take responsibility when appropriate and understands the consequences of missing deadlines. Applicant described the basic elements of a plan for avoiding similar situations.

3—Describes situation in some detail. Answer indicates applicant realizes that missing the deadline was a problem and that a better plan of action is needed in the future. Applicant took responsibility for own role in missing the deadline.

2—Describes situation in some detail. Applicant took some responsibility for missing the deadline but primarily blamed it on other circumstances, even though description of situation suggested otherwise. Applicant did mention that perhaps better planning could have occurred.

1—Applicant had to be prompted to answer the question. Applicant gave numerous excuses for why deadline was not met, taking no responsibility for his/her role in the missed deadline even though it was obvious that poor planning had some impact on the outcome.

---

likely to get higher ratings, attractive applicants are rated more highly, and personality characteristics such as extraversion can positively impact interview outcomes.[35]

Reference Checks, Background Checks, Credit Reports, and Honesty Tests

The manager of staffing administration for Continental Airlines is involved in hiring more than 600 people on average each month for multiple locations worldwide. And before any of the applicants can be hired, somebody has to do a background check on each one of them. Continental worked with an employee screening vendor to come up with a plan to make the process as efficient as possible. Computer technology played a large role in the new plan. The vendor created a dashboard—an interactive display panel for summarizing information—and built-in databases so that screening procedures for different job codes could be easily followed.[36]

Employers use a variety of means to do employee screening, with the goal of ensuring that applicants are providing complete and truthful information in the employment process and that they are not likely to steal from the company or commit another crime. These methods include reference checks, background checks, credit reports, and honesty tests. The amount and type of information collected to verify an applicant's credentials differs by type and level of job. An entry-level job where an employee doesn't handle cash or have other access to company money would require only a reference check. The job of bank manager, though, would require a complete background check and honesty test because someone filling that job would have direct access to company funds. Many organizations warn job candidates that if they are hired, and it is later discovered that they provided false information during the hiring process, they will be dismissed.

Reference checks require applicants to provide the names of individuals the potential employer can contact to verify information provided by the applicant and who can provide additional information about the applicant. Often names of current or former supervisors are given for this purpose. The questions asked of the reference typically focus on the applicant's education, work, and related experiences. Oftentimes, companies ask the reference provider to offer a judgment about the applicant's qualifications for the open position.

Employers often find themselves in a Catch-22 when it comes to reference checks: They need to conduct them to collect information about applicants; however, they are reluctant to give reference-check-related information about their own current or former employees for fear of being sued for *defamation of character*.[37] Defamation of character occurs when someone makes written or verbal comments about that person that are not true. Consequently, it's extremely important that any information an employer gives out about a current or former employee be true and verifiable. In addition, hiring employers should require applicants to sign release forms granting permission for information to be gathered about them and should request only job-related information, using a structured questionnaire.

Because of the risk of defamation of character, many companies have policies limiting the amount and type of information they can provide about former employees. Some policies prohibit personnel from divulging any information whatsoever. Other policies limit the information provided. For example, often company employees are allowed only to confirm whether the person actually works or worked for the company, the dates of the person's employment, and the individual's salary.[38] Some states have passed "Good Samaritan" laws to encourage employers to provide reference information. The laws protect reference providers from being sued if they provide verifiable information in good faith.[39]

The purpose of a *background check* is to verify information provided during the application process and/or to obtain additional information about some aspect of the applicant's life from a reliable source. Approximately 99% of large companies and 92% of small and midsize companies conduct some type of background check. They either conduct the checks themselves or hire a third-party firm that specializes in background screening to do it for them. The Internet has made conducting background checks much easier and more affordable.[40] Regardless of the type and extensiveness of the background check a company conducts, it is important to have a policy describing what will be done, who will be involved, how the information obtained will be handled, the consequences to the applicant of a negative report, and how an applicant can appeal a negative employment decision that was based on background check information.

Information collected as part of a background check can range from verification of college degrees to criminal background checks to credit reports. An applicant's eligibility to work in the United States is the most common piece of information verified by prospective employers.[41] Organizations know that under the *Immigration Reform and Immigrant Responsibility Act of 1996 (IRCA)*, they can be fined for failing to verify this information. Recall that we discussed the IRCA in Chapter 3. Exhibit 7.8 provides a list of the acceptable documents for verification.

Negligent hiring occurs when an employer does not conduct a background check on an employee and that person commits a crime at work similar to a crime he or she committed in the past. One source indicates that employers lose about 72% of all negligent hiring lawsuits.[42]

Despite the risk of being sued for negligent hiring, a Society for Human Resource Management (SHRM) survey found that only 68% of respondents said that they conduct criminal background checks on applicants. However, employers must be cautious in using any negative information they obtain. The information should affect the hiring status of the applicant only if the criminal behaviors identified are related to the job tasks and duties. Learning that an applicant was convicted of manslaughter because of a driving incident could affect a firm's decision to hire that person as a driver. However, the information would be less relevant for a job that didn't involve driving for the company, such as the job of an assembly-line worker.

negligent hiring

The situation that occurs when an employer does not conduct a background check on an employee and that person commits a crime at work similar to a crime he or she committed in the past.

Exhibit 7.8 ▶ List of Acceptable Documents for Verification

LIST A Documents that Establish Both Identity and Employment Eligibility OR	LIST B Documents that Establish Identity AND	LIST C Documents that Establish Employment Eligibility
1. U.S. Passport (unexpired or expired)	1. Driver's license or ID card issued by a state or outlying possession of the United States provided it contains a photograph or information such as name, date of birth, gender, height, eye color, and address	1. U.S. Social Security card issued by the Social Security Administration *(other than a card stating it is not valid for employment)*
2. Permanent Resident Card or Alien Registration Receipt Card (Form I-551)	2. ID card issued by federal, state or local government agencies or entities, provided it contains a photograph or information such as name, date of birth, gender, height, eye color, and address	2. Certification of Birth Abroad issued by the Department of State *(Form FS-545 or Form DS-1350)*
3. An unexpired foreign passport with a temporary I-551 stamp	3. School ID card with a photograph	3. Original or certified copy of a birth certificate issued by a state, county, municipal authority, or outlying possession of the United States bearing an official seal
4. An unexpired Employment Authorization Document that contains a photograph (Form I-766, I-688, I-688A, I-688B)	4. Voter's registration card 5. U.S. Military card or draft record	4. Native American tribal document 5. U.S. Citizen ID Card *(Form I-197)*
5. An unexpired foreign passport with an unexpired Arrival-Departure Record, Form I-94, bearing the same name as the passport and containing an endorsement of the alien's nonimmigrant status, if that status authorizes the alien to work for the employer	6. Military dependent's ID card 7. U.S. Coast Guard Merchant Mariner Card 8. Native American tribal document 9. Driver's license issued by a Canadian government authority	6. ID Card for use of Resident Citizen in the United States *(Form I-179)* 7. Unexpired employment authorization document issued by DHS *(other than those listed under List A)*
	For persons under age 18 who are unable to present a document listed above: 10. School record or report card 11. Clinic, doctor or hospital record 12. Day-care or nursery school record	

Illustrations of many of these documents appear in Part 8 of the Handbook for Employers (M-274)

Form I-9 (Rev. 06/05/07) N Page 2

Many jobs require employees to handle cash or securities or grant employees access to corporate bank accounts. A *credit check*, or review of an applicant's credit report, is job related in such cases. The employer needs to ensure that employees are not in a bad personal financial situation that might motivate them to steal from the company. The *Fair Credit Reporting Act (FCRA)* permits employers to collect information about applicants' and employees' credit. The act requires applicants or employees to provide written authorization for an employer to legally access their credit information prior to doing so, however. Emplkoyers are also required to notify applicants if their credit reports keep them from being hired and give them the contact information for the credit reporting agency that provided the information.[43]

Many employers used polygraph tests to screen job applicants until problems with inaccurate results led to the passage of the *Polygraph Protection Act of 1988*. Specifically, the problem was related to false-positives and false-negatives. *False-positive* results on a polygraph test indicate that the person taking the test is lying when in fact he or she is not. *False-negatives* indicate that the person taking the test is not lying when he or she actually is. False-negatives can be just as costly to organizations as false-positives, but they are less likely to occur.

After the general use of the polygraphs became illegal, employers still wanted and needed a way to predict whether an applicant would engage in illegal behavior. *Honesty tests*, also called *integrity tests*, serve that purpose. There are two basic types: overt honesty tests and personality tests.[44]

An *overt honesty test* is just what it sounds like: a test that is designed specifically to predict honesty and integrity. This type of test measures the frequency of a person's stealing or how lenient one's attitude is toward theft. An overt honesty test might include questions such as: "Have you ever told a lie?" or "Do you think most people would steal something if they thought they wouldn't get caught?" These types of questions are written in such a way that the same belief is assessed with multiple questions, making it more difficult for the respondent to "beat" the test.

A *personality test* asks questions in a more disguised way to identify traits known to be related to counterproductive behaviors. These traits include insubordination, substance abuse, and other discipline problems. Questions on these tests are less direct and may ask the test taker to respond to questions about his or her relationships with parents, spouse, or co-workers as well as about the individual's own state of being, such as "Do you ever think you are losing your mind?"[45]

Using tests of these types for prescreening applicants is preferable to using them with current employees who are likely to become upset if they feel their integrity is being challenged. Also, if an employment decision is made about employees who score poorly on one of these tests, those employees might file a lawsuit against the company if their behavior is not counterproductive.[46]

No employment decision should be made on the basis of only an honesty or integrity measure, however. Just as polygraphs result in false-positives and false-negatives, so too can these tests. Some states have laws that limit the use of honesty tests, so it is important to check the laws in your state before administering these tests.

Assessment Centers

Assessment centers put job candidates through a series of simulations designed to assess their ability to perform aspects of the jobs they're seeking. Most often, the jobs are managerial or professional positions. Oftentimes, the assessments are conducted to make *internal* promotion decisions. Typical simulations include:

- *An in-basket exercise*—Candidates sort through and respond to letters, memos, and reports within a specific time frame and within a specified context.
- *A leaderless group discussion*—Candidates are given a problem to solve together with no one person designated as the leader.
- *Role plays*—Candidates play out job-related situations, usually involving solving a problem.

assessment center

A selection process, often focused on internal promotions, in which candidates participate in a series of simulations designed to determine their ability to perform aspects of the jobs they are seeking.

biodata (short for biographical data)

A standardized questionnaire based on the premise that past behavior is the best predictor of future behavior and used with job applicants as part of a selection process to gather personal and biographical information to be compared with the same information for successful employees.

Trained evaluators, often managers from within the company, observe how applicants perform during these simulations and rate their performance on a defined scale for each job-related dimension. Among the dimensions frequently assessed are oral and written communication, decisiveness, adaptability, initiative, delegation, and planning and organization. An assessment center can last for several days and be expensive to administer. The costs include setting up the process and the time the firm's managers must spend rating candidates. Some companies have their own in-house assessment centers; other companies send job applicants to outside assessment centers for testing.[47]

BIODATA Biodata is short for *biographical data*, a standardized questionnaire that asks applicants to provide personal and biographical information. The questions might focus on candidates' hobbies, experiences in high school or college, preferred supervisor characteristics, and so forth. The information candidates provide is then compared to the information provided by a firm's successful employees. The outcome is a prediction of how likely the employee is to succeed at the company, based on the idea that past behavior is the best predictor of future behavior.[48] Procter & Gamble (P&G) is one company that uses biodata in its selection process.[49]

Biodata questionnaires are expensive to develop. Extreme care must be exercised to ensure that the questions asked are job related, particularly because many personal and biographical questions do not appear to be job related at first glance. Employers should also verify the information candidates provide to the extent that they can.[50]

Drug Tests

The *Drug-Free Workplace Act of 1988* requires all federal contractors to develop policies to ensure that their employees are drug free. Since the passage of this act, many employers have implemented policies requiring all applicants to pass a drug test before being hired. Most employers also prohibit the use of alcohol at their workplaces and discipline employees who come to work under the influence of alcohol or drugs.

The trend for companies to do drug testing appears to be changing. In the past few years, companies have been moving away from drug testing of applicants due to concerns over the cost of testing ($25 to $150 per applicant, with hair follicle testing at the higher end of the cost range) and a belief that fewer people are using drugs.[51] It is important to remember, however, that research has shown that employees who abuse drugs are more likely to miss work, be tardy, be involved in workplace accidents, and file workers' compensation claims.[52] Therefore, the decision of whether to test is a serious one.

An employer using drug testing needs to have a written policy about its use that is in compliance with federal, state, and local laws. Generally, a candidate must sign a consent form before being tested, too.[53] Employees who are currently using drugs or alcohol are not protected under the ADA. Recovering drug users and alcoholics are covered. Therefore, an employer can refuse to hire someone who is using illegal substances or shows up at the interview under the influence of alcohol. The employer cannot refuse to hire someone recovering from a drug or alcohol problem if that is the reason for the decision.[54]

Medical Examinations

Prior to the passage of the ADA, employers could require a medical examination as a condition of employment. Now, the ADA specifies that a medical examination can be required only after an offer of employment has been made. Employers requiring a medical examination of an employee should provide a copy of the job description to the examining physician. If the results of the medical examination indicate that the person cannot perform the job requirements, and there is no reasonable accommodation that would allow him or her to do so, the company does not have to employ that individual. Generally, a medical exam can lead to disqualification of an applicant if that individual would be a direct threat to the health or safety of self or others.[55]

CHOOSING AMONG SELECTION METHODS

You have learned about a lot of selection methods. Exhibit 7.9 provides a summary of the selection methods discussed so far. Keep in mind that each serves a different purpose. Which method(s) should you use and when? Companies report that interviews are the most frequently used selection method, followed by applications and resumes.[56] (Recall that interviews are more valid when they are carefully structured and interviewers are carefully trained to ensure that interviews are correctly administered.) That said, depending on the type of position you're hiring for, these three methods might not result in the best hiring decision. The best, most appropriate methods depend on the job for which you're hiring and the goals and objectives your organization is trying to achieve. Bottom line: Use the methods that will provide the most relevant information you need to collect about applicants.[57]

Before beginning the selection process, you need to make sure you know what information you need, how you can best collect it, and how you will use it to make a final selection decision. This last part is more challenging than it might appear. Each person is likely to have different strengths and weaknesses. Very few individuals will excel in all areas. Some candidates will score well on one or more selection measures and lower on others. The challenge for you as a manager is to determine how to use all the information you obtain to make the best hiring decision. Several approaches are available for helping you make this determination.

Compensatory Approach

In most of your classes, if you don't do well on one assignment, you have the opportunity to offset that grade by doing well on another assignment. This model is known as a **compensatory approach**. Theoretically, during the selection process, a candidate could score low on one measure, perhaps a written test, but do exceptionally well on another part, such as the interview. The outcome of the interview could offset the lower score on the written test or vice versa, depending on how you "weight" the different scores. Measures that correlate more highly with on-the-job success should be more heavily weighted. Exhibit 7.10 shows an example of how the compensatory approach works. For this particular job, the organization doing the hiring has determined that the second interview should receive the highest weight (45%), followed by the written test (35%), and the initial interview (20%). Each applicant's score on each measure is multiplied by the weight assigned to the measure to arrive at a score for the measure. These scores are then summed to come up with a total score for the applicant. When scores are close, you can ask applicants to provide additional information or have them return for another interview.

compensatory approach

A process for deriving a final score for each candidate in the selection process by weighting outcomes on multiple selection measures differentially so that some items are weighted more heavily than others and a high score on one part can offset a low score on another part.

Exhibit 7.9 ▶ Selection Methods

Initial screening: Methods used to decide which applicants should continue to be evaluated during the selection process	
Application blanks and resumes	*Application*—Standardized form for collecting job-related information about an applicant
	Resume—Applicant-supplied data sheet that provides information, including the person's contact information, education, previous work experience, and special skills and interests
Screening interviews	Short interview to collect additional information about an applicant, assess his or her interest in position, and verify information previously provided by applicant

(continued)

Exhibit 7.9 ▶ Selection Methods *(continued)*

Final screening: An extensive review of candidates' qualifications prior to making a final hiring decision		

Employment tests: Ability tests		***Cognitive ability test***—Measures the general intelligence or level of specific aptitudes of an applicant
		Physical ability test—Measures an applicant's physical attributes, such as endurance, strength, or general fitness
	Achievement tests	***Work sample***—Assesses how well an applicant can actually perform some aspect of a job
		Knowledge test—Measures how well an applicant has mastered the content required to perform a job
	Personality inventories	Measures the extent to which applicants possess characteristics required to do the job
	Interviews	***Unstructured Interview***—Questions asked without a specific plan for so doing
		Structured Interview—Standardized set of questions asked based on the requirements of a job
		Situational Interview—Questions that focus on how an applicant would handle job-related situations
		Behavioral interview—Questions that focus on how an applicant actually handled job-related situations in the past
	Reference and background checks	***Reference check***—Process of contacting an applicant's past employers and other persons, such as teachers, to inquire about the candidate's qualifications for the job
		Background check—In-depth investigation to verify the accuracy of the information provided by an applicant and ensure that there is nothing in the applicant's past that would disqualify the person
		Credit reports—Review of an applicant's credit history to reduce the likelihood of theft
		Honesty/integrity tests—Assessment of an applicant's beliefs, values, or personality to identify the potential of the person to engage in counterproductive behaviors on the job
	Assessment centers	Series of simulations to assess the ability of candidates to perform certain aspects of a job

Biodata	Standardized process of collecting biographical and personal data from candidates and comparing it to the same type of information collected from a firm's successful employees
Drug tests	Assess whether or not applicants have recently used drugs
Medical tests	Physical examinations conducted by physicians to determine whether applicants are able to do the job

Multiple-Hurdle Approach

In the multiple-hurdle approach, applicants have to successfully pass each step (hurdle) to continue on in the selection process. Staying with the selection techniques shown in Exhibit 7.10, an applicant would have to reach a minimum score on the written test (hurdle 1) to be scheduled for a first interview (hurdle 2). If the applicant does well in the first interview, he or she can then proceed with the last hurdle (interview 2). Company Spotlight 7.2 provides an example of how the Wynn Las Vegas Casino used a multiple-hurdle selection process when it first opened.

multiple-hurdle approach

The final selection decision making approach that requires applicants to successfully pass each step (hurdle) to continue on in the selection process.

Multiple-Cutoff Approach

With the multiple-cutoff approach, an applicant has to reach a minimum score on each measure to remain in the running for a particular job. This approach differs from the multiple-hurdle approach in that applicants go through all steps of the process. After all applicants have completed all steps, those who meet the minimum score on all parts are considered eligible for the job, and the selection decision is then made from that group.

multiple-cutoff approach

The final selection decision making approach that requires applicants to make a minimum score on each measure to remain under consideration for a particular job.

Choosing a Scoring Method

Each scoring approach has advantages and disadvantages. The compensatory model works best when there are no absolute requirements that a candidate has to meet. If you are hiring a project manager, and there are six qualifications the successful candidate should have but no one qualification is a make-or-break factor in the decision, then the compensatory approach would work well. The multiple-hurdle approach works well when there are absolutes. For example, if a candidate for a project manager's position needs to have each qualification you're measuring, and you can order the qualifications from most critical to least critical, then the multiple-hurdle approach would be a good choice. If all the qualifications need to be met at a minimal level, then the multiple-cutoff approach would work.

For some jobs, a company might use a combination of a multiple-hurdle approach and another approach. Suppose, for example, that a company needs an accountant who is a certified public accountant (CPA). In this situation, it would be logical to use the CPA credential to make the first cut. After that cut, a compensatory or multiple cutoff, or even further hurdles could be used.

Assessment Tool	Weight	Applicant 1	Applicant 2
Written test	35% ×	70 = 24.50	85 = 29.75
Interview 1	20% ×	80 = 16.00	75 = 15.00
Interview 2	45% ×	90 = 40.50	95 = 42.75
Total score		81.00	87.50

◄ **Exhibit 7.10**
Example of Compensatory Approach for Selection Decision Making

7.2 Using a Multiple-Hurdle Selection Process at the Wynn Las Vegas

Not too many employers receive 67,000 applications in response to a single newspaper ad. But that was the number of applications the Wynn Las Vegas resort received after the company ran a help-wanted ad for just one day in a Las Vegas newspaper in 2004. The Wynn needed 9,000+ employees to run its new operation in the city. The jobs it hired for ranged from serving food to making up beds to dealing cards. Not surprisingly, wading through all those applications to find the right people was not an easy task.

Fortunately, Arte Nathan, the chief human resources officer for Recruitmax, a recruiting software maker, had many years of experience working with the developer of the Wynn. Nathan knew a lot about how to approach the problem. Recruitmax's system let Wynn managers search applications by job title to find out how much experience applicants had and where they had worked. Applicants could use a pull-down menu showing the names of the other resorts in Las Vegas to indicate which ones they had worked for, and they could log on to www.wynnjobs.com and find out where they stood in the selection process.

Nathan also realized that some folks interested in applying might not have computers, be computer literate, or even speak English. Consequently, he made sure there were other ways for these people to apply for jobs with the Wynn. This included establishing a hiring call center staffed with employees who could speak eight different languages, including Korean, Spanish, and even Tagalog, one of the major languages spoken in the Philippines. One of the links on the Wynn's hiring Web site provided answers to frequently asked questions in Spanish, further showing the company's commitment to diversity.

The Recruitmax system computed a rating score for applicants based on the information they provided about their previous work experience. Applicants meeting a minimum cutoff score continued on in the selection process. Applicants who made it through the first interview also had to take a drug test. Additional steps included interviews and a process whereby people seeking card dealer positions "auditioned" for jobs.

The application system developed by Recruitmax focused on making the application and review process as easy as possible and totally eliminated paper applications. Along with the multiple-hurdle selection process, the well-designed system made it possible for the Wynn to hire the employees it needed in a relatively short period of time: In November 2004, the resort began taking applications. A month later, it began reviewing the tens of thousands of applications it had received. Three months later, it began making job offers. The following month, April 2005, the Wynn opened its doors, fully staffed.

Sources: Berkshire, J. C. The countdown is on at Wynn Las Vegas. *Workforce Management,* March 2005, pp. 65–67; Wynn Resorts recruiting Web page, www.wynnjobs.com; and Stutz, H. Board backs license for Wynn Hotel: Gaming Commission to consider matter. *Knight Ridder Tribune Business News,* March 10, 2005, p. 1.

SELECTION IN PRACTICE: ORGANIZATIONAL DEMANDS

Now that you have a good understanding of the fundamentals of the selection process, we focus on the types of decisions managers must make on a regular basis when designing the process and selecting employees. Exhibit 7.11 outlines many of these decisions. We have already established how the requirements of a job and a firm's recruitment efforts affect the employee selection process. Let's now look at how organizational demands, environmental demands, and regulatory issues affect the decisions you will make as a manager when you're selecting employees to work for you.

Strategy and Selection

The role of the selection process is to help you hire the "right" employees. The best widget in the world won't be designed, made, or sold without the right people thinking up the idea, developing the design, setting up a production process for it, and manufacturing and marketing it. People and the competencies they possess matter greatly to a firm's success. But different competencies matter more or less for different strategies. Remember that a

Exhibit 7.11 ▶ Selection in Practice

Context	Employee Competencies Chapter 7, "Selection"
Organizational Demands	
Strategy drives . . .	• Selection criteria for person–job fit • Core competencies needed
Company characteristics determine . . .	• Degree of formalization of process • Availability of funds for designing and implementing process • Criteria used for selection • Willingness of applicants to accept jobs offered
Culture establishes . . .	• Selection criteria for person–organization fit • Practice of promotion from within • Who is involved in selection process
Employee concerns include . . .	• Perceptions of fairness/justice • Impact of job offered on work/family balance
Environmental Demands	
Labor force influences . . .	• Types of applicants available for selection • Willingness of applicants to accept jobs
Technology affects . . .	• Process of selection • Need to verify the legitimacy of credentials
Globalization impacts . . .	• Focus of selection process • Characteristics of applicants
Ethics/social responsibility shapes . . .	• Concerns about privacy • Amount and type of information given to applicants
Regulations *guide...*	• Definition of who is an applicant • Decisions about what is legal and nondiscriminatory

company's strategy is its plan for gaining a competitive advantage over its rivals. As a manager involved in hiring employees, you need to understand the company's strategy and the core competencies that the strategy requires of all employees. Those competencies, along with the specific criteria to ensure that there is a good person–job fit, determine what you focus on when you're selecting employees. Your firm's strategy also determines the choice of methods you use for collecting information about applicants.

CORE COMPETENCIES Core competencies differ from company to company. Focusing on your company's strategic competencies when you're setting up the selection process helps ensure a strong match between what employees can do and what the company strategy requires. Companies that compete based on low costs often design jobs to maximize employee efficiency and productivity. The result is often jobs with a narrow range of tasks and limited employee discretion. These companies are much less concerned about competencies such as creativity and flexibility than they are about competencies such as efficiency, dependability, and cooperativeness. A company pursuing a differentiation strategy focused on customer service will look for different competencies than a company pursuing an innovation strategy.

Certainly there can be overlapping competencies among firms with different strategies. Trustworthiness, one of IBM's foundational competencies,[58] would likely be valued by all firms, regardless of their strategic focus. The important point to remember is that the core competencies assessed during the selection process should be a function of a company's strategy. Therefore, it is important for you as a manager to know what these competencies are as you participate in the process of hiring new employees.

SELECTION CRITERIA FOR PERSON–JOB FIT Core competencies are usually broadly defined because they apply across jobs within a company. KSAs, on the other hand, are job specific and are determined by the design of a job. A company's strategy, like its core competencies, will determine the specific KSAs each employee needs in order to do his or her job. Remember the cooks we described at the start of Chapter 4? The cook in the fast-food restaurant needs different skills than the cook in a fine-dining establishment. Likewise, an accountant in a major accounting firm will have different job requirements than an accountant who works in a low-cost retail chain. The two jobs will share some requirements, but the strategy of each organization results in additional and specific job requirements that need to be considered during the selection process.

METHODS OF SELECTION The type and number of selection methods used are driven by a company's strategy. If your company has a low-cost strategy, you will want to find the most efficient selection methods possible. A simple application and one short interview might be all that is used. Or, if the company typically needs a lot of people to do the same job, it may be more cost-effective to develop a selection test specifically for that job. Employees can be selected in an efficient manner with a standardized process.

A company with a differentiation strategy that focuses on high-quality service will be especially interested in how well future employees respond to situations involving others. Including role plays, situational interviews, or behavioral interviews in the selection process will provide a way to assess how well applicants respond to such situations. If the differentiation strategy is one of innovation, the selection methods might include a simulation in which the applicant has to do something unique or "think outside the box." Behavioral interviews and references can also reveal how "innovative" applicants have been in the past.

Company Characteristics and Selection

The size and stage of development of a company are often highly correlated. These characteristics of a company will determine the structure of its selection process and the substance and form of the process for designing and implementing the process. Whether the firm is large or small, new or old, wealthy or struggling, as a manager, you will be able to use the information you are currently learning to conduct a successful selection process within those parameters.

DEGREE OF STRUCTURE Selection processes range from highly structured to highly unstructured and from a few steps to many steps. Some processes are very informal and include perhaps only an application and an interview, whereas others are very formal and involve multiple steps and extensive, structured interviews. Larger, more established companies, such as Lockheed Martin, generally have more resources and can afford to utilize more extensive selection methods. Many of these organizations also develop their own selection processes. They also recognize that the more applicants they have, the greater the risk there is that an informal and/or unstructured process will be viewed by applicants as subjective and biased. Thus, a structured and validated process is more likely to be in place in firms such as these.

Keep in mind that exceptions always exist. A company may have grown quickly and not taken the time to develop good selection processes, and even some long-established companies might not have good processes. Some firms—for example, JetBlue—have always understood the importance of a well-designed selection process.[59]

SUBSTANCE AND FORM OF THE SELECTION PROCESS A company's industry has a big impact on the type of employees the firm needs as well as the selection norms it will tend to use. How a defense contractor selects employees will obviously be very different from how a restaurant selects employees: Defense contractors must conduct extensive background checks of applicants to meet government security regulations. Restaurants may do background checks but they are not as extensive.

An industry's norms can be either implicitly or explicitly conveyed. For example, major business consulting firms, such as Accenture and KPMG, have similar, highly structured selection processes. They typically use extensive interviews and case studies to narrow down the number of acceptable candidates for their open positions. These are large, established firms, but because of the norms of the industry, even the small boutique consulting firms use the same type of selection processes.

Specific practices also exist within occupations. Some occupations, such as accounting, law, and medicine, require licenses or certifications. Other occupations do not require certification but have it available. Human resources is an example. Companies use the credentials as a signal of the competencies an applicant will bring to the job. As a result, fewer additional steps may be needed during the selection process than for occupations that do not have similar credentials.

Culture and Selection

Will the culture of a company matter to you when you are applying for jobs? We expect that it will. When setting up a selection process, it is important for you to be familiar with your company's culture and decide how to determine whether an applicant will fit in with it.

PERSON–ORGANIZATION FIT   A company's strategy and characteristics influence the criteria managers rely on to maximize person–job fit. **Person–organization fit** involves how well a person fits within the broader organizational culture.[60] Recall that a firm's culture is a function of the basic assumptions, values, and beliefs of the organization's members.[61] Each company's culture is unique and influences the selection process. Company Spotlight 7.3 provides an example of how the selection process at CDW was changed to better reflect the corporate culture.

A company's culture can also be a primary reason applicants accept job offers at the firm. Starbucks is a good example of this. It believes its corporate culture is the reason it is able to attract and retain good employees. The company mission and vision statement emphasize a work environment that is positive and respectful. Starbucks hires employees who are adaptable, passionate, and dependable team players. The company's interview guidelines provide examples of questions interviewers can ask applicants to discern whether they have these attributes. Companies such as Starbucks know that a match

person–organization fit

The extent to which the potential employee fits well within the broader organizational culture and values.

COMPANY spotlight   7.3 Culture and Selection at CDW

Many companies attribute their success to their corporate culture. Companies such as these take their culture into account when they design their selection processes. CDW, a technology products and services provider, did just that. The company has been experiencing rapid growth over the past few years. For instance, in 2006, its reported revenue was up 7.8% from 2005. In the first three months of 2007, the company hired more than 300 new account managers.

CDW spent over a year revamping its approach to human resources management, reviewing and revising its recruitment and selection processes and its orientation and retention strategies. A big part of the revamping involved examining the relationship between the selection system and the desired culture to make sure that they were in alignment.

This company knows that if it does a better job of hiring, turnover will go down. The new process uses a three-minute realistic job preview video to ensure that applicants understand the nature of the jobs for which they are applying. The new selection approach is customized for CDW jobs and includes a behavioral interview. The manager to whom the applicant is likely to report, if hired, conducts this interview. This early interaction provides a way for the managers to begin to build relationships with potential hires and to communicate and model key points of the corporate culture.

Sources: Adapted from Hansen, F. Overhauling the recruiting process at CDW Corp. *Workforce Management* online, April 11, 2007, www.workforce.com/archive/feature/24/85/32/index.php; and CDW Web site, http://www.cdw.com/webcontent/inside/career/default.asp.

between the values of their employees and those fostered by the organization increases employee productivity and contributes to success.[62]

It should be noted that some candidates might have the necessary competencies to do a particular job but still not fit in with a company's culture. Other candidates might share the values and beliefs of an organization but lack the competencies to succeed in a particular job. That's why, as we have explained, both the person–job and person–organization fit are important.

PROMOTION-FROM-WITHIN POLICY   Culture affects the extent to which a company has an internal versus external hiring mindset. Many companies are quite loyal to their employees. When a job vacancy occurs, these companies promote current employees rather than look outside the organization. A firm's current employees are already familiar with the company's culture when the cultural values are continuously reinforced. Of course, there is also a downside to this practice. Without "new blood" coming into the organization on a regular basis, the company runs the risk of becoming stagnant. Therefore, carefully weighing the pros and cons of promoting from within is important before the practice becomes too entrenched.

WHO PARTICIPATES IN THE SELECTION PROCESS   The norms about who participates in the selection process are established, at least in part, by company culture. In a team environment where employee input is valued, all members of the team are likely to be involved in some aspect of the selection process. In more traditional, hierarchical organizations, only employees in higher-level positions will be involved in selecting new employees.

Employee Concerns and Selection

During the selection process, prospective employees want to be treated fairly and equally to other applicants. They also want to gather as much information as possible about the job so they can decide how it will affect their lives.

FAIR AND EQUAL TREATMENT   The psychological contract between an employee and an employer begins to be established during the recruitment process and is reinforced in the selection process. How applicants are treated during this time gives them an idea about how they will be treated as employees. Reducing bias in the selection process and treating applicants in a consistent manner positively affects applicants' perceptions of the organization.

We all have personal preferences and stereotypes that can affect our decisions. Acknowledging this is the first step in preventing the use of those factors to make decisions. A well-designed selection process helps hiring managers clearly understand the factors that *should* affect their hiring decisions versus those that shouldn't. As we've explained, a structured selection process and training help reduce the likelihood of bias and ensure equal treatment of all applicants. Many companies train their employees on diversity issues and how to select employees. Providing hiring managers with a scoring key for rating candidates' answers to their interview questions will also reduce the risk of bias occurring. Also, remember that as a manager you are ultimately responsible for ensuring that your employees participating in the hiring process understand how they should go about making unbiased judgments about candidates. This should be the case whether the company you work for is large or small, new or established, affluent or struggling, your own company or part of a conglomerate.

IMPACT OF JOB ON WORK/LIFE BALANCE   In Chapter 3 we discussed the concept of realistic job previews (RJPs). Recall that RJPs provide candidates with information about the demands of the jobs they're applying for, including the time expectations, working conditions, and possible stressors related to the jobs. As a manager, you might have an applicant you really want to hire, and you may be fortunate to convince that person to come to work for you. However, if he starts work only to find that the job is going to require more travel than he was told, or longer work hours, and if those requirements interfere with his family responsibilities, he is likely to find another job as soon as possible and not be very productive in the interim.

SELECTION IN PRACTICE: ENVIRONMENTAL INFLUENCES

A number of environmental influences directly affect the selection process. The labor market influences both who is available for employment and who is willing to work for the company. Technology affects the design and implementation of the selection process, and it creates new challenges for selection. Globalization affects a firm's decisions about hiring employees at home and abroad. Ethics and social responsibility concerns shape privacy issues, including what information and how much of it the organization should communicate to applicants. We discuss each of these issues in some detail.

Labor Market and Selection

For selection purposes, we are interested in both the larger labor market and relevant labor markets for particular jobs. The labor market influences both the type of applicants available for selection and the willingness of applicants to accept jobs. As a manager, you will be confronted at some point with labor market challenges and have to decide to what extent those changes affect the selection process you use.

TYPES OF APPLICANTS AVAILABLE   The applicant pool changes as the demographics of a country or region change. The age of applicants is one demographic that today has a direct impact on the hiring of employees. Many older workers are finding themselves having to work to make ends meet after retiring. Often these workers are highly qualified applicants who may want to work part time and bring valuable skills and information to the workplace. Employers need to be open to what these potential employees can contribute and ensure that age doesn't become an explicit or implicit factor in selection. In fact, many companies are realizing that an aging workforce means they have to be proactive and embrace the employment of older workers to maintain a sufficiently large workforce.

In the past in the United States, teenagers often filled low-skilled, entry-level service jobs. Now, teens either don't have to work because of their parents' affluence or have lots of choices of places where they can work. As a result, they are less willing to work in fast-food jobs, discount retail jobs, or other service jobs that people in this age group would have more willingly accepted a few decades ago. Instead, the applicants for these jobs have increasingly become immigrants to the United States who may need skills and language training so they can communicate with customers. The selection process has to be modified to accommodate these applicants. For example, you may need to have your

A diverse workforce at a fast-food restaurant.

applications translated into various languages if your target applicants lack the ability to read and write English, and English is not an essential job requirement. Interviewers may need to speak multiple languages.

A number of specific occupations have experienced shifts in their applicant pools. School districts are using alternative selection measures to determine a potential teacher's qualifications in fields where there is a shortage of qualified teachers, for example. Sometimes when teachers are hired, they are given a timeline by which they must acquire certain credentials to remain employed. Hospitals have had to look outside their domestic borders to find qualified nurses because fewer people are choosing nursing as a career at the same time that the population is aging and more health care professionals are needed. The selection process has to be modified in these situations to identify and process applicants. Managers have to recognize that qualifications they are looking for today might not look exactly like those they traditionally searched for in the past.

WILLINGNESS OF APPLICANTS TO ACCEPT JOBS A *loose labor market* presents the best of all possible worlds for employers. When there are more qualified employees available than job openings, an employer has the luxury of being very selective about who is hired. Applicants have fewer offers and are going to be less selective. But what happens when there are too few qualified employees in the labor market? In a *tight labor market*, employers don't have the luxury of being very selective. An employer may actually eliminate all but the most essential steps in the selection process (keeping application, background check, and interview) and use resources formally earmarked for selection to train new employees to do the job. Applicants may have multiple offers in this labor market, so much of the selection process becomes "selling" the job. Company Spotlight 7.4 discusses how one medical center handled a tight labor market.

Technology and Selection

Technology has had a significant impact on how selection is managed. The two most prominent advances are the increased use of computer technology to perform part of the selection process and to verify candidates' credentials. We will first discuss technology's impact on the process of selection.

TECHNOLOGY AND THE PROCESS OF SELECTION Apply for a job at Target, Garden Ridge, or Wal-Mart, and you will most likely find yourself completing an application at a computer kiosk. At this kiosk, applicants can be asked to complete a personality or situational judgment questionnaire that serves the same purpose as a screening interview.

COMPANY *spotlight*

7.4 How St. Bernardine Medical Center Handled a Tight Labor Market

During a tight labor market, employers often get very creative in order to convince applicants to accept their job offers rather than other firms' offers. When St. Bernardine Medical Center in San Bernardino, California, decided it had to do something to attract and retain nurses, it began a series of marketing campaigns: Prospective nurses were offered up to $12,000 in assistance, home closing costs, and up to $10,000 for car lease payments if they would sign a two-year contract.

This might sound like a lot of money to offer job candidates. However, the hospital reports that marketing efforts such as these over the past few years have actually improved St. Bernardine's bottom line by $10 million. Why? Because replacing a nurse costs about 1.5 times the position's annual salary. The overall gains for the hospital result from reduced turnover, less need to rely on temporary nurses, increased employee morale, and increased market share for the hospital.

Source: Adapted from Tucker, D. M. Nursing shortage causes headaches; Incentives attract nurses to open slots. *Knight Ridder Tribune Business News,* February 7, 2005, p. 1.

The information collected supplements the information job seekers put on their applications and provides the companies with a preliminary idea of how well the applicants will fit the job and organization.[63] In other organizations, an applicant might be directed to call a specific phone number to respond to similar questions. Computer kiosks and phone systems used for initial screening save a lot of time and paperwork for the company, and the information entered by applicants can become part of a company's applicant tracking system. Look back at Company Spotlight 7.2 on the Wynn Las Vegas. The spotlight provides an example of how the Wynn found online applications invaluable when it needed to hire more than 9,000 employees in a short period of time.

Companies are also using online selection tests, which raises questions about how equivalent these tests are to traditional paper-and-pencil versions. If the two versions are not highly equivalent, the Internet test may have to be validated separately. Testing conditions, such as whether a test is timed if it is online, may make a critical difference in terms of equivalency.[64]

VERIFICATION OF CREDENTIALS   Employers are finding it easier, faster, and more cost-effective to do reference and background checking now that much of it can be done online. Applicants often fail to disclose information that paints them in a less-than-favorable light, such as information about having been fired from a previous job. Sometimes applicants omit information about their previous work experience simply because they're afraid it will make them look overqualified. Other information submitted by applicants is simply false. Staffing experts report that anywhere from 30% to 43% of job applicants misrepresent information on their resumes.[65] Electronic processing of reference and background checks may make it more difficult for applicants to lie about their past. Nonetheless, employers need to exercise due diligence to ensure that the information they're collecting electronically is coming from reliable sources and is accurate.[66]

Technology may be making it more difficult for applicants to conceal or falsify information, but at the same time, it can make it easier, too. For example, some job applicants have gone so far as to hack into university computers and add their names to graduation lists. A candidate for a director position at Korn/Ferry, an international executive search firm, did just that. (He was found out, and he didn't get the job.) In addition, technology makes it much easier for candidates to forge documents indicating that they have certain credentials when they actually lack them.[67]

Globalization and Selection

Many organizations find themselves involved in global selection activities in one of four ways:

1. Hiring increasingly large numbers of international employees to work in their domestic operations
2. Selecting internal candidates to send to other countries to work
3. Hiring host-country nationals to work in their companies' operations in host countries
4. Hiring international employees to work for the company abroad

Each of these activities creates unique challenges and opportunities related to selecting employees. Next we discuss these practices.

LABOR MARKET AT HOME   The most carefully constructed selection process is ineffective if applicants aren't available to apply for the jobs. During the end of the twentieth century and the beginning of the twenty-first century, the U.S. economy was booming, and job growth was on the rise. High-tech and other companies began to rely more and more on immigrants for their staffing needs as a result, especially given the shortage of math and science majors in the United States and the increasing need for workers with those backgrounds. However, after the terrorist attacks on September 11, 2001, the amount of information, time, and cost required to obtain visas for immigrants to work in the United States increased, and the number of available H-1B visas decreased, too. The need for such workers did not decrease in the same proportion, however. For instance, on April 2, 2007, the U.S. Citizenship and Immigration Services (USCIS) had received 150,000 petitions for H-1B visas, which exceeded the cap on available visas by 85,000.[68] The United States has become the third most "challenging" country in which to relocate employees.[69]

H1-B is a classification used for nonimmigrant aliens who are employed to work temporarily in very specific occupations, such as engineering, math, law, theology, architecture, physical sciences, and medicine. In 2008 and 2009, only 65,000 aliens could receive these visas. This cap was put in place in 2004. In previous years, that number was higher: 195,000 H1-B visas were available in the years 2001 through 2003. Employers seeking to hire workers with the H1-B status have to complete a labor condition application with the Department of Labor and pay a fee. The workers can be on H1-B status for only six years at a time.[70]

LABOR MARKET ABROAD   If you are staffing an international operation, you will need to decide whether to staff with parent-country nationals, host-country nationals, third-country nationals, or some combination of the three. The choices you make are critical for the success of your operation.

Companies send **parent-country nationals (PCNs)** on international assignments to control how the business abroad is run and to instill the company culture in the foreign location. They also use PCNs when there is a real or perceived lack of skilled workers in the host country. Selecting the right PCN for an assignment is challenging but essential because when PCNs fail (return to their home countries earlier than planned), it is very costly for organizations.

PCNs are often selected for assignments abroad because of their technical skills. However, research suggests that companies need to focus on other factors that can affect the ability of PCNs to work successfully abroad, such as the ability of PCNs to adapt and of their family members to adapt to foreign cultures.[71] When hiring for domestic positions, most U.S. employers do not include the families of candidates in the selection process. However, because it can often be difficult for families to relocate abroad and adjust to conditions there, international selection decisions should focus on candidates' families, too. This focus can be justified as job related because of research that supports the importance of the family's adjustment to PCN success. In fact, companies in Sweden and Switzerland routinely include families in the selection process for assignments abroad.[72]

It is important to remember that EEO laws apply to U.S. employees working abroad. Therefore, when selecting employees for international assignments, you need to make sure you do not discriminate. Some employers argue that they can send only men to certain countries. We will use the United Arab Emirate (UAE) as an example of such a country. Women in the UAE, like women in other Middle Eastern countries, are limited in terms of the types of jobs they are allowed to hold in the country due to cultural forces that require women to follow a "code of modesty" and be segregated from men. As a result, women work in traditional female roles, such as in schools.[73] So, how does that affect the types of U.S. employees U.S. firms can send abroad to work? Title VII of the Civil Rights Act prohibits U.S. employers from discriminating on the basis of gender; however, if the host country's laws and customs prohibit employment of a woman in the job that your company has available, the host country laws and customs overrule the U.S. law. Employers need to make sure that what they think is true about laws and customs in another country is actually true and not merely an impression with no real basis.

Some multinational organizations staff their operations abroad with **host-country nationals (HCNs)**. More senior positions are often still reserved for PCNs, at least initially.[74] Staffing with HCNs makes a lot of sense. HCNs know the local culture and resources, and they are usually much less costly to employ, at least in developing countries. Companies that are going to be hiring HCNs need to be aware of differences in selection practices across countries, though. Here are some examples. **Graphology** is an accepted selection method in France. Graphology involves evaluating handwriting to infer personality attributes and like many other assessments is more art than science. Using this practice for selection purposes is discouraged in the United States because of the lack of a strong scientific basis for the inferences made, yet the French see it as a valid measurement based on long success with its use. Selection tests are used more frequently in Belgium and France than in Germany and the United Kingdom. Assessment centers and situational tests are more likely to be used in the Netherlands, Germany, and the United Kingdom. Other differences exist around the globe.[75]

When selecting HCNs for an international assignment, multinational firms often employ HCN human resources directors to ensure that the selection processes used conform to local laws. If the company doesn't have a human resources professional in-house, it is often advantageous to hire the services of a local consultant to ensure that the selection practices are appropriate for the host country and that the company doesn't violate host country laws relative to selection.

Increasingly, employees are willing to work wherever in the world the best opportunities exist. This willingness is good news for employers because there are not always enough qualified employees from a company's home or host country to staff a new or even an existing operation.[76] **Third-country nationals (TCNs)** are foreign nationals who work in countries other than their home countries or their parent company's home country. Many of the same selection practices that apply to PCNs apply to TCNs. Ensuring that a TCN has good technical skills is not enough to ensure the person's success on the job. Attention should also be paid to the ability of the person and his or her family to adapt to the country to which they are relocating.

third-country national (TCN)

A foreign national who works in countries other than his or her home country or the parent company's home country.

Ethics and Employee Selection

A number of ethical and social responsibility issues exist in employee selection. We will focus on two of these: concerns about privacy and the amount and type of information provided to applicants.

CONCERNS ABOUT PRIVACY Honesty tests, background checks, credit reports, drug tests, and medical exams are among the selection methods that applicants consider highly invasive.[77] These and related selection methods should be used only when they can be shown to be job related and no other less-invasive alternative is available. If a drug test is needed, collecting a hair or saliva sample from a candidate is likely to be perceived as less invasive than collecting a urine or blood sample.[78] If invasive methods are used, well-defined policies should be in place to ensure that applicants are treated fairly. The tests should be consistently administered across all candidates being considered for the same job. The rationale behind the tests should be explained to candidates as well, and the reliability and validity of the tests should be established. By far the most invasive selection method an employer could use is genetic testing. This type of test is done to find out if an employee is predisposed to certain medical conditions or diseases that could affect work performance and cause increases in company medical insurance rates. Some states have prohibited employers from genetically testing candidates to protect them from being discriminated against based on diseases they might or might not develop.[79]

AMOUNT AND TYPE OF INFORMATION GIVEN TO APPLICANTS As a manager, you might find yourself in a dilemma about what information and how much of it you should provide to job applicants. If you're not careful, you might inadvertently omit information to make a job seem more attractive to applicants, especially applicants you really want to hire. Or, you might inadvertently omit information about the hazards related to a job or activities your company engages in that applicants might find questionable. It is, therefore, important for you and your organization to think through what information is ethical and responsible for you to divulge before you start the selection process. Realize, too, that you and your company will face consequences as a result of the choices you make. Remember that RJPs have the added benefit of yielding more satisfied and productive employees.[80]

SELECTION IN PRACTICE: REGULATORY ISSUES

In this section, we focus on two regulatory issues of particular importance to the selection process for managers: (1) procedures for using selection measures and (2) the determination of who is an applicant.

Procedures for Using Selection Measures

In 1978, the EEOC, Civil Service Commission, and U.S. Labor Department issued guidelines for the legal use of employee selection procedures. Those guidelines, the *Uniform Guidelines on Employee Selection Procedures*,[81] describe in detail how organizations can legally use tests and other selection methods. The *Uniform Guidelines* are given great deference by the courts. They also describe the recordkeeping procedures employers should follow with regard to their selection activities. Required records include information on the demographics of applicants as well as test validation information. A complete description of these guidelines is beyond the scope of this book, but it is important that you know that the guidelines exist. They are an invaluable reference when it comes to setting up a selection process. For instance, they offer guidance on what to do if your selection practices result in adverse impact and define what constitutes biased, or unfair, selection procedures.[82]

Definition of an Applicant

You might be wondering why we even need to discuss the definition of an applicant. After all, we are finally arriving at the end of this chapter. And didn't we already define the term? Yes and no. We gave you a generic definition of the term. Recently, the EEOC found a need to clarify who is an applicant. So, in addition to the concept being important for this chapter, it also serves as an excellent example of how regulatory issues affect employee management practices.

According to the *Uniform Guidelines on Employee Selection Procedures*:

The precise definition of the term "applicant" depends upon the user's recruitment and selection procedures. The concept of an applicant is that of a person who has indicated an interest in being considered for hiring, promotion, or other employment opportunities. This interest might be expressed by completing an application form, or might be expressed orally, depending on the employer's practice.[83]

This definition does seem fairly straightforward; however, with the rapid growth of computer technology, the ways in which applicants and employers interact has changed. As a result, the EEOC published *Questions and Answers: Definition of "Job Applicant" for Internet and Related Electronic Technologies* in March 2004.[84] The Equal Employment Opportunity Commission voted in March 2008 not to finalize this document but it has already become the standard for defining a job applicant for Internet and related electronic technologies.

The old definition still applies to traditional methods of application, and the new guidelines deal with online applications. When it comes to electronic technologies, such as e-mail, applicant tracking systems, employment Web pages, and the Internet, an individual is considered an applicant if:

1. The employer is acting to fill a specific position.
2. The applicant has followed the procedures described by the employer for applying for a job.
3. The applicant actually has indicated interest in a specific position.[85]

This definition is quite important in the event of a discrimination charge. Without it, an individual could just make an e-mail inquiry about a possible job and then decide to charge the company with discrimination if he didn't get the job.

Even prior to issuing the new guidelines, many employers had already established policies for determining who was actually an applicant. The policies resulted in part from efforts by the EEOC to find employers who were discriminating. To do this, the EEOC sent "testers"—individuals who were not actual applicants—to apply for jobs in an attempt to identify unlawful discrimination practices.[86] Employers have responded to the use of testers by specifying that they do not accept unsolicited applications. Managers need to ensure that everyone who is involved in the selection process has been carefully trained in terms of how to conduct the process and what records to maintain.

SUMMARY

Selection is the systematic process of deciding which applicants to hire to achieve your organizational goals. Selection involves making predictions about which job applicants will be able to perform a job successfully. Matching a person to a job will lead to more satisfied and productive employees.

The selection process is basically the same for external and internal hires. Job analysis information is used to determine the required KSAs a successful job incumbent should have. This information is then used to decide on the most appropriate methods for selecting from the pool of job applicants.

Selection methods need to be reliable, valid, and unbiased. Reliability means that the methods used are consistent over time and across raters. Validity means that the methods are actually measuring what they were designed to measure. Unbiased means that the personal characteristics of applicants and impression management efforts by applicants do not affect the selection decision. Unbiased also means that selection decisions are made based on how applicants perform during the selection process and not on how well one applicant performs relative to another applicant or how well an applicant does on only one part of the selection process.

The selection process typically consists of two parts: initial screening and final screening. Initial screening includes reviewing applications and resumes and conducting an initial interview. Final screening reduces the number of job candidates down to the number of employees needed for the job. Final screening methods include ability tests; achievement/competency tests; work samples; personality inventories; reference checks, background reports, credit reports, and scores on honesty/integrity tests; and interviews, assessment centers,

and biodata. Drug tests can be used also. A medical examination can be requested by a firm only after it has extended an employment offer to a candidate.

The final selection decision can be made in one of four ways: via the compensatory approach, multiple-hurdle approach, multiple-cutoff approach, or a combination approach. Each approach has advantages and disadvantages.

From an organizational design perspective, strategy drives the core competencies candidates need and the person–job fit criteria, as well as which methods are used to select employees. Company characteristics determine how structured the selection process is, the substance and form of selection methods used, and how much discretion individual managers have in terms of designing and implementing the process. Culture establishes the person–organization fit criteria, whether there will be a promotion-from-within policy, and who participates in the selection process. Applicant concerns include the right to fair and equitable treatment and the impact of one's job on one's family life.

Various environmental demands affect the design and outcome of the selection process. The labor force influences the characteristics of applicants who will be interested in job openings and the willingness of applicants to accept jobs. Technology affects how the selection is done and also the process of verifying applicants' credentials. Globalization affects the composition of domestic and foreign labor markets. Two ethical issues that have to be addressed during the selection process are concerns about privacy and what and how much information to provide to applicants. Finally, regulations guide the procedures used for selecting tests, keeping records, and defining who is an applicant.

KEY TERMS

achievement/competency tests *p. 193*

assessment center *p. 199*

behavioral interview *p. 195*

biodata *p. 200*

cognitive ability test *p. 192*

compensatory approach *p. 201*

concurrent criterion-related validity *p. 218*

construct validity *p. 219*

content validity *p. 218*

contrast effect *p. 189*

criterion-related validity *p. 218*

devil's horns effect *p. 189*

final screening *p. 190*

graphology *p. 212*

halo effect *p. 189*

host-country national (HCN) *p. 212*

impression management *p. 189*

initial screening *p. 190*

multiple-cutoff approach *p. 201*

multiple-hurdle approach *p. 201*

negligent hiring *p. 197*

panel interview *p. 195*

parent-country national (PCN) *p. 212*

person–job fit *p. 186*

person–organization fit *p. 207*

physical ability test *p. 193*

prediction *p. 184*

predictive criterion-related validity *p. 218*

reliability *p. 187*

selection *p. 184*

situational interview *p. 195*

structured interview *p. 195*

subject matter experts (SMEs) *p. 218*

third-country national (TCN) *p. 213*

unstructured interview *p. 195*

validity *p. 188*

work sample *p. 193*

DISCUSSION QUESTIONS

1. In what ways can a firm's employee selection procedures affect its performance?
2. Describe what has to take place if a company wants to increase the likelihood of achieving a good person–job fit when hiring a new employee.
3. Why are reliability and validity so important to the selection process?
4. What is the difference between initial and final selection methods? Why are both needed for most jobs?
5. Discuss when you would use a multiple-hurdle process as opposed to a compensatory process for making a final employment decision.
6. Suppose you are an assistant manager at a five-star luxury hotel, and you have been asked to create a structured behavioral interview for the job of bell captain. What role should your organization's culture play in terms of the interview questions you create? What might be an appropriate question to include? If you aren't sure what this particular job entails, visit O*NET (http://online.onetcenter.org) and read about it.
7. Identify and describe ways technology can be used to enhance the selection process.
8. How is the term *applicant* defined for selection purposes?

LEARNING EXERCISE 1

Identify a company that you would like to work for when you graduate. Research how that company handles the selection process. Use your networking skills to contact someone at the company who can tell you about the selection process. As you answer the following questions, keep in mind that the list is not exhaustive, so you will need to identify additional questions.

1. What is involved in the selection process for jobs at this company? (Be sure to identify the company in your response.)
2. Is the same process used for all jobs? If not, how does the process differ?
3. Does the company use initial and final screening methods?
4. Based on what you have learned about employee selection procedures, how effective do you think this company's selection process is likely to be?

LEARNING EXERCISE 2

Find a job description for a job that you would like to have. You can obtain many generic job descriptions online simply by typing the job title into a search engine. Based on the job description chosen, complete the following activities.

1. Design a selection process to use for both the initial screening and final screening of applicants. Indicate why each selection method included is appropriate.
2. Prepare two behavioral interview questions for the job. Specify which aspects of the job you are assessing with each question. Include a rating scale with the questions.
3. Discuss how you would change the selection process for the job selected if the company were small (under 50 employees) versus large (thousands of employees). Indicate why those changes would be appropriate and what other variables could affect the design of the selection process.

CASE STUDY # 1 — SELECTION AT FIRST APPAREL

For the past few years, First Apparel, a company headquartered in Spartanburg, South Carolina, has been evolving its business. Instead of only making cloth for designer apparel, First Apparel has begun to produce and offer for sale many types of fabric products, including canvas awnings and fabric for upholstery. The company has recently used nanotechnology to develop stain-resistant fabrics that are increasingly popular in skilled nursing facilities and hospitals because of their durability and ease of care.

The company has grown from 150 employees working at one plant in Spartanburg to 700 employees working in three plants in the United States and one in China. Some of the corporate jobs at First Apparel are marketing analyst, executive assistant, designer, sales representative, customer service specialist, purchasing manager, attorney, research scientist, and accountant. The company values integrity, relationships, innovation, and change. Its mission statement emphasizes the importance of putting the customer first:

At First Apparel, we strive to be the number-one provider of high-quality, high-performance designer fabrics. We believe in always putting the customer first, valuing our employees, and maintaining the highest ethical standards.

As First Apparel has grown, it has begun to experience a problem with turnover. Last year, the turnover rate was 45%. The turnover rate for comparable organizations in its industry and location is less than 20%.

The selection process at First Apparel has not changed from the time the company was started until now. Basically, the HR department prepares and posts an advertisement for whatever job is available, collects the applications and resumes, calls applicants of interest, and has them come in for a one-hour interview, followed by an interview with the supervisor of the position, regardless of the job.

DISCUSSION QUESTIONS

1. Discuss how the change in First Apparel's business strategy has likely affected the focus of its selection process for new employees.

2. Do you think the turnover problem could be related to selection? Discuss your answer.

3. How might First Apparel use technology to enhance its selection process?

4. How does the culture at First Apparel affect its selection process? How could it? How should it?

5. As First Apparel continues to grow its business, what are some other changes that need to occur in the selection process?

CASE STUDY # 2 — VIRTUAL SELECTION AT NATIONAL CITY CORPORATION

National City Corporation, a multistate banking firm with headquarters in Cleveland, Ohio, employs around 32,000 people. The company has been named one of "The Top 100 Employers" by *The Black Collegian* magazine. National City, founded in 1845, is one of the nation's largest financial holding companies.

National City uses a computerized simulation of specific job-related tasks known as "Virtual Job Tryout" to select candidates for jobs. In effect, job candidates get to audition for the job they want. The company believes that this type of assessment does more than help the company select the right people. The process also gives National City Corporation a distinctive recruiting experience that creates a unique impression on applicants and helps build the employer brand of the company.

National City worked with a consulting firm to develop several virtual simulations. The simulations have audio and video interactivity and are quite appealing to younger job applicants such as Gen Y'ers. Call center applicants, for instance, are given scenarios requiring them to solve customer service problems. Branch manager applicants have to demonstrate their skills at developing client relationships and making quick personnel decisions. Of course, these online assessments are just part of the overall selection process, but they are the next step in getting hired after completing the application process.

The firm believes that this part of its selection process is an educational tool that helps potential employees learn about the company. According to one of the consultants involved in the development of the simulation, innovative companies are looking for unique experiences such as this one to make their selection process stand out.

DISCUSSION QUESTIONS

1. Discuss the pros and cons of using virtual assessment for employee selection. To answer this question, you may want to do further research on the concept of virtual assessment for selection.

2. What concerns would you have about this selection process if you were an applicant?

3. Describe the steps the company would need to take to ensure that the selection process is nondiscriminatory and fair.

4. Do you think all types of employees would react the same to virtual assessment? Why? Why not?

5. For what type of skills is the virtual assessment best suited (e.g., hard, soft, business, engineering, other)? Explain your response.

6. Are there jobs for which this type of assessment would not be appropriate?

Sources: Adapted from Ruiz, G. Job candidate assessment tests go virtual. *Workforce Management* Online, January 2008; Shaker Consulting Web site, www.shakercg.com/hr/analytical-assessment. html#VJT, and National City Corporation Web site, www. nationalcity.com.

APPENDIX
Reliability and Validity

This appendix provides you with more detailed information about the concepts of reliability and validity. As you have already learned, if selection methods are not reliable and valid, you cannot be assured that they are useful for making good selection decisions.

RELIABILITY

In this chapter, we defined *reliability* as how well a selection measure yields consistent results over time or across raters. But how do you really know the degree of reliability of a selection technique such as a test or an interview? Answer: By computing a reliability coefficient. The coefficient expresses the degree of relationship between two variables. A higher reliability coefficient means the test is more reliable. Reliability coefficients can range from 0 to 1.00. A rule of thumb is that the reliability coefficient should be at least .85, and preferably .90, for the test to be considered reliable for selection purposes.[87]

VALIDITY

As discussed in the chapter, reliability alone does not ensure that the selection method is going to predict success on the job. Remember that *validity* is the extent to which a selection method measures what it is supposed to measure and how well it does so—or, simply, the job-relatedness of the selection measure. There are three ways to show that a selection method is valid: content validity, criterion-related validity, and construct validity.

Content Validity

Subject matter experts (SMEs)—individuals with skills, knowledge, and expertise related to a particular job—identify questions to include in selection tests and interviews to ensure that what needs to be measured is measured. A test developed by SMEs is considered to have **content validity**. For example, suppose a company has an opening for an electrical engineer. If the hiring manager decides to use a test to measure how much knowledge of electrical engineering applicants already have, he could either purchase a test designed to measure electrical engineering concepts or develop such a test. In either event, SMEs with expertise in electrical engineering should participate in the development of the test. In fact, if the company wants to purchase such a test, it is important to ask the vendor, "Who were the SMEs who prepared the test?" in order to determine whether they really were appropriate SMEs.

Most managers don't have to develop entire selection tests, but they may be called upon to provide questions for use in such a test, based on their expertise in a particular area and their knowledge of the job for which the test will be used. Also, as mentioned earlier, managers are required to interview prospective employees. As with tests, the closer the questions reflect the job, the greater is the content validity of the interview.

Criterion-Related Validity

Content validity provides support that a test measures what it is designed to measure based on how well the information in the test reflects the job requirements it is designed to measure. **Criterion-related validity**, also referred to as *empirical validity*, provides additional evidence of the validity of the measure by establishing a statistical relationship between the selection test and some measure of job performance, such as performance appraisal scores or quotas for production of work. Criterion-related validity is determined by correlating the selection test scores with scores on the criterion—the performance measure. If there is a positive relationship, the test is said to be a valid predictor of a person's performance on the job. Consider this example: Jane, Mark, Jorge, Abbie, Jie, Aron, and Darius all took a test as part of the selection process for managerial jobs, and all were hired for the jobs. After they had worked for the company for six months, the performance of each employee was evaluated, and a correlation coefficient computed between each person's test scores and performance appraisal scores. The results indicated that the test predicted how well each person would perform on the job. Thus, assuming that the test is reliable, it is also a valid predictor and can be used in the future to select among job applicants. Now let's look at two types of criterion-related validity: predictive criterion-related validity and concurrent criterion-related validity.

This following example demonstrates **predictive criterion-related validity**. Suppose job applicants are given a selection test that is not used to select employees. The scores on the test are filed away until the sample of test takers who are actually hired is sufficiently large (usually well over 100 test takers; the more test takers, the better). At that time, an evaluation of the performance of these employees is conducted, and the correlation between the scores is computed.

Another approach is **concurrent criterion-related validity**. This type of validity involves administering the selection test and collecting performance measure scores concurrently. The correlation between the two—the test score and performance measure scores—are computed and correlated to determine whether the test predicts how well people will perform on the job. Instead of filing away the scores, as in the previous example for predictive criterion-related validity, the scores are correlated with performance evaluation results collected at approximately the same time.

Exhibit A7.1 provides general guidelines for interpreting validity coefficients. As you can see, unlike reliability coefficients, validity coefficients don't have to be as high to be beneficial. And because a person's on-the-job performance depends on many factors, no single selection tool will perfectly predict one's performance.[88]

Exhibit A7.1 ▶

General Guidelines for
Interpreting Validity
Coefficients

Validity Coefficient Value	Interpretation
Above .35	Very beneficial
.21—.35	Likely to be useful
.11—.20	Depends on circumstances
Below .11	Unlikely to be useful

Source: U.S. Department of Labor. *Testing and assessment: An employer's guide to good practices*. Washington, DC: U.S. Department of Labor, Employment and Training Administration, 2000, p. 3–10.

Construct Validity

Construct validity is how well a selection tool, such as a test, measures the job-related characteristic—the construct—that it claims to measure. Constructs are abstract qualities or traits a person can possess, such as conscientiousness or a customer service orientation. An example will help to make this concept clearer. A bank call center needs employees with a customer service orientation. The bank can use a test to select employees with this orientation as long as the test is valid. To judge the construct validity of the test, the bank needs to:

1. Define exactly what it means by the term *customer service orientation*.

2. Show that the content of the test to be used reflects a customer service orientation (that is, has content validity).

3. Provide evidence that the test correlates with other measures of the customer service orientation construct.

4. Demonstrate that the test predicts a person's job performance (empirical validation).[89]

As with criterion-related validity, empirical evidence needs to be collected to show that the test exhibits construct validity.

chapter 8

TRAINING
AND
DEVELOPMENT

1. Explain the purpose of training and development. *(222)*

2. Use a needs assessment to determine training gaps. *(225)*

3. Describe commonly used training methods. *(231)*

4. Discuss types of training needed in organizations. *(236)*

5. Develop a way to measure the effectiveness of training. *(238)*

6. Make decisions about training within the context of organizational demands. *(241)*

7. Design training programs that address environmental influences. *(246)*

8. Ensure that a firm's training and development activities are legally compliant. *(251)*

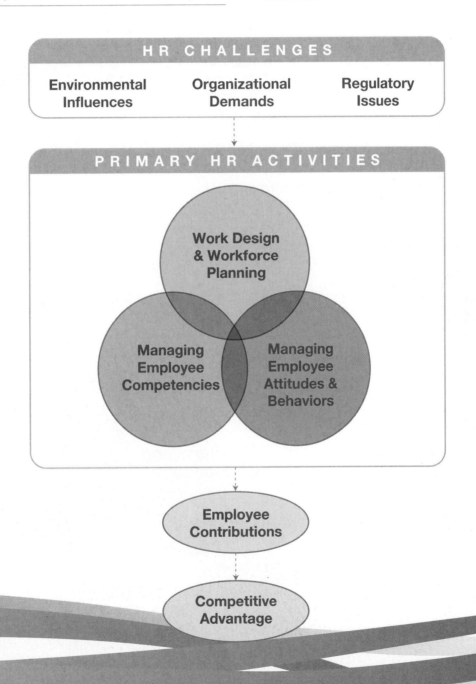

HR CHALLENGES

Environmental Influences Organizational Demands Regulatory Issues

PRIMARY HR ACTIVITIES

Work Design & Workforce Planning

Managing Employee Competencies

Managing Employee Attitudes & Behaviors

Employee Contributions

Competitive Advantage

THE PURPOSE OF TRAINING AND DEVELOPMENT

From the time you were born, you have been in training. Take a few minutes to think about everything you have learned over the years . . . how to dress yourself, how to get your homework done, how to drive, how to perform tasks at work . . . the list is endless. Now, think about how you learned to do all those things. Did you have a teacher? Did you learn in a classroom setting? Did you get it right the first time or make some mistakes and have to start over? Did you learn everything all at once or over time?

Chapter 4 introduced you to workforce planning, and in Chapter 5 you learned about job design and job analysis. Recall that job design and analysis define the tasks employees need to perform as well as the competencies they need to successfully do those tasks. Managers use that information to determine the training their employees need and to identify or develop effective training programs for them.

In Chapters 6 and 7, we examined the first two aspects of managing employee competencies, the highlighted circle in Exhibit 8.1. These chapters addressed employee recruitment and selection, both of which also affect training and development activities, the third aspect of managing competencies. At a basic level, training and development are needed to

Exhibit 8.1 ▶

Framework for the Strategic Management of Employees

ensure that workers recruited and selected are able to do their jobs well and that they will be prepared for future jobs in the company. If the labor market is flush with many highly qualified workers, managers will more easily be able to hire employees with the skill sets required to be immediately productive in their jobs. As a result, these workers will need less training and development. Conversely, fewer qualified workers in the labor force will mean new employees will need more training to ensure that they have the necessary competencies.

Training and development, therefore, are critical activities for ensuring the success of a company. In addition, training frequently appears as one of the top three benefits that employees want from their employers.[1] Providing the appropriate training and development opportunities for employees will increase their satisfaction and help them perform at a higher level, making the company more likely to achieve its goals.

In this chapter, we discuss the essential components of the training and development process and describe the methods used to train and develop new and current workers. We refer to Chapter 4 to demonstrate how the tasks, duties, and responsibilities of a job affect the amount and types of training employees need to perform their jobs well. We wrap up the chapter by discussing how organizational demands, environmental factors, and regulatory issues affect the decisions managers have to make about employee training and development.

But, before we discuss the specifics of training and development, we want to introduce you to two special types of training programs that organizations are paying more attention to as they focus more on employees as human capital critical to organizational success. These programs are orientation and onboarding. The same planning that we will describe as important for other training and development activities also applies to these programs.

EMPLOYEE ORIENTATION.   Employee orientation ensures that new employees know and understand company policies and procedures. When done well, these programs help employees understand how their jobs fit in with the goals of the organization. Orientation helps employees get off to a good start and improves their retention rates.[2] The Container Store views employee orientation as a key training activity. Over the years, the company's orientation has evolved into a weeklong program called "Foundation Week." For one full day during Foundation Week, store managers talk to new employees about the philosophy of the company. On other days, the employees learn about how the store operates, including how products come into the store and get shelved. Employees also learn about the various parts of the store, are taught selling techniques, and learn how to perform other functions in the store, such as properly greeting customers and running the company's store systems. By the review session on the last day, the employees are ready to start work, and do so prepared to deliver the high level of customer service that's put The Container Store among the top companies on the list of FORTUNE's "100 Best Companies to Work for in America." The company believes that its orientation program, coupled with its ongoing employee training programs, have definitely helped it retain its employees. Employees who understand how the company works as well as how to perform their jobs are more likely to be retained over time.[3]

employee orientation

A process designed to ensure employees understand the policies and procedures of the company when they first begin work, as well as understand how their job fits with the goals of the company.

Container Store employees participate in an extensive orientation program when they join the company.

onboarding

The hiring and integration process used to ensure a smooth transition of new employees, especially mid- and upper-level executives, into their jobs and the company, including helping them acclimate to the culture and goals of the organization.

ONBOARDING. For many companies, new employee orientation is only one part of a larger program referred to as onboarding. Onboarding refers to the hiring and integration process used to acclimate new employees, especially mid- and upper-level executives. Employees involved in onboarding at Randstad North America, one of the world's largest temporary and contract staffing agencies, job shadow other employees for 16 weeks. During that time, they receive training to do a number of activities, such as administer knowledge tests to job candidates and conduct performance reviews. The goal is to get the employees acclimated to the organization and job as quickly as possible.[4] Because up to 4% of new employees quit after a bad first day[5] and up to 40% of senior managers hired externally fail within 18 months,[6] programs that create a welcoming environment are critical. Formal programs bring new employees up to speed. They ensure that employees have the information they need or know where to get it, have someone to go to with questions and problems, and receive the training needed to be successful on the job.

Now, let's take a close look at the process of designing and implementing training and development programs. We start by providing a definition of training and development.

TRAINING AND DEVELOPMENT DEFINED

training

The systematic process of providing employees with the competencies—knowledge, skills, and abilities—required to do their current jobs.

Training is the systematic process of providing employees with the competencies—knowledge, skills, and abilities—required to do their current jobs. For instance, an employee might need to learn to use new computer software to do his job. This employee would need to be trained on the new software. Training can take many forms. Employees can obtain the KSAs on the job, by attending classes either online or in a classroom setting, by participating in role plays or simulations, or through a combination of these and other methods (discussed later in this chapter).

high-potential employees

Employees with the greatest likelihood of being successful and making significant contributions to organizational goal achievement.

development

Learning experiences that are focused on the future and aimed at preparing employees to take on additional responsibilities in different jobs, usually at a higher level.

In addition to training employees for their current jobs, companies also invest a lot of resources in developing employees for other jobs. For instance, Lockheed Martin invests a lot of resources in leadership development to prepare high-potential employees (employees with the greatest likelihood of being successful and making significant contributions to organizational goal achievement) for new and more significant jobs in the future. The purpose of training is to improve how well employees perform their current jobs. Development, in contrast, is future focused and aims to prepare employees to take on additional responsibilities in different jobs, usually at a higher level.

Both training and development help an organization equip its workforce to gain a sustained competitive advantage. Good managers make sure their employees participate in both. For example, many companies that invest a lot of money in skills training are also investing heavily in leadership development programs designed to prepare workers for higher-level jobs in their firms. One reason they are doing so is because as the baby boomers retire, other workers will need to be ready to step into their jobs.

The importance of training and development cannot be overemphasized. In fact, companies that treat training and development as a fundamental requirement for achieving their goals have been rewarded for this philosophy. One study of 500 publicly traded companies found that the ones that invested the most in training and development programs for their employees returned significantly higher returns to their shareholders than did the others.[7] That outcome is why in 2007 companies spent $16.38 billion on training products and services and why the overall U.S. corporate learning market was valued at $58.5 billion.[8]

Of course, appreciating the potential value of training and development is only part of the equation. Effective managers understand that training and development activities must be carried out properly to be effective. Designing an effective process requires making a lot of decisions, including deciding what training is needed, where the training is needed, who should be trained, and how to best carry it out. Although our discussion focuses directly on the training process, keep in mind that the same basic principles apply to designing effective development programs.

DESIGNING AN EFFECTIVE TRAINING PROCESS

Effective training programs result from following a systematic process, shown in the flowchart in Exhibit 8.2, that consists of (1) needs assessment, (2) design, (3) implementation, and (4) evaluation. Each part of the training process is critical. As a manager, the input you provide for each part will be key. If your organization has a training department, you will provide job information to the department to use in designing the programs. You will also need to provide information about where training is needed, who should be trained, and the types of training that should be delivered. In addition, you will be responsible for providing your employees with on-the-job training (OJT). (We describe OJT later in the chapter.) In smaller organizations, you might bear complete responsibility for each part of the training process. Let's take a look at each part of the process.

Part 1: Needs Assessment

Training has tremendous potential to improve the performance of employees, but it is often costly and time-consuming. Consequently, wise managers conduct a training needs assessment to understand where training activities can have the most impact within their organizations. A **needs assessment** identifies where gaps exist between what employees should be doing and what they are actually doing.[9] Training is used to fill these gaps.

Remember that training should support the company's strategic goals. With this in mind, Rockwell Collins, an aviation electronics and communication company serving government and private-sector customers, developed a training needs assessment form to ensure that training requests from managers were in keeping with strategic goals, the training was actually needed, and no alternatives to training existed.[10] An analysis such as this ensures that managers request training programs that will add value to their companies. When done effectively, a training needs assessment involves three separate, but equally important, analyses: organization analysis, task analysis, and person analysis. As you read about each of these analyses, you will understand more about the types of data needed to identify the gaps we described between what employees should be doing and what they are actually doing.

ORGANIZATION ANALYSIS   The needs assessment begins with an **organization analysis** to determine a firm's progress toward achieving its goals and objectives. Scanning the environment for opportunities and threats and evaluating the strengths and weaknesses

needs assessment

A means to identify where gaps exist between what employees should be doing and what they are actually doing.

organization analysis

An assessment used to determine a firm's progress toward achieving its goals and objectives.

◄ Exhibit 8.2

Flowchart for Designing an Effective Training Program

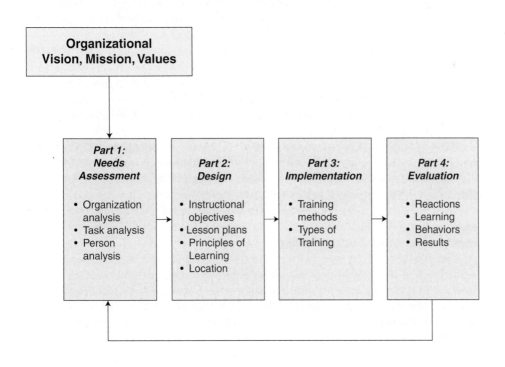

internally will help you identify training gaps. Is the company doing what it set out to do? If it isn't, is it because its current employees need better training? How do the organization's performance metrics, such as meeting its production goals, look? Do these metrics suggest that there are performance gaps that could be reduced with training? By answering questions such as these, companies will know where in the organization to provide training.

Along with determining where training is needed, the organization analysis involves determining the external and internal factors that affect what a company is trying to do and how it can do it. In the external environment, the demographics of the labor market determine the availability of workers with the skill sets needed to achieve the company's goals. New technologies present an opportunity for more efficient and effective processes. However, managers will need to determine whether there is a gap between the KSAs their employees have and the ones they need in order to make the most of the new technologies. When new laws are passed, employees need to be trained to comply with them. New business initiatives undertaken by the firm require its managers to consider whether the company's employees have the capabilities to take advantage of those opportunities. If a downturn in the economy forces a company to lay off employees, the employees who remain often need additional training as they take on new responsibilities.

In the internal environment, employee grievances, absenteeism, turnover, and accidents can indicate a need for training. Grievances often indicate that employees' supervisors need training or that their co-workers need compliance training related to illegal behaviors such as sexual harassment. High absenteeism rates can occur when employees are highly stressed because of a lack of training—a problem that can lead to high turnover rates as well. Accidents often happen because employees have not received proper safety training.

We will talk about external and internal factors in more detail in the second half of the chapter. For now, Company Spotlight 8.1 provides a good example of the importance of identifying and addressing skills and knowledge gaps. When IBM changed its strategy, the shift led to gaps between what the company's employees were used to doing and what the organization's new direction required them to do. The change in direction determined where IBM needed to provide training.

task analysis

An analysis used to identify gaps between the knowledge, skills, and abilities needed to perform work required to support an organization's objectives and the current KSAs of the employees.

TASK ANALYSIS After the organization analysis, the next step is to conduct a **task analysis**. The purpose of a task analysis is to identify gaps between the (1) KSAs needed to perform the work required to support an organization's objectives and (2) its employees' current KSAs. An organization analysis focuses on identifying training gaps across a company's workforce. A task analysis focuses on identifying the specific training content needed to close the gaps between what employees know and are able to currently do and the KSAs they should possess to actually make value-added contributions to their firms. Employees cannot be expected to perform at their highest levels until those gaps are addressed.

Gaps exist for a variety of reasons. The employees a firm hired might not have the right KSAs. Perhaps a job was not properly analyzed before the hiring process began, so the employee was hired for the wrong skill set. Perhaps the organization itself has changed direction, and the job needs to be restructured. Or, employees with the right skill set may not have been available in the labor market. A task analysis will reveal the discrepancies between the KSAs needed and the KSAs employees have.

KSA gaps can surface in a number of ways. For instance, problems in meeting production requirements, low levels of performance among knowledge workers, an increase in accidents, and an increase in customer complaints about service are all possible signals that employees may not have the required KSAs to perform their jobs. This gap analysis should be an ongoing process. And any time major changes are made in an organization that affect what employees do, a task analysis should be conducted to ensure that employees are prepared to assume their new responsibilities.

Consider the following situation: The CEO of a midsized financial services firm decided to hire a consultant to provide its employees with customer service training. However, after the consultant conducted an organizational needs assessment, she determined that the firm's customer service was actually a key source of its competitive success. What the firm really needed was more training for employees on a new computer system. The new system had some bugs that needed to be worked out, and the training on the new system had been limited. As a result, employees kept going back to their old manual system

COMPANY spotlight   8.1 How Training Helped IBM Change Its Focus

Training magazine ranked IBM as the number-one company for developing human capital on its 2005 "Training Top 100" list. From 2003 to 2004, IBM increased its expenditures on training and learning by 32%. In 2005, IBM projected that it would spend over $700 million for learning-related activities and that employees would spend more than 15 million hours on training initiatives. Several years earlier, IBM had decided to realign its business strategy, operational, and organizational models to be more agile and adaptable in order to better meet its customers' needs. This necessitated a major change in the firm's culture. IBM knew it needed to determine what its clients needed and base the expertise its employees needed on that information. Consequently, the company identified 522 roles in the company and the expertise employees needed to perform each role.

In addition to classroom training, IBM began to pay more attention to how employees learn through their work. The company believes that most learning—80% of it, in fact—takes place *outside* classroom training programs. IBM's "On Demand Learning" program is a result of its organization analysis. The "On Demand Learning" program includes face-to-face courses, Web-based courses, and on-the-spot learning.

The program works like this: As an employee works on a project, learning opportunities appear on her computer screen to support what she is working on at the time. Additional learning opportunities are provided, including a link connecting the employee with experts on topics related to the project, an invitation to discuss the situation with IBM's other employees online, and online learning modules. With this approach, learning is more personalized, embedded in employees' work, and available when and where needed.

A learning team member is intimately involved in the annual strategic planning process for each business unit of IBM. This team member's role in the planning process is to ensure that he understands the unit's strategic direction and the implications of the firm's training plans. Its training programs have become so successful that IBM now sells some of its learning programs to other organizations.

Sources: Based on IBM Web site. IBM ranked #1 in training. http://www-304.ibm.com/jct03001c/services/learning/ites.wss/us/en?pageType=page&c=a0004380; Davenport, R. A new shade of BIG BLUE IBM reinvents its workforce. *T + D* 59:34–40, 2005; and Speizer, I. IBM builds a new business on its training program. *Workforce Management*, July 2005, p. 59.

to service customers. The firm's top managers mistakenly believed employees' preference for the old system meant that they needed more customer service training, which was not the case: Because the employees knew how to provide a high level of customer service, they used the system that worked! The moral of the story is to keep in mind that the "apparent" problem you're trying to solve might not be the actual problem—and not identifying the right gap can result in wasted training time and money.

PERSON ANALYSIS   A **person analysis** involves deciding which employees actually need to participate in training programs. The information needed to make this decision can come from a variety of sources, including observation, performance appraisals, supervisor recommendations, and employee skills inventories. Individual production records and skills tests also help determine which employees need training.

Regardless of the source of the information, it is very important to make sure that training is what is needed to address any gaps between an individual's performance and desired outcomes. Employees who are unhappy at work and not performing well might actually have the right qualifications but not be willing to use them. This highlights a key point about person analysis and training effectiveness. In general, person analysis is a great tool to use to identify situations in which employees simply are not properly trained. It does not, however, usually overcome problems of employee motivation or effort. When employees are not motivated to perform tasks that they are able to perform, performance management rather than training is the necessary course of action. In these circumstances, the resources spent to train the person are not likely to result in a high payoff; they will just increase the training costs.

Managers should also remember that when an employee is not performing well, the problem might not be a lack of skills or a lack of motivation. Rather, the person's manager

person analysis

An assessment of the gap between an individual's performance and desired job outcomes.

might not be communicating to the person what the organization's expectations are. As a result, the employee might not need training but rather might need to have his or her job responsibilities clarified.

Part 2: Design

The information from the needs analysis tells managers where in the organization training is needed (organization analysis), what the focus of the training initiatives should be (task analysis), and which employees should participate in the training programs (person analysis). And while this is critical information, training must also be effectively designed to be of value.

A clear understanding of the goals of the program at the beginning of the design process helps ensure that the training program is results oriented and supports the mission of the organization.[11] Effectively designing a training program includes establishing the program's instructional objectives, developing the lesson plans for it, and incorporating principles of learning. We will now review each of these elements.

INSTRUCTIONAL OBJECTIVES Do you like to get in your car and just drive? When you don't have to be anywhere by a specific time, doing so can be quite relaxing, especially if the traffic is light and the weather is good. But when you have to be somewhere by a certain time, you are likely to carefully plan your trip to ensure that you arrive at your destination on time. A lot of training programs aren't successful because they are more like the first journey than the latter. Take the case of the manager of a small dry cleaning establishment. He decided to put in some new dry cleaning equipment last year. He knew he would have to teach his six employees how to use the equipment. However, instead of thinking about what specifically they would need to know, he randomly relayed information to them as he thought of it. Only when customers began to complain about their dry cleaning did he realize that he wasn't doing a good job of training his employees. In large or small organizations, providing training that has clearly defined objectives saves a lot of time and energy, and it often results in superior customer service or higher-quality products.

What the manager in our story missed was an understanding of the need for a focused training plan. Writing effective instructional objectives is a first step in designing the training program. **Instructional objectives** describe the purpose of the training program and what it will accomplish. The objectives should be linked to the organization's goals and conveyed to employees so they understand what they should learn from the training and how they can use it on the job.

You probably noticed that we have listed objectives at the beginning of each of the chapters. These, in fact, are instructional objectives. They served as a guide as we wrote this book to make sure we were providing you with the information you need relative to each topic. The objectives also serve as a guide for you as you read the chapters. Before we wrote the objectives, we thought about who our audience would be (students studying business), the level of course for which the book is targeted (college students), and what our audience would need to know relative to each topic. Had the dry cleaning manager taken the time to do the same thing, he likely would have had few, if any, customer complaints because he would have made sure the employees were properly trained. Even on-the-job training, as you will learn later in this chapter, needs to be well designed.

LESSON PLANNING School teachers are intimately familiar with the concept of a lesson plan. They routinely map out what they will do during their class sessions to achieve their instructional objectives. Corporate training requires the same type of planning. If you work in a company that has its own training department, you likely will be asked to provide information about the content that should be covered during training. As we have already mentioned, in a small business, you will often be responsible for designing and carrying out the entire training program. Having a lesson plan is critical in either case.

Whereas instructional objectives guide the content of training, **lesson plans** provide a map of what should be done during each training session to achieve the objectives. This map includes what will be covered, who will cover it, how the material will be taught, where it will be taught, and how long each part will last.

instructional objective

Statement that describe what is to be accomplished in a training program and, therefore, drive the design of the program.

lesson plan

A map of what should be done during each training session to achieve objectives.

PRINCIPLES OF LEARNING   Even the best lesson plan will fail if the trainer doesn't understand that people do not all learn in the same way or at the same pace. Some people can learn how to do something by having it described to them. Others need to see it demonstrated. Many people have to actually perform the task to learn how to do it. Each of us has a preference for how we learn best, even though we can usually adapt to other teaching methods. When you're designing and providing informal as well as formal training and development programs for your employees, how you deliver the material can be as critical as the material itself. We will now discuss some principles of learning related to learning styles, learning agility, self-efficacy, interest in learning, and training location that improve the likelihood that employees will learn during training.

Learning Styles.   If you have to find your way to a new place, would you rather have someone: (1) tell you the directions, (2) draw you a map, or (3) take you there the first time? Learning styles affect how people prefer to absorb and process new information. A number of ways to categorize learning styles exist. One often-cited approach categorizes learners as auditory, visual, tactile, or kinesthetic.[12] Auditory learners hear information and are able to process and remember it. Lectures and discussions are good training methods for these learners. Visual learners need to see the information, and they often prefer seeing it in a picture format, such as a map or table. They learn well in training programs using a lot of visual and audiovisual demonstrations. Tactile learners need to interact with the material they're learning. They are likely to underline what they are reading and take notes when listening to others. They prefer training programs that include writing activities and other experiences that keep their hands busy. Kinesthetic learners need to be actively involved in the learning experience by actually doing something rather than by hearing or seeing the material. They relate well to role plays and other experiential-based training methods. We all learn in multiple ways but usually have a preference for one style of learning over another.

So, what does all this mean in terms of employee training? Think about your experiences in class. Have you learned better when the teacher used hands-on exercises or just lectured? Your employees, like you, are most comfortable with a particular learning style. Basically, you need to acknowledge these differences.[13] By being aware that differences exist, you will be more likely to use a variety of training approaches with your employees, and you may even learn to target your on-the-job training style to the learning styles of the employees. The result will be better trained and more satisfied employees. For instance, visual learners will be less frustrated and have less difficulty learning if most of the training is visual rather than auditory. The opposite is true for auditory learners. Incorporating all four learning styles in training programs will reduce the frustration of trainees with different styles and increase the learning that results.

Learning Agility.   Employees high on **learning agility** seek new experiences and opportunities to learn new knowledge and skills. They are then willing and able to incorporate that information into how they perform their job. Employees high on learning agility are also believed to be high-potential employees[14] (mentioned earlier in this chapter). While we don't recommend just using learning agility as a selection criterion, being aware of the impact of this aspect of learning during the selection process is a good thing.

Self-efficacy.   Having confidence that you can do something means you have **self-efficacy** with respect to that task. If you have self-efficacy, you will more likely succeed at doing that task. In the context of training, employees who have higher self-efficacy with regard to the training are more likely to perform well during the training and are more likely to then use that training on the job.[15] There is a possible downside, however. Employees with high self-efficacy might not be as diligent in the training process as those with low self-efficacy. High self-efficacy could lead employees to think they can rush through the training activity. Low self-efficacy can cause employees to work harder to learn the material and/or skill to overcome their lack of confidence.[16]

Interest in a Training Program.   Everything we need to learn in order to do our jobs well is not equally interesting to us. A manager needs to understand the importance of carefully choosing the right training program for employees. In general, the effectiveness of training is likely to increase when employees are genuinely interested in the content of the

---

learning style

How people prefer to absorb and process new information.

learning agility

The willingness to seek new experiences and opportunities to learn new knowledge and skills.

self-efficacy

The confidence that a person has that he can perform a particular task.

Exhibit 8.3 ▶

Training Adult
Learners

Adults need to:

1. See the big picture of what they are learning at the beginning of the training program

2. Be intimately involved in the training activities

3. Have spaced practice (learning opportunities spread out over a period of time) when learning something new rather than having everything thrown at them in one long session

4. Be allowed to relate their past and current experiences to the training

Source: Based on Hager, P. Lifelong learning in the workplace? Challenges and issues. *Journal of Workplace Learning* 16:22–32, 2004.

training and are motivated to learn.[17] Charismatic trainers and engaging and fun learning experiences heighten participants' interest in the training process. If you want to ensure that employees complete their training programs and remember what they were taught, making the training program interesting is important. But even more important is helping employees see how they can personally benefit from participating in the program. Understanding how their job performance will improve, for example, is likely to stimulate their interest in learning the material presented. Exhibit 8.3 provides ideas for enhancing the learning experiences of adult learners. As you will see, these ideas should work well with learners of all ages, even though they are based on research of adults.

Location. Would you learn better in a large auditorium or as part of a small group, sitting around a conference table? How about sitting at home at your computer or at a retreat center with co-workers and a dynamic trainer? Perhaps you could learn in a number of these settings. Location is important for training success. Just think about the basics, such as heat, light, and comfortable seating. A room that is too warm might put trainees to sleep; a room that is too cold will distract attendees as they try to keep warm. When deciding on the location, little things do matter. Many companies take employees offsite for training programs or send them to programs sponsored by other organizations. These companies know how easily distracted employees can become by the daily routine and unexpected events related to their jobs if they are returning to their offices during breaks. Having employees in another location reduces their distractions, although with the proliferation of handheld computers, this is getting more difficult. Regardless of whether it's onsite or offsite, the training location should be carefully selected to ensure that the environment is conducive to learning and disruptions are minimized.

Part 3: Implementation

As toddlers, we learned to feed ourselves and put on our clothes. This learning took place "on the job" because our job at the time was to learn to take care of ourselves. As we entered school, we learned in the classroom, often through a variety of teaching methods. Our teachers lectured to us, led discussion groups, and had us engage in exercises to reinforce the concepts we were learning. You probably experienced different types of computer-aided learning as well. The ways you have been trained to do things in the past are not that different from how you will train your employees to do things in the future.

If you were a manager at Booz Allen, a rapidly growing professional services firm that provides consulting to private companies and government agencies, you would have a large array of training resources available for your employees. They could participate in traditional classroom training as well as in a virtual, online campus; they could take "stretch" job assignments that required them to do new and challenging tasks, participate in university partnership opportunities, and have a mentor and/or coach.[18] Those examples are just some of the many methods available for delivering training. As you read about the different methods, you will likely note that some of them require little to no computer or audiovisual technology and can therefore be described as "low tech." There is minimal interpersonal interaction during

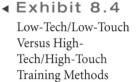

	Low Tech	High Tech
High Touch	OJT Classroom training Coaching	OJT Simulation Blended learning
Low Touch	Printed materials	E-learning Audiovisual Simulation

Low tech = Limited or no use of computers and/or audiovisual technology
High tech = Training depends on use of computers and/or audiovisual technology

Low touch = Minimal or no interaction with others
High touch = Training involves extensive interpersonal interaction

the training as well, so they are "low touch." Other methods can be classified as "high tech" and "high touch." Exhibit 8.4 provides a summary of the methods we discuss within the high-tech/high-touch dimensions. The content of the training determines whether it should be high tech or high touch, and some content calls for both. We have categorized the methods where they are most likely to fall on the chart. This list is by no means exhaustive but gives you a good idea of what is available and what is most commonly used.

TRAINING METHODS As a manager, you will constantly be making decisions about how well your employees are doing their jobs and whether additional training is needed to improve or upgrade their skills and knowledge. Making sure the method of training delivery is appropriate for the content and audience will increase the value that the training adds. In this section we discuss the most common training methods. We provide a brief overview of each method, along with some discussion of the advantages and downsides of each. Keep in mind that there are many more methods for training than are described here. We end this section with a discussion of blended learning, an approach that many organizations are now using to reinforce learning concepts.

On-the-Job Training. On-the-job training (OJT) occurs when a manager or co-worker teaches an employee how to perform some aspect of a job in the actual job location rather than in a separate training location. OJT is frequently used and can be cost-effective.

on-the-job training (OJT)

Training that occurs when a manager or coworker teaches an employee how to perform some aspect of a job in the actual job location rather than in a separate training location.

Employee training comes in many forms including using a ropes course for team building.

A primary benefit is that while employees are learning, they are being productive. The employee doesn't have to take time away from the job to attend a training program. OJT works best when the trainer is selected carefully and understands that all trainees will not learn in the same way.

On the other hand, OJT can be costly. If the person providing the training is not adequately trained to perform the job, then the new employee will not learn the right way to perform the job tasks or might not learn all the information needed to perform tasks successfully.[19] If you have ever been in a store when an employee was just learning the job, on the job, you know that an employee-in-training often takes more time to assist you than an experienced employee would take. This slowness causes delays and irritates customers. And mistakes made can be costly, especially if the customer leaves and never returns.

In a more extreme example, think of the potential costs to an airline that chooses to use on-the-job training for pilots as the primary training method. You probably would not want to fly on that airline! Therefore, a manager needs to think through the costs as well as the benefits of OJT and remember that costs include loss of productive time, loss of customers, and loss of property—at a minimum. For OJT to be effective, it is important to ensure that the trainers have a framework for conducting training. Using the guidelines listed in Exhibit 8.5, along with making sure there are well-written training materials and measurable performance objectives, will enhance the likelihood of training success.

Three specific types of OJT programs are apprenticeships, internships, and cooperative education programs. *Apprenticeships* have long been an established method for teaching skilled trades. Learning a skilled trade, such as carpentry, requires "hands-on" learning under the tutelage of a master tradesperson. But there are other types of apprentice programs as well. For instance, the National Information Technology Apprenticeship System (NITAS) is a collaborative effort by the U.S. Department of Labor Office of Apprenticeship and employers of information technology workers. The program provides tools and resources to train, certify, and mentor IT workers in seven types of IT jobs.[20]

Internships are a type of OJT that is familiar to many students. An internship involves a student working at an organization for a specified period of time for the purpose of learning what a job is like and seeing the relationship between information learned in the classroom and practice in an organization. A large number of universities have begun to require students to complete internships before they graduate in disciplines as diverse as finance and human services. These internships can be paid or unpaid, and they can be completed for college credit or not for credit. For a student, an internship provides a way to try out a job of interest. For an employer, internships provide a mechanism for recruiting top students. Interns who do well during their time at the company often receive full-time

Exhibit 8.5 ▶

Steps to Increase the Effectiveness of OJT

The trainer should:

1. Conduct an orientation to ensure that the trainee understands the objectives of the training.

2. Establish rapport with the trainee to reduce anxiety on the part of the trainee and increase learning.

3. Demonstrate the task for the trainee and discuss how the task is important for the job.

4. Coach the trainee to reinforce the training and address any questions.

5. Observe the trainee performing the task and give feedback, as needed, about the performance.

6. Debrief the trainee to further reinforce the importance of the training and schedule follow-up times.

Source: Based on Walter, D. Training and certifying on-the-job trainers. *Technical Training*, March/April 1998, pp. 32–35.

job offers when they graduate. It is worth noting that high school students have begun to complete internships as well.

Engineering and a few other disciplines offer *cooperative education programs* for students. These coop programs, as they are known, are also a form of OJT. Students typically work for one semester and then attend school for a semester. A coop can also be done while a student is taking classes. The student goes to school part of a day and works the other part. The purpose of a coop is the same as the purpose of internships. Students and employers get to find out if they are a good fit for each other while the student learns practical application of information being learned in school.

Operations and Procedures Manuals. Almost everything you buy these days comes with some kind of operations manual. The same is true for many tasks that employees do on their jobs. Often employee operations and procedures manuals outline company policies and practices as well. Because procedures and task guidelines are written down and available on the job, employees can refer to them as often as needed for clarification or if they forget something. The manuals can also be readily copied and distributed to a large number of employees or put online. The downside is that not all manuals are well written or address all potential problems or issues employees will encounter. This can result in frustrated employees who have trouble getting their questions answered and frustrated customers who can't get their questions answered.

Classroom Training. We are all familiar with **classroom training** by virtue of having been students for many years. However, lecturing to employees is one of the least effective ways to train them because it does not always engage people (and it is not really effective for most students, either!). Lectures can be an effective way to disseminate simple information, but they do not necessarily facilitate behavioral change. Including role plays, discussions, and other experiential activities along with lectures as part of the classroom training experience will increase its effectiveness.

Until recently, classroom training was often an economical way to provide training for a large number of employees. Now, computer technology has made training more efficient and more economical in many cases, even allowing companies to create virtual classrooms that bring together employees from different locations. When classroom training does occur, it lasts for a shorter period of time, perhaps one day instead of five.[21]

E-learning. **E-learning** involves using the Internet, computers, and other electronic tools to deliver training programs. Advances in computer technology and its accessibility have probably changed the training process more than any other innovation in history.[22] Now, training can be delivered online, on demand, 24/7, regardless of an employee's location. Companies can train more employees more efficiently, faster, and at less cost to the company than with traditional classroom-type training programs. At Caterpillar, the cost of online training is about one-third the cost of traditional training, and the more employees who receive training, the greater the savings.[23]

E-learning can take several forms:

- *Web-based training.* With **Web-based training**, employees can log on to a secure Web site and take a course or participate in a Webcast.
- *Desktop training.* Employees use computer software programs to learn new information or skills. **Desktop training** differs from Web-based training in that the training program is housed on the employee's personal computer or on a server.
- *Podcast training.* **Podcasts** are digital recordings that can be downloaded and played back later. They are part of the latest training wave. Capital One, a financial services company, bought 3,000 iPods for its employees so that they could download more than a dozen lessons on topics the company wants all employees to know. The goal of the program was to reduce the time employees spend in a classroom and to reduce the costs of bringing employees to Capital One's McLean, Virginia, location.[24] Of course, audio learners are the most drawn to this training approach. The U.S. government has also made use of podcasts to keep employees trained on the latest developments of importance to their jobs. The government has even used radio commercials to encourage employees to download its podcasts to stay current on workplace changes.

classroom training

Traditional learning that includes lectures, role plays, discussions, and other experiential activities.

e-learning

Using the Internet, computers, and other electronic tools to deliver training programs.

Web-based training

Learning experiences that are accessed through a secure Web site, such as online courses and Webcasts.

desktop training

A training approach in which employees access a software program housed on their computers or on a server.

podcast

A digital recording that can be downloaded and played back later.

Exhibit 8.6 ▶

Tips to Increase
E-learning
Participation

- Provide guidance for selecting courses.
- Include a rating and recommendations tool with the course listings.
- Award certification or provide a certificate of achievement upon completion of a course or series of courses.
- Offer benefits such as points redeemable for gifts or products.
- Reward managers who promote e-learning.
- Use online ads or guided tours to increase familiarity with e-learning.
- Provide live demos to increase awareness.
- Use organizational communication to familiarize employees with programs.
- Ensure that programs are user friendly and that support is readily available.
- Employ multiple techniques to engage learners.

Source: Based on Carliner, S. Ten tips for getting learners to take e-courses. *ASTD Learning Circuits*, 2008, www.learningcircuits.org/0108_Carliner.html.

One reason e-learning is often more economical than classroom training is that participants don't need to travel to a training site.[25] The downside of e-learning is that employees have more control over how long and how often they practice the material—which can be bad for people who tend to skip parts or move quickly through the material.[26] Before embarking on an e-learning program, a company needs to weigh the pros and cons of this type of training[27] and pilot the program with a small group of employees to make sure it achieves desired goals. Exhibit 8.6 lists tips that have been found to increase the likelihood of employee participation in e-learning courses.

audiovisual training

Providing instruction to employees by having them watch a video presentation.

Audiovisual Training. Audiovisual training involves providing instruction on a topic to employees by having them watch a video presentation. The presentation is often stored on a DVD, although VHS and CD-ROM formats are also still widely available. Presentations can be viewed in an individual setting or in a group setting, the choice of which should depend on the goals for the training. Using video training to teach a computer skill can be done individually. Using video training to teach team building is best done in a group setting so that the employees can practice what they are learning from the video. Group training sessions are facilitated by an expert on the topic who can be either a company employee or an external consultant. Video training provides an economical way to ensure that all employees receive the same information. Organizations can either prepare their own audiovisual training materials or buy programs off the shelf. The downside is that preparing a custom video for a company can be quite expensive initially, and off-the-shelf programs can also be costly because they sometimes involve a per-participant charge each time they are used.

simulation

A training activity that replicates the work employees will be doing without the safety and cost concerns often associated with various jobs.

Simulations. Simulations, which replicate the work the employees will be doing, were first used by the military to train pilots and for weapons training. Airlines use flight simulators to teach pilots to fly and to handle an airplane in typical situations they are likely to encounter. This approach to training is much less expensive and much safer than waiting until a pilot actually encounters a hazardous situation and hoping that a lot of OJT happens quickly. Now, simulations are used in other work environments to train employees.[28]

Good simulations are engaging, fun, and challenging. Unlike static online training programs, simulations lead to a high rate of completion by keeping the "players" involved in the learning process.[29] A downside is the complexity involved in developing a simulation that accurately mirrors the job, especially when the job is less structured than the one in our pilot example. Company Spotlight 8.2 provides yet another example of how IBM is innovative in its approach to training.

COMPANY *spotlight* 8.2 Gaming as Training Tools

Any gamer is familiar with the concept of Avatars and other aspects of virtual worlds. IBM and Sun Microsystems are just two of many companies that have found their own use for the virtual world that Avatars inhabit when providing training for employees.

IBM is using Second Life, a virtual world in which an employee can create her own image—as close to or different from the real one as she wishes—as a training tool for employees. In 2006, IBM announced that it would use video game technology and three-dimensional virtual space as a training forum for its employees around the world, specifically for new employee orientation and employee mentoring.

The company believes that using virtual space for training will appeal to the generation of employees who have grown up playing virtual games. And, since employees see this approach to training as more of a game than traditional learning, they may be willing to take more risks and be more flexible in the learning process.

Sun Microsystems wanted to find a way to improve its onboarding process for new employees. In October of 2007, Sun introduced a game called "Dawn of the Shadow Specters" to teach new hires about Sun's core businesses, mission, and

values. In the futuristic world of the game, employees fight evil foes that are trying to destroy Sun's network.

The game serves two purposes: teaching employees about Sun Microsystems and more quickly engaging them in the culture of the company. In fact, new hires can log onto a company Web site even before they start work and play a virtual game to learn about the company. Sun has also revamped other aspects of the onboarding process to make the process more high tech and high touch, such as changing the welcome gift from a t-shirt that usually faded fast to a nice Sun Microsystems backpack, and printing the new hire paperwork on brighter paper. While these may seem like small things, they have a positive impact on first impressions which ensures the employment relationship gets off to a good start.

Sources: Based on IBM Learning Programs Get a 'Second Life'. By: Frauenheim, Ed, *Workforce Management,* 12/11/2006, Vol. 85, Issue 23, p. 6; and Klaff, L. New Emphasis on First Impressions. *Workforce Management* Online, March 2008. URL: http://www.workforce.com/archive/feature/25/41/58/index.php?ht=virtual%20training%20avatar%20virtual%20training%20avatar

Blended Learning. Probably the most frequently used form of training now is blended learning, which refers to the use of multiple modes of training to accomplish a training goal. DaimlerChrysler, for example, decided to use behavioral interviewing to improve the quality of the firm's hiring decisions. Because the company had to find a way to train all managers involved in the hiring process, it created a two-part program. Part 1 was required and could be taken online or in a full-day class. The training focused on identifying competencies, developing and practicing behavioral interview questions, and learning how to score the interviews. Part 2 was optional and focused on skill building. As with Part 1, Part 2 was delivered in two ways: Trainees could attend a class, conduct mock interviews, and receive feedback, or they could arrange to do a telephone interview and receive feedback.[30]

Another global organization invested $3 million in training for 30,000 employees in North and South America, Europe, and Asia. The training on new system technology and business processes took place over four weeks. The training was done by using a blended learning approach involving e-learning and exercises and activities in a classroom learning lab. The cost to the company was only $100 per employee which was far less than the cost of classroom training alone.[31] The downside of blended learning is often the time and resources required to put the training components together; however, the payoff is generally worth the expense. Company Spotlight 8.3 describes how Marriott Corporation used blended learning to prepare employees for a new corporate initiative.

College and University Programs. Mitre, a not-for-profit research firm, provides up to $20,000 and bonuses for employees to obtain advanced degrees.[32] Mitre recognizes that some of the training and development that employees need can be provided through taking courses and completing degrees at educational institutions; therefore, Mitre offers tuition reimbursement. Companies that offer tuition reimbursement usually have

blended learning

The use of multiple modes of training, often with one part being online, to accomplish a training goal.

COMPANY spotlight

8.3 Marriott's Shared Services Initiative

Marriott Corporation differentiates itself by ensuring that its employees throughout the hotel chain are well trained. One of Marriott's recent strategic initiatives has involved consolidating all the finance operations of its hotels worldwide at what it calls a "Shared Services Center." The firm's decision to do so meant that the company needed to train 8,000 of its employees around the globe to use the new system at the center.

All 8,000 users received computer-based training. Hotel property managers received instructor-led process training. Employees assigned to the center received blended training in the form of computer-based and instructor-led training as well as a day of training designed to simulate the actual work environment. The design of the course was chosen because it was the quickest way to effectively train a large number of users.

Marriott reports that the training program was a success—the most successful distance-learning program the company has ever offered, in fact. The firm's managers say that it helped get the new center open on schedule so that Marriott could continue to deliver high-quality customer service, in keeping with its mission.

Source: Prescott, C. A. Marriott redefines the shared services model. *Accenture Outlook Journal: Case Study, 1*, 2002, http://www.accenture.com/NR/rdonlyres/E9EA5BDA-D8A2-4A5A-9C73-ED871B32EE92/0/Marriott.pdf.

---

restrictions on how much they will pay and for what kinds of education they will pay. Often the coursework has to be directly job related. The amount of reimbursement can vary from full reimbursement to reimbursement of only a portion of the cost. Reimbursement can also be contingent on achieving a certain grade in a class. For instance, the firm might reimburse 100% of the cost if a grade of A is earned but only 80% for a B grade.

Coaching and Mentoring. Employee coaching is often used as a form of employee development, but there is a training element to it as well. Coaching is a billion-dollar business that started out in organizations as a way to help problem employees become better performers. Now, much of the coaching that occurs is with executives, to groom them for future opportunities.[33] One of the problems with coaching, however, is that the concept is often confused with mentoring. Coaching is primarily about performance improvement, usually short term, and usually relative to a specific skill or ability. For instance, a manager who is having trouble gaining the cooperation of his subordinates might be coached on how to better communicate with his employees. Mentoring is a longer-term relationship that involves a more senior employee teaching a junior employee how the organization works and nurturing that person as she progresses in her career.

Coaching is better at supporting different learning styles than a lot of other types of training and development because coaching is almost always done one-on-one—one coach and one employee.[34] It can be done by members of the organization, if they're appropriately trained, as well as by external coaches. One hospital in London provides 22 hours of coaching during the year for its directors and heads of departments. The head of training and development there sees this as an important part of the hospital's leadership and management program.[35] The growth in the coaching industry has led to the call for standards to ensure that employees and organizations are treated ethically and fairly.

Now that we have looked at some of the most frequently used methods of training, we can discuss types of training programs.

TYPES OF TRAINING Training can generally be grouped into four categories: compliance, knowledge, basic skills, and behavioral. We discuss each briefly.

Compliance Training. In Chapter 3, we provided a lot of information about the regulations that affect employee management. It is important for you, as a manager, to ensure that your employees, especially those with supervisory responsibility, know these regulations. Compliance training includes both legal compliance training and diversity training. Legal compliance training ensures that a firm's managers and employees know what they can and cannot do from a legal standpoint. Sexual harassment training and ADA

coaching

Short-term training provided one-on-one and primarily focused on performance improvement relative to a specific skill or ability.

mentoring

A longer-term relationship that involves a more senior employee teaching a junior employee how the organization works and nurturing that person as she progresses in her career.

legal compliance training

Training that ensures that a firm's managers and employees know what they can and cannot do from a legal standpoint.

training are examples. **Diversity training** helps reduce discrimination by making employees more aware of discrimination that occurs overtly and covertly in the workplace. Next, we discuss each type of training in more detail.

Compliance training ensures that employees know what they can and cannot do from a legal standpoint. Some laws specify that certain training must occur. For example, California Assembly Bill (AB) 1825, which was signed into law in 2004, required California firms with 50 or more employees to provide sexual harassment training to all their supervisors by 2006. AB 1825 went so far as to specify the length of the training, the format in which it had to be presented, and the topics discussed—the relevant federal and state laws, remedies available to victims, and so forth. Connecticut has a similar law.[36] Even in states that do not have such laws, sexual harassment training is necessary to reduce the likelihood of such behavior occurring in the workplace and to reduce an employer's liability should it occur. In fact, the federal guidelines for reducing sexual harassment in the workplace include guidance on providing training.

The case of *Cadena v. Pacesetter Corp.*, 224 F.3d 1203 (10th Cir. 2000), highlights both the need for training and the need for employers to carefully select trainers to cover topics such as sexual harassment. In this particular case, the jury awarded $300,000 in punitive damages to the plaintiff, and the 10th U.S. Circuit Court of Appeals upheld the award. Apparently, the employer could not verify that the trainer used for sexual harassment training was actually qualified to do the training. The trainer had answered some questions incorrectly during the training session.[37]

Different jobs require different types of compliance training. All supervisors need to be familiar with all the employee laws that deal with discrimination. Employees who manage compensation plans and payroll need to know the guidelines outlined by the U.S. Fair Labor Standards Act (discussed in detail in Chapter 10) as well as antidiscrimination laws. Supervisors who work in manufacturing facilities need to know about the laws related to workplace safety. These are just a few of the examples of how the context of a job affects the need for compliance training.

Most companies recognize that providing diversity training for employees is an important complement to EEO compliance training. A study of 2,500 North American senior HR executives, conducted by the Boston-based consulting firm Novations, reported that for 2008, diversity training was projected to be more important than training in areas such as sales, information technology, customer service, project management, and basic skills. In fact, one in four respondents indicated that they planned to increase their budget for diversity and inclusion training.[38]

In addition to making employees more aware of how stereotypes can be destructive in the workplace, diversity training can also help them understand that differences among people are actually good for a company that wants to be competitive. Different viewpoints lead to more and often better ideas. Diversity training can focus on people's individual attitudes or involve major initiatives to change the corporate cultures of firms. The more comprehensive a program, the more effective it's likely to be.[39] Exhibit 8.7 provides benchmarks to use to ensure that diversity training is successful.

Knowledge Training.   Every job has a knowledge component. In fact, knowledge has been recognized as a key—if not *the* key—for firms that want to achieve a competitive advantage in today's global business environment. The knowledge can be either technical or practical. Examples of technical knowledge are information on how an engine works and federal regulations that govern banking. Examples of practical knowledge are theories of what makes for good customer service or different approaches to project management. A firm's job descriptions should describe the knowledge employees need, and training programs can then be planned to address any gaps identified.

Skills Training.   In addition to knowledge, all jobs require some type of skills. Skills can range from how to change an electrical panel for an electrician, to how to read an annual report for a financial analyst, to how to register a guest for a hotel front desk clerk. If you visit the Web site for the National Institutes of Health (NIH) Training Center, for example, you will find an online course catalog with a list of the types of skills training available. Courses cover a wide array of skills, such as how to prepare purchase card logs and computer skills.[40]

diversity training

A type of training designed to help reduce discrimination by making employees more aware of the value of differences in the workplace and the problems associated with stereotypes.

Exhibit 8.7 ▶

Benchmarks for
Effective Diversity
Training

Research shows that effective diversity training requires:

- Strong support from top management
- Customization to the organization
- Linkage to the central goals of the organization
- Qualified trainers
- Involvement of all levels of employees in the organization
- Focusing on discrimination as a general process that can affect anyone
- Explicitly focusing on individual behavior
- Appropriate changes in human resource practices
- A match with corporate culture

Source: Based on Bendick, M., Egan, M., & Lofhjelm, S. Workforce diversity training: From anti-discrimination compliance to organizational development. *Human Resource Planning* 24:10–25, 2001.

A well-written job description will provide information about the skills a person needs to successfully do a job. A person analysis provides information about the extent to which employees have those skills. When both pieces of information are available, a plan can be developed to provide training to address any skills gaps.

Behavioral Training. Employees need training on the behavioral aspects of their jobs. Behavioral training focuses on the "how" of getting a job done. For example, employees whose jobs require working as part of a team might need to be taught more effective team skills.

Team training, leadership development, time management, project management, customer service, diversity, and sensitivity training are examples of training designed to change the behaviors of employees. Customer service training is designed to change how employees interact with customers. Consulting firms are sometimes hired to teach employees how to dress and interact with clients. Many companies provide their managers with behavioral training to ensure that they treat their employees fairly and equitably; research has shown that such training does work.[41] Most jobs have some behaviors that are standardized across the organization and that can be taught or have behaviors that need to be reinforced through training.

Part 4: Evaluation

The final component of a successful training program is evaluation. Training programs are expensive, so it is critical to make sure they are delivering results. Training professionals have identified four levels of evaluation. We next discuss each level. In addition, Exhibit 8.8 provides information about the levels of evaluation for determining return on investment for training costs.

LEVEL 1: REACTION[42] The first level of evaluation focuses on how employees react to the training program. At the end of each term, your professors probably ask you to complete course evaluations. These evaluations usually ask you to rate on a scale of 1 to 5 the extent to which you learned in the course, found the course challenging, felt the instructor motivated you, and would recommend this instructor to other students. Basically, the evaluation measures your reaction to the course—how you feel about the learning experience. The same type of evaluation is also used for company training programs. The primary advantages of this level of evaluation are that the ratings are fairly easy to obtain and the information can be useful in terms of identifying problems with particular trainers or training content.

If participants only rate the trainer, without providing specific feedback on the person's strengths and/or areas for improvement, the information is only marginally useful. Vague questions on the evaluation form exacerbate this problem. Consider the question

Exhibit 8.8 ▶ Levels of Evaluation for Determining Return on Investment (ROI)

Level	Objective of Measurement	Tool or Technique	Comments
1. Reaction (and planned action)	Participant's reaction to and satisfaction with the content and delivery of training.	Participants complete evaluation forms and/or develop action plans for implementing new knowledge.	Subjective but has some usefulness. If follow-up is scheduled, participant's action plans will be more realistic.
2. Learning	Skills, knowledge, or attitude changes as a result of training program.	Tests via paper and pencil or computerized format.	Tests must be assessed for validity and reliability.
3. Behavior	Changes in behavior on the job as a result of training.	Performance reviews and observations.	Assumption is that if the skills are applied, results will follow.
4. Results	Impact of training on business activities and processes.	Cost reduction, productivity increases, improved quality, reduced labor hours, decreased production/processing time, etc.	Critical tasks are isolating the effects of training and capturing appropriate data.
5. ROI	Compares the costs of the training program with monetary results and is usually expressed as a percentage.	Detailed, comprehensive data collection and analysis of costs and benefits. Accounting expertise is helpful. The time value of money is a factor.	This is the most comprehensive and objective evaluation technique, but the process can be very costly and time-consuming.

Source: Adapted from Lily, F. Four Steps to Computing Training ROI, 2001. SHRM

"How would you rate the effectiveness of this instructor?" with an accompanying scale ranging from 1 (totally ineffective) to 5 (extremely effective). Think for a minute about how you would interpret the word *effective*. Some participants might think about how the trainer conveyed the material, whether it was understandable, and whether they learned something. Other participants might think about whether the trainer was entertaining in her delivery of the material. As you can see, simply gauging participants' reactions won't tell you how much they learned and therefore how effective the training program was; it only tells you whether they liked it.

LEVEL 2: LEARNING   The goal of training is to impart new information or skills in such a way that the trainee leaves able to transfer the new knowledge or skills to the job. A pre-training–posttraining assessment is the easiest way to determine whether learning has occurred during training. If the scores on the pre- and posttests are not appreciably different, then the organization needs to review the training program. Perhaps the wrong employees were trained (they didn't need the training), the training needs assessment itself was not reliable or valid, or the trainer simply didn't deliver.

LEVEL 3: BEHAVIOR   Training should help employees perform at higher levels or do new things. If a firm conducted a thorough training needs analysis, and the right employees were trained, their performance should improve. They are more likely to improve when there is a high degree of transfer of training. Transfer of training refers to the degree to which the information covered in the program actually results in job performance changes.[43] The more related the training content is to the tasks the employee has to perform on the job, the greater the transfer of training will be. The knowledge an employee acquires on how to prepare a computer spreadsheet should transfer quite well to a job that requires such work. If the training takes place on exactly the same type of software that the employee will use on the job, the transfer of training will be even greater. Not all training

transfer of training

The degree to which the information covered in a training program actually results in job performance changes.

Exhibit 8.9 ▶

Checklist for
Designing a
Training Program

_____ Have the gaps that need to be addressed with the training program been identified?

_____ Are the objectives for the training process clearly defined?

_____ Do the lesson plans support the instructional objectives?

_____ Has the audience been considered?

    _____ Differences in learning styles

    _____ Willingness/readiness of audience to learn

    _____ Audience's belief in their ability to learn the material

    _____ Audience's interest in learning the material

    _____ Adult learners' needs

_____ Are the training methods selected appropriate for the content of the training?

_____ Does the type of training fit with your firm's organizational needs?

_____ How will the effectiveness of the program be evaluated?

mirrors this closely the job tasks being taught. Nonetheless, there should be a measurable improvement in how well employees perform following the training.

LEVEL 4 AND LEVEL 5: RESULTS AND RETURN ON INVESTMENT Companies have struggled for years with how to demonstrate that training really matters when it comes to a firm's bottom line. Almost everyone knows that it should, but evidence used to be hard to come by. Booz Allen makes extensive use of many types of training methods. This company has found a way to demonstrate the actual return-on-investment (ROI) of its training programs. Booz Allen conducted an ROI study of an executive coaching program and found the ROI to be nearly $3 million per year, which equated to a 689% return on their investment in training![44]

Many measures can be used to evaluate the ROI of training programs. Measures can include:

- Total cost of training including facilities charges, course materials, and instructor fees,
- Per participant training costs,
- Savings generated such as reduced waste, fewer errors, and increased customer service,
- Costs compared to savings, and
- Projected savings from conducting the training.[45]

Exhibit 8.9 is a checklist that managers can use when designing a training program.

CAREER DEVELOPMENT

We have noted a number of times already that many of the same principles that apply to training also apply to career development. However, there are a few points we would be remiss in omitting from a discussion of career development. We start by providing an example of some of the options available to employees through the career development program at the NIH and then discuss effective career development practices.

Recall that we discussed skills training at the NIH earlier in the chapter. The NIH also provides opportunities for employee career development. Employees have to meet eligibility requirements to participate, and they take part in a rigorous selection process. Once selected, candidates are expected to fulfill all the requirements of the program. The overall philosophy for career development at the NIH is to provide participants with a systematic approach for professional growth and self-improvement. The activities increase job-related competencies and support career planning for the employee. An example of a specific career development program is the Senior Leadership Program for senior scientists and administrators. The focus of the program is on developing competencies needed for taking on leadership roles at the NIH.[46]

Most large companies have well-designed career development programs. In small and medium-sized companies, an employee will likely have to take responsibility for his or her own career development. We will now take a look at a few concepts that affect career development activities in firms.

Competency Analysis

We have discussed the concept of competencies a number of times already in this book. Recall that competencies are the knowledge, skills, abilities, and other characteristics that an employee needs in order to perform a job. The NIH and many other organizations use the results of their competency analyses to design career development programs. A competency analysis assists an organization in creating career paths that are logical for employees to follow and assists in identifying what experiences employees need to acquire along the way. Individual employee performance assessments can be used to determine what gaps employees have between their KSAs and the competencies needed for jobs in their career path.

Career Development Activities

Managers, mentors, coaches, and career counselors play a role in assisting individual employees in acquiring the competencies needed. Employees can also take part in assessment centers (see Chapter 7), job rotation (Chapter 4), and career workshops and related programs to gain information on where they are relative to the competencies needed to move into other jobs. Succession planning and replacement charts, discussed in Chapter 5, serve as roadmaps to determine which paths employees follow and what career development activities are needed.

BAE Systems, an aerospace and defense company, uses job rotation to prepare high-potential employees for leadership roles. This select group of employees participates in a three-year program in which each employee switches to a new job each year and participates in challenging assignments. Employees are forced to learn new skills and information; for example, an engineer may work in financial accounting and then in operations.[47] Successful career development plans such as this one provide clear guidelines for employees relative to participation requirements, expectations, and outcomes.

TRAINING AND DEVELOPMENT IN PRACTICE: ORGANIZATIONAL DEMANDS

Now that you have read about the basics of training theory and methods, we turn to a discussion of how different organizational demands require different decisions about investment and practice in training and development. Some of the decisions that have to be made are included in Exhibit 8.10. For the sake of simplicity, we once again primarily refer to training in this section, but keep in mind that the same contingencies apply to providing development opportunities. Remember that a company's mission should drive all of its decisions. As an informed manager, you are the person most equipped to decide how much and what types of training and development are appropriate for your employees to help your firm achieve its goals and have a competitive advantage. Directly or indirectly, you are held accountable for achieving results. Effective training for you and for your workforce can help you achieve those results.

Strategy and Training

We have already noted that training and development are expensive. Resources need to be deployed where they will yield the most return on the investment while achieving the goals of the company. Considering a company's business strategy provides insight into

Exhibit 8.10 ▶
Training in Practice

Context	Employee Competencies Chapter 8, "Training"
Organizational Demands	
Strategy drives . . .	• Level of investment in training • Type of investment in training
Company characteristics determine . . .	• Where training is offered • Type of training needed • How training is provided • Content of training
Culture establishes . . .	• Focus of training (e.g., customer service, change, technology) • Willingness of employees to participate in training
Employee concerns include . . .	• Access to and availability of training • Focus of training (e.g., work/life balance, stress reduction)
Environmental Demands	
Labor force influences . . .	• Mode of delivery • Type of training
Technology affects . . .	• Mode of delivery • Content of training • Communication of training options
Globalization impacts . . .	• Where training is delivered • When training is delivered • How training is delivered • Who receives training
Ethics/social responsibility shapes . . .	• Obligation to train • Content of training • Use of training to change behaviors
Regulations *guide* . . .	• Accessibility of training and employee development opportunities • Type of training needed

both the level and type of training investments companies should make to realize their strategic objectives.

Level of Investment

U.S. organizations spent about $129.60 billion on employee training and development in 2006.[48] That's a lot of money for training. The decision about how much to spend for employee training and development will depend upon your company's strategy. If your company is pursuing a low-cost strategy, you will focus on minimizing the cost of training. Fred's, which describes itself as "America's favorite hometown store," is a discount department store that started in Mississippi in 1947 and now has more than 600 stores.[49] The strategy at Fred's is to keep costs down so the company can offer lower product prices to consumers. Because cost considerations are a major component of all of Fred's organizational decisions, the firm's training approach differs from the approach taken by a company such as Nordstrom, a leading high-end retailer known for delivering a very high level of customer service.[50] Nordstrom understands that great customer service requires that all the employees of the company be extensively trained with regard to the firm's philosophy and the products it sells. As a result, the company's training costs are likely to be greater than Fred's. Nordstrom is operating on

Nordstrom focuses on high-level customer service training for all employees.

the assumption that the return on that investment will result in greater customer satisfaction and high customer retention rates.

Deciding how much money is available for training should be factored into an organizational needs analysis. If little money is available for formal training, the company will have to use other means to ensure that employees are trained to do their jobs. More selective hiring is one alternative to training. That is, the company could focus on hiring employees who are already fully trained. Firms pursuing a low-cost strategy often train their employees as quickly and cost effectively as possible. This is not to say that training is not carried out: A company might hire many unskilled employees and give them the minimum level of training needed to do their jobs. This approach costs less than paying higher wages for workers who are already trained. Some companies view expensive training initiatives as a mechanism to actually save money in the long run via increased employee productivity, safety, or teamwork. That said, cost-oriented firms are likely to view training activities as a necessary expense that needs to be minimized. Sometimes they minimize their costs by using more mechanized systems in their workplaces.

In contrast, companies following differentiation strategies do not focus on cost as much as on some source of differentiation, such as innovation or customer service. These companies believe that extensively training their employees in areas directly relevant to their sources of competitive advantage is critical. This doesn't mean that the companies provide unlimited training to all their employees; the trade-offs in terms of costs versus benefits still have to be considered, and decisions need to be made about which employees will receive training and where.

Emphasis of Investment

A company's strategy influences the type of investments it is willing to make in terms of training its employees. Because each company is unique, achieving its strategic objectives means a company has to train its employees in a way that adds the most value possible to the firm. The reality is that when managers have limited training dollars, they have to prioritize their training needs. For companies that try to compete by achieving high customer satisfaction levels, training programs that focus on customer service skills, product knowledge, and teamwork are likely to have more strategic relevance. A company emphasizing high levels of employee productivity and efficiency, in contrast, might gain more from training initiatives that focus on helping employees improve their individual talents and expertise in their particular jobs. Moreover, not all employees are as critical to train on the core competencies of the business as others. For example, support staff who do not interact with customers might need less, or different, training than frontline employees.

Of course, many training programs aren't optional for companies because *not* delivering them can actually result in increased costs and other problems. For example, failing to provide a sufficient amount of safety training for employees is likely to result in more employee injuries, higher medical costs for the firm, and government fines. These are the direct costs of failing to train employees. Indirect costs can include recruiting and hiring expenses related to replacing employees who are injured and can no longer work or who quit because they believe their workplace isn't safe.[51] Similarly, ensuring that employees understand any regulatory restrictions or requirements they must adhere to will dramatically decrease a firm's long-term legal problems. Therefore, managers need to remember that no matter what the company strategy, there are certain types of training that have to occur, regardless of the cost.

Company Characteristics and Training

In addition to strategic and financial resources, other organizational factors influence training. The size and stage of development of a company influence where training is done, who does the training, the type of training needed, and how the training is provided.

WHERE TRAINING IS DONE An increasing number of companies have created their own training centers, known as corporate campuses or corporate universities. They bring their employees to these locations for much of their training because they want to ensure that all employees have the same training experience. They also want to maintain control over the content and delivery of the training programs and/or see a need that can be filled in-house. McDonald's calls its corporate program Hamburger University. About 75,000 employees have gone through this worldwide management training program, located in Oak Brook, Illinois, since McDonald's started the program in 1961. McDonald's ensures greater consistency in the operations of its restaurants by using this training approach. Some of the courses at Hamburger U. are accredited, and some of the credits will even transfer to traditional colleges and universities.[52]

Younger and smaller companies might need to use more on-the-job training in order to maximize the productive time of employees. As companies become older and grow, they often have more resources and can invest in other methods of training, including sending employees to training programs or investing in e-learning that can be done in-house. These companies also have more employees to train and may be more concerned about the consistency of their training.

WHO HANDLES TRAINING A company's stage of development influences who does the training. Managers in small businesses are likely to have to do much of the training, or make a strong case for why resources should be used to send employees to special training programs. Larger and more mature companies are more likely to have training departments that can help identify appropriate training opportunities and resources. As a manager in such a firm, you will be responsible for providing information to your training department about the type of training your employees need to perform at a high level.

TYPE OF TRAINING In small businesses, employees may wear many hats. These employees are often hired for one particular role but take on additional duties as the company begins to grow. In more established, larger organizations, jobs are likely to be more specialized. Managers of employees with expanding job responsibilities need to ensure that these employees receive the type of training needed to perform the new job responsibilities. And all employees, regardless of the stage of development and size of the company, need training on topics such as sexual harassment, the company pension plan, and other issues that could lead to liability for the company. Managers have an obligation to the company and to their employees to make sure this training occurs, preferably in a formal manner so that participation can be documented in case a problem occurs—especially in case of a legal challenge.

In newer, fast-growing companies, employees are being added quickly, and some of the training that should occur doesn't. You, as a manager, have a responsibility to ensure that the training is done no matter what. Remember that employees who are well trained add greater value to the organization because they are more effective, more efficient, and more satisfied. Unfortunately, managers today are often so busy that they fail to pay attention to how well their employees are performing until there is a problem. Many times problems result from lack of training.

HOW TRAINING IS PROVIDED In very large companies, many employees perform the same type of job. Consider large retail chains such as Michaels, Sears, and Safeway. A considerable number of employees in these organizations serve as cashiers or customer service representatives. Efficiency in training these employees is easier to achieve than in smaller organizations, due to economies of scale. A standardized training program can be designed for a large number of employees at a lower cost because one set of materials is developed and used many times. If you have to train only one or a few employees, as is usually the case in small businesses and startup companies, the cost per employee is greater. Therefore, companies with a lot of employees who have to receive the same training will gain more return on their training investment by developing materials in-house—and they have both the human capital and financial capital to do so. Companies with few employees might be forced to send them to outside training programs because doing so is less expensive than developing their own programs. Or these companies might simply resort to OJT. E-learning has made external types of training more accessible, but, again, cost and time are factors that can limit the use of e-learning.

Culture and Training

Some companies have a culture of training and development. Employees in these companies understand the importance of continuous learning. Remember from Chapter 2 that culture is about shared values and meanings. A company's culture influences the decisions it makes about the focus of its training programs and affects the willingness of its employees to participate in training. Managers who appreciate the value of training and development are more likely to provide the resources needed for these activities. They know that the result of doing so leads to higher employee performance, and that, in turn, leads to higher firm performance.

FOCUS OF TRAINING   We have already noted that Nordstrom and Marriott are two companies known for their high levels of attention to customers. Ameriprise Financial, formerly known as American Express Financial Advisors, also focuses on customers. The organization believes that it is better to keep customers satisfied than to have to find new ones. This philosophy infuses the company's corporate culture, both in terms of how employees treat customers and how Ameriprise Financial treats its employees.[53] All three companies have a customer service culture and provide training to support that culture. A company that values innovation will have a different training focus than these companies.

A change in the strategic direction of a company can also lead to a change in the culture, which leads to new training initiatives. Training can be used to change from a culture that doesn't value diversity to one that does,[54] from a culture that doesn't understand quality to one that does, and from a culture that doesn't appreciate the importance of being frugal to one that does. However, getting buy-in from your employees is essential to making the change happen; otherwise, no amount of training will change behavior or performance. If employees believe that the changes are simply the "flavor of the month," they may go through the motions during training but transfer very little of it to their jobs.

EMPLOYEES' WILLINGNESS TO PARTICIPATE IN TRAINING   A firm's reward structure is a very important part of its culture. What it signals to employees about the importance of training and development may be the chief motivator that determines whether employees are willing to participate in the programs. In companies where rewards can be obtained easily, without participating in training, employees are much less likely to seek out or participate in training, especially if it means they have less time to do those things that are rewarded. Also, when employees undergo training, they are more likely to transfer what they learned if they understand that the behaviors matter.[55]

Small businesses and startup companies are less likely than larger, more established companies to spend money for formal employee development activities. Small businesses have few opportunities for employees to move upward in their organizations or to even move vertically. When openings do exist, they are usually given to employees who have been at the company the longest. Any new knowledge needed to perform a higher-level job is acquired by employees on the job or via training and education they pay for themselves.

Many small businesses also miss the boat with regard to employee development. Often they fail to prepare a successor to take over if the owner dies or is otherwise unable to continue operating the business. So, although employee development is very important in small firms, it is not as likely to occur there as it is in larger, more mature firms. In startup companies, the speed with which change occurs often precludes time and resources being set aside for employee development. As these companies grow, employee development becomes more important because more job opportunities are created, and employees need to be ready to step into new roles.

Employee Concerns and Training

As with other employee management areas, employees want to be treated fairly and equitably in terms of training opportunities.

FAIRNESS AND EQUITY   In Chapters 6 and 7, we talked about the importance of fairness and equity when it comes to managers' selection decisions. Employees also evaluate training and development opportunities and requirements in terms of these factors. Consider a situation in which you, as a manager, have to decide which of two employees to send to a training program. Both employees hold the same position. One employee is in his 50s and has been a solid performer at the company for 10 years. Another employee is in her 30s and has been with the company for 5 years. She has been a solid performer as well. Which employee should you send if you can send only one? What factors would you consider? If the training will be seen as a reward or as a signal of future opportunities, what factors do you need to consider? As a manager, you need to have a job-related reason for deciding who participates in training. You might consider which employee has most recently been given a training opportunity, future job changes anticipated for each employee, and a host of other job-related reasons. Even if the employees were the same age, you would need to have a logical reason for selecting one for training over the other and then be prepared to defend that decision.

Employees pay attention to situations where perceived equity issues exist. They expect you to honor the agreements you make to provide them with training; if you don't, they are less likely to exhibit good citizenship behaviors. Employees also expect to be paid commensurate with the training they received and perceive anything less as unfair and not equitable.[56]

WORK/LIFE BALANCE Training can affect the work/life balance of employees in a number of ways. Some employers offer training to help their employees find a better balance between their work and personal lives. Stress and time management training are two such programs. Providing opportunities for telecommuting helps address the work/life balance needs of some employees, especially in areas where commutes tend to be long. Also, supervisors need to be trained to manage employees who telecommute.

Companies also have to consider work/life balance issues with regard to participation in their training programs. Employees might be required to travel away from home to take part in a training or development program. For employees with children or elder-care responsibilities, the required travel can present several challenges, including a lack of child care. Companies need to work with employees to assist them with these challenges. For example, a company might allow an employee to postpone training because of child-care obligations, but only if the required training can be obtained at a later time. Or, the company might allow the family to travel with the employee, as long as doing so will not interfere with the employee's focus during the training activities.

TRAINING AND DEVELOPMENT IN PRACTICE: ENVIRONMENTAL INFLUENCES

In this section, we explore how environmental factors relate to training and development. Managers have to constantly scan the environment to make sure that their plans for employee training and development take into account changes in the labor market, technology advances, increased globalization of the company, and the growing need for ethics training.

Labor Market

The labor market influences the decision about which employees need to be trained as well as the type of training needed. Changes in the labor market also affect organizations' training requirements.

Who Needs Training

As part of a workplace forecast, HR managers were asked what they were doing to address changing demographic trends in the workforce. The majority of them—82%—indicated that they were investing more in training and development to improve their employees' skill levels.[57] There are many reasons for this response. For example, in a loose labor market, companies have more flexibility in making decisions about which applicants to hire and are more likely to find employees with the skill sets they seek. Consequently, there would be no need to provide training to bring these new employees up to the minimum job standards. In contrast, in a tight labor market, individuals who don't meet all of a job's requirements are more likely to be hired. In this case, either the job requirements need to be changed or training needs to be provided to the new employees.

Type of Training

A diverse labor market requires employers to think about the type of training needed. Employees might be functionally illiterate and/or immigrants with little English-speaking ability, for example. In both of these cases, employers will most likely have to provide basic English reading and writing training. This type of training is also "good business." By providing literacy and English-language skills to employees, a company is not only equipping them to do their jobs but also helping improve their lives. As a manager, you can be instrumental in determining which employees need these basic skills and identifying ways to provide them. The training can come through company programs or through community-based programs that you identify.

Wyndham Hotels has a program called *Sed de Saber* ("Thirst for Knowledge") to teach its non-English-speaking employees how to speak English. The training is geared for employees who do not have a lot of guest contact and is done through battery-operated LeapPads, which resemble talking books. The interactive tutorial Wyndham employees complete on their LeapPads includes pictures, sounds, and activities. The company also plans to use LeapPads to teach Spanish to its English-speaking employees.[58]

Technology

Changes in technology have made it easier to keep track of who has taken part in various training and development opportunities. Advances in technology have also changed training methods and affected how training information is communicated to employees.

SKILLS INVENTORIES Given the cost of training, it is important to be selective about who really needs training. However, keeping track of employee training participation is a big job. Software has made that job much easier. Now managers can search skills inventories of current employees to identify what types and how much of it employees already have. Managers can also search the inventories to identify employees who have completed training that would make them eligible for job openings. This tracking process expands the options for employees and makes the manager's job easier when seeking employees internally. Moreover, skill inventories reduce the likelihood of selecting for training programs people who don't need to attend them.

METHOD OF DELIVERY Technology has had a great impact on how training is delivered. Earlier in the chapter, we discussed the various methods for delivering training. Later in the chapter, we discussed how Wyndham Hotels is using LeapPads to teach English to its workers. Not all organizations have the same technology capabilities, however, and not all employees have equal access to technology for training purposes. Employees working on an assembly line are not likely to have ready access to complete e-learning training sessions on the job. Companies can set aside lab space and provide time away from the factory floor for the employees to do such training. Before doing so, managers have to determine whether the employees have the computer skills needed to participate in the e-learning and make sure those skills are provided, if needed.

COMMUNICATION OF OPTIONS Technology has enhanced the ability of firms to provide information about their training and development programs to their employees. For example, managers and employees can request that they be contacted by their firm's training department when certain types of opportunities are going to be offered. This notification can be done easily, thanks to advances in software programs that can automatically notify individuals when specific information is input into the system. Employees can select programs that would be beneficial to them, and managers can identify training programs to which they need to send employees. They can also use the Internet to identify external training options.

Globalization and Training

Companies doing business globally have to recognize that a "one size fits all" training program is not likely to work. Sure, the process for determining where training is needed will be the same: Conduct an organization analysis, a task analysis, and a person analysis. Even the content of the training program may be the same. What will differ is the design and implementation. Think about the challenges of designing training programs in a developing country such as Bangladesh. Access to technology will be limited, training materials will have to be translated into the appropriate languages, and even the values of the Bangladeshi culture must be considered. Where training will be offered, when it will be offered, how it will be offered, and who will be trained are all considerations in a global economy.

WHERE TRAINING WILL BE OFFERED   Companies used to have two choices of where to train employees on global assignments: bring them back to the headquarters or send a trainer to them in their location abroad. These are still the best choices for some types of training, such as OJT. Increasingly, however, by using online and other technology-oriented training programs, employees can complete a training program sitting on the beach in Hawaii rather than back in the office in Minneapolis or Hong Kong. Costs will be a major consideration in where and how you do training. For example, if you are training many HCNs, sending a trainer to where the employees are located will likely be less expensive than bringing the employees to the trainer. On the other hand, if the training can be done online, that may be the least expensive alternative.

WHEN TRAINING WILL BE OFFERED   Employees need training to bring them up to speed when they're hired, and they need training when their job tasks change. Because the cost to the firm when expatriates return early from assignments is high—estimated to be well over $300,000 per employee,[59]—making sure these expatriates receive needed training is critical. For expatriates, there are three timeframes in which training needs to be offered: before departure, in the assignment, and as part of repatriation.

Pre-departure training sets the stage for an expatriate's experience abroad. And, given the extensive research showing that a main cause of expatriate failure is inability of the expat's family to adjust to the location, including the family in the pre-departure training is important. A lot of research has focused on the pre-departure training needs of expats and has concluded that it should include setting realistic expectations for them in terms of both the living conditions abroad and how a nation's culture affects what goes on in the workplace. Pre-departure training should address issues related to language, religion, culture, business practices, and safety. Training can be done by a former expatriate or a consulting firm that specializes in expatriate pre-departure training. Numerous Web sites and training videos are also available to address issues related to living abroad and can be incorporated into the training program. For instance, the U.S. Department of State offers extensive information on its Web site (www.state.gov/travelandbusiness and www.state.gov/countries) to help prepare for doing business and living abroad.

Once an expatriate is on assignment, the training should focus on what the employee needs to know to do the job. If you are the manager of an expatriate at your firm's corporate headquarters, it can be easy to miss knowing that the person doesn't have some of the KSAs needed to successfully complete his or her assignment abroad. Therefore, developing an ongoing communication process and having an open exchange of dialogue to encourage the expatriate to share such information earlier rather than later is important.

When an employee is repatriated (brought back to the firm's headquarters on a permanent basis), she and her manager need to assess whether she should have additional training for her new job assignment. Forgoing this assessment sets the expatriate up for failure at a time that is stressful anyway. The expatriate already has to adjust to being in a different culture than the one she has known in her assignment abroad. Consequently, her manager needs to make sure that further stress does not result from a lack of training.

HOW TRAINING WILL BE OFFERED   Before beginning the training process for HCNs, managers need to consider factors such as how the country views education in general, the role of teachers in the culture, the extent to which status matters, and willingness to take risks and experiment. Briscoe and Schuler have researched the type of training methods that work best in different cultures based on two cultural dimensions: power distance and uncertainty avoidance, along with a third dimension, preferred learning format. They found, for instance, that Guatemala, Greece, and Portugal, countries that are high in power distance (hierarchy matters), strong in uncertainty avoidance (don't like risk), and prefer a more didactic learning format (classroom setting) prefer training that involves assigned readings and lectures. Switzerland, Australia, and Singapore, countries that are nearer the other end of these three continua and are therefore lower in power distance, lower in uncertainty avoidance, and have a preference for a more experimental learning format prefer training that includes simulations, role play, and structured exercises.[60]

If OJT is used, decisions have to be made about whether an HCN will be the trainer or whether an expatriate can fill that role. One particular element of culture to consider is whether employees are comfortable giving feedback and asking questions.[61] In addition, the training materials may have to be translated into multiple languages and adapted in other ways to fit the local culture in which the training will occur.

WHAT TRAINING WILL BE OFFERED Much of the training content and development issues for expatriates and HCNs will be little different than what we have already discussed. After all, the content of training derives from the organization, task, and person analyses. A few additional types of training and development may need to be added, however. Cross-cultural training may be necessary to ensure that problems in the workplace are not the result of either the expatriate or HCN misunderstanding why things are done a certain way. Training such as this also creates an environment in which employees can openly exchange their concerns about cultural differences. Company Spotlight 8.4 describes how Sony Corporation has used cross-cultural training to overcome misunderstandings among employees in their global work-groups. Expatriates are also likely to need ongoing training on changing host country laws and regulations as well as development opportunities to prepare them for new assignments.

Ethics and Training

A London *Financial Times* article focused on ethical behavior for professional education for chartered accountants[62] highlights a growing concern for firms today: How can they ensure that their employees understand what is and is not ethical behavior? To help answer this question, we discuss the fact that firms have an obligation to train, the content of the training, and the use of training to change behavior.

COMPANY spotlight 8.4 Cross-Cultural Training at Sony

Sony Corporation is a Japanese firm that has long understood the importance of teaching employees about cultural differences. Sony moved the design function for one of its flat-screen televisions to San Diego from Tokyo. The move placed the firm's design personnel nearer to its marketing, sales, and manufacturing personnel. More than 13 cultures were represented in this group, including Japan, Paraguay, Russia, and the United States.

When the employees at the San Diego manufacturing plant wanted to speed up the production time for flat-screen TVs, Sony provided a team of about 35 people with classes on how to interact with their colleagues from other cultures. U.S. and Japanese employees were put in separate groups by nationality and instructed to list the rewards and challenges of working with the other group. They then returned to the training session and shared the information—with very positive results. Each group was validated by the positive things the others saw in them.

Sony also uses coaching to reduce conflict. When conflict occurs, cross-cultural consultants coach the two sides to overcome their misunderstandings. And, in the United Kingdom, Sony's training managers have developed an employee survey to assess the success of the firm's cross-cultural training. All these efforts are typical of how Sony uses cross-cultural training and coaching to improve its performance.

Source: Based on Ryst, S. Sony's cross-cultural training aims to foster workplace Zen. *Workforce Management* online, April 2005, http://www.workforce.com/archive/article/24/00/82.php?ht=sony%20cross%20cultural%20training%20sony%20cross%20cultural%20training.

OBLIGATION TO TRAIN Creating an ethics statement alone is not sufficient:[63] Employers have an obligation to train employees about ethical behavior. Corporate scandals, such as those at Enron and the accounting firm Arthur Andersen, have underscored this obligation, as has recent legislation in the United States, such as the Sarbanes-Oxley Act. That said, companies should train their employees about what constitutes ethical behavior even absent corporate scandals and regulations. A company that wants to ensure that all its stakeholders—employees, customers, and shareholders—are treated ethically can't just issue a statement about ethics and believe that all employees will live by it. It must be proactive in providing the right environment for ethical behavior to be valued.

CONTENT OF TRAINING The content of ethics training can range from orientation to the company's values and beliefs to intensive training on the topic of ethics relative to one's profession. Accountants need to understand what are and are not acceptable practices, just as physicians need to understand what constitutes ethical medical practice. Often ethics training is combined with other training programs. However, it should always be a part of the company's orientation process for new employees. A one-time training course on ethics is not likely to be sufficient, either. In fact, most, if not all, employee training programs should touch on related ethical issues. Obviously, there are ethical issues related to diversity training. But what about leadership development programs and safety training programs? The reality is that there is just as great a need to incorporate discussions about ethical issues in these latter types of training as in the former. The more employees hear about the company's view on ethical behavior and see it modeled by management, the more likely they are to comply.

Organizations have several additional ethical issues to address relative to training. First, they have an ethical obligation to ensure that supervisors and co-workers don't discriminate. Second, they have an ethical obligation to ensure that all employees have equal access to the training appropriate for their jobs and roles in the company. This is especially important given that greater training is often associated with higher wages. Finally, companies have an ethical obligation to ensure that employees have the training needed to do their jobs effectively and safely. Recall that we discussed regulations related to fair treatment of employees in Chapter 3; therefore, we don't elaborate further on that topic here but rather remind you of its importance from an ethical standpoint.

We have not yet discussed the obligation to train employees to do their jobs. A number of court cases have involved charges by clients or customers that they were harmed in some way because employees lacked training. For instance, a precedent-setting case relative to failure to train for police officers is *City of Canton v. Harris*. In this case, Harris was arrested by the Canton, Ohio, police and taken to lock-up. She fell several times during booking and responded incoherently to a query about the need for medical attention, which she did not then receive. The Supreme Court ruled that a municipality can be held liable for failing to adequately train employees. In other words, had the police officers been appropriately trained, they would have made sure that Harris received the medical attention that she needed.[64] The ruling in this case applies to nongovernment organizations as well.

USE OF TRAINING TO CHANGE BEHAVIOR A former dean of the Yale School of Management once noted that business schools will not be able to turn a dishonest person into an honest one. All schools can do is teach students about making appropriate value judgments in situations that are obviously right or wrong.[65] The same is true of companies. Unfortunately, many companies that have been found to be in violation of ethical practices have had ethics programs in place, including codes of ethics.

If employees see their managers behaving ethically, they are more likely to do so. Although the former dean of the Yale School of Management was right about the fact that, in your role of manager, you can't change a dishonest person into an honest one, you can clearly set the expectations for how you expect the firm's employees to behave and hold them accountable for their behaviors.

Raytheon is a company that does just that and has been recognized for its ethics training. This company requires every employee, including the CEO, to participate in ethics training.[66] Training mandates such as this signal to employees that the company is concerned about ethics. In addition, if the firm's top leaders model the behavior the company seeks, employees are more likely to follow suit.

TRAINING AND DEVELOPMENT IN PRACTICE: REGULATORY ISSUES

Companies spend a lot of training resources on compliance issues to reduce or avoid liability.[67] As noted earlier, this type of training covers everything from EEO laws to the Sarbanes-Oxley Act. Because information covered in compliance training is fairly standard across organizations, this type of training lends itself particularly well to off-the-shelf purchases of training materials. E-learning also works well for compliance training.[68] Just remember that the courts will look at whether the training is designed and delivered by trainers qualified to teach the topic.

As you learned earlier in the chapter, managers cannot discriminate when it comes to deciding who should or should not receive training: An employer cannot provide training just to women or just to Asians. Likewise, it would be inappropriate to require only men to take part in a training program with an outdoor physical component. (If outdoor training is necessary, then women need to be required to participate also.) In other words, employees should be selected for training programs based on job-related reasons, and individuals should be treated equally, regardless of their race, color, religion, sex, national origin, age, disability, or veterans' status, unless laws specifically provide for doing so.

Accessibility of Training and Employee Development Opportunities

Because firms have to make their training programs available to all qualified employees, this effectively means that managers have to ensure that all employees have access to the training they need to do their jobs. For example, intentionally or not, managers might believe that younger employees deserve more opportunities for training. They may rationalize that younger workers "will be around" longer, so the training investment will be more worthwhile, whereas spending training resources on the "old guys" who are closer to retirement is a waste of resources. There are a couple of flaws in such a plan, not to mention the fact that it violates the Age Discrimination in Employment Act (ADEA). First, there is no guarantee that the younger workers will stick around after they complete the training and development programs they receive. Second, an underlying presumption is that older workers are not as capable of learning and/or are not interested in training and development. This thinking is based on generalizations with little if any basis in reality.

Another accessibility issue relates to the Americans with Disabilities Act (ADA), which requires employers to make reasonable accommodations for employees with disabilities. This includes employers' training programs. The accommodations might include changing the training location to make it accessible to disabled employees or providing special computer equipment so disabled employees can participate in e-learning activities. In some cases, a signer for the hearing impaired might be required.

Type of Training Needed

As regulations are passed or amended, government agencies develop new guidelines to help managers interpret the laws. Companies have an obligation to provide that information to their employees and to make sure they know what it means. Managers, in particular, need to understand the roles they need to play to ensure that their employees comply with the laws. This includes training their new employees as well as their current employees when laws change.

Here is an example of the need for compliance training: As in most other firms, compliance issues are a big concern for financial services call centers. When Wachovia set up its call center in Columbia, South Carolina, it assigned a full-time compliance manager to the center. This person has responsibility for making sure all employees are trained on compliance issues and that they understand that compliance is everyone's responsibility.[69] For example, all employees in the call center who work with customers or customer data need to understand compliance requirements such as deposit account disclosure rules and alternative identification procedures. Both of these requirements help ensure that customer data are protected. These are just two of the many compliance issues with which call center employees must be familiar.

SUMMARY

Training prepares employees to do their current jobs, whereas development prepares employees for future jobs. The two activities together ensure that employees can help their organization achieve its goals in the present and in the future. Some companies view training and development as critical to their success and invest money in the programs accordingly. Other organizations do not value training and development as highly and spend little money on the two activities.

Effective training programs are systematic. They begin with a needs assessment of the organization, its tasks, and personnel. This process identifies gaps between what the firm's employees are doing and what they should be doing for the company to be successful. At this point, managers can begin to identify which employees need training or development.

Successful training and development programs are built around solid learning strategies: clearly identifying instructional objectives for the training, creating appropriate lesson plans, understanding the principles of learning, appreciating the impact of learning agility, and getting learners interested in the material. Learning self-efficacy affects outcomes as well. Also, trainers need to understand the nuances associated with adult learners. Finally, training in the most appropriate location plays a part in ensuring that the training is successful.

Managers have a number of training delivery methods from which to choose. The methods include on-the-job training, using printed materials, classroom training, e-learning, audiovisual training, simulations, blended learning, college and university options, and coaching. Employee orientation and onboarding programs help new employees learn a company's policies and procedures and understand how their positions fit in with the firm. Employee development programs provide employees with new knowledge, skills, and abilities that will help them successfully move into lateral jobs or be promoted.

The last part of the training process is to assess how well the programs have worked. Training evaluations gauge participants' reactions to the training program, the extent to which learning occurred, whether the training led to behavior changes on the job, and how the training affected the company's bottom line.

A firm's organizational strategy determines the amount and type of investment the company makes in its training programs. The size and age of the company affect where training is done as well as the type of training and how it is provided. The firm's organizational culture influences the focus of training and whether employees are willing to participate in it. Employees need to perceive that their firm's training and development opportunities and activities are managed in a fair and equitable manner.

The same environmental factors that affect other employee management activities affect training and development decisions. The nature of the labor market affects who needs training when they are hired and the type of training they need. Of all the environmental factors, technology has perhaps had the greatest impact on the training and development activities of organizations. Computer technology advances have provided a way for companies to track the activities of their employees, changed how training is delivered, and made it easier to train more employees and make them aware of training opportunities available to them. Technology has also made it easier to provide standardized training to employees scattered around the globe and affected where and how training programs are offered.

Companies have an ethical obligation to ensure that their employees are properly trained to do their jobs, especially when there are safety or legal concerns. Ethics training is becoming more commonplace. Overlapping with ethical concerns are regulatory issues such as making training and development opportunities accessible to employees based on job-related reasons and the type of training they must have to comply with the law.

KEY TERMS

audiovisual training p. 234

blended learning p. 235

classroom training p. 233

coaching p. 236

desktop training p. 233

development p. 224

diversity training p. 237

e-learning p. 233

employee orientation p. 223

high-potential employees p. 224

instructional objectives p. 228

learning agility p. 229

learning style p. 229

legal compliance training p. 236

lesson plan p. 228

mentoring p. 236

needs assessment p. 225

onboarding p. 224

on-the-job training (OJT) p. 231

organization analysis p. 225

person analysis p. 227

podcast p. 233

self-efficacy p. 229

simulation p. 234

task analysis p. 226

training p. 224

transfer of training p. 239

Web-based training p. 233

DISCUSSION QUESTIONS

1. Discuss why some companies view training as a value-added activity whereas other companies see it simply as an expense.
2. Explain the difference between an organization analysis, a task analysis, and a person analysis. How are the three related? Why should all three types of analyses be conducted to determine a firm's training needs, no matter how large or small the organization?
3. Suppose you're the manager of a five-star hotel and that you have to ensure that all your employees perform at a very high level. What do you think will be the greatest challenges in training the front desk staff? The housekeeping staff? How would you overcome these challenges?
4. How would you measure the effectiveness of a training program designed to increase the accuracy of a company's audits? How would you measure the effectiveness of a training program designed to improve loan processing in a financial services institution?
5. How does having an employee development program help a firm?
6. Your firm has a culture that values teamwork and innovation. What role would training play in terms of ensuring that these two values are instilled in all employees?
7. Use the Web to research topics likely to be covered in a pre-departure training session for expatriates. Do the topics differ based on the countries to which the expatriates are being sent? Or are they the same?
8. What does it mean to say that training must be accessible to all employees? Why does this matter? What might happen if it's not?

LEARNING EXERCISE 1

Choose an activity that you are good at doing. The activity can be related to sports, music, a hobby—virtually anything. Prepare a plan for teaching someone how to do that activity. Apply the concepts you have learned in this chapter about effective training in putting together your plan.

1. What type of assessment will you use to prepare for this training?
2. What methods and types of training will you use?
3. What role will principles of learning play in your training program?
4. How will you determine whether the training has been successful?

LEARNING EXERCISE 2

Develop a training program for a job with which you are familiar. Work through the following steps to prepare your training program:

1. Obtain a copy of a job description for the job or prepare one.
2. Include a description of the organization in which the job is done. Include the mission statement for the organization.
3. Identify the competencies (KSAs) that should be the focus of training and describe why you selected each of the KSAs.
4. Describe the specific types of training that will be used, including the training content, how the content supports the company's organizational goals, who will deliver the training, when and where it will occur, and the specific methods that will be used.
5. Discuss the outcomes the company can expect the training to produce.

CASE STUDY #1 — PROJECT MANAGEMENT AND NEXT STEPS AT HP

When Hewlett-Packard's (HP's) Services division decided to focus more on external IT consulting, Ron Kempf, the director of project management competency and certification at HP, brought together the firm's various stakeholders to conduct a needs assessment to determine what type of training would be needed to achieve the new goal. HP's decision to expand its consulting and integration business meant that 2,500 client-focused project managers and support staff around the world would need to improve their skills.

Based on cost of the training and the resources it could provide, ESI International was chosen to train Kempf's division so employees could achieve the "project management professional" designation. The designation has become a standard in the industry, and clients ask for the certification when requesting project bids. As a result, HP needed its project managers to be certified for the company to be competitive. Kempf worked with ESI to provide training in various formats to meet the needs of the worldwide workforce. The training methods included using HP's knowledge management system, networking participants so they could learn from each other, e-learning, self-paced instruction, and formal training conducted at a "project management" university.

The training initiative, which has been refined as needed over the years, has been very successful. Kemp credits it with boosting HP's profit margins and keeping projects within budget. Now, however, HP needs to decide on the "next steps" to ensure that it doesn't lose its competitive edge since many other companies have the same certifications for their project managers. Also, about 20% of the first group of employees who were trained will retire in five years.

DISCUSSION QUESTIONS

1. Discuss the role that a needs assessment played in planning the training program for project management staff.

2. What are the issues HP now faces? What role, if any, will training need to play in addressing those issues?

3. How would you begin the process of creating a new training plan? Who should be involved? What would be the desired outcome of this training?

4. HP is a very large company. How might the planning process for training be different if HP were a much smaller company?

Source: From Barron, T. It's all about alignment: Training managers are getting creative in the quest to align organizational learning with broader business objectives and they're being helped by growing recognition of training's value. *T&D*, November 2003, p. 57.

CASE STUDY #2 — QUALITY AND CUSTOMER SERVICE AT MICHAEL'S COFFEE AND DESSERTS

Providing the highest-quality products and the highest level of customer service are two of the core values of Michael's Coffee and Desserts. This chain of gourmet coffee and pastry shops was started in Spring Green, Wisconsin, by a mother-and-son team. The vision for the concept came after the son despaired of finding pies "just like mom makes" when he had to travel on business. Now, the company has shops in 30 states and is considering opening shops in a couple of foreign countries. The company plans to continue expanding by adding at least two new shops each quarter for the next three years. Each shop has one manager and 6 to 10 associates.

The company recognizes the need to ensure that training on quality and service is delivered consistently across all operations. The owners see this training as a key ingredient in achieving their vision of "being the favorite place to meet for dessert and coffee." Further, in addition to training shop managers and associates, Michael's wants to put together a program to ensure that current shop managers will mentor and develop future shop managers. Associates are typically high school and college students and retirees. The current goal of the management team is to develop a training and development program for Michael's shop managers and shop associates that will be the best in the industry and that will be offered around the globe.

DISCUSSION QUESTIONS

1. Do you agree with the owners that training is needed? Discuss your answer.

2. What should Michael's do first in setting up this training program?

3. What unique challenges need to be addressed in designing the training program, given the wide range of ages of the employees and the cultural differences in different parts of the U.S. and abroad? How would you manage these challenges?

4. How should the owners evaluate training effectiveness?

Part III
PROSPERA EXERCISES

At the end of Part Two, you developed job descriptions for three jobs commonly found at Visions Optical. In this part of the book, you have learned about the importance of managing employee competencies. Recruiting, selection, and training and development ensure that the right employees are in place and prepared to do their jobs. Develop a staffing plan for each of the three jobs. The staffing plan should include information about how and where recruiting for each position will take place and should provide a structured interview process for each job.

Section I: Developing a Recruiting Process

The recruiting message affects how many and what type of employees apply for available jobs. Using the information from Chapter 6 and additional recruiting information you find at the Prospera Web site (www.prospera.com), develop a recruiting plan for the jobs from Part Two. Be prepared to justify your decisions, indicating how your plan will help reduce the turnover problem at the company.

Section II: Creating the Structured Interview

A well-structured interview will help you hire the right employees when there are openings to fill. Use the resources at the Prospera Web site and the job descriptions from Part Two to develop an interview guide, including a candidate evaluation form. The evaluation form provides a consistent way to track information about each candidate. Be prepared to justify the choice of questions you have included in the interview guide.

Section III: Ensuring a Smooth Onboarding Process

Using the "Welcome New Employees" feature at the Prospera Web site, create a checklist for an orientation process for new employees at Visions Optical. Pay particular attention to including items that send signals to employees about what is valued at the company (e.g., competencies). Add new items if you feel that the list is not inclusive enough.

Section IV: Integrating the HR Activities in the Case

Discuss how the recruiting, selection interview, and onboarding process you have designed will affect business at Visions Optical. Be specific in describing the relationships among the activities as well as with the Visions Optical mission and the HR mission.

MANAGING EMPLOYEE ATTITUDES AND BEHAVIORS

PERFORMANCE MANAGEMENT

1. Describe the different purposes of performance management. *(261)*

2. Describe the components of an effective performance management system. *(261)*

3. Discuss how to develop useful performance measures. *(262)*

4. Discuss the advantages and disadvantages of the different approaches used to evaluate the performance of employees. *(264)*

5. Compare and contrast the usefulness of different sources for employee performance data. *(269)*

6. Develop an effective approach for providing employees with performance feedback. *(273)*

7. Describe the merits of alternative approaches to disciplining employees. *(275)*

8. Explain how an organization's demands affect its performance management system. *(277)*

9. Discuss how a firm's environment affects its performance management system. *(283)*

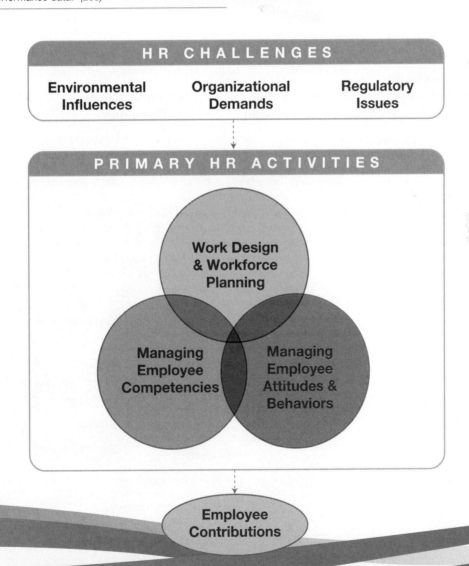

WHY PERFORMANCE MANAGEMENT IS SO IMPORTANT

As a manager, you are dependent on your employees. When your employees work hard and achieve their objectives, you receive accolades. When they perform poorly, you are blamed. Put simply, your job performance is tied directly to theirs. How well your employees perform is, to a large extent, a function of the effort they expend. Your goal therefore is to motivate them to work hard and continually improve what they do. As shown in Exhibit 9.1, one of *the primary HR activities* is to manage employee attitudes and behaviors. One way managers do this is by using performance management programs. **Performance management** involves two related activities: (1) evaluating the performance of your employees against the standards set for them and (2) helping them develop action plans to improve their performance.

Part of a good performance management program is being able, as a manager, to answer questions such as these:

- How can I best measure the performance of my employees?
- What's the best way to give my employees developmental feedback to improve their performance?

performance management

The process of: (1) evaluating employee performance against the standards set for them and (2) helping them develop action plans to improve their performance.

Exhibit 9.1 ▶

Framework for the Strategic Management of Employees

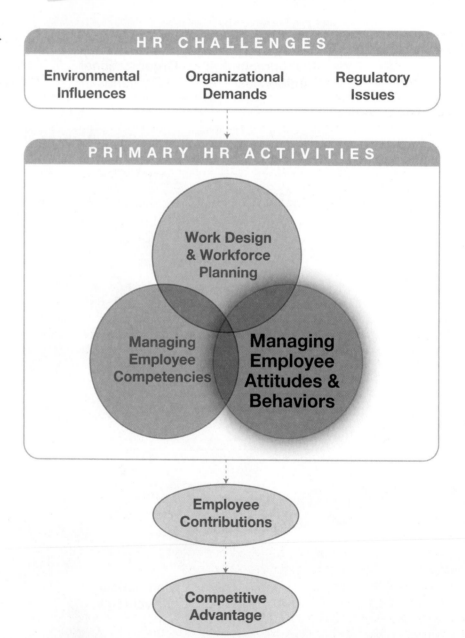

- How should I communicate that information to employees?
- How should I manage poorly performing employees?

After reading this chapter, you should be in a better position to design and implement a performance management system that motivates your employees to display the necessary attitudes and behaviors at work to help your company achieve a competitive advantage.

PURPOSES OF PERFORMANCE MANAGEMENT

In general, performance management activities may be used for administrative and/or developmental purposes.[1] The first purpose is *administrative* in nature because it directly affects a firm's administrative decisions regarding its workforce. As we will discuss in Chapters 10 and 11, firms use performance evaluations to make decisions regarding their employees' salary adjustments, merit raises, and incentive rewards. For example, how do you know how much raise to give an employee? For many companies, this decision is based on the employee's performance evaluation.

As we discussed in Chapter 5, managers must make decisions regarding the promotions, demotions, transfers, terminations, and even layoffs of individuals. On what basis are these decisions made? Understanding your employees' current performance as well as their potential to perform will help you make decisions about the movement of employees throughout, or out of, your organization. Managers also use performance evaluation data for disciplinary purposes—that is, to reinforce the attitudes and behaviors employees should display on a daily basis.

The second purpose of performance management is *developmental* in nature—using performance evaluation information to help employees improve their performance in order to add more value to the company. Performance evaluations serve a vital role in terms of identifying employees' training needs, for example. Even if employees are not performing at a satisfactory level, a developmental emphasis strives to find out if there are areas in which employees are able to improve their performance and then identify a course of action to help employees meet their potential. A developmental approach may also involve disciplinary actions to signal to employees that current actions or behaviors may not be acceptable. A developmental approach can also be part of succession planning or just employee career development in general.

When you understand how to use performance evaluations for different administrative and/or developmental purposes, you can start to think about how to better manage the performance of your employees. As shown in Exhibit 9.2, there are five steps related to developing and implementing a good performance management process, starting with identifying performance dimensions.

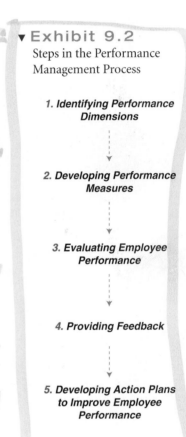

▼ Exhibit 9.2
Steps in the Performance Management Process

1. Identifying Performance Dimensions

2. Developing Performance Measures

3. Evaluating Employee Performance

4. Providing Feedback

5. Developing Action Plans to Improve Employee Performance

STEP 1: IDENTIFYING PERFORMANCE DIMENSIONS

If you were asked to evaluate the instructor for one of your courses, what would you say? Would you say your instructor is "good," "average," or "poor"? Or would you think about it for a minute and break down different aspects of your instructor's performance and evaluate each one of them separately? You might rate your instructor as "good" in terms of being prepared for class, "average" for maintaining student interest during lectures, and "good" for grading fairly. If you focus on a single overall evaluation of your instructor, you are relying on a **global performance measure**—a single score to reflect overall performance. If you choose to separate different parts of the instructor's performance, you are identifying **performance dimensions.**

Performance dimensions relate to the specific tasks and activities for which employees are responsible. Although an individual's performance can be evaluated using a global performance measure, the jobs people perform generally consist of multiple performance

global performance measure

The use of a single score to reflect an individual employee's overall performance.

performance dimension

The specific tasks and activities for which employees are responsible.

dimensions.[2] For example, suppose you have to measure the performance of two of your employees. Now suppose that both employees exhibit similar performance levels overall (average), but they excel at different dimensions of their jobs. One employee might excel at helping his co-workers, whereas another might excel at working with her customers. But if you didn't break their performance down into different dimensions, you wouldn't be able to identify areas that the individuals should focus on to improve their performance. The first step in a successful performance management system is to determine the performance dimensions you should evaluate.

A job's performance dimensions should reflect the reasons it exists in the first place. For example, it wouldn't make much sense to evaluate a receptionist on the number of innovative products developed by his company because a receptionist is not likely to be directly involved in developing products. Rather, he's likely to be responsible for greeting customers, answering inquiries via the telephone, and the like. These tasks reflect the essential functions of the job that should be evaluated. A primary source of information for identifying performance dimensions is job analysis. As we discussed in Chapter 4, each job within a company exists to perform certain tasks, duties, and responsibilities. The performance dimensions should reflect these tasks, duties, and responsibilities. Understanding the concept of performance dimensions serves as a starting point for developing an effective performance management system. As a manager, you need to understand what performance dimensions are important for a job; that is, what are the tasks, duties, and responsibilities that define the essence of the job.

STEP 2: DEVELOPING PERFORMANCE MEASURES

Knowing what performance dimensions should be evaluated does not necessarily translate into an effective performance management system. Rather, you have to be able to measure an employee's level of performance on the dimensions you have identified.[3] Effective performance evaluation systems use performance measures that are valid, have clear standards, and are specific. Let's look more closely at each of these criteria.

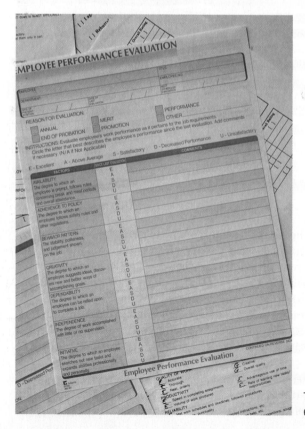

There are many different performance evaluation forms managers may use.

Valid Measures

Performance measures must be reliable and valid. In our discussion of selection decisions in Chapter 7, we brought up the concepts of reliability and validity. Reliability refers to how well a measure yields consistent results over time and across raters. Validity is the extent to which you are measuring what you want to measure and how well that is done.[4] Essentially, validity means that your performance measures reflect the actual performance of your employees.

Sometimes, however, performance evaluations go awry because the measures used are deficient or contaminated. A performance measure is said to be **deficient** when important aspects of an individual's performance are not measured. For example, measuring only the number of phone calls made by a sales representative to potential clients fails to recognize an additional and important aspect of her job: actually making, or closing, sales. A performance measure is said to be **contaminated** when it captures information that is irrelevant to an individual's job performance.[5] Considering our sales representative example again, if the person's manager evaluates the rep's typing speed or the neatness of the employee's desk, the overall measure of her performance is likely to be contaminated by irrelevant information. In other words, you have to make sure the performance measures you use reflect all the essential performance dimensions a job and only those dimensions.

deficient performance measure

An incomplete appraisal of an individual's performance when important aspects are not measured.

contaminated performance measure

The reliance on information that is irrelevant to an individual's job performance.

Performance Measurement Standards

One key consideration in developing performance measures is clarifying the level of expected performance, or **performance standards**.[6] Consider an automobile salesperson. Is selling 10 cars in one month a good, average, or poor performance? Without a standard, or benchmark, just knowing the person's level of performance won't give you enough information to evaluate the employee's effectiveness.

Managers can use a number of standards. For example, they might rely on some objective performance measure, such as number or dollar amount of sales, number of mistakes, quantity of output, and the like. Performance standards can also be qualitative. Managers might evaluate employees on whether they performed some task successfully, using a yes-or-no format. They might assess the degree to which employees performed some tasks successfully using a scale ranging from unsatisfactory to above average or excellent.

Standards must be clear and reflect the entire performance spectrum. An evaluation will not be of much use if the typical employee receives the highest possible rating because average performers and outstanding performers would receive the same ratings. At the same time, however, the standards cannot be so high that they are unattainable. If employees do not feel they can reasonably reach the standards set for them, their motivation to do so will likely diminish.

performance standards

The level of expected performance.

Specificity

Performance evaluations are most effective when the standards are associated with high levels of **specificity**. Whereas validity focuses on the extent to which the performance standards reflect the actual tasks, duties, and responsibilities employees are responsible for in their jobs, specificity refers to the clarity of those performance standards. For example, when evaluating the dimension of customer service, a performance standard that simply focuses on evaluating whether employees provide "excellent" customer service is much less specific than a performance standard that is more narrowly construed—for example, one that evaluates whether employees help customers determine which products or services they most want or need.

Greater specificity affords firms two benefits.[7] First, it makes a standard clearer, and managers are likely to be more consistent when they evaluate employees on that standard. This helps improve the reliability of the performance management process. Moreover, greater specificity means that a wider array of job tasks is likely to be evaluated rather than focusing on some overall global assessment.[8] As a result, companies are

specificity

The clarity of performance standards.

likely to have a better idea about how different employees are performing different aspects of their jobs. Second, greater levels of specificity help employees understand how different aspects of their job should be performed.[9] Telling an employee he has poor customer service skills does not provide the same level of developmental potential as identifying for the employee specific aspects of customer service in which his performance is lacking.

STEP 3: EVALUATING EMPLOYEE PERFORMANCE

Managers can evaluate the performance of their employees in a number of ways. They can compare and rank order them, rate them against preset standards, or evaluate the results, or outcomes, of their performance. These methods vary in several important ways. First, some methods focus on measuring performance outcomes (e.g., quantity, speed, sales), whereas others focus on employee traits or behaviors.[10] Traits refer to employees' attributes, such as their knowledge, courtesy, or some attitudinal measure. In contrast, methods that focus on behaviors strive to capture the extent to which employees display the desired behaviors related to doing their jobs. The various methods also differ in terms of their usefulness for meeting the administrative or developmental purposes of a firm's performance management system.

Individual Comparisons

Perhaps the simplest form of performance evaluation is to compare employees to one another to discern their relative standing along some performance dimension. In a simple ranking approach, managers rank order employees from best to worst along some performance dimension or by virtue of their overall performance. For example, a manager might rank order employees based on their sales volume for a month. The person with the highest sales would be ranked number 1; the person with the second highest sales would be ranked number 2, and so on. When managers have quantitative performance data, rankings are quite easy to do.

A variation of the ranking approach is the paired comparisons method, whereby each employee in a business unit is compared to every other employee in the unit. The rater then assigns a point value to the "better" individual in the pair being compared. After all individuals are compared to one another and their points added up, they are then ranked from the most points to the least. Exhibit 9.3 shows how a paired comparison works. For example, Bob's performance is evaluated as being better than Sue's, John's, and Anil's. As a result, Bob receives a point total of three. In contrast, Anil's performance is rated as better than Sue's, John's, Magni's, and Karen's, giving him a point total of 4. After all employees are evaluated,

ranking approach

An evaluation approach in which employees are evaluated from best to worst along some performance dimension or by virtue of their overall performance.

paired comparisons

An evaluation approach in which each employee in a business unit is compared to every other employee in the unit.

Exhibit 9.3 ▶

Example of a Paired Comparison

Employee for Paired Comparison	Employee Being Rated					
	Bob	Sue	John	Anil	Magni	Karen
Bob	—				✓	✓
Sue	✓	—		✓	✓	
John	✓	✓	—	✓		✓
Anil	✓			—		
Magni		✓		✓	—	
Karen		✓		✓	✓	—
Point Total	3	2	1	4	3	2

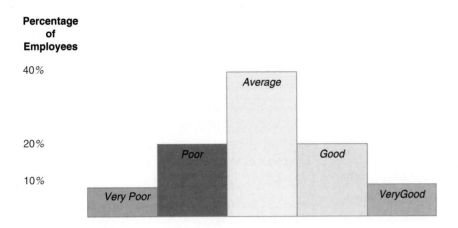

◄ Exhibit 9.4

Example of a
Forced Distribution
Performance
Evaluation

PRINCIPLES

Anil has the highest ranking, with 4 points. Bob and Magni have the second-highest ranking, with 3 points. Sue and Karen have the second-lowest ranking, with 2 points each, and John has the lowest ranking, just 1 point.

Another form of individual comparisons is the **forced distribution** approach, whereby managers are forced to distribute employees into one of several predetermined categories. Exhibit 9.4 shows an example of a forced distribution. In this example, a manager would be required to rate 10% of his employees as "very good," 20% as "good," 40% as "average," 20% as "poor," and the remaining 10% as "very poor." Thus, if the manager had 100 employees, she could give only 10 of them a "very good" rating. Forced distribution systems prevent managers from rating all employees as outstanding, average, or poor. They must use the entire range of the performance scores. This forces managers to be more critical in terms of which employees truly are exceptional, average, or poor.

Of course, all three of these individual comparisons have some advantages and disadvantages. On the one hand, using individual comparisons is a relatively easy approach to design and implement. Managers simply need to determine a basis for the comparisons or rely on an overall global assessment, and then they need to compare individuals to one another. In addition, the comparisons can be used for administrative purposes, such as determining who to promote and how to disseminate merit raises. If a company is forced to lay off employees, these methods may help them decide who to let go. As shown in Company Spotlight 9.1, GE has used forced distributions to differentiate high performers from those who need to improve or look elsewhere for work.

On the other hand, there are some drawbacks to using comparison approaches. For example, what do you do if two employees display equal performance levels, but you must rank order them? Similarly, what if 20% of your employees deserve to be rated as very good or outstanding, but you are forced to limit this rating to only 10% of your employees? In such a case, you will have to make distinctions among your employees that don't truly reflect their performance.[11] Ranking employees also gets considerably more difficult as business units grow in size. What if you have to compare 200 employees or 2,000 employees to one another? Aside from the time constraints, managers might not have enough information to do so with a high level of confidence in their evaluations.

Finally, although comparative approaches are often helpful for administrative purposes, they are not as useful for developmental purposes. Rankings and distributions boil down to a single overarching rating for employees that often does not capture the specifics of why they are performing at certain level. In other words, being ranked "5" as an employee simply reflects your current performance; it doesn't tell you much about what you can do to be ranked 1, 2, 3, or 4.

Absolute Approaches: Measuring Traits and Behaviors

Rather than comparing or ranking their employees against one another, many companies use **absolute approaches** to evaluate the performance of their employees. This involves comparing employees against certain "absolute" standards (rather than against each other) along a number of performance dimensions (rather than simply making a global assessment

forced distribution

A form of individual comparisons whereby managers are forced to distribute employees into one of several predetermined performance categories.

absolute approach

The evaluation of employees' performance by comparing employees against certain "absolute" standards (rather than against each other) along a number of performance dimensions (rather than simply making a global assessment about them).

COMPANY spotlight 9.1 Forced Distributions at GE

While many companies use a forced distribution approach, perhaps the best known is the system that GE uses for evaluating managerial and professional staff. Under the guidance of former Chief Executive Jack Welch, GE focuses on 4 Es when ranking managers and executives: high *energy* level, ability to *energize* others around common goals, the *edge* to make tough yes/no decisions, and the ability to consistently *execute* and deliver on promises. Once assessed, individuals are allocated into three groups—a top 20%, a middle 70%, and a bottom 10%. If employees are placed in the bottom 10%, there is a good chance they will be told to look elsewhere for employment. As Welch noted, "A company that bets its future on its people must remove that lower 10 percent, and keep removing it every year—always raising the bar of performance and increasing the quality of its leadership." Bill Conaty, chief HR officer at GE, said, "It's not so much rankings; it's differentiation. We believe that we need to recognize and reward our very best performers and we need to let our least effective performers know where they stand and give them a chance to improve or look for other opportunities outside of GE."

Sources: Marquez, J. GE's people power: Conaty made Jack Welch a believer. *Workforce Magazine*, July 23, 2007, pp. 26–30; Lawler, E. E., III. The folly of forced rankings. *strategy+business*, Third Quarter, 2002, http://www.strategy-business.com/press/16635507/20290; Grote, D. Forced ranking: Making performance management work. *Harvard Business School Working Knowledge Archive*, November 14, 2005, http://hbswk.hbs.edu/archive/5091.html; and Abelson, R. Companies turn to grades, and employees go to court. *New York Times*, March 19, 2001. http://www.nytimes.com/2001/03/19/business/19GRAD.html?ex=1209096000&en=2b922e98d45290e0&ei=5070.

about them). Each employee is assessed in terms of how well he or she performs a myriad of performance dimensions based on some predetermined standards of performance. As a result, each employee's evaluation is independent of other employees' evaluations. In theory, all employees could score high, average, or low. Absolute approaches are also conducive to evaluating employees in terms of their traits, or attributes, as well as their behaviors. Next we discuss these two types of approaches.

graphic rating scale

A method of evaluating employees based on various traits, or attributes, they possess relevant to their performance.

ATTRIBUTE-BASED APPROACHES The most common attribute-based approach is the graphic rating scale. Using **graphic rating scales**, raters evaluate employees based on various traits, or attributes, they possess relevant to their performance. Exhibit 9.5 shows an example of a graphic rating scale. As shown, a rater might be asked to evaluate the extent to which an individual is cooperative when performing his job—for example, to rate the person as "poor," "below average," "average," "above average," or "outstanding." The performance dimensions that can be used in a graphic rating scale are really only limited to the imagination of the managers using the scale.[12] For example, employees might be evaluated

Exhibit 9.5 ▶

Example of a Graphic Rating Scale

Evaluate employee performance on the following performance dimensions. Circle the most appropriate rating to reflect the employee's performance on each performance dimension.

Performance Dimension	Rating				
	Poor	Below Average	Average	Above Average	Outstanding
Courteous	1	2	3	4	5
Cooperative	1	2	3	4	5
Knowledge	1	2	3	4	5
Quality of work	1	2	3	4	5
Quantity of work	1	2	3	4	5
Product knowledge	1	2	3	4	5
Creativity	1	2	3	4	5

in terms of the extent to which they possess certain traits, such as product knowledge, creativity, and the like. Because the graphic rating approach provides a format for breaking down performance into a number of attributes, it is more suitable for developmental purposes than the comparative approaches. Employees and their managers can see which attributes they scored high or low on and thereby identify areas for improvement.

Graphic rating scales suffer from some limitations. Perhaps the most serious limitation is that if the scales are poorly designed, they can be ambiguous, and the performance standards can be interpreted differently by raters—especially if the dimensions being rated are not described in some detail, and definitions for outstanding, average, good, and superior ratings are not provided. For example, what does it really mean to be "above average" on a trait such as being cooperative? One manager might rate an employee as "above average" in terms of the person's cooperativeness, and another manager might rate the employee just as "average."

BEHAVIOR-BASED APPROACHES   Attribute-based approaches overcome some of the limitations of comparisons approaches because they rely on a variety of performance dimensions and evaluate employees along a range of performance standards. However, focusing on workers' attributes alone can be somewhat misleading. Some attributes truly reflect an employee's job performance. However, it is more likely that the attributes predict the person's *potential* to perform well rather than his or her actual performance. Put simply, possessing some attribute does not necessarily mean that an employee is using it to perform better. To overcome this limitation, some companies rely on behavior-based approaches that emphasize examining the extent to which employees actually display certain behaviors on the job. The most common approaches are the critical incident approach, forced-choice approach, behaviorally anchored rating scales, and behavioral observation scales.

In the **critical incident approach**, the evaluation criteria consist of statements or examples of exceptionally good or poor performance employees display over the course of the evaluation period. One of the primary advantages of focusing on critical incidents is that they focus on actual behaviors rather than traits employees display on the job. Because of this, raters have clear examples to refer to when evaluating employees. However, to effectively use a critical incident approach, managers must keep track of employees' behaviors. Although this might be easy to do when a manager is responsible for only a few employees, it grows exponentially more difficult as the number of employees being evaluated by a manager increases. In addition, raters might not be in a good position to monitor employee behaviors throughout the day or over time. Sales managers are a good example. Often their representatives work remotely. In cases such as this, an employee is likely to exhibit many behaviors the rater simply isn't around to observe.

When managers use the **forced-choice approach**, they must choose from a set of alternative statements regarding the ratee. As Exhibit 9.6 shows, each statement is designed to be equally favorable or unfavorable. The rater is forced to choose the statement that is most reflective of the individual's job performance. In many cases, the statements viewed as "higher" from the company's point of view might not be known to the rater; the rater simply picks the most accurate statement. The idea here is to mitigate the chances of bias creeping into the evaluation—that is, the chances a manager will rate people either particularly high or low or otherwise fall prey to other rating errors.[13] However, each statement actually has a predetermined value assigned to it, reflecting its relative value to the organization and distinguishing exceptional employee behaviors from poor employee behaviors.[14] After a manager has chosen among the statements, each employee is scored to determine his or her overall evaluation of the individual's performance.

critical incident approach

A behavior-based approach where the evaluation criteria consist of statements or examples of exceptionally good or poor performance employees display over the course of the evaluation period.

forced-choice approach

A behavior-based approach where managers must choose from a set of alternative statements regarding the person being rated.

(1) _____ Is effective	(OR) _____ Is efficient
(2) _____ Follows directions	(OR) _____ Takes the initiative
(3) _____ Turns in work on time	(OR) _____ Turns in high-quality work

◄ **Exhibit 9.6**

Example of the Forced-Choice Approach

Exhibit 9.7 ▶

Example of a
Behaviorally Anchored
Rating Scale

Performance Dimensions		**Prepared for Class:** The extent to which the professor is well prepared to lead a class discussion on a particular topic and address students' concerns.
High	5	Professor has examples from recent news stories relevant to the topic. Professor is familiar with the assigned reading material. PowerPoint slides are well developed prior to class discussion.
	4	PowerPoint slides are well developed prior to class discussion, and professor is familiar with the assigned reading material.
Average	3	Professor is familiar with the assigned reading material and has some PowerPoint slides prepared for class.
	2	Professor is familiar with the assigned reading material but does not have PowerPoint slides prepared for class.
Low	1	Professor does not have any PowerPoint slides prepared for class discussion and is not familiar with the assigned reading material for the lecture

behaviorally anchored rating scales (BARS)

A behavior-based evaluation approach where raters must evaluate individuals along a number of performance dimensions with each performance rating standard anchored by a behavioral example.

One approach that integrates some of the advantages of the graphic rating scales and the critical incident approach is the use of **behaviorally anchored rating scales (BARS)**. Similar to graphic rating scales, BARS require raters to evaluate individuals along a number of performance dimensions. However, a BARS goes beyond a graphic rating scale by anchoring each of the rating standards with a particular type of behavior that warrants a particular rating. So, instead of simply choosing between "below average" and "above average" ratings, the rater associates each rating score with a specific example of an actual behavior that typifies below average, average, or above average.[15] Exhibit 9.7 shows an example of a BARS used to evaluate how prepared college professors are for their classes.

One of the major advantages of the BARS approach is that it gives all raters a frame of reference for evaluating each dimension of an employee's performance.[16] Thus, the consistency of performance ratings across different raters should improve. The main disadvantage of the approach is that it takes more time and effort to develop the behavioral anchors for a BARS. Although information for a BARS can be collected from many sources, including the ratee,[17] doing all the information collecting as well as writing and scaling the critical incidents for each dimension of all of a firm's jobs can be too time-consuming for some managers and companies.[18] Moreover, BARS are job specific. As a result, their use across jobs requires the creation of distinct BARS evaluation forms for each job.

behavioral observation scales (BOS)

A behavior-based approach that requires raters to evaluate how often an employee displays certain behaviors on the job.

Whereas the BARS approach requires raters to evaluate whether an employee displays certain behaviors on the job, **behavioral observation scales (BOS)** require raters to evaluate how *often* an employee displays certain behaviors on the job. Similar to BARS, BOS are based on critical incidents that differentiate high and low job performance. The primary difference is that raters are able to assess the frequency by which a wide array of different behaviors, related to specific performance dimensions, are displayed on the job. Exhibit 9.8 shows an example of a BOS used to evaluate how prepared professors are for class.

Results-Based Approaches

Rather than an attribute or a behavioral approach, some companies use results-based methods that rely on objective performance dimensions such as production or quality measures. The measures are not necessarily tied to the job analysis but, rather, to the outcomes employees achieve.[19] There are two primary results-based methods: the direct measures approach and management by objectives.

direct measures approach

A results-based evaluation in which managers gauge the outcomes of employees' work, such as their sales, productivity, absenteeism, and the like.

With a **direct measures approach**, managers gauge the outcomes of their employees' work, such as their sales, productivity, quality, and the like. Because the approach focuses on quantifiable outcomes, it is very clear and meaningful when the right measures are evaluated. For example, sales revenues generated are clearly an important indicator of an employee's sales performance in a retail establishment.

Performance Dimensions					
Prepared for Class: The extent to which the professor is well prepared to lead a class discussion on a particular topic and address students' concerns.					
	Almost Never		Sometimes		Almost Always
Professor has examples from recent news stories relevant to the topic.	1	2	3	4	5
Professor is familiar with the assigned reading material.	1	2	3	4	5
Professor's PowerPoint slides are well developed.	1	2	3	4	5
Professor's PowerPoint slides are prepared prior to class's discussion.	1	2	3	4	5

◀ **Exhibit 9.8**

Example of a Behavioral Observation Scale

However, there are several limitations to the direct measures approach. First, not all jobs are associated with an objective outcome measure. For example, what objective outcomes exist for a guidance counselor, a mentor, a receptionist, or even a manager? Should receptionists be evaluated based on how many calls they answer? Or should they be evaluated on a more subjective behavioral dimension, such as how they handle the calls? Second, focusing solely on certain outcomes can lead to other outcomes being neglected. For example, overemphasizing sales in a retail outlet might create a disincentive for the store's employees to help one another out. They might figure that if they take the time to help one another, their sales will suffer.

Management by objectives (MBO) is another results-based approach. Rather than focusing on direct measures of performance, managers using the MBO approach meet with their employees and jointly set goals for them to accomplish during a particular time period. Ideally, the goals that are specified are objective in nature and easy to measure. At the end of the evaluation period, the rater and the ratee meet again to discuss the ratee's performance during the review time period. If the ratee met or exceeded the goals, the evaluation is positive; if the ratee failed to meet the goals, the evaluation is less favorable. As you might imagine, some jobs are not very conducive to the MBO approach because they lack objective or quantifiable goals employees need to strive to meet. Another potential problem is that if the goals are set too narrowly, employees are likely to strive to meet only those targets and neglect other aspects of their jobs that are not directly evaluated. Despite its drawbacks, the MBO approach is a powerful method for helping raters and ratees agree on what goals are most important and the performance levels needed to meet them.

management by objectives (MBO)

A results-based approach where managers meet with their employees and jointly set goals for them to accomplish during a particular time period.

Sources of Performance Data

There are many different sources of data to use for a firm's performance management system. Next we discuss each.

SUPERVISORS   Because supervisors are ultimately responsible for the performance of the employees they oversee, it's logical that they would be a key source of performance data. Indeed, supervisors are often in a good position to provide such data. However, as we have explained, this depends on the opportunities they have to observe their employees perform. Put simply, managers might not have the time to constantly monitor what their employees do throughout the day. Nor do they always work in close proximity to them. As a result, the data they provide generally include only the data that they were able to observe—not data that necessarily represent the full picture of an employee's performance.

CO-WORKERS In a team work environment, or when employees perform interdependent tasks and have related responsibilities, their peers are often in a unique position to comment on certain aspects of their performance. For example, they may be more able to comment on how well employees cooperate and support others as well as their actual task performance than their supervisors. People's co-workers are also likely to have a solid understanding of the particular challenges associated with their jobs. Managers face several potential downsides when they try to collect performance data generated by co-workers, however. First, if the co-workers are close friends, or if they do not like each other, their interpersonal relationships might influence their ratings of one another. Second, there are also concerns when peer evaluations are used in an administrative context. If employees have to rate each other, and those ratings are used to make decisions about raises or promotions, co-workers will have an incentive to rate each other lower to make themselves look better. That's why many firms use co-workers' evaluations for developmental purposes rather than administrative purposes.

self-appraisal

An evaluation done by an employee that rates his or her own performance.

SELF-APPRAISALS A **self-appraisal** occurs when an employee evaluates his or her own performance. People are generally very aware of how they are doing their jobs on a daily basis. As a result, self-appraisals can be a useful source for data. Of course, the obvious drawback of using self-appraisals is that employees will have an incentive to artificially inflate their own evaluations, particularly if the data are to be used for administrative purposes. At the same time, however, asking individuals to reflect on their own performance can be a very useful starting point and developmental tool to help them improve their performance.

SUBORDINATES Many jobs in organizations require the supervision and oversight of others. In these positions, it is important to assess how well the supervisor is doing in terms of managing his or her employees. Another source of performance data is to ask subordinates to rate their supervisors. Understanding how the people being managed by a person view their manager is useful information to which a firm's middle or upper managers might not have ready access. As you can imagine, however, there are challenges related to using these data. For example, subordinates may fear that their managers will retaliate against them if they say anything negative about them. The problem is likely to be magnified if the information subordinates provide isn't kept anonymous or they think their managers might be able to associate their comments with them[20]—which can happen if a manager has only a few subordinates. Second, it is important to be sure to separate how well liked a supervisor is from how good he or she is at supervising. A supervisor might be very well liked by her subordinates but not very good at getting them to work as hard as possible. Third, if the evaluations provided by a manager's subordinates are weighted too heavily, the manager will have an incentive to put the satisfaction of his employees first rather than put the firm's goals first.

CUSTOMER EVALUATIONS Employees' customers are a good source of performance data. Automobile manufacturers, hotels, restaurants, and many other service industries often try to gather customer information regarding the performance of their employees, supervisors, and business units. Because customers' satisfaction is a critical determinant of a company's success, it makes sense to ask customers for input. However, you need to consider several challenges related to gathering customer-generated data. First, the data might not be equally relevant for all jobs. Consider a restaurant: Gathering data from customers related to the performance of waiters is clearly appropriate—after all, waiters directly affect the quality and enjoyment of customers' dining experiences. However, gathering data from customers related to the performance of the restaurant's dishwashers might not be as appropriate (unless there are problems with dirty dishes). Second, trying to reach out to busy customers and provide them an incentive to take the time to complete a survey or answer questions about the performance of employees can be time-consuming and expensive. Moreover, if some customers don't respond to your questions or surveys, you're less likely to get a complete picture of your employees' performance. Customers with particularly bad or particularly good experiences with your firm are more likely than others to provide information. Despite these challenges, incorporating customer data into your performance management

Name:		(Optional)
Day Phone:		(Optional)
Evening Phone:		(Optional)
E-Mail:		

	Excellent	Good	Fair	Poor
1. How would you rate our facility overall?	○	○	○	○

	Yes	No	No Opinion
2. Were the charges explained to your satisfaction?	○	○	○
3. Was the repair work done to your satisfaction?	○	○	○
4. Were our personnel knowledgeable, courteous and efficient?	○	○	○
5. Was your car ready when we promisied?	○	○	○
6. Would you use our facility again?	○	○	○

Additional Comment:

[Send Form] [Reset]

Home | Contact & Find Us | Service History | Request an Appointment | Our Services
Auctions | Employment Info |

Employee's customers are a good source of performance data.

process is often an excellent idea. It's important to ensure that a representative sample of customers participate in the process.

360-DEGREE APPRAISALS   As you have learned, there are many different sources for performance data, each with advantages and disadvantages. In an attempt to try to capture all the relevant data from different sources, some companies use **360-degree appraisals**, which involve gathering performance data from as many sources as possible—supervisors, peers, subordinates, and customers. Because this approach tends to be very comprehensive, the performance of employees is more accurately depicted. As you can imagine, however, sorting through all the performance data can be cumbersome. Indeed, one of the primary disadvantages of the 360-degree appraisal approach is the time it takes managers to make sense of the different, and sometimes conflicting, information. After all, different raters are likely to observe different dimensions of an individual's performance or have in mind different standards of effectiveness when rating the person.[21] For example, a person's peers might think the individual is performing well in terms of his or her cooperation. Meanwhile, the employee's subordinates and supervisors might be less enthusiastic about the individual's productivity. Whose perspective is more accurate? Despite these problems, many companies have jumped on the 360-degree appraisal bandwagon.

360-degree appraisals

A comprehensive measurement approach that involves gathering performance data from as many sources as possible—supervisors, peers, subordinates, and customers.

Weighting Performance Criteria

One thing to consider when evaluating the performance of employees is the relative importance, or *weight*, of each performance dimension. In every organization, each job differs in terms of how it adds value to the company. In some jobs, the *quantity* of products produced is most important, whereas in other jobs, the *quality* of the products produced is of utmost concern. Some jobs require high levels of employee cooperation and teamwork, whereas other jobs require high levels of creativity and innovation. To complicate matters further, each job comprises multiple performance dimensions that vary in terms of their relative importance.

Recall our performance evaluation for a college professor. What are the key performance dimensions of a good professor? Being prepared for each class is certainly an important

▶ **Exhibit 9.9** Example of the Impact of Different Weights in Evaluations

Performance Dimension	Employee Ratings	Equal Weight	Scores	Example 1: Adjusted Weights	Scores	Example 2: Adjusted Weights	Scores
Clearly conveys course material	1	20%	.2	30%	.3	50%	.5
Is prepared for class	3	20%	.6	30%	.9	20%	.6
Maintains an entertaining class	5	20%	1	20%	1	10%	.5
Provides excellent feedback	5	20%	1	10%	.5	10%	.5
Grades fairly	3	20%	.6	10%	.3	10%	.3
Total Score			*3.4*		*3*		*2.4*

Evaluation Ratings: 1= poor, 2 = slightly below average, 3 = average, 4 = slightly above average, 5 = outstanding

dimension of teaching, but is it enough? What about the quality of the lecture? You also have to consider how responsive the professor is to students' questions as well as how fairly the professor grades exams. How much weight should each performance dimension carry?[22] Should being an entertaining teacher be as important as conveying knowledge in a way that enhances students' learning? Both are relevant, but are they equally relevant?

Exhibit 9.9 provides an example of how decisions you make regarding the relative weights of different performance dimensions affect an employee's evaluation. As you can see, the overall score for a single employee will vary, depending on how the performance dimensions are weighted. In this example, the college professor would receive the highest evaluation score when all the performance dimensions are weighted equally. When the weights are adjusted as in examples 1 and 2, the professor's summary score varies as well. These adjustments obviously have important implications for administrative issues such as promotion decisions and merit raises for employees. As a result, employees are likely to be particularly sensitive to how the different dimensions of their jobs are weighted. In fact, employees may have an incentive to focus their energies on some job dimensions at the expense of others. For example, in example 2 in Exhibit 9.9, if clearly conveying course material is half the evaluation score, it is reasonable to expect that employees may disproportionately focus their energies on that aspect of their job, perhaps at the expense of grading fairly or providing excellent feedback to students. Given that most jobs are multidimensional, managers need to take the time to think about which dimensions, if any, are more important than others and adjust the relative weight placed on each accordingly.

Performance Measurement Errors

As discussed in Chapter 7, when people make hiring decisions, certain biases can creep into the process.[23] The same is true when it comes to the performance management process. A manager commits the **halo error** when his overall positive view of an employee's performance biases the ratings he gives the person on the individual criteria that make up his or her performance.[24] In contrast, a manager commits the **horn error** when his overall negative view of an employee biases his ratings such that the individual receives lower ratings on specific performance dimensions than he or she really merits. The **contrast effect** occurs when a manager artificially inflates or deflates an employee's rating after comparing the person to another individual. For example, an employee with average performance might get a higher rating than he deserves if he is compared to an employee with poor performance. Or an employee with average performance might get rated lower than she deserves if she is compared to an employee with outstanding performance.

halo effect (also halo error)

The bias that occurs when a positive characteristic of a person affects the evaluation of the person's other attributes.

horn error

A performance evaluation error that occurs when an overall negative view of an employee's performance that biases the ratings such that the individual receives lower ratings on specific performance dimensions than he or she really merits.

contrast effect

Bias that results when an evaluation of one or more persons is artificially inflated or deflated compared to the evaluation of another person.

There are several additional potential errors worth noting. The **primacy error** reflects situations in which a rater's earlier impressions of an individual bias his or her later evaluations of the person. For example, if a rater has an early positive impression of an employee, the rater might pay particular attention to later performance information that is consistent with that impression and discount information that is inconsistent with that impression. In contrast, a **recency error** reflects situations in which a rater narrowly focuses on an employee's performance that occurs near the time of the evaluation. **Similar-to-me errors** occur when managers more highly rate employees who resemble them in some way. For example, if the manager and ratee both went to a particular college, have similar opinions, or simply have similar personalities, the manager might artificially inflate her evaluation of the individual because of the similarity. Put simply, there is a tendency for individuals to be more favorable of others who are more like them than different, and this tendency can creep into their measurements.

Some raters may also commit restriction of range or distributional errors. As noted earlier in this chapter, raters often must evaluate individual performance along some scale. For example, raters may be asked to assess the extent to which individual employees are "poor," "average," or "outstanding." Sometimes raters have a tendency to commit leniency, strictness, or central tendency errors. Raters commit the **leniency error** when they consistently rate employees on the higher end of the scale—that is, rating everyone as a 4 or a 5 on a 5-point scale.[25] In contrast, they commit the **strictness error** when they consistently rate employees on the low end of the scale—such as rating everyone as a 1 or a 2 on a 5-point scale. When raters evaluate everyone as average, regardless of their actual performance level, they commit the **error of central tendency**, which reflects the unwillingness of raters to rate individuals as very high or very low. In these situations, for example, a manager may rate all her employees as a 3, or "average," out of 5 rating options.

There are several steps companies can take to reduce the chances that these biases will occur. As noted earlier in this chapter, one approach is to incorporate more specificity into the rating formats. Defining more precisely what is being evaluated helps raters focus more on the relevant performance dimensions. A second approach is to train raters—to familiarize them with the errors that can occur and encourage them to avoid them.[26] A third approach, called **frame-of-reference training**, aims to help raters understand performance standards as well as performance dimensions.[27] It helps raters understand and identify different standards or levels of performance. In essence, it is intended to "calibrate," or "align," different raters to reach a consensus on varying levels of performance[28] in order to help raters develop common evaluation standards.[29] Finally, companies can use multiple raters. If one rater exhibits bias, having multiple raters will help smooth out the bias. This is one of the reasons firms use 360-degree appraisals.

STEP 4: PROVIDING FEEDBACK

The fourth step in an effective performance management system involves providing feedback to employees to help them improve their performance.[30] To be effective, the feedback must be provided in a timely manner and in a professional and positive way.

When to Appraise Employees

Companies vary in terms of how often they provide performance feedback to their employees. Most supervisors are required to formally appraise their employees every six months or once a year. Providing feedback to your employees on an ongoing basis, however, is ideal. If you don't do this as a manager, the feedback you give them during their formal appraisals will be far less effective. After all, how useful is it to tell your employees in a single meeting that they did something wrong six months ago or that they have consistently been underperforming? Moreover, failing to let your employees know immediately that they did something wrong is implicitly telling them that their performance is satisfactory. In other words, they may not even realize that their performance is less than satisfactory. And, of course, the longer managers wait to discuss performance problems with their employees, the longer they and their firms will be forced to have to deal with the substandard behavior. Unfortunately, managers are typically very

primacy error
A performance evaluation error that occurs when a rater's earlier impressions of an individual bias his or her later evaluations of the person.

recency error
A performance evaluation error that occurs when a rater narrowly focuses on an employee's performance that occurs near the time of the evaluation.

similar-to-me errors
A performance evaluation error that occurs when managers give a higher rating to employees who resemble them in some way.

leniency error
A performance evaluation error that occurs when employees are consistently rated on the higher end of a performance evaluation scale.

strictness error
A performance evaluation error that occurs when employees are consistently rated on the low end of a performance evaluation scale.

error of central tendency
A performance evaluation error that occurs when raters are unwilling to rate individuals as very high or very low on a performance evaluation scale.

frame-of-reference training
Training that aims to help raters understand performance standards as well as performance dimensions.

comfortable providing employees with positive feedback but are more reluctant to provide them with negative feedback, even though these are the employees who are likely to benefit most from clear feedback and a plan for improving their performance.

The Feedback Meeting

In addition to deciding when to formally appraise your employees, as a manager, you need to consider several factors, described in the following sections, when conducting appraisal meetings with them.

SEPARATING EVALUATION FROM DEVELOPMENT Recall that from an administrative perspective, performance evaluations help managers make decisions regarding employees' salary adjustments, merit raises, and other incentive rewards. Managers also use performance evaluation information to help their employees develop and improve their performance. The problem is that it's not likely that your employees will want to talk about how they can improve their performance while they are simultaneously lobbying you for a raise during a performance appraisal. As a result, some companies schedule two separate feedback meetings at different points in time—one to help employees improve their performance and a second to make administrative decisions based on their performance.

TARGETING BEHAVIORS OR OUTCOMES RATHER THAN THE INDIVIDUAL
A second major consideration for a feedback meeting is to separate the behaviors or outcomes of an employee's performance from the employee him- or herself. For example, telling an employee she didn't handle customer complaints well is more constructive than telling her she is a bad employee. By focusing on specific behaviors and/or outcomes, managers are more likely to be able to help employees identify specific areas to improve. And if managers do not label employees as bad or good, employees are more likely to be more open to their managers' suggestions as to how they might improve.

BEING BALANCED IN YOUR APPRAISAL Recall that jobs generally consist of multiple performance dimensions. In most cases, employees' performance on their respective job dimensions will vary. It is quite likely that they will excel at some dimensions and have room for improvement on others. During an appraisal meeting, it is important to discuss the full spectrum of these dimensions. Even if an employee's overall performance rating is not satisfactory, you don't want to diminish the positive contributions the person has provided. In fact, you want to encourage the person to continue to excel in those areas while improving those in the dimensions that aren't at a satisfactory level.

ENCOURAGING EMPLOYEE PARTICIPATION When employees are active, rather than passive, participants in the appraisal process, they are likely to view the process as more fair and useful. It is particularly helpful to ask employees to reflect on how well they performed different aspects of their job, as well as what factors may have helped, or constrained, their job performance. By doing so, you are signaling to an employee that your agenda is not simply to judge him but to help him improve. And by engaging him and considering his thoughts and concerns, you are taking positive steps toward creating an open dialogue regarding the person's development. This is a critical component for the last step of the performance management process—developing an action plan.

STEP 5: DEVELOPING ACTION PLANS TO IMPROVE EMPLOYEE PERFORMANCE

Simply providing employees with feedback about their performance is not enough to improve it. Rather, effective managers take another step: They work with their employees to diagnose the source of any performance problems they might have and help devise strategies to remedy them. Doing so, however, requires a clear understanding of the nature of the performance deficiency, the development of a plan to address the performance problems, and, when necessary, effective discipline of employees.

Understanding the Causes of Poor Performance

As Exhibit 9.1 shows, the contributions employees make are a function of their competencies, attitudes and behaviors, and work environments. Performance deficiencies can therefore be related to any of these three factors. For example, a performance problem might not be due to the amount of effort an employee is exerting but the fact that she lacks certain knowledge, skills, and abilities. Punishing employees for performing poorly when they want to perform well and are working as hard as they can yet fail to deliver is not likely to be an effective way to help improve their performance.

Performance problems can stem from factors related to an employee's work environment. For example, salespeople in rural areas often have to drive long distances to call on their customers. As a result, the number of sales calls they're able to make per day will be fewer than, say, the number that salespeople located in New York City are able to make. Obviously, this is a factor related to their work environment—not their performance—and is out of their control. There may also be something related to the design of employees' jobs, the technology they use, or the support or performance of their co-workers that prevents them from achieving excellent performance levels.

Sometimes, however, the root of the problem does, indeed, stem from the amount of effort an employee is exerting. Dealing with lack of effort or motivation requires a different approach than dealing with skill deficiencies or the work environment as the source of poor performance. When this is the case, the person's managers can respond in a variety of ways. For example, one way is to tie employees' annual raises to their performance reviews. Another is to provide employees with explicit goals and certain rewards if they reach those goals. As we will discuss in Chapter 11, this type of incentive model can be quite effective at maximizing employees' performance. Alternatively, as a manager, you may work jointly with each employee to develop a plan of action to help improve his or her performance.

The feedback meeting is an important part of the performance management process.

Taking Action

With a clear understanding of where performance deficiencies exist and a discussion with your employee about the potential causes of those performance deficiencies, you are in a position to jointly develop an action plan to help improve their performance.

The first step is to examine ways to remove barriers to employee success—obstacles that make it difficult for employees to be successful in their jobs. If the performance evaluation and appraisal meetings identify competencies as the leading cause of poor performance, for example, then training and development activities may be a viable solution. As discussed in Chapter 8, managers can use training and development programs to address skill deficiencies that may contribute to poor performance. Coaching and mentoring are two training tactics that are particularly useful in helping employees improve their performance. Coaching typically focuses on an employee's performance improvement, usually short term and usually relative to specific skills. Mentoring involves a longer-term relationship in which a more senior employee teaches a junior employee how the organization works and nurtures that person as she progresses in her career.

If the cause of poor performance is a result of the work environment, the solution may rest in aspects of the work design. As discussed in Chapter 4, some factors to consider are the design of the job, the competencies of co-workers, and technological considerations that constrain what employees are able to do in their jobs. It might be the case that an employee is being asked to perform more tasks than is possible to complete in a single workday. Alternatively, the technology in place may limit how well she can perform on the job.

If the cause of poor performance isn't a result of competencies or the work environment but rests with level or quality of an employee's performance, the following are some actions you may pursue:

- **Review the performance dimensions with your employee.** Are your employees clear about what they are expected to do to be successful? Sometimes employee performance is not a function of competencies, the work environment, or even motivation but lack of clarity on what is expected. Employees may simply not have a full understanding of all the aspects of their job. When this is the case, a review of the job description should provide clarity as to what employees are to do in the course of their

workday. You might also clarify which performance dimensions you measure to signal to an employee what aspects of their jobs are most important.

- **Review the standards of performance with your employee.** Sometimes employees understand what is expected of them, but they do not have a firm grasp on what it means to be successful at each task. Your employees should be clear on the types of performance that are considered poor, average, and good for each performance dimension. This might be accomplished through discussion of the different evaluation measures and the types of attitudes or behaviors that are indicative of each potential rating. This is a major benefit of the BARS evaluation form: It has clear behavioral anchors that identify the differences between the ratings for the performance dimensions.

- **Ensure that the performance measures are accurate.** The performance evaluation may be contaminated, deficient, or inaccurate. In such a case, you might discuss with an employee ways to more accurately evaluate his or her performance on the job. You may also consider adjusting what is evaluated to make sure your measures reflect the full array of behaviors important to your firm.

- **Evaluate potential role concerns.** In Chapter 4 we discussed role conflict, role overload, role underload, and role ambiguity. If these are present, they may lead to diminished performance. Employees may have conflicting pressures from their supervisor, customers, and colleagues that prevent them from effectively performing all their tasks. If this is the case, it might be useful to consider how to provide additional support to help balance these roles or to consider how the job might be redesigned to allow employees to succeed in their job.

The second component of an action plan is to reach agreement on performance targets and timelines for achieving improved performance. For example, establishing clear targets of improvement such as to decrease error rates by 10% or to increase sales by 10%, and to do so by a particular point in time, provides a clear goal for employees. This is much more constructive than simply telling employees to improve, and it provides employees with a benchmark to judge their improvements to see how they are progressing. In addition to using formal targets and timelines, effective managers also engage in informal feedback and regular discussions with employees to see how they are doing in their jobs and take steps to work with them to continuously improve.

As a manager, you want to be supportive of the development of your employees, and if the steps you have taken are successful, the result will be a happier and more productive workforce. At the same time, however, it is important to recognize that employees must perform at an acceptable level, and failure to reach that level of performance over a reasonable period of time may indicate that an employee is not a good fit for the job. In such situations in which the tactics we have discussed fail, managers may resort to discipline.

Disciplining Employees

You probably think of discipline as negative actions taken by managers, with actions such as excessive tardiness, absenteeism, dishonesty, theft, and violence warranting serious and immediate discipline. However, discipline can also be positive in nature because it's designed to encourage employees to behave appropriately at work. A useful way to think about discipline is that it sends a strong signal to employees about how they should behave or otherwise perform at work. There are two prominent approaches to discipline: positive discipline and progressive discipline.

progressive discipline

A process by which an employee with disciplinary problems progresses through a series of disciplinary stages until the problem is corrected.

PROGRESSIVE DISCIPLINE Progressive discipline refers to a process by which an employee with disciplinary problems progresses through a series of disciplinary stages until the problem is corrected.[31] As shown in Exhibit 9.10, there are typically four steps in this process. In the first step, the employee receives a verbal warning stating that his or her behavior or performance is not acceptable. The second stage involves writing up a reprimand, giving it to the employee, and documenting it in his or her personnel file. If the problem remains, the third stage of the progressive discipline is suspension. Finally, if the problem continues, the final stage is termination. Of course, companies bypass these stages if the

	Progressive Discipline	Positive Discipline
Step 1	Verbal warning	The employee and manager verbally agree as to how the employee must improve.
Step 2	Written reprimand	The manager and employee hold a follow-up meeting and outline a new action plan; written documentation is kept.
Step 3	Suspension	Employee is given a final warning of termination.
Step 4	Termination	Termination occurs.

◀ **Exhibit 9.10**
Steps of Progressive and Positive Discipline

problem is gross misconduct at work. Stealing, fighting, drug use, violence, and the like often result in immediate termination rather than progressive discipline being administered.

The primary advantages of progressive discipline are that it clearly informs employees that there is a problem and provides them with the opportunity to improve their performance. If a problem is corrected, there is no need to take further disciplinary steps. One criticism of progressive discipline is that it puts a priority on punishment rather than corrective action. Therefore, some companies instead use positive discipline.

POSITIVE DISCIPLINE With positive discipline, the disciplinary process is not punitive; rather, it focuses on constructive feedback and encourages employees to take responsibility for trying to improve their behaviors or performance at work. The key to positive discipline is to help employees identify their problems early on and address the causes of their problematic behavior. As Exhibit 9.10 shows, like progressive discipline, positive discipline also consists of four steps. The first step involves getting the employee and his or her manager to verbally agree as to how to improve the problem. The second step involves another meeting to explore why the problem was not corrected and to arrive at a new action plan. At this stage, there is written documentation of the meeting and a plan to address the problem. The third step involves a final termination warning. If the problem is not rectified, the final step, termination, occurs.

The steps in Exhibit 9.10 appear to be similar for both progressive and positive disciplinary procedures. However, positive discipline utilizes employee counseling, a problem-solving approach instead of punishment. The advantages of positive discipline are that the meetings are more constructive for employees, and employees feel that they are being treated with respect. The disadvantage, however, is that it requires more time and effort by managers to administer the process. Moreover, not every manager is adept at functioning in a counseling role.

A few caveats are worth noting regarding discipline: First, employees must clearly understand the rules, regulations, and procedures for any discipline to be effective. In other words, they need to know they are doing something wrong. As discussed in the previous section, this may be addressed simply by having a performance appraisal with an employee to discuss the situation. Doing so may avoid unnecessary discipline by helping to effectively manage performance expectations. Second, the discipline should happen swiftly. Why? When employees aren't disciplined immediately for a problem, they often don't know the problem exists, and it may be unreasonable to expect them to correct it.

positive discipline

The disciplinary process that is not punitive but rather focuses on constructive feedback and encourages employees to take responsibility for trying to improve their behaviors or performance at work.

PERFORMANCE MANAGEMENT IN PRACTICE: ORGANIZATIONAL DEMANDS

As shown in Exhibit 9.11, while the basic principles of performance management apply to all companies, how performance management systems are designed and implemented are likely to vary across contexts. Because each company is unique and operates in a distinct

▶ **Exhibit 9.11**   Performance Management in Practice

Context	Employee Attitudes & Behaviors Chapter 9, "Performance Management"
Organizational Demands	
Strategy drives . . .	• Which performance dimensions are emphasized • The performance evaluation method used
Company characteristics determine . . .	• Which performance evaluation method is used • Who carries out the process
Culture establishes . . .	• The objective of the performance management system • Which evaluation approach is used • Effectiveness of performance management approaches
Employee concerns include . . .	• Perceptions of procedural and distributive justice • Employees' responsiveness to performance feedback • Achieving work life balance
Environmental Demands	
Labor force influences . . .	• Accuracy of performance evaluations • The need to evaluate diversity efforts
Technology affects . . .	• The performance management process • How telecommuters are evaluated
Globalization impacts . . .	• What is evaluated • The acceptability of the performance management system • Who provides performance data
Ethics/social responsibility shapes . . .	• Employees' perceptions of the performance management system • How employees react to surveillance and monitoring • How ethically employees behave at work
Regulations *guide...*	• Efforts to reduce discrimination in the performance management process • The importance of documenting employee performance

context, it is important to examine how firms use performance management systems in light of their strategies, company characteristics, cultures, and employee concerns. We'll start with these organizational demands.

Strategy and Performance Management

A firm's strategy affects the specific performance dimensions the company emphasizes and the methods it uses to evaluate its employees. Let's look at each of these factors more closely.

WHICH PERFORMANCE DIMENSIONS ARE EMPHASIZED   Earlier in this chapter, we discussed the fact that each job within a company comprises multiple performance dimensions. However, the importance of each dimension is likely to vary, based on the company's strategy. A key task for a manager is to consider his or her company's strategy when deciding how much weight to place on the different performance dimensions to reflect how jobs add value to the company. Consider the job of a sales representative in a call center in a company with a strategy that emphasizes low costs and high sales call volumes. Now compare this job to one in a call center in a company whose strategy emphasizes customer service. In the cost-oriented company, the call center representatives will add more value when they make more phone calls. In contrast, in the company with a customer service strategy, the quality of the interaction between a representative and a customer is likely to be of utmost concern. As a result, managers in the two call centers are

COMPANY spotlight 9.2 Targeting Customer Service at Trader Joe's

In the grocery store industry, Trader Joe's has emerged as a trendy place to shop. Unlike other grocers, it doesn't have everything in stock that you might look for. What it does offer customers, however, is the ability and willingness to meet their requests. While this certainly depends on having products that customers are willing to pay for, it is also about creating an environment where shopping is a fun experience. In large part, this is a result of how Trader Joe's manages its workforce. Everything the company does reinforces the importance of having employees who provide excellent customer service. A recent job posting on the company Web site for a crew member, for instance, stated that the ideal candidate:

> works with a sense of urgency, loves food, enjoys a physically active work environment and has a fun, positive personality. Crew Members should have the ability and desire to create a fun, warm and friendly shopping experience.

Once on board, employees are reviewed frequently—every three months—to help reinforce the importance of customer service. Employees are evaluated on some traditional measures of performance, such as punctuality and thoroughness, but also on more subjective performance dimensions, such as being friendly, creating a fun shopping experience, engaging customers, greeting and asking customers if they need assistance, and promoting high morale in the store. With low employee turnover and a loyal customer based, Trader Joe's serves as a reminder that hiring the right people and evaluating them based on how they add value can go a long way toward company success.

Sources: Speizer, I. Shopper's special. *Workforce Management*, September 2004, pp. 51–54; Trader Joe's. *Job descriptions*, www.traderjoes.com/job_descriptions.html; McGregor, J. Leading listener: Trader Joe's. *FastCompany.com*, October 2004, www.fastcompany.com/magazine/87/customer-traderjoes.html; and Armstrong, L. Trader Joe's: The trendy American cousin. *BusinessWeek* online, April 26, 2004, www.businessweek.com/magazine/content/04_17/b3880016.htm.

likely to weight each performance dimension related to a sales representative's performance differently.[32] Company Spotlight 9.2 highlights how Trader Joe's uses performance evaluations to recognize outstanding customer service among its employees.

THE PERFORMANCE EVALUATION METHOD USED In addition to which performance dimensions are emphasized, a company's strategy also influences the performance evaluation method used. Recall that managers can use a comparative approach, an absolute approach, or a results-based approach. Each approach affects how employees do their jobs. Consider the job of a salesperson. How might the three different performance evaluation approaches affect how a salesperson performs her job? A comparative approach is likely to foster a competitive climate in which employees strive to achieve a high ranking by outperforming their co-workers at the expense of helping each other. With an absolute approach, each salesperson is evaluated based on his or her attributes (extroversion, knowledge of the products, etc.) and behaviors (engaging with customers, making many cold calls to potential customers, etc.), so strife among employees may be less of a problem.

Which approach should be used? The strategy of a company might lead its managers to emphasize one approach over another. If total sales are the primary objective, the firm's managers might be inclined to use a comparative approach to signal to employees the importance of making sales. However, if total sales and teamwork are important, a comparative approach might give employees a disincentive to help one another out, although it might result in high sales. And if a customer service is the strategy, a behavioral approach might allow managers to evaluate their employees based on how many sales they make as well as how they work with each other. We can imagine similar concerns in other jobs as well. In a production facility, for example, the extent to which employees focus on production volumes, the quality of production, or teamwork will reflect the strategic priorities of the company and affect which evaluation approach is used.

Company Characteristics and Performance Management

Which performance evaluation approach is used and who carries out the performance management activities are influenced by a company's size and stage of development.

WHICH PERFORMANCE EVALUATION APPROACH IS USED The size of a company directly influences the feasibility of using the different performance evaluation approaches. As discussed earlier, one of the major advantages of a comparative approach is that it allows managers to rank order employees. It's easier for managers in small companies to realistically know how well employees perform relative to one another. However, as companies grow and hire more employees, comparing each of them to one another becomes less feasible. Consider the challenges of using a comparative approach in a company with 10 employees versus in a company with 1,000 employees. With 10 employees, most managers could probably rank order the employees with a pretty high level of accuracy. But the addition of each employee exponentially increases the number of comparisons that have to be made. In addition, managers will be in less of a position to closely monitor their employees. As a result, the accuracy of the rankings is likely to diminish.

Larger companies are in a better position than small companies to use absolute performance evaluation approaches. Doing so also provides employees with more specific information about how well they are doing along a variety of performance dimensions. However, developing an absolute performance evaluation system is often time-consuming and expensive. For example, it might not be a wise for a small firm with only three employees to incur the expense associated with designing a BARS. However, a company with a greater number of employees may be able to realize a greater return on the investment. Spreading the costs of developing the system across 1,000 employee evaluations is much more feasible than with 3 employees. Moreover, larger companies and more mature companies are likely to have more financial resources at their disposal to allocate to develop absolute performance evaluation systems.

WHO CARRIES OUT THE PROCESS A company's size affects who carries out the performance evaluation process. Smaller and less-well-established companies are less likely to have support staffs or HR departments to help design and implement their performance management systems. Rather, in these organizations, line managers are likely to be expected to perform these duties. This generally changes as companies grow and become more mature. This isn't to say that managers in larger organizations don't participate in the performance management process; rather, the amount of administrative support available to them is simply likely to be greater.

Culture and Performance Management

A company's culture influences its performance management in several ways. First, it influences the likelihood that managers will use the different performance evaluation approaches. Second, how employees perceive the firm's cultural values will affect how they react to those approaches. Let's now look at each of these facets.

THE OBJECTIVE OF THE PERFORMANCE MANAGEMENT SYSTEM Suppose you work for a company that has a highly competitive culture, and managers emphasize that employees either succeed or look elsewhere for work. In an environment such as this, an administrative approach to performance management might be consistent with the firm's culture. In contrast, in cultures that prioritize the well-being of employees and their long-term employment managers may be more likely to focus on developmental approaches.[33]

WHICH EVALUATION APPROACH IS USED Given its culture, which performance evaluation approach should a firm use? Each of the primary performance evaluation approaches (comparative, attribute, behavioral, results) has different attributes. In a highly competitive, cutthroat culture such as that of the National Football League, a comparative approach may be preferred—and expected. In contrast, in a culture characterized by a concern for employee welfare and employee loyalty, absolute approaches may be preferred.

COMPANY spotlight   9.3 Shaping the Culture at Yum Brands, Inc.

How do you create a culture? This is exactly the issue Yum Brands faced when it split from PepsiCo in 1997. Pepsi had a culture that emphasized hard, financial-oriented measures of performance. Breaking away to focus solely on the restaurant industry, executives at Yum wanted to also break away from the numbers-driven culture at Pepsi and cultivate a culture that was customer focused. After all, their success or failure ultimately hinges on keeping their customers happy and attracting new ones. To achieve this goal, they implemented a 360-degree performance management system that emphasizes attributes such as cleanliness, hospitality, speed, and enthusiasm among their employees. The feedback from the 360-degree appraisals provides insights into how well the managers know their customers and how well they go about exceeding customer expectations. Managers are also evaluated on their ability to coach their employees to adhere to the customer focus. According to Yum's vice president of people development, they wanted to "put a yum, or smile, on customers' faces. We want to do that on every transaction." And by considering multiple perspectives, Yum has created a climate where everyone expects excellent service.

Source: Shuit, D. P. Yum does a 360. *Workforce Management*, April 2005, pp. 59–60.

A not-for-profit organization such as the Red Cross is an example of such an organization. Similarly, focusing solely on results rather than how employees perform their jobs may run counter to a culture that strives for continuous improvement in employee performance. 3M, a company that prides itself on innovation, is a good example. Some of 3M's best products were actually created by accident.[34]

EFFECTIVENESS OF PERFORMANCE MANAGEMENT APPROACHES Any discrepancy between a firm's cultural values and how its performance management system is designed can result in negative reaction by employees as well as lower morale and greater turnover on their part. However, when a firm's performance management systems are consistent with its cultural values, the result is more likely to be a reinforcement of those values and a renewed focus on what is necessary for the company to succeed. As highlighted in Company Spotlight 9.3, for example, Yum Brands has reaped many benefits from the implementation of a 360-degree performance management system that was consistent with the customer-focused culture it was trying to create among its workforce.

Employee Concerns and Performance Management

An important perspective to consider in the performance management process relates to employee concerns. A major goal of performance management is to encourage employees to work as hard as possible to help the company achieve its goals. When employees perceive that their performance management system is effective, they will be motivated to perform at a high level. For this perception to exist, a number of concerns need to be addressed when the system is designed or revised, including perceptions of procedural and distributive justice, the existence of potential conflicting interests, and the impact of the performance management system on the work/life balance of employees.

PERCEPTIONS OF PROCEDURAL AND DISTRIBUTIVE JUSTICE The performance management process is one particular management activity that is subject to many instances of employee justice perceptions. From a distributional justice perspective, when employees perceive that performance evaluations reflect their true performance during the evaluation period, they are more likely to accept the evaluation and work toward the company's goals. And when employees understand the rationale regarding why they received the performance evaluations they did, as well as what it would take to improve their performance, they are more likely to accept the evaluations and take steps to sustain or improve their performance.

Even if they agree with their evaluations (distributional justice), employees might disagree with different aspects of the performance management process (procedural justice), if it's not designed right. Employees' perceptions of procedural justice can be affected throughout the performance management process. For example, if they feel that their performance evaluations were deficient and failed to reflect the true scope of performance dimensions they perform, or if they feel that their performance evaluations included performance dimensions that were beyond their control or irrelevant in their job (contamination), they may view their evaluations as unfair. It is also possible that they may believe that the performance standards set for them were too hard or that the process was biased. They might also question whether different raters were truly in a good position to evaluate their performance.[35] Alternatively, they might not feel that they were provided with sufficient guidance as to how they would be evaluated or how performance problems they experienced would be handled.[36] Finally, they might not believe they were given enough feedback to understand how to improve their performance or know which performance dimensions they should have focused on.[37]

As this discussion suggests, managers have to be concerned with both distributional and procedural justice in the performance management process. When distributional and/or procedural justice concerns emerge, the impact on employees may be significant. Most directly, when employees disagree with the evaluation, or have concerns about how different stages of the evaluation process are carried out, the performance evaluation process is less likely to motivate them. Over time, this can lead to feelings of mistrust and anger, and it can affect employees' loyalty to the company.[38]

EMPLOYEES' RESPONSIVENESS TO PERFORMANCE FEEDBACK   In addition to perceptions of procedural and distributive justice, how employees respond to performance management feedback can vary, too—especially if they and their managers have different objectives for the performance evaluation process. As noted earlier, performance management systems can be used for developmental or administrative purposes. Both purposes are valuable to a company's success. However, they can lead to conflicting responses, particularly during performance reviews. On the one hand, managers might be required to rely on performance management systems to make decisions about promotion, merit raises, layoffs, and the like. On the other hand, employees might want to focus on the feedback and developmental functions of the performance management system to help improve their performance and earn higher ratings in the future.[39] Although employees might be open to critical feedback used for developmental purposes, they are less likely to be as open to the same feedback being used for administrative purposes, particularly when the evaluation is tied to their pay, job security, and the like.[40]

ACHIEVING WORK/LIFE BALANCE   Throughout the previous chapters, we have explored how achieving work/life balance is an increasing concern for many employees. We have also talked about the steps that companies can take to help employees realize this balance through activities such as flexible work schedules. The performance management system a company uses can reinforce or conflict with the other activities it implements to support the work/life balance needs of its employees. This can be the case if the amount of time employees need to put into their jobs to meet their performance standards requires them to spend less time at home or enjoying other personal activities.

A somewhat related concern stems from how the performance management process works when employees telecommute or work flexible hours. Traditionally, supervisors and employees work similar hours in the same location, providing their supervisors with the opportunity to observe them regularly. But how do supervisors or other evaluators gather performance data about employees if they aren't at work all the time? Employees might be concerned that their raters don't understand or appreciate the work they do offsite or might think that there is a bias against individuals who work remotely or work different schedules. Alternatively, employees might discover that even though they've been given the opportunity to telecommute or modify their work schedules to accommodate their personal activities, if they take advantage of these programs, they are less likely to be evaluated highly by their managers.

PERFORMANCE MANAGEMENT IN PRACTICE: ENVIRONMENTAL INFLUENCES

Influences in the external environment play a role in performance management. In particular, labor force trends, technology, globalization, and ethical considerations strongly influence the decisions managers must make about how the performance management processes in their firms should be implemented. Next we discuss these facets.

Labor Force Trends and Performance Management

As the workforce becomes more diverse, the performance management system used within a company may need to be reevaluated in terms of both the accuracy of the performance evaluations being administered and what is being evaluated.

ACCURACY OF PERFORMANCE EVALUATIONS

Because workforces are becoming more diverse, people may be concerned about the accuracy of performance evaluations—especially because some firms use subjective evaluation approaches. Given this subjectivity, there may be concerns regarding ethnic, gender, or age biases.[41] For example, in one study, male employees reacted more unfavorably to performance appraisal feedback from female supervisors than from male supervisors.[42] Interestingly, another study found that as the proportion of a company's workforce became more racially diverse, the effects race had on the company's performance ratings decreased.[43] This suggests that as the workforce becomes more diverse, the influence of diversity on performance management may diminish. Nevertheless, the concern is that managers may adhere to biases such as the similar-to-me bias in which they more favorably evaluate individuals who are more like them than individuals who are dissimilar. Fortunately, there are steps companies can take to improve the accuracy of their evaluations. As noted earlier in this chapter, companies can incorporate more specificity into their rating formats, train raters to help them avoid biases,[44] and help raters understand the specific performance evaluation dimensions that need to be emphasized.

THE NEED TO EVALUATE DIVERSITY EFFORTS

If firms are going to take steps to embrace diversity and increase it within their organizations, they must also hold managers accountable for their diversity efforts,[45] as do companies such as Procter & Gamble, Sara Lee, Allstate, and Texaco.[46] There are several ways to include diversity efforts in the performance management process. For example, companies can track the number of women and minorities they have in managerial positions or positions targeted for diversity initiatives. The ability to develop employees with diverse backgrounds for higher-level positions can also be included as part of managers' performance evaluations. Alternatively, a company using a behavioral approach could ask a person's co-workers, subordinates, and supervisors to relate incidents that show how well the person works with and/or manages women and minorities. Although doing so can take some time and effort, it can help employees identify areas for improvement and increase their ability to work in a diverse environment.

Technology and Performance Management

Advances in technology affect performance management in several ways. Managers must rethink how they evaluate employees who telecommute, how employee performance data are collected, and how employees receive feedback. Next, we discuss each of these aspects.

THE PERFORMANCE MANAGEMENT PROCESS

Companies use a wide array of technologies to monitor different aspects of the performance of their employees, such as the number of keystrokes they type or the number of calls they make and receive. Managers can also use the Internet or their companies' intranets to administer online surveys to gather additional performance data from an employee's co-workers, vendors, subordinates, and even customers. Once all the data are collected electronically, the manager then can tabulate the results for a wider array of feedback to improve the accuracy of the performance evaluation.

COMPANY *spotlight*   9.4 Using Technology at Applebee's

What type of performance management system would you use if you had to evaluate thousands of employees scattered across different stores in various locations? At Applebee's, the solution to this issue involved technology. Applebee's developed a Web-based performance management program called ApplePM (for "people management") that provides standard information for managers and executives to identify employee performance and effectiveness at retaining their top performers. The system provides numeric data such as data on turnover, sales, and profits as well as more subjective data, such as customer satisfaction and performance reviews. Through the system, managers can track their own monthly scorecards that show how they are performing on the key performance dimensions by which they are judged. "We keep looking for new ways to use this powerful system," says Chief People Officer Lou Kaucic. "With 1,600 restaurants, it's not like we have one factory where I can walk around the floors. Having a good method of communication and feedback becomes critical, and that's where a Web-based system has really helped us."

Source: Dalton, A. Applebee's turnover recipe. *Workforce Management* online, May 2005, http://www.workforce.com/archive/article/24/05/60.php.

Technology can also be used to provide employees with instant feedback about how they're doing in their jobs. At Red Hat, Inc., a Linux operating system developer located in North Carolina, all employees are able to access the firm's performance management system from any computer. The system allows employees to see their performance evaluations and track how well they are progressing toward goals.[47] Considering the fact that many companies provide formal employee feedback only semi-annually or annually, the ability to dramatically increase the frequency with which feedback is given is certainly a valued improvement in the performance management process. As shown in Company Spotlight 9.4, technology has played a vital role in increasing the communication and feedback for employees at Applebee's.

HOW TELECOMMUTERS ARE EVALUATED   In earlier chapters, we discussed how technological advances have made it possible for many employees to telecommute. Telecommuting can complicate performance management: If employees are not at work, how are they evaluated? After all, managers have less direct communication and face-to-face interaction with telecommuters than they have with in-house employees. This gives the managers less opportunity to personally evaluate the performance of telecommuters, which has several implications.[48] First, managers can simply rely on traditional evaluation techniques and do their best to gauge the performance of telecommuters. Of course, with limited ability to observe the performance of their telecommuters, the quality of the data that managers gather and the feedback they provide them are likely to suffer.[49] A second option is to modify how employees are evaluated. For example, managers might try to focus on the outcomes, or results, telecommuters achieve rather than observe their behaviors.[50] A word of caution is in order here: Shifting to an outcome-oriented evaluation approach might work for some jobs that have clearly identifiable and objective outcomes, but for many jobs, how employees do their work is just as important as, or more important than, any outcome measure. Consider customer representatives who work from home: Should they be evaluated based on how many customer calls they handle or based on the degree to which they satisfy customers?

Globalization and Performance Management

When designing an international performance management system, a key issue is whether individuals on an international assignment should be evaluated based on dimensions and standards used in their home country or those adjusted to reflect the host country's culture. A second key issue is what is the best way to evaluate international assignees? The reality is that working internationally creates a number of challenges regarding both the content of the performance management system and the process by which it is carried out.

WHAT IS EVALUATED In the United States, many companies evaluate their managers and employees on quantifiable criteria such as efficiency, quantity of production, and sales. However, elsewhere in the world, the ability of a firm's employees to maximize their performance on the same dimensions can be affected by local conditions related to the political environment, union relations, country, infrastructure, social norms, and cultural differences.[51] For example, an employee's ability to increase his firm's sales at an international facility might be limited by the local economic conditions, currency valuations, or level of poverty in the country. If the employee's company fails to consider such factors, it is relying on a performance evaluation system that doesn't reflect the challenges the employee faces. Thus, the different dimensions of the job need to be reviewed to ensure that they capture the relevant aspects of an individual's performance.

Companies must also clearly communicate the standards of performance for the performance dimensions for which employees are held accountable. What does it mean to be successful on each performance dimension? While improving sales might be an important dimension in both the home and host countries, the level of sales improvement in an international culture that is possible can vary dramatically. In addition, how long does it take to reach the objectives? If an employee is assigned to a new facility, it may take considerably longer for the person to reach her performance expectations than if she is assigned to an established facility. What is achievable in six months in one location may take more or less time in another location. The performance standards need to reflect these potential differences.

THE ACCEPTABILITY OF THE PERFORMANCE MANAGEMENT SYSTEM Cultural differences can influence the acceptability of different performance management systems.[52] Some countries, for example, tend to be more individualistic, whereas others are more collectivistic. Holding employees accountable for the how they individually perform is generally quite acceptable in individualistic countries such as the United States. However, the practice may not be as accepted in countries that place a higher value on social relations, teamwork, and helping each other succeed.[53]

In addition, the means by which performance standards are achieved can vary. In some cultures, it might be more critical to a company's success for its employees to spend more time developing relationships with the unions, communities, and local leaders there than focusing solely on aspects within the company.[54] In other words, it's quite possible that for an international assignment to be a success, an employee stationed abroad might have to utilize different mechanisms than he would need to use in his home country.[55] Thus, managers evaluating employees in such situations must be certain to consider which performance dimensions are most relevant, what the appropriate standards of performance are, how the employees will interpret the performance dimensions based on their cultural experiences, and how they may need to work differently to reach their performance objectives.

WHO PROVIDES PERFORMANCE DATA Who should provide the data related to how well an expatriate is performing? Should the person's manager at the company headquarters compile the data? Or should the manager rely on raters in the foreign country to which the expatriate is assigned? There are two factors that influence who should provide performance data. First, raters from different cultures are likely to interpret an employee's behaviors differently. They will be inclined to rely on their own cultural values, which may or may not be consistent with the values of the employee or the home culture.[56] For example, aggressiveness might be a valued employee trait in the home country but disdained by people in the host country.

However, if employees adjust their behaviors to fit the cultures to which they are assigned, how will their performance look to raters in their home countries? Or should the employees be evaluated by raters in their host countries? Whose perspective is likely to be more accurate?[57] The second factor relates to the opportunity to observe employees when the home country managers of expatriates, for example, are located in a different country than the expatriates. Obviously, the ability of managers to observe employees in this situation will be severely compromised.[58] Thus, it is unwise to rely on one rater to evaluate an international assignee, given the potential biases that can emerge as well as the limited opportunity the person's supervisor will have to observe the employee's performance. A more appropriate approach is to rely on multiple raters from both countries.[59]

Ethics and Performance Management

The performance management system a firm has in place affects the perceptions the company's employees have about whether they are being treated ethically, whether the evaluation process is ethical, and how ethically employees act on the job.

EMPLOYEES' PERCEPTIONS OF THE PERFORMANCE MANAGEMENT SYSTEM

Because performance evaluations can significantly affect a firm's employees, as a manager, you need to ensure that your performance management system is ethical. Not surprisingly, there is considerable overlap between employees' perceived fairness of the performance management system and their views on the ethicality of the system in place. Employees will view a system that has both procedural and distributive fairness as being more ethical. Whether employees are allowed to participate in the performance management process can also affect their perceptions of how ethical it is. In particular, providing employees with a channel to voice their concerns about the process, the opportunity to challenge or disagree with the ratings they receive, and a chance to meet with their supervisors to discuss any discrepancies will improve the perceived fairness and ethicality of the system.

HOW EMPLOYEES REACT TO SURVEILLANCE AND MONITORING

Because technological advances have given companies new ways to monitor and control their employees, privacy issues have emerged—particularly when it comes to employees' use of the Internet and e-mail. Using computer programs such as Cyber Snoop, WebSpy, or NetChatSpy, companies are able to monitor what Web sites their employees visit.[60] Xerox and Compaq are among the companies that have used technology such as this to monitor how much time their employees spend surfing the Web.[61] Some companies also record their employees' phone conversations, and track their numbers of keystrokes. Although these actions are legal, how employees, managers, and society view them from an ethical point of view is open to debate. Moreover, it is possible that the use of these systems, even when done for legitimate reasons, can lead employees to believe that their managers don't trust them. If employees have ethical concerns about invasion of privacy or excessive surveillance, they may not respond in a positive way to these forms of monitoring. Clearly, this is a controversial topic that needs to be pursued with caution.

HOW ETHICALLY EMPLOYEES BEHAVE AT WORK

Meltdowns at companies such as Enron and Tyco have made people more aware of corporate ethics (or a lack of ethics). Indeed, a firm's performance system can affect whether its employees engage in behaviors that other stakeholders consider unethical. For example, a company that relies on a com-

Some companies use technology to monitor employee behavior at work.

parative evaluation approach for its employees might unintentionally be fostering a climate in which employees are willing to cheat or stab the backs of their co-workers. Similarly, a performance management system that solely evaluates a corporation's financial performance might inadvertently encourage managers to engage in unethical (and perhaps illegal) accounting practices in order to improve the firm's bottom line. Managers might also fail to fill vacant positions or repair on-the-job safety problem because doing so might incur more costs and hurt their chances of reaching their financial targets and earning incentive pay. Furthermore, if administrative decisions made about promotions, layoffs, and the like are significant, the performance management system may help prompt employees to engage in unethical behaviors to maximize their potential income, protect their job security, or enhance their career progressions.

PERFORMANCE MANAGEMENT IN PRACTICE: REGULATORY ISSUES

Of course, managers need to consider legal ramifications when they're designing and implementing their firms' performance management systems. Two issues that are directly related to regulatory issues are discrimination in the performance management process and the importance of documentation.

Efforts to Reduce Discrimination in the Performance Management Process

In response to several lawsuits, Ford paid out $10.5 million over forced ranking-related discrimination claims on the basis of age, gender, and race.[62] Goodyear changed its forced distribution model, in part due to concerns about the presence of discrimination in the ranking of employees.[63] Other companies, such as Microsoft, Wal-Mart, and Conoco, have faced legal action based on concerns of discrimination stemming from their employee performance management systems.[64]

These lawsuits serve as an important reminder that the performance management system you use must not be discriminatory. And while some discriminatory actions in the performance evaluation or appraisal process may be intentional, managers may also unintentionally discriminate against employees. Sometimes these actions occur through biases such as similar-to-me error that managers unknowingly commit. They may also stem from evaluation approach used. Evaluating employees on outputs is much more objective than ranking employees based on some general category such "level of performance." Some of the evaluation approaches, such as BOS and BARS, that explicitly identify performance dimensions and levels of performance among those dimensions are conducive to helping raters focus on the performance of their employees without discriminatory considerations. As a manager, you need to remember the importance of job-relatedness, highlighted in Chapter 3. Striving to maximize validity, specificity, and clarity in performance standards are steps in the right direction to eliminating bias in the performance management process. The key is to rely on evaluations that truly reflect employee attributes, behaviors, and/or outcomes that differentiate levels of actual job performance.

The Importance of Documenting Employee Performance

Considering the potential consequences of performance evaluations, it should be obvious that you need to be sure to maintain documentation of decisions and actions throughout your performance management process. This involves documentation of the evidence—the factors—that led to your decision to assign a particular performance rating for an employee. Without documentation of an employee's performance, how do you know if they deserve a 3 or a 4 on your 5-point rating scale? Without proper documentation, how can you be certain you don't commit biases such as recency bias because you can't remember the entire review period for an employee? Without documentation, how can you be sure you are not confusing events and perceptions of performance among 5 or

10 employees over the past six months? Taking the time to document events and incidents isn't easy. But doing so will provide you with much more accuracy in your ratings as well as assurance that you are providing the correct ratings for your employees. Given the implications these ratings may have for the careers and financial well-being of your employees, it is only fair to be as thorough and accurate as possible. In addition to documenting the incidents that led to your evaluation, it is equally important that you document all discussions and steps taken to help improve your employees' performance, as well as any disciplinary actions. If you encounter a situation in which you must suspend or terminate an employee, it is important that you be able to provide a timeline of the steps that you have taken to try to correct the person's performance.

SUMMARY

Performance management is the process of evaluating the performance of your employees against the performance standards set for them and then helping them develop action plans to address any gaps identified. There are two primary purposes of performance management systems. First, they serve an administrative function by providing information managers use to make decisions about merit increases, layoffs, and the like. Second, they serve a developmental purpose by providing employees with information they can use to improve their performance in order to add more value to the company's success.

Managers must take five steps to design and implement an effective performance management system. First, they must identify a job's relevant performance dimensions. The performance dimensions of a job reflect the reason it exists. They help pinpoint the specific tasks and activities employees are responsible for in their jobs. Once the performance dimensions are identified, managers then turn to the second step: developing performance measures that serve as the basis for evaluating the performance of their employees. To be effective, performance measures must be valid, be associated with clear performance standards, and be specific.

The third step focuses on evaluating employees' performance. There are several different approaches managers can take. (1) They can take a comparison-based approach in which employees are ranked according to how well (or how poorly) their performance compares to the performance of their co-workers. (2) Managers can evaluate their employees against certain preestablished standards of performance rather than evaluate them relative to their co-workers. This absolute approach requires managers to evaluate the extent to which employees possess certain traits, such as being leaders, or exhibit certain behaviors, such as being prepared for work or helping solve customer problems. (3) Using a direct approach, managers can evaluate their employees based on the outcomes of their work, such as volumes they produce or sales they generate. (4) With a management by objectives approach, managers can evaluate their employees based on the extent to which they meet the objectives jointly developed for them.

The third step managers need to take to develop an effective evaluation system is to determine which sources of performance information to draw on. Managers can rely on information from the employees themselves, their co-workers, supervisors, and even customers. The choice of which source of information to use should be based on the ability of the source to provide useful and valid information about the employee's performance.

The last two steps of an effective performance management system involve providing employees with feedback about their levels of performance and developing action plans to improve their performance. When an employee performs poorly because of a lack of effort rather than ability, the manager may need to resort to discipline. Managers can use either progressive or positive discipline to help employees understand their performance deficiencies and improve. Progressive discipline is a process by which employees who have disciplinary problems progress through a series of disciplinary stages until the problem is corrected. Positive discipline is not punitive; rather, it focuses on constructive feedback and encourages employees to take responsibility for improving their behaviors or work performance.

The choices managers make regarding the various options in the performance management system they use is influenced by organizational demands, environmental influences, and legal requirements. The organizational demands of a firm, such as its strategy, company characteristics, culture, and employee concerns, will affect the performance evaluation approaches managers use, the performance dimensions they emphasize, employees' responsiveness to the performance feedback they receive, and the like. Environmental factors require managers to look at how labor force trends, technology, globalization, and ethics impact the performance management system. Finally, because of legal considerations, managers need to try to reduce error and bias in the performance management process and to avoid wrongfully discharging employees.

KEY TERMS

360-degree appraisals *p. 271*

absolute approach *p. 265*

behavioral observation scales (BOS) *p. 268*

behaviorally anchored rating scales (BARS) *p. 268*

contaminated performance measure *p. 263*

contrast effect *p. 272*

critical incident approach *p. 267*

deficient performance measure *p. 263*

direct measures approach *p. 268*

error of central tendency *p. 273*

forced-choice approach *p. 267*

forced distribution *p. 265*

frame-of-reference training *p. 273*

global performance measure *p. 261*

graphic rating scale *p. 266*

halo error *p. 272*

horn error *p. 272*

leniency error *p. 273*

management by objectives (MBO) *p. 269*

paired comparisons *p. 264*

performance dimension *p. 261*

performance management *p. 260*

performance standards *p. 263*

positive discipline *p. 276*

primacy error *p. 273*

progressive discipline *p. 276*

ranking approach *p. 264*

recency error *p. 273*

self-appraisal *p. 270*

similar-to-me error *p. 273*

specificity *p. 263*

strictness error *p. 273*

DISCUSSION QUESTIONS

1. What are the two primary purposes of performance management? When should each purpose be emphasized?
2. Explain the major components related to an effective performance management system.
3. What are effective performance measures? What should you do to ensure that your performance measures are useful?
4. What are the advantages and disadvantages of the different sources of information used to evaluate the performance of employees?
5. Explain the major steps in progressive and positive discipline procedures. Why are the steps included in the procedures?
6. How do an organization's demands influence its performance management process?
7. Explain how environmental circumstances affect the design and implementation of a firm's performance management system.
8. What legal aspects must you must consider when designing and implementing a performance management system?

LEARNING EXERCISE 1

As a manager, you have a number of choices to make regarding your evaluation approach to managing the performance of your employees. First, you can use a ranking-based approach such as a straight ranking, forced distribution, or paired comparison. Second, you can use an attribute-based approach that focuses on evaluating your employees' traits via a graphic rating scale or your employees' behaviors via behaviorally anchored rating scales and behavioral observation scales. Finally, you can use a results-based approach that measures direct employee outcomes or uses a management by objectives approach.

1. What are the advantages and disadvantages of using ranking, absolute-trait, absolute-behavior, and results-based approaches to evaluate your employees' performance?
2. When should each approach be used?

LEARNING EXERCISE 2

Working in groups, obtain a job description for a job. After reading the job description, develop a performance management evaluation form that you might use to evaluate someone performing that job. In this task, it is important that you do the following.

1. Identify the performance dimensions to be evaluated.
2. Explain any weights you might assign to the performance dimensions.
3. Identify any standards you might create for the performance dimensions.
4. Create a form that might be used to assess the jobholder based on your responses to the first three questions.
5. Identify which source(s) of data would be best positioned to evaluate the jobholder.

CASE STUDY # 1 — A NEW SYSTEM AT ADDILLADE AND PARTNERS

Addillade and Partners is a private medical practice with a full-time staff of about 15 nurses. Until now, the performance management system at Addillade has been based on a direct evaluation approach. The partners would simply rate how well each nurse they interacted with over the course of the year performed. However, some of the nurses have complained that the system isn't fair. One of the criticisms is that some managers are known to be good ones to work for—their nurses tend to receive high ratings and, as a result, high rewards. Other managers don't really provide any feedback; each nurse is simply given a score at the end of the review period, without any insights into why they received their score or what they could do to improve.

Because Addillade relies so extensively on its nurses, the partners have decided to take steps to improve their perceived fairness of the system. In doing so, the partners are considering using the following graphic rating scale to evaluate the nurses:

DISCUSSION QUESTIONS

1. From an administrative perspective, what are some of the potential problems with this evaluation form? What are some of the potential problems from a developmental perspective?

2. What recommendations would you make to improve the evaluation form?

3. Is there another type of evaluation form you would suggest? Why?

Evaluate the employee's performance on the following performance dimensions. Circle the most appropriate rating for each.

Performance Dimension	Rating				
	Poor	Below Average	Average	Above Average	Outstanding
Courteous	1	2	3	4	5
Cooperative	1	2	3	4	5
Knowledgeable	1	2	3	4	5
Quantity of work	1	2	3	4	5

CASE STUDY # 2 — KAY JOHNSON AT HUMAN CAPITAL CONSULTANTS (HCC)

Kay Johnson is a strategic consultant for Human Capital Consults (HCC). HCC is a modestly sized consulting firm located in Chicago. It provides consultancy services regarding HR issues and specializes in strategic alignment and corporate change. HCC has 30 consultants, 3 junior partners, and 3 senior partners. The firm has a fairly friendly, laid-back culture. Turnover at HCC is extremely low; when the right people join the firm, they tend to stay because of the close-knit, familial atmosphere.

When John Yeoung, the lead senior partner of HCC, initially recruited Kay to join the firm, Kay was skeptical. She knew that the culture at HCC was very team oriented and not very supportive of individualism or competitiveness among consultants. Kay's hesitation stemmed from the fact that she was well aware that she had a strong individual personality. As a result, she worried that she would not be a good fit and might be better off in her current job as an independent consultant, in which she had a lot of leeway to act on her instincts and make final decisions.

After a lot of consideration, along with pressure from John and a lucrative compensation package, Kay joined HCC as a senior HR consultant. Her primary job is to bring in new business and lead small project teams of three to four individuals working with clients. When John hired Kay, he told her that if she did well, she would be on the fast track to becoming a junior partner in the consulting firm.

In the course of her first year, Kay has been routinely commended for her work. Her clients love her, and word of mouth of her abilities in the industry has generated new business for HCC. John is very pleased with the job she has done and acknowledges that she has been more successful in this job than any of her predecessors.

The problem is that while the clients are happy, Kay's colleagues are not. Many people don't want to work with her on projects. John hears concerns from a number of her colleagues that Kay's style is abrasive, volatile, and lacking team-player skills. In fact, several co-workers have suggested to John that if they have to continue working with her, they will consider leaving for another company. Moreover, some of the other partners have pulled John aside to state their displeasure with Kay's work style.

It is now time for John to give Kay her first annual performance review. John knows that Kay will inquire about the possibility of being promoted to junior partner.

DISCUSSION QUESTIONS

1. What are the major problems John is facing in this case?

2. How would you evaluate Kay's performance during her first year?

3. What recommendations would you make to John? Should Kay be promoted? Should Kay be fired? What are the implications for each of these decisions?

4. If your recommendations were implemented, what impact would they have for HCC and Kay?

COMPENSATING EMPLOYEES

1. Describe the purpose of compensation. *(294)*

2. Discuss the importance of equity relative to a firm's compensation decisions. *(296)*

3. Understand the process and rationale for establishing internal alignment of pay systems. *(298)*

4. Explain how a firm ensures that it is externally competitive in what it pays. *(301)*

5. Identify alternative compensation approaches that companies can use. *(305)*

6. Describe the impact organizational demands have on a firm's compensation decisions. *(308)*

7. Discuss environmental factors that affect the compensation firm's offer. *(314)*

8. Outline the regulations that affect how employees are compensated. *(318)*

HR CHALLENGES

| Environmental Influences | Organizational Demands | Regulatory Issues |

PRIMARY HR ACTIVITIES

Work Design & Workforce Planning

Managing Employee Competencies

Managing Employee Attitudes & Behaviors

Employee Contributions

Competitive Advantage

PURPOSE OF COMPENSATION

If you will come to work for us, we will pay you $30.00 per hour for the first 40 hours you work each week and $35.00 per hour thereafter. Will you work for us? What would you want to know before you make your decision? Would the type of work matter? Would you want to know how much other people are making doing the same kind of work? Is what we are offering violating any pay laws?

In previous chapters, we discussed how companies design and plan for work and how they ensure that employees have the competencies needed to achieve organizational goals. Then, in Chapter 9, we began a discussion of how to manage employees' attitudes and behaviors by describing the performance management process. However, employees most likely will not be motivated to help you achieve company goals unless they feel that they are properly compensated for their performance. This chapter is about how pay decisions are made and what you, as a manager, need to know and do to ensure that the pay will attract, motivate, and retain employees. Thus, this chapter is also about the Managing Employee Attitudes and Behaviors circle in Exhibit 10.1. In this chapter, we discuss a

Exhibit 10.1 ▶

Framework for the Strategic Management of Employees

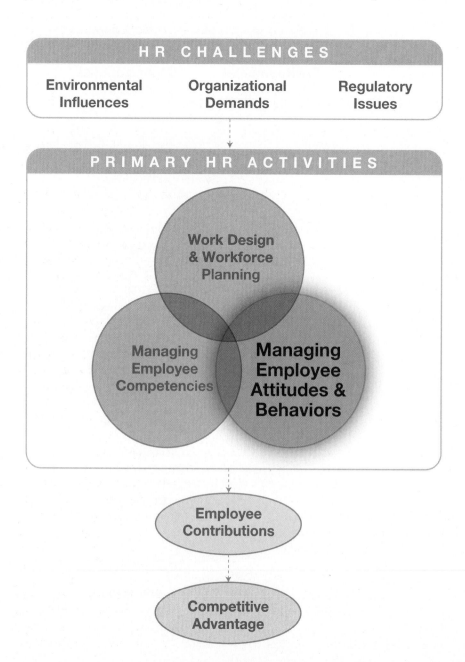

number of questions that are important to consider when making compensation decisions, including the following:

- What factors should you consider when determining the salary range for a job?
- What is the best way to determine how much employees should be paid?
- How much of that pay should be guaranteed, and how much should be based on incentives?

In this chapter, we will discuss pay equity and the decision-making processes used to establish pay rates and to assign pay to jobs and to individuals. As with the previous chapters, the second half of this chapter will help you understand some of the complex decisions that managers face because of organizational demands, environmental influences, and regulatory issues. As you study this chapter, keep in mind that the decisions you make about the pay for employees in your organization will affect how likely your company is to achieve and maintain a competitive advantage in the marketplace. As a manager, you will have input at various stages of the decision-making process. Thus, it is important for you to understand some of the theories related to compensation decisions as well as the mechanics of how these decisions are made. And it is equally important that you understand the legal implications of the decisions you make. Before we get into the specifics, we need to define what we mean by compensation.

TOTAL COMPENSATION

Compensation refers to the monetary and nonmonetary rewards employees receive in exchange for the work they do for an organization. In exchange for these rewards, employees are expected to be loyal and committed to their firms. Compensation can be either direct or indirect. Direct compensation includes the hourly wages or salaries paid to employees, as well as any incentives, including merit raises and bonuses or commissions they receive. Direct compensation can be fixed (wages) and/or variable (commissions). Indirect compensation includes the benefits and services employees receive, such as their health care insurance, vacations, lunches, company-paid training programs, and other "perks." This chapter focuses on direct compensation in terms of base pay and introduces the other components of a total compensation package. In later chapters, we discuss variable pay, such as incentives, and benefits and other forms of indirect pay.

Over the past decade or so, many organizations have begun to refer to the total compensation package they provide as **total rewards**. The word *rewards* is believed to better reflect the many aspects of a compensation package (base pay, incentives, benefits, perks, and so forth) and to signal to employees that they are receiving more than just base pay. The goal behind this thinking is to motivate employees by helping them understand everything they are receiving from the organization in exchange for the work they do.[1] CH2M HILL is a global full-service engineering, construction, and operations firm that was on *Fortune*'s list of the "100 Best Companies to Work For" in 2006, 2007, and 2008. The company emphasizes its total rewards package in its online recruitment information, noting the competitive pay and benefits offered as well as solutions to help with work and personal life balance. Benefits range from educational opportunities to pet care![2]

The key to a successful compensation plan is a compensation philosophy that supports the goals of the organization. Exhibit 10.2 describes the compensation philosophy of PMI, one of the largest private mortgage insurers in the United States, Australia, New Zealand, and the European Union, and the largest mortgage reinsurer in Hong Kong.[3] With a clear idea of the compensation philosophy and its objectives, a carefully constructed pay system can be developed that is aligned with the overall strategy of the organization, taking into account internal alignment, external competitiveness, and employee contributions. When these factors are addressed and the program is administered well, the compensation program will assist the firm in achieving a competitive advantage.[4] In the following sections, we discuss these concepts and your role as a manager in making pay decisions. First, however, you need to have a solid understanding of equity theory. Consequently, we discuss it next.

compensation

The monetary and nonmonetary rewards employees receive in exchange for the work they do for an organization.

total rewards

The sum of all the aspects of a compensation package (base pay, incentives, benefits, perks, and so forth) that signals to current and future employees that they are receiving more than just base pay in exchange for their work.

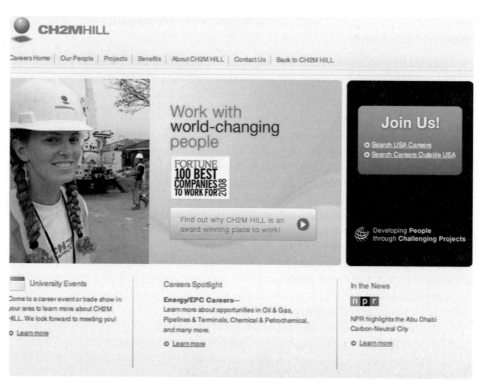

Employees at CH2M HILL receive an exceptional total rewards package.

Exhibit 10.2 ▶

PMI's Rewards &
Recognition
Program

Compensation Philosophy

PMI puts the spotlight on performance.

At PMI, we place a high value on high performance, and compensate for it accordingly. We believe that our rewards and recognition programs are essential to communicating performance expectations, improving productivity, and acknowledging contributions to the company's success.

The objectives of our compensation programs are to:

- Achieve a performance-driven work culture that generates company growth.

- Provide clear focus and measurement on key objectives with a meaningful link to rewards.

- Provide competitive compensation that attracts and retains top performers, focusing on external competitiveness as the primary driver of pay opportunities.

Source: http://www.pmi-us.com/about_pmi/comp_philosophy.html

EQUITY THEORY

Compensation is important to employees beyond the simple fact that most of us need money to pay our bills and buy the things we need and want. Employees also perceive that their compensation reflects how their firms and people around them value them as individuals. Compensation, therefore, is very important to employees and serves to motivate them at work. You probably already have studied a number of motivation theories in other classes, such as psychology. We introduced motivation theory in Chapter 4, when we described the job design process, and in Chapter 9, when we discussed performance management, and we will talk more about motivation in Chapter 11, when we discuss incentive pay. In this chapter, we introduce another theory of motivation: equity theory.

Consider this scenario. You began working at a company eight years ago, and you gradually climbed the corporate ladder to arrive at your current midlevel management position. You think your salary is reasonable; you have gotten nice raises for your performance each year and for each promotion. You work hard because you have a strong work ethic and feel that your employer deserves a fair day's work for the salary you are receiving. In a casual conversation, a colleague in a similar job at the same level as you mentions his salary, which is considerably higher than yours. You know for a fact that this guy doesn't work nearly as hard as you do. After your initial shock, what is your response likely to be? Do you think you will continue working as hard as you were but ask for a raise? Do you think you will quit working as hard? What if you don't get a raise? Do you think you will stay with the company? Would your response be the same or different if the colleague worked for another company but in a comparable job?

The situation just described involves a question of equity. According to **equity theory**, you and your employees will be motivated to work harder (provide inputs) when you believe that your compensation (outcome received) is at the right level for the work you are doing. As shown in Exhibit 10.3, people compare their input and outcome levels to those of other people in similar situations. If employees know, or even just believe, they are not receiving an appropriate level of compensation for their work (outcome), they will experience "disequilibrium." The disequilibrium, or inequity, can be either positive or negative. When the inequity is negative, employees believe they are not getting as much out of their jobs as they are putting into them relative to other people.

Faced with this situation, employees are likely to try to resolve the inequity. They can do this in several ways. One way is by asking for a raise or a bonus. If that doesn't work, they can adjust their inputs to make their inputs to outcome ratio more equitable. In other words, they can stop working as hard as they once did, perhaps by putting in fewer hours, taking longer breaks, and so forth. Employees can also adjust their psychological perspective by rationalizing why there is inequity. They may try to explain the situation by seeking some other reasons for the difference, such as education, experience, or even political connections within the organization. If the reason they identify seems logical to them, they may reduce their feelings of inequity. A final option for employees is to quit their jobs if they feel that the inequity is too great and cannot be altered.

As a manager, you might not have much say about the actual pay structure within your firm. However, you are likely to have a great deal of input about how to reward your employees within that structure. Thus, it is important that you be aware of the importance of pay equity as you make recommendations for pay increases for your staff.[5]

To make matters more complicated, there are actually two labor markets in which inequities can exist: (1) the labor market within your firm and (2) and the labor market outside your firm. Companies try to develop compensation systems that are equitable both internally and externally. We focus predominantly on the job-based approach because many companies use this method to balance internal and external equity. We also discuss some of the newer forms of pay, such as skill-based pay, competency-based pay, and market pricing, as alternative approaches for designing compensation systems. We describe all these approaches within the context of how they are used to address a firm's internal alignment and external competitiveness.

equity theory

The theory that employees compare their input (work effort) and outcome (wages) levels to those of other people in similar situations to determine if they are being treated the same in terms of pay and other outcomes.

Self   Comparative Other

Input Outcome = Input Outcome

◀ **Exhibit 10.3**

Equity Theory

INTERNAL ALIGNMENT

internal alignment (for compensation)

When each job in a company is valued appropriately relative to every other job in terms of its ability to help the firm achieve its goals.

Internal alignment occurs when each job in a company is valued appropriately relative to every other job in terms of its ability to help the firm achieve its goals. An example will help you understand this concept: Assume that you are a manager in a financial services firm with two jobs reporting to you. One job involves working with clients daily to help them with their financial needs. The other job is an accounts payable position—making sure that company's vendors get paid on time. Both jobs are important, but the first job is directly related to the purpose of the organization, which is selling financial services. The other job plays a supporting role. Which job do you think adds the most value to the company? If your answer is the sales job, you are correct. Therefore, in establishing a relative worth hierarchy for determining salaries, the sales job would be ranked higher than the accounts payable job and would receive a higher rate of pay.

Now, let's take a look at how companies establish internal alignment among their jobs. Keep in mind that as a manager, the more you understand the terminology we will be using, the better able you will be to understand and explain to employees the internal pay structure within your organization. This information can also help you when you are negotiating your own pay.

Traditionally, companies have established pay rates for jobs, not for individuals performing the jobs. This point is important to remember as we examine the various types of job evaluation approaches used by companies. We tend to think that pay rates are established for employees rather than for tasks they perform, but it is the other way around. As you will learn in the following sections, a relative worth structure is developed for jobs, and then pay rates are assigned to those jobs.

Before a company can begin to establish the relative worth of its jobs and the pay associated with each, it must first have information available about the tasks, duties, and responsibilities for each job. Recall that in Chapter 4 we described the job analysis process. The information derived from a job analysis is vital for establishing the relative worth of the jobs within the company through a systematic process called **job evaluation**.

job evaluation

The systematic process of determining the relative worth of jobs to a company.

The four most common job evaluation approaches are job ranking, job classification, point factor, and factor comparison. The first two approaches, job ranking and job classification, are qualitative approaches. Point factor and factor comparison are quantitative approaches to job evaluation. Next we give a brief overview of each approach. As you read about each one, consider the importance of having a well-defined job description resulting from a careful job analysis before you can effectively apply any of the approaches.

Job Ranking

job ranking

A type of job evaluation that involves reviewing job descriptions and listing the jobs from highest to lowest in worth to the company.

Job ranking involves reviewing job descriptions and listing the jobs in order, from highest to lowest worth to the company. This process is fairly easy to do when there are only a few jobs in the company. Accurately ranking jobs in a large company is much more difficult than ranking jobs in a small company. If you have only five jobs to evaluate, you probably know the jobs well, even without their associated job descriptions. But what if you had to rank 25 jobs? In this case, you would be less likely to know a great deal about all of the jobs. Second, you would need some type of framework just to process all the information found in the 25 job descriptions. You would probably be able to decide which jobs were the most valuable and which jobs were the least valuable without too much trouble. However, you would likely find it difficult to evaluate the jobs that fall somewhere in the middle. Such a system is also more difficult to justify to employees because ranking jobs is largely subjective. That is, the order is just a manager's opinion about which jobs are more valuable to the firm than others.

Job Classification

job classification

A type of job evaluation that involves the development of broad descriptions for grouping jobs that are similar in terms of their tasks, duties, responsibilities, and qualifications for the purpose of assigning wages.

The **job classification** approach involves developing broad descriptions for groups of jobs that are similar in terms of their tasks, duties, responsibilities, and qualifications. The job description for a particular job is then compared to the classification descriptions, and a decision is made about which description best fits the job. A wage range is attached to each classification, reflecting the relative worth of the jobs slotted into that classification.

The federal government has used a variation of the job classification system for many years. Visit www.opm.gov/fedclass/, and you will find a lot of information about how the federal classification system works. Unlike with some other job classification systems that involve a solely subjective process of matching jobs to classifications, the government provides factor descriptions that can be used to develop scores for jobs to help slot them into the appropriate classifications, based on score. The standards are meant to serve as a guide—not a replacement for the judgment of skilled compensation professionals and/or the knowledge of managers who make job classification decisions.[6]

In the federal government, the classification levels are referred to by the prefix GS, which stands for General Schedule, followed by a number. The higher the number, the greater the complexity and responsibility associated with the job, and the greater the qualifications required for performing the job. Naturally, the pay range is higher for jobs with higher GS numbers than for those with lower numbers; more senior jobs fit into an entirely separate pay schedule.

Sometimes managers want to reclassify jobs so that they can give a particular employee who merits it a large raise and/or because a job's duties have changed. The manager can then compare the revised job description to the classification guide to determine in which grade the job falls. The classification descriptions can also be used as inputs for preparing the new job description.

One criticism of the job classification system is that parts of the job being evaluated might fit into one job grade in the system, whereas other parts might fit into another grade. A decision then has to be made about which classification is the most appropriate. Because the pay range will differ, depending on the decision, the outcome of the evaluation process is extremely important.

Point Method

The most commonly used type of job evaluation is the **point method**. This quantitative approach uses a point value scheme that yields a score for each job. The scores for various jobs are then compared to determine their relative worth. The point method is developed by first identifying a set of factors for which the company is willing to pay. These **compensable factors** are chosen because they represent aspects of jobs that a company needs in order to achieve its goals. Typically companies use compensable factors such as skill, effort, responsibility, and working conditions, but they can add other factors, such as innovativeness. Remember that we are focusing on evaluating a job, not a person performing a job, so compensable factors should be elements that appear in varying degrees across many jobs within the company.

With the point method, a point manual is used to determine the relative worth of jobs. The point manual contains a general description of each compensable factor along with a description of each degree of the factor. Exhibit 10.4 defines a factor in a point method of

point method

A quantitative method of job evaluation that involves assigning point values to jobs based on compensable factors to create the relative worth hierarchy for jobs in the company.

compensable factor

Aspects of jobs, such as skill, effort, responsibility, and working conditions, that exist across jobs in a company, are needed by employees for the firm to achieve its objectives, and for which the company is willing to pay.

◄ **Exhibit 10.4**
Definition of
Responsibility Factor

Responsibility—This factor measures the type and level of responsibility associated with performing the duties of the job.

- *1st degree*—Minimal responsibility expected, such as following directions as provided and reporting completion of duties.

- *2nd degree*—Limited responsibility, including ensuring that all policies and procedures are followed and that all tasks are completed in a timely manner.

- *3rd degree*—Responsibility for timely and accurate completion of assigned parts of projects.

- *4th degree*—Oversight responsibility for various aspects of the work, including some supervision of other workers and accountability for quality of outcomes.

- *5th degree*—Complete responsibility for ensuring that tasks are performed from start to finish, including providing supervision of other workers, managing budgets, and ensuring that finished projects are completed on time and with the highest quality.

► **Exhibit 10.5**   Point Values

Factor	1st Degree	2nd Degree	3rd Degree	4th Degree	5th Degree
Skill					
• Job knowledge	20	40	60	80	100
• Experience	35	45	55	65	75
Effort					
• Mental demand	55	70	75	80	85
• Physical demand	20	25	30	35	40
Responsibility	70	85	100	115	130
Working conditions	30	40	50	60	70

job evaluation. An example of factor and point values is shown in Exhibit 10.5. The points assigned represent the relative weight of the factor in terms of its importance to the company. Any number of total points can be assigned, but 500 points is often used. And, although five is a typical number of degrees assigned, the number can be greater or smaller. The descriptions need to be carefully written to ensure that two different individuals evaluating the same job on the same compensable factors will arrive at the same results. In other words, clearly describing the compensable factors and defining what each degree represents will lead to a more reliable and valid process.

Once the point manual is ready, job descriptions for **benchmark jobs** can be compared to the factor descriptions, and the appropriate points can be assigned for the jobs. Benchmark jobs are used to represent the range of types of jobs in the company. These jobs need to be:

- Stable over time in terms of their responsibilities
- Well known and recognized
- Clearly and concisely described
- Accepted in the external labor market for setting wage rates
- Currently at an appropriate wage rate

The points assigned for each factor are added together into a score for the job. This score provides a way to compare jobs with each other to determine which jobs should be paid more and which less. Often this process is conducted by a compensation committee to ensure that the results are reliable and valid.

As you can see, the point method brings more objectivity to the job evaluation process. The key to its success is threefold: (1) properly identifying the compensable factors and selecting the benchmark jobs, (2) assigning appropriate weights to each factor, and (2) accurately using the point manual.

Once the points are assigned, **job grades** are created to reflect the hierarchy of jobs within the company. Jobs with comparable points are grouped together to create the job grades. A company may have one job grade plan for all jobs. Typically, however, a company develops different structures for professional, technical, and other categories of jobs, such as clerical and skilled-trade jobs. Non-benchmark jobs can then be evaluated and slotted into the hierarchy.

Factor Comparison

Factor comparison is a quantitative type of job evaluation that involves ranking benchmark jobs in relation to each other on each of several factors, such as mental requirements, physical requirements, skill, responsibility, and working conditions. A determination is then made about how much of the hourly rate for a job is associated with each factor, as illustrated in Exhibit 10.6.

The factor comparison approach is actually a hybrid method for job evaluation that combines aspects of job ranking and the point method, but it also breaks down the wage into smaller parts. Unfortunately, although this method can be quite accurate, it is also quite complex and would be challenging to explain to managers and employees.[7] Managers also

---

benchmark job

A job that represents the range of the types of jobs in the company and is used for comparison with jobs in other companies to establish salaries internally.

job grade

Grouping jobs with comparable points together to reflect the hierarchy of jobs within the company and establish pay rates.

factor comparison

A quantitative type of job evaluation that involves ranking benchmark jobs in relation to each other on each of several compensable factors, such as mental requirements and responsibility, and then assigning a portion of the hourly rate for the job to each factor.

Job	Hourly Rate	Skill	Responsibility	Working Conditions
Carpenter assistant	$12.00	$ 7.00	$ 2.00	$3.00
Carpenter	$18.00	$10.00	$ 5.00	$3.00
Senior carpenter	$25.00	$12.00	$ 8.00	$5.00
Supervisor	$30.00	$15.00	$10.00	$5.00

◄ **Exhibit 10.6**
Factor Comparison Method of Job Evaluation

need extensive training to properly use the method. And, because the monetary rates are included, as the market changes the data, the method used has to be updated frequently.[8] As a result, the factor comparison approach is used less often than other approaches.

EXTERNAL COMPETITIVENESS

External competitiveness ensures that jobs in a company are valued appropriately relative to similar jobs in the company's external labor market. Companies make decisions about what they want to pay relative to the external market, and these decisions affect how attractive the firm is to potential employees. They also affect the attitude and motivation of current employees.

To begin our discussion of how a company uses market data to set its pay rates, we first describe the process used to collect market data. We then discuss how to combine that information with the job evaluation process results to arrive at wage rates for jobs.

external competitiveness

Jobs in a company are valued appropriately relative to similar jobs in the company's external labor market.

Salary Surveys

Salary surveys provide a systematic way to collect information about wages in the external labor market. However, salary surveys must be carefully constructed to ensure that the data gathered are reliable and valid. Managers can either conduct their own surveys or purchase survey data from a number of different sources, including professional organizations and human resources consulting firms. If you decide to purchase data, it is important to ask a lot of questions about the process used to collect the data, including the types of organizations included and the jobs analyzed. If your human resources department provides the data for you, it is still important that you do due diligence and ask the same questions about the data provided.

Typically, salary survey data will come from companies in the same industry. For many jobs, it is also important to collect data from companies in other industries that might be competing with you for employees. A hospital and an airline operate in different industries, but both require accountants, marketing professionals, and other types of employees. The data should also come from the appropriate geographic labor market, which can be local, regional, national, or global, depending on the type of job.

Salary surveys should collect data for an organization's benchmark jobs because it would be too expensive and time consuming to try to collect data for every job in the company. Plus, there will be jobs in your company for which there are no comparable jobs in other organizations. Exhibit 10.7 contains a list of questions to consider when preparing to either conduct a salary survey or purchase one.

salary survey

A systematic way to collect information about wages in the external labor market.

Job Pricing

When the data collection for a salary survey is complete, the pricing of jobs begins. **Job pricing** is the systematic process of assigning monetary rates to jobs so that a firm's internal wages are aligned with the external wages in the marketplace. It is during this process that the organization's pay policy relative to the market is developed.

Job pricing is a multiple-step process. It begins with managers plotting the results of a salary survey for the benchmark jobs within their firm. To illustrate how the external data translate into internal compensation decisions, we will assume that the managers are using

job pricing

The systematic process of assigning monetary rates to jobs so that a firm's internal wages are aligned with the external wages in the marketplace.

Exhibit 10.7 ►

Questions to Ask to
Conduct Effective
Salary Surveys

1. What organizations should be included in the survey? Consider the industry, number of employees, and types of jobs.

2. How many organizations should be included? Too few organizations will reduce the validity of the data, whereas too many organizations will lead to redundant data being collected.

3. What specific information should be collected? Consider information about the jobs' base pay, incentive pay, benefits, and so forth.

4. For what key jobs will the data be collected?

Source: Based on Caruth, D. L., & Handlogten, G. D. *Managing compensation (and understanding it too): A handbook for the perplexed.* Westport, CT: Quorum Books, 2001.

the point method to evaluate jobs. (Later in the chapter, we discuss alternative approaches to making pay decisions.)

As you can see from Exhibit 10.8, the *x* axis represents the evaluation points associated with different jobs that are used to map their importance to the firm. The *y* axis represents the salaries the external labor market is paying for those jobs. The result of combining the data for the jobs is a scatterplot. Notice that you can almost draw a straight line from the bottom-left corner to the top-right corner of the graph. In fact, that is what actually happens. The market line, also known as the **wage curve** (which may be a straight line but is more likely to be curved), is drawn to represent the relationship between the job evaluation points and the salaries paid for the jobs. The wage curve can be drawn by hand through the points so that about as many points are above the line as are below the line, or a statistical regression process can be used to draw the line. (The regression approach is, of course, most accurate.)

The next step is to plot the actual salaries paid for the benchmark jobs in the company and compare that result with the results from the market. Once again, the job evaluation points are used. Any difference between the wages the company is paying and the wages being paid in the marketplace is noted. In short, the wage curve shows how similar the pay within a firm's job structure is to how the jobs are being paid in the labor market.

The next step is to plot the actual salaries paid for the benchmark jobs in the company and compare that result with the results from the market. Once again, the job evaluation points are used, but this time, the salaries are the actual salaries in the company for the benchmark jobs used in the survey. The difference between the company wages and the wages paid in the market provides information about how the company is currently paying for these benchmark jobs relative to pay in the labor market. Exhibit 10.9 describes the job pricing process.

wage curve

The market line that represents the relationship between the job evaluation points and the salaries paid for the jobs.

Exhibit 10.8 ►

Results of Point
Method of Job
Evaluation

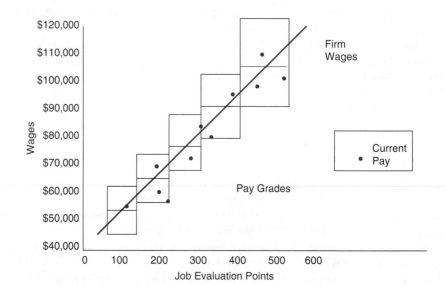

Company Pay Policy

If a company's wage curve is below (or above) the market wage curve, then decisions have to be made about whether to move the wages for those jobs up to the line, leave them as they are, or move them above the line. The company's pay policy will determine what is done and is driven by the strategic objectives of the firm's compensation policy.

Firms can decide to pay *at the market* (follow), *above the market* (lead), or *below the market* (lag). Most firms decide to pay at the market. Think for a minute about why this makes sense. If your company pays above the market, it might be incurring unnecessary labor expenses if there is a sufficient supply of workers willing to work at market wages. In contrast, if a company pays below market, it will have a harder time attracting employees.

Some firms choose to pay at the market but offer benefits that exceed what is typically offered for comparable work at other companies. An additional approach is to match to the market the wages of as many jobs as possible. This approach is used when a company's main focus is on external competitiveness rather than internal alignment.

Pay Grades and Pay Ranges

Determining the actual pay rates for individual employees is governed by the pay range within which their jobs fall. Employees in a particular job should not be paid less than the minimum amount of the pay range nor more than the maximum amount of the range. To set pay ranges, managers decide which jobs are similar according to the job evaluation results and group those jobs into job grades. Often there will be natural breaks in the point spread for the benchmark jobs that make it easy to decide which jobs logically should be grouped together into pay grades. The jobs in each pay grade will have the same pay range. Each pay grade will have a minimum and maximum number of job evaluation points (which appear on the horizontal axis), as well as minimum and maximum wage rates (which appear on the vertical axis).

If you once again refer to Exhibit 10.8, you will see that each range has a midpoint as well as a minimum and a maximum. The midpoint of the range typically represents what an employee who is fully qualified and functioning at an acceptable level of performance should make and is drawn relative to the pay line the company intends to pursue. In the case of our example, the company is using the market line as its new pay line. The minimum represents what an entry-level employee would make, and the maximum represents what a highly qualified, longer-term employee would make. Wage ranges for high-level jobs can be 30% to 60% above or below the midpoint, whereas entry-level wage ranges might be within 5% to 15% of the midpoint.[9]

When establishing wage ranges, an important consideration is the degree of overlap of pay ranges. A small amount of overlap between two grades means that there is a great deal of difference between the salaries paid for the two jobs. In other words, less overlap means that there is more difference between jobs in each grade. The overlap decision is affected by the nature of the job (clerical versus professional) and other factors, such as what the firm wants to signal to employees in terms of upward mobility. When there is a lot of overlap, employees in a lower grade might actually have the same salary as employees in a higher grade. Thus, internal equity as well as external equity is a concern in determining the overlap of pay ranges.

Grades and ranges give managers some degree of flexibility when it comes to compensating employees who have different amounts of seniority, skills, and productivity levels. For example, an employee with one year of experience who is still learning the job would be paid lower within the pay range than would someone with five years of experience and a high level of performance.

Once the pay grades are determined, non-benchmark jobs can be evaluated and slotted into the appropriate pay grades. Exhibit 10.9 summarizes the job pricing process. It is unlikely that you, as a manager, will have to actually collect the data, develop the wage curves, and determine job grades and ranges unless you choose a career in human resources. (And, by the way, jobs in compensation typically pay very well!) You do need, however, to understand the process and the implications of the process. In the event that you are called on to actually use a job evaluation manual to make decisions about the point

Exhibit 10.9 ▶

Job Pricing Process

1. Conduct a salary survey.

2. Plot the salaries for benchmark jobs using job evaluation points for each job.

3. Draw the market line.

4. Decide on your company's line based on its pay policy.

5. Create wage ranges for your firm's job grades.

6. Adjust the wages for jobs within each grade, as needed, to match your company's pay policy.

values for new jobs or restructured jobs within your firm, having this understanding will be invaluable. Most likely, unless you are in a small business, you will be given guidance from a human resources department regarding how to set the salary for your employees within their appropriate pay grade range. Exhibit 10.9 describes the job pricing process.

Broadbanding

broadbanding

An approach used to reduce the complexity of a compensation system by consolidating a large number of pay grades into a fewer number of broader grades (or bands).

In recent years, companies have worked to identify ways to reduce some of the complexity involved in the job pricing process. An approach that has worked well for some companies is **broadbanding**. Broadbanding consolidates a large number of pay grades into a few "broad" bands—usually 3 to 10 bands, or grades, as opposed to the larger number traditionally used. Company Spotlight 10.1 describes the role of broadbands at JCPenney.

The maximum pay for a particular band can be as high as 100% to 400% above the band's minimum pay.[10] For example, at your company, one person in the middle band might earn $10,000 per month, while another person in the same band might earn $18,000 per month, a 180% difference. The jobs in this band are all professional jobs at the company, ranging from comptroller to marketing manager. The jobs in the band are similar to one another in that they require approximately the same level of education and experience as well as have similar levels of responsibility.

Reducing the number of grades by using bands makes managing the system much easier, too, because the bands are typically wide enough that changes in the market don't require managers to adjust the bands as frequently. Another plus for broadbanding is that the pay range for a band gives you, as a manager, more flexibility to set the starting

COMPANY spotlight   10.1 Career Banding and Market Pricing at JCPenney

When JCPenney realized that it needed a different business model to compete in its industry, the company decided to change its model. Doing so required that the company change its compensation system as well.

To make the company more competitive, JCPenney went from a pay model that rewarded employees' time on the job and efforts to one that rewarded their results. Part of the change also included hiring the best applicant for a job, whether that person was external or internal. Hiring from the external labor market meant that the company had to pay attention to market pricing as well.

The company used job evaluation information to get a clear idea of what its jobs involved. Similar jobs were

grouped into broadbands, which JCPenney refers to as *career bands.* The company used the information to match its jobs to jobs in the external market. The goal was to make the company more externally competitive than it had been in the past and to give managers a clearer idea of what jobs were really worth.

Employees, known as associates, received personalized letters explaining the bands they were in and the market data related to their jobs. So far, the results of the new system have been positive.

Source: Based on How JCPenney uses salary surveys for market pricing jobs. *IOMA's Report on Salary Surveys* 4:1, 2004.

pay for one of your employees and more room for you to give raises to your existing employees without going outside a band. Both IBM and Marriott have adopted broad-band pay systems, thereby giving greater salary management responsibility to their line managers.[11]

If bands are used, it is important to ensure that there is some logical reason why jobs are in the same band. Managers also need to understand how the bands work and how to properly assign salaries within the bands. Otherwise, employees might believe that the company's salary decisions aren't based on objective criteria. Also, the flexibility in pay ranges afforded by bands can lead to higher wages overall for the company if processes are not in place to manage how increases are instituted.

PAY FOR INDIVIDUAL EMPLOYEES

Remember that until this point, we have been talking about how to determine pay for jobs, not pay rates for individual employees. Once you have decided on the pay ranges for jobs, it is time to decide what to pay the employees performing the jobs.

The initial pay for a new employee will be based on a number of factors, including the person's previous work experience, education, and training, and the person's negotiating skills. Better negotiators often start at higher salaries. For current employees, salary increases can be tied to meeting quotas, completing projects, providing high levels of customer service, or the results of their performance appraisal.

Chapter 11 describes incentive pay in greater detail, including merit raises and sales commissions. This topic is an important one because the decisions managers make about performance-based pay affect employees' perceptions about how fairly they are being treated, their motivation levels, and the company's bottom line. Companies are giving greater emphasis to performance-based pay in response to stakeholder concerns about the overall firm performance and in acknowledgement of the substantial contributions employees make to achievement of company goals. Even the U.S. federal government has adopted a pay-for-performance plan for many of its agencies.[12] This plan is in part the result of employee frustrations with a system that rewarded seniority more than contributions and the growing concerns about attracting top talent to government jobs.

Other issues have to be addressed in determining compensation for current employees as well. You may have an employee whose job is *red circled* or *green circled*. Red-circled jobs are those for which the person in the job is being paid above the maximum wage for that pay grade. In such an event, the manager can freeze the person's pay until the range catches up, reduce the person's salary (not a smart move unless you really want to get rid of the employee), reevaluate the job to make sure the job evaluation was done properly the first time, or upgrade the person's job description so that her job is evaluated in a higher grade. In the event of a green-circled job, the person's salary is below the minimum of the range. The manager can leave the salary where it is (again, not a good move unless you want to get rid of the employee), reevaluate the job, reclassify the job into a lower grade, or give the person a raise. If there is a big difference between the person's current pay and his or her new pay range, the raise may be awarded in increments over time.

ALTERNATIVE COMPENSATION APPROACHES

The job-based compensation approach is the predominant model used in most companies. However, some companies have experimented with alternative approaches for compensation plans. These companies often recognize that the human capital the employee brings to the job is critical for their organization's success. Paying a person makes more sense than paying for a particular job in that context.

In contrast, paying for the job performed rather than what a person brings to the job makes more sense when job duties and responsibilities are relatively unchanging. In fact, job-based pay, especially when seniority is a big factor, is less likely to motivate employees to develop the knowledge, skills, and abilities the firm needs for the future, and it doesn't recognize that the high level of knowledge and performance provided by employees makes a value-added difference. Of course, one central problem in moving to more employee-based pay systems is the need for good metrics to use as the basis of pay decisions.[13] Addressing the metrics issue is critical to reducing perceptions of inequity if a manager has control over setting the pay rates.

Some of the alternatives to the traditional job-based structures are skill- or knowledge-based pay, competency-based pay, direct market pricing, and broadbanding (which we have already described).

Skill-Based Pay and Knowledge-Based Pay

skill-based pay

A pay system that requires employees to acquire certain skills or knowledge in order to receive a pay increase.

knowledge-based pay

A pay system that requires employees to acquire certain skills or knowledge in order to receive a pay increase.

Skill-based pay and **knowledge-based pay** systems require employees to acquire certain skills or knowledge in order to receive a pay increase. The skills or knowledge are arranged in a hierarchy. An employee demonstrates mastery of each level of skill or knowledge by passing a test, passing a class, or serving in an apprentice role. Once the level has been passed, the employee receives a pay raise. The goal of this type of pay plan is to ensure that a sufficient number of employees have the skills and knowledge an organization needs to succeed. The process also makes it clear to employees what they have to do to increase their pay.

These pay systems are not without problems, however. Some companies have found that they end up with more employees at higher levels of mastery than they need. This outcome is expensive. Passing the test at each level automatically leads to a raise, so employees are getting

▶ **Exhibit 10.10** Comparison of the Types of Pay Structures

	Job Based	Skill Based	Competency Based
What is valued **Quantify the value**	• Compensable factors • Factors degree weights	• Skill blocks • Skill levels	• Competencies • Competency levels
Mechanisms to translate into pay	• Assign points that reflect criterion pay structure	• Certification and price skills in external market	• Certification and price competencies in external market
Pay structure	• Based on job performed/market	• Based on skills certified/market	• Based on competency developed/market
Pay increases	• Promotion	• Skill acquisition	• Competency development
Managers' focus	• Link employees to work • Promotion and placement • Cost control via pay for job and budget increase	• Utilize skills efficiently • Provide training • Control costs via training, certification, and work assignments	• Be sure competencies add value • Provide competency-developing opportunities • Control costs via certification and assignments
Employee focus	• Seek promotions to earn more pay	• Seek skills	• Seek competencies
Procedures	• Job analysis • Job evaluation	• Skill analysis • Skill certification	• Competency analysis • Competency certification
Advantages	• Clear expectations • Sense of progress • Pay based on value of work performed	• Continuous learning • Flexibility • Reduced work force	• Continuous learning • Flexibility • Lateral movement
Limitations	• Potential bureaucracy • Potential inflexibility	• Potential bureaucracy • Requires costs controls	• Potential bureaucracy • Requires cost controls

Source: Milkovich, G. T., & Newman, J. M. Compensation. New York: McGraw-Hill/Irwin, 2005, p. 175.

paid at higher salaries than are really appropriate, given their jobs. And, even though they have received a raise, employees are frustrated because they can't use the skills they have acquired.

On the other hand, because highly trained employees (for example, consultants, IT professionals, lawyers) have specific credentials (MBAs, JDs, or certain computer certifications, for example), firms can charge customers higher rates. As a result, their companies encourage them to acquire the training needed to obtain the higher-level credentials.

Competency-Based Pay

Similar to skill- or knowledge-based pay, **competency-based pay** plans identify the competencies (for example, attitudes, behaviors, abilities) employees need to master to be eligible for pay raises. The competencies are identified for the firm as a whole or for a particular work unit, and they are the competencies that are believed to be the most critical if the firm is to achieve its goals. For instance, the competencies might focus on customer service delivery, teamwork, ability to motivate others, problem solving, and creativity and innovation.[14] Employees receive higher compensation when they demonstrate that they have a higher level of the competencies valued by the company.

For a competency-based system to be successful, managers need to clearly define the competencies employees need to have and outline a valid process for determining whether they do. One plus of this system is that it keeps employees focused on continuous learning. The disadvantages are similar to the ones discussed for skills-based pay: Employees can obtain more competencies than their current jobs merit, leading to higher labor costs for a firm, and they can become frustrated because they aren't using their additional training to advance within the organization. Exhibit 10.10 summarizes the differences between job-based, skill-based, and competency-based pay.

Direct Market Pricing

Employers can use **direct market pricing** to make employee compensation decisions. Market pricing involves collecting salary information from the external labor market first rather than starting with the development of an internal structure based on the value of the jobs within the

competency-based pay
A highly structured pay system that identifies the competencies employees need to master to be eligible for pay raises.

direct market pricing
Collecting salary information from the external labor market first rather than starting with the development of an internal structure based on the value of the jobs within the company.

COMPANY *spotlight*   10.2 Market Pricing at Marriott

When Marriott decided to adopt a new corporate strategy designed to manage its entire hotel market as one business, the company's compensation system had to change also. Marriott credits the changes that were made with helping to revolutionize the company's approach to pay and performance and with reshaping employee loyalty.

At the time the changes were being made, Marriott had 2,600 properties staffed by 140,000 employees. In addition to the namesake hotel, Marriott brands included Ramada International, Courtyard, Residence Inn, and Fairfield Inn. Each brand targeted a different market and operated separately from the other brands. Employees saw themselves as employees of the brand, not of Marriott Corporation. Consequently, employees tended not to move across brands.

The new compensation system integrates compensation, performance management, and career development. Before moving across brands became commonplace, Marriott actually paid managers a bonus to move across brands. In the new

system, each job has a market reference point equal to the competitive rate for that job in the relevant labor market. Managers have the authority to pay within 25% above or below that reference point, based on the experience and performance of an employee. For a market reference point of $40,000, for example, the manager can pay from $30,000 to $50,000. When an employee moves up to a higher-level position, managers know they can give from 0% to 15% promotional increases. Supervisors oversee the pay decisions.

Each employee—not just managers—receives six hours of training on the program, follow-up communications, and information about how he or she fits into the new career bands and competency models. Marriott feels that the market pricing pay plan creates an environment of opportunity and gives the company a competitive advantage in its marketplace.

Source: Based on Hansen, F. Power to the line people. *Workforce,* June 2003, pp. 70–75.

company. Data are collected on as many jobs as possible, with the remaining jobs included in the final pay structure. This approach came into vogue in the 1980s, in part because jobs were changing rapidly as the use of technology became more prevalent.[15] The approach works well as long as the data are accurate. Ignoring small sample sizes and other measurement problems can lead to incorrect inferences about the actual market pay rates for a particular job.[16]

Company Spotlight 10.2 describes Marriott's compensation strategy, which includes a market pricing system.

ADMINISTERING COMPENSATION

Regardless of which compensation plan you use, it has to be carefully administered. A handbook for the job evaluation process, skill- or competency-based plan, market pricing, or broadbanding is only one part of effective administration of a compensation program. Three other key elements are needed: the training of managers, communication, and evaluation. We discuss each of these aspects next.

Anyone involved in making employee pay decisions needs to receive training on how the process works. Topics to cover would include how pay rates are set at the company and how frequently they are reviewed, how pay raises are determined, and what can and cannot be communicated to employees about the firm's pay system. When a point method is used, managers need training on how to use the job evaluation handbook to score jobs, slot them into grades, and decide how much to pay for them.

Companies also have to decide how much information they should share with their employees about the compensation system. Most companies have *closed* pay systems. With a closed system, the details about individual pay rates are not made public, except as required by law for high-ranking executives of publicly traded companies. The law requires publicly traded companies to include in their annual reports a breakdown of the components of the total compensation package. Public organizations in many states are required to disclose what they pay their employees. These organizations have *open* pay systems.

Companies that voluntarily make their pay information public believe that transparency is important and that the more information employees have, the more equitable the system will be perceived to be. Companies that use a closed system believe that there are many reasons pay differences exist and that some of those reasons are difficult to explain to employees. These firms believe it is therefore better to not make too much information available. A company's compensation philosophy will guide these decisions.

With both open and closed systems, however, all companies and managers need to carefully consider what employees are told about their pay and how they are told that information. Information that is carelessly conveyed can have a long-term negative effect on employee morale and productivity, while a carefully crafted, honest, and thoughtful communication will enhance employees' perceptions of equity and justice.

The company also has to regularly review its compensation system. Without such a review, you might not know when external market salaries might rise, and your company would be at a competitive disadvantage. Keeping salary information current is only one reason for a regular review of the company's compensation system, however. The system also needs to be evaluated to ensure that employees in protected classes are being equitably paid, to ensure that managers are being trained as to how the compensation system works and properly rewarding employees, and to ensure that any changes in the company's values or strategic objectives are reflected in the firm's compensation system.

COMPENSATING EMPLOYEES IN PRACTICE: ORGANIZATIONAL DEMANDS

As with all other employee management decisions, compensation decisions have to be made within the appropriate context of a firm's organizational demands and environmental influencers. Exhibit 10.11 lists some of these demands and influencers. In this section,

▶ Exhibit 10.11 Compensation in Practice

Context	Employee Attitudes & Behaviors Chapter 10—"Compensating Employees"
Organizational Demands	
Strategy drives . . .	• Internal value of jobs • Compensation mix
Company characteristics determine . . .	• Ability to provide compensation • Types of compensation
Culture establishes . . .	• Priorities of the firm's compensation policies • Employees' expectations and attitudes toward compensation
Employee concerns include . . .	• Equity versus equality • Fairness of reward
Environmental Demands	
Labor force influences . . .	• Level of compensation • Form of compensation employees desire
Technology affects . . .	• Ease of collecting compensation data • How compensation is tracked and delivered • What is considered compensable work
Globalization impacts . . .	• Where compensation decisions are made • Acceptableness of compensation • Pay rates
Ethics/social responsibility shapes . . .	• What compensation signals to employees • Attitudes about the living wage and comparable worth
Regulations include . . .	• Davis-Bacon Act • Walsh-Healey Public Contracts Act • Fair Labor Standards Act

we examine how a company can manage employee compensation within this context so that it achieves the objectives of attracting, maintaining, and retaining the employees needed for the firm to have and maintain a sustained competitive advantage. We will also emphasize your role as a manager in making decisions about compensation. As with the first half of this chapter, we focus more on the broader topic of compensation in general, with an emphasis on base pay. Chapter 11 addresses organizational demands and environmental influencers relative to incentive pay, and Chapter 12 addresses benefits as well as safety to round out our discussion of total compensation. As a manager, you are in a critical position to understand how the organizational demands and environmental influencers affect both how the company pays employees and their perceptions about that pay.

Strategy and Compensation

A firm's strategy directly affects the internal value of its jobs, the wages it pays, and the pay mix it uses.[17] Next we discuss each of these aspects of a compensation system.

INTERNAL VALUE OF JOBS   A company's strategy will determine the tasks, duties, and responsibilities it considers most valuable for achieving its goals. Jobs that involve those tasks, duties, and responsibilities will receive the highest rewards. However, because the strategies of firms differ, as explained earlier in the chapter, the same job can be valued differently from one company to another. Keep in mind, too, that if a company's strategy changes, the compensation system will need to change as well to ensure that it continues to help the firm achieve its overall goals. Now, let's look at some examples.

Consider a company that develops new pharmaceutical products, such as Pfizer. Their focus is on developing safe medicines for prevention and treatment of serious medical

Research scientists at work.

conditions.[18] This company has a differentiation strategy and focuses on innovation. Jobs that are core for the company include research and sales representative positions. Research has shown that a firm's innovation strategy influences the relative pay level for those employees who will be held most accountable for innovation.[19] So the firm will pay more for those jobs than for support jobs (accounting, for example). The core jobs have a bigger impact on the company's bottom line. In fact, the company likely will pay wages higher than the market to attract the very best research and sales staff. The firm might even offer more variable pay as a way to further enhance employees' salaries and make the company an attractive employer.

Now consider a firm, such as Deloitte & Touche, that pursues a differentiation strategy by providing an exemplary level of audit and tax services to its clients. Many of the core jobs in this firm are accounting jobs, and employees in these jobs receive the highest pay. As you can see, the same job—the job of accountant in this case—can be valued differently, depending on the business of the company and its strategy.

Consider another example. In many fast-food restaurants, such as Wendy's, the focus is on maintaining low costs, standardization, and efficiency. Most of the core jobs will be very specialized and require low skills. As a result, the pay for these jobs will be low. A manager in an organization with a low-cost strategy would be tasked with ensuring that costs are kept down, that employees are efficient, and that employees follow the standards of the company. The manager would be paid to achieve these goals.

COMPENSATION MIX A firm's strategy will affect the pay mix it offers employees. Many companies are reconsidering the amount of base pay versus variable pay that is included in employee compensation packages. A problem with base pay is that it ties the firm to a fixed dollar amount that becomes larger as cost-of-living adjustments and merit pay are added to the base. So, before we discuss the compensation mix further, we need to discuss the concepts of cost-of-living adjustments and merit increases. These are two common methods of increasing employee base pay.

cost-of-living adjustment (COLA)

A pay adjustment for employees to offset the increases in the prices of goods and services they purchase and to keep salaries from lagging behind the external market.

As a result of inflation, many firms give their employees **cost-of-living adjustments (COLAs)** to offset the increases in the prices of goods and services they purchase and to keep salaries from lagging behind the external market. The consumer price index (CPI) is used as the basis for determining the amount of a COLA. The CPI consists of a market basket of goods and services that are regularly consumed by urban households, and it includes fees for water and sewer as well as sales and excise tax. The data to calculate the CPI comes from 87 urban areas in the United States and about 23,000 retail and service establishments and 50,000 landlords or tenants.[20]

merit pay increase

A compensation adjustment based on the results of an employee's performance evaluations.

Merit increases are not automatic. **Merit increases** are awarded based on how well an individual has performed. Like a COLA, however, a merit increase permanently raises a person's wages. Even if the worker's performance declines, the previous merit increase still remains a part of his of her base pay. To offset the "permanency" of merit raises, quite a few firms are increasing the amount of variable pay they offer to employees. In fact, a lot of managers believe that offering employees more variable versus base pay can effectively shape their behavior.[21] Variable pay can include bonuses, commissions, stock options, and other forms of monetary rewards that do not become a permanent part of a person's base pay. Chapter 11 provides more discussion of these types of pay. For now, we will discuss the value of variable pay.

A company such as Pfizer, the pharmaceutical company in our earlier example, would have to consider whether more of the pay it offers its employees should be in the form of direct base pay or whether a large percentage of it should be variable. The research staff might receive bonuses based on their individual performance and/or department's performance or the company's performance as a whole. The sales reps are likely to receive commissions (variable pay) tied to their ability to convince physicians to write prescriptions for the company's drugs. They may or may not receive base pay as well. You will learn more about how sales commissions work in the next chapter.

At McDonald's, which has a low-cost strategy, the most significant part of the compensation package for employees is base pay.[22] In contrast, Zensar Technologies, a global software solutions provider, includes both a fixed and a variable component in its total compensation package. The company's performance and individual performance determine the variable part of the pay package.[23] By setting up its pay mix in this way, Zensar can better

COMPANY spotlight 10.3 The Top 10 Reasons to Work for Stew's

Stew Leonard's started out in 1969 as a small dairy store with seven employees. Today, Stew's claims to be the world's largest dairy and grocery store, with annual sales of over $300 million and more than 2,000 employees. The dairy store has been called the "Disneyland of Dairy Stores," by the *New York Times* and was featured in a groundbreaking book on business excellence titled *A Passion for Excellence and Thriving on Chaos.* Stew's has also been included in *the Guinness Book of World Records* for "the greatest sales per unit area of any single food store in the U.S."

The owners of Stew Leonard's know that they would not be successful without the right employees and that they need to take care of their employees. Hence, they offer an extensive pay and benefits program. Team members receive top pay, with time-and-a-half paid for all Sunday work, overtime or not.

Benefits include flexible hours for working moms so they can be home when their children are home, social events, referral rewards program, scholarship for college work, English as a second language classes, and a full range of other benefits, including 100% coverage of health insurance premiums, dental and vision plans, legal services, 401(k) retirement savings plan, profit sharing, and much more. Promotional opportunities round out the total rewards program for Stew's employees. Stew Leonard's understands that employees expect more than just a paycheck from their employer.

Sources: Based on Stew Leonard's. *Top 10 reasons to work for Stew's,* www.stewleonards.com/careers/careers.cfm; and 100 best companies to work for 2007, *Fortune,* http://money.cnn.com/magazines/fortune/bestcompanies/2007/full_list/

manage the direct costs associated with employees' salaries yet still give them an incentive to perform at higher levels. Research has shown, for instance, that managers and employees who receive stock options behave in ways that are more beneficial to their firms because part of their pay (the stock options) is linked to the performance of their firms.[24] Keep in mind that we are only talking about manager and employee pay at this point. We will discuss issues related to stock options and executive pay, a much more complex topic, in Chapter 11.

Overall, a company's strategy will determine the mix of base pay and variable pay and the mix of monetary and nonmonetary rewards it offers. Managers need to understand how this works so they can make appropriate decisions about pay. A firm's strategy also determines the extent to which other types of rewards, in the form of benefits, are available. Company Spotlight 10.3 describes the various types of pay and benefits provided by Stew Leonard's, which *Fortune* has included on its list "100 Best Companies to Work For" seven years in a row. Chapter 12 provides more discussion of the topic.

Company Characteristics and Compensation

Along with strategy, the characteristics of a company have a major impact on its compensation decisions in terms of what the firm is able to offer its employees and the type of compensation provided. The age and stage of development of the company, as well as other characteristics, such as its size, play key roles in these decisions.

ABILITY TO PAY Why might a firm pay less-than-market wages? Startup and small firms might not be in a position to do otherwise. This situation could create some problems relative to attracting employees, but this is not always the case. Microsoft paid lower wages when it first started but was still able to attract highly qualified employees because the work they would be doing was cutting edge, and Microsoft gave shares of the company to the employees. The employees were betting on eventually making a lot of money by forgoing higher wages in the beginning of their careers with the firm. We all know the rest of that story.

More established companies have more resources and can pay at or even above the market wage. If a company is profitable, it will more likely offer higher salaries relative to the market. Keep in mind, however, that age and size of the company are subordinate to the company's pay philosophy and that the company strategy should drive the pay philosophy. A new, small startup company might actually pay above-market wages for its size, age, and industry to ensure that it starts off with top talent. As a manager, part of your job will be to help employees understand your company's pay philosophy and why it exists.

Larger companies and more established companies generally have greater resources and can pay higher wages. Companies such as Lockheed Martin, for example, are large, established firms known for paying above-market wages. Keep in mind that even in these companies, some jobs are paid at the market and some are paid above, as discussed in the earlier section on strategy. Whether a job is a core job or a support position affects the decision about level of pay.

TYPE OF COMPENSATION   The size and age of a firm plays a major role in determining the type of pay it offers. As mentioned earlier, startup firms often give stock options to their employees to offset their inability to pay market wages. Older, more established firms focus on finding the best balance between base pay and variable pay. Larger firms generally have more complex pay systems, in part because of the many different types of jobs they have and the differing degrees to which those jobs contribute to the profitability of the firms. Larger firms can also offer more benefits and services to employees because of economies of scale. Generally speaking, the more employees at the firm, the better deals the firm is able to strike with third-party benefit and service providers. Also, larger firms, overall, pay more than smaller firms.[25]

Culture and Compensation

The culture of an organization has a major impact on the compensation decisions its managers make. Specifically, culture establishes the priorities for the pay policy of the firm. It also plays a large role in terms of employees' expectations and attitudes about the rewards offered them. Let's take a look at each of these issues.

PRIORITIES OF A FIRM'S COMPENSATION POLICY   An organization's culture impacts the pay policy of the firm both directly and indirectly. Overall, the pay policy of a company should compliment its culture. In thinking about culture and rewards, it is important to remember that even the best intentions can lead to unwanted outcomes. If the culture is one of competition with individual rewards given, employees will be less interested in collaboration and being part of a team and more interested in maximizing their own rewards.[26] If the organization values teamwork, then the pay policy needs to make it clear that teamwork will be rewarded. If the culture values innovation, the pay policy should emphasize that the company will provide higher rewards for employees who exhibit this value.

EMPLOYEES' EXPECTATIONS AND ATTITUDES TOWARD COMPENSATION   An organization's culture sends a message to the firm's employees about what rewards they can expect to receive. For example, in a culture that values learning, employees will expect to receive higher pay for engaging in learning activities. Employees in cultures in which they know they are valued tend to have a more positive attitude toward their compensation than those in harsh and competitive cultures. In the latter environment, employees tend to be suspicious and distrustful of the compensation decisions managers make.[27] In turn, a firm's compensation system sends a message to employees about the company's culture by rewarding the types of behaviors desired in the culture.[28] Company Spotlight 10.4 describes how IBM used compensation to change its culture.

As a manager, you might not be able to change the entire corporate culture of your firm. However, you can do a lot to inform your employees about how pay decisions are made within it and what employees need to do to achieve higher pay levels. You are also in the best position to know what types of rewards are valued by your employees.[29] For example, if employees greatly value higher base pay, trying to offset a lower-pay plan with perks such as employee recognition programs isn't likely to motivate workers.

Employee Concerns and Compensation

How your employees perceive the "psychological contract" they have with your firm will, in large part, be due to the company's pay decisions—both in terms of what the firm's compensation system communicates is valued and how the process is implemented. Thus,

COMPANY spotlight

10.4 IBM's Compensation Strategy

IBM knows that what gets rewarded determines what gets done. Consequently, over the past decade, IBM has reoriented its reward strategy to sustain and renew "the highest performing, most effective culture in the business." The reward strategy focuses on investing in programs that recognize results, not just tenure.

The design of the overall compensation strategy at IBM is on providing market-based pay that is performance driven across all segments of the company. The highest contributors are the most rewarded, and the rewards come in the form of base salaries and variable bonuses that are performance driven. The base pay consists of competitive wages determined by using market rates from the IT industry while taking into account geographical differences in employee locations.

Source: Based on IBM. *Compensation and benefits*, www.ibm.com/ibm/responsibility/pdfs/ibm_crr_comp_053105.pdf.

---

significant employee concerns relative to compensation center around equity and fairness issues. You should be familiar with both of these issues by now. Let's take a look at how they play out relative to compensation.

EQUITY VERSUS EQUALITY Earlier in the chapter, we discussed equity theory: Employees compare their inputs to their outputs and contrast them against those of people who are similarly situated to them either within the company or outside it. If there is a perception that the rewards are not equitable, then the person will seek a way (or ways) to rectify the situation.

Consider what happens in an egalitarian organization where the goal is to compensate all employees at the same level. The idea is that doing this eliminates status differences and will foster a more cooperative work environment. The reality, however, is that not all jobs require equal knowledge, skills, and abilities or have equal levels of responsibility or accountability, and not all employees have the same motivation to perform their jobs. Thus, while having an egalitarian pay structure appears to be more objective than some other types of pay structures and appears to reduce equity concerns, such a system fails to address differences that are legitimate reasons for pay variability among employees.

In setting a pay structure, managers must carefully consider their decisions and acknowledge the consequences of the choices made. As a manager, you need to understand these and other employee concerns about compensation so that you can address them appropriately.

FAIRNESS OF REWARDS When it comes to compensation decisions, employees are particularly sensitive to justice issues. If employees believe there is distributive justice, they might be less concerned about procedural justice. Typically, however, employees want to understand that both the process and the outcomes are fair. Employees know that even if they get a good outcome such as a good raise, they might not the next time around if the process is poorly designed.

In addition, interactional justice is important. If an employee feels that he doesn't have a good relationship with you, as his manager, he will be concerned about the fairness of decisions you make, including those that relate to his compensation. Therefore, as a manager, it is your responsibility to make sure that your employees understand the pay process and how their pay was determined and that they know that you are treating them fairly.

Another fairness issue is **salary compression** (also referred to as *pay* or *wage* compression). Salary compression occurs when the pay for jobs in the external marketplace rises faster than the pay for jobs inside the organization. Let's look at the job of college professor as an example. In the late 1980s, the numbers of students enrolling in business schools increased exponentially. As a result, universities needed to hire qualified faculty to teach these students. In order to attract and hire faculty in what had become an increasingly tight labor market, pay rates began to increase faster than the pay rates for faculty already employed. Faculty fresh out of Ph.D. programs started their academic careers making much higher salaries than faculty who had been at the schools for a long time. We have

salary compression (also pay or wage compression)

A situation that occurs when the pay for jobs in the external marketplace rises faster than the pay for jobs inside the organization, resulting in new employees receiving higher salaries than existing employees.

used an academic example, but the same situation occurs in many other occupations across all types of organizations. Anytime there is a shortage of workers in the labor market, organizations end up paying higher salaries to attract needed employees, and it is often not economically feasible for the company to increase the salaries of existing employees to the same levels. Thus, salary compression happens, and with it come concerns about internal equity. When firms decide to make salary adjustments for a job to address equity issues, they have to decide whether all of the longer-term employees in that particular job should be raised to the market level or not. Doing so implies that these employees would be able to obtain new jobs in the marketplace at market wages.

COMPENSATING EMPLOYEES IN PRACTICE: ENVIRONMENTAL INFLUENCES

Along with organizational demands, environmental influences are a determining factor in how organizations set up their compensation systems. Labor surpluses and shortages affect pay levels, for instance. Technology has made administering systems easier and has made access to compensation data more available to people. Globalization has increased the complexity of pay decisions. In this section we take a closer look at these and related environmental influencers.

Labor Force and Compensation

Think back to what you learned in your economics courses relative to supply and demand. As the supply of a good or service increases and demand decreases, what happens to its price? What about the reverse—when the supply declines and demand increases? Wages for jobs work the same way as prices for products. From a company perspective, then, the ideal world is one in which the labor supply far exceeds the demand for labor. In that environment, companies can keep wages down and still attract, maintain, and retain highly qualified workers. The opposite is also true: When the labor market is tight, companies have to use more of their profits to attract, maintain, and retain employees. Overall, the labor market influences the level of compensation firms offer, the form of the compensation, and market wages.

THE LEVEL OF A FIRM'S COMPENSATION   What would you do if you had seven McDonald's restaurants in Billings, Montana, and were finding it difficult to attract quality applicants? When actually faced with this problem, the owner of these restaurants had to begin offering higher-than-minimum wages to attract workers. With lots of service jobs available, and few applicants to fill them, wages in Billings have continued to go up. The McDonald's franchiser is paying upwards of $7 per hour, but other employers in the area are advertising as much as $15 per hour, plus benefits, for service jobs. Thus, trying to maintain the lower wages that are part of McDonald's low-cost strategy is hard in Billings.[30] This example shows how labor market supply and demand have a huge impact on market wages. By now you are very familiar with how important it is that a firm decide whether to follow, lead, or lag the market and some of the organizational demands that influence that decision.

Obviously, we do not know everything about the impact of the various pay level decisions. We do know, however, that leading the market helps a firm attract better-qualified workers (and more of them), helps retain workers, and reduces pay dissatisfaction. Paying at the market rate results in attracting and retaining employees, containing labor costs, and reducing pay dissatisfaction. And, while lagging the market helps contain labor costs, it makes an organization less attractive to prospective employees and leads to greater pay dissatisfaction. Thus, the decisions you make about your firm's pay relative to the external labor market are indeed important ones. Often a hybrid policy may be the best approach. Jobs that are more critical to the firm can receive above-market wages, whereas less-critical jobs receive market or below-market wages. Jobs in high demand in the labor market may require higher compensation as well.

In reality, a firm may actually use a combination of pay strategies for a single job structure, depending on the availability of workers. If there is an abundance of workers for the entry-level jobs in the structure, their pay could be below or just at market. At the same time, a smaller supply of workers for higher-level jobs in the structure might necessitate paying above-market wages for those jobs.[31]

FORMS OF COMPENSATION EMPLOYEES DESIRE Researchers have found that people have specific pay preferences and that individuals in the labor market will be more attracted to organizations with pay practices that match their pay preferences.[32] For example, one study found that college students preferred high pay that was based on what they individually contribute, fixed instead of variable pay, and job based rather than person based pay, along with flexible benefits. When the labor market is loose, preferences such as these are less of a concern to firms because people looking for work will be less demanding. In contrast, people become more demanding in terms of the pay and other rewards they expect when the labor market is tight.

Technology and Compensation

Technology has vastly reduced the challenges of managing complex compensation systems but created new challenges. It has made it easier to collect salary data and deliver pay. It has also affected what is considered compensable work. Let's take a look at each of these issues.

EASE OF COLLECTING SALARY DATA Before the Internet, employers had to collect salary survey data with paper and pencil methods and then compile it—a slow process at best. Now, employers can access online salary surveys, and they can conduct salary surveys online. Both of these activities—accessing salary surveys and conducting surveys—have increased the speed with which employers and workers can access the most current salary information.

In addition to salary surveys provided by professional organizations and job sites such as Monster.com, sites such as Salary.com have grown in terms of the accuracy and comprehensiveness of information they provide. Before you make any decisions based on salary data from sites such as these, make sure you research how and when the data were collected to ensure that they accurately represent the jobs of interest to you. Think about the consequences of using incorrect data if you are using these data to negotiate your own salary or if you are negotiating salary with an employee you are hiring.

HOW COMPENSATION IS TRACKED AND DELIVERED With the advent of sophisticated database programs and expert systems, employers have been able to develop and implement computer programs to simplify the job evaluation process and to maintain all their compensation records. Employees have greater access to their pay information through their companies' employee portals as well.

Many companies are able to have employees input their work hours, with the data going directly into the company's accounting software, thus saving the firms even more processing time. When the employees are consultants, lawyers, or other professionals who get paid based on the number of hours they bill clients, this ability to input data directly into the system has another advantage: It allows customers to more readily gain access to what their charges will be. For mobile professionals, the ability to input their time records directly online for compensation purposes helps ensure that they will be paid in a timely manner.[33] And, with online banking, companies can deposit employees' paychecks directly into their accounts so they don't have to worry about when and where to pick them up.

WHAT IS CONSIDERED COMPENSABLE WORK When employees telecommute, managers need to put in place clear policies that communicate what constitutes compensable work time. This way, employees understand what time they will be compensated for and what constitutes unauthorized "off-the-clock" work. To control off-the-clock work, managers should require employees to complete timesheets and certify that they are correct, in accordance with the company's telecommuting policy. Supervisors also need to verify the accuracy of the timesheets. The company's telecommuting policy should also be consistently enforced, and any disciplinary measures should be outlined.[34]

Globalization and Compensation

Global organizations have to decide whether they want to centralize or decentralize their compensation systems. That is, they have to decide where pay decisions will be made—either at headquarters or in the countries in which they are operating.[35] In addition, the laws and norms of countries will affect the extent to which certain pay practices are accepted by employees. Let's now look at each of these two issues.

WHERE PAY DECISIONS ARE MADE   Centralized compensation structures appear to be increasing. Global companies with centralized compensation systems are more satisfied with them and view them as more effective than companies with decentralized processes. Centralized systems provide a consistent link between results and rewards and provide a greater likelihood of internal and external equity being achieved. In addition, these firms are more likely to have a global compensation strategy and have job grades and job bands that they apply globally. The trend does not, however, mean that regional and country-specific differences in compensation are not considered, only that they are integrated within a single framework.[36]

Beckman Coulter, a California-based biomedical company, provides the same international incentive arrangements to all its employees, regardless of where they're located. Non-U.S. employees receive the same proportion of variable pay as U.S. employees, subject, of course, to the firm's local and regional performance standards being met.[37]

Another approach to global compensation is that adopted by Dow Chemical Corporation in response to changes at the corporate level. Pay levels for employees are determined by managers in a global exercise each January. Dow establishes guidelines for global pay planning, and pay is set for large groups of employees at a market-median (midpoint) position based on data from a premier group of companies. Managers can then use individual performance differences in deciding on employee pay within these broader guidelines. Base pay, bonuses, and long-term incentives are all included in this planning. Employees and managers give the system high marks because the system is clear about what is valued.[38]

ACCEPTABLENESS OF COMPENSATION   Comparative studies of compensation in various countries have found some similarities and some differences in the acceptability of various forms of compensation. For instance, in a study of compensation preferences in Hong Kong and in China, several differences were identified. In Hong Kong, workers were interested in profit sharing and mortgage assistance, whereas in China, workers were interested in individual bonuses and a housing provision.[39]

For expatriates, the picture is even more complicated, partly because companies have tightened their approach to global staffing and, in so doing, have made changes that affect how employees perceive the acceptability of their compensation. Globally, companies are just as concerned as U.S. companies with how well their compensation packages attract, maintain, and retain employees, whether those employees are host-country nationals (HCN), third-country nationals (TCN), or parent-country nationals (PCN).

Paying PCNs is perhaps the most complicated aspect of global compensation. HCNs and TCNs will often be paid the host country wage, while companies traditionally have tried to keep PCNs "whole." That means that PCN salaries have been adjusted upward to account for the higher living costs in some countries versus the comparable costs in the home country. The converse is not true. Wages are not adjusted downward if living costs are actually less. Hence, when a PCN is from a country with considerably higher wages than the host country wages, the PCN can be making a significantly higher wage than an HCN or a TCN in a comparable job, creating equity concerns.

One way to manage the compensation of PCNs is to use the balance sheet approach. This approach involves looking at what the PCN was making prior to the international assignment and adding in incentives for taking the foreign post and any pay adjustments needed to keep the employee at the same income level she was experiencing. The adjustments can include incentives for hardship assignments (assignments to countries with poor living conditions), dangerous assignments (say, to war-torn countries), or primitive assignments (assignments to countries or regions that are remote, such as the Australian outback). Therefore, the compensation for a global assignment typically would involve adding current base pay and benefits to incentive and equalization adjustments.[40]

PAY RATES   There are still significant pay rate differences around the world—and even within countries. HayGroup's *World Pay Report* in 2007 found that managers in the United States are ranked 24th out of the 46 countries included. The buying power of the U.S. managers was equal to $104,905 compared to Saudi Arabia and United Arab Emirates managers who were at the top of the list, at $220,000. Managers in the emerging countries of Russia, Turkey, and Mexico had average salaries of $150,000.[41] In Vietnam, wages traditionally have been extremely low. In January 2008, the minimum monthly wage for unskilled laborers who work for foreign and international organizations was set at $62 USD or one million VND in the urban areas of Hanoi and Ho Chi Minh City. Wages vary throughout Vietnam based on whether the area is suburban or urban and whether the jobs are in the state sector or private.[42]

Many U.S. companies doing business abroad have been criticized for paying low wages relative to American wages. But is the comparison appropriate? Take China, for example. In March 2004, the Ministry of Labor and Social Security in China issued minimum wage regulations for the first time.[43] In June 2007, the highest minimum wage in China was in Shenzhen and equal to $106 USD a month. The lowest was $35 USD a month in the eastern province of Jiangxi. Average minimum wages in China have been growing in double-digit percentages for the past several years.[44] In the United States, the minimum wage is $6.55 per hour, for a monthly wage of $1,135; the minimum wage is scheduled to increase to $7.25 per hour, or $1,257 per month, on July 24, 2009. Although the difference between the minimum monthly wages in China and the United States sounds quite significant, the minimum wage in China might actually have equal or greater buying power compared to the minimum wage in the United States. Therefore, before generalizations are made, many factors, such as cost of living, have to be taken into consideration. That fact doesn't, however, justify taking advantage of workers and paying them less than the minimum wage or just the minimum wage when a company can afford to pay more.

Ethics/Social Responsibility and Compensation

Perhaps as much as or more than any other HR activity, compensation is surrounded by ethical and social issues. What compensation decisions signal to employees about their firms' values, and what people's attitudes are about living wage and comparable worth issues are just a few of the ethical and social responsibility challenges associated with compensation. Next, we discuss these issues.

WHAT COMPENSATION DECISIONS SIGNAL TO EMPLOYEES   The old adage that "what gets rewarded is what gets done" carries strong ethical implications. Enron and related scandals raised the consciousness of many people about how compensation practices can lead to unethical behavior. By setting up a system that rewarded employees for goals that were short term and easily manipulated, employees with less-than-strong moral grounding (and even some who had been more grounded) found themselves engaging in unethical behavior to achieve the rewards. Managers who tie compensation to performance need to think long and hard about the possible consequences of their decisions about what to compensate.

ATTITUDES ABOUT THE LIVING WAGE AND COMPARABLE WORTH   An issue that has been oft debated in Congress and in state legislatures that relates to ethics and social responsibility is a concept called the **living wage**. The concept is generally described as providing a fair wage to a person so that basic living needs can be met. Much controversy surrounds this concept, however, because of the differences in opinion that exist about what minimal amount of income would constitute a living wage and about whether it is the employer's obligation to ensure that employees make a living wage. Employers must pay the legally mandated minimum wage but have difficulty with the idea that they have to pay more than that for low-skilled jobs.

A few local governments have been able to enact living wage legislation. The City of Brookline, Massachusetts, has living wage bylaws that require certain employers to pay $11.15 per hour for wages. In Syracuse, New York, the Living Wage Ordinance requires certain employers to pay $10.08 per hour if employees receive health care benefits and $11.91 if they do not.[45]

living wage

The concept that employees should be paid a wage that ensures that their basic costs of living are met.

Exhibit 10.12 ▶

Sample of Wage
Inequities Identified
in 2006 Reports

Minnesota Female Salaries Adjusted to be Comparable to Males with Same Job Evaluation Ratings, Comparable Length of Service and Performance

Position	Hourly Wage "Before"	Hourly Wage "After"	Difference
Admin. Asst.	19.00	23.15	4.15
Asst. Cook	13.63	16.53	2.90
City Clerk	12.71	14.00	1.29
Community Dev. Dir.	26.17	29.51	3.34
Head Librarian	14.75	16.96	2.21
Liquor Store Clerk	13.00	16.51	3.51
Office Manager	14.77	16.83	2.06
Teacher Aide	9.72	11.51	1.79
Typist	9.60	11.28	1.68

Source: Based on Minnesota Department of Employee Relations. *Minnesota local government pay equity compliance report*, January 2007, www.doer.state.mn.us/lr-peqty/payequity.pdf.

comparable worth

Eliminating inequity in wages by ensuring that jobs that require similar levels of education and experience and have other characteristics in common are paid at a similar wage regardless of gender.

Should these two employees receive a comparable wage?

Davis-Bacon Act

An act that requires contractors and subcontractors with contracts in excess of $2,000 with the federal government to pay their workers a minimum wage that is at least equal to the local prevailing wages and to provide them with the local prevailing benefits.

Comparable worth has been another hotly debated topic. Comparable worth focuses on eliminating the gender inequity in wages because jobs held by women traditionally have been underpaid relative to similar jobs held by men. With comparable worth, jobs in the organization would be valued relative to other jobs within the organization, regardless of whether they are traditionally "male" jobs or "female" jobs. This process ensures that the value to the company is the driver in establishing wages, rather than the labor market being the determinant. Exhibit 10.12 provides a brief overview of the results of a 2006 compliance study for the comparable worth policy adopted by the state of Minnesota. Before the adjustments made as a result of the study, females were paid 81% of the wages paid to men in jobs with comparable job evaluation ratings. The inequities most often found in the city governments were between city clerks and maintenance workers. In the schools, a number of "female" jobs—jobs for secretaries, food service workers, and teacher aides—were paid less than "male" jobs for custodians.[46]

As you can imagine, the idea of comparable worth has had only limited success. Employers are concerned with the added direct labor costs associated with reclassifying jobs. The Equal Pay Act only requires equal pay for jobs that are substantially the same.

COMPENSATION IN PRACTICE: REGULATORY ISSUES

In Chapter 3, we discussed one piece of legislation that is directly related to compensation, the Equal Pay Act. Recall that the purpose of this act is to ensure that males and females are paid equally when they perform jobs similar in terms of their skill requirements, responsibilities, working conditions, and so forth. In the following sections, we cover additional legislation that affects compensation decisions. Specifically, we discuss the Davis-Bacon Act, the Walsh-Healey Act, and the Fair Labor Standards Act (FLSA).

Davis-Bacon Act

The **Davis-Bacon Act**, passed in 1931, requires contractors and subcontractors with contracts in excess of $2,000 with the federal government to pay their workers a minimum wage that is at least equal to the local prevailing wages and to provide them with the local prevailing benefits. This act is administered by the Department of Labor.[47] Even minimal presence of a union in the local area can result in a higher prevailing wage because union wages are typically higher than nonunion wages.[48]

Walsh-Healey Public Contracts Act (PCA)

The **Walsh-Healey Act**, passed in 1936, applies to contractors with contracts over $10,000 who are involved in either manufacturing or providing goods and services to the U.S. government. The Wage and Hour Division of the U. S. Department of Labor enforces the law. These firms must pay their workers the federal minimum wage for the first 40 hours they work in a particular week and 1.5 times the minimum wage for any additional hours they work during the week.[49]

Fair Labor Standards Act (FLSA)

The **Fair Labor Standards Act (FLSA)** is the most significant piece of legislation governing what can and cannot be done with regard to compensation. Congress passed this act in 1938 to improve labor conditions for workers by ensuring that they would earn enough to have a minimum standard of living. The FLSA regulates the use of child labor, specifies what types of workers must be paid the minimum wage, and stipulates the pay rate for overtime work.[50] The Department of Labor oversees compliance with the FLSA. As a manager, you need to be sure that decisions you make are in compliance with this law, so let's take a look at the most significant parts of this act.

MINIMUM WAGE At the time of this writing, most employees in the United States are entitled to a **minimum wage** of $6.55 per hour, effective July 24, 2008, and is scheduled to go to $7.25 an hour on July 24, 2009. In addition, each state has the option of setting its own minimum wage. If that wage is higher than the FLSA minimum, employers operating in that state must pay the higher wage. For example, West Virignia has a minimum wage of $7.25 per hour if there are six or more employees at one location, and Washington has a minimum wage of $8.07 per hour. The U.S. Department of Labor Web site contains a link to information about the minimum wage laws of the various states: www.dol.gov/esa/minwage/america.htm.[51]

There are some exceptions to the minimum wage requirement. People under the age of 20 can be paid less than the minimum wage during their first 90 consecutive days of employment; employees who receive more than $30 in tips per month may be required by their employer to count their tips as wages under the FLSA requirements (although the employer must still pay at least $2.13 per hour in wages to these employees); and full-time students employed in colleges and universities, retail or service stores, and agriculture can be paid from 85% to 100% of the minimum wage if their employer has obtained a special certification.[52]

EXEMPT VERSUS NONEXEMPT EMPLOYEES Managers need to know if their employees are exempt or nonexempt. **Exempt employees** do not receive overtime pay for hours worked over 40 in a workweek, while **nonexempt employees** do receive overtime pay. Executive, administrative, professional, and outside sales employees who receive salaries are typically considered to be exempt employees. In addition, Congress has specified that certain computer professionals are also exempt if they earn at least $27.63 per hour.[53] The FairPay Overtime Initiative, which went into effect in 2006, clarified which employees were eligible to be classified as exempt and resulted in jobs at many companies being reclassified. This initiative strengthened overtime rights for approximately 6.7 million American workers, 1.3 million of whom were low-wage workers who did not get overtime under the old rules.[54]

OVERTIME Nonexempt employees who work more than 40 hours in a week are considered to be working **overtime** and are entitled to receive pay at the rate of 1.5 times their regular pay for that additional time. Managers can use the Department of Labor's guidelines and its Web site to determine whether employees must be compensated for rest and meal breaks (rest breaks, yes; meal breaks, usually no), whether employees "on call" must be compensated, and whether employees attending training programs must be paid for that time.

CHILD LABOR The last significant part of the FLSA we need to discuss is the child labor provision. Prior to the passage of the FLSA, it was not uncommon for young children to work long hours, often in dangerous conditions in factories. Today, youths under the age of 16 can work on a restricted basis: Those who are ages 14 and 15 can work after school hours

Walsh-Healey Act

An act that applies to contractors with contracts over $10,000 who are involved in either manufacturing or providing goods and services to the U.S. government and requires these firms to pay their workers the federal minimum wage for the first 40 hours they work in a particular week and 1.5 times the minimum wage for any additional hours they work during the week.

Fair Labor Standards Act (FLSA)

An act that governs what employers can and cannot do in regards to compensation, including regulating the use of child labor, defining the difference between exempt and non-exempt employees, setting a minimum wage, and stipulating the pay rate for overtime work.

minimum wage

The lowest hourly wage rate an employer can pay.

exempt employee

A worker whose job classification does not require the payment of overtime pay for time worked in excess of 40 hours a week.

nonexempt employee

A worker who receives overtime pay for time worked in excess of 40 hours a week.

overtime

Work hours that exceed the number of hours established as the normal workweek.

(after 7 A.M. and before 7 P.M.) during the school year, but no more than 3 hours on a school day and no more than 18 hours per week; they can work 8 hours during a non-school day and 40 hours during a non-school week. Between June 1 and Labor Day, they can work until 9 P.M. Youths 16 years and older have no work-hour restrictions, but they cannot work in hazardous jobs if they are under age 18. Examples of hazardous jobs include those involving driving a motor vehicle, doing wrecking and demolition work, operating saws, and being exposed to radioactive substances.[55]

RECORD KEEPING　Employers must keep certain information for each nonexempt employee, including the person's:

- Full name and Social Security number
- Address
- Birth date, if the employee is younger than 19
- Gender
- Occupation
- Time and day when the person's workweek starts
- Daily hours worked
- Total weekly hours worked
- Basis and rate of pay
- Overtime earnings
- Additions and deductions from pay
- Total wages by pay period
- Date of pay and pay period[56]

SUMMARY

Compensation refers to the monetary and nonmonetary consideration employees receive in exchange for the work they do. The compensation can be direct, such as hourly wages and salaries, or indirect, such as benefits. When designing compensation packages, often referred to as total rewards, companies try to balance internal and external equity issues.

Internal equity is addressed by designing a process of internal alignment to ensure that jobs are properly valued relative to their worth to each other and to the company. The job evaluation process is used to do this. Job ranking and job classification are two qualitative job evaluation processes used. They are based on global evaluations of jobs. The point method and factor comparison method are two quantitative job evaluation approaches. They involve identifying and defining compensable factors and using benchmark jobs to set up the relative worth hierarchy of the jobs. In the point method, points are assigned to each degree of each compensable factor. In the factor comparison method, dollar amounts are assigned to each degree of each factor. Both approaches result in a job hierarchy.

External equity is addressed by ensuring that a company's pay is competitive with pay for similar jobs outside the company. This goal is accomplished by collecting salary information for benchmark jobs and comparing it to what the firm is paying for those jobs. Adjustments are then made to the pay, depending on the organization's chosen compensation policy.

Companies can decide to pay at, below, or above the market for some or all of their jobs.

The process for deciding how much to pay individuals under the traditional job-based structure requires first grouping jobs into grades based on job evaluation results; establishing a minimum, midpoint, and maximum dollar amount for that grade, based on market data and the firm's pay policy; and, finally, slotting individuals into the appropriate grades. Companies use an approach called broadbanding to reduce some of the complexity of this process. Reducing the number of grades and increasing their size in terms of minimum and maximum dollars gives managers more leeway when it comes to setting the pay for their employees.

A number of alternative compensation approaches have evolved to address some of the complexity and challenges of the traditional job classification approach. Skill and knowledge-based pay systems require employees to acquire certain skills or knowledge to receive pay increases. Lower-level skills or knowledge must be mastered before higher-level ones. Competency-based pay works in a similar way. This type of pay is based on employees mastering competencies that have been identified as supporting the firm's success. Firms also use direct market pricing, which involves collecting salary information from the external labor market first rather than starting with the development of an internal structure based on the value of the jobs within the company.

Successful compensation plans are well designed and carefully administered. A handbook describing the process and training for managers who will be using the process are critical. A decision also has to be made about whether the pay system will be open or closed. Finally, the compensation plan should be reviewed regularly to ensure that information, including market salary information, is current and relevant to the goals of the company.

Organizational demands, environmental influencers, and the legal environment affect how compensation systems are designed and administered, as well as how they are viewed by employees. The strategy of a firm drives the internal value of jobs and the compensation mix offered employees. Company characteristics determine the firm's ability to pay and the type of compensation offered. Organizational culture plays a key role in establishing priorities for compensation policies and influencing employees' expectations about their firm's compensation. Employee concerns include equity versus equality issues and the fairness of the rewards offered.

The labor force influences the level of compensation firms must pay employees, the form of compensation desired by prospective employees, and market wages. Technology affects the ease with which data are collected, how compensation information is tracked and pay is delivered, and even what is considered compensable work. Globalization affects where compensation decisions are made, the acceptableness of different compensation systems, and pay rates. What compensation decisions signal to employees about their firms' values and what people's attitudes are toward the living wage and comparable worth are just a few of the ethical and social responsibility challenges associated with compensation.

Finally, the regulatory forces affecting compensation decisions are driven in the United States by laws that include the Davis-Bacon Act, the Walsh-Healey Act, and the Fair Labor Standards Act.

KEY TERMS

benchmark jobs *p. 300*

broadbanding *p. 304*

comparable worth *p. 318*

compensable factors *p. 299*

compensation *p. 295*

competency-based pay *p. 307*

cost-of-living adjustment (COLA) *p. 310*

Davis-Bacon Act *p. 318*

direct market pricing *p. 307*

equity theory *p. 297*

exempt employee *p. 319*

external competitiveness *p. 301*

factor comparison *p. 300*

Fair Labor Standards Act (FSLA) *p. 319*

internal alignment *p. 298*

job classification *p. 298*

job grade *p. 300*

job evaluation *p. 298*

job pricing *p. 301*

job ranking *p. 298*

knowledge-based pay *p. 306*

living wage *p. 317*

merit pay increase *p. 310*

minimum wage *p. 319*

nonexempt employee *p. 319*

overtime *p. 319*

point method *p. 299*

salary compression *p. 313*

salary survey *p. 301*

skill-based pay *p. 306*

total rewards *p. 295*

wage curve *p. 302*

Walsh-Healey Act *p. 319*

DISCUSSION QUESTIONS

1. Why is compensation so important to employees? What role does it play in their lives? What role does it play for companies?

2. Describe how you can ensure that a compensation process is equitable for employees.

3. Why is it important for some jobs in a company to be paid more and some less?

4. An employee of yours makes an appointment to discuss his salary with you. He feels that he is not being paid "at market." What does the employee mean? How would you validate that he is or is not being paid at market currently?

5. What are the advantages and disadvantages of compensation approaches such as skill-based pay and competency-based pay? How can the disadvantages be overcome?

6. What is the relationship between compensation and organizational culture? Discuss whether compensation can be used to change a company culture.

7. Spend some time researching either the living wage or the comparable worth issue and prepare a one-page summary indicating whether you support the idea. Justify your position, citing the research you examined. Include a reference list with the paper.

8. Go online and research what happens to a company that violates the FLSA. Why might a company violate the FLSA?

LEARNING EXERCISE 1

As a manager, you will have employees come to you and tell you that they think they are underpaid. Assume that has just happened. The employee in this case is an accountant who works for you in Seattle, Washington, in a luxury hotel. The employee's current base salary after three years with the company is $42,000. The company tries to pay at market. Develop a plan of action for how you would respond in this situation.

1. Identify the information you would need to have to determine whether the employee's concerns are valid.

2. How would you resolve the situation if you were in a large company with a compensation staff in the human resources department? How would you resolve it if you were a small business owner?

3. Find salary data for the job for the relevant labor market. Discuss how you decided on the relevant labor market, where you obtained the data, and whether there is a significant difference between what the employee is making and the relevant labor market salary for that job.

LEARNING EXERCISE 2

You will graduate from college soon and have been offered two jobs. Both jobs involve conducting financial research and both are a good fit for you. One job is with a major Wall Street investment firm located in New York City. The other job is for a large financial services firm in Charlotte, North Carolina. The salary for the New York City job is $70,000 with a $5,000 starting bonus. The second job is at $55,000 with no starting bonus.

1. How would you research the cost-of-living differences between these two cities?

2. What factors are considered in determining cost-of-living differences?

3. Given that both jobs are a good fit for you, which job should you take? Describe your decision process.

4. As an employer, what should you do to address cost-of-living issues that limit the number of job candidates willing to sign on to work for you?

CASE STUDY # 1 — AN ETHICAL DILEMMA?

Due to growth in your biopharmaceutical company, you have just added two new research scientist positions. After some investigation, you have determined that the least amount you could offer candidates for the job is $135,000. Because most of your employees have been with the company for a long period of time, you are particularly interested in hiring some research scientists who have recently completed their graduate work. In the past, you have had problems hiring employees because your company is not yet well known, and it is located in South Dakota. After the first round of interviews, you identify a candidate who is from the area, who wants to stay in the area, and who has acceptable, though not exceptional, credentials. She is an acceptable candidate who will do a good job but who doesn't meet your need for "fresh" ideas in the same way as would a recent graduate. You offer her the job, with a salary of $105,000, and she accepts, without negotiating for any increase in the salary. Shortly thereafter, you interview a male candidate who is just completing his degree and who has exactly the credentials you are seeking. During the course of the interview process, you learn that he has two other offers, he has two other interviews scheduled, and his offers are both considerably higher than what you are going to pay the person you just hired. You are pretty sure the latter candidate will accept the job if you offer him $135,000. What are you going to do?

DISCUSSION QUESTIONS

1. Identify the issues in this case.

2. Make a decision about what to do.

3. How should you respond to the female employee if you hire the male employee for more money and she finds out that you did so?

CASE STUDY # 2 — COMPENSATION AT W. L. GORE

W. L. Gore & Associates is a company well known for its GORE-TEX fabric for protective outerwear. In 2006, the company ranked fifth on *Fortune*'s list "100 Best Companies to Work For." It was the eighth year in a row the firm had made the list. One of Gore's hallmarks is innovation. Rather than job titles, bosses, and organization charts, Gore uses a team approach, with leaders, sponsors, and team members.

The goals of Gore's compensation plan are internal fairness and external competitiveness. Gore uses two approaches to achieve these goals. The first is straightforward and typically used by companies: comparing pay at Gore with pay for comparable jobs at other companies. That takes care of the external competitiveness part. It is the internal competitiveness part that is different at Gore. The process works like this: Associates (co-workers) on the same team rank each other based on contributions to the company for the year. Team members can provide comments to support their rankings and identify strengths or areas for improvement of the associates they rank. This information is then used for determining raises.

DISCUSSION QUESTIONS

1. Provide a critique of the compensation practices at Gore, indicating the pros and cons of each approach.

2. Do you think that Gore can achieve its goals of internal fairness and external competitiveness with the two approaches used?

3. Would you want to work for this company? Why or why not?

Sources: Based on W. L. Gore & Associates Web site, www.gore.com; and 100 best companies to work for 2006, *Fortune*. http://money.cnn.com/magazines/fortune/bestcompanies/snapshots/1542.html.

INCENTIVES
AND REWARDS

1. Explain the theories behind how incentive plans motivate employees. *(327)*

2. Compare and contrast the different types of individual incentives. *(328)*

3. Discuss the major team- and group-based incentive plans. *(333)*

4. Compare and contrast the relative merits of the different types of group-level incentive plans. *(333)*

5. Explain how to design an effective incentive plan. *(336)*

6. Describe how organizational demands affect a firm's incentive plans. *(337)*

7. Explain how environmental factors affect a firm's incentive plans. *(341)*

HR CHALLENGES

| Environmental Influences | Organizational Demands | Regulatory Issues |

PRIMARY HR ACTIVITIES

Work Design & Workforce Planning

Managing Employee Competencies

Managing Employee Attitudes & Behaviors

Employee Contributions

Competitive Advantage

WHY ARE INCENTIVE PLANS IMPORTANT?

Why do some employees work harder than others? This question is admittedly simple but important. Most of us, at some time, have worked with people who did not work as hard as their abilities would indicate they could. Managers face this problem constantly. What should they do? After all, as a manager, much of your personal success or failure, not to mention that of your company, rests on the performance of your employees.

As Exhibit 11.1 shows, employee competencies—their KSAs and other characteristics— affect their performance. That is, employees who have the competencies needed to excel at their jobs will able to perform at a much higher level than employees without those competencies, Beyond competencies, the structure of the work environment—how jobs are designed and the effectiveness of a firm's workforce planning efforts—also affect the quality, type, and amount of effort individuals put into their work.

Beyond knowing what to do, the ultimate purpose of incentives is to motivate—to motivate employees to work as hard as possible to reach certain goals by rewarding them

Exhibit 11.1 ▶

Framework for the Strategic Management of Employees

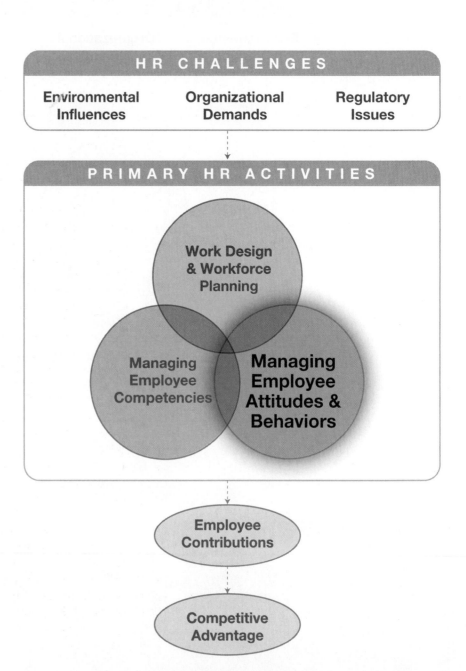

when they do what is desired. Managers face a host of decisions that affect their incentive plans. For example, as a manager you have to answer questions such as:

- What actions or outcomes should we base our incentives on?
- What types of incentives should we use?
- Should we focus on individual performance, team performance, company performance, or some combination of the three?

In this chapter, we look at how companies use the rewards associated with incentive plans to motivate their employees. We then discuss a variety of incentive plans that you, as a manager, can use to encourage your employees to engage in different types of behaviors.

HOW INCENTIVES WORK

Let's look, for a moment, at how various incentive plans work in light of different motivational theories of behavior. Reinforcement theory, goal setting, expectancy theory, and agency theory will help you understand how different incentive plans affect employees' attitudes and behaviors.

Theories of Motivation

According to **reinforcement theory**,[1] when people experience positive consequences after they do something, they are likely to repeat those actions. This, of course, includes employees when they are rewarded under a company's incentive plan for what they do. In short, reinforcement theory suggests that individuals are more likely to repeat certain behaviors when they are rewarded for them than when they are not rewarded for them. As noted by Diane Allessi, director of training development at the American Bankers Association in Washington, DC, "By recognizing employees in front of their peers, it not only reinforces the behavior in the individuals, it telegraphs to everyone around them that this is the conduct you expect and value."[2]

A second theory regarding why incentives may prove to be motivating is **goal setting theory**. When employees are committed to specific, challenging, but attainable goals, the goals serve as an anchor to focus their efforts on as well as for the amount of effort needed.[3] By setting challenging goals rather than simple goals, employees are encouraged to push themselves to achieve their objectives. And when individuals have specific goals rather than vague goals, they have a clear sense of the objective they are trying to realize and are more likely to focus their efforts toward that goal than other irrelevant or less relevant activities.[4] Setting a target for employees to decrease error rates by 10%, for example, provides more guidance than telling them to work harder to help company performance. Finally, goals must be attainable to exert any influence on employee effort.[5] If employees perceive that there is no possibility of achieving a goal, they are not likely to work toward attaining it.

Another useful theory regarding the potential motivating impact of incentives is expectancy theory. According to **expectancy theory**,[6] employees make decisions regarding how to act at work based on which behaviors they believe will lead to their most valued work-related rewards and outcomes.[7] As shown in Exhibit 11.2, three factors influence how incentives influence employees' motivation on the job: expectancy, instrumentality, and

reinforcement theory
The theory that when people experience positive consequences after they do something, they are likely to repeat those actions.

goal setting theory
The theory that when employees are committed to specific, challenging, but attainable goals, the goals serve as an anchor to focus their efforts on as well as for the amount of effort needed.

expectancy theory
The theory that employees make decisions regarding how to act at work based on which behaviors they believe will lead to their most valued work-related rewards and outcomes.

Performance incentive: Employees who exceed their past year's sales targets by 20% will receive a 10% bonus at the end of the year		
Expectancy →	**Instrumentality** →	**Valence**
Whether employees believe that the performance goal can be achieved	Whether employees believe they will actually be rewarded if they meet the goal	The extent to which the reward (10% bonus) is valued by employees

◀ **Exhibit 11.2**
Example of Expectancy Theory

expectancy

The degree to which employees believe that, if they work toward a certain performance objective, they will be able to achieve that objective.

instrumentality

The degree to which employees believe that achieving a performance objective will be rewarded.

valence

The degree of value employees place on different rewards.

agency theory

The theory that managers can motivate their employees to act in certain ways by aligning their interests with the interests of the firm's other stakeholders.

valence. **Expectancy** refers to the degree to which employees believe that, if they work toward a certain performance objective, they will be able to achieve that objective.[8] If employees don't believe they are capable of achieving the objective, their motivation to work toward it will diminish. **Instrumentality** reflects whether employees believe that achieving an objective will be rewarded. Employees will be less motivated to achieve an objective when there is not a direct or consistent link between the achievement and being rewarded for it. **Valence** is the degree of value employees place on different rewards. Employees will be more motivated to achieve incentives they value than ones they don't. For example, some employees might be more motivated by the potential to earn a week-long vacation to Hawaii than an equivalent cash bonus. For other employees, the reverse will be true.

According to **agency theory**, managers can motivate their employees to act in certain ways by aligning their interests with the interests of the firm's other stakeholders—typically the company's owners. When one person (the principal, or owner) hires another person (an agent, or employee) to make decisions and work on his or her behalf, conflicts can occur. Agency problems may emerge if the two parties have different interests and goals. For example, a company's owner (principal) has an interest in maximizing the firm's profitability. In contrast, an employee (agent) has an interest in maximizing his or her own well-being, perhaps with "perks" such as higher pay and generous benefits. Of course, these benefits will reduce the firm's profitability. Creating incentives to align the interests of principals and agents can help firms overcome agency problems such as this. For example, if employees are rewarded with a significant share of a company's profits, they will be more likely to take steps to improve the firm's performance. In other words, when properly designed and implemented, incentive systems reward employees and managers for acting in the best interests of a company's owners.

TYPES OF INCENTIVE PLANS

Based on theories about how incentive plans work, companies have devised a wide variety of plans to encourage their employees to work toward certain goals. One of the major distinctions among the different types of incentive plans is the level of their focus. Some incentive plans encourage superior individual performance. Other plans encourage entire groups to achieve some goal or even focus on the performance of an entire company. A second distinction is whether incentives are used as an add-on to employees' base pay, or if they are used in place of some, or all, of an employee's base pay. We discuss these next.

Individual Incentive Plans

There are several common individual incentive plans that companies use: merit pay programs, lump-sum bonuses, piecework plans, standard hour plans, spot awards, and sales incentive plans.

merit pay increase

A compensation adjustment based on the results of an employee's performance evaluations.

MERIT PAY PROGRAMS Recall that we first discussed merit pay programs in Chapter 10. Merit pay programs reward employees for achieving certain levels of performance over a predetermined time in the past. The logic for this approach is straightforward: Employees who perform at higher levels should receive greater rewards.[9] With a typical **merit pay increase**, employees receive a compensation adjustment based on the results of their performance evaluations. The performance ratings they receive are then used to allocate merit pay increases to them. For example, employees with a low rating of 1 (on a 5-point rating scale) might receive a merit increase of 0% or 1%. As performance ratings increase, so too does the amount of merit increase allocated to the employees. The highest performers receive the greater percentage increases to their base pay. Someone receiving a score of 3 might be rewarded with a 3% to 4% increase while someone with a score of 5 might be rewarded with a 5% increase, or even more.

While merit pay increase plans are commonplace, they are not without problems. First, the increases are tied directly to employees' performance ratings, and this can be a problem if the ratings are not always accurate or reliable. And, as we discussed in Chapter 9, biases can creep into the evaluation process and threaten the accuracy of the ratings. When this occurs, employees will doubt the equity and fairness in their incentive systems. Second, because merit pay increases permanently raise the base salaries of employees, a company's labor costs can quickly escalate. Third, merit pay increases are backward focused: They reward employees for their past performance rather than provide them with an incentive to work toward future goals. Moreover, because the increases are rolled into their base pay, the actual impact on an employee's weekly paycheck might not seem significant to employees. For example, a $2,000 raise spread out over 52 paychecks amounts to just over $38 per week—before taxes are deducted. As a result, it may be difficult for employees to differentiate merit pay increases from cost-of-living adjustments. Finally, when merit increases occur year after year, employees may view the pay as an entitlement rather than as a motivator.[10] As a result of these drawbacks, many companies use other types of incentive plans.

A variation of the merit pay increase is the **lump-sum merit bonus**. Like traditional merit pay programs, lump-sum bonuses are often based on an employee's level of performance. The primary difference is that lump-sum bonuses are not rolled into employees' salaries—they are a one-time payment. This is an important difference. Compared to merit pay plans, bonuses generally cost companies less because the payouts don't increase their labor costs permanently.

lump-sum merit bonus
A one-time payment based on an employee's level of performance.

As Exhibit 11.3 shows, there are several important cost differences between merit pay increases and lump-sum bonuses that accumulate over time. The most notable difference is that merit pay is permanently rolled into the base pay, resulting in a higher level of base salary for an employee throughout his or her tenure with an organization—even if the employee earns the payment only once. Second, the amount of the employee's compensation increases each year, even if the person continues to perform at the same level. For example, suppose the employee receives a 5% merit raise in year 1, which amounts to $2,000. If this level of performance holds steady over time, in year 4, a 5% merit increase would translate into $2,315.25. In contrast, with a lump-sum bonus plan, the incentive payments are distributed separately from the base pay. Further, because the costs of the payments are not rolled into the base pay of employees, companies can keep their salary levels lower and, instead, allocate higher lump-sum payments only to employees who meet the goals that have been set for them.

PIECEWORK INCENTIVE PLANS   As we have suggested, merit pay increases and lump-sum bonuses reward employees based on their past performance efforts. In contrast,

		Merit Pay Increase	Lump-Sum Bonus
Year 1	Base salary	$40,000	$40,000
	Performance rating salary increment for year	5%	5%
	Payout at end of year 1	$2,000	$2,000
Year 2	New base salary	$42,000	$40,000
	Performance rating salary increment for year	5%	5%
	Payout at end of year 1	$2,100	$2,000
Year 3	New base salary	$44,100	$40,000
	Performance rating salary increment for year	5%	5%
	Payout at end of year 1	$2,205	$2,000
Year 4	New base salary	$46,305	$40,000
	Performance rating salary increment for year	5%	5%
	Payout at end of year 1	$2,315.25	$2,000
Year 5	New base salary	$48,620.25	$40,000

◄ **Exhibit 11.3**
Merit Pay Increases Versus Lump-Sum Bonus Payments

Individual incentive plans can be used for many jobs.

straight piecework plan

An individual incentive plan in which employees receive a certain rate of pay for each unit produced.

differential piecework plan

An individual incentive plan in which the level of pay employees receive per unit produced or delivered changes at certain levels of output.

piecework incentive plans are more forward looking because they reward employees for their future performance levels. Under a **straight piecework plan**, employees receive a certain rate of pay for each unit they produce. Calculating a straight piecework plan is very simple. For example, a salesperson might be compensated $1.00 for every call made to a potential customer. The more calls a salesperson makes, the more he or she earns. Under a **differential piecework plan**, the pay employees receive per unit produced or delivered changes at certain levels of output. Returning to the salesperson example, a company might implement a differential piecework plan in which employees who make more than 10 calls in one hour receive $1.10 for each of the calls compared to $1.00 per call for those failing to meet or exceed 10 calls.

A key advantage of piecework plans is that they focus employees' efforts directly on tasks that are valuable for company success. Piecework plans also very clearly tell employees what types of behaviors they need to exhibit. They know if they perform well, they will receive higher levels of compensation. The simplicity of these plans, and the ease of computing the anticipated compensation for different levels of productivity, makes them easy to communicate to employees.[11]

There are some potential problems associated with piecework systems. To be most effective, piecework plans depend on firms having clear, objective job outcomes on which to base their incentives. Unfortunately, not all jobs are so clear-cut. Many jobs require employees to perform a wide array of tasks that are difficult to measure. If, as a manager, you implement a piecework plan for this type of job, employees may focus their efforts on the parts of the job that are rewarded by the plan and ignore other important aspects of their jobs. As a result, piecework systems are generally most effective for jobs that are narrow in scope and involve the frequent performance of certain objective tasks. Manufacturing jobs, like those highlighted in Company Spotlight 11.1, are a good example. Second, piecework plans place a premium on volume. Without adequate controls, a firm might experience a high volume of products of diminished quality being produced. A third challenge is determining the firm's productivity standards that trigger the higher levels of incentive pay. The standards should be challenging for employees yet attainable. Finally, if the amount of work an employee can produce depends on the work of other employees or on the amount of equipment a firm has, for example, the person's output is less likely to be under his or her direct control. If this is the case, a piecework plan will be less motivating to the employee.

standard hour plan

An individual incentive plan in which employee's pay is based on how much time an employee is expected to need to complete some task.

STANDARD HOUR PLAN Standard hour plans focus employees' attention on how quickly they can perform their tasks. With standard hour plans, a pay rate is set based on how much time an employee is expected to need to complete some task. If employees are able to complete their tasks in less time than expected, they still receive the full rate of pay for the task performed.[12] For example, if the standard time to install a new computer and associated software is 2 hours, and a computer technician performs the job in 1.5 hours, he will receive his hourly rate for the full 2 hours. Likewise, if employees are able to complete

PRINCIPLES

COMPANY spotlight   11.1 Lincoln Electric

Lincoln Electric, a $1 billion maker of arc-welding equipment, is a model of efficiency and productivity within its industry. What has been the key to the Cleveland, Ohio-based company's success? If you ask anyone at Lincoln, they will likely point to the company's piecework incentive system, which has been in place since 1934. With this system, an employee can earn, on average, between $10,000 and $20,000 in annual bonus pay. When coupled with the company's policy of not laying off an employee after he or she has been with the company for three years, it is clear how Lincoln Electric has been able to build and retain such a talented workforce.

As company spokesperson Roy Morrow says, "If you have a labor force that's highly productive and skilled, you want to do what you can to keep them."

Sources: Lincoln Electric Web site, www.lincolnelectric.com; No layoff payoff. *Corporate Meetings & Incentives* 21:12, January 2002; and Eisenberg, D., Sieger, M., & Greenwald, J. Where people are never let go. *Time*, 157(24):48, June 18, 2001.

more tasks than they're expected to in a given time period, they will receive a premium for their higher level of work. For example, suppose a salesperson is paid $10.00 per hour and is expected to make 10 calls per hour. As Exhibit 11.4 shows, this translates into 6 minutes per call. Over the course of an 8-hour workday, she would be expected to make 80 calls. If it takes her only 45 minutes to make 10 calls, she would receive her $10 pay for the 45 minutes. Over the course of a day, if the salesperson actually makes 100 calls, she would be compensated for 10 hours worth of work during those 8 hours. According to the standard hour plan, she would receive the equivalent to $12.50 per hour for that day, rather than $10 per hour if she had simply met expectations. This translates into a 25% incentive premium for her performance.

The primary advantage of the standard hour plan is that it encourages employees to work as quickly as possible to complete their tasks. And if they are very efficient, they are able to perform more tasks than expected in a typical day, thereby increasing their take-home pay. Another benefit of standard hour plans is that, compared to piecework systems, they can be used to motivate employees doing more complex jobs—that is, those that involve different tasks or projects that are not necessarily standardized or simplified.[13] Automobile mechanic and attorney are examples that may work with a standard hour plan. At the same time, however, employees need some sort of motivation to pay attention to the quality of their work, not just their speed. It doesn't do any good for a company, or the customer, to have employees working very quickly but committing many mistakes. Some companies even require employees to correct their work on their own time if the quality of their work is low.

AWARDS   Spot awards are an incentive that companies use to encourage their employees to work toward specific outcomes. Managers give the awards (often cash) to employees "on the spot" when they exhibit certain behaviors or achieve certain outcomes associated with excellent performance. Spot awards give managers flexibility because they can be linked to a variety of employee actions at any time. Unlike merit raises and lump-sum bonuses, they don't depend on performance evaluations over the course of the review period. For example, a manager might give a cash award to the employee with the most

spot award

An incentive that companies use to encourage their employees to work toward specific outcomes.

	Standard Performance for Eight-Hour Day	High Performance for Eight-Hour Day
Base pay per hour	$10.00	$10.00
Performance level	80 calls	100 calls
Incentive premium	0%	25%
Final pay per hour	$10.00	$12.50
Final pay	$80.00	$100.00

◄ **Exhibit 11.4**

Sample Standard Hour Plan for a Salesperson

Commission plans are used extensively for sales employees.

straight commission plan

A plan that pays employees a percentage of the total sales they generate.

straight salary plan

A plan where employees receive a set compensation, regardless of their level of sales.

mixed salary/commission plan

A plan where employees receive a lower base salary, perhaps only 50% or 70% of what would be offered under a straight salary plan, with the remaining percentage commission-based.

sales, the employee who makes the fewest mistakes, or the employee with the highest customer satisfaction ratings. The strength of spot awards is that they can be tied directly to specific performance dimensions of employees' jobs and are paid only when desired performance levels are met. Given the flexibility of spot awards, it shouldn't be a surprise that near 80% of companies in a recent survey said they use short-term incentives to reward high-performing employees.[14]

Companies can use non-cash awards as incentives, too. Vacations, merchandise, gift certificates, and paid time off from work are examples of some of the types of awards employees might be offered for achieving certain levels of performance. At the restaurant chain Golden Corral, employees can win a trip for two to anywhere in the world for achieving outstanding performance.[15] At BP Retail, a leading fuel retailer in the United Kingdom, store managers are permitted to reward their employees with retail vouchers.[16] Recognition programs, such as employee-of-the-month programs, are another type of reward firms use to motive their employees. A survey conducted by Forum for People Performance Management and Measurement at Northwestern University indicated that 66% of companies use gift certificates or gift cards and 57% use merchandise incentives.[17] Even though programs such as these often aren't associated with monetary rewards, they can still be powerful motivators.[18]

SALES INCENTIVE PLANS   Salespeople have an obvious impact on the performance of their firms. The more sales these employees generate, the more business their companies enjoy. As a result, companies benefit from providing extensive sales-based incentives to these employees. There are three primary types of sales incentive plans. The first type is a commission-based sales plan. A **straight commission plan** pays employees a percentage of the total sales they generate. For example, an employee working on a 1% straight commission plan who generates $1 million in sales would receive $10,000. If the person generated $10,000,000 in sales, he would receive $100,000 in compensation.

The primary benefit of this type of system is that high-performing employees receive high payouts, and companies pay employees only for what they sell. However, employees working under these plans face a considerable amount of financial risk in terms of what they potentially earn: If a person sells nothing or very little, he or she receives little or no compensation under these plans. Another problem is that employees operating under commission-based pay systems can become so obsessed about their sales levels that they are hesitant to help their co-workers unless they are able to get a part of their commissions. This may be particularly problematic when sales environments depend on collaboration and teamwork among employees. Given these concerns, some companies, including the electronics retailers Best Buy and Circuit City, have replaced their commission-based pay systems with systems that are more team oriented.[19]

Some companies, including HomeBanc corporation, rely on **straight salary plans** for their salespeople[20]: Employees receive a set compensation, regardless of their level of sales. As you can imagine, employees working under these plans might not be as motivated to sell as much as they can. However, the systems do provide employees with much greater personal income security. And because these plans remove the strong incentive to focus only on sales, employees might be more willing to spend time providing quality service to customers or working with existing customers. For example, in the financial services industry, there have been concerns about the practice of *churning*—investment brokers inflating their own commissions by increasing the number of transactions they make on a client's account, even if the transactions are not in the client's best financial interests.

In an attempt to capitalize on the benefits of both commission and salary incentive plans, some companies use a **mixed salary/commission plan**. In these systems, employees receive a lower base salary—perhaps only 50% or 70% of what would be offered under a straight salary plan. The remaining percentage is commission based. For example, if an employee would normally make $50,000 under a straight salary plan, under a 70/30 plan (70% salary, 30% commission), she would earn a base salary of $35,000, and the rest of her compensation would be based on 30% of her former commission plan (1% of sales). If she sells $5 million, she would earn $35,000 in salary plus 30% of $50,000 (1% of $5 million), or $15,000, resulting in a total salary of $50,000. If she sold $10 million, she would earn $35,000 in salary plus $30,000 in commission.

Group/Organizational Incentives

Rather than focus solely on individual incentive plans, companies can also implement group or organizational incentive plans. Group incentive plans are intended to get employees to work as a collective unit. The group might consist of a couple of individuals, an entire department, or an entire company.

TEAM INCENTIVE PLANS   When a company relies on teams, it is important to foster a collective sense of identity and cooperation among the team members. One method of doing so is to provide team-based incentives. In fact, piecework plans, standard hour plans, bonuses, awards, and merit pay can all be applied to entire teams as well as individuals. If a team reaches or exceeds its target objective, all its members are rewarded equally, and if the team fails to meet its goals, none of the members receive the incentive.

Team incentives make most sense when employees perform tasks that are highly interdependent on one another and when cooperation and collaboration are required for the team to be successful. The primary downside of team incentives, as with other group incentive plans, is the potential for free riders. **Free riders** are individuals who do not work as hard as the others on their teams. In other words, they are getting a free ride from the work their teammates are doing. When this occurs, the hardworking members are likely to feel they are getting a bad deal, and the team will tend to become dysfunctional. One solution to this problem is to have team members evaluate the contributions of each other through a peer appraisal or a 360-degree performance evaluation. Another option we will discuss later in the chapter is to rely on a mixed-level system that rewards individual effort as well as team effort.

free rider

An individual who does not work as hard as the others on their teams.

GAIN SHARING PLANS   **Gain sharing plans** are designed to help increase an organization's efficiency by increasing the productivity of the company's employees and/or lowering the firm's labor costs. Under these plans, employees earn a share of the gains of their productivity with the company. The gains may be realized in one of two ways. First, if the firm's collective productivity improves and the employees exceed some predetermined productivity level, they receive part of the monetary value of the increased productivity. Second, if employees are able to maintain the same level of productivity but do so with fewer costs, they share the gains of their increased efficiency. Two common plans that are used to realize these gains are Scanlon plans and Improshare plans.

gain sharing plan

A plan designed to help increase an organization's efficiency by increasing the productivity of the company's employees and/or lowering the firm's labor costs.

A **Scanlon plan** can help reduce a firm's labor costs without corresponding decreases in productivity levels. Under a Scanlon plan, employees make suggestions for how to improve a firm's productivity and offer those suggestions to a review committee for its consideration for implementation. If the review committee accepts the plan and its implementation results in increased efficiency, the gains of that efficiency are shared with employees. The incentive is based on improving the relative level, or ratio, of the firm's labor costs to the sales value of the products it produces. For example, a firm might have a target ratio of .1. In this case, if the company expected to do $1 million in sales, it would strive to keep its labor costs to $100,000. If employees are able to achieve the same sales value of production with a ratio that's lower than .1, they share the gains of that increased efficiency with their company. For example, if the firm's workforce were able to realize $1,000,000 in sales with only $90,000 in labor costs, the $10,000 in savings would be split among the employees and their firm. By providing employees with a portion of any savings they help realize through participation and suggestions, companies are directly rewarding employees for taking steps to increase their productivity levels and working harder toward their companies' goals.[21]

Scanlon plan

A group based incentive plan used to help reduce a firm's labor costs without corresponding decreases in productivity levels based on employee suggestions for increased efficiencies and productivity.

A somewhat different approach to gain sharing is the **Improshare plan**. Improshare plans are based on the number of hours a firm expects to take to reach a certain level of output. In essence, it is not based strictly on cost savings but on time savings per unit of production. To implement this type of plan, companies must first establish the expected hours per unit of productivity for a group of employees. If the employees are able to achieve a set level of productivity in fewer hours than expected, they receive an equal share of the hours saved in the form of pay.[22] Similar to the standard hour plan at the individual level, the primary impact of an Improshare plan is that it encourages employees as a group to produce a greater quantity of output.

Improshare plan

A group based incentive plan based on the number of hours a firm expects to take to reach a certain level of output.

The primary advantages of gain sharing plans are that they help foster a participative environment in which employees are able to help improve productivity and are rewarded for making useful suggestions. Because these plans operate at a group or plant level, all employees within the unit are encouraged to help one another succeed.[23] An additional advantage of gain sharing plans is their instrumentality—that is, there a clear link between the effort employees expend and the rewards they receive.[24] As with team incentive plans, however, one potential problem is the existence of free riders in a group. An additional potential problem is that the plans may be too complex for employees to understand,[25] or they may be viewed as unattainable, particularly in situations in which employees already operate at very high levels of efficiency.

PROFIT SHARING PLANS   Under **profit sharing plans**, company profits are shared with employees. Procedurally, profit sharing can be distributed to employees as cash or can be deferred. Under a **deferred profit sharing plan**, the incentive money paid an employee is put into a retirement account for the person. The plan has a tax advantage because the income the employee earns is deferred until he or she retires. And after people retire, their earnings are generally lower, so the income withdrawn from the retirement account is taxed at a lower rate.

There are several other advantages of profit sharing plans. First, profits are obviously an important component of a company's success. Thus, implementing these plans helps keep employees focused on activities that are truly important. Moreover, by focusing everyone's efforts on the performance of the entire company rather than solely on their own performance, profit sharing encourages collaboration and teamwork among employees. A final benefit of profit sharing is that employees are paid only when a company is doing well, a mechanism that helps maintain control over labor costs.

In some instances, however, employees may be doing exceptionally well in their jobs and helping their co-workers excel, but their company's overall performance goal may not be being realized. The point here is that the profitability of a company is influenced by a multitude of factors, many of which are outside the control of employees. Competition, changes in consumer preferences, industry trends, and the like affect a company's profitability. With profit sharing plans, it is conceivable that employees might not be rewarded by their incentive plans even though they have done everything they can to help their company succeed. A second potential problem with profit sharing plans is that employees might not see the fruits of their labor for a long time. It may take a while for the efforts of employees to translate into company profits. If this occurs, the gap between when performance occurs and when the reward is realized might be significant, thereby diminishing the motivating impact of these plans.

OWNERSHIP PLANS   Whereas profit sharing plans tie employee incentives to the profitability of a firm, ownership plans tie employees' incentives to the performance of a company's stock in the marketplace. Companies use two primary types of ownership plans: stock option plans and employee stock ownership plans.

Stock option plans provide employees with the right to purchase shares of their company's stock at some established price (often its market value) for a given period of time. During that period of time, employees can exercise this right, and they can subsequently sell their shares. For example, an employee might be provided with a stock option plan to buy shares at $10 per share for 5 years. If the stock price rises above this to $30 per share, and the employee exercises her rights to purchase and sell the shares during the 5-year period, she would realize a gain of $20 per share. **Broad-based stock option** plans are plans that apply widely to a firm's employees. More than 50% of a firm's non-executive employees are included in broad-based plans.[26]

Under an **employee stock ownership plan (ESOP)**, a company contribute shares of its stock to a trust set up for its employees. In a **leveraged ESOP**, the trust borrows against the company's future earnings, and as the debt is repaid, employees receive shares of the stock held by the ESOP in employee accounts.[27] During the course of their employment, workers are updated as to the value of their stock accounts. When they retire or leave the company, they can then sell their stock to the company or on the open market. One of the major benefits of ESOPs is that employees are not taxed on the accumulated stocks until they receive

---

PRINCIPLES

profit sharing plan

A group based incentive plan where company profits are shared with employees.

deferred profit sharing plan

A group based incentive plan where the incentive money paid an employee is put into a retirement account for the person.

stock option plan

A group based incentive plan that provides employees with the right to purchase shares of their company's stock at some established price (often its market value) for a given period of time.

broad-based stock option

A stock purchase plan that applies widely to a firm's employees.

employee stock ownership plan (ESOP)

A group based incentive plan where the company contribute shares of its stock to a trust set up for its employees.

leveraged ESOP

A group based incentive plan that allows a trust to borrow funds against the company's future earnings, and as the debt is repaid, employees receive shares of the stock held by the ESOP in employee accounts.

their distribution upon separation from the company. Similarly, the company also receives a tax deduction of the value of the stock transferred to the trust.[28] Remember when we discussed agency theory earlier in the chapter? If employees continue to accumulate considerable shares of company stock, they may adopt more of the perspective of the firm's owners in terms of how they do their jobs. Ownership plans can therefore increase how committed employees are to the success of their companies.[29] Indeed, research suggests that ESOPs are associated with higher productivity and higher survival rates in companies.[30]

One of the primary benefits of ownership plans is that they may serve to align the long-term interests of employees with those of the company. Because they do this, employees may be more inclined to exert the necessary effort in their jobs to maximize their value-added contributions. In addition, ownership plans do not require employees to use their own savings to participate. At the same time, however, there is still risk for employees: If employees rely on ESOPs as the main source of income for their retirement, their investment portfolios won't be well diversified. So, for example, if the company's stock does not perform well, its employees might end up holding worthless stock. This is exactly what happened to Enron's employees. Employees who were once worth millions on paper by virtue of what was in their ESOPs were suddenly worth nothing after Enron's demise.[31] And, as is the case with other group-oriented plans, the risk of free riders is a problem. An additional potential problem with ownership plans is that employees might not feel that they can really make a difference or that the ultimate measure—the stock price of their firms—is within their control.

Mixed-Level Plans

Under a **mixed-level plan**, employees are exposed to multiple incentives. For example, at the restaurant chain Bubba Gump, one-quarter of a manager's bonus is based on the person's individual goals, and the remaining portion is based on his or her store's performance.[32] The logic for using multiple incentive plans at different levels is that doing so can maximize the benefits of each plan while discouraging the downsides of each. Rewarding employees for their individual performance, as well as the performance of their teams or companies, encourages them to maximize their own performance but not in a competitive manner or to the detriment of their co-workers. Employees who don't work well with their co-workers diminish their chances of realizing one of their incentives.

mixed-level plan

An incentive plan where employees are exposed to multiple incentive plans.

Executive Compensation: Pay and Incentives

No aspect of compensation has been as controversial or received as much attention in recent years as executive compensation. It is almost impossible to pick up a newspaper or business magazine without seeing an article about problems with executive compensation or about unethical practices executives have participated in to enhance their own personal wealth. As shown in Exhibit 11.5, relative to average workers, average CEO pay has skyrocketed. In 1980, CEOs earned 42 times the average worker. In 1990 that figure was 107, and in 2006 it was 364—which means that for every $1 an average worker earns, the CEO is paid $364.[33]

Greater attention from shareholders and new and proposed legislation have led companies to reconsider how they provide executive compensation. Generally, a larger proportion of the pay mix for executives is being tied to the performance of their firms. In fact, a 2006 survey of 350 firms by the *Wall Street Journal* and Mercer Human Resource Consulting found that over 84% of CEOs' compensation was at risk or dependent upon their firms meeting either their short- or long-term goals.[34]

Executive compensation includes the same components as other compensation packages—base salary, short- and long-term incentives, and benefits and services. Short-term incentives often include rewards based on financial measures of company performance. Long-term incentives such as stock options are used to encourage executives to try to improve their company's performance for a long period of time. This is done by aligning their pay with the long-term success of the company. Executive compensation differs in the magnitude and mix of these components as well as the perquisites not offered to other employees. The perquisites can include the use of a company plane, a car and driver, country club memberships, and even a bodyguard.

Exhibit 11.5 ▶

Average CEO: Worker
Pay Ratio, 1990–2006

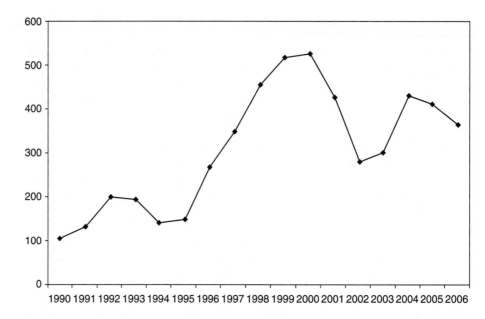

Source: United for a Fair Economy. *CEO pay charts, 1990–2006.* www.faireconomy.org/news/
ceo_pay_charts.

A CEO's pay is typically established by a compensation committee made up of members of the firm's board of directors, who are often high-ranking executives from other companies. A major concern about the use of compensation committees to establish executive pay is the extent to which they can be unbiased. The members of the committee understand very well how the labor market works in terms of wages. As CEOs or vice presidents themselves, they know that market pay rates can be influenced by one company paying higher wages. Thus, these people have an incentive to provide greater rewards to the CEO of the company on whose boards they sit. In other words, what goes around, comes around; they know the higher wages they award will eventually pay off for themselves.

It is worth mentioning that a number of CEOs are very aware of the controversial nature of their pay relative to their workers and have made adjustments in their pay in response. In fact, a number of high-profile CEOs have sacrificed their salaries in favor of performance-based pay. Steve Jobs of Apple, Eric Schmidt of Google, James Rogers of Duke Energy, Richard Fairbank of Capital One Financial, Terry Semel of Yahoo, and John Mackey of Whole Food Market have all agreed to $1 per year in base salary.[35] This is not to suggest that these executives don't reap the benefits of their efforts. Rather, they are tying their own financial gains to those of their companies. If their companies make money, they make money.

WHAT MAKES AN INCENTIVE PLAN EFFECTIVE?

As a manager, you have a wide array of incentive plans to choose from. To be effective, however, the plans need to meet several criteria:

- **Link to your firm's strategic objectives.** First, you have to know what exactly you are trying to accomplish with your incentive plan. Piecework systems, for example, are quite effective in settings that place priority on volume and efficient employee productivity. Commission plans help encourage employees to maximize their sales. Gain sharing plans encourage groups of employees to think about ways to improve the efficiency of their firms.
- **Have clear standards.** Effective incentive plans have clear standards of performance that employees strive to reach. One of the reasons piecework systems, sales incentives, and standard hour plans are effective is that they offer a clear link between pay and achieving some predetermined level of performance. Says Judy Irwin, vice president of

human resources and training at the Golden Corral Corporation, "If you don't give people the right things to focus on, they can't do well."[36]

- **Sample the full performance domain.** Effective incentive plans must give employees an incentive to excel in all aspects of their jobs. Managers must be careful not to focus solely on one performance aspects while neglecting others.
- **Be attainable.** The standards by which incentives are triggered must not only be clear, they must also be attainable. Recall goal setting theory and expectancy theory. If employees work hard and consistently fail to attain the incentives they hope to receive, the power of the incentive plan designed to motivate them will diminish.
- **Be easy to understand.** Incentive plans must be easy to understand. If employees don't know how to realize the incentives offered under a plan, the plan's motivational power will be weak.
- **Provide meaningful incentives.** Incentive must be meaningful to employees. The more employees desire an incentive, the harder they will work to attain it.
- **Be evaluated regularly.** A final criterion for effective incentive plans is that they must be regularly evaluated to ensure that they are actually motivating people to work toward the appropriate individual, team, and company goals.

INCENTIVES AND REWARDS IN PRACTICE: ORGANIZATIONAL DEMANDS

As shown in Exhibit 11.6, the rewards and incentives plans used by companies are likely to vary as they cope with different organizational demands, environmental influences, and regulatory issues. We start with how organizational demands—strategy, company characteristics, company culture, and employee concerns—affect how incentive plans are designed and implemented as well as how effective they are.

▶ **Exhibit 11.6** Rewards and Incentives in Practice

Context	*Employee Attitudes & Behaviors* Chapter 11, "Incentives and Rewards"
Organization Demands	
Strategy drives . . .	• What is rewarded • Which incentive plans are used
Company characteristics determine . . .	• Feasibility of different incentive plans • Impact of incentives on employees
Culture establishes . . .	• Incentive plans managers choose • Employees' acceptance of incentive plans
Employee concerns include . . .	• Fairness of incentive plan standards • Likelihood of receiving incentives • Acceptability of incentive payouts
Environmental Demands	
Labor force influences . . .	• Using incentives to increase diversity • Desirability of different rewards
Technology affects . . .	• How incentives are managed • Incentive plans for a virtual workforce
Globalization impacts . . .	• What is rewarded • Acceptability of incentives
Ethics/social responsibility shapes . . .	• Ethical employee behavior • How employees and communities view executive incentive plans
Regulations *guide* . . .	• Bias and discrimination • Stock option backdating

Strategy and Incentives

Strategy influences incentives in several important ways. First, the strategic goals and direction of a company affect the types and levels of employee performance the company targets and the incentives it uses. Second, strategy influences which incentive plans are used for different groups of employees within companies.

WHAT IS REWARDED   In our discussion of job design in Chapter 4 and performance management in Chapter 9 we noted that each job comprises multiple tasks and responsibilities. However, not all job duties are equally important for different strategic objectives. The strategic focus of a company should influence which tasks or behaviors are targeted with incentives.[37] A company with low costs as its strategic focus would likely reward different employee behaviors and outcomes than a company focusing on strategies such as customer service, innovation, or quality. In companies with a cost focus, managers are more likely to target employee behaviors that directly contribute to the efficiency of the companies' operations. In contrast, a company pursuing a customer service strategy will be more concerned with encouraging attitudes and behaviors that lead to increased customer satisfaction, retention, and repeat business. A key task for managers is to consider their company's strategy when deciding which performance aspects to target. Ideally, they should be the ones that maximize the amount of value added to a company. And, as we have indicated, you need to consider the full array of tasks that your employees perform. If you implement an incentive plan that is one dimensional and focuses on only a limited subset of tasks and behaviors, your employees may focus only on those tasks directly rewarded and neglect performance of other important responsibilities.[38]

WHICH INCENTIVE PLANS ARE USED   The strategy of a company is related to the incentive plans used to motivate employees. If a company competes on a strategy that requires cooperation and teamwork among employees, group- or company-wide plans might be more appropriate than individual incentive plans. Of course, individual incentive plans can be quite effective when other strategies are used. If customer service is the objective, a merit-based incentive may be more appropriate than, say, a standard hour plan or a piecework system that rewards employees for how fast they complete their tasks rather than how satisfied they leave the firm's customers. Alternatively, in a company with a cost-focused strategy, incentive plans such as standard hour plans or gain sharing plans may effectively encourage employees to reach and sustain certain productivity and efficiency levels.

To be effective however, an incentive plan must be tailored in terms of how different employees add value to the organization. For example, production employees may add value through efficiency, sales employees may add value through generating sales, and R&D employees may add value through the creation of new products. Each of these employees therefore needs to be provided with a distinct incentive plan that reflects how he or she contributes to the organization's strategic objectives. This means that within a single firm, managers might have to design multiple incentive plans to motivate different employees to maximize their efforts in specific ways. Trying to use a single incentive plan for all employees may not reflect differences in the nature of their contributions.

Company Characteristics and Incentives

A company's stage of development and its size have a bearing on which incentive plans are feasible to use. A company's characteristics also affect the impact its incentive plans will have on its employees.

FEASIBILITY OF DIFFERENT INCENTIVE PLANS   In our previous discussion, we highlighted how the strategy of a company influences which incentive plans managers choose to use to motivate their employees. These choices are also influenced by a company's characteristics. Not all companies are in a position to use all the incentive plans. For example, a small startup company might not have enough financial slack to provide high levels of merit pay to its employees. Rather, the firm might be more inclined to use incentives that are paid only if the firm's employees improve the company's financial performance. In these cases, profit sharing plans, lump-sum bonuses, awards, or piecework

11.2 Increasing Productivity and Reducing Turnover at FirstMerit Bank

Faced with high turnover among staff, FirstMerit Bank turned to a new incentive program to motivate its check-proofing operators. At FirstMerit Bank, proof operators perform the critical task of keying in the amount of money to be moved between bank accounts. In an effort to reward employees for excellent performance and keep employees happy and motivated, FirstMerit implemented a two-part incentive system. In this plan, proof operators are rewarded for speed and accuracy of their keystrokes. The outcome? High-performing employees were able to significantly raise their take-home pay. And with employees more satisfied with the rewards for their efforts, turnover is down dramatically. In fact, the higher productivity has allowed FirstMerit to reduce the number of proof operators needed to cover the workload. The result is a more efficient and motivated group of employees.

Sources: FirstMerit Bank Web site, www.firstmerit.com; and Dalton, A. Pay-for-performance plan helps shrink bank's turnover. *Workforce Management* online, http://www.workforce.com/archive/article/24/02/86.php.

plans—which are paid out only if the company benefits from the increased performance—may be more feasible than guaranteed salary increases.

IMPACT OF INCENTIVES ON EMPLOYEES   The size of a company can affect how well its incentive plan motivates its employees. Consider the impact of a profit sharing plan in a company with 20 employees versus a company with 20,000 employees. In the smaller company, employees are more likely to have a clear line of sight regarding how their individual performance affects the performance of the entire company.[39] This is likely to increase their instrumentality; they believe there is a stronger link between their efforts and the profitability of the company. When an employee is only one of thousands of employees, however, the direct link between his or her efforts and their company's overall profitability is likely to be, or at least perceived to be, much weaker. These employees might believe that their performance simply does not make that much difference. As a result, the motivating impact of the incentive plan might be weaker than if the plan were used in a smaller company.

Culture and Incentives

A company's culture affects the use of incentives in several ways. First, it influences the likelihood that managers will use the different incentive plans. Second, the shared perceptions among employees regarding the firm's cultural values influence their acceptance of incentive plans.

INCENTIVE PLANS MANAGERS CHOOSE   A manager is likely to be most comfortable implementing an incentive plan that is consistent with the values of his or her company. In a company with a culture that encourages employees to work together to meet their departmental or unit goals, managers are likely to be more comfortable with a team-based incentive plan than with individual incentive plans. In contrast, in a high-performance culture that strongly values the accomplishments of individual employees, managers might be more comfortable with individual incentive plans. Different incentive plans send different signals to employees about what they should do at work, as well as how they should do it. The choice of which incentive plan you implement must reflect the cultural values of your company. Company Spotlight 11.3 highlights the impact of misalignment and alignment between incentives and culture at R.F. Moeller Jewelers.

EMPLOYEES' ACCEPTANCE OF INCENTIVE PLANS   The culture of a company influences how employees perceive the appropriateness of the incentive plans it adopts. Any discrepancy between the design of a firm's incentive plan and a company's cultural values will result in a negative reaction from the employees. If inconsistencies exist between the plan and the culture, the result may be decreased, rather than increased, motivation to work toward your company's goals. Consider the options available for incentive plans for

COMPANY spotlight   11.3   When Everyone Quits

When Mark Moeller took over the family jewelry business from his father, he decided to change the incentive system to encourage the salespeople to increase their productivity. Mark wanted to implement a mixed salary/commission plan to replace the straight salary plan under which the employees had been working. Shortly after he implemented the new system, however, all the non-family employees quit. The employees thought the personal risks with the pay-for-performance plan were too great (the plan reduced their base salary and provided them with 20% of the gross profit on the jewelry they sold). Over time, however, Moeller hired new employees who were not scared away by the sales-driven incentive plan. And once the right people were in place, sales took off. In fact, after a few years, the sales associates were put on straight commission to reward their outstanding efforts.

Source: Spector, B. When everyone quits. *JCK* 172(6):258–264, June 2001.

salespeople. As a manager, you can choose from a straight commission, a straight salary, or a mixed salary/commission plan. Which one should you choose?

One factor to consider is the underlying culture of your organization. If your company's culture is an individual performance-oriented culture, a straight commission system might be most appropriate. If your firm is more paternalistic and values taking care of employees, a salary or salary/commission mixed plan that provides employees with greater financial security is likely to be more consistent with your culture. Recall the sales force reaction in Company Spotlight 11.3: The incentive plan was ineffective under the existing culture and worked only when all the non-family employees were replaced with employees open to a more performance-oriented culture.

A similar concern relates to how employees feel about the amount of compensation they have at risk—that is, the amount of their compensation that is based on incentive pay. With standard hour plans and piecework systems, for example, the financial security of employees is tied directly to their productivity. Employees do not earn incentives unless they hit certain performance targets. In contrast, plans such as merit-based pay and gain sharing do not carry this risk. The rewards are added to the employees' regular paychecks. The extent to which employees are willing to embrace these risks may be influenced by the cultural values of the company. For example, a company with a paternalistic history might face more resistance from its employees for shifting to an incentive-based pay plan than a company with a more performance-oriented culture might face.

Employee Concerns and Incentives

In Chapter 10 we discussed the importance of employee concerns of fairness in a compensation system. Employees want to make sure that the level of their pay and the process for determining pay levels are fair. This includes their incentive pay, too. Specifically, employees can be concerned about the procedural justice related to their firms' incentive plans, the likelihood of their receiving the awards associated with the plans, and the actual incentive levels they receive.

FAIRNESS OF INCENTIVE PLAN STANDARDS   One design issue that influences employee perceptions of fairness relates to the standards that are set as part of their firms' incentive plans. Managers might develop very high standards for achieving particular incentives, bonuses, or awards such that very few people achieve them. Alternatively, performance standards may be set at a lower level that is easily attainable by many employees in a company. Consider a piecework system in which the average employee produces 20 units per hour. How would employees react if the standard for the higher incentive premium per unit were raised to 40 units per hour? If employees don't believe they can realistically produce 40 units per hour or more, they will view the plan as unfair.

A similar problem can exist with other incentive plans. The time standard in standard hour plans might be too short, for example, to allow employees to actually receive the incentive bonus. Likewise, individual or team incentives might be tied to goals that are unrealistic. Scott Testa, CEO of Mindbridge Software, learned the importance of employee concerns and incentive system plans when he implemented a new incentive program for his sales force. Employees were rewarded with long weekend trips to any destination, as long as the trips didn't cost more than $3,000. The problem was that the performance standard was unattainable. Salespeople who generated $200,000 per month in revenues had to bring in more than $500,000 per month in revenues for an entire year simply to qualify for the trips.[40] The idea for sales incentives and rewards has potential, but it must be attainable to have the desired impact on employees.

LIKELIHOOD OF RECEIVING INCENTIVES   Employees are concerned about the instrumentality of a plan. As explained earlier, instrumentality refers to the perceived link between one's performance and receiving the reward or incentive payment promised. When this perception is compromised, employees will question the procedural justice of their incentive plans. For example, profit sharing plans and ownership plans are influenced by factors beyond the control of the employee. Employees operating under a profit sharing plan might be legitimately concerned that even if they work as hard as possible and meet or exceed their individual goals, they might not necessarily be rewarded.[41]

ACCEPTABILITY OF INCENTIVE PAYOUTS   Beyond concerns about the process of how incentive plans operate, employees can also have concerns about the actual incentive payouts they receive. These distributive justice concerns can surface when either individual or team incentive plans are used.

When it comes to individual incentive plans, employees can be concerned about the amount of differentiation between high and low performers. Consider a merit pay program in which a high performer receives a 7% raise, and an average performer receives a 3% or 4% raise. While this might sound like a big difference, when spread out over the course of a year, the actual dollar amount between these raises might not be that great. Thus, the high performers might not feel like their outstanding efforts are reflected in their incentive pay.[42]

A closely related concern has to do with incentive pay being rolled into employees' base pay over time. Lower-performing employees who earn modest annual merit raises can earn more than high-performing employees who have less tenure. Of course, over time, the differences will lessen as the high performers acquire more tenure and merit pay. However, in the short term, the high performers might believe their base pay is insufficient in light of their outstanding performance.

Finally, distributive fairness concerns can also arise with regard to team- and group-level incentive plans. As noted earlier in this chapter, free riders are individuals in a work group who rely on their teammates to put in more effort for the team to achieve success. As a result, they achieve team success for free. In addition to free riders, social loafing can be a problem with group-based incentive plans.[43] **Social loafing** refers to situations in which the motivation of individuals to exert effort diminishes when their outputs are combined with those of others.[44] One reason for this particular phenomenon is that their individual efforts are less likely to be noticed in a team setting compared to when they perform alone. As a result, they don't feel their efforts will be rewarded, and this compromises their motivation to work hard. To overcome problems with social loafing, managers might turn to incentives that are able to reward both individual and team success. If controls are not in place to deal with nonproductive team members or free riders, high performers might ultimately look to move on to other teams or another company.

social loafing

A situation in which the motivation of individuals to exert effort diminishes when their outputs are combined with those of others.

INCENTIVES AND REWARDS IN PRACTICE: ENVIRONMENTAL INFLUENCES

The external environment affects incentive systems within companies. In particular, labor force trends, technology, globalization, and ethical considerations affect the decisions managers make when deciding which incentive plans to use.

Labor Force Trends and Incentive Plans

Labor force trends in the environment affect the use of incentives in companies in several ways. First, managers need to think about how to reward employees in ways that support and embrace diverse workforces. Second, diversity can affect the types of incentive rewards different employee groups desire.

USING INCENTIVES TO INCREASE DIVERSITY Throughout this book, we have discussed how different tools can be used to help employees and managers embrace diversity initiatives within companies. Recruitment and selection activities may help target underrepresented employee groups, and training programs may help employees appreciate and embrace co-workers with diverse backgrounds. Moreover, managers may be evaluated on how many women and minorities they have under their supervision.

If companies are truly serious about diversity, they need to reward their managers for embracing diversity efforts.[45] For example, companies can provide spot awards to managers who are able to recruit and retain employees from diverse backgrounds. Similarly, companies can include diversity measures as part of a manager's merit pay program and provide bonuses to managers who are outstanding mentors and coaches to diverse employees. A portion of a manager's incentive pay may be based on input from peers and subordinates regarding how well they work with and develop members of diverse backgrounds. At Georgia Power and Southern Company, for example, executives' incentives are linked to a diversity goal to increase the number of minorities and women in leadership positions.[46] Similarly, Lehman Brothers implemented an incentive pool for employees tied to efforts to reach out to women and minorities.[47]

DESIRABILITY OF DIFFERENT REWARDS As we have explained, the relative desirability of various incentive plans can vary. Moreover, it is likely to change as the composition of the workforce changes. For example, rather than merit bonuses, some employees might prefer time off via additional vacation, shorter workdays, and so forth. The types of rewards offered may prove more or less valuable, depending on the age of the workforce. Younger employees may be more open to a greater emphasis on stock option programs that are associated with greater risk compared to older individuals who are closer to retirement.[48] Also, with a growing presence of women in the workforce, as well as a greater presence of dual-career families, some individuals may be more motivated by nonfinancial incentives such as time off from work or flexible scheduling compared to straight cash-based rewards. Similarly, the values of Generation X and Y are different from those of older employees, and these differences influence what rewards and incentives they value. A recent study by Sloan Work and Family research network of Boston College indicated that Generation X workers place greater priority on personal and family goals than on career goals. For these employees, rewards that provide flexibility to address work/life balance may be more motivating than more traditional cash bonuses.[49] Jenny Floren, CEO and founder of Experience, a leading provider of career services for college students and alumni, suggests that learning and growth are more important than simply money for Generation Y employees. As Floren noted, "The focus for these individuals is less about the compensation and more about the advancement, the improved capabilities and the recognition of achievement marked by a new position. Offering Generation Y employees a raise while keeping all other factors the same will not have the same impact as giving them new challenges."[50]

Technology and Incentives

In addition to labor force trends, technological advances affect incentives in organizations. One impact of technology is how incentives are managed. A second influence relates to incentives for virtual employees.

HOW INCENTIVES ARE MANAGED Technology influences the management of incentive systems. The most notable implication of technology on the incentive process is the use of online incentive plans. With online incentives, much of the administration of the plans is coordinated electronically. Online incentive plans are a great tool for managers because they serve a number of useful purposes. First, online incentive plans are ideal for standard recognition programs related to service awards or the completion of projects. When managers are in charge of a large number of employees, it might be difficult to remember each employee's anniversary or when each project is completed. Online incentive plans can be designed to send managers e-mail notices for service awards and track the progress of employees as they reach their incentive targets.

A second benefit of online incentives is the speed of recognition for employee accomplishments. Too often, incentive rewards are acknowledged at the end of the year or the end of the quarter. One of the major benefits of online incentive plans is that they help managers provide rewards when they are most powerful—right when they are earned. Says Shelly Potter of the Global Communications and Benefits division of the technology firm Nortel, "By providing recognition at the time an employee completes a project, instead of waiting for weeks or months for an annual award, we're able to reinforce the reward's effect."[51] As noted earlier, in our discussion of reinforcement theory, quicker recognition is one of the key principles of encouraging employees to display desired behaviors.

Technology can also reduce the cost of administering incentives. Fewer people have to be involved in the oversight of the program because the technology takes care of many of the details. And with fewer staff needed to oversee the incentive plans, firms potentially have more money to put toward their incentive programs.[52]

Finally, online incentive plans allow companies to reward their employees with the types of rewards they want. Companies can choose the types of awards they offer their employees and allow employees to use online tools to select those they most value. For example, Hewlett-Packard (HP) uses its eAwards program to help reach its 150,000 employees across 178 countries. Using the system, supervisors around the globe can nominate and award employees for their outstanding work. The rewards can include cash, HP products, merchandise, and so forth.[53] By allowing employees input into the types of rewards they want, online incentive systems may help increase the valence of the rewards, thereby increasing the motivational power of the incentive plan. Of course, employees must have access to online incentive systems in order for them to be most useful. Although arranging computer access for all your employees might involve some initial startup costs, the costs may be offset by the lower overall costs of administration and other benefits.

INCENTIVE PLANS FOR A VIRTUAL WORKFORCE   Technology has influenced which incentive plans are used for virtual employees. Because of the difficulty tracking how employees perform their jobs when working offsite, many companies rely on outcome-oriented incentive plans. However, this is most appropriate when employees have clearly identifiable tasks or projects, and the completion of these tasks or projects is clear. The plans can also be team based for virtual teams. Piecework approaches, for example, may be used on an individual or team basis.

In contrast, behavioral-based incentive plans, such as merit pay increases, can prove more difficult. As we discussed in Chapter 9, one concern is that it is hard for supervisors to directly observe virtual employees. How do supervisors or other evaluators gather performance data if employees are not at work all the time? Virtual employees might worry that their raters do not understand or appreciate the work they perform offsite or that there is a bias against individuals who work remotely or who work varied schedules. Given these difficulties, it is not surprising that for virtual employees, companies may be forced to use more results-oriented incentives.

Globalization and Incentive Plans

Globalization affects the use of incentives in several ways. The decision to send employees to locations around the globe requires the use of different incentives for expatriate employees. At the same time, cross-cultural differences influence the acceptability and effectiveness of incentives as a motivational tool.

WHAT IS REWARDED   In a global company, different units around the globe may have different objectives. A manager on assignment in Europe might be assigned to help penetrate an emerging market, whereas a manager on assignment in Asia might be tasked with

Cross-cultural differences influence the acceptability and effectiveness of incentives as a motivational tool.

improving the efficiency of an establishment. These different objectives should be reflected in the incentive plans used for these different managers.

Moreover, the ability of employees to meet incentive targets can depend on local conditions such as union relations in a country, the country's infrastructure, or social norms.[54] As a result, it may not be realistic for companies to establish a global incentive plan for their employees. Rather, the plans might be more effective if they are customized to fit different regions or countries.

ACCEPTABILITY OF INCENTIVE PLANS   When we discussed performance management, we looked at how cultural differences affect the acceptability of different evaluation approaches. A similar concern exists when we consider incentives from a global perspective. For example, as noted earlier in this chapter, incentives can be designed to reward individuals or larger groups of employees. In countries that are highly individualistic, employees might prefer incentives that reward their individual efforts. In contrast, in countries such as Japan that more highly value social relations, teamwork, and helping each other succeed,[55] employees might prefer incentive plans that do not force them to compete with one another. In addition to employee acceptance, managers in international locations might also be reluctant to implement certain incentive systems. In these situations, a company's plan might not be implemented at all or might be implemented in principle but not fully embraced.

Firms also have to be sensitive to standards of living in different locations. For example, in China or India, it takes roughly $20 to buy what $100 buys in the United States.[56] As a result, a company with a global incentive program might have to make some adjustments to reflect such regional differences. What triggers those rewards may have to be modified as well. For example, country managers at McDonald's located around the world are provided with a menu of business principles such as customer service, marketing, or restaurant reengineering to focus on as part of the company's "Plan to Win" program. Each country manager, in turn, identifies three to five areas he or she needs to focus on for the local market. At the end of the year, the country's incentive pool is based on how the region met its targets as well as each unit's operating income.[57]

Ethics and Incentive Plans

The fourth environmental challenge, ethics and social responsibility, also comes into play when firms develop their incentive plans. First, the plans can directly affect how ethically employees and managers behave. Second, there is a growing concern regarding the ethics associated with the use of incentives for executives.

ETHICAL EMPLOYEE BEHAVIOR   By this point, it should be clear that incentive systems can have a strong impact on how employees behave at work. It is important to keep in mind, however, that incentive systems must be designed such that they encourage ethical behavior. What is rewarded might not always lead to ethical behavior among employees.[58]

Consider the use of piecework systems. Under these plans, employees have a strong incentive to increase the volume of their productivity. However, without appropriate quality controls, defective products of low quality or that are potentially hazardous to consumers might be produced. Likewise, a heavy emphasis on commissions could lead employees to steal customers away from one another to help their own sales figures. In other words, an incentive system that solely evaluates outcomes such as volumes, sales, or financial metrics might not take into account how those results are achieved. It is important for you, as a manager, to realize that your incentive plans can inadvertently encourage employees to engage in questionable or unethical behaviors to improve their chances of earning rewards.

Similar problems hold for incentive plans at the managerial level. Many managers are evaluated based on short-term financial performance measures, such as a company's return on assets (ROA). ROA provides a snapshot of how efficiently a company is using its assets to generate its revenues. The logic for this incentive is that it motivates managers to try to earn more revenues per dollar the company has invested in assets. But it is conceivable that managers could improve their ROA not by increasing revenue but by lowering assets via firing employees, failing to fill vacant positions, or even neglecting to repair defective products because doing so might incur more costs that hurt their chances of earning their bonuses. If this approach were followed, a manager could earn a bonus based on improving her company's ROA but could potentially do so at the expense of the company's long-term health.

HOW EMPLOYEES AND COMMUNITIES VIEW EXECUTIVE INCENTIVE PLANS As we have indicated, how employees and communities view the incentives corporate executives receive has become a big issue. Consider the situation with CEO Hank McKinnell of Pfizer. Between 2001 and 2006, Pfizer's shares lost more than 40% of their value while McKinnnell received $79 million in pay, with a guaranteed pension of $83 million when he retires.[59] As you can imagine, employees, shareholders, and members of the community take exception to high payouts such as these being given to executives when the performance of their firms is lackluster. And these perceptions are even stronger when executive compensation grows while employees do not receive significant increases in their own pay or when companies engage in downsizing activities or other workforce reduction tactics. Given these concerns, many companies have increased their use of long-term incentives that directly link executive pay with company performance.

INCENTIVES AND REWARDS IN PRACTICE: REGULATORY ISSUES

Regulatory issues affect incentive plans. Two issues that are of particular importance are eliminating bias and discrimination related to incentive plans as well as how stock options are managed.

Bias and Discrimination

Like a firm's other practices, its incentive plans must be neutral with regard to discrimination and bias. Members of protected classes need to have equal access to incentive plans and be assured that the design and implementation of those plans are based on performance rather than something illegal or discriminatory. This might sound simple, but it is not. One study, for example, found that more than one-third of the pay differences earned by men versus women were due to gender differences in the performance-based pay plans they participated in rather than differences in their education, experience, occupations, or job levels.[60] In other words, men and women may not have equal access to pay-for-performance plans within companies. Clearly, the criteria used to allocate incentives must be free from bias. For example, because merit-based incentive plans are based on subjective performance evaluations, any biases that exist in the performance management process will carry over to a firm's incentive system.

Even when more objective measures are used for incentive plans, employees need to have an equal opportunity to excel at those aspects of their jobs that drive their incentive payouts. If there is unequal access based on biases or discrimination in the tasks employees perform, that unequal access may carry over into more results-based or objective indicators of performance. For example, if women are denied opportunities to assume positions associated with commission-based pay or are excluded from jobs that are eligible for stock option plans, that might prove discriminatory. It is important that you, as a manager, take steps to ensure that all employees have the opportunity to excel in the incentive system and that the system does not unfairly discriminate against particular groups of employees.

Stock Option Backdating

One reason for increased skepticism regarding executive incentives relates to the use of stock option awards for executives. A potential problem with stock option plans is the practice of **backdating.** With backdating, companies pick a date when the company stock is low to be considered the date of the award. With backdating, the recipient of the stock option immediately realizes a profit—simply by changing the date of the option. For example, a manager might be issued a stock option plan on June 1, when the stock price is $20. If the company backdates the stock option date to a time when the stock was priced lower— perhaps $15, the recipient automatically realizes a $5 profit per share when she sells her shares.

The motive for using stock options is to provide an incentive to managers and executives to help improve the value of the stock in the market. Backdating, however, adversely affects the motivation of executives to perform well because they are guaranteed a profit, even if their companies don't improve their performance. As noted by Senate Finance Committee Chairman Charles E. Grassley, "It's one thing for an executive to make big profits because he's improved his company, but it's a whole different thing to make big profits because he's playing fast and loose with the dating of stock options."[61] SEC Chairman Christopher Cox echoed this sentiment when he noted, "What makes the option work as a powerful motivational tool is that, unlike a bonus, it isn't so much a reward for prior performance as it is an incentive for future performance. That's why the undisclosed backdating of options is such as serious potential problem."[62]

backdating

Choosing the date of a stock award based on when the stock price was low rather than the exact date the stock award was issued, thereby creating an immediate profit for the individual.

SUMMARY

Incentive plans are important tools managers have at their disposal to motivate superior performance by employees. Drawing on goal setting theory, reinforcement theory, agency theory, and expectancy theory, incentives are powerful motivators in organizations because they explicitly reward employees when they do something desired by their firms.

Incentive plans can be categorized based on whether they emphasize the efforts of individual employees or collective efforts, such as those expended by teams, departments, or the company as a whole. Merit-based incentive plans are some of the most common plans in organizations. However, these plans reward employees based on their past performance. Other plans include individual incentive plans such as lump-sum bonuses, piecework incentive plans, standard hour plans, awards, and sales/commission-based incentive plans.

Gain sharing plans reward employees for improving the efficiency of their organizations. Profit sharing plans reward employees for increasing their companies' profits. Ownership plans give employees partial ownership of their firms by

awarding them company stock. If the company's market performance increases, employees benefit from the increases in the value of the stocks they hold.

The choices managers make regarding which incentive plans to use depends on the organizational demands their firms face, environmental factors, and legal requirements. A firm's strategy, company characteristics, culture, and employee concerns are organizational factors that affect the appropriateness of using different incentive plans, which criteria are emphasized to receive the incentives, and whether employees view their incentive plans as being fair. Environmental pressures force managers to consider how factors related to labor force trends, technology, globalization, and ethics affect the design and implementation of various incentive plans. Finally, legal considerations necessitate that managers take steps to ensure that their incentive plans are free from bias and discrimination and that they comply with legal requirements regarding the distribution of stock options.

KEY TERMS

agency theory *p. 328*
backdating *p. 346*
broad-based stock option *p. 334*
deferred profit sharing plan *p. 334*
differential piecework plan *p. 330*
employee stock ownership plan
  (ESOP) *p. 334*
expectancy *p. 328*
expectancy theory *p. 327*
free rider *p. 333*

gain sharing plan *p. 333*
goal setting theory *p. 327*
Improshare plan *p. 333*
instrumentality *p. 328*
leveraged ESOP *p. 334*
lump-sum merit bonus *p. 329*
merit pay increase *p. 328*
mixed-level plan *p. 334*
mixed salary/commission plan *p. 332*
profit sharing plan *p. 334*

reinforcement theory *p. 327*
Scanlon plan *p. 333*
social loafing *p. 341*
spot award *p. 331*
standard hour plan *p. 330*
stock option plan *p. 334*
straight commission plan *p. 332*
straight piecework plan *p. 330*
straight salary plan *p. 332*
valence *p. 328*

DISCUSSION QUESTIONS

1. Why do incentive plans work or not work?
2. We discussed the fact that Circuit City and Best Buy have moved away from commission-based incentive plans to team-oriented incentive plans. How do you think this change will affect these companies?
3. What are the advantages and disadvantages of the different types of group- and organizational-level incentive plans firms use?
4. How do the organizational demands a firm faces affect the incentive plans it uses?

5. What type of incentive plan would you use in a company pursuing a cost strategy? What about in a company pursuing a quality or customer service strategy?
6. Explain how different environmental factors influence the incentive systems companies use.
7. Explain how employees' perceptions of procedural fairness and distributional fairness are affected by the incentive plans under which they work.
8. What legal factors do companies have to consider when they're designing their incentive plans?

LEARNING EXERCISE 1

As a manager, you have a number of choices to make regarding which incentive plan(s) you use. What are the advantages of the different types of incentive plans discussed in this chapter? Research companies that have successfully used these plans and complete the following grid, based on your analysis of each plan and when it should be used:

	Advantages?	Disadvantages?	Company Examples?	When Should This Plan Be Used?
Merit Pay Program Lump-Sum Bonus Piecework Incentive Plan Standard Hour Plan Awards Sales Incentive Plan				

LEARNING EXERCISE 2

As noted in the chapter, a key component of effective incentive plans is that employees need to accept the plan. Otherwise, they are not likely to be motivated to work to their highest levels of performance. Put yourself in the position of the employees you might manage. How would you feel if you were working as an employee in a company under each of the different individual and team/group incentive plans discussed in this chapter?

1. What would be your concerns? Why?
2. What aspects of each incentive plan would you find attractive? Why?
3. What recommendations would you make to a company to address your concerns to maximize your motivation for each plan?

CASE STUDY # 1 — A NEW INCENTIVE SYSTEM AT THE AUTO DEALER

You've been hired by a relatively large local automobile dealer to design a new compensation and incentive system for several positions that make up the bulk of the firm's workforce. These positions are:

- **10 administrative positions**—These positions involve the day-to-day operational facets of running the dealership—answering phones, working at the customer service desk, filing paperwork, pulling records on cars, and so forth. These employees are currently paid on an hourly basis. The turnover rate is about 30% for these positions. There have been several complaints about the courtesy and helpfulness of employees occupying these positions.
- **15 sales positions**—The employees occupying these positions are primarily focused on selling cars and are paid entirely on commission. The turnover among these employees is fairly high (about 80% leave each year), although a few of the sales staff have been with the dealership for a number of years.
- **10 service positions (mechanics)**—The mechanics occupying these positions are paid on a standard hour plan (that is, their pay is based on how much time it is should take to perform each repair). The turnover among these employees is very low. As in any other dealership, there have been some complaints about the quality of the service the firm's mechanics have delivered. A number of customers have had to bring their vehicles in several times before their auto problems were properly repaired.

The goals of the dealership are primarily to make money on the sale of new and used cars, although the service department does generate a modest amount of income. There are several challenges you must consider before you make your recommendations:

- The dealership's profitability is fundamentally influenced by the number of cars sold and the prices of those cars. In addition, the dealership's profitability is enhanced by (a) repeat business and (b) the company's reputation. Historically, repeat customers represent a sizable amount of business; the dealership gets to sell their used cars they traded in and also sells them new cars. Moreover, customer loyalty matters a lot because word-of-mouth advertising generates business.
- Service quality in terms of the sales process as well as the service department (mechanics) is a critical component of customer satisfaction and affects the amount of repeat business dealerships get.
- The income salespeople earn is directly related to the profitability of each car they sell. The prices on the cars are somewhat negotiable. Under the current system, the sales staff and the dealership split the profits 50-50 from every transaction.

DISCUSSION QUESTION

1. What incentive system(s) would you establish for these three groups of employees?

CASE STUDY # 2 — EXECUTIVE COMPENSATION AT AB3D

AB3D Industries is a company with six manufacturing facilities that produces a variety of plastic-based children's toys. The company was founded in 1983 by Edward Pistrom, who served as the chief executive officer until 1995. Since then, several CEOs have filled the post quite successfully—continuing to meet the demand for safe and durable children's toys.

AB3D Industries has approximately 2,400 employees throughout the facilities. Each facility is run by a general manager and has staff who address the relevant employee and customer needs of those in key positions. The general managers of each facility report to the corporate staff, which consists of the CEO (chief executive officer), the COO (chief operating officer), and the directors of Human Resources, Legal, Sales, and Marketing. Since its founding, the company has maintained a healthy rate of growth in sales as well as in financial returns related to return on investments (ROI) and return on assets (ROA).

Despite the prosperous history of AB3D, over the past four years, the company's performance has declined. Of the six manufacturing facilities, four have failed to post any gains in productivity or revenue, while two have posted slight gains in productivity despite diminished levels of revenue at the

facilities. Put simply, the performance of the facilities and the company as a whole has been poor. The CEO for the past three years was fired due to this poor performance.

Over the past three months, a consulting company has worked with AB3D top management to identify potential candidates for the CEO position. After a lengthy search and extensive interviews, AB3D is excited about the prospect of one candidate in particular—Andrew Reason. Andrew essentially grew up in this industry. Over the past 16 years, he has worked his way up from the manufacturing floor through operations and marketing positions to assume a director of operations position at a competing firm. Based on numerous discussions, it is clear that Andrew is interested in the prospect of helping turn around the performance of AB3D industries. His main concern is that AB3D must be able to provide a compensation package compelling enough for him to take on the CEO role. The consulting company has suggested that the market average for base compensation for CEOs in this industry should be approximately $1,000,000. In addition to base pay, CEOs in this industry expect lucrative short-term and long-term incentives to reward them for exceptional performance. What should you offer to this top candidate?

DISCUSSION QUESTIONS

1. What factors are you considering in setting the executive compensation package for this potential hire?

2. What compensation/incentive package would you recommend for the new CEO? Be sure to identify the base pay as well as the forms of short-term and long-term incentives you would recommend. Why would you recommend this package?

3. What implications, if any, would this package have for the workers at AB3D industries?

chapter

12

EMPLOYEE BENEFITS AND SAFETY PROGRAMS

1. Understand how a firm's benefits and safety programs shape its employees' attitudes and behaviors. *(352)*

2. Describe the major characteristics of each of the mandatory employee benefits that firms must provide their employees. *(354)*

3. Discuss the different types and major characteristics of voluntary benefits. *(356)*

4. Outline the key components of effective benefits administration. *(370)*

5. Explain the key components of an effective safety program. *(372)*

6. Discuss how a firm's organizational demands affect its benefits and safety programs. *(374)*

7. Identify the environmental factors that affect the benefits and safety programs firms implement. *(379)*

8. Describe the regulatory issues related to benefits and safety. *(383)*

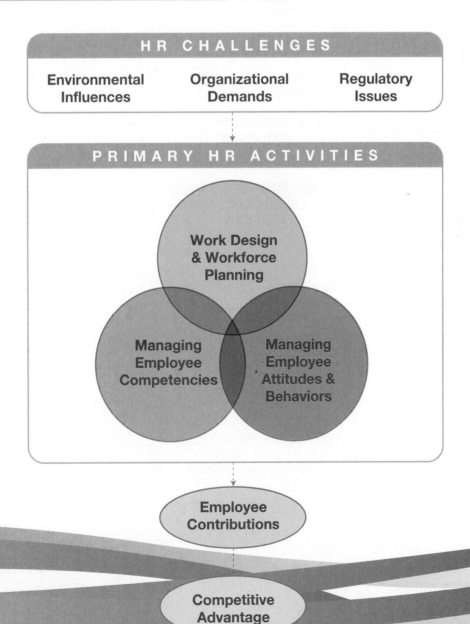

351

EMPLOYEE BENEFITS AND SAFETY PROGRAMS

In Chapter 1, we asked if you would be more willing to work for a company that had an attractive benefits program with coverage for dental care, vacation time, tuition assistance, and the like, or a company that did not offer these options. Most likely you answered that you would want to work for the company with the benefits. If you did, you are not alone. In a 2006 compensation and benefits study of 10,001 workers by Hudson, a professional staffing and outsourcing firm, 49% of respondents indicated that they would not even consider working for an employer if health benefits were not offered. And 20% of the respondents indicated that they would be happier with their current total compensation package if it offered better benefits.[1]

One conclusion from this research is that benefits affect how employees feel about their company and their job. Many employers understand this fact and use benefits as one way to manage employee attitudes and behaviors. Managing employee attitudes and behaviors, as you know by now, is an important part of the framework for managing employees for competitive advantage as shown in Exhibit 12.1. Benefits offerings can take a variety of

Exhibit 12.1 ▶

Framework for the Strategic Management of Employees

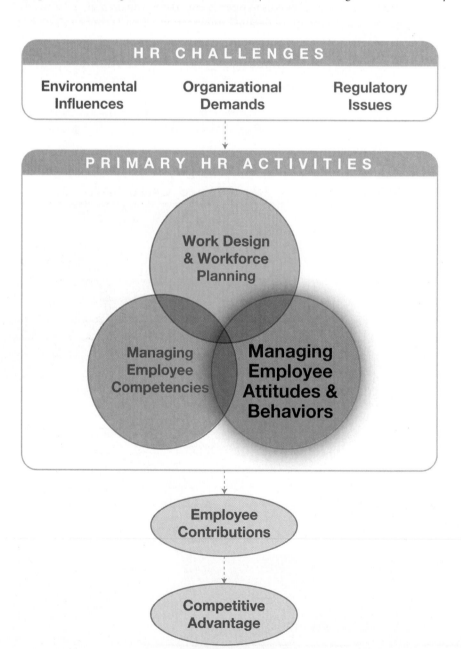

forms to address health and wellness, including health insurance, employee assistance programs, health promotion programs, health risk appraisals, and work and family balance programs.

In this chapter, we also discuss safety in the workplace, a topic intimately related to health and wellness. Overall, we will address questions such as the following that managers will need to be able to answer:

- Which benefits programs are most appropriate for your workforce?
- What are the regulatory requirements regarding benefits programs?
- How can you ensure the safety of your employees?

On a personal level, having an understanding of the different practices we discuss in this chapter will help you make informed decisions when choosing a new employer and choosing among the benefits offered to you.

As you read this chapter, keep in mind, too, that internal equity, external competitiveness, and proper administration of your firm's safety and benefits programs are just as important as they are for the monetary portion of employee compensation. So, even though your role as a manager may not require that you develop benefits and safety policies or make decisions about which benefits to offer to employees, you do need to know what is available and how and where more detailed information about these programs can be obtained in the company.

Take a minute to read Company Spotlight 12.1 to learn about the "outrageous employee benefits" at Vitale Caturano & Company, a company that understands the short- and long-term value of an exceptional benefits program.

12.1 "Outrageous Employee Benefits" at Vitale Caturano

COMPANY spotlight

Vitale Caturano & Co. (VCC) is among the top 100 accounting and consulting firms in the United States. Located in Boston, VCC has been recognized by the *Boston Business Journal* as one of the city's best places to work. The firm offers a wide range of employee benefits. Along with medical, dental, group term life, and disability insurance, VCC offers a 401(k) plan, a college savings plan, tuition reimbursement programs, in-house continuing professional education, an employer referral program, and health club membership discounts.

Complimentary fruit, continental breakfast, coffee, cappuccino, and soda are available all day, and VCC's own chef prepares fresh, nutritious, and delicious lunches. The chef sends out an e-mail with the day's menu, and staffers order their sandwiches, burgers, and salads electronically. When the staffers are ready to eat, their meals are waiting for them. Employees also have access to a full-time concierge service to help them with their work-related errands, dry-cleaning pickup and delivery, and more. During the firm's busy season, VCC even provides complimentary dinners and free child care on Saturdays.

VCC frequently refers to the "outrageous employee benefits" it offers. The company's managers firmly believe those benefits have led to the firm's rapid growth and its low employee turnover. VCC's education program alone costs about $400,000 per year, but it generates about $625,000 in additional revenue. Why? The company can charge clients more when its employees have advanced educational credentials. Or, take the lunch program: It costs VCC about a $100,000 a year to run the kitchen, but the company recovers the money through increased productivity. Employees get back to work faster than if they go out for lunch. In fact, about one-third to one-half of VCC's employees use the service all year long. An extra hour a week of work for one-third of the company's employees at $100 per hour equals about $520,000 in savings for VCC. The firm invests in its human capital by providing these outrageous benefits because it knows that motivated, happy employees are more likely to stay with the company and are more productive.

Sources: Vitale Caturano & Co. Web site, www.vitale.com; and Hayes, M. Outrageous employee benefits: A strategy to keep your people happy is sound business. *Journal of Accountancy* 199:32–37, 2005.

BENEFITS AND SAFETY PHILOSOPHY

A firm's benefits and safety philosophy drives the decisions it makes as to what it offers beyond what is mandatory. In developing such a philosophy, a firm needs to understand the needs and preferences of its workforce. For instance, you are probably familiar with Maslow's hierarchy of needs. According to this theory of motivation, individuals are motivated by five levels of needs. Starting with the lowest level and climbing to the highest, they are physiological, safety and security, belongingness, self-esteem, and self-actualization needs. Motivational theories such as this one help companies understand that employees all have some basic needs but that their needs differ, depending on each employee's current circumstances. An employee who needs food, housing, and transportation is going to be more concerned about fulfilling those needs than achieving a certain level of status within his firm, for example. Employees who have their basic physiological needs met will be more interested in benefits such as life insurance and retirement accounts that provide a safety and security net for them. Thus, a firm's benefits and safety philosophy needs to account for these differences.

In addition to understanding that employees have different needs, depending on their life circumstances, companies have to decide how much they are willing to invest in benefits and safety programs for their employees beyond what the law requires. Of course, the decisions a firm makes about these programs sends a signal to employees about what the company values. A firm's philosophy should support the mission, vision, and values of the firm. We now provide an overview of the mandatory benefits that firms are required by law to provide. Following that discussion, we will discuss voluntary benefits and safety programs.

MANDATORY BENEFITS

In the United States, mandatory employee benefits include Social Security, workers' compensation, unemployment compensation, and family and medical leave. We discussed the Family and Medical Leave Act (FMLA) in Chapter 3; let's now take a look at the purpose and requirements of the other mandatory benefits.

Social Security

The idea of social insurance began in Europe in the nineteenth century. At its core, social insurance protects people against job-related risks—disability, death, unemployment, and so forth. The goal of social insurance is to improve not just the lives of individual participants in social insurance plans but society as a whole.

The **Social Security Act** was one of the first social insurance programs implemented in the United States. President Roosevelt signed it into law in the United States in 1935, and it went into effect in 1937. The act created the Old-Age and Survivors Insurance (OASI) program (which later became the Old-Age, Survivors, and Disabilities Insurance program [OASDI]). Its purpose was to provide retired workers with a continuous stream of income after their retirement. Later, other provisions would be added to cover dependents and survivors of covered workers, as well as disabled workers and their dependents, and to provide health insurance coverage for the elderly.[2]

The Social Security Act was passed in the United States in part because workers were becoming less likely to have extended families to care for them in their later years as more people moved from the family farms to the cities to work in industry. At the time he signed the law, President Roosevelt stated, "We can never insure one hundred percent of the population against one hundred percent of the hazards and vicissitudes of life, but we have tried to frame a law which will give some measure of protection to the average citizen and to his family against the loss of a job and against poverty-ridden old age."[3]

Social Security is funded by payroll taxes. In 2008, the Social Security tax rate was 12.40% of an employee's salary, shared equally between the employee and employer on earnings up to $102,000. Employers withhold Social Security taxes from employee paychecks and submit the funds to the Internal Revenue Service. This tax is the OASDI

Social Security Act

A social insurance act put into effect in 1937 and funded by employer and employee contributions to provide old age, survivors, disability, and death benefits.

portion of the Federal Insurance Contributions Act (FICA) tax that is withheld from employee paychecks. Most people have to work for at least 10 years to receive full credit, which accrues at the rate of about four credits per year, depending on a person's earnings. The amount of Social Security income retirees receive is a percentage of their average lifetime earnings. However, lower-income workers actually receive a higher percentage than upper-income workers. It is important to keep in mind that Social Security was meant to supplement people's retirement or disability income, not fully replace it.[4]

Medicare is the health insurance portion of Social Security for retirees age 65 or older and for disabled workers; it is the second part of the FICA tax and became law in 1965. Your Social Security credits count toward Medicare eligibility. Employers and employees contribute equally to the Medicare taxes.[5] The tax rate for Medicare for 2008 was 1.45% of a worker's total earnings. Therefore, in 2008, the total FICA tax rate for employees for Social Security (OASDI) and Medicare combined was 15.30%, paid equally by employee and employer.[6]

Medicare

The health insurance portion of Social Security for retirees age 65 or older and disabled workers.

Unemployment Insurance (UI)

The **Federal–State Unemployment Insurance (UI) program**, created by the Social Security Act of 1935, provides temporary financial assistance to eligible workers who lose their jobs through no fault of their own. Almost all workers are covered by the program, although the eligibility requirements are determined by state laws. Railroad workers, veterans who have recently served, and civilian federal employees are covered by other, similar programs.

Because UI is a partnership between the states and the federal government, states must meet the federal guidelines developed for the UI program. In all but three states, funding for this benefits program is based on an unemployment tax that employers are required to pay. Employers must pay a minimum amount of federal unemployment tax if they have one or more employees in each of at least 20 calendar weeks or paid $1,500 or more in wages in any calendar quarter. The tax rate each employer pays is determined by the individual states and based on the number of unemployment claims filed against the employer. Three states—Alaska, New Jersey, and Pennsylvania—actually collect taxes from employees to fund the program.[7]

Public employment offices or other approved agencies pay out the compensation to unemployed workers, who are required to demonstrate that they are actively seeking reemployment. Workers can typically receive UI for a maximum of 26 weeks. When unemployment in the United States is high, the federal government sometimes increases the number of weeks. For instance, when Eastern Airlines closed in 1991, the former employees of this once major international airline received unemployment benefits for over a year if they remained eligible for the benefits. Funding for an extended time period is shared between the states and the federal government. In the fourth quarter of 2007, approximately 4.9 million workers filed for UI benefits. The amount of benefits paid in that quarter was around $7.9 million.[8] Exhibit 12.2 outlines what you would need to do to collect unemployment benefits if you were laid off from your job.

Unemployment Insurance (UI) program

Created by the Social Security Act of 1935 and administered by the states, this program provides temporary financial assistance to eligible workers who lose their jobs through no fault of their own.

- Meet state eligibility requirements
- File a claim at the appropriate state unemployment insurance agency
- Follow the guidelines for continued eligibility for benefits including reporting income and job offers
- Register with your state's employment service for reemployment assistance and/or training program information

◄ **Exhibit 12.2**

Requirements for Collecting Unemployment Insurance Benefits

Source: Based on Employment Training Administration, U. S. Department of Labor. *State unemployment benefits*, http://workforcesecurity.doleta.gov/unemploy/uifactsheet.asp.

workers' compensation

A social insurance program that provides cash benefits and medical care to workers when they suffer injuries or illnesses related to their employment.

Workers' Compensation Insurance

Workers' compensation was actually the first type of social insurance developed widely in the United States. The program was started in 1908 to cover civilian employees of the federal government. That coverage has now been expanded to other employees and provides cash benefits and medical care to workers when they suffer injuries or illnesses related to their employment. It also provides survivor benefits to dependents of workers who die due to work-related incidents. Workers who receive these benefits are not permitted to sue their employers for damages of any type.[9] All 50 states as well as the District of Columbia, Puerto Rico, and the Virgin Islands have workers' compensation programs. The federal government has its own program and also administers the Longshore and Harbor Workers' Compensation Act, which covers all longshore and harbor workers in the United States. The Black Lung Benefits Act of 1972 covers coal miners who have black lung disease, and the Energy Employees Occupational Illness Compensation Act of 2000 covers employees, employees' survivors, contractors, and subcontractors of the Department of Energy (DOE) exposed to beryllium as well as private companies that provided beryllium to the DOE.[10] In most states, employers are required to have a workers' compensation program, regardless of the number of people they employ.[11]

The federal government has no involvement in the administration or financing of workers' compensation programs, nor does it have reporting requirements or standards for determining what constitutes a "tax-qualified" plan. Thus, information about actual costs of workers' compensation and the number of workers covered under the various state and U.S. territory plans is not always readily available.[12]

Workers' compensation begins paying for an employee's medical care immediately after a workplace injury occurs. After a waiting period of three to seven days, it pays temporary disability benefits, and it pays permanent partial and permanent total disability to workers with permanent disabilities caused by their work. Other costs covered include rehabilitation and training for employees who cannot return to their pre-injury jobs and benefits to survivors of employees whose work-related injuries lead to death.[13]

Employer costs for workers' compensation include insurance premiums and deductibles that have to be met. If an employer is self-insured, meaning the employer funds the workers' compensation plan rather than buying insurance from a provider, the costs of the plan equal the administrative costs related to it plus any benefits paid out to employees.[14] Employers can reduce their share of these costs by focusing on strategies such as educating employees about wellness and safety, ensuring that the workplace is free of hazards that could lead to injuries or illnesses, establishing "return-to-work programs" to get employees back on the job faster, and doing a better job of tracking claims to identify where health and safety problems in their companies might be present.[15] The sharing of electronic data among the government, employers and employees, and third-party administrators also helps reduce the costs related to workers' compensation.[16] Later in the chapter, we talk more specifically about regulations for employee safety programs.

VOLUNTARY BENEFITS

voluntary benefits (also discretionary benefits)

Benefits that an employer voluntarily chooses to offer to its employees.

Voluntary benefits, sometimes referred to as discretionary benefits, are those that an employer voluntarily chooses to offer its employees. Voluntary benefits primarily focus on health, wellness, and welfare; life management; and retirement. Many of these benefits would be extremely expensive for employees if they had to purchase them outside the group plans provided by their employers. Even if employees have to pay a portion of the cost, a group plan lowers that amount considerably.[17] In this section, we discuss health and wellness programs, life management, and retirement programs. These categories cover most of the types of voluntary benefits typically offered by firms.

Health and Wellness Programs

Traditionally, companies have provided health insurance benefits to employees. Now, many companies have expanded their health-related benefit offerings to include benefits that focus on both health and wellness. These benefits often include health care

J.B. Hunt understands that the demands on a truck driver require special attention to health and wellness.

plans, prescription drug plans, vision and dental care, and mental health and substance abuse benefits.

Companies have recognized the importance of integrating benefit offerings to contain rising costs. For example, J. B. Hunt Transport Services was awarded The Best Health Benefits Solution in 2006 for its Better Health for Life program. Truck drivers have a job that lends itself to poor health habits: Eating unhealthy food at truck stop diners and other eating establishments, sitting in the truck cab all day, and smoking can lead to increased incidence of high blood pressure and obesity. Add to that the time away from home and family for long periods of time and infrequent contact with others, and you have a recipe for serious health problems. After reviewing medical claims histories for drivers, J. B. Hunt came up with the Better Health for Life plan, which stresses exercise, weight management and proper diet, smoking cessation, and disease management and personal health coaching. After only two years, the company saw a measurable, positive impact due to better health of its drivers and the associated lower health care plan payouts.[18] In the next sections, we describe various types of health and wellness programs provided by employers.

HEALTH CARE PLANS The cost to employers to provide health care benefits continues to increase. Employers have to absorb the costs themselves, pass more of them along to their employees, or cut the number and type of benefits offered. In 2007, employers paid an average of $7,211 per employee for health care, a 2-percentage-point drop from 2006, while health care costs continue to rise at twice the rate of inflation.[19]

Health care costs are increasing for a variety of reasons. Individuals are living longer and working longer. Whether we like it or not, there is often a correlation between one's age and the need for health care. And newer medical technologies and newer drugs for treating everything from headaches to cancer are often costly.[20] Companies employ a number of different approaches to maintain health care costs. These approaches include traditional plans, managed care, high-deductible health care programs, generic and mail-order drugs, and wellness programs. Next, we discuss each.

Traditional Health Care Plans. *Traditional plans* include those available through insurance carriers, community-based plans such as Blue Cross/Blue Shield, and employer self-insurance. Under these traditional fee-for-service plans, an employee typically has to meet a deductible before the insurance plan pays for most medical services—and even then, the plans sometimes pay only 80% or less. Employees can choose the doctors they want and usually don't have to live in a certain geographic location to participate. The plans generally do not pay for preventive care and pay only part of the costs of diagnostic tests.

Managed Care Plans. *Managed care plans* are the oldest of the approaches to health care cost containment and include health maintenance organizations, preferred provider organizations, and point-of-service plans. Major differences in the three types of plans include how payments are made and the way medical costs are determined.[21] These plans provide health care to members for a set monthly fee for a comprehensive set of services. Primary care physicians serve as gatekeepers.[22]

health maintenance organization (HMO)

A type of managed care health insurance program that requires employees to designate a primary care physician and have any visits to specialists referred by the primary care physician.

preferred provider organization (PPO)

A type of managed care program in which the employer negotiates with health care providers, usually in a network, for discounts and services for healthcare coverage for employees.

copay

The minimum amount employees must pay for health care as determined by their health insurance plan.

point-of-service plan (POS)

A hybrid of an HMO and a PPO where individuals can also receive treatment outside the network but must pay a higher deductible.

consumer-driven health plan (CDHP)

An alternative type of health care plan that puts more of the decision making under the control of employees by letting them choose whether they prefer a plan with a higher deductible or other more expensive alternatives, how much to put into a savings plan for health care purposes, and which health care provider to use.

high-deductible health plan (HDHP)

(also called a **catastrophic health plan**) A type of managed-care health insurance plan that costs the employer and employee less per month because they require the employee to pay the first few thousand dollars of medical costs each year and pays medical costs only when the employee has a major medical problem.

Health maintenance organizations (HMOs), the first type of managed care programs, originated in 1973 when the Health Maintenance Organization Act became law and allowed *third-party payers* to participate in health care payments. Third-party payers are companies, insurers, or other entities that negotiate health care options for employees rather than the employees doing so directly.[23] HMOs became very popular in the 1980s. They often require that the employees live within a designated service area and use doctors and facilities that are specified by the HMO. The plan pays for medical services if the health care providers are designated in the plan. Each employee identifies a primary care physician and goes to that person, who can then refer the employee to a specialist within the HMO if needed. Employers with 25 or more employees must give employees the opportunity to join a federally qualified HMO.

A second approach to managed care is the use of **preferred provider organizations (PPOs)**. In a PPO, an employer negotiates with health care providers, usually in a network, for discounts. The providers must follow strict standards about the number of diagnostic tests they order and must adhere to other cost controls. The employer also gives its employees an incentive to use the preferred providers because when they do, the rates they pay are lower. Thus, employers save money on their health care costs, employees have a greater choice of doctors than they do with an HMO, and doctors are assured a flow of patients. If employees use a doctor not in the PPO network, they pay a higher **copay**. A copay is the minimum amount an employee must pay for health care, including a doctor's visit, a prescription, or diagnostic test.[24]

The third type of plan is a **point-of-service plan (POS)**. This plan can be described as a hybrid of an HMO and a PPO. In a POS, the employee can decide which plan to use, as needed. The employee might use the HMO component to see a primary care physician but receive treatment following a referral through an in-network physician in the PPO. Individuals can also receive treatment outside the network but must pay a deductible of $500 or more.[25]

The HMO and POS options tend to have lower premiums (costs to belong to the plan) than PPOs because they require that the primary care physician decide whether an employee should be referred to a specialist. They also have had lower premium increases than PPOs as a result of this requirement, although in the past couple years, that has been changing. There are, however, a number of criticisms that have been raised regarding HMOs and POSs. One concern is that in these plans, physicians act as gatekeepers to the care of patients. Due to the way physician payments are structured, the plans can give physicians an incentive to limit their patients' access to specialists and/or certain diagnostic procedures. In fact, as a result of consumer and government pressures, HMOs and POSs have been approving more patient referrals in recent years, even though the practice drives up costs.[26] Another criticism of HMOs and POSs is that the plans limit how much employees have to pay out-of-pocket for costs. Consequently, employees may not be as careful about taking care of their health as they would if they had to pay more of their health care costs themselves.[27]

Employers have adopted a variety of alternative approaches to address the concerns about health care plans. These alternatives come under the rubric of **consumer-driven health plans (CDHPs)**. CDHPs put more of the decision making under the control of employees. (The main idea behind CDHPs is that giving employees more responsibility for their health care costs will cause them to pay more attention to their health and their health care–related treatments and plans.) A 2008 Watson Wyatt survey found that the number of companies offering CDHPs had nearly doubled in the preceding two years. The survey also found that companies with at least 50% of their employees enrolled in a CDHP had health cost increases that were about half those of companies with traditional health coverage.[28] Under a CDHP, employees have choices about whether to select a plan with a higher deductible or select other alternatives that are more expensive, how much to put into a savings plan for health care purposes, and which health care providers to use. Exhibit 12.3 shows what employers can do to help their workers choose wisely among different CDHP plans.

In the past several years, more employers have turned to **high-deductible health plans (HDHPs)** as a way to manage the costs of employee health care plans. HDHPs are also referred to as *catastrophic health plans* because they don't pay for the first few thousand

- Share actual health care costs with employees

- Provide alternative health care options to employees

- Share a portion of the costs related to the health care plans

- Give employees assistance in understanding their options

- Provide information and tools to help employees know how to select doctors, specialists, hospitals, tests, and prescriptions on a cost and quality basis

Source: Based on Aita, S. A rational approach to consumer-directed health care: Engaging consumers and providers in controlling costs. *Compensation & Benefits Review* 36:40–47, 2004.

◄ Exhibit 12.3
Helping Workers
Make Good CDHP
Choices

dollars of a person's medical costs each year. Thus, they pay only when the employee has a major medical problem. Because of their high deductibles, these plans are less costly for employers, and employees' monthly premiums are lower, too.

Employees in a HDHP can also participate in a health savings account. **Health savings accounts (HSAs)** were created as part of the Medicare Prescription Drug Improvement and Modernization Act of 2003. HSAs provide a way for employees to pay for their immediate health care expenses and save money on a tax-free basis. Exhibit 12.4 shows how HSAs work. The employee in the example is 42 years old, married, and wants to include his spouse on his health care plan. He has two choices of plans provided by his employer. In the company health plan, a traditional plan, he has to pay $700 per month for his share of the plan versus only $300 a month for his share if he chooses the HDHP. However, his deductible for the traditional plan is $500 versus $4,000 for the HDHP. So, what is the best choice? The difference in the two annual premiums is $4,800, $800 more than the $4,000

health savings account (HSAs)

A special account established through employers, banks, credit unions, insurance companies, and other approved financial institutions into which an employee puts aside money pre-tax to help pay for his or her health care expenses.

◄ Exhibit 12.4
Example of How an
HSA Works

Coverage for an employee, age 42, and his or her spouse

	Deductible	Monthly Cost	Employee's Annual Cost
Company Health Plan	$500	$700	$8,400
HDHP	$4,000	$300	$3,600
Employee's Savings			$4,800
− HDHP Deductible			4,000
Difference			$ 800
Contribution to HSA		$4,000	
Annual spending on health care		1,000	
Savings		$3,000	

$3,000/year saved until age 65, 8% gain = $200,000 saved for retirement

Rules:

- Qualified health care expenses during the year would be paid from the employee's HSA

- Any amounts not spent roll over to the following year

- The savings are tax deferred and can be used for the employee's future qualified health care or retirement needs

Source: Lavis, B. Health savings accounts: Has the revolution begun? *Compensation & Benefits Review* 36:48–52, 2004.

deductible under the HDHP plan. And, because he can put the $4,000 for the deductible into an HSA pretax and let it accumulate if not spent, he has the potential to have a nice sum at retirement if the money is invested well.

As you can see from the example, the basic idea behind an HDHP is that you save money on the cost of the HDHP compared to having a health care plan with a lower deductible, and you can put aside the difference to cover medical costs you incur. In 2007, the maximum annual HSA contribution for a single person was $2,850 and for a family was $5,650. These amounts increase annually to account for inflation. In 2007, the minimum deductible for an HDHP by law had to be at least $1,100 for an employee and $2,200 for family coverage. The annual maximum out-of-pocket copay could not exceed $5,500 for an employee or $11,000 for a family.

HSAs can be established through employers, banks, credit unions, insurance companies, and other approved financial institutions. Following passage of the act, about a half million people participated in HSAs, and that number has soared. In fact, the Treasury Department expects there to be 21 million participants by 2010. Many participants are individuals who currently do not have employer-provided health insurance and small businesses that had not previously provided health care options for their employees.[29]

health reimbursement account (HRA)

An account into which an employer puts money to reimburse employees for qualified medical expenses.

Health Reimbursement Accounts. Health reimbursement accounts (HRAs) are another mechanism for paying for the health care costs of employees. There are several differences between HSAs and HRAs, even though the purpose of both is to reimburse employees for qualified medical expenses. An employer, an employee, or an employee's family member can put money into an HSA. In contrast, only the employer sets aside money in an HRA. Employers can deduct the costs of HRAs on their taxes in the same way they can deduct the costs of the health care insurance they provide their employees. When an employee leaves the company, whether for retirement or other reasons, funds left in the account are accessible to the employee. However, the accounts are not portable; they remain with the employer that provided them, and they cannot be used for retirement income. In an HSA, the funds belong to the employee and can be rolled over to the next plan year and withdrawn for retirement, subject to a penalty if the withdrawal occurs before age 65. With only a few exceptions, employees who have an HRA cannot have an HSA.[30]

The 2006 Watson Wyatt/National Business Group on Health study found that companies that used a combination of an HDHP with an HSA or an HRA were the most successful at controlling costs. They found that of the 585 midsized and large companies in the study, 29% were offering CDHPs, and an additional 33% planned to do so in the next year. These companies believe that the CDHPs cause employees to be more discerning about their health care choices. With CDHPs, the insurance is designed to protect against catastrophic medical costs and provide for preventive care, and the HSA or HRA is there to cover the other costs.[31]

Self-Funded Plans. Instead of contracting with an insurer such as Blue Cross/Blue Shield or Cigna to design and deliver all or part of their benefits programs, companies can decide to *self-fund* their programs (self-insure). Many large employers and a growing number of medium and small employers make this decision each year. By self-funding, employers avoid having to pay premiums and taxes on those premiums, and they avoid some of the state requirements for benefits. When employers self-fund, they typically employ the services of a third-party administrator to oversee the plan. Because these plans are not subject to state mandates, they actually offer employers more flexibility, which is one of their attractive features. Self-funding can save a company money, but it is not without risks. For example, if a number of the firm's employees suffer catastrophic illnesses, the fund may end up with greater costs than income for a year. By self-funding, a company is assuming that the money that it sets aside for employee medical costs, including what the employees pay into the fund, will be sufficient to cover all costs incurred.[32]

Prescription Drug Benefits. Prescriptions are a major expense for health care plans. In fact, many prescription costs have increased more than other health care costs. Companies reduce prescription costs by requiring employees to purchase *generic drugs* rather than brand-name drugs.[33] Generic drugs have the same formulas as brand-name drugs, but many employees prefer the brand name. Caterpillar Inc. has coined a term for this preference, "the purple pill syndrome," named after Nexium, which is widely advertised as "the purple pill". Because of extensive advertising by the manufacturer patients ask their doctors to prescribe it for them.

In 2005, Caterpillar spent about $156 million on prescription drugs, an amount equal to 25% of its health care costs. To reduce these costs, Caterpillar first tried a two-tier and then a three-tier copay system. In a two-tier system, brand-name drugs cost more than generic drugs. In a three-tier system, insurance companies have different payment schedules for brand-name drugs, generic drugs, and drugs on a formulary list. A formulary list identifies drugs that the insurance company has decided are the most cost-effective for treating certain conditions. About 78% of companies use a three-tier system. When the three-tier system didn't cut costs as much as Caterpillar wanted, it chose to go to a "step therapy" program, whereby employees have to pay the full cost of brand-name drugs if a generic is available unless their doctors require the brand name. One concern with this approach, however, is that employees might end up not getting prescriptions they need and then experiencing health problems that affect their productivity and the health care costs of their firms.[34]

Another way to cut prescription costs is to require employees to obtain their prescriptions through a mail-order service. The prescribing physician writes the prescription so that the medicine can be dispensed for three months at a time. The firm and its employees receive volume discounts as a result, and administrative costs are reduced. Other cost-saving strategies include deciding whether "lifestyle" drugs, such as Viagra, will be covered by a company's insurance plan and/or if employees need to get prior authorization from their firms' insurers before certain drugs can be dispensed to them.[35]

Vision and Dental Insurance.   Many employers include dental and/or vision coverage in their regular health plans or offer them as separate options. These plans can be offered through HMO or PPO plans, and they can also be included as part of traditional fee-for-service plans.

Employers' dental plan costs have remained fairly stable in recent years, while other insurance plans have experienced double-digit increases. Better dental hygiene products and better care starting at a younger age, fluoridation, and awareness programs have led to less tooth decay and gum disease and helped hold down costs. Dental coverage usually includes basic and major restorative care, and orthodontia, with a large percentage of the cost of preventive care being covered.[36] Employers often pay a portion of the premium costs and require their employees to pay the rest. Sometimes the plans include certain restrictions, such as the minimum amount of time an employee has to have participated in the plan before certain procedures, such as root canals, are covered. When selecting a dental plan, employers typically look for carriers with broad networks of doctors in terms of their locations and the services they provide, generous discounts, and high service quality.[37]

Vision insurance can also be included as part of a firm's health care options, with the employer and employee both paying for the coverage. Managed care vision companies provide employees with a network of optometrists and ophthalmologists from which to choose. Usually vision plans pay at least partially for eye exams, glasses or contact lenses, and, occasionally, LASIK surgery.[38]

WELLNESS PROGRAMS   Workplace problems such as absenteeism and injuries on the job are often correlated with employee health and safety issues and lead to increased insurance costs. Because lifestyle choices such as smoking, excessive drinking, overeating, not wearing safety equipment, and not exercising are responsible for 50% to 80% of health care expenditures, it isn't surprising that companies have devised a number of programs to keep employees healthy.[39] These programs, known as **wellness programs**, range from smoking cessation to weight loss management programs and even include memberships in fitness centers. The purpose of these programs is to reduce health insurance costs by encouraging employees to become educated about their own health and to participate in programs to improve their health in general as well as their health and safety on the job.

Wellness programs typically include the following:[40]

- A health-risk assessment to identify employees at risk for chronic diseases
- The identification of programs and incentives to motivate employees

wellness program

An employer provided program to keep employees healthy through a range of offerings, ranging from smoking cessation to weight loss management to membership in a fitness center.

COMPANY spotlight 12.2 Wellness Program Success at Lincoln Plating

Lincoln Plating, located in Nebraska, is a good example of a company that has reaped rewards from incorporating a wellness program into its corporate culture. In 2005, the company was named a Top 50 Best Small and Medium Company to Work For by the Great Place to Work Institute. The company reports a 6-to-1 total return on its investment in wellness and has health insurance costs that are 50% less than the U.S. average. Lincoln Plating is quick to point out that this savings did not occur overnight. In fact, the firm started with a first aid cart and blood pressure checks back in 1970. Awareness and education followed in the 1980s; in the 1990s, a cross-functional wellness committee was formed, and later a full-time wellness manager was hired.

Employees receive free, on-the-job initial and annual blood profiles and mandatory blood pressure screenings, flexibility tests, and weight/body fat analyses each quarter. Pocket wellness cards give workers a way to track the information and wellness tips. Employees cannot smoke on the company's premises, and employees who don't smoke get insurance discounts. Every employee receives a pedometer and is strongly encouraged to walk 10,000 steps each day. Gym memberships are reimbursed, as are the costs of other fitness-related activities. A nutritionist and Weight Watchers personnel are available, and wellness outings—including activities such as mountain climbs, short and long bike rides, and short and long walks—are regular events.

As a result of its programs, Lincoln Plating has been able to lower not only its health care costs but its turnover and absenteeism, too. In fact, in 2004, the company saved $900,000 in direct health care costs and $200,000 in related savings (workers' compensation, turnover, and absenteeism), for a total cost savings of over $1 million. That equaled a 6-to-1 return on the company's investment (ROI) in the programs.

Sources: Miller, S. Developing a cutting-edge wellness program. *SHRM Compensation & Benefits Focus Area*, July 2005, www.shrm.org/rewards/library_published/benefits/nonIC/CMS_013248.asp; and Lincoln Industries Web site, www.lincolnindustries.com.

- Education and awareness programs to promote the wellness effort
- Efforts that encourage employees to take responsibility for their own health
- An evaluation of the program's outcomes

Company Spotlight 12.2 describes how Lincoln Plating, a Nebraska company, made wellness a part of its culture.[41] In addition, Exhibit 12.5 lists some of the key ingredients for a successful wellness program.

Because wellness programs make employees more aware of health and safety risks and educate them about how to stay healthier, companies that use the programs expect to realize substantially lower health insurance costs. Unfortunately, the employees who usually

Exhibit 12.5 ▶

Keys to a Successful Wellness Program

- The support of the firm's senior-level managers
- Assessment and planning that involves employees across the organization and goes beyond what's legally required
- A wellness team or committee to administer and promote the program
- A clear plan for the program's implementation, including a sufficiently large budget and communications strategy
- An incentive program to encourage employees to use the program
- Organizational culture change

Sources: Rosenfeld, M. Workplace wellness: Take it up a notch. *SHRM Compensation & Benefits Forum*, February 2005, www.shrm.org/rewards/library_published/benefits/nonIC/CMS_011093.asp; and Cestnick, K. Quality and healthy workplaces: HR must play a critical role. *Canadian HR Reporter*, 19:10–11, 2006.

participate are the ones who are already a firm's healthier employees. Thus, companies have found that just having a wellness program is not enough to change the behavior of employees. Instead, firms are using incentives to encourage their employees to participate in their wellness programs.[42] When Sprint saw its health care costs increasing by $45 to $50 million per year, it decided to offer each of its employees $45 to take a health assessment. In addition, the firm gave away more than two dozen $500 American Express gift cards in a raffle for employees and dependents who took the assessment.[43] Similarly, IBM offers $150 cash rebates to employees who participate in the company's physical activity programs. Employee participation in the programs increased from 10,000 to 100,000 employees with this new incentive.

One criticism of wellness programs is that they don't typically take into consideration the design and furnishing of an employer's workplace. Health hazards such as poorly ventilated heating and cooling systems and non-ergonomically designed work setups can create health problems for employees.[44] However, safety programs, which we discuss later in this chapter, often do address these issues. Another criticism relates to concerns of discrimination and privacy when employees are required to participate in health assessments. The concern here is that information obtained might be used in a discriminatory manner. For instance, let's assume that an employee has gone for a health screening as part of a wellness program. During the screening, the physician identifies a health problem that could be labeled a disability, but the disability does not affect the employee's ability to perform his job. If that information is shared with the supervisor, who then uses it in a negative way against the employee, the company is violating the ADA.[45]

EMPLOYEE ASSISTANCE PROGRAMS Conditions such as anxiety and depressive disorders can result from work or family situations or a combination of the two. Regardless of the cause, problems such as these have cost employers an estimated $146 billion per year.[46] To help employees cope with mental health issues, substance abuse, and life challenges, companies offer **employee assistance programs (EAPs)**. EAPs were started in the 1970s, primarily to provide a resource for managers dealing with employees who had or appeared to have substance abuse problems. When Ford Motor Company launched its EAP in 1976, it had one purpose: to combat workplace alcohol abuse because about 40% of workplace injuries were related to substance abuse. Today, Ford's EAP addresses a broad array of issues, ranging from helping employees locate day care to financial planning.[47]

EAPs have indeed evolved from their early focus on substance abuse. Today, an employee can use an EAP to consult an attorney, find out about child-care and elder-care options, get information on budgeting, and seek family counseling. Managers who suspect that an employee has a substance abuse or other personal problem can refer that employee to the company's EAP. Exhibit 12.6 explains what a manager should do if he or she thinks an employee has a substance abuse problem. Company Spotlight 12.3 shows how Caesars Entertainment uses both an EAP and a wellness program.

SHORT- AND LONG-TERM DISABILITY INSURANCE Many companies offer their employees the opportunity to participate in short- and long-term disability insurance plans. These plans pay a percentage of the employee's salary during the time the employee is out of work due to a disability. Typically, a **short-term disability** plan will pay you half to two-thirds of an employee's salary for 13 to 26 weeks' time, depending on the plan. (Usually there is a maximum benefit per month, called a *cap*, that high-income-earning employees can collect.) The benefits usually start immediately for an injury and within 14 days for an illness; however, these guidelines vary from employer to employer.[48]

Long-term disability (LTD) typically kicks in after a specified number of days (typically 30 to 90 days) from the time of a disability and pays a portion of the employee's salary until retirement age. Employers traditionally have maintained health insurance for their disabled employees who were collecting LTD payments. However, some firms have begun to discontinue this practice due to rising health insurance premiums. One study reported that about half of U.S. firms now terminate a person's health care benefits as soon as the person goes on LTD.[49]

Many employers are instituting *return-to-work programs* to get employees back on the job as soon as possible. These programs typically specify when an employee is eligible to return to work and under what conditions. These programs are important to the employer

employee assistance program (EAP)

A resource for employees dealing with personal problems that provides services such as attorney consultation, child-care and elder-care options, budgeting information, and family counseling.

short-term disability

An insurance plan that will pay a portion of an employee's salary when the employee is out of work for a limited time due to a disability.

long-term disability (LTD)

An insurance plan that typically kicks in after 30 to 90 days from the time of a disability and pays a portion of the employee's salary until retirement age.

PRINCIPLES

Exhibit 12.6 ▶

What You Should Do
If You Suspect That
an Employee Has a
Substance Abuse
Problem

Watch for indicators. Note if the employee:

- Frequently misses work because of an "illness," especially on Mondays or Fridays
- Is involved in frequent accidents at work
- Returns from lunch with glassy eyes or smelling of alcohol
- Changes his attitude toward his co-workers and you

As a manager you should:

- Confront the employee about his behavior, making sure to focus only on the problems at work
- Let the employee know that you are going to be closely monitoring his behavior
- Stress that your concern is that the employee's job is not getting done or is not being done properly and that this situation has negative consequences for the organization
- Make the employee aware that your organization has an EAP and that information shared through the EAP is confidential
- Set a time to follow up with the employee to see if the person's performance has improved

COMPANY *spotlight*

12.3 Health and Wellness at Caesars Entertainment, Inc.

Caesars Entertainment, Inc., has 52,000 employees working at 21 properties in three countries. In 2005, it merged with Harrah's Entertainment to become the world's largest gaming company. The company recognizes that employee health and wellness matter. Consequently, it takes an integrated approach to reducing the costs associated with its health and wellness problems.

Caesars has opened onsite health care clinics in four of its markets, and more clinics are coming. It also has onsite physical therapists and pharmacies. The goal of the program is to save employees money and reduce the amount of work time they lose when they are sick. An extensive employee assistance program (EAP) helps employees identify financial, legal, educational, child-care, elder-care, and pet-care resources so they can maintain a good work/life balance. Caesars offers this program as part of its total compensation package, alongside a wide range of traditional benefit offerings, such as medical insurance and group term life insurance.

Having a wide array of options available allows the company to take a holistic approach to health and wellness. For example, Caesars recognizes the negative health effects of obesity and is willing to pay for bariatric surgery for any employees who could benefit from it. Before the company will agree to pay for the surgery, however, employees have to consult with the company's EAP and visit a behavioral health specialist as well as agree to work with a company wellness center coach. Caesars also notifies its disability insurer early in this process, before the surgery is performed. The overall goal of these programs is to provide as many resources as possible to employees to ensure that lifestyle changes occur.

Sources: Harrah's Entertainment. *Health & wellness*, www.harrahs.com/harrahs-corporate/careers-life-at-harrahs-benefits-health-wellness.html; Fine, A. A different approach to wellness programs. *Managed Care Quarterly* 13:24, 2005; and Roberts, S. Caesars betting onsite pharmacy will yield savings. *Business Insurance*, May 3, 2004.

▶ **Exhibit 12.7**   Return-to-Work Stipulations Under the FMLA, ADA, and Workers' Compensation Act

Requirements	FMLA	ADA	Workers' Compensation Act
Reinstatement	Required unless the employee's position is eliminated or the employee is unable to perform the essential functions of the job.	Required if the employee can return to work with reasonable accommodation that does not impose undue hardship on the organization.	Required in some states. Check individual state regulations.
Reassignment	Allowed if employee is reassigned to an equivalent position with pay and benefits equivalent to the previous job.	Creating a new position is not required, but reassignment is allowed if the employee is qualified for another position.	Allowed. Reassignment to light duty can help reduce the overall costs and length of disability.
Fitness-for-duty evaluation	Allowed only if evaluation is required for all employees returning from similar leaves. The employee must be informed at the beginning of the leave that the evaluation will be required.	Allowed if it is job related and consistent with business necessity. The evaluation is also permitted to determine whether a worker has a disability and to identify an appropriate accommodation.	Allowed. Some states require an order from the commissioner.
Light duty/modified duty	Allowed. However, the employer cannot force employees to accept light/modified duty instead of FMLA.	Allowed. The employer need not create a light/modified duty position or make it permanent.	Allowed. Reassignment to light duty can help reduce the overall costs and length of disability.

Source: Ahrens, A. Is a Return-to-work program right for your organization? *SHRM Information Center White Paper*, 2003, www.shrm.org/hrresources/whitepapers_published/CMS_000188.asp.

for productivity reasons and are important to employees as well: Work provides a sense of order and purpose for most people. Before rolling out a return-to-work program, however, employers need to carefully think how legal requirements such as those of the ADA, FMLA, Pregnancy Discrimination Act, workers' compensation, and the FLSA will affect the program. Exhibit 12.7 outlines the return-to-work stipulations required under the FMLA, the ADA, and the Workers' Compensation Act.[50]

Employers considering such programs need to have a good understanding of the costs of having employees out on leave, have an organizational philosophy and policies about how leave should be managed, and ensure that employees are not put in a position to have to return to work too early.

ACCIDENTAL DEATH AND DISMEMBERMENT (AD&D)   Accidental death and dismemberment insurance (AD&D) is designed to compensate employees for the loss of a body part or to compensate the employee's family if an employee suffers the loss of a limb or dies accidentally at work. The insurance usually specifies how much will be paid for the loss of each body part or for an accidental death, and it is likely to be more valued by workers in manufacturing and skilled-trade jobs than by white-collar workers.

accidental death and dismemberment insurance (AD&D)

An insurance plan designed to compensate employees for the loss of a body part or to compensate the employee's family if an employee suffers the loss of a limb or dies accidentally at work.

Life Management Benefits

Many employers offer a wide variety of life management services to employees. These services are typically referred to as work/life benefits. However, we have labeled them as *life management benefits* to more accurately reflect the idea that work is part of life rather than separate from it. Designed to help employees achieve a balance between their home and work responsibilities, these benefits include paid time off, child-care and elder-care assistance, financial planning, and concierge services. Many of the life management benefits that companies offer today were instituted in an attempt to retain women in the workforce. But the programs can certainly help retain both male and female employees. When employees know that the company will be responsive to accommodating their personal needs, they will, in turn, be loyal, committed employees. IBM has 50 different life management programs; Bank of America has 30.[51] In the following sections, we provide an overview of some of the ones most frequently offered. Keep in mind that there are many other types of benefits available, ranging from commuter benefits to onsite dry cleaning and hair-care services to personal shoppers and pet boarding.

PAID TIME OFF When employees are able to get away from the workplace for rest and renewal, they are more productive when they return. Also, employees need to know that when they are sick, they can (and should) stay home. To accommodate the needs of employees for time away from the job, employers provide paid time off in the form of vacation, sick leave, bereavement leave, personal leave days, and holidays. Instead of breaking down leave into all these categories, some employers give employees a certain number of days per year to take as *paid time off (PTO)*. PTO leave can be a specified number of days per year and/or accrued on a monthly basis, based on the length of time a person has been employed. Employees observe different religious holidays. PTO gives them the flexibility to take off the religious holidays of their choice rather than holidays firms have traditionally designated.

Even though employees know they have PTO, they do not always use it. One study found that employees in the United States gave back over 574 million vacation days in 2005, which amounts to 4 unused days per adult worker. Respondents in the study said they didn't use the time because they were too busy at work, the vacation had to be scheduled in advance, and they preferred the money instead of the vacation time if their company pays employees for all or a portion of the PTO they don't use.[52] Some employers allow their employees to contribute their unused time off pay to a pool from which employees who are out of work for medical reasons can draw after they have used up their own leave.

EDUCATIONAL ASSISTANCE One study found that 86% of companies in the United States offer some type of educational benefit to their employees and collectively spend about $10 billion annually to educate their workers.[53] These employers either pay directly for their employees to attend school or reimburse them for all or a portion of their educational costs. Employers believe that when their employees acquire more education, they bring more human capital to the workplace and are, therefore, more valuable on the job. Some employers will reimburse their employees only if they make a certain grade in their courses. Some employers require their employees to agree that they will remain with the company for a set period of time after completing their education. As long as certain requirements outlined by the IRS are met, an employee can receive up to $5,250 per year from his or her employer without having to pay taxes on that money. The IRS requires employers to document the details of their educational assistance plans and ensure that access to them isn't limited to highly compensated employees.[54]

CHILD CARE AND ELDER CARE Baby boomers—people born between 1946 and 1964—are most likely to feel the effects of child-care and elder-care responsibilities; hence, this group is sometimes referred to as the "sandwich generation." It's been estimated that the absenteeism and lower productivity that employees who are caregivers experience costs employers anywhere from $11 billion to $29 billion per year. Providing long-term care insurance options to employees is one to way to keep caregivers in the workplace. We discuss this option next.

long-term care insurance (LTCI)

An insurance plan that provides assistance to aging, disabled, and ill persons who need daily help with tasks such as dressing, eating, or bathing for an extended time period.

LONG-TERM CARE BENEFITS Long-term care insurance (LTCI) provides assistance to aging, disabled, and ill persons who need daily help with tasks such as dressing, eating, or bathing for an extended time period. Often employers offer LTCI to the extended family members of their employees, including their parents and in-laws. Generally, employees pay for the premiums for this insurance themselves. Making this benefit available to your employees can give them peace of mind; when they are at work, they know that their loved

PRINCIPLES

ones are being cared for. If employers pay some or all of the cost of the LTCI, the cost is fully tax deductible. The LTCI benefits that employees receive are also tax free.[55]

LIFE INSURANCE Life insurance provides financial protection, or income, for an employee's family in the event of the employee's death. Thus, life insurance has been described as "a basic pillar for retirement saving because it provides psychological comfort."[56] Employer plans are often limited to $50,000 of coverage,[57] although some employers offer an amount equal to 1.5 times the employer's annual salary or more or allow the employee to purchase greater coverage than the employer provides. A lot of plans allow employees to buy insurance to cover their spouse and/or children at a group-rate cost as well.

FINANCIAL PLANNING Financial planning services increase the financial literacy of employees and can help them achieve financial security. For example, employees with debt problems often experience stress and anxiety. They may also look for a higher-paying job and leave the company.[58] Employees who take advantage of the financial planning programs their employers offer have a better understanding of how to manage their finances, gain more confidence about their future financial situation, and tend to be more supportive of and satisfied with their companies.[59] Other outcomes of financial education programs are reduced absenteeism and increased productivity.[60]

Some employees provide access to professional certified financial planners directly, whereas others make the information available to their employees via online financial portals or Web sites. Using the portals, employees can calculate how much money they need for retirement, how much money they need to save to send their children to college, and how much mortgages and loans will cost. Employers need to make sure that any financial planning information they provide to employees, whether through a financial planner or through a financial portal, does not violate laws regarding financial advice.[61] For instance, employers can only make recommendations to the employees—not tell them what to do— and should make sure to provide employees with the pros and cons of various options.

LEGAL SERVICES Darden Restaurants, owner of the Olive Garden and Red Lobster restaurant chains, offers legal services as one of its voluntary benefits for employees, and may other companies also do so. This benefit provides employees with access to attorneys for assistance with everything from estate planning and adoption to legal representation if they are sued. Employees at Darden pay the full cost of the premiums associated with the services. The premiums generally run less than $20 per month per employee, and employees can make the payments through their payroll deductions. Aside from some initial enrollment costs for the company and some administrative costs, the plans cost employers nothing and are very appealing to employees. Each plan specifies the types of services that are provided and what additional costs apply beyond the monthly premium. A typical plan gives employees access to legal consultation through phone calls with lawyers in the plan's network and discounted legal fees for certain services.[62]

Retirement Benefits

A goal for most of us is to one day be able to retire from our jobs and to have time for travel, hobbies, and whatever else we don't get to do today because we're busy earning a living. If we want to do these things, we have to carefully plan for our retirement. In this section we

Company pension plans make it more likely for retirees to enjoy their retirement without financial concerns.

describe the Employee Retirement Income and Security Act (ERISA) and then describe the most frequently offered types of retirement accounts.

The **Employee Retirement Income and Security Act of 1974 (ERISA)** is a federal law that protects retirees in the private sector.[63] Just a few of the benefit plans covered under ERISA are pension, health, disability, life and accidental death and dismemberment, and cafeteria plans.[64] Under ERISA, private employers must have written plans documenting the pension benefits they provide their employees. The plans must specify what the benefits are, who is eligible to receive them (as well as when and how), and how the plans can be terminated by employers. ERISA's major function is to ensure that firms treat their employees fairly with respect to their retirement accounts. We now describe some of the major provisions of ERISA.

Vesting refers to the time required before you own part or all of your retirement funds. The money you pay into your retirement funds plus interest earned on that money is 100% vested immediately. This means that you have a nonforfeitable right to those funds, even if you leave your employer before you reach retirement age. Your employer can require you to fulfill certain service requirements before you are vested in the money it contributes to your retirement. ERISA provides minimum standards for vesting; your employer can use a different standard, as long as the ERISA minimum is met.[65]

There are two ways in which employees become vested: *cliff vesting* and *graded vesting*. Under cliff vesting, employees become fully vested when they have three years of service. This means that employees own the employer's contributions to their retirement funds after three years of working for the employer. An employer has the right to allow the employee to be fully vested before three years of service but cannot require a longer vesting time if it uses cliff vesting. The other option, graded vesting, is a phase-in plan. Under a plan such as this, an employee must be fully vested—that is, entitled to her firm's contributions—within six years: After the second year of service, the employee must be vested at 20% of the employer's contribution, with the percentage increasing by 20% each year thereafter until 100% vesting is reached at the end of six years of service.

CONTRIBUTORY AND NONCONTRIBUTORY RETIREMENT PLANS Some employers make retirement plans available to their employees but require them to fund their own accounts. However, most employers that offer plans such as these either make the entire contribution, provide some type of matching funds, or do some combination of the two. A **noncontributory retirement plan** is one in which the employer puts funds into an employee's account without requiring the employee to make contributions. A **contributory retirement plan** is one in which the employer and employee both put money into the retirement account.

An employer can have both types of plans—noncontributory and contributory. George Washington University (GW) offers such a plan. Here's how it works: GW puts 4% of an eligible employee's annual salary into a retirement fund, without requiring the employee to put anything into the account. GW also offers to match some or all of the money the employee puts into the account at 1.5 times the total, up to a maximum of 6%. So, if the employee puts in 4% of her annual earnings, GW puts in 6% (4% × 1.5 = 6%). With the noncontributory amount (4%) and the contributory amounts (4% contributed by the employee plus 6% contributed by her firm), 14% of the person's total salary would be going into her retirement account annually.

DEFINED BENEFIT PENSION PLANS A **defined benefit pension plan** provides an annuity to eligible employees upon their retirement. The annuity is either a specified dollar amount each month or is based on a formula that usually involves multiplying the number of years an employee worked at a company by a designated percentage by the employee's last or highest salary. The salary amount can also be an average of a number of years' salaries—for example, the average of the person's salary for the last three years he or she worked for the firm. Under this type of pension plan, the employee is promised an annuity that increases the longer the person has been with the company. For example, consider an employee who has worked for a company for 30 years and was making $70,000 at her retirement. If the company has designated the percentage for determining the retirement income of its employees to be 3% (a typical amount), then the employee's retirement

---

Employee Retirement Income and Security Act of 1974 (ERISA)

A federal law that protects benefits for retirees in the private sector.

vesting

The time required before employees own part or all of their retirement funds.

noncontributory retirement plan

A pension plan in which the employer puts funds into an employee's account without requiring the employee to make contributions.

contributory retirement plan

A pension plan in which the employer and employee both put money into the retirement account.

defined benefit pension plan

A pension plan that provides an annuity to eligible employees upon their retirement with the amount paid per year based on a formula that usually includes a company-determined percentage, the number of years worked, and either the last salary or some average of previous years' salaries.

income each year would be computed as follows: 30 years × $70,000 × 3% = $63,000. Her retirement income would be 90% of her pre-retirement salary.

Companies such as GM and Ford have used defined benefit plans for many years. The plans were designed to entice employees to stay with the employer for a longer period of time so they could increase the value of their retirement income. Unions are particularly fond of these plans because their members are assured of good retirement income. The downside for companies, however, is that when a lot of employees retire at the same time, a lot of money has to be paid out. If the company funds have not been carefully managed and/or are underfunded because fewer employees subsequently paid into the plan (or for some other reason), the company has to make up the difference.

The economy plays a major role in the success of these plans. Low, long-term interest rates, a stock market that isn't climbing rapidly, extensive regulations, and global competition from firms that don't provide retirement programs such as these create a huge financial burden on firms that are trying to manage their defined benefit plans.[66] Even companies that are financially strong and have fully funded defined benefit plans, such as IBM, have frozen their defined benefit pension plans. Beginning January 1, 2008, no IBM employees could accumulate additional benefits in their defined benefit plans. This change is expected to result in a $3 billion savings over five years.[67]

In the past five years, a large number of companies have turned their pension programs over to the **Pension Benefit Guaranty Corporation (PBGC)**, a not-for-profit organization created by the federal government that insures defined benefit plans.[68] Employees who receive their pensions under the auspices of the PBGC (because the pensions of their firms are either underfunded or insolvent) are limited to a maximum amount per year. That amount was $47,659 in 2006.[69]

For many years, the predominant type of retirement or pension plan for older, established firms in the United States has been the defined benefit plan. That is no longer the case. In 2006, only about 21% of U.S. workers were covered by a plan of this type.[70] Many companies have frozen, terminated, or closed access to defined benefit plans for new hires and instead offer a defined contribution plan. In 2004, 96 *Fortune* 1000 companies had at least one plan that was not available to new hires for one of these reasons. In 2006, that number had jumped to 162.[71]

DEFINED CONTRIBUTION PLANS   Defined contribution plans have found favor with employers over the years as an alternative to defined benefit plans. Under a defined contribution plan, the amount of retirement income is a function of how well the money put into the plan was invested. The employer specifies where the money is to be deposited, sometimes providing several options of places, and often gives employees the power to decide how that money is invested within a place. Research of employee participation in 401(k) plans, a type of defined contribution plan described in the following section, has found that employees are most likely to participate in defined contribution plans when the company matches their contributions, when they can borrow from the plan, and when they have choices about how to invest in the plan.[72] Next we describe two types of defined contribution plans in more detail: 401(k) plans and cash balance plans.

401(k) Plans.   A study by Hewitt Associates, a leading HR outsourcing and consulting firm, found that almost two-thirds of 450 large companies in 2005 indicated that **401(k) plans** were the primary retirement savings plans for their employees.[73] A 401(k) plan, named after the section of the IRS code that permits these plans, allows employees to defer receiving some of their compensation until retirement. The money contributed by the employee is taken out of the person's paycheck pretax, and it accumulates tax free until the person retires. Only when a person begins withdrawing the funds upon retirement is he or she taxed. There is a dollar limit on how much can be deferred each year, however. In 2008, the limit was $15,500 for traditional and 401(k) plans. And, the IRS has a provision that permits employers to include an elective deferral provision for individuals over the age of 50 to make catch-up contributions.[74]

Cash Balance Plans.   A **cash balance plan** is a type of defined benefit plan that operates like a defined contribution plan because it defines the benefit a person receives upon

Pension Benefit Guaranty Corporation (PBGC)

A not-for-profit organization created by the federal government that insures defined benefit pension plans.

defined contribution plan

A pension plan in which the employer specifies where the money will be deposited and often gives the employee the power to decide how the money will be invested with the retirement income being a function of how well money put into the plan was invested.

401(k) plan

A retirement plan that allows employees to defer receiving some of their compensation until retirement with contributions to the plan taken out of the employee's paycheck pretax and the funds accumulating tax free until retirement begins.

cash balance plan

A type of retirement account in which the employer credits the participants' retirement account with a pay credit and an interest credit and the employer bears the risk because the employee, when fully vested, is entitled to receive the stated account balance upon leaving the company or retirement.

retirement in terms of a cash payout. What does that mean? The employer credits the participants' accounts with a pay credit and an interest credit. The pay credit might be a percentage, for instance 5%, of the employee's compensation, whereas the interest credit can be either a fixed or variable rate tied to an index. One index that might be used is the one-year U.S. Treasury bill rate. The employer bears the risk in this plan because the employee is entitled to receive the stated account balance. If an employee is vested in the plan, she can take the account balance in a lump-sum payment upon leaving the company or at the time of retirement. Or, if she is retiring, she can draw an annual payment, referred to as an annuity, from the account.[75]

Pension Protection Act (PPA)

An act passed in 2006 and designed to strengthen the U.S. pension system by tightening rules relative to employer responsibilities for funding pension accounts and for administering and terminating pension funds.

PENSION PROTECTION ACT OF 2006   When it was passed in 2006, the **Pension Protection Act (PPA)** was referred to as historic and groundbreaking. The legislation resulted in large part from the increase in the number of firms that were turning their pension plans over to the U.S. Pension Benefits Guaranty Corporation because they could not afford to pay the pensions. The act was designed to strengthen the U.S. pension system. In essence, the PPA tightened rules relative to employer responsibilities for funding pension accounts and for administering and terminating pension funds.[76] The act requires employers to pay more attention to how they are managing these funds, particularly if they have underfunded their pension plan. It also raises caps so that employers can set aside more money when the economy is doing well to offset the fact that less money goes in at other times. For employees, the act makes sure more information is provided to employees, especially regarding their choices for their pension funds.

RETIREE HEALTH PLANS   A study by the Employee Benefits Research Institute (EBRI) found that a couple who retires at age 65 and lives to an average life expectancy will need $295,000 for the cost of health insurance and nonreimbursed medical expenses.[77] This news comes at a time when more and more companies are finding it prohibitively expensive to provide health insurance for retirees. In 1988, about 66% of firms with 200-plus employees provided medical benefits to their retired employees. By 2006, the percentage was half that. Companies are either eliminating these benefits altogether or capping them at a specified dollar amount. Some companies allow employees to purchase health care benefits at employee group rates, and others also allow employees to carry over medical spending account funds into their retirement, as noted earlier.[78]

BENEFITS ADMINISTRATION

Adequately and effectively communicating benefits, wellness, and safety program information to employees is critical to the success of these programs. Studies have shown that when firms do a better job of this, their employees are more knowledgeable about their programs and participate in them more frequently, and the service quality of the programs improves.[79] In fact, in a study done in the United Kingdom, two-thirds of the 1,357 workers surveyed indicated they thought companies should be required to include information about employee benefits in job advertisements. Forty-two percent of the managers surveyed agreed that providing the information would be useful for applicants as they compared potential employers.[80]

Indeed, workers often don't know how much money their employers are spending on their benefits. In one study, employees indicated that they thought the employer probably spent less than $1,000 per year rather than the actual $7,000 for family coverage and $3,000 for individual health care coverage.[81] To address this issue, an employer often provides a detailed listing of how much each benefit or service is costing the company in addition to the employee's basic salary. Doing so provides the employee with a more realistic picture of what he or she is actually making at the company. When considering changing jobs, employees can use this information to compare the total rewards packages other employers are offering.

When putting together a benefits package, an employer has to decide which employees will receive the benefits, how much the employer will pay versus how much the employee will contribute, and how much choice among available alternatives the employee should be given.[82] Exhibit 12.8 contains a list of the types of issues managers need to address when they are putting together a firm's benefits package.

1. Length of probationary period before employee is eligible to receive each type of benefit

2. Availability of coverage for:
   - Dependents of employees
   - Retirees and their dependents
   - Survivors of deceased employees
   - Employees suffering from a disability
   - Employees during a layoff, leave of absence, or strike
   - Part-time and temporary employees

Source: Based on Parmenter, E. Employee benefit compliance checklist. *Compensation & Benefits Review*, May/June 2002, pp. 29–39.

◄ **Exhibit 12.8**

Issues to Consider When Designing a Benefits Package

The age, marital status, number of children, and other demographics of an employee affect the person's preferences for different benefits. To assist their employees with different types of needs, employers have developed a number of flexible benefit plans. **Flexible benefit plans,** also known as *cafeteria plans*, allow employees to choose which benefits they want to purchase from a menu of benefits. Some companies require all their employees to receive certain benefits, usually health insurance, but can allow them to choose which others they want to purchase. Some companies provide a set amount of money or credits for each employee for benefits. Vanguard, the company featured in Company Spotlight 12.4, provides its employees with credits to use for benefits. Employees decide how to distribute the allotted money, or credits, among the benefits they choose, sometimes with certain restrictions. For example, an employer might require its employees to have health insurance but allow them to choose among different health plans. There may even be choices within each type of benefit. An employee might be able to select from among an HMO, a PPO, and a traditional health insurance plan.

flexible benefit plan (also called a cafeteria plan)

This plan allows employees to choose which benefits they want to purchase from a menu of benefits.

COMPANY spotlight   12.4 FlexCare at Vanguard

Each year Vanguard gives its crew members (employees) FlexCare credits that they can use to purchase benefits. If the cost of the benefits a crew member chooses exceeds the allotted number of FlexCare credits, the crew member can pay the balance as a pretax contribution. If the crew member doesn't use all her credits, the remaining cash value is added to her paycheck, and she is taxed on that amount.

Crew members can choose to use their FlexCare credits for the following benefits:

- Medical (required to choose one of available comprehensive plans)
- Dental (choose among two dental plan options)
- Vision
- Prescription (employees receive reduced price for prescriptions)
- Health care and dependent care reimbursement accounts
- Legal services
- Retiree medical benefits

- Basic life insurance (including options for purchase for spouse or child)
- Short-term disability
- Long-term disability

Vanguard also understands that wellness programs can cut down on medical costs and lead to a more productive workforce. Its wellness programs include the following (some for free, and some for a fee):

- Blood pressure and cholesterol screening
- Mammography screenings
- Weight Watchers at Work
- Lunchtime seminars on health topics
- Supervised day trips for school-aged children on some school holidays

Source: Based on Vanguard. *FlexCare*, https://careers.vanguard.com/pljb/vanguard/vgcareers/applicant/VG/rewards_benefits_flexcare.shtml.

Integrating benefit plans is often one of the greatest challenges for merged companies. When Sears and K-Mart merged in 2004, a major concern of retired employees was whether they would still have a health plan after the merger went into effect. They did get to keep their plan but had to start paying the full price of the premium if they were under age 65.[83]

SAFETY PROGRAMS

One way organizations address worker health and wellness is through safety programs. Safety is regulated in the workplace by the Occupational Safety and Health Act (OSH Act). Of course, many companies have developed their own safety practices that go beyond those of the OSH Act. For the moment, however, let's look at what the act requires. Safety starts with hiring employees who are more likely to be safe on the job and rewarding employees for following safety standards.[84]

Programs Related to the Occupational Safety and Health Act

Occupational Safety and Health Act of 1971 (OSH Act)

This act requires employers to provide a safe workplace for all employees, and provides a process for investigation of complaints of unfair practices as well as provides for work-site inspections.

The mission of the **Occupational Safety and Health Act of 1971 (OSH Act)** is to "send every worker home whole and healthy every day."[85] The act covers private-sector employers and employees in all 50 states and certain territories and jurisdictions of the United States through the federal act or through state-approved programs.[86] Since the passage of the act, occupational illness and injury rates have declined by 40%, and workplace fatalities have been reduced by 62%. The Occupational Safety and Health Administration (OSHA) enforces the OSH Act and other safety and health regulations in the workplace; provides outreach programs, education, and compliance assistance to employers; and develops partnerships with employers and other groups interested in safety issues.[87]

OSHA requires an employer to provide a workplace that is free of known hazards to health and safety that complies with OSHA guidelines. Compliance officers have the right to inspect businesses and can issue citations when health and safety hazards are discovered. Such a citation lists the OSHA violation, the financial penalty for the violation, and the time period within which the violation must be corrected. Employers can contest these citations before a hearing board.

Employers are responsible for notifying employees about OSHA standards, and employees are responsible for following the standards. Employees have the right to report their concerns to OSHA and can even request an inspection without their employer finding out they made the request. Employees have the right to know how their complaints are handled and to be advised of any actions taken. They can also request an informal review of a decision to not inspect an employer.[88]

INSPECTION PROGRAMS Because of the sheer number of workplaces that OSHA has authority to inspect, it has developed a system for inspection priorities. The administration's top priority is to inspect reports of imminently dangerous situations. The second priority is to investigate fatalities and catastrophes that have resulted in five or more employees being hospitalized. The third priority is to respond to employees' complaints about unsafe or unhealthy working conditions. OSHA also conducts planned inspections of high-hazard industries or occupations. Following the inspections, OSHA conducts follow-up and monitoring inspections to make sure any hazards are eliminated and employees are safe.[89]

PARTNERSHIP PROGRAMS OSHA has developed a number of programs to recognize employers who are committed to ensuring that their workplaces are safe and healthy. The Strategic Partnership Program enables OSHA and its partners—employers, employees (and their unions and associations), and other stakeholders—to develop a written, signed agreement to work together to address critical safety and health issues and to measure the results.[90] Another OSHA program is the Voluntary Protection Program (VPP), which focuses on establishing a cooperative relationship between OSHA and companies that have comprehensive safety and health programs. The program recognizes the outstanding efforts of such companies.[91]

OSHA is also available for consultation services, to help employers establish workplace safety and health programs. When a firm requests a consultation, OSHA will appraise its mechanical systems, physical work practices, environmental hazards, and current safety and health programs.

REPORTING REQUIREMENTS   Employers have eight hours following the work-related death of an employee or a work-related accident leading to the hospitalization of three or more employees to report the information to OSHA.[92] Firms are required to use OSHA Form 300 to log their work-related injuries and illnesses and OSHA Form 301 to provide specific details about incidents leading to injuries or illnesses.

Workplace Violence Programs

Workplace violence might not be a topic you typically associate with workplace safety, but it is an important one. Did you know that homicide is the fourth-leading cause of fatal occupational injuries?[93] The National Institute for Occupational Safety and Health (NIOSH) has identified a number of risk factors for violence in the workplace. These include having contact with the public; delivering passengers, services, or goods; working alone or in small numbers; exchanging money; and working with unstable or volatile persons, such as in health care, criminal justice, or social service settings.

Violence in the workplace can be prevented in a number of ways. The environmental design of the workplace can be changed to maximize its visibility and lighting, and companies can install security devices and erect barriers between employees and customers. Administrative controls can be implemented to reduce the chances of workplace violence occurring. This can include reviewing the firm's staffing plans to ensure that the company's employees are not working alone or required to transport or store money. Providing conflict-resolution training to employees can also help employers diffuse situations that could become violent. This type of training is an example of an employee behavioral change companies can pursue.[94]

Ergonomic Programs

Employers can increase safety in the workplace through **ergonomics**. (Recall that in Chapter 4 we discussed the concept of ergonomics, which is the science of understanding the capabilities of humans in terms of their work requirements.) An ergonomically designed workplace is one that is designed for the safe and efficient completion of tasks. The height of employees' chairs, their visual distance from their computer screens, and the way in which they should lift heavy objects are all examples of ergonomically related issues about which employers need to be concerned. Improperly designed workspaces or work processes lead to injuries, which in turn affect employee productivity.

In 2002, the Department of Labor initiated a four-pronged comprehensive approach to workplace ergonomics. This approach focuses on developing industry- and task-specific guidelines, enforcing the guidelines, providing outreach and assistance for businesses, and chartering a national advisory committee to identify gaps in research related to ergonomics in the workplace. The overall goal of the program is to "quickly and effectively address musculoskeletal disorders (MSDs) in the workplace."[95] The program was first rolled out for the nursing home industry, and other industries are being added.

Managers concerned with identifying conditions that can contribute to musculoskeletal disorders can start by reviewing the injury and illness records they submit to OSHA, as well as their firm's workers' compensation claims, group health insurance records, first-aid logs, absentee and turnover records, and employee complaints and grievances. By using

ergonomics

The science of understanding the capabilities of humans in terms of their work requirements.

these information sources, you can identify incidents of MSDs such as carpal tunnel syndrome, tendonitis, and bursitis and categorize them by job, department, division, task, and so on in order to determine whether there are injury patterns or trends occurring within your company and, if so, where.[96]

EMPLOYEE BENEFITS AND SAFETY PROGRAMS IN PRACTICE: ORGANIZATIONAL DEMANDS

We have provided a lot of information in this chapter already, and by now it goes without saying that decisions about employee management practices must take into account the organizational demands, environmental factors, and legal issues affecting firms. We have outlined significant issues to address in Exhibit 12.9. We start this section by discussing organizational demands and how those demands affect the benefits and safety programs companies design for their employees.

Strategy, Benefits, and Safety Programs

An organization's strategy has clear implications for the design and delivery of the company's benefits and safety programs. The strategy determines the role these programs play in terms of the total rewards the firm offers its employees as well as the funds available for the programs.

ROLE OF PROGRAMS IN TOTAL COMPENSATION PACKAGE As noted in Chapter 10, when we discussed compensation, decisions have to be made about the composition of a total compensation package. These decisions include how much of the compensation will be in the form of fixed versus variable monetary compensation and nonmonetary compensation

▶ **Exhibit 12.9** Employee Benefits and Safety Programs in Practice

Context	**Employee Attitudes and Behaviors** Chapter 12, "Benefits and Safety Programs"
Organizational Demands	
Strategy drives . . .	• Role in total compensation package • Funds available for programs
Company characteristics determine . . .	• Types of programs • Availability of programs
Culture establishes . . .	• Attitudes toward benefits and safety • Who gets nonmandatory benefits
Employee concerns include . . .	• Perceptions of the fairness of the firm's benefits • Safety in the workplace
Environmental Demands	
Labor force influences . . .	• What benefits need to be offered • What safety modifications and training should occur
Technology affects . . .	• How benefits information is delivered • Concerns about safety for telecommuters
Globalization impacts . . .	• Types of benefits offered • Policies about benefits equalization • Norms relative to safety
Ethics/social responsibility shapes . . .	• Management of benefits • Comprehensiveness of safety programs
Regulations *guide* . . .	• What happens when workers change jobs • Protection of employee medical information

in the form of benefits and services. The decision is driven, in large part, by the firm's strategy. Firms with a low-cost strategy will minimize the amount of funds they spend on nondirect compensation. Generally speaking, they might offer full-time employees a few basic benefits, such as reduced premiums on their medical insurance. However, they will be less likely to offer more elaborate benefits, such as legal services. Nonetheless, the companies will still offer safety programs because they know they the programs may be legally required and because they recognize that providing safer workplaces for their employees saves money in the long run.

Firms with a low-cost strategy can still appreciate the broader cost savings that come from providing benefits to improve the health of their employees. When they have this longer-term view, they are more likely to offer wellness programs and life management benefits to employees. Wal-Mart, a company we have mentioned several times because of its well-known low-cost strategy, actually offers more than 50 health benefit options to employees.[97] Offering the benefit options does not mean that Wal-Mart pays for all of them, or even that every employee has a chance to receive or purchase them, however. For example, many of the benefits are not available to Wal-Mart's large group of part-time employees, and the company's full-time employees have to pay all or a portion of their insurance premiums. Wal-Mart uses its buying power to bargain with benefits providers just as it bargains with its other suppliers. However, it is important to remember that many other low-cost employers do not have the same amount of bargaining power when it comes to their benefits providers as Wal-Mart does.

Firms with a differentiation strategy recognize that they need to offer higher levels of benefits to attract the human capital needed to achieve a sustained competitive advantage. These companies emphasize the value of employees in the development of their corporate values and design "state-of-the-art" benefits programs. They recognize that employees are as attracted to firms by the benefits they offer as they are by the monetary compensation.

FUNDS AVAILABLE FOR BENEFITS The overall strategy of an organization affects how much money the company is willing to spend on employee benefits and safety programs. Companies that adopt a low-cost strategy will, obviously, want to minimize these expenditures. Companies with a differentiation strategy will weigh the pros and cons of offering various benefits and wellness programs and decide which are most likely to attract, motivate, and retain the types of employees the firms need. Managers can—and should— play a critical role as providers of information to decision makers about the programs that are most attractive to potential and current employees.

A firm's strategy also affects how much it will invest in safety programs, although that decision is often easier to make than deciding how much to invest in benefit options. Some firms that pursue a low-cost strategy pride themselves on having an excellent safety record and fund such programs generously. These companies want to avoid fines, reduce downtime, and reduce or eliminate the other negative effects workplace safety violations and incidents can have.

Company Characteristics, Benefits, and Safety Programs

The stage of a company's development, size, and industry affect the types of benefits and safety programs it offers, too. We take a look at each of these issues next.

TYPES OF BENEFIT AND SAFETY PROGRAMS Many startup firms in the software industry in the 1990s offered a wide range of benefits to employees to attract and retain them. In fact, these firms had a lot to do with the increase in the types of life management programs available to employees today. The employees targeted most by these firms wanted to work hard and play hard, and they were in short supply. Hence, firms got very creative when it came to designing their benefits programs, offering employees everything from concierge services to meals at their workplaces. Google is a good example of such a company. The company offers a wide array of benefits, including free gourmet food (breakfast, lunch, and dinner), a 24-hour gym, an in-house doctor and nutritionist, dry cleaners, and massage services, along with traditional benefits such as health insurance.[98] In order to compete for the best employees, many larger, older employers found that they needed to be more creative with the benefits they were offering, too. Employees in medium to large companies tend to have greater access to health care benefits in particular. However, because

12.5 Badger Mining Corporation, The Best Small Company to Work for in America

Badger Mining Corporation is a privately held, family-owned international company that manufactures industrial silica sand, limestone, and other aggregates. In 2006 and 2007, the firm, which is based in the midwestern United States, was recognized as The Best Small Company to Work for in America by the Society for Human Resource Management and the Great Place to Work Institute. Badger has 180 employees in the United States and 25 in Poland. The company emphasizes both safety and health care. In fact, it spends about 10% of its annual budget on safety training and sees safety as a collaborative effort. Spending on safety has paid off for the company. In 2005, Badger experienced no lost time because of work accidents. The company also pays for the full premium for health insurance for its employees and provides personalized health coaching through its wellness program.

Sources: Shea, T. Badger Mining stages an encore. *HR Magazine*, 52: 44-45, 2007; Shea, T. Badger Mining debuts at the top. *HR Magazine*, 51: 56-57, 2006; and Badger Mining Corporation. *BMC honored nationally as best small company to work for in America*, June 27, 2006, www.badgerminingcorp.com/news/news_detail.cfm?id=24.

small employers often choose to offer fewer benefits, or choose to participate in insurance pools with other small employers in their community, these employers might actually experience less of an impact of higher benefit costs due to an aging workforce than will large employers that have their own company-provided insurance plans.[99]

Small and midsized businesses have been less likely to offer LTCI options to their employees. Fewer than 25% of companies with 2 to 49 employees and fewer than 50% of companies with 50 to 199 employees provided LTCI options to their employees in 2005, whereas 75% of companies with more than 5,000 employees provided LTCI.[100] However, smaller companies have done a better job of offering flexibility to their workers. Moreover, employees consider flexibility one of the most prized benefits because it allows them to better manage their work and life responsibilities. As a result, smaller firms may have an edge over larger employers because of their greater willingness and ability to adapt to their employees' needs. Ward's Furniture in Long Beach, California, for example, believes its ability to adapt to the needs of its employees is the main reason many of its 17 employees have worked for the company for 10 to 20 years.[101] Company Spotlight 12.5 describes how one small company recognized that benefits and safety matter.

AVAILABILITY OF PROGRAMS The industry in which a company operates affects the benefits to which the company's employees have access. Employees in goods-producing industries are more likely to have access to retirement benefits than employees in service industries. Government employees receive the highest level of benefits of employees in any industry, followed by firms in the education and large nonprofit sectors and firms in the utilities, mining, and pharmaceutical and medicine manufacturing industries. Each of these industries offers a higher percentage of benefits than the national median percentage.[102] When it comes to providing retirement benefit options, overall, smaller firms have lagged behind large corporations. At the end of 2005, for instance, 97% of large companies offered their employees access to defined contribution plans, whereas only 15% of firms with 100 or fewer employees did so.[103]

All companies, regardless of their size, have to be concerned with following OSHA safety guidelines. OSHA's *Field Inspection Reference Manual (FIRM)* does, however, allow OSHA's inspectors to adjust the penalties for violations imposed on firms based on their size: A 60% penalty reduction can be given to firms with fewer than 25 employees, a 40% reduction to firms with 26 to 100 employees, and a 20% reduction to firms with 101 to 250 employees. These reductions reflect the fact that larger employers typically have greater resources available to address safety issues and should, therefore, be penalized accordingly.[104]

SAS Corporation provides many benefits for its employees, including a state-of-the-art workout center.

Company Culture, Benefits, and Safety Programs

A company's culture plays a key role in determining how the firm's employees will react to the benefits and safety programs the company implements and which employees will receive the nonmandatory benefits the firm provides.

EMPLOYEES' ATTITUDES TOWARD THEIR FIRM'S BENEFITS AND SAFETY PROGRAMS SAS Corporation, a privately owned multi-billion-dollar company located in Cary, North Carolina, provides a good example of how a company's culture can affect how employees feel about their benefits. SAS believes that "if you treat employees as if they make a difference to the company, they will make a difference to the company." SAS ensures employees know they make a difference through the extensive benefits and wellness programs it makes available. Onsite child-care centers, elder-care information, an onsite employee health care center, wellness programs, and a 58,000-square-foot recreation and fitness facility are just some of the benefits the firm offers. Programs such as these have kept SAS in the top 20 companies on *Fortune*'s 100 Best Companies to Work for in America list for 11 straight years.[105]

Employees' attitudes toward safety are greatly affected by the safety culture of the firms for which they work. Company Spotlight 12.6 describes how UPS changed what its

COMPANY spotlight   12.6 UPS Turned Upside-Down

United Parcel Service (UPS) has traditionally used a top-down management approach. But when the company found itself struggling with how to reduce its rising rate of on-the-job injuries, it decided to make a radical change. Instead of approaching its managers as it had traditionally done for 90-plus years, its managers went to UPS's employees—the drivers and parcel handlers—to seek their help in developing a new approach to safety.

The goal of UPS's new safety program, called Comprehensive Health and Safety Process (CHSP) is to ensure that every employee makes safety a personal value. There are about 2,400 CHSP committees throughout the company. Each committee has at least five members who represent management and nonmanagement. The committees investigate accidents, counsel employees about safety on the job, and audit facilities and equipment.

CHSP has led to a decrease in injuries and an increase in safety awareness for UPS. The rate of injuries per 200,000 hours worked decreased from 27.2 when the program began in 1996 to 10.2 by the end of 2004. Another byproduct of the program has been lower employee turnover. In 2005, UPS was honored with an Optimas Award for the innovation that went into improving its safety record.

Source: Based on Shuit, D. A left turn for safety at UPS. *Workforce Management*, March 2005, pp. 49–50.

employees thought about safety in the workplace. UPS reduced injuries on the job and reduced turnover as a result of a safety awareness and training program led by employees. A U.K. construction company, Frank Haslam Milan Ltd. (FHm), has done even better than UPS. This company had a goal of zero reportable accidents and achieved it. The company credits its success to employees and even customers who are involved in safety awareness and training programs. The firm's programs cover everything from first aid to driver awareness to control of substances that are hazardous to human health.[106]

Some of the methods used to educate employees about safety are safety posters, slogans, training sessions, incentives, and contests. These programs help remind employees of the responsibility they have to be safe on the job. It's an idea that works: The payoff to companies that use programs such as these can be as high as $3 to $6 for every dollar spent.[107] By creating a culture of safety and ensuring that safety is a core value of a firm's senior managers, employers can reduce their workers' compensation claims, medical expenses, and liability for negligence.[108]

WHO RECEIVES NONMANDATORY BENEFITS The degree of hierarchy in a firm's corporate culture influences decisions about who receives nonmandatory benefits and services. Consider a CEO who has access to a private jet, has a golf club membership, and has a personal assistant to run errands. These amenities are there to make the life of the executive less stressful. At the same time as the CEO is enjoying these benefits, the lower-level employees in the company may be worrying about how they can afford the higher insurance premium the company is requiring them to pay.

Employees' Concerns About Their Firm's Benefits and Safety Programs

Employers who understand their employees' concerns relative to the benefits and safety programs offered to them have an advantage in terms of both recruiting and retaining employees. Two of the major employee concerns are the perception of fairness when it comes to how the benefits are distributed and how safe employees feel in the workplace.

PERCEPTIONS OF THE FAIRNESS OF THE FIRM'S BENEFITS Earlier in this chapter, we noted that diversity in the workplace has led to the need for a larger group of religious holiday options for employees. Diversity also plays a critical role in employee preferences for everything from type of health care options to educational benefits to retirement options and perceptions of fairness of benefit offerings. Consider the many different demographic groups in the typical workplace: They represent differences in age, gender, marital status, ethnicity, and number of children (if any). In recent years, more companies have begun to offer domestic partner benefits, regardless of sexual orientation and marital status. Controversy surrounds the practice, though. Other benefit issues frequently debated range from whether it is fair for employees with children to be given time off from work to care for them (when employees without children don't get equal time off) and whether employees with pets but no children, for example, should get benefits for pet care since employees with children get child-care options.[109]

One area in which the need for fairness clearly intersects with antidiscrimination law is age discrimination and benefits. As employees get older, the cost of providing benefits—such as health care, disability, and pensions—to them increases. These costs can, ultimately, impact the firm's ability to be competitive in the global marketplace.[110] However, older employees are also longer-tenured employees who provide much value to employers because of their knowledge, well-honed job skills, and conscientiousness. To retain these employees, treat all their employees fairly, and comply with the law, employers have found that they need to pay the extra costs associated with providing benefits to older workers. In fact, following the outcome of the U.S. Supreme Court case *Public Employees Retirement System of Ohio v. Betts*, 109 S.Ct. 256 (1989), Congress passed an amendment prohibiting discrimination against older workers "in all employee benefits except when age-based reductions in employee benefit plans are justified by significant cost considerations."[111] This amendment is known as the **Older Workers Retirement Protection Act.**

Finally, research has shown that procedural justice generally is a better predictor of satisfaction with benefits than distributive justice. However, in an open culture, characterized by giving employees a lot of information about the company and their role in the company, distributive justice predicts satisfaction with the cost of benefits.[112]

SAFETY IN THE WORKPLACE News reports about safety in the workplace typically focus on sensational cases in which large numbers of employees are injured or killed. It goes without saying that employees expect a workplace in which they are not in imminent danger. But that is not their only concern about safety. Employees expect, at a minimum, to have equipment that is well maintained and functioning properly, ergonomically designed work areas, and protective gear if they're working in hazardous situations. An employer is responsible for providing these for employees and for training all employees about the proper operation of the equipment, use of protective gear, and their responsibility to keep the firm's workplace safe and free of hazards. Falls because of slippery floors are a major cause of injuries in the restaurant industry. Researchers have found that factors related to the environment—for example, the friction of a restaurant's floors—affect whether employees report the floors as being slippery. And they have also found that factors related to employees themselves—for example, a person's age and recent experience with slipping—affect the likelihood of such reports being made.[113] This research provides a good example of the importance of training employees about safety in the workplace.

EMPLOYEE BENEFITS AND SAFETY PROGRAMS IN PRACTICE: ENVIRONMENTAL INFLUENCES

The labor market, technology, globalization, and ethical and social responsibility issues all influence benefits and safety in the workplace. We explore each of these influencers in the following sections.

The Labor Market and Benefits and Safety Programs

The labor market affects what benefits employers need to offer to attract workers as well as the need for safety modifications and training. As the labor market becomes tight, offering more benefits to attract workers may be more cost-effective than trying to lure them with higher wages, for example.

WHAT BENEFITS NEED TO BE OFFERED We have already discussed how important it is for employers to be aware of the demographics of their employees to determine the benefits they should offer. The same is true for the labor market. Younger applicants will have different benefit expectations and needs than older applicants. For example, younger applicants are likely to be more interested in education and child-care benefits, whereas older workers are more likely to be focused on long-term care insurance and retirement benefits. Gender, marital status, and ethnicity affect applicant preferences for benefits. Also, in a tight labor market, employers have to be more creative in terms of the benefits they offer to attract workers. In contrast, in a loose labor market, they can offer fewer benefits and still attract qualified workers.

NEED FOR SAFETY MODIFICATIONS AND TRAINING An older workforce and having more individuals with disabilities in the workforce create challenges for workplace safety, but these challenges are not usually insurmountable. In fact, managers who recognize the contributions these groups can make are often willing to make modifications to ensure their safety. Let's once again use age as an example.

As we start to age, there are changes in our bodies that affect how we respond to situations that require strength and flexibility, postural steadiness, visual capacity, and mental processing. Employers who recognize the value of their older workers also

Older Workers Benefit Protection Act

An amendment to the Age Discrimination in Employment Act prohibiting discrimination against older workers relative to their benefits except when reductions in employee benefit plans based on age are justified by significant cost issues.

recognize that many of the work modifications needed to reduce injuries in older workers are also important for preventing injuries in workers of other ages. That's why many firms encourage employees to participate in exercise programs that focus on strength and flexibility as well as using techniques such as modifying one's work by using mechanical lifts to do the heavy lifting. Providing employees with education about changes in their visual capacity as they age so that they can receive the proper treatment, providing appropriate lighting for their tasks, and ensuring that materials to be read are easily viewable by older eyes are minor modifications that can help make the workplace safer and more "senior friendly."[114]

Technology and Benefits and Safety Programs

Computers have greatly enhanced the ability of companies to manage their benefits programs themselves as well as made it easier to outsource the task. In addition, technology plays a significant role when it comes to monitoring and managing workplace safety. The safety of telecommuters has also become a concern for employers.

employee self-service (ESS) applications

Web-based programs accessed via a company's intranet where employees can review their benefits information and make changes during open enrollment periods.

HOW BENEFITS INFORMATION IS DELIVERED   Employee self-service (ESS) applications have redefined how employees access and manage their benefits. These applications are Web-based programs accessed via a company's intranet. Using ESS, employees can review their benefits information and make changes during *open enrollment periods*, the time during which company employees are authorized to make changes to their benefit preferences. Research shows that ESS enhances the service delivery of a firm's benefits programs and improves employee communication while significantly reducing operating costs for companies.[115] In fact, employees have become so used to doing their banking and other business online that they expect to be able to access their benefits information online, too. Yet in a 2005 study by MetLife, only 34% of the companies surveyed used the Internet or an intranet for benefits enrollment. Most companies were still relying on the traditional paper-and-pencil approach.

Companies with high numbers of blue-collar employees can provide computer kiosks if they are concerned about these workers not having access to computers to enroll in the benefits program. Online benefits management reduces the time a firm's HR personnel has to spend administering changes to the benefit status of employees—for example, if a worker marries or has a child. Web-based systems increase an employer's ability to manage the firm's liability by providing an easier way for the company to disseminate and track information related to programs such as COBRA and HIPAA, which we discuss later in this chapter. They also ensure that information such as this is consistently communicated to all of a firm's employees.[116]

TELECOMMUTING AND SAFETY   While technology enables employees to work from home, it also raises concerns about workers' safety. In 2000, OSHA issued a policy specifically addressing home offices. OSHA indicated that it would not conduct inspections of employees' home offices, nor would it hold employers liable for home offices, and it does not expect employers to inspect these offices. It did, however, reaffirm that employers have a responsibility to report all work-related illnesses and injuries, regardless of where they occur.[117]

Workers' compensation laws typically do not distinguish between home offices and other work sites. Employers need to include information in their telecommuting policies, including the hours employees are required to work and identification of the areas of their homes that are their home offices. The policy should state that workers' compensation coverage applies only when employees are performing their jobs during their work times and in their home offices. An employer should also provide its telecommuters with guidelines explaining how to ensure that their home offices are safe. The guidelines should address issues ranging from proper ventilation and lighting to comfortable and safe office furniture.[118]

Globalization and Employee Benefits and Safety Programs

Globalization has caused employers to look for ways to reduce labor costs to maintain their competitive advantage (or to gain such an advantage). Two main costs employers are cutting are health care costs and retirement benefits. Health care costs in the United States are much higher than in other countries. For instance, in 2003, the most current year for which data were available, the total expenditures on health care in the United States amounted to 15% of the country's gross domestic product. The next highest percentage was 11.5%, in Switzerland. In Korea, the percentage was only 5.6%. Employers can reduce their health care and retirement costs by, for example, reducing the number of employees, selecting different benefits to offer to employees, and changing which employees are eligible for benefits.[119] Thus, globalization affects the types of benefits offered and policies about benefits equalization, as well as the norms for benefits and safety programs.

TYPES OF BENEFITS OFFERED Laws and norms differ among countries with regard to the types of benefits required or expected by employees. For instance, in Ireland and New Zealand, pension is not tied to preretirement earnings but rather is based on a flat rate while in the United States and Canada pensions are tied more directly to preretirement earnings.[120]

One study that looked at national cultures and employee benefits reported that the cultural characteristic of uncertainty avoidance—that is, being uncomfortable in unknown, unstructured environments—was a major determinant of the managerial decision to offer welfare plans such as cafeteria plans, supplemental employment plans, and temporary disability plans. Those plans provide some degree of security to employees. The study further reported that there are benefits that are so commonly offered that no cultural differentiators were found, suggesting that managers have little discretion in deciding to offer them. These include death, dental, health, life, long-term disability, and severance benefits.[121]

However, the Social Security–type programs in many developed countries, including the United States, need to be reformed because many older workers are retiring, and there are fewer workers paying into the programs to support them. Sweden, Germany, and Canada—three countries that have traditionally provided their citizens with strong social insurance programs—have adopted policies encouraging people to wait longer until they retire. Gradual retirement, partial retirement, and credit for caregiving activities are among the new practices in these countries. When older workers stay employed longer, the tax base for their contributions into Social Security–type programs remains stronger.[122]

Major differences also exist among countries in terms the amount of paid time off employees receive. The average number of days for vacations in the United States is 14. In Great Britain and Germany, workers typically receive 24 and 27 days off, respectively. In France, they receive 39.[123] Another global concern is health care costs, which are rising around the world. Even in countries that have traditionally had government-financed health care programs, multinational companies are finding it necessary to offer supplemental health plans to employees to make up for the difference in what the governments provide and what the employees have to pay out of pocket. Canada and France are two of the other countries, in addition to the United States, where the percentage of health care expenditures is increasing for employers.[124]

One benefit not typically needed in the domestic workplace is kidnap and ransom insurance. More than $1 billion in ransom has been paid out since 1980 for kidnapped executives. Typical kidnap and ransom insurance covers a wide variety of things: security company fees, fees for professional negotiators and their travel costs, the bodily injury and lost salaries of abductees, psychological counseling for them and their families, and the cost of ransom money. The standard coverage amount is $1 million for a multinational employee, and it can be higher for executives.[125] The U.S. Department of State Web site (www.state.gov) maintains updated information on its Travel & Business tab about countries where it is not safe to travel. The site includes "Travel Alerts" and "Worldwide

Caution," both of which provide information about where not to go. For instance, since the United States invaded Iraq, the terrorist attacks on expatriates in the Middle East have increased, leading to greater risk for expatriates in that area.

POLICIES ABOUT BENEFITS EQUALIZATION   Benefits practices for expatriates vary around the globe and are more complex than even compensation for expatriates. Some companies take a benefits equalization approach to try to keep an expatriate "whole" relative to the benefits the person would have received if assigned to her home country. For instance, expatriates might not have a choice of whether to enroll in a country's social insurance program, and if they are required to enroll, the employer will pay the cost. Expatriates are also often provided with benefits beyond what they would receive at home. Annual leave time, educational expenses for their children, and family travel are just a few examples of these benefits.

Just as with compensation, with provision of benefits, decisions have to be made about using the going rate approach or using a balance sheet approach. The laws of a country can affect this decision. Antidiscrimination legislation passed in Hong Kong in 2006, for example, made it illegal for private companies to discriminate on the basis of ethnicity or race. Consequently, a company could not provide greater benefits to an expatriate of Western descent than to other employees in the operation in Hong Kong who were not of Western descent unless the company could show that the Westerners possessed unique skills and abilities.[126] Pensions are another benefit subject to differences around the world. Among countries that are members of the Organization for Economic Co-operation and Development (OECD), the most widespread type of pension plan is a defined-benefit plan. This type of plan is found in 17 countries. The factors used to determine the benefit vary from country to country. Some of the other OECD countries have defined-contribution plans. In Australia, companies are required to pay 9% of their employees' earnings into a defined-contribution plan. In Mexico, employers pay 6.5% with the government also paying 5.5% of the minimum wage into the accounts. By contrast, the mandatory amount that Danish companies must pay is 1% of earnings.[127]

Similarly, laws vary from country to country regarding heath and safety, and so do countries' safety records. New Zealand, for example, has a higher incidence of work-related injury, disease, and death than most of the other industrialized nations.[128]

NORMS RELATIVE TO SAFETY   Although you might expect safe working conditions to be the norm worldwide, that is not always the case, even in the United States. Most countries have safety standards, but they differ greatly in terms of how well those standards are enforced. In Brazil, for instance, Fundacentro, a division of the Ministry of Labor and Employment, establishes occupational, health, and safety standards. These standards are compatible with international norms. Due to insufficient resources, however, Fundacentro cannot always enforce these standards. This lack of enforcement in addition to the corruption known to exist in the system results in delays in resolving complaints about safety.[129] Generally, however, more developed countries have better workplace safety practices.

Ethics, Social Responsibility, Benefits, and Safety Programs

Ethics and social responsibility concerns relative to employee benefits have gained a lot of attention since Enron collapsed and so many of its workers were left without retirement income. This scandal and the others have raised awareness about the need for ethical and socially responsible behavior regarding the benefits that firms promise employees.

MANAGEMENT OF BENEFITS   Downsizing, mergers and acquisitions, pension fund underfunding, and health screening programs may seem like somewhat of a random list of corporate issues. What connects them is the impact they have on the benefits employees receive and the opportunities they present for companies to exercise ethical and responsible behavior in this regard.

When companies downsize, decisions have to be made about who stays and who goes and also about what happens with the benefits of those who leave. Will health insurance continue to be available to individuals who take early retirement offers or whose jobs are eliminated? What happens to their retirement accounts? And what constitutes a "fair" early retirement offer?

What about when a merger or acquisition occurs? Which company's benefits plan will be continued, and how will any negative consequences of this decision for the employees of the other company be managed? Ethical issues relative to employee benefits also arise when employers require employees to participate in health screenings to receive certain benefits. Managers have to consider what is appropriate and what infringes on the rights of the employee.

COMPREHENSIVENESS OF SAFETY PROGRAMS Hazards in the workplace can range from those created by a company's manufacturing processes to those created by such things as toxic fumes from new carpet. Managers have to make ethical and socially responsible decisions about how much information to share with employees about potential workplace hazards as well as how to manage those hazards. Tyson Foods, a company that processes poultry, has had a number of workplace problems, ranging from charges of discrimination to charges of dangerous work conditions. To address its need to exercise more social responsibility, Tyson developed the Team Member Bill of Rights, which specifies that employees have rights to a safe workplace, adequate equipment and facilities, and continuing training.[130]

EMPLOYEE BENEFITS AND SAFETY PROGRAMS IN PRACTICE: REGULATORY ISSUES

We have already discussed many of the regulations that affect benefits and safety programs in the workplace. In this section, we discuss amendments to ERISA that affect what happens with some benefits when employees change jobs as well as the protection of their medical information.

What Happens When Workers Change Jobs

Two amendments to ERISA are particularly important for workers who leave an employer. They are the Consolidated Omnibus Budget Reconciliation Act and the Health Insurance Portability and Accountability Act.

The **Consolidated Omnibus Reconciliation Act (COBRA)**, was passed in 1986. It provides for employees and their families who participate in a group health plan sponsored by an employer that has 20 or more employees to continue their group health insurance coverage, including their dental and vision coverage, when they are terminated for a *qualifying reason*. For an employee, a qualifying reason is a layoff or a reduction in the number of hours the person works for a reason other than his gross misconduct.[131] For up to 18 months after the employee leaves his job, he can pay the premiums to continue his health insurance coverage. Spouses and dependent children of an employee can qualify for coverage for up to 36 months if the spouse is eligible for Medicare, if the employee and spouse experienced a divorce or legal separation, or if the employee dies. When a child can no longer be classified as a dependent because of age and/or no longer being enrolled in school full time, the child can obtain coverage for up to 36 months.[132]

President Clinton signed the **Health Insurance Portability and Accountability Act (HIPAA)** into law in 1996. HIPAA makes it easier for workers to maintain their health care coverage when they change employers because it specifies that coverage under a prior employer's health plan counts for meeting a preexisting condition requirement under a new plan—as long as coverage is transferred within 63 days of the date that the person's coverage ended under his or her old plan.[133]

Consolidated Omnibus Reconciliation Act (COBRA)

This act, passed in 1986, provides for employees and their families who participate in a group health plan sponsored by an employer with 20 or more employees to have the option to continue their group health, dental, and vision insurance coverage for up to 18 months when they are terminated for a qualifying reason as long as they pay the full cost of the premium.

Health Insurance Portability and Accountability Act (HIPAA)

An act passed in 1996 that makes it easier for workers to maintain their health care coverage when they change employers because it specifies that coverage under a prior employer's health plan counts for meeting a preexisting condition requirement under a new plan.

Protection of Employee Information

In addition to HIPAA's portability protections, the act also has provisions designed to ensure that only individuals who have a right to a person's medical information can access it. Employer group health plans come under the HIPAA guidelines. The plans cannot share information about you without your permission. In addition, under HIPAA, you have a right to see and to get a copy of any of your health records, and you can request that your communications with the record-keeper be kept confidential. This last provision means that you could specify that your doctor call you at your home rather than your office, if you wish, and the doctor would have to comply with any reasonable requests of this sort.[134]

SUMMARY

Employee benefits and safety programs serve a critical role when it comes to firms attracting, motivating, and retaining workers. Managing the costs of these programs is a challenge for companies, especially in light of the escalating costs of health insurance, the most frequently offered employee benefit. However, firms that want to maintain a competitive advantage recognize that providing their employees with benefits and a safe workplace far outweigh the costs.

The law requires employers to provide employees with Social Security, unemployment compensation insurance, workers' compensation, and family and medical leave. Beyond these mandatory benefits, many employers provide benefits that address employees' health and wellness, retirement, and life management issues. Health insurance, a primary benefit that most employees want, can take the form of a traditional plan, an HMO, a PPO, or a POS. Many employers have moved to consumer-driven health plans (CDHPs), often with a high-deductible health plan (HDHP) and health savings account (HSA).

Some of the most frequently offered types of retirement plans are defined benefit, defined contribution, and cash balance plans. Employers are moving away from defined benefit plans and relying more on defined contribution plans, such as 401(k) and cash benefit plans. Benefits designed for life management include employee assistance programs (EAPs), educational benefits, financial planning, and child-care and elder-care plans. ERISA provides guidelines for how many of the benefits, particularly retirement plans, are to be managed. In addition, HIPAA regulates employee benefits and ensures that employees' medical information is kept confidential.

The OSH Act requires employers to provide a safe workplace for all employees. The OSHA oversees the OSH Act and partners with companies through various programs to ensure that workplaces are safe. OSHA also investigates complaints about workplace safety violations and fines employers who are out of compliance.

Organizational demands, such as a firm's strategy, company characteristics, and culture, as well as the concerns of its employees, affect how a company manages its benefits and safety programs. Successful managers recognize that these factors dictate the benefits and safety programs their firms offer. For instance, a small startup firm with a differentiation strategy and a culture that views employees as the firm's most critical resource will make different benefits choices than a larger, more established firm with a low-cost strategy and a hierarchical culture. Environmental factors, including regulations, influence decisions about benefits and safety programs as well. In order to compete for talent in a tight labor market, employers often have to offer workers more benefits than they do in a loose market. Technology has made it easier for companies to provide more and better information to employees about their benefits and safety. Globalization has forced employers to consider the types of benefits they offer to expatriates, host-country nationals, and third-country nationals, which are often affected by host country regulations, and whether they will equalize benefits for expatriates. Also, firms have to make decisions about how they will manage workplace safety because norms differ around the globe.

KEY TERMS

401(k) plan *p. 369*
accidental death and dismemberment insurance (AD&D) *p. 365*
cash balance plan *p. 369*

Consolidated Omnibus Reconciliation Act (COBRA) *p. 383*
consumer-driven health plan (CDHP) *p. 358*
contributory retirement plan *p. 368*

copay *p. 358*
defined benefit pension plan *p. 368*
defined contribution plan *p. 369*
employee assistance program (EAP) *p. 363*

DISCUSSION QUESTIONS

1. You are a manager and have been assigned to a task force to consider discontinuing a number of the employee benefits your firm currently offers. What issues should you address in making this decision?

2. What can managers do to try to reduce the misuse of the workers' compensation benefits or the Family and Medical Leave Act? (Choose one tactic and discuss it.)

3. Choose one type of voluntary benefit you are not very familiar with but would like to receive as an employee. Then research that benefit and prepare a one-page summary of your research. Write the summary as if you were explaining the benefit to a new employee.

4. Your company is going to announce a new benefit for employees. Outline the points that need to be addressed before the announcement and as part of the announcement.

5. Visit the OSHA Web site (www.osha.gov). Identify and briefly describe two types of cooperative programs available through the Occupational Safety and Health Administration. Discuss why these alliances are important.

6. The culture in your company emphasizes making money more than it does safety. However, you know that a safe workplace will save the firm money in the short run and the long run. How would you make a case to senior management that developing a culture of safety would yield high returns for the company?

7. Choose a country in which you would like to live some day. Then research the types of benefits typically provided to employees in that country.

8. Research the privacy issues associated with requiring employees to participate in health screenings to receive employee benefits.

LEARNING EXERCISE 1

You are a manager for a software developer in Salt Lake City, Utah. A number of your employees have come to you and told you that they should receive additional benefits. Your company currently offers the following: health care insurance for which the employee pays one-third of the premium and the company pays two-thirds, dental insurance and vision care at no cost to the employee, and reduced-cost parking. Also, employees receive accidental death and dismemberment insurance and long-term disability insurance at no cost to them. Most employees receive 8 sick days per year that can be used only for illness and 10 vacation days after three years at the company. The employees want you to provide the following:

- Reduced-cost child care
- Legal resources
- Long-term care insurance
- Short-term disability

- Twenty personal leave days that they can take at anytime in lieu of the current sick days and vacation days

The employees are telling you that these benefits are provided by other companies in the area. Develop a plan of action for how you would respond in this situation.

1. Outline what steps you would take, including where you would find relevant information and the options that would be available to you if you are (1) in a large company with a compensation and benefits staff in a human resources department and (2) if you are a small business owner.

2. Provide documentation of the research you do to find benefits data for the software industry and the specific location.

3. Are there additional benefits you identified that some companies are offering that you could/should also offer?

LEARNING EXERCISE 2

Your boss has asked you to develop a plan to reduce health care costs for the company. Currently, your company offers employees the choice of an HMO or a PPO. You are aware that one reason health care costs are on the rise in the company has to do with the long-term costs of employee smoking, obesity, and an older workforce. At least 10% of the 350 employees in the company currently smoke (which they have to do outside the building). You believe that at least that many of the employees are obese, but that estimate is probably low. The average age of the employees is 52.

1. What can you legally do to address the health concerns regarding the effects of smoking and obesity on long-

term costs of health care for the company? Are there any ethical concerns with what you have identified as being legal to do? Are there any ADA concerns?

2. How can age be taken into consideration in this situation without violating the ADEA?

3. What are some other ways in which health care costs could be reduced?

4. How would you communicate this information to your employees?

CASE STUDY # 1 — KEEPING UP WITH ACUITY

As a manager at a mutually owned property and casualty insurer, you like to stay on top of what companies in your industry are doing. You have just read that ACUITY Insurance, another mutually owned property and casualty insurer, has been recognized as a great place to work for the past three years. ACUITY has over 700 employees and more than half of them have been with the company for more than six years. ACUITY is located in Sheboygan, Wisconsin. Your company is located in a neighboring town and has about half that many employees.

The article about ACUITY noted that employees receive free onsite massages, and they eat lunch with company officers on a regular basis. The company offers flextime, access to a fitness center, and generous wellness benefits, including health and dental insurance, a vision plan, an EAP, and more. These benefits and perks are just a few of the ones that helped ACUITY gain recognition by the Society for Human Resource Management and the Great Place to Work Institute as one of the Best Small and Medium Companies to Work for in America. The CEO and president of ACUITY, Ben Salzmann, believes that spending money on employee benefits and perks pays off in the long run.

The benefits are part of the overall culture at ACUITY that ensures employees know they matter to the company. When Salzmann arrived at ACUITY in 1999, that wasn't the case.

Turnover was high and morale was low. That has now been turned around and the company frequently receives accolades for its employee practices and turnover is less than 2% annually.

DISCUSSION QUESTIONS

1. What potential returns might ACUITY yield by providing so many types of benefits and perks to its employees? (In responding, you may want to review motivation theory, including the discussion of motivation in Chapter 4.)

2. Currently, your company provides only basic benefits to its employees: a health insurance plan (for which the company pays half the premium) and a 401(k) plan that is funded solely by the employees. What issues would you need to consider before deciding to increase the benefits offerings at your company?

3. Prepare a one-page memorandum to your company's CEO, explaining the value of providing additional benefits. Identify what some of those benefits would be and explain your rationale for choosing them.

Sources: ACUITY toasts a successful culture. *HR Magazine*, 49: 48, 2004; Tyler, K. Leveraging long tenure. *HR Magazine*. 52: 54-60, 2007; and and ACUITY. *Careers related topics*, www4.acuity.com/acuityweb/careers/relatedtopics.

CASE STUDY # 2 — CREATING A SAFETY CULTURE AT CUSTOM TRANSPORTATION

Custom Transportation, located in Elgin, Illinois, is a company that specializes in the delivery of medical equipment and supplies to hospitals, clinics, and medical supply companies in the Midwest. The majority of employees at Custom Transportation are sales representatives, warehouse staff, and truck drivers. Currently, most of these workers are over age 40.

As a result of ongoing expansion, the company will grow from 225 employees to more than 500 employees in the next three years. Several government contracts have already been signed, and more are anticipated. The company has recently hired you as the warehouse manager. Part of your job is to oversee all safety programs for the company. These duties had been handled primarily informally by the chief financial officer (CFO) prior to your coming onboard.

On your first day, the CFO calls you in and gives you the following directives and information:

- Safety in the warehouse is becoming a real issue. The accident rate has tripled since last year. Something has to be done.
- Absenteeism has increased, especially on Fridays and Mondays.
- The company is spending 25% of its payroll costs on workers' compensation claims. Many of the claims are related to cumulative trauma disorders.
- You need to get rid of an employee in the warehouse who is reported to have AIDS.

DISCUSSION QUESTIONS

1. How would you would respond to each of the directives from the CFO? What steps would you take to instill a culture of safety in this warehouse?

2. Do you think a wellness program makes sense for this company? Provide support for your answer.

3. What do you think will be the biggest challenge in increasing safety and health at this facility?

4. How will you address the issue of the employee with AIDS?

Source: Based on Gowan, M. *eHRM*. New York: Prentice Hall, 2001.

Part IV

PROSPERA EXERCISES

In this part of the book, you have studied how performance appraisals and compensation, benefits and safety, and incentives affect employee attitudes and behaviors. Recall the situation at Visions Optical: Turnover is high, resulting in reduced productivity. You have been involved in setting HR strategy to support the company mission and have designed a process to manage competencies. With the right people onboard, it is time to look at how to manage attitudes and behaviors and, as a result, reduce turnover and improve productivity.

Section I: Creating Performance Appraisals

In the "REVIEW" area of the Prospera Web site (www.prospera.com), find the "Create Performance Appraisals" feature. Work through the feature to create a performance appraisal for each of the three jobs for which you have developed job descriptions. Think about the purpose of a performance appraisal, the goals of the company, and the problems that the owners of Visions Optical have had with employee turnover and reduced productivity as you create the performance appraisals. Remember that you can add information and change the wording of items and responses.

Section II: Determining the Compensation

Setting the salary for a job is an important task and can affect whether an employee stays or leaves the organization, as well as how invested the employee is in his or her job while at work. Using the information in the "COMPENSATE" area of the Prospera Web site, determine the starting salary for each of the three jobs you have been working with. Note that the Prospera Web site provides data from PayScale™ as well as the Bureau of Labor Statistics. Be sure to look at both sets of data. Discuss how the percentile selected as the starting salary for each job supports the goals of the company. What factors might result in paying less than the median as a starting salary? What might be the consequences for Visions Optical of doing so? What might be the consequences for paying at the 75th percentile? Think about these questions from both the individual and business perspectives.

Section III: Establishing Exempt Status

An employee's exempt or non-exempt status determines whether she will receive overtime pay. Work through the "Determine the FLSA Status" feature in the "COMPENSATE" area of the Prospera Web site for each of the three jobs at Visions Optical.

Part V

SPECIAL TOPICS

13

c h a p t e r

LABOR UNIONS AND EMPLOYEE MANAGEMENT

1. Explain why labor unions exist. *(392)*

2. Describe the main purpose and key points of the laws regulating labor relations. *(394)*

3. Discuss unfair labor practices. *(396)*

4. Understand the different types of unions and union shops. *(398)*

5. Explain the steps in the process of organizing a union. *(400)*

6. Describe the collective bargaining process. *(402)*

7. Explain the grievance process used in a union environment. *(404)*

8. Discuss issues in managing labor relations in the future. *(406)*

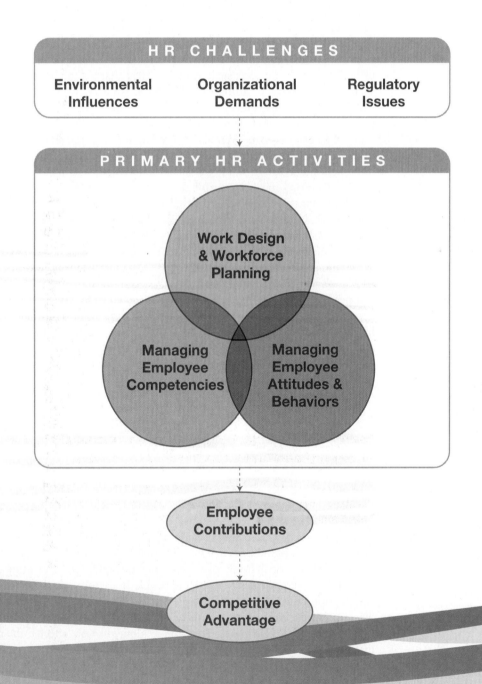

HR CHALLENGES

Environmental Influences   Organizational Demands   Regulatory Issues

PRIMARY HR ACTIVITIES

Work Design & Workforce Planning

Managing Employee Competencies

Managing Employee Attitudes & Behaviors

Employee Contributions

Competitive Advantage

LABOR RELATIONS OVERVIEW

In the late 1700s, a group of businesses that made and sold boots decided to form a guild to protect themselves against unfair competition. The bootmakers who worked for these employers decided that they needed to look out for themselves as well. They formed a society to bargain for wages and to restrict who could work for their employers. These actions ultimately led to the first labor case recorded in the United States. In this case, the Commonwealth of the State of Pennsylvania brought charges against eight bootmakers for conspiring to coerce their employers to increase their wages.

Why did the case occur? In 1798 in Pennsylvania, employers had reduced the wages paid to bootmakers from $2.75 per pair for custom boots and $2.50 per pair for stock orders to $2.25 per pair for both types of boots. The bootmakers subsequently went on strike and successfully managed to restore their wages to their previous levels. The next year, employers reduced the bootmakers' wages again. When the bootmakers went on strike this time, their employers got together and decided to lock them out of their jobs. These events led to growing concern that workers were organizing, so the employers responded by taking steps to suppress such activities. They charged the bootmakers with conspiracy against the employers. Ultimately, the eight bootmakers were found guilty of conspiracy and fined $8 each. The outcome in this case gave states the impetus to squelch union activity in the United States for the next 36 years or so.[1]

The labor movement eventually picked up momentum, and it has played a key role in securing better working conditions, wages, and benefits for workers, particularly in the manufacturing sector. In recent years, labor union membership in traditional industries such as manufacturing has been on the decline in the United States and in other developed countries. At the same time, efforts have increased to unionize groups of employees who have not typically been targeted by unions. These groups include adjunct faculty members and graduate students at universities, service workers in various industries, and information technology professionals and other knowledge workers. And, as less developed countries bring in more industry, unions have turned their attention to improving working conditions for laborers there. Consequently, whether you are working domestically or globally as a manager, you need to be familiar with the laws that regulate labor union activity, the processes of unionization and collective bargaining, and the trends in labor relation activities. After a brief history of the union movement in the United States, we discuss each of these topics. Labor relations affects many aspects of the framework shown in Exhibit 13.1. The presence of a union determines the work design and workforce planning, how employee competencies are managed, and employee attitudes and behaviors.

BRIEF HISTORY OF LABOR UNION MOVEMENT IN THE UNITED STATES

Workers join unions for many reasons, such as higher wages, better health and accident benefits, contractual provisions that ensure a safer workplace, greater job security, and a voice in the workplace.[2] Skilled craftspeople were the first workers to unionize. Remember the bootmakers described at the beginning of the chapter? The society they formed was the first labor union in the United States. The first unions in Sweden were formed by printers. In Great Britain, the first unions were formed by building and printing trade workers. All these unions were formed because the people in these trades were concerned about the competition they faced.[3] For example, as the transportation of products in the United States improved, bootmakers in Philadelphia found themselves competing for the first time with bootmakers in New York. This competition adversely affected their wages. Combine that situation with the advent of mass production, in which skilled workers were no longer needed, and the foundation was laid for increased unionization.

In some trades, the ability of the skilled workers to move from one location to another affected wages within their industries and led to the formation of local unions. The local unions prevented tradespeople from other parts of the country from coming into a certain locale and bringing down wages. (You will better understand the situation described here if

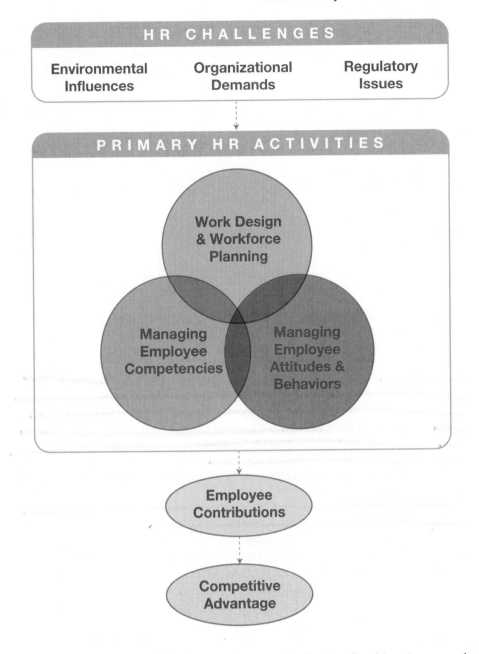

Framework for the
Strategic Management
of Employees

you think about how many Americans today resent the fact that illegal immigrants to the
United States are often willing to work for lower wages than U.S. citizens will accept.)[4]

Since the early days of labor unions, strikes have been used to achieve a union's objectives. Workers who continued to go to work during a strike became known as *scabs*, and
their names were shared among local unions in an effort to ensure that they were not
employable. Union members refused to work with nonunion members and would even
refuse to interact socially with them or live in the same boarding houses with them.[5]

By 1873, union membership had reached 300,000 in the United States. By 1878, however, membership was down to 50,000 due to a depression. Then, in 1886, the American
Federation of Labor (AFL) was formed, and unionism began to increase once again. Still, it
wasn't until about 1933 that unions became firmly entrenched in the manufacturing sector.
This helped fuel an upturn in union membership. A pro-union U.S. president, Franklin
Delano Roosevelt, and new legislation that made it easier for workers to unionize also
played a part in the upsurge.[6] Exhibit 13.2 shows the rise and fall of union membership in
the U.S. private sector from 1900 until 2005. As you can see, the number of union members
reached a peak of 18.5 million in 1974, and it has been declining since then.[7]

Many reasons exist for the decline in union membership. The reasons are largely
systematic. Globalization has resulted in many traditional union jobs being moved

Exhibit 13.2 ▶

U.S. Private-Sector
Union Membership

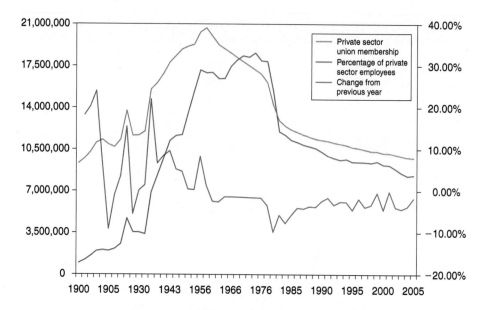

Source: The Public Purpose. *US private sector trade union membership*, www.publicpurpose.com/lm-unn2003.htm.

to other countries. Manufacturing has been particularly hard hit. As manufacturing has moved abroad, U.S. job growth has occurred in the services sector and in small businesses, sectors of the economy that have historically been less likely than others to organize. Add to that the reluctance of local unions to spend money on organizing efforts—something that has traditionally been their responsibility—and you have a recipe for the decline of unions in the United States.[8] The decline in union membership is not just a U.S. phenomenon, though. Later in the chapter, we will look at unionization in other parts of the world.

Critics of unions say that employees don't support unions today because they are able to individually reap the benefits unions used to provide for them. Research suggests otherwise. Some studies have found that union members are paid 15% to 27% more in terms of their pay and benefits than are nonunion members. Other studies show that 89% of union members have health care benefits compared to just 67% of nonunion employees. Union members pay 1% to 2% of their salaries to their unions; that's a small price to pay relative to the benefits members reap.[9] Now, let's take a look at some of the regulations related to labor unions.

GOVERNMENT REGULATION OF LABOR UNIONS

Two of the earliest pieces of labor legislation were the Railway Labor Act of 1926 and the Norris-LaGuardia Act of 1935. This legislation was followed by the passage of three acts: the Wagner Act of 1935, the Taft-Hartley Act of 1947, and the Landrum-Griffin Act of 1959. Jointly, the acts are referred to as the National Labor Code.

Railway Labor Act of 1926

Prior to the nineteenth century, five laws had been enacted to handle rail labor disputes. Nonetheless, labor unrest in the railroad industry continued. Violent strikes and lockouts interrupted the rail transportation of people and goods in the United States, adversely affecting the economy. The **Railway Labor Act (RLA)** was passed in 1926 to try to provide a peaceful way for railroads and their employees to resolve their disputes. The RLA applies to common-carrier rail service and commercial airline employees (the latter of whom were included in the act through provisions passed by Congress in 1936).

Railway Labor Act (RLA)

The act that provides a peaceful way for railroads and their employees to resolve their disputes; also applies to common-carrier rail service and commercial airline employees.

Union workers on strike.

Besides providing a way for employees and railroads to peaceably resolve their differences, the RLA allows rail and airline employees to join labor unions. The act also distinguishes between minor and major disputes. Boards such as the National Railroad Adjustment Board settle minor disputes. Employees can engage in strikes for major disputes but not minor ones. Employers can use lockouts for major disagreements. The act spells out provisions for handling major disputes, including collective bargaining guidelines, and it created the National Mediation Board (NMB) to handle these disputes and help parties resolve them.[10]

Norris-LaGuardia Act of 1932

Congress passed the **Norris-LaGuardia Act** in 1932 to make it easier for employees to engage in union-organizing activities. Before the passage of the act, employers had all of the power when it came to how workers were treated. They could have federal courts issue injunctions in cases involving or resulting from labor disputes if employees wanted to strike or otherwise interfere with the flow of work.[11] The act also outlined the process to be followed for hearings, granted workers the right to collective bargaining, and stated that neither officers of a union nor the union itself would be held liable for unlawful activities of its members that could not be proven to have been instigated or approved by the union.[12]

Wagner Act (National Labor Relations Act)

Even after the passage of the Norris-LaGuardia Act, relations between labor and management continued to deteriorate because management in many companies refused to allow unions to represent labor. These poor labor/management relations cut across many industries, from automotive to textile, from steel to trucking. In 1934, the country was in the midst of the Great Depression, and 1.5 million workers went on strike. Many of the strikes became violent. A large number of the strikes were about wage increases, but one-third of them were over the right of unions to be recognized.[13]

Congress subsequently passed the **National Labor Relations Act (NLRA)**, known as the **Wagner Act**, in 1935. This act is often regarded as the most important piece of labor relations legislation. It was passed for three main reasons: (1) to protect the rights of employees and employers, (2) to encourage these parties to engage in collective bargaining, and (3) to control their activities so the economy wouldn't be adversely affected.[14] The Wagner Act established the National Labor Relations Board (NLRB) to oversee compliance with the act. Let's take a look at some of the specific provisions of the act relative to employee rights, unfair labor practices, workers not covered by the NLRA, and the establishment of the NLRB.

EMPLOYEE RIGHTS   The NLRA protects private-sector employees from employer and union misconduct such as attempts by employers to prevent unions from organizing and attempts by unions to coerce employees into joining them. The NLRA also ensures that

Norris-LaGuardia Act

This act makes it easier for employees to engage in union-organizing activities.

National Labor Relations Act (NLRA) (also called the Wagner Act)

This act protects the rights of employees and employers, encourages these parties to engage in collective bargaining, and controls their activities so that the economy won't be adversely affected by their actions.

employees have the right to organize a union where none currently exists. The specific rights provided under the NLRA to employees include the following rights:

1. To form, or attempt to form, a union at their workplace
2. To join a union, even if it's not recognized by their employer
3. To assist in union-organizing efforts
4. To engage in group activities (collective bargaining) such as attempting to modify their wages or working conditions
5. To refuse to do any or all of the above unless a clause requiring employees to join the union exists[15]

unfair labor practices (ULPs)

Violations of the NLRA that deny rights and benefits to employees.

UNFAIR LABOR PRACTICES   Unfair labor practices (ULPs) are violations of the NLRA that deny rights and benefits to employees. Such violations include threatening to take jobs or benefits from employees who attempt to form a union, reassigning workers to less attractive jobs than their current ones if they are involved in union activities, and telling employees they will receive greater benefits if they don't join a union. Labor unions violate the NLRA when they tell employees they will lose their jobs if they don't join the union or, when union employees are on strike, they bar nonstrikers from entering an employer's premises.[16]

Specifically, the act defines the following ULPs:

1. Interfering with, restraining, or coercing employees in the exercise of their rights guaranteed in Section 7 of the act
2. Dominating or interfering with the formation or administration of any labor organization, or contributing financial or other support to it
3. Discriminating against employees in terms of their hiring, tenure of employment, or any other term or condition of their employment, so as to encourage or discourage them from becoming members in a labor organization
4. Discharging or otherwise discriminating against employees because they file charges or give testimony under the act
5. Refusing to bargain collectively with the duly chosen representatives of employees

Although the act identified these practices as "unfair," it did not make them crimes or impose any penalties or fines on people or organizations for their occurrence.[17]

National Labor Relations Board (NLRB)

An agency of the U.S. government created by Congress to administer the NLRA.

NATIONAL LABOR RELATIONS BOARD (NLRB)   The National Labor Relations Board (NLRB) is an agency of the U.S. government that was created by Congress to administer the NLRA. This agency has two main functions. One is to prevent and remedy unfair labor practices on the part of either labor organizations or employers. The second is to decide whether groups of employees want labor union representation so that they can engage in collective bargaining. This decision is based on the results of secret-ballot elections the NLRB conducts for employees.[18]

The two components of the agency are the board and the general counsel. The board is made up of five members, appointed to five-year terms by the president of the United States and approved by the U.S. Senate. Their role is quasi-judicial and involves making decisions in administrative proceedings. The president also appoints the general counsel (an attorney) to investigate and prosecute unfair labor practices and supervise the NLRB field offices as they process cases.[19] The general counsel is appointed for a four-year term and must be approved by the Senate as well.

Taft-Hartley Act of 1947

Labor Management Relations Act (also the Taft-Hartley Act)

This act protects the rights of employees and makes the NLRB a more impartial referee for industrial relations.

For the 12 years after its passage, the NLRA was perceived by many as giving too much power to the unions. In response, Congress passed the **Labor Management Relations Act** of 1947, commonly known as the **Taft-Hartley Act.** President Truman subsequently vetoed the act, but Congress overrode his veto. The main purpose of the act is to protect the rights of employees and make the NLRB a more impartial referee for industrial relations rather than having it serve as an advocate for organized labor.[20] The following are some of the provisions of the act:

1. To promote the full flow of commerce
2. To prescribe the legitimate rights of employees and employers in their relations affecting commerce
3. To provide orderly and peaceful procedures for preventing employees and employers from interfering with the legitimate rights of the other party
4. To protect the rights of individual employees in their relations with labor organizations
5. To protect the rights of the public in connection with labor disputes affecting commerce[21]

This act increased the reach of government regulation of collective bargaining (which is discussed in detail later in this chapter) and added new sanctions for violations in addition to those already existing under the Wagner Act. Specifically, these sanctions included criminal penalties in the form of fines and imprisonment, injunctions, and private suits for damages.[22] The Taft-Hartley Act also specified that the Bureau of Labor Statistics (BLS) would maintain a file of collective bargaining agreements. The BLS now collects agreements that cover 1,000 or more workers. These files are accessible through the BLS office in Washington, DC.

Next, we provide an overview of three outcomes of the Taft-Hartley Act: permissible types of union membership, national emergency strikes, and the Federal Mediation and Conciliation Service.

UNION MEMBERSHIP   Among the most significant outcomes of the Taft-Hartley Act was the provision that employees cannot be forced to join a union. Twenty-two states (see Exhibit 13.3) have passed **right-to-work laws** to prevent workers from having to join a union as a condition of employment, be forced to not join a union as an employment condition, or be forced to pay dues to a labor union or be fired for not paying such dues. Organizations such as the National Right to Work Legal Defense Foundation and the National Right to Work Committee work to ensure that these rights of workers are not violated. The role of the foundation is to work through the courts to support individuals who have been victims of forced unionism. The committee lobbies state legislatures and Congress to eliminate forced unionism and works to educate people about right-to-work laws.[23]

Regardless of whether a state is a right-to-work state, the Taft-Hartley Act has led to safeguards for workers who do not wish to be forced to become union members and redefined what types of union shops are legal under collective bargaining agreements. The most

right-to-work laws

Laws that prevent workers from having to join a union as a condition of employment, be prevented from joining a union as a condition of employment, or be forced to pay dues to a labor union or be fired for not paying such dues.

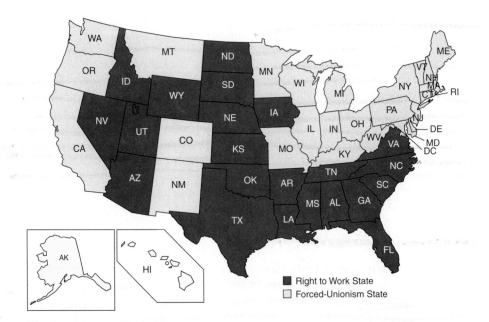

◄ Exhibit 13.3
Right-to-Work States

■ Right to Work State
□ Forced-Unionism State

Source: National Right to Work Legal Defense Foundation, Inc. *Right to work states*, www.nrtw. org/rtws.htm.

closed shop

This type of union shop was outlawed under the Taft Hartley Act and is considered the most extreme form of union membership because it requires workers to join a union before they can be hired and requires employers to go to the union first to hire new employees.

union shop

An arrangement under which all workers except managers in an organizational unit represented by a union have to become members of that union within a certain period of time after being hired or at least pay the equivalent of union dues.

agency shop

A labor union arrangement under which employees cannot be required to join a union but can be required to pay an agency fee for purposes such as initiation.

national emergency strike

A strike or lockout prevented by the government because it affects an entire industry or a substantial part of it and/or national health and safety are imperiled.

Landrum-Griffin Act

This act protects union members from being abused by unions and outlines the responsibilities of union officers as well as the rights of union members via a bill of rights.

extreme form of union membership is a **closed shop**, which requires workers to join a union before they can be hired and requires employers to go to the union first to hire new employees. Only if union employees are not available can the employer recruit nonunion employees. The Taft-Hartley Act generally outlawed closed shops and ended the right of unions to decide who could be members of the union.[24]

Under a **union shop** agreement, all workers except managers in an organizational unit represented by a union have to become members of that union within a certain period of time after being hired or at least pay the equivalent of union dues. This type of agreement is referred to as a "union security clause." Union shops are illegal in right-to-work states.[25]

Under an **agency shop** agreement, employees cannot be required to join a union but can be required to pay to a union an amount equivalent to initiation fees and dues that are considered to be a tax or service charged and are referred to as an *agency fee*. In exchange for these payments, the union acts as the bargaining agent for the employee. In reality, workers who are not union members can only be required to pay an amount equivalent to reduced union dues solely for the purpose of supporting the collective bargaining, contract administration, and grievance resolution services the union provides.[26]

NATIONAL EMERGENCY STRIKES The Taft-Hartley Act included a provision that allows the president of the United States to direct the appropriate state attorney general to issue an 80-day injunction against a strike or lockout when the following conditions are met: (1) An entire industry or a substantial part of it is affected and (2) national health and safety are imperiled. When a strike is considered to constitute a **national emergency strike**, the U.S. president appoints an inquiry board to determine whether the two conditions are met. Specific steps exist for obtaining the injunction and following up after the injunction is ordered. After the 80-day injunction ends, the union can strike, and management can lock out the union. Basically, the 80 days are to serve as a "cooling off period" for both parties, with the hope that the strike or lockout will not end up occurring.[27]

FEDERAL MEDIATION AND CONCILIATION SERVICE The Taft-Hartley Act established the Federal Mediation and Conciliation Service (FMCS). The FMCS provides both unions and employers free mediation, conciliation, and voluntary arbitration for labor-management disputes. Its primary purpose is to prevent labor-management disputes from impeding the free flow of commerce. The agency also provides education and training programs designed to improve the working relationships between labor and management. FMCS reports that about 85% of all mediated contract disputes in recent years have reached agreements.[28]

Landrum-Griffin Act of 1959

Whereas the NLRA gave employees the freedom to join labor unions, the Taft-Hartley Act protects employers from certain labor union practices. The last part of the National Labor Relations Code, the **Landrum-Griffin Act**, protects union members from being abused by unions. It outlines the responsibilities of union officers as well as the rights of union members via a "bill of rights" that gives union members the right to free speech and due process, the opportunity to be involved in the nomination process for the election of union leaders, the right to receive copies of their collective bargaining agreements, and the right to sue their unions.[29] The act also gives union members the right to vote on any increase in their union dues and requires unions to provide annual financial reports to the U.S. Secretary of Labor. Exhibit 13.4 provides an overview of union member rights.

TYPES OF UNIONS

We now provide an overview of the different types of unions and discuss why they exist and how they are related. The types of unions have evolved over time and include local unions, city and statewide federations of local unions, and international unions. Local unions later joined together to form city and statewide federations. Statewide federations joined together to form national unions, and many of these have now become international unions.

◄ Exhibit 13.4
Overview of Union
Member Rights
Provided for in the
Labor-Management
Reporting and
Disclosure Act
(LMRDA)

Union Member Rights

Bill of Rights

Union members are guaranteed democratic rights that include:

- **Equal rights and privileges** for involvement in union elections and union business, subject to reasonable rules in the union constitution and/or bylaws

- **Freedom of speech and assembly** with regard to criticizing union officials, expressing different viewpoints, and holding meetings

- **Right to secret ballot vote** on rates of dues, initiation fees, and assessments

- **Protection of right to sue** the union, without reprisal

- **Protection from improper union discipline** and right to due process in disciplinary situations

Other rights:

- To receive a copy of the collective bargaining agreement

- To review union reports, constitutions, and bylaws

- To be involved in union elections including running for office

- To have elected union officers removed for misconduct

- To be protected from certain discipline in violation of law

- To be protected from violence

Sources: The Association for Union Democracy. *The LMRDA and the Union Members' Bill of Rights*, www.uniondemocracy.org/Legal/lmrda.htm#bill%20of%20rights; and U.S. Department of Labor. *Compliance Assistance—The Labor-Management Reporting and Disclosure Act of 1959, as amended (LRMDA)*, www.dol.gov/esa/regs/compliance/olms/compllmrda.html.

Local Unions

Local unions protect the interests of workers in a particular craft/trade or industry. For instance, Local No. 1 of the International Union of Operating Engineers is located in Denver, Colorado. Its members are in the stationary/skilled building maintenance trades. Members' dues are used to pay for worker representation and collective bargaining efforts and are set through a vote of the members.[30] Today the lines between craft unions and industrial unions are blurring, but there are still some distinctions. **Craft unions** are organized to represent the interests of members with specialized craft skills. The United Association of Journeymen and Apprentices of the Plumbing and Pipe Fitting Industry of the United States and Canada Local 344 is an example of a local craft union in Lawton, Oklahoma. This union represents skilled plumbers and pipe fitters. **Industrial unions** have traditionally represented semiskilled and unskilled workers in a particular industry. For example, United Paperworkers International Union Local 1342 represents workers in the paperwork industry in Panama City, Florida.

Local unions are voluntary associations of workers who have banded together because of their shared economic interests. They might work for the same employer or for several employers. In any case, the members recognize that the union provides them with a greater voice with respect to their employers than they would have alone. Each member is entitled to one vote, and decisions are made by a majority vote. Elected officers and an executive board are empowered to act on behalf of the union. Members remain in good standing as long as they pay their dues and other required fees and follow the guidelines for union membership. The goal of most local unions is to improve the wages, benefits, and working hours of members. A local union also provides a grievance mechanism for its members with the employer. We describe the grievance process later in this chapter.

craft union

A union organized to represent the interests of members with specialized craft skills.

industrial union

A union that has traditionally represented semi-skilled and unskilled workers in a particular industry.

union steward

A union member elected to serve as a liaison between the rest of the employees and the leadership of the union.

After a local union is organized at a company, the union elects a **union steward** to serve as a liaison between the rest of the employees and the leadership of the union. The union steward is an employee of the company who serves in the role voluntarily. Typically the formal agreement between the union and the employer will specify the role of the union steward, including the amount of work time that the steward can spend on union activities.

International Unions

international unions

Federation of local unions.

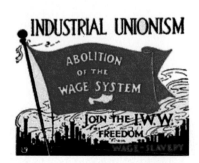

A poster used to recruit union members.

International unions are federations of local unions. In essence, an international union is a "parent" for the local unions. Workers are members of the local union rather than the international union. However, the local union pays dues to the international union. International unions hold regularly scheduled conventions in which delegates from local unions participate. The international union elects officers and an executive board from among these delegates.

International unions provide services to local unions that would be more costly and/or difficult for them to provide individually. For instance, the federation is in a better position to lobby for legislation on behalf of the local unions than are the individual local unions. The Industrial Workers of the World (IWW) is an example of an international union. Its goal is to organize all industries into a single, worldwide union that cuts across industries and crafts.[31]

One of the fastest-growing and largest unions in North America is the Service Employees International Union (SEIU). In 2006, the SEIU had 1.8 million members from the United States, Canada, and Puerto Rico. Members work in hospital systems, long-term care organizations, property services, and public services.

Many U.S. and international unions have been part of a voluntary federation known as the AFL-CIO (formerly the American Federation of Labor–Congress of Industrial Organizations). The AFL-CIO consists of 54 unions that have voluntarily joined together "to solve problems, build stronger workplaces, and give working families a real voice."[32] The AFL-CIO has long been a force in the United States. However, that is changing.

The SEIU and the International Brotherhood of Teamsters were the first groups to split from the AFL-CIO in 2005. The leaders of these two unions were concerned that the AFL-CIO was not doing enough to stop the decline in union memberships and was not making the labor movement a force to be reckoned with in the modern workplace.[33] These two unions joined with five others to form the Change to Win (CTW) coalition. CTW's purpose is to become the leading voice for the labor movement in the United States. The organization believes a radical change is needed if U.S. unions are to survive.[34] These seven national unions represent about 6 million workers while the AFL-CIO has 9 million members.[35]

THE UNION-ORGANIZING PROCESS

bargaining unit

The group of employees designated by the NLRB or identified by the union and employer together as eligible to participate in a union election.

union authorization card

A document indicating that a worker is interested in being represented by a particular union.

When a group of employees decide they would like to be represented by a union, their first step is to file a petition with the NLRB. Employees in the designated work unit, referred to as the **bargaining unit**, provide a dated signature on either a **union authorization card** or a signature sheet, indicating that they are interested in being represented by a particular union. At least 30% of the eligible employees must provide this card for the NLRB to consider the petition. The NLRB then assigns an agent from the appropriate regional field office to process the petition. The regional office of the NLRB holds a secret-ballot election, usually at the workplace. A majority vote in favor of the union is all that is required. The NLRB then certifies that the union represents the employees for collective bargaining purposes and requires their employer to bargain with the union.[36] Exhibit 13.5 provides an overview of the steps required in the union certification process.

One of the most challenging parts of the certification process is determining who is actually eligible to sign the card. The bargaining unit can consist of workers in a single location or from multiple locations. The bargaining unit can also be limited to a specific group of craft workers or a single department. The NLRB determines who is eligible to be part of the bargaining unit, or the union and the employer jointly make this decision. Regardless of who makes the decision, the company is required to supply to the NLRB a list of names and

Step 1: Workers decide they want to be represented by a specific union.

Step 2: Thirty percent of eligible workers in the bargaining unit sign cards petitioning the NLRB for secret-ballot election.

Step 4: A representation certification petition is filed with NLRB.

Step 5: The regional office of the NLRB holds a secret-ballot election.

Step 6: The NLRB tallies the votes to determine if a majority of the workers voted for the union.

Step 7: The union is certified if the vote was positive.

Step 8: The employer is required to bargain with the union.

◄ **Exhibit 13.5**
Labor Union
Certification
Process

addresses for employees who are eligible to vote in the representation election within seven days after the NLRB has indicated that an election will be held.[37] This list is known as the *Excelsior* list. Here is an example of just how important this list is in a union election. In 2004, the adjunct faculty at George Washington University (GWU) successfully voted to be represented by SEIU, Local 500. The university challenged the outcome of the vote because it felt that some of the employees who had voted were not eligible to vote, and because they had been allowed to vote, some other employees should have been allowed to vote as well. The NLRB said the appeal was without merit, and the federal appeals court agreed.[38]

Excelsior list

A list of names and addresses for employees who are eligible to vote in the representation election within seven days after the NLRB has indicated that an election will be held.

Role of Employees, Employers, and Union Organizers

Guidelines exist for what employees, employers, and union organizers can do during a unionization attempt. Employees can lobby co-workers to vote in favor of the union, but they can only do so during lunch and other break times. The employer gets to decide where the union literature can be distributed by employees. Employers can also require employees to attend company meetings so that management can present its view about the union being formed. These meetings can be held on company premises and during work hours. However, no meetings can be held in the 24 hours immediately preceding an election. Supervisors are permitted to have one-on-one meetings with employees about the union issue and can give employees written information as well.

Union organizers work for the unions and are not company employees. These organizers are not allowed to campaign for the establishment of a union on company property unless the workplace is remote, such as a logging camp. Organizers can distribute information in public areas at the work location or in public areas of the city. They can also call employees and visit them at their homes.[39]

Card Checks and Neutrality Agreements

Conducting a union election costs about $1,000 per worker, whether the union wins or loses. In recent years, unions have won about 55% of NLRB-administered elections. In 2003, there were 2,133 NLRB-conducted certification elections, down from more than 7,000 per year in the 1960s.[40]

In an attempt to reduce the cost of certification elections and to counter employers' attempts to quash the formation of unions, union leaders have been pushing for the acceptance of card checks and neutrality agreements. A **card check** is a process whereby a company recognizes a union once the union has produced evidence that the majority of workers have signed authorization cards indicating that they want the union to represent them. No election is held. Under a **neutrality agreement**, a company agrees that it will not express its views about unionization during the time when signatures are collected.

Unions prefer card checks and neutrality agreements because the NLRB does not become involved in the union certification process, and management loses its right to speak out about the possible effects of unionization. The AFL-CIO reports a more than 70% success rate when card checks and neutrality agreements are used.[41] Because the

card check

A process whereby a company recognizes a union once the union has produced evidence that the majority of workers have signed authorization cards indicating that they want the union to represent them.

neutrality agreement

An arrangement whereby a company will not express its views about unionization during the time when signatures are being collected.

NLRA does not require secret-ballot elections, these activities are not illegal. However, under a card check, more than 30% of the eligible employees may have to sign the authorization cards or petition for the bargaining unit to be recognized.[42]

COLLECTIVE BARGAINING

collective bargaining
The process that labor unions and employers use to reach agreement about wages, benefits, hours worked, and other terms and conditions of employment.

Collective bargaining is the process that labor unions and employers use to reach agreement about wages, benefits, hours worked, and other terms and conditions of employment. In this section we discuss this process.

Good Faith Bargaining

good faith bargaining
The process that requires the parties to meet at a reasonable time and come to the bargaining table ready to reach a collective bargaining agreement.

The NLRB requires that employers and unions bargain in good faith. **Good faith bargaining** requires the parties to meet at a reasonable time and come to the bargaining table ready to reach a collective bargaining agreement. **Mandatory bargaining topics**, those that must be negotiated, include compensation and benefits, hours of employment, and other conditions of employment. Pensions, insurance, grievance processes, safety, layoffs, discipline, and union security have also become mandatory bargaining topics. The law does not require an employer and a union to actually reach an agreement on the topics—only that they bargain in good faith.

mandatory bargaining topics
Topics that must be negotiated, including compensation and benefits, hours of employment, and other conditions of employment.

The bargaining process can also address issues such as employee rights, managerial control, and benefits for retired union members. However, these topics are not mandatory and are referred to as **permissive topics**. With the fast-changing global economy, job security has become a critical component for collective bargaining.[43] No measures can be discussed that would be unlawful. For example, the two parties couldn't discuss a situation in which only union members could be hired. Nor can the parties discuss discriminating against employees based on their membership in a protected class.

permissive topics
Nonmandatory issues, such as employee rights, managerial control, and benefits for retired union members, that are often part of the collective bargaining negotiations and agreement.

Bad Faith Bargaining

bad faith bargaining
Entering into a collective bargaining situation with no intention of reaching an agreement or in some other way violating the protocol for appropriate collective bargaining, for instance bargaining with individual employees rather than with union representatives or refusing to meet at reasonable times to engage in bargaining.

Among the actions that constitute **bad faith bargaining** are bargaining with individual employees rather than union representatives, refusing to meet at reasonable times to engage in bargaining, and "going through the motions" of bargaining without the intent of reaching an agreement. Other activities that may or may not be considered bad faith bargaining include not being willing to schedule enough bargaining sessions and applying economic pressure to the other party.[44]

Negotiating the Agreement

As a manager, you will find that there are many times when you are involved in negotiations. You will have to negotiate with customers, vendors, and/or employees. And, even if you do not actually represent your company in collective bargaining negotiations (assuming that you work in a union environment), you might be asked to provide those who do with certain information. Regardless of the type of negotiation, there are a few critical steps that should be followed to reach the best possible solution for all parties involved. Those steps apply to the collective bargaining negotiation process as well: (1) being prepared, (2) knowing the interests of the other party, and (3) understanding the consequences of not reaching an acceptable agreement. We briefly discuss each of these components within the context of the collective bargaining negotiation process, and we discuss the major types of negotiation that are likely to occur.

PREPARING TO NEGOTIATE   Both parties involved in the negotiation—labor and management—spend considerable time preparing to negotiate. It is important that each side have current and accurate data to address the topics for negotiation. For instance, as noted previously, wages are a mandatory topic for negotiation in a collective bargaining agreement. Both parties will want to gather data about prevailing wage rates in the relevant labor market and be ready to make an offer during the negotiation that is reasonable based

A collective bargaining session.

on that information. Of course, each side will seek to find wage information that is most advantageous for its part of the negotiation. The union will want data to support higher wages, while the company will want data to support lower wages.

If one party in the negotiation indicates that it is unable to make a concession, it is important that the party be able to substantiate its claims. For instance, if a representative of the company indicates that the cost of the benefits desired will adversely affect the operation of the company, the representative needs to be prepared with the appropriate financial data to support this argument. It is also imperative for the parties to know what their objectives are in order to make sure that they have the information they need to bargain well.

As you can see, preparing to negotiate requires paying careful attention to a lot of issues. In addition, preparation is an ongoing activity. As soon as a collective bargaining agreement is signed, it is time to start thinking about the one that will come next. During the preparation stage, the first-line supervisor can be a critical source of information about what employees are really expecting and desiring.[45]

KNOWING THE INTERESTS OF THE OTHER PARTY

Being prepared means entering into negotiation with some idea of what the other party will expect with regard to the final outcome. Understanding the interests of the other party—what the other party sees as critical relative to the outcome—puts the negotiator in a stronger position to bargain for concessions. Learning the interests of the other party takes a lot of time and effort, but the payoff is worth it.

Two commonly used types of negotiation strategies in labor negotiations are distributive and integrative bargaining. When a **distributive bargaining strategy** is used, there is a winner and a loser. The goals of one party are in direct conflict with the goals of the other party, and often each party wants to claim a fixed set of limited resources as its own or at least maximize its share. Each party takes a defensive position during the bargaining sessions. In an **integrative bargaining strategy**, each party is more cooperative and works to make the outcome win–win. In this situation, one party can pursue its goals without precluding the other party from doing the same. Both sides cooperate to reconcile their differences and reach a mutually agreeable solution.[46]

Interest-based bargaining (IBB) is basically an extension of integrative bargaining. In this situation, each party looks for common goals in order to meet the interests of the other party. Brainstorming, information sharing, and other techniques are used to ensure that the lines of communication between the two parties are kept open. The goal is to reach consensus so that both parties "win."[47]

UNDERSTANDING THE CONSEQUENCES OF NOT REACHING AN ACCEPTABLE AGREEMENT

What happens if the parties to a union negotiation can't reach an agreement? Often the result is either a strike by workers, a lockout of the workers by managers, or arbitration, with a third party making the decisions. The situation in which both parties have made their final offers and are not willing to make further concessions is referred to as an **impasse**.[48]

When an impasse occurs, the parties have several options. First, an impartial outside party such as the Federal Mediation and Conciliation Service, discussed earlier, can be called in to facilitate the negotiation. This facilitation can take the form of **conciliation**, which involves keeping the parties working on the agreement until they can resolve the issues at hand. The facilitation can also take the form of **mediation**, which involves the outside party working with each side to reach an acceptable agreement. Finally, **arbitration** can be used to resolve the issues. Unlike conciliation and mediation, in which a third party acts as an intermediary, arbitration involves a third party actually making the decision about the issue. Recall that in Chapter 3 we introduced the concept of mediation and arbitration. More and more companies are using mediation and arbitration to resolve employee discrimination complaints and other grievances. Employees and unions also are using arbitration to resolve their disputes with individual employees. And labor arbitration or mediation is increasingly used by employers and unions to resolve collective bargaining labor-management disputes because this approach is more cost-effective and timely than taking the dispute to court.[49]

distributive bargaining strategy
The negotiation strategy used when the goals of one party are in direct conflict with the goals of the other party and results in a winner and a loser.

integrative bargaining strategy
The negotiation strategy used when each party cooperates and works to reach a win-win outcome.

interest-based bargaining (IBB)
An extension of integrative bargaining in which each party looks for common goals in order to meet the interests of the other party.

impasse
The situation in which both parties have made their final offers and are not willing to make further concessions.

conciliation
A type of facilitation used when an impasse occurs in a collective bargaining session so that both parties keep working toward an agreement until they can resolve the issues at hand.

mediation
The arrangement whereby an outside party works with each side in a negotiation to reach an acceptable agreement.

arbitration
A method of resolving disputes in which a third party acts as an intermediary and actually makes the decision about how the issue should be resolved.

THE GRIEVANCE PROCESS

grievance process

The formal steps that must be followed to settle disputes between labor and management.

grievance

A charge by one or more employees that management has violated their contractual rights.

Most collective bargaining agreements outline formal steps that must be followed to settle disputes between labor and management. These steps make up the **grievance process**. Officially, a **grievance** is a written charge by one or more employees that management has violated their contractual rights. Exhibit 13.6 lists the typical steps for employees to follow if they believe their rights have been violated.

The grievance process typically works as follows. First, the problem is reported to one's immediate supervisor, who is obligated to investigate the matter and try to resolve the problem. The report can be written or oral, but it is usually written. The supervisor should then work with the union steward to resolve the problem. If the union steward does not believe that the problem is a legitimate grievance, no further action is taken. If these efforts do not result in a resolution, it goes to the next level of supervision. This time, the employee filing the grievance is represented by the union. Failure to resolve the grievance at this stage within the time allotted in the collective bargaining agreement (usually 5 to 15 days) results in the grievance being taken to a higher level of management, such as a plant manager or even the executives of the company. The highest level for the resolution of a grievance is spelled out in a union contract. If the grievance is still not resolved, the final step in the grievance process is to call in an arbitrator, who reviews the facts of the case and makes a determination about what action should occur. At this stage, the company and the union are both represented by high-level managers and union officials. If the union contract calls for binding arbitration, and most do, the arbitrator has the final say in the case.[50]

The employee's right to have a union representative involved in the process of disciplinary hearings resulted in large part from the 1975 landmark U.S. Supreme Court case *NLRB vs. Weingarten, Inc.* In this case, the Supreme Court ruled that a union representative could be present when a supervisor conducted an investigatory interview to gather information that could result in the employee being questioned or disciplined, or when an employer asks an employee to defend his or her actions. As a result of this case, managers have to notify union representatives of the purpose of the interview. In addition, the employee has the right to select which union employee will be present.[51]

Exhibit 13.6 ►

Steps to Follow if Rights Have Been Violated

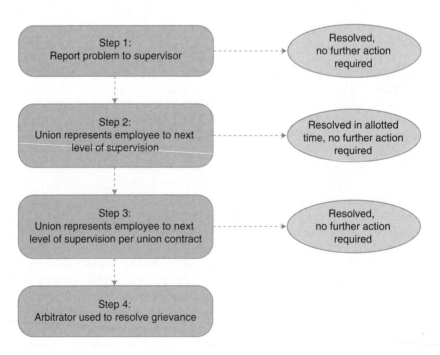

Source: Based on Society for Human Resource Management (SHRM). Module 5: Employee and labor relations. *The SHRM Learning System*. Alexandria, VA: SHRM, 2007.

Managers need to be very familiar with the requirements of union contracts and understand the types of actions that lead to grievances. By doing so, they reduce the likelihood that they will have to participate in a grievance process. If a grievance is reported, the proper care and handling of it is critical. Conducting a fair and timely investigation, keeping your supervisor informed, and carefully documenting all activities related to the grievance are just a few ways to minimize the likelihood of the grievance going to an arbitration hearing.

THE NLRB'S ROLE IN UNFAIR LABOR PRACTICES

When an unfair labor practice charge is filed with the appropriate NLRB field office, an investigation ensues to determine whether there is reasonable cause to believe that the National Labor Relations Act has been violated. If cause is found, the field office makes an attempt to help the parties involved reach a settlement agreement. If a settlement cannot be reached, a formal complaint is filed, and the case goes to the NLRB administrative law judge. The judge then issues a written decision, which can be appealed to the NLRB. If one of the parties believes the NLRB decision is not acceptable, it can file an appeal with the U.S. Court of Appeals. About 25,000 charges of unfair labor practices are filed each year with the Court of Appeals. About one-third of these are found to have merit, and more than 90% are settled.[52]

DECERTIFICATION

decertification
The process of terminating union representation in collective bargaining.

If employees in a collective bargaining unit decide that they no longer want to be part of a union, they can petition the NLRB for decertification. **Decertification** means that the union will no longer represent the employees or engage in collective bargaining on their behalf. The decertification petition can only be filed within 90 days of the expiration of the collective bargaining agreement currently in force. As with certification, at least 30% of the employees in the bargaining unit must indicate that they no longer want to be represented by the union. A secret-ballot election is a requirement for decertification. Between April 2007 and September 2007, 125 successful decertification elections occurred in the United States.[53]

CORPORATE CAMPAIGNS

corporate campaign
Tactical strategies designed to identify and exploit opportunities to interfere with the normal operation of a business and affect its reputation.

In the 1970s, unions began to use a strategy known as a corporate campaign to increase their presence and role in companies. A **corporate campaign** involves tactical strategies designed to identify and exploit opportunities to interfere with the normal operation of a business and affect its reputation. The goal is to create so much pressure on the company that it gives in to the union's demands. These campaigns begin with a power structure analysis aimed at identifying the vulnerabilities in stakeholder relationships that are critical to a company. The tactics used as part of the campaign range from sophisticated governance and financial initiatives to psychological warfare. Unions have used tactics such as introducing shareholder resolutions that restrict management and director authority, filing unfair labor practice claims that are not valid, and getting union-paid organizers hired to work for the company so that they can organize employees. This latter practice is known as "salting."[54] Corporate campaigns are an attempt to get around the NLRB's normal union certification procedures. Companies that have been targeted by campaigns such as these include Comcast, Borders, Sodexho, Taco Bell, and Nike.[55]

We don't want to give the impression that the unions are the only ones that don't play fair. Employers also engage in unfair and inappropriate activities to try to prevent unionization from occurring, as discussed earlier in this chapter. In a study in Canada, researchers found that the majority of the companies included had engaged in overt or covert tactics to keep the unions out. Among the reported activities were dismissing union activists and issuing threats or promises that were inappropriate. Interestingly, these actions did not have any effect on the certification process but did affect collective bargaining success and retention of the certification two years later.[56]

PUBLIC-SECTOR LABOR RELATIONS

Civil Service Reform Act

An act passed in 1978 that set up the Federal Labor Relations Authority (FLRA) as the oversight agency for labor-management issues at the federal level.

Federal Labor Relations Authority (FLRA)

The oversight agency for labor-management issues at the federal level.

Prior to 1962, federal employees were not allowed to form unions. This prohibition was lifted by an executive order signed by President John F. Kennedy. It gave federal workers limited rights to unionize and bargain for nonwage items. The **Civil Service Reform Act** of 1978 set up the **Federal Labor Relations Authority (FLRA)** as the oversight agency for labor-management issues at the federal level. Other state and local laws protect government employees who want to participate in unions.

Unions such as the National Education Association (NEA) provide representation for specific groups of public employees. The NEA represents approximately 3.2 million members working in public kindergarten through grade 12 schools across the United States. Other unions, such as the Washington Federation of State Employees (WFSE), represent all employees in a particular state. These unions are also affiliated with the American Federation of State, County, and Municipal Employees (AFSCME), which is affiliated with the AFL-CIO.

TRENDS IN LABOR RELATIONS

We end the chapter by noting a number of trends in labor relations in the United States and elsewhere. Specifically, we address changes in union activities, new forms of employee organizations, and global unionization trends.

Changes in Union Activities

Do labor unions have a place in the twenty-first century?[57] As we have indicated, in the United States, unions have been on the decline for some time, both in terms of the number of unions and the number of union members. The scope of unions is also changing. Employees are pulling away from the mega-national unions they believe do not fully represent their cause.

The decline of unions has prompted unions to reach out to prospective members via innovations such as union credit cards, smaller unions that represent less than 50% of the workforce, and greater organizing efforts, consolidations, and mergers. The AFL-CIO, for example, is actively working to create state and local solidarity charters that will keep the union movement united at the local level.[58] Unions are also considering adopting new strategies. For instance, some unions are using variable pay plans to protect employees' wages during difficult economic times. Recall from Chapters 10 and 11 that variable pay plans often include a portion of the salary that is fixed and a portion that is dependent on achievement of some goal, such as a production quota. With a variable pay plan, the percentage of the pay that is fixed is lower than in a traditional pay plan, where all the salary is fixed; thus, there is more flexibility relative to what the company has to pay when the business is not doing well. Such plans also enable greater union/employee involvement in decision making relative to production issues, lead to improved communication between unions and management, and increase the input of unions into organizational strategy. Although seemingly anathema to the traditional philosophy of unions, which was to reduce the employment risks their members face, about 20% of U.S. collective bargaining agreements now include variable pay plans.[59]

In addition to the corporate campaigns discussed earlier in this chapter, there are a number of other trends among labor unions, including the following:

- Developing stronger ties with public officials and increasing support for political candidates who are pro-union

COMPANY spotlight

13.1 The Industrial Areas Foundation of San Antonio

The Industrial Areas Foundation (IAF) is a network of community organizations with affiliates throughout the country. Originally founded in Chicago, the IAF works to bring change to low- and moderate-income neighborhoods by revitalizing the local democracies within them. Its mission is to train people to take responsibility for their communities, thus getting citizens involved in public life by providing them with leadership and development training, for example. Often 10 to 20 people meet at a member's home to talk about issues and schedule conferences.

Many IAF members are churches, which typically give 2% of their annual budgets to the IAF. One such church is Valley Interfaith, in the Rio Grande Valley. It consists of a network of about 45 churches and 16 schools and represents more than 60,000 people. Labor unions and community organizations such as health centers can also join the IAF. By focusing on institutional rather than individual members, the IAF ensures the continuity of the membership.

In 1974, another organization affiliated with the IAF, Communities for Public Service (COPS), began in San Antonio. Now there are COPS organizations in about 30 cities in the Southwest. Other organizations have since joined with COPS. The Southwest IAF (SWIAF), which serves Texas, New Mexico, Nebraska, Arizona, and part of California, is made up of 24 community-based organizations. This group has helped get bonds and other regulations passed to clean up and manage the spread of *colonias*, residential areas located on the U.S.–Mexican border that lack even basic infrastructure. The SWIAF has also worked successfully to implement school reforms and labor market programs.

Sources: Chambers, E. T. *Roots for radicals*. New York: Continuum International Publishing Group, 2003; and Osterman, P. Community organizing and employee representation. *British Journal of Industrial Relations* 44:629–649, 2006.

- Engaging in outreach to underrepresented and minority populations to educate them about union membership
- Leveraging technology, including designing sophisticated Web sites targeted at particular groups such as Generation Xers and using data mining to identify and reach out to potential union members
- Consolidating and merging to pool union resources
- Offering members more options, such as credit cards and other perks, to involve more employees in the labor movement[60]

New Forms of Employee Organizations

As unions have continued to decline in membership, other groups have formed within organizations to represent employees. They include affinity groups, such as those focused on race, gender, or lifestyle and that lobby for the fair treatment of their members; worker centers that provide services, such as legal resources, to employees; and professional associations and guilds that provide services to their members. All these groups attempt to ensure that members have a voice in the workplace. Community-based organizations have also begun to provide a voice for workers. These community networks often rely on churches and other neighborhood institutions to represent workers and advocate for them.[61] Company Spotlight 13.1 describes a network based in San Antonio, Texas.

A worker–management committee is another type of employee group. These groups originated in part out of the quality management and continuous improvement movement that occurred in the United States in the late 1980s. The movement's goal was mainly to increase the communication between workers and managers and aid in productivity improvements. These groups have been ruled illegal, however, when they engage in activities such as setting wages and establishing conditions of employment. When they do so, they are considered to have crossed the line and are viewed as attempting to become labor organizations, which can only be certified by the NLRB. If you want to establish a worker–management committee, you need to make sure that its purpose is to share information and that all workers—not just union members—have the right to participate in the process.[62]

Global Trends

The United States is not the only country that has experienced a reduction in its union membership. In 2005, the labor union participation rate in Korea reached an all-time low of 10.3% of employed workers—down from 25.4% in 1977. Some people speculate that the rate dropped because workers felt that the large unions representing them were doing a poor job.[63]

In Great Britain, the birthplace of the modern labor union, membership has been declining since 1979. The changing structure of the British economy is believed to be the root cause. As manufacturing industries have declined in the country, so, too, has the membership of the unions. Today more of the United Kingdom's public sector than private sector is unionized, and more women than men are union members.[64] Unions in Great Britain still have a voice in the workplace, but their economic impact has been significantly reduced.[65]

The impact of unions is felt around the world, in developing countries as well as developed countries. About 70% of workers in Mexico are union members. In Mexico, unions have led to increased job training and greater productivity per worker as well as improved the ratio of fringe benefits to total compensation and the value of benefits per worker. While these trends are positive, higher worker turnover has also been associated with union presence in Mexico.[66] However, the wage rates there haven't readily adjusted to market levels in the past. Mexico actually has a complex system of unions that has existed for some time and is intricately connected to the government. Some people believe this relationship between the unions and the government is one reason wages have remained lower than they might otherwise be.[67]

Globally, a number of laws and organizations affect what workers are permitted to do when it comes to joining unions. The UN's Universal Declaration of Human Rights and other conventions issued by the International Labour Organization (ILO) set forth the rights of workers to form and join trade unions. Some of the conventions specify that governments cannot interfere with this activity, whereas others protect workers from anti-union discrimination by employers.

Of course, just because such declarations exist does not mean that they are followed. For instance, there is a labor union in China, but it is the All China Federation of Trade Unions and is a product of the Chinese Communist Party. Collective bargaining does not occur because representing labor rights is secondary to serving the party. New labor legislation that went into effect January 1, 2008, appears to be making a difference. This legislation, known as the Law of the People's Republic of China on Employment Contracts allows workers to have labor contracts and has led to an increase in wages. There was an unintended consequence, however. The higher wages have led to higher production costs, which have to be passed along to the consumer and in turn makes the products less competitive in the marketplace.[68]

Laws such as this one in China begin to address some of the issues surrounding such companies as Nike relative to their fair trade practices. Specifically, Nike and other companies have been accused of exploiting workers by not paying them a fair wage and not providing better overall working conditions for them. Much of the debate concerns whether companies have an obligation to pay a "living wage." Recall that we discussed the concept of a living wage in Chapter 10 and noted that it is a complicated concept. However, the need for improved worker conditions and fair pay creates an opportunity for unions to provide a voice for workers in these developing countries.

Finally, large confederations of unions now exist that cut across country and continent borders. For instance, the European Trade Union Confederation (ETUC) includes unions from eastern and western Europe, and the International Confederation of Free Trade Unions (ICFTU) includes 125 million workers from 145 countries and territories and 215 national unions.

SUMMARY

Labor unions exist to provide a collective voice for workers in bargaining with employers for higher wages, better benefits, safe and fair working conditions, and other conditions of employment. Labor union membership has been on the decline in the United States as a result of many traditional union jobs in manufacturing moving to other countries. Yet research continues to show the benefits of union membership, including higher wages and better benefits for employees.

A number of regulations exist to govern labor/management relations. These include the Railway Labor Act of 1926, which provided a way for employees and railroads to handle differences, and the Norris-LaGuardia Act of 1932, which made it easier for employees to engage in union-organizing activities. The most significant legislation affecting labor and management relations was the Wagner Act, also known as the NLRA, which gave employees the freedom to join unions, defined unfair labor practices that were impermissible, and created the NLRB to administer the NLRA.

In 1947, Congress passed the Taft-Hartley Act to protect the rights of employees and employers because of a perception that the NLRA had given too much power to the unions. The Taft-Hartley Act protects employers from certain labor union practices that impede their business. The Landrum-Griffin Act was passed in 1959 to protect union members from abuse by unions. The act outlines an employee bill of rights that gives union members, among other protections, the right to freedom of speech, the right to secret ballots, and the right to sue the union.

Unions exist in various forms. Local unions protect the interests of workers in a particular craft/trade or industry. A union steward serves as a liaison between the employees and the leadership of a union. International unions are federations of local unions and have stronger bargaining power and greater ability to lobby for legislation on behalf of union members.

The union-organizing process begins when workers decide to be represented by a specific union. If 30% of eligible employees indicate their desire to be represented by that union, a representation certification petition is filed with the NLRB, and a secret-ballot election is held. If the ballot passes, the union is certified, and the employer is required to engage in collective bargaining with that union.

Collective bargaining is the process of the employer and union reaching agreement about wages, benefits, and working conditions. Employers and unions are required to bargain in good faith on these mandatory bargaining topics. Collective bargaining agreements define the grievance process for resolving disputes between workers and management. These processes include involvement of a union steward or other union representative on behalf of or alongside the employee. Arbitration is the final step in resolving such disputes. If employees decide they do not want to be represented by the union any longer, they can initiate a decertification process. Federal employees can unionize and bargain for nonwage items. The Civil Service Reform Act of 1978 set up the Federal Labor Relations Authority as the oversight agency for the federal employee labor/management issues.

With the decline in union memberships, unions have sought new ways to reach out to prospective members. These new approaches range from being open to variable-pay rather than fixed-pay plans; offering members more benefits, such as union credit cards; developing stronger ties with public officials and political candidates who are pro-union; and consolidating and merging to pool union resources. New forms of employee organizations have developed as well. These can be in the form of affinity groups and community networks designed to provide support and resources for employees not protected by unions to ensure that they have a voice in the workplace.

Globally, union membership is declining in some countries such as Great Britain but growing in developing countries such as Mexico. The UN's Universal Declaration of Human Rights and other conventions issued by the International Labour Organization define the rights of workers relative to forming and joining trade unions, but not all countries follow these conventions.

KEY TERMS

agency shop p. 398

arbitration p. 403

bad faith bargaining p. 402

bargaining unit p. 400

card check p. 401

Civil Service Reform Act p. 406

closed shop p. 398

collective bargaining p. 402

conciliation p. 403

corporate campaign p. 405

craft union p. 399

decertification p. 405

distributive bargaining strategy p. 403

Excelsior list p. 401

Federal Labor Relations Authority (FLRA) p. 406

good faith bargaining p. 402

grievance p. 404

grievance process p. 404

impasse p. 403

industrial union p. 399

integrative bargaining strategy p. 403

interest-based bargaining (IBB) p. 403

international union p. 400

Labor Management Relations Act (also the Taft Hartley Act) p. 396

Landrum-Griffin Act p. 398

mandatory bargaining topics p. 402

mediation p. 403

national emergency strike p. 398

National Labor Relations Act (NLRA) p. 395

National Labor Relations Board (NLRB) p. 396

neutrality agreement p. 401

Norris-LaGuardia Act p. 395

permissive topics p. 402

Railway Labor Act (RLA) p. 394

right-to-work laws p. 397

Taft-Hartley Act (Labor
  Management Relations Act) *p. 396*
unfair labor practices (ULPs) *p. 396*

union authorization card *p. 400*
union shop *p. 398*
union steward *p. 400*

Wagner Act (National Labor
  Relations Act [NLRA]) *p. 395*

DISCUSSION QUESTIONS

1. Labor unions were much more powerful and larger during the Industrial Revolution than they are today. Discuss why this is so and what type of issues unions need to address to be more of a force in the current knowledge age.
2. Summarize the purpose of each of the three components of the National Labor Relations Act. Discuss why three laws were necessary and why they likely occurred in the order in which they were passed.
3. Prepare a short presentation to teach managers who work for you about the actions that constitute unfair labor practices to ensure they understand what they can and cannot do in case employees attempt to unionize the company.
4. Go to the Web site for the Change to Win labor federation (www.changetowin.org) and identify the affiliated unions.

Choose one of them and research its purpose, history, and current membership. Identify how many local unions belong to the affiliated union you selected.
5. What role can you, as a manager, play in a union-organizing effort?
6. If you were asked, as a manager, to provide input for the purposes of a collective bargaining process, what type of information would you provide?
7. One of your employees has come to you with a written statement indicating that his work hours are not fair. The employee is a member of the recognized union in your company. Describe how you would handle this complaint.
8. Spend some time researching the pros and cons of the Employee Free Choice Act. Prepare an argument for or against the act.

LEARNING EXERCISE 1

Visit the following Web sites plus another one about a country-specific union federation you identify:

Singapore (National Trades
  Union Congress): www.ntucworld.org.sg
United States (AFL-CIO): www.aflcio.org
Australia (Australian Council
  of Trade Unions): www.actu.asn.au

Prepare a table that compares and contrasts the focuses of these federations. Answer the following questions about each federation as you prepare your table.

1. What year was the federation started?
2. How many members does it represent?

3. Who is eligible to join the federation?
4. What is the focus of the federation?
5. What benefits are promised to members?
6. Do workers join local unions or just the national union?
7. Based on the information you collected, summarize the similarities and differences among unions around the world. Note whether patterns emerge, such as differences between unions across countries versus within countries.

LEARNING EXERCISE 2

Identify and interview someone who is a member of a union to learn more about the benefits of union membership. In your interview, address at least the following questions.

1. How long have you been a member of the union?
2. Why did you join the union?

3. How has being a union member affected your job, including what you are required to do and your promotion opportunities?
4. Would you advise other workers to join the union? Why or why not?

CASE STUDY # 1 — TIME FOR A UNION AT STARBUCKS?

The Industrial Workers of the World (IWW) was founded in 1905 for the purpose of representing unskilled workers who had low wages and who felt oppressed in their jobs. By the 1920s, the IWW had 100,000 members. The membership is currently around 2,000 members.

Starbucks was founded in 1971 in Seattle, Washington. The company has more than 12,400 coffee shops throughout the United States and 35 other countries. Most Starbucks locations are company owned, but a significant number are operated through licensees and franchises.

In 2007, the IWW targeted a Starbucks store in Rockville, Maryland, as a place to gain a union foothold. A number of coffee servers, or baristas, served the assistant manager with a declaration requesting union membership. They also provided the assistant manager a letter listing a number of grievances, including an allegation that the baristas did not earn a "living wage" and grievances related to their work schedules. They also complained that baristas who were possibly involved in union-organizing efforts had been fired.

At the time, none of the 8,000 Starbucks locations in the United States were unionized, even though the IWW had been trying to organize a union at Starbucks since 2004. According to Starbucks, the union-organizing effort had not been successful because most baristas were satisfied with the company. The company said it believes in the importance of having a good working relationship with its employees and addresses their concerns as they occur.

DISCUSSION QUESTIONS

1. Describe the steps that employees at the Starbucks in Rockville, Maryland, should have taken for the IWW to be officially recognized as the bargaining unit for employees there.

2. If employees believe they have been fired for trying to unionize, what recourse do they have?

3. What can Starbucks legally do to keep employees from unionizing?

4. What would you do if you were a Starbucks manager and some of your employees approached you with a list of grievances and indicated that they wanted to unionize?

Sources: Adapted from Mook, B. Regular, decaf or wobbly? IWF labor union targets Starbucks in Rockville *The Daily Record*, January 24, 2007, p. 1; and Hoovers Starbucks Corporation Information.

CASE STUDY # 2 — NOT SO GRAND EMPLOYEE MORALE AT THE GRAND LIMITED HOTEL

For years, the Grand Limited has been known as the hotel to work for in the metropolitan area in which it is located. The hotel has even received a number of awards for being a best place to work and for its family-friendly policies. It is not uncommon for workers to have been with the hotel for 25 years.

Now the hotel is faced with new management and numerous retirements among its 500 employees. And, with a downturn in the economy, the new management of the hotel has decided to offer a lower wage structure and fewer benefits for new employees than it has offered in the past. The hotel is still paying the market rate for jobs similar to others in the area, and so far it has been able to attract new employees. Unfortunately, the hotel managers have failed to take into consideration that many of the local hotels are unionized. Now, there are rumblings that the newer employees are considering asking the local service industry union to represent them to bargain for better wages and benefits, as well as better working conditions. Not feeling like they are treated equitably with the employees who have been around for a long time, the newer employees are feeling disenfranchised and have little loyalty to the hotel. As you can imagine, these issues are starting to spill over into the level of customer service provided to guests of the hotel.

You have been asked to serve as a consultant for the hotel to address these labor issues. A goal of management in bringing you in is to stop the employees from having a vote to be represented by a union.

DISCUSSION QUESTIONS

1. As the consultant, take a stand either for or against what management has done to date. Review the facts of the case and use them to support your argument as well as indicate any assumptions that you are using.

2. Describe what you would do to assist management in blocking the union. Be sure to address legal issues inherent in attempting to block a union effort.

3. Can you identify any value that could actually come from having the employees represented by a union?

4. Make a final recommendation to management about how to proceed in handling this situation.

14

CREATING HIGH-PERFORMING HR SYSTEMS

1. Explain the principle of external fit. *(415)*

2. Explain the principle of internal fit. *(416)*

3. Explain how HR systems can be aligned with the contributions employees make. *(417)*

4. Discuss how to manage an employment portfolio. *(419)*

5. Explain what strategic performance drivers and HR deliverables are. *(424)*

6. Evaluate the external alignment of your HR system. *(424)*

7. Evaluate the internal alignment of your HR system. *(425)*

8. Create a plan to change your HR system to make it more effective. *(427)*

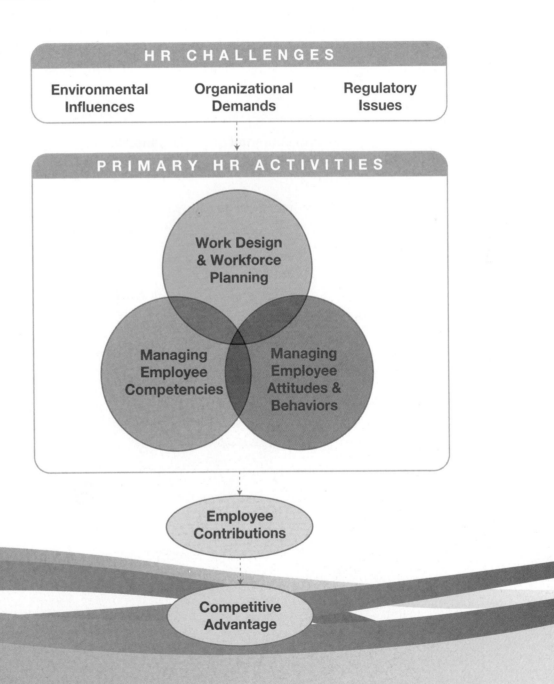

In the beginning of Chapter 2, we introduced three axioms for effectively managing employees:

1. No two companies are the same.
2. There is no one best way to manage employees.
3. Using the wrong practice, or using the right practice poorly, can cause more harm than good.

After reading the previous chapters, you should have a pretty good idea about why these axioms are so important. As Axiom 1 states, each company is unique. Companies may compete for similar customers, offer similar products, and even have similar technologies. But their cultures, sizes, stages of development, workforce compositions, and the like are unique. In addition, companies often face similar environmental challenges and regulatory issues, but the relative impact they have on each company is different. Figure 14.1 shows that these HR challenges influence the management of employees.

Axiom 2 highlights the fact that when managing employees, you can select from a wide array of HR activities. Consider how you select an employee. You may use interviews, personality tests, physical ability tests, or a number of other options. The best choice, however, depends on a number of factors—first, how the company is set up and how it competes in

Exhibit 14.1 ▶

Framework for the Strategic Management of Employees

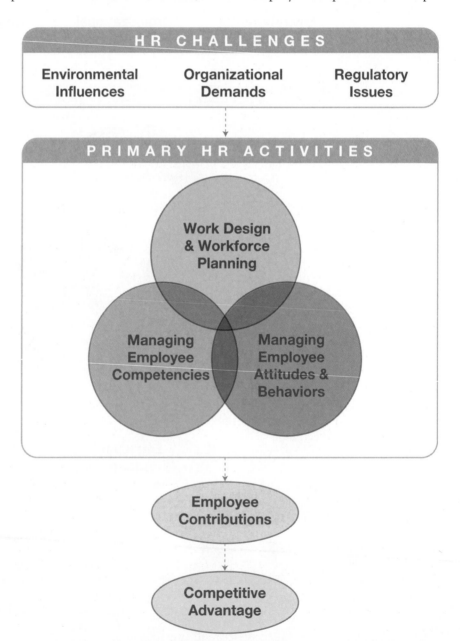

its market (see Axiom 1) and, second, how the firm internally aligns itself. These factors, in turn, are directly affected by the HR challenges that you, as a manager, face. In other words, as a manager, you need to understand how and when to use the different HR practices.

Axiom 3 shifts our focus to issues of design and implementation: A firm will experience problems if it designs and uses the wrong HR practices to manage its employees. Sometimes managers choose the wrong practice because they don't know enough about the different tools they have at their disposal. Even if a firm chooses the right practices, how those practices are implemented can be problematic. For example, a team-based incentive-pay plan might work well with project teams, but it is not likely to be as effective in a company in which employees work independently.

Although there is no single best system with which to manage your employees, several fundamental principles can help guide your decisions and, in turn, determine whether your firm will have a high-performing HR system or a less effective system. In the next section, we focus on the key principles of high-performing HR systems.

PRINCIPLES OF HIGH-PERFORMING HR SYSTEMS

In Chapter 1, we defined HR system alignment as a situation in which a firm's primary HR activities reinforce one another. When they do, a firm's employees have the skills they need as well as exhibit the right attitudes and behaviors. The firm is also able to manage and allocate its work to make sure the right people are doing the right things when they need to be done.[1] There are really two forms of alignment to consider. The first—**external alignment**—means that managers must select HR activities that help their companies meet their organizational demands, cope with environmental factors, and comply with regulatory issues. A second form of alignment—**internal alignment**—focuses on how well a firm's employee management practices support one another. Next, we discuss both of these aspects in more detail.

External Fit: Aligning HR Activities with HR Challenges

Throughout this book, we have emphasized the importance of choosing employee management practices in light of a number of challenges that managers face. We have focused on three sets of challenges: organizational demands, environmental influences, and regulatory issues. The key point of these influences is the importance of external fit. External fit refers to the alignment between the three primary HR activities and the HR challenges.

Each of the challenges affects which practices are used within companies as well as the effectiveness of those practices. For example, a company's strategy influences how its jobs are designed, which workforce planning tactics are most appropriate for it to use, the recruitment and selection practices it chooses, the types of training and development it needs, and the performance evaluation methods it uses. Also affected by the firm's strategy are how the company compensates employees in different jobs, the incentive plans it chooses, and the decisions it makes about the benefits and safety and wellness plans it designs and offers. Companies that emphasize customer service, such as Nordstrom and Macy's, rely on different practices to manage their employees than companies that place greater emphasis on competing on the basis of costs, such as Wal-Mart, Costco, and Target.

At the same time, the other HR challenges, such as company characteristics, labor force trends, ethics, and regulatory issues, influence these same practices, albeit in potentially different ways. Some challenges affect which HR practices a firm needs in order to cope with changes in the environment. For example, the increasing diversity of the labor force affects how employees react to the use of different employee management practices. Similarly, the growing need for ethical and social responsibility on the part of firms affects which practices people and communities view as socially acceptable. Other challenges affect how employee management practices are carried out. Laws and regulations affect the wages employees must be paid, the types of interview questions prospective candidates can be asked, what companies must do to ensure that their workplaces and employees are safe, and the like.

external alignment

The extent to which the three primary HR activities that a company uses help them meet their organizational demands, cope with environmental factors, and comply with regulatory issues.

internal alignment

The extent to which specific practices used *within* each HR activity are consistent with one another as well as aligned *across* the primary HR activities.

Nordstrom emphasizes customer service among their employees.

Some of these challenges present opportunities for how to manage employees; others constrain which options a company is able to choose; still other challenges affect how a firm's HR practices will affect the company's ability to meet its goals. Adopting practices that facilitate the management of employees in light of these challenges is the first step toward designing an effective system for managing employees.

Internal Fit: Aligning HR Activities with One Another

Throughout this text, we have covered a lot of material regarding HR activities and the practices that comprise those activities. And, although we have focused on the primary practices individually in each chapter, the reality is that HR practices are rarely, if ever, used in isolation of one another. Rather, employees are exposed to multiple practices simultaneously, and the impact of one depends on the impact of the others.[2] For every job that exists within an organization, decisions are made regarding how the job should be designed or whether the job should be staffed by a full-time employee or through the use of contingent labor. Who occupies the job, as well as the person's knowledge, skills, and abilities, is a result of decisions managers made regarding the recruitment and selection process as well as training and development activities. Decisions about the performance management process, how much to compensate employees, what types of incentive plans to implement, and which benefit programs to offer also have to be made to encourage the right attitudes and behaviors.

Although these might seem to be independent decisions, each decision influences other choices companies make about managing employees as well as the effectiveness of those choices. To achieve internal alignment, you must first make sure that the specific practices used *within* each HR activity are consistent with one another. To be able to effectively manage employee competencies, it is important to ensure that the recruitment, selection, and training practices you use are reinforcing rather than conflicting with one another. For example, a state-of-the-art selection test will be useless if the firm's recruitment process fails to generate qualified candidates for a job. In turn, the quality of a firm's recruitment and selection procedures will affect the types of training programs employees need.

Beyond alignment among the practices within each primary HR activity, there must also be alignment *across* the primary HR activities. Each of the three activities described is critical; however, none is effective in isolation. As Exhibit 14.2 shows, work design and workforce planning; identifying, acquiring, building and retaining employee competencies; and encouraging the right employee attitudes and behaviors must align with each other if they are to be effective.[3] A very low selection standard limits the job design options and

Exhibit 14.2 ▶

Aligning a Firm's
Internal HR Practices

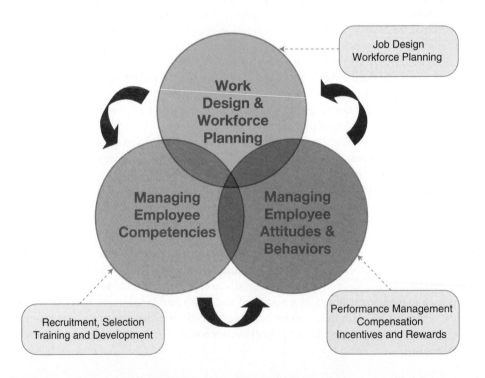

affects how employees should be evaluated and rewarded. Similarly, if a company hires truly outstanding employees but then uses a forced-ranking performance evaluation method, the firm's managers might be forced to make arbitrary distinctions among employees that don't accurately reflect their performance. As a result, lower employee satisfaction and increased turnover could occur.

The degree of internal alignment determines whether companies realize synergies among their HR practices. Synergies occur when the combined use of specific HR practices is more powerful than the sum of their individual effects.[4] When we talk about synergies among HR practices, however, it is important to recognize that there can be positive synergies as well as negative synergies.[5] Deadly combinations and powerful connections are two ways to categorize what can happen with various configurations of employee management practices.

DEADLY COMBINATIONS   Deadly combinations occur when managers rely on HR practices that seem appropriate but present problems when combined with other HR practices to manage employees.[6] There is a long list of deadly combinations that may potentially exist among the HR practices used to manage employees. The following are some situations that may potentially elicit deadly combinations:

- If employees are motivated to work toward important goals but do not possess all the competencies to do so, the results will be diminished employee performance and reduced organizational productivity.
- If employees possess the skills they need but lack sufficient motivation, their contributions to the company's success will be limited.
- If employees are capable and motivated but are limited in what they can do or are shorthanded due to poor job design or poor workforce planning, their ability to contribute to the organization will be limited.

POWERFUL CONNECTIONS   Powerful connections occur when HR practices are used in combinations that support and reinforce other practices that are in place.[7] For example, the use of a commission-based incentive system will reinforce the use of a performance management system that evaluates employees based on their sales levels. Using either one of these practices alone—the commission-based incentive system or the performance management system that evaluates employee sales—might encourage employees to achieve high sales levels. However, using the two practices together reinforces the importance of this objective for employees and is likely to be more effective than either practice alone. Google, for instance, engages in extensive recruitment and selection activities to ensure that it has great talent within the organization. Once on board, employees are exposed to a fun work environment that is conducive to creativity and are reward with attractive compensation and rewards to work as hard as possible toward the company's goals.[8]

deadly combination

HR practice that seems appropriate but presents problems when combined with other HR practices to manage employees.

powerful connection

HR practices used in combinations that support and reinforce other practices that are in place.

Aligning HR Systems with Employees' Contributions

As noted in Chapter 2, a company has a competitive advantage when it is able to create more economic value than its competitors. This is achieved by providing greater value to customers relative to the costs of making a product or providing a service.[9] A competitive advantage can stem from a variety of sources. For example, it can result from holding protected assets, having extensive financial resources, maintaining state-of-the-art manufacturing technologies, providing excellent customer service or great product quality, or some other feature that separates a company from its competitors.

An effective management system helps align the contributions employees make so as to give the firm a competitive advantage. To do so, however, you need to have a clear understanding of how your employees add value in your particular company. Employees add value to their firms in different ways. Consider a firm that pursues a cost leadership strategy, for example. Cost advantages relative to competitors may stem from efficiency manufacturing, low-skilled labor, or very efficient highly skilled labor. The implications for how to manage employees may vary, depending on the source of the competitive advantage to realize cost leadership. Suppose a firm has three different groups of employees: production workers, research and development employees, and customer service representatives. The value production workers add relates to their individual and collective contributions

Google aligns its HR practices to hire and motivate talented employees.

toward achieving manufacturing efficiency for their firm. The research and development employees contribute to their firm by improving the technological superiority of the company's production process and product designs. Finally, the customer service representatives add value by maximizing the satisfaction of the firm's customers.

Although a cost leadership strategy might be the overarching focus of the company, because the firm's different employees contribute to that advantage in various ways, managing them all effectively is critical to achieving the competitive advantage. An effectively managed R&D group alone cannot lead to achievement of company goals any more than an effectively managed group of production employees alone can lead to success. This also has implications for the design of HR systems to maximize employee contributions. As Exhibit 14.3 shows, the HR system you use to manage different groups of employees must reflect how they add value to your company.

Notice in Exhibit 14.3 that we have three groups of employees in a company. Because each group adds value in different ways, the HR system that maximizes their contributions must vary as well. To be most effective, the HR system needs to have a target or an objective (employee contributions); otherwise, employees will be left with no direction for how to focus their efforts. This target should reflect employees' contributions to the source of competitive advantage.

Indeed, research has shown that HR systems targeted toward certain company objectives are more effective than others. One study, for example, focused on how to design HR systems to improve employee safety. The study found that a system that included selective hiring and extensive training (managing competencies), contingent compensation (managing behaviors) and employment security, information sharing, high-quality work, teams and decentralized decision making (work design and workforce planning) was associated with a positive safety climate, improved safety orientation, and lower injury incidences.[10]

Exhibit 14.3 ▶

Aligning HR Systems with Employees' Contributions

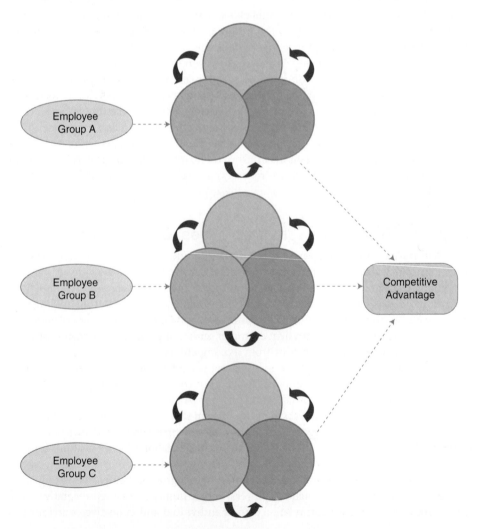

Likewise, research has shown that HR systems can be designed to encourage employees to provide high levels of customer service. In firms such as this, the HR system should be designed to provide employees with the skills and resources to be successful and to provide them with the discretion they need to meet their customers' demands immediately and reward workers for doing so.[11] One of the key strategic goals of Trader Joe's is to create an excellent shopping experience for customers. One way the company accomplishes this is through its hiring and evaluation practices. Trader Joe's recruits and hires people who love food and have fun, engaging personalities. Once on the job, employees are frequently evaluated based on customer-oriented metrics such as friendliness, helpfulness, and promotion of high team morale.[12]

As these sample HR systems point out, HR systems may be designed to target a variety of different employee contributions, such as safety, customer service, productivity, creativity, quality, and the like. The key point is that to realize its intended impact, a system must align the three primary HR activities with employee contributions.

Trader Joe's hires people with engaging personalities and an interest in food.

MANAGING THE EMPLOYMENT PORTFOLIO

Up to this point, we have highlighted three key components of effective HR systems and how managers should go about aligning them. First, managers must take into account the HR challenges that exist within and outside companies. Second, effective managers strive for synergy among the three primary HR activities. Finally, effective managers target the employee management systems to maximize employee contributions to company success.

Beyond these three factors, however, managers have to consider the fact that different types of HR systems involve different types of costs and benefits. For example, training programs to develop employees' skills involve the costs related to the instruction, the lost labor productivity during the training, and the like. Although your firm might be able to make these investments, the question is whether it should. There are certainly financial considerations, but these decisions also reflect strategic considerations for the potential benefits that stem from those investments. From a strategic point of view, the key question is whether the investments in HR systems and the resulting employee competencies and motivation will actually help your company realize and sustain a competitive advantage. One way to make this determination is by taking a "portfolio" perspective of your employees' contributions. This involves considering two factors: the strategic value and uniqueness of the contributions they make.

Strategic Value

Strategic value refers to the fact that employees contribute different things to their firms. The question is How much do their contributions add to the company's success? Are the contributions a key component of how the company competes, or are they more peripheral to the company's competitiveness?[13]

strategic value

The extent to which the contributions of employees are of value for organizational success.

As Exhibit 14.4 shows, the strategic value employees contribute to a firm affects a whole host of choices managers make, including whether to retain employees internally or turn to external sources, such as outsourced or contingent labor. In Chapter 5, we defined *outsourcing* as the practice of sending work to other companies. Increasingly, companies are realizing that it is prohibitively expensive, and not realistic, for a firm to be a world-class leader in all aspects of its operations. Because external service providers often focus on a single service and provide their services to many different companies, they are often able to attain greater efficiency in the performance of those tasks than a company could realize if it maintained the services in-house. And by outsourcing tasks that are not strategically valuable, companies may be able to focus their efforts on activities that serve as a source for their competitive advantage.[14] For example, Wheeling-Pitt was able to save $170,000 in transportation costs by outsourcing the oversight of its trucking of steel coils to Pittsburgh Logistics Systems, Inc.,[15] and was able to focus more extensively on developing better steel products.

Beyond outsourcing, companies may also turn to contingent labor—employees who are hired on a temporary or contractual basis, as opposed to being hired on a full-time or permanent basis—to perform certain tasks and responsibilities.[16] Similar to outsourcing, relying on contingent labor and other forms of alternative labor is a way to achieve cost savings and strategic focus. Turning to external work doesn't appear to be a trend that is slowing. In fact, in the first quarter of 2006, U.S. companies employed a record 2.8 million temporary and contract workers.[17] According to a recent survey by Aberdeen Group, the top two benefits from using contract labor are the flexibility it gives a firm to quickly adjust its workforce (70% of respondents) and the ability it gives a firm to quickly hire workers with specialized skills (66% of respondents).[18]

When considering strategic value, the question is whether your company needs to have full-time employees perform certain tasks internally or whether some external provider of these services could perform them more effectively or more efficiently. When employee contributions have a greater potential strategic impact, their companies are encouraged to make sure these positions are nurtured in-house so as to leverage their potential.[19] Given the importance of these positions, companies are often reluctant to outsource them or turn to contingent workers.[20] In contrast, as the strategic value of an employee's contributions decreases, the potential return from his or her contributions relative to the costs of maintaining the full-time employee internally diminishes. This is when it makes sense to turn to external sources.

Of course, the strategic value employees contribute to their firms varies across companies. Different strategies emphasize different internal business processes for competitive advantage. By extension, the strategic value of potential employee contributions oriented toward different business processes is likely to vary. For example, a company competing on costs might put a priority on operational efficiency. In a firm such as this, jobs in supply-chain management, logistics, and industrial engineering may be particularly valuable for facilitating efficiencies. In contrast, in companies competing on innovation, jobs related to product development, research and development, and external collaboration might be most important. In companies competing on customer service, jobs related to customer relations and sales and marketing may have priority. As a result, a highly valuable employee group in one company might be less valuable in another company, even when they are performing the same job.[21]

Uniqueness

Uniqueness refers to the extent to which the contributions employees make, and the necessary competencies to realize those contributions, are specialized or unique to a company and not readily available in the open labor market.[22] When employees make unique contributions to a company, they can set it apart from its competitors. In these cases, companies are more willing to invest in employees to realize those contributions. In contrast, when the uniqueness of their contributions is based on competencies that are widely available in the labor market, there will be little incentive for a company to invest extensively to develop those skills.[23]

Of course, all employees require some degree of investment. The question that uniqueness raises is what type of investment to make. In general, the type of investment companies make depends on the nature of the relationship they have with their employees. This investment spans a continuum ranging from transactional to relational.

Transactional relationships are best described as *quid pro quo*, or "a fair day's work for a fair day's pay."[24] Transactional relationships are economic in nature and focus on both parties meeting the basic terms of the contract they have with one another. These relationships tend to focus narrowly on the performance of the necessary tasks, duties, and responsibilities that must be performed during a predetermined time period. In contrast, **relational relationships**

Exhibit 14.4 ▶
Strategic Value of
Employee
Contributions

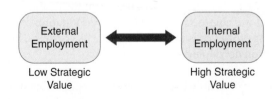

External Employment ◀▬▶ Internal Employment

Low Strategic Value   High Strategic Value

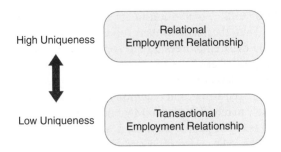

◄ **Exhibit 14.5**

Uniqueness of
Employee
Contributions and the
Employment
Relationship

involve a much greater commitment to the individual by the company and vice versa. Relational relationships contain more of an emotional or social component that translates into a higher level of concern the parties have for one another. As Exhibit 14.5 shows, when employees make unique contributions, their companies tend to focus on building relational relationships with them. When they don't, companies tend to maintain transactional relationships with them.[25]

Mapping Your Employment Portfolio

It is possible to map the contributions employees make based on the strategic value and uniqueness of their contributions. As we have noted, the strategic value of certain positions influences whether a company will retain those positions internally or turn to external labor sources for them. Uniqueness influences the types of relationship that companies have with different groups of employees. The potential combinations of these two variables results in four types of employment groups: core employees, job-based employees, contract workers, and alliance partners. In addition, four different approaches to HR investments emerge to manage each group: commitment-based, productivity-based, compliance-based, and collaborative-based HR systems. These are highlighted in Exhibit 14.6.

CORE EMPLOYEES   Based on their highly unique and valuable contributions, **core employees** are most likely to contribute directly to a firm's core competencies on the basis of what they know and how they use their knowledge.[26] As a result, these employees tend to be employed internally and treated as core workers in whom companies invest for their long-term success. The HR system used to manage these employees involves practices that support a **commitment-based HR system**. For example, a company may invest extensively in the development of core employees' competencies, empower them to use their competencies in the performance of their jobs, and encourage their full participation in decision making and discretion on the job. Likewise, a firm might offer long-term incentives (stock ownership, extensive benefits, and so forth) to ensure that its core employees receive continued and useful feedback and adopt a long-term orientation to help the company achieve success.[27]

core employee

Person who directly contributes to a firm's core competencies and competitiveness.

commitment-based HR system

A system of investing extensively in the development of core employees' competencies, empowering them to use their competencies in the performance of their jobs, and encouraging their full participation in decision making and discretion on the job.

◄ **Exhibit 14.6**

Diagram of an
Employment Portfolio

	External Employment	Internal Employment	
High	*Alliance/ Partners* HR System: Collaboration	*Core Employees* HR System: Commitment	*Relational Relationship*
Low	*Contract Workers* HR System: Compliance	*Job-Based Employees* HR System: Productivity	*Transactional Relationship*

Uniqueness

Low   High
Strategic Value

job-based employee

Individual employed internally but does not contribute in a unique manner.

productivity-based HR system

A system that involves standardized jobs, selection of people from the external labor market who can contribute immediately in these jobs, rewards based on efficiency and productivity improvements, and results-oriented performance management system.

contract worker

External employee whose contributions are not unique and are limited in strategic value.

compliance-based HR system

A system that focuses on meeting preset rules, regulations, and/or procedures with an emphasis on short-term productivity and the efficient performance of tasks that are limited in scope, purpose, or duration.

collaborative-based HR system

A system of managing external labor on a long-term basis through alliances or partnerships. The longer-term relationships help preserve continuity and ensure trust among partners, and they engender reciprocity and collaboration between external individuals and internal employees through the use of group incentives, cross-functional teams, and the like.

alliance partner

External employee who makes unique contributions but whose contributions are limited in terms of strategic value.

JOB-BASED EMPLOYEES In addition to core employees, **job-based employees** also create value for firms. Thus, the positions these individuals hold tends to be held within the firm. However, because these employees do not contribute in a unique manner, there are likely to be a fairly large number of them in the external labor market. As a result, companies do not have the same level of incentive to extensively invest in job-based employees' long-term development, well-being, and retention as they do for core employees.[28] Rather, managers are more likely to rely on a **productivity-based HR system**—a system that involves standardized jobs and selecting people from the external labor market who can contribute immediately in these jobs.[29] The types of rewards and incentives that are used for employees in positions such as these tend to focus on efficiency and productivity improvements. And, of course, companies are less likely to expend a great deal of money to develop people in these positions. Instead, they are more likely to emphasize a short-term, results-oriented performance management system.[30]

CONTRACT WORKERS When the tasks a firm needs done are neither strategically valuable nor unique, the company may turn to **contract workers** to do these tasks.[31] Because of the limited uniqueness in these employees' contributions, external workers are often used to perform these tasks. And with limited strategic value, these employees do not contribute as much as core and job-based employees, and there is usually a good supply of them in the labor market. When managing contract workers, firms tend to emphasize **compliance-based HR systems**—systems that focus on meeting preset rules, regulations, and/or procedures. For example, these systems focus on short-term productivity and the efficient performance of tasks that are limited in scope, purpose, or duration. The job descriptions for positions such as these are likely to be standardized, and the training and performance management for these positions, if conducted, is likely to be limited to ensuring that the company's policies, systems, and procedures are met.[32] In addition, the compensation for employees in these positions is likely to be based on hourly wages and the accomplishment of specific tasks or goals.[33]

ALLIANCE PARTNERS The fourth group of employees are those who make unique contributions but whose contributions are limited in terms of strategic value. Because the contributions of these employees are not directly central to a firm's strategy, companies often look externally for these individuals. However, the contributions of these individuals are also unique to a company. To manage this group of employees, companies focus on establishing a **collaborative-based HR system** and turn to external labor on a long-term basis through alliances or partnerships.[34] While companies may be reluctant to invest in these **alliance partners** directly, there is investment in the relationship with these individuals. For example, many companies hire consultants to serve as an external source of knowledge for a particular project. Although some consulting relationships last only a short while, many constitute a partnership such that the external consultant works with internal employees on an ongoing basis. While both alliance partners and contract workers are external to a company, they contribute in different ways, with alliance partners applying their competencies in some unique capacity over a longer time frame. The longer-term relationships help preserve continuity and ensure trust among partners, and they engender reciprocity and collaboration between external individuals and internal employees.[35] Given the need for ongoing exchange, alliance partners are more likely to be managed with group incentives, cross-functional teams, and the like.

Many companies are under pressure to keep their HR costs down. From a strategic perspective, not all forms of employee contributions are equally critical to a company's success. While there are certainly many ways a firm can structure and manage its employment portfolio, adopting an architectural perspective helps managers make decisions regarding the level of investment in different employee groups to align their potential contributions with the long-term success of the company.

The first step is to evaluate the contributions of different employees of your firm, based on their levels of strategic value and uniqueness. This involves rating each group individually to arrive at a relative scoring for all employee contributions within your company. The second step involves mapping out your employees' contributions. Once you have done this, you will see how different employee groups contribute to your company's success. Exhibits

◀ Exhibit 14.7

Constructing an
Employment Portfolio:
Evaluating the
Contributions of Your
Employees

Business Strategy_____Customer Service

_____

Evaluate the extent to which each employee group provides strategic value and
is unique.

1	No value added
5	Modest level strategic value
10	High level of strategic value

Employee Group	How Much Value Added?	How Much Uniqueness?
Manufacturing	NA	NA
R&D	NA	NA
IT	1	2
Distribution	8	2
Legal	1	7
Marketing	8	5
HR	5	7
Customer Service	10	9
Sales	9	7
Finance	2	4
Logistics	3	3
Other: _____	NA	NA

14.7 and 14.8 provide a hypothetical evaluation of strategic value and uniqueness of a company's employee contributions. Exhibit 14.7 shows that in this case, customer service and
sales add the most value, given this particular firm's strategic priority of providing good customer service. In contrast, the contributions of employees working in the firm's IT, logistics,
and finance departments are not key factors for this company.

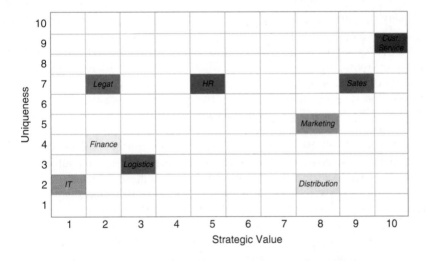

EVALUATING YOUR HR SYSTEM:
THE HR SCORECARD

Effectively creating a high-performing HR system involves evaluating the system. Is the HR
system in place helping the company achieve its strategic objectives? Although there are a
variety of ways to evaluate HR systems, one approach that has gained tremendous popularity is to build an HR scorecard. Pioneered by Professors Brian Becker, Mark Huselid, and

Dave Ulrich, an HR scorecard[36] helps assess the degree to which the links within HR systems and the contributions employees make to their firms actually help them realize a competitive advantage. To create an HR scorecard, you need to take the following steps:

1. Identify your firm's strategic performance drivers
2. Evaluate your firm's external alignment
3. Evaluate your firm's internal alignment

Step 1: Identify Your Firm's Strategic Performance Drivers

strategic performance drivers

Activities that enable a company to realize the potential of its source of competitive advantages.

Earlier in this chapter, we discussed the fact that a company's competitive advantage can stem from a variety of different sources, such as low costs, product quality, customer service, and the like. **Strategic performance drivers** are the activities that enable a company to realize the potential of its source of competitive advantages. Companies pursuing a low-cost leadership strategy, for example, rely on operational excellence and cost controls to attain or maintain their position of cost leadership. Some key strategic performance drivers might be improved operational efficiency, reduced overhead, and increased productivity. Similarly, in a company with an innovation-based differentiation strategy, the key strategic performance drivers might be an increase in patent applications or a greater percentage of sales from new products. A company with a quality-based differentiation strategy might emphasize strategic performance drivers such as reduced scrap rates or fewer customer returns.

To translate a firm's strategic objectives into actionable activities, the source of a company's competitive advantage must be translated into strategic performance drivers. Senior managers within companies are often responsible for identifying their companies' strategic performance drivers.

Step 2: Evaluate Your Firm's External Alignment

The second step in creating an HR scorecard is to evaluate your employee management system to assess the alignment of your primary HR activities with the source of your competitive advantage. Doing so involves two activities: translating your firm's strategic performance drivers into *HR deliverables* and evaluating the effectiveness of those deliverables.

HR deliverables

What is needed from a firm's HR activities, or the mechanism by which an HR system creates value for a company.

TRANSLATE THE STRATEGIC PERFORMANCE DRIVERS INTO HR DELIVERABLES **HR deliverables** are what is needed from a firm's HR activities, or the mechanism by which an HR system creates value for a company.[37] Consider the strategic performance driver high-quality customer service. To realize high levels of customer service, companies need to attract and retain talented employees who are able to build and sustain long-term relationships with customers. As a result, the HR deliverables for the strategic driver high-quality customer service might be employment stability and high-quality employees. Similarly, consider the strategic performance driver increasing new product offerings. What types of HR deliverables would be needed for this driver? Employee collaboration and creativity could be the HR deliverables that would enable companies to realize a strategic performance driver of new products.

Most strategic performance drivers incorporate elements of employee contributions, either directly or indirectly. A key strategic performance driver in a manufacturing plant, for example, might be the quality of the technology used in a production process and the efficiency of the employees. Employee productivity is an HR deliverable that is directly linked to achieving low costs, and the ability of employees to work with technological advancements may be an indirect contributor that enables the realization of technologies in place.[38] In other words, some HR deliverables are directly related to strategic performance drivers, and others serve as "enablers" to the drivers.

Exhibit 14.9 shows a hypothetical example of a company's assessment of the effectiveness of its strategic performance drivers. The company illustrated in this exhibit has identified three strategic performance drivers that are believed to help the company improve its competitiveness: improved customer service, improved product quality, and more new product offerings. To achieve these three strategic performance drivers, the firm has determined that employment stability, employee creativity, high-quality employees, and employee collaboration are the HR deliverables that, if fully realized, would maximize the strategic performance driver.

▶ **Exhibit 14.9** Evaluating the Alignment of a Firm's HR Deliverables

Please indicate the degree to which each HR deliverable in the chart below would currently enable each strategic driver, on a scale of −100 to +100. Empty cells indicate this is not a "key" deliverable for a particular driver. Examples of the extremes and midpoints on that continuum are as follows:

−100: This deliverable is **counterproductive** for enabling this driver.
0: This deliverable **has little or no effect** on this driver.
+100: This deliverable **significantly enables** this driver.
DNK: Don't know or have no opinion.

	HR Deliverable			
Strategic Performance Driver	**Employment Stability**	**Employee Creativity**	**High-Quality Employees**	**Employee Collaboration**
1. *Improve customer service*	−80		+30	
2. *Improve product quality*	−20		+20	−20
3. *Increase new product offerings*	−10	+30	+30	+10

Source: Adapted from Becker, B., Huselid, M., & Ulrich, D. *The HR scorecard*. Cambridge, MA: Harvard Business School Press, 2001.

EVALUATING THE ALIGNMENT OF HR DELIVERABLES WITH THE STRATEGIC PERFORMANCE DRIVERS The second part of the second step in creating an HR scorecard is to evaluate the effectiveness of the HR deliverables. This is done by rating the extent to which the HR deliverables actually contributed to the strategic performance drivers. In Exhibit 14.9, for example, we can see some positives and some negatives for the company whose HR system we're evaluating. On the positive side, the company's ability to attract high-quality employees is a positive contributor to all three strategic performance drivers. However, the firm's employment stability is troubling because its turnover is a negative contributor to sustaining all three performance drivers. In addition, employee collaboration is positively related to the creation of new product offerings, as is employee creativity. At the same time, however, employee collaboration is not contributing to the realization of improving product quality. Clearly, some adjustments are needed to improve this company's odds of competing based on its strategic performance drivers.

Conducting an evaluation such as this will help you determine whether your HR deliverables are successful as well as identify areas of your company that are underperforming. You can then target the deliverables that are unsatisfactory. To do so, however, you will have to further explore the HR practices that are used to manage employees. Step 3 of evaluating the HR system builds on the information from step 2 and focuses on examining how well or how poorly the practices used within the three primary HR activities are in alignment with the needed HR deliverables.

Step 3: Evaluate Your Firm's Internal Alignment

The third step in creating an HR scorecard is to evaluate the degree of alignment between the firm's HR practices and its HR deliverables as well as to evaluate the degree of alignment among the various HR practices themselves.

EVALUATING THE ALIGNMENT OF THE HR PRACTICES WITH THE HR DELIVERABLES One of the key objectives of the third step of the HR system evaluation process is to determine whether the practices you are using for your primary HR activities (work design and workforce planning, managing employee competencies, and managing employee attitudes and behaviors) are helping or hurting the achievement of your firm's HR deliverables. This type of evaluation is easy to conduct. Exhibit 14.10 shows an example of such an assessment. Completing this assessment involves evaluating each practice on a scale of −100 to +100 in terms of whether the practice enables the HR deliverables.

▲ **Exhibit 14.10** Evaluating the Alignment of a Firm's HR System with Its HR Deliverables

Please indicate the degree to which the following elements of the HR system facilitate the HR deliverables shown, on a scale of –100 to +100. Examples of the extremes and midpoints on that continuum are as follows:

–100:   This dimension is **counterproductive** for enabling this driver.
0:   This dimension **has little or no effect** on this driver.
+100:   This dimension **significantly enables** this driver.
DNK: Don't know or have no opinion.

HR Deliverable	Job Design	Workforce Planning	Recruitment	Selection	Training and Development	Performance Management	Compensation	Incentives	Benefits
Employment stability	0	0	0	–20	+10	–30	+30	–30	–40
Employee creativity	+40	0	0	0	+20	–30	0	–40	0
High-quality employees	0	–20	+20	+30	–20	–20	+20	–20	0
Employee collaboration	+20	0	+20	+30	–20	–40	0	–60	0

Source: Adapted from Becker, B., Huselid, M., & Ulrich, D. *The HR scorecard.* Cambridge, MA: Harvard Business School Press, 2001.

426

In Exhibit 14.10, we can see that some of the practices are contributing in a positive way to the HR deliverables. For example, the activities associated with training and development and with compensation are helping to foster employment stability among the workforce. At the same time, the activities associated with selection, performance management, incentives, and benefits are negatively related to employment stability. With regard to selection, it may be the case that the company is failing to hire workers who are a good fit for the jobs for which they are being hired and/or the firm's culture. As discussed in Chapter 9, it is possible that the performance management process is contributing to employee turnover because employees perceive that there is a lack of distributive or procedural fairness with regard to their performance evaluations. Similarly, the firm's incentive systems might be misaligned such that what is rewarded is not what employees value. Finally, the benefits package provided to employees might not meet the company's needs or be attractive compared to what other companies are offering.

Of course, these are simply speculations. But they do provide valuable information by showing areas of alignment and misalignment. When misalignments are identified, managers can look for ways to adjust the firm's HR activities to improve the realization of the company's HR deliverables and, ultimately, the firm's strategic performance drivers.

EVALUATING THE ALIGNMENT AMONG THE FIRM'S HR PRACTICES   It is important to evaluate the alignment among a firm's HR practices themselves. As we have discussed, it is possible that the failure to achieve a firm's HR deliverables is due to negative synergies, or "deadly combinations," among the company's HR practices. As Exhibit 14.11 shows, evaluating the alignment among a firm's HR practices is done by assessing the degree to which each HR practice is consistent with each of the other practices.

In Exhibit 14.11, for example, we can see examples of positive connections and deadly combinations. On the positive side, the firm's training and development activities are consistent with how its jobs are designed and with the company's recruitment and selection activities. However, although the firm's performance management system and the incentive system are aligned with one another, they are inconsistent with how the company's jobs are designed and how employees are recruited, selected, and trained. Comparisons like these illustrate that managers can face numerous alignment issues among their firms' HR practices, which, in turn, can affect their firms' HR deliverables. When areas of misalignment are identified, this provides a focus for discussion among managers to identify the sources of the problem. This diagnostic also pinpoints specific practices that are inconsistent with practices that are effective in achieving the desired HR deliverables.

BUILDING YOUR OWN HIGH-PERFORMING ORGANIZATION

As you can probably tell, evaluating your HR system is a critical component of effectively managing your workforce. After all, if you don't conduct an evaluation, how do you really know if you are managing your employees as effectively as possible? In addition, organizations and environmental conditions continually evolve. As a result, it is important to continually assess the ability of your HR system to meet your company's changing needs.

Conducting such an evaluation is not enough, however. You must also think about what to do with the information you acquire during the evaluation. Often, this involves reassessing and redesigning the practices you use to manage your employees so they contribute more to your organization's competitive advantage. An HR scorecard is also an excellent starting point for redesigning how you manage your employees. You can use an HR scorecard to effectively redesign your HR system by doing the following:

1. Customizing your HR scorecard
2. Being consistent
3. Being specific
4. Following up on the implementation of the redesign

Next, we discuss how you go about doing these things.

▶ **Exhibit 14.11** Evaluating the Internal Fit Among a Firm's HR Activities

In the chart below, please estimate the degree to which the various HR management subsystems work together harmoniously, or "fit" together. Think of the degree of fit and internal consistency as a continuum from −100 to +100, and assign a value in that range to each relationship. Examples of the extremes and midpoints on that continuum are as follows:

−100: The two subsystems work at **cross-purposes.**
0: The two subsystems have **little or no effect on one another.**
+100: Each subsystem is **mutually reinforcing and internally consistent.**
DNK: Don't know or have no opinion

	Job Design	Workforce Planning	Recruitment	Selection	Training and Development	Performance Management	Compensation	Incentives	Benefits
Job design	—	−30	0	−20	+10	−20	+20	−50	0
Workforce planning		—	0	−10	−20	0	0	0	0
Recruitment			—	+20	+20	−40	−10	−40	−10
Selection				—	0	−20	0	−10	−20
Training and development					—	−10	+10	−10	−10
Performance management						—	0	+20	0
Compensation							—	+50	0
Incentives								—	—
Benefits									—

Source: Adapted from Becker, B., Huselid, M., & Ulrich, D. *The HR scorecard.* Cambridge, MA: Harvard Business School Press, 2001.

Customizing Your HR Scorecard

The first step in using an HR scorecard to redesign your HR system is to customize your firm's HR scorecard by following the three steps outlined earlier. Take a moment to identify the source of your company's competitive advantage. Is it productivity, product quality, customer service, product innovation, or some other strategic performance driver? Once you have identified the firm's strategic performance drivers, you can determine which HR deliverables are necessary to help achieve those drivers. Then you have important strategic anchors to evaluate the effectiveness of the practices you use to manage your company's employees. You are also in a position to identify any misalignments among the firm's HR practices.

Sysco increased its employee performance by adjusting its pay.

Sysco Corporation, for example, found that paying its delivery employees based only on the hours they worked wasn't helping create value for the firm. As Ken Carrig, Sysco's executive vice president of administration, said, "The model didn't necessarily provide better customer satisfaction or profitability."[39] To align Sysco's HR practices with the employee contributions it was seeking, the company shifted to a pay system that rewarded its delivery employees for making more deliveries, making fewer mistakes, and improving safety.[40]

Being Consistent

A key point to remember is that much of the success of HR systems comes down to consistency. The presence of powerful connections or deadly combinations rests directly on the degree of alignment among your HR practices. In other words, you need to be sure that all the practices used to manage your employees reinforce, rather than counteract, one another. If employees are assigned to teams, for example, your performance management and incentive systems should involve a team component. Rewarding team members based solely on their individual accomplishments will undermine the power of the system. If your HR practices are not consistent, employees won't accurately interpret the messages the firm is sending them and thus may not behave in expected ways.[41] In contrast, when the practices are consistent with one another, they create an environment in which employees share a common interpretation of what behaviors are important, expected, and rewarded. This, in turn, will motivate them to work toward the business objectives the firm is trying to achieve.

Being Specific

Employees need to have a clear understanding of what it is they need to do to help their company succeed. In many ways, the various practices we have talked about in this text may be viewed as communications between management and employees. Practices determine the competencies of the workforce—how employees are expected to interact as well as how they are to act in the performance of their jobs. One prominent part of understanding HR system effectiveness is that companies use different practices in an attempt to elicit needed role behaviors from employees, given different considerations regarding strategy, technology, and the like.[42] Telling employees to make fewer mistakes on the job is not likely to be as powerful as explaining to employees how the number of mistakes they make affects company performance. If employees don't have a clear objective, they are not likely to reach that objective. Thus, implementing an effective HR system requires managers to be specific about what they expect from their employees and what the company needs them to do.

In many ways, implementing an effective HR system comes down to good communication. One of the keys of the successful implementation of an incentive program at FirstMerit Bank is providing very clear, specific guidance to check-proofing operators. Under this system, employees are evaluated on both the speed and accuracy of their keystrokes. By making this incentive scheme a considerable portion of employee pay, FirstMerit Bank was able to provide specific guidance to employees on how to focus their energies in ways that help the company maintain its success.[43]

First Merit Bank.

Following Up on the Implementation of a Redesign

Just because a company designs a particular HR policy doesn't mean the policy will be carried out as it should.[44] In other words, what should be done might not be what is actually done.[45] For example, a company might institute a merit-based pay program to reward employees for their outstanding efforts. However, if the firm's managers rate all employees equally high on their performance evaluations, the pay program will fail to differentiate high versus medium or low performers. One outcome from this disconnection between the design and implementation of the program might be a decrease in motivation among the high performers. Similar situations may exist for other practices as well. A company policy for increased empowerment may be interpreted differently by different managers, resulting in inconsistency in its implementation throughout an organization. Some managers may view this as soliciting input from employees, while others may actually push decision making down to employees.

This discussion highlights an important component of implementation: A company must take the time to help its managers understand how to implement a practice. Failure to follow up on the actual implementation of the policies that are intended to be used to help realize employee contributions will dramatically decrease their effectiveness in improving company performance.

SUMMARY

One of the key themes of this chapter, and of this entire book, is that there is no single best way to manage employees. Rather, how employees should be managed depends on several HR challenges related to organizational demands, environmental influences, and regulatory issues. In addition to these considerations, there are several principles of high-performing HR systems that separate successful companies from not-so-successful ones. First, high-performing companies look at how their HR activities fit with the three HR challenges—organizational, environmental, and regulatory—they face. Second, high-performing companies internally align their HR practices to realize synergies from them. Third, high-performing HR systems target specific employee contributions that are critical for helping companies achieve a competitive advantage in the marketplace.

In addition to these three key principles, companies must also consider the costs and benefits related to maximizing the contributions their employees make. Different types of HR systems and activities involve different types of investments and costs. The key question is whether a particular investment will help a company achieve and sustain a competitive advantage. One approach to making tough investment decisions

such as these is to view your workforce as an employment portfolio. By assessing the strategic value and uniqueness of their firm's different employee groups, managers are in a better position to evaluate the potential benefits that could stem from making those investments in terms of employee contributions. From a strategic point of view, will the investments in HR systems, and the resulting employee competencies and motivation, help the company realize a sustainable source of competitive advantage?

Many companies are now using HR scorecards to help evaluate the effectiveness of their HR systems. By identifying a firm's strategic performance drivers and key HR deliverables, an HR scorecard helps managers focus their attention on value-added activities. In addition, the scorecard helps managers evaluate the alignment between their firms' HR practices and HR deliverables. An HR scorecard provides managers with a clear snapshot of how well or how poorly they are managing their employees. This helps managers pinpoint specific practices that are inconsistent with one another and practices that reinforce one another and lead to the HR deliverables their firms desire.

KEY TERMS

alliance partner *p. 422*
collaborative-based HR system *p. 422*
commitment-based HR system *p. 421*
compliance-based HR system *p. 422*
contract worker *p. 422*
core employee *p. 421*

deadly combination *p. 417*
external alignment *p. 415*
HR deliverable *p. 424*
internal alignment *p. 415*
job-based employee *p. 422*
powerful connection *p. 417*

productivity-based HR system *p. 422*
relational relationship *p. 420*
strategic performance driver *p. 424*
strategic value *p. 419*
transactional relationship *p. 420*
uniqueness *p. 420*

DISCUSSION QUESTIONS

1. What is meant by external fit? In terms of HR systems, what are the major challenges associated with achieving external fit?
2. Explain the principle of internal fit.
3. How can knowing how your employees contribute to your firm's ability to achieve a competitive advantage help you better manage them?
4. Choose three sources of competitive advantage (cost, innovation, etc.). After you identify your sources of competitive advantage, identify the potential strategic performance drivers that are critical for realizing those sources of competitive advantage. How does how you manage employees affect your ability to achieve those strategic performance drivers?
5. What are the advantages and disadvantages of managing different employee groups in an employment portfolio using different HR systems—for example, a system that is collaborative for the firm's alliance partners and a system that is commitment based for a firm's regular, full-time employees?
6. Identify a company you are familiar with. How would you describe that company's strategy? Given its strategy, what do you think are the firm's strategic performance drivers? What are the firm's HR deliverables?

LEARNING EXERCISE 1

As a manager, you have a number of choices to make regarding how you manage your employees. Throughout this book, we have focused on three primary HR activities: work design and workforce planning, management of employee competencies, and management of employee attitudes and behaviors. The question you need to answer is when to use the various practices that make up the three HR activities. Use the following table to compare and contrast how a complete HR system might differ across four companies pursuing different strategies:

		Cost Leadership Strategy	Innovation Strategy	Quality Strategy	Customer Service Strategy
	Which group of employees is likely to be viewed as "core"?				
Work Design and Workforce Planning	Job design				
	Workforce planning				
Managing Employee Competencies	Recruitment				
	Selection				
	Training				
Managing Employee Attitudes and Behaviors	Performance management				
	Compensation				
	Incentives				
	Benefits, health, and wellness				

LEARNING EXERCISE 2

Companies are increasingly acknowledging that their employees are a potential source of competitive advantage. At the same time, however, companies are increasing their reliance on external employees, such as contract labor and temporary workers.

1. As a manager, how would you strike a balance between the number of employees you retain internally and the number of external workers you employ?

2. Develop a strategic plan to identify when companies should rely on internal employees versus when they should turn to external labor.

3. What implications do you think your decisions would have for the morale, commitment, and effort of your employees?

CASE STUDY # 1 — THE PUZZLING CLIMATE AT DIGITAL GAMING

Sitting at his desk, Bob Menendez is distraught over his current situation. Bob is the founder of a relatively young, small company called Digital Gaming (DG), which designs computer games. He has personally earned a lot of money and has a strong reputation in the electronic gaming industry for his vision and creativity. His computer games are routinely best sellers and rated among the top products in the industry, particularly for being lifelike, creative, and challenging. Recently, however, several industry analysts have noted that DG's games are not as creative as they once were and that occasionally the company's software contains glitches. Bob knows there is something true about these reviews. As an avid gamer himself, he sees that his products, although still high quality, have slipped a notch. Bob is equally concerned about the climate at DG. In the early years of the company's history, employees were highly engaged, full of energy, and completely committed to the company's success. Recently, however, Bob has noticed that some of the 100 programmers he employs seem distant and disengaged. Moreover, the turnover rate of his top programmers has more than tripled from its seven-year average of 10% to a point where DG continually has to hire new programmers. Interestingly, absenteeism and employee complaints are not a problem, and employees put in long hours.

Bob is confused: People are leaving his firm, but he doesn't really know why. As he tries to figure out what is causing the diminished product quality and increased turnover in his company, he wonders if how he is managing his employees is the problem. He goes out of his way to hire the best and brightest job candidates. He doesn't recruit at top-notch schools because, in his experience, many of the really gifted programmers do not bother with school. Instead, he focuses on referrals from current employees, word of mouth, and advertisements in the top trade outlets. Rather than give applicants a typical employment test or interview, he simply asks them to do some programming on a computer in order to showcase their creativity and skills. Bob usually hires people with potential right on the spot, and he provides them with very attractive signing bonuses.

Once hired, DG employees typically work long hours. However, they have a lot of control over how they work. DG has a very informal culture. Some people show up for work in shorts and T-shirts, and many people work odd hours. For example, some programmers work all night and take the afternoons off. Employees are also given liberal training budgets that they personally manage to help stay on the cutting edge of their business.

The pay package Bob offers is also fairly generous. Base pay for employees is roughly the market average, but they can earn considerably more based on the amount of programming code they complete each month. Employees' computers are monitored by electronic software, not necessarily to evaluate what they do while they work, but to track how much work they finish by the end of the week. Bob then divides a monthly bonus among the programmers based on the volume of code they have completed. Each employee can access the company's intranet to see the status of his or her volume relative to that of DG's other programmers. As shown in the table below, employees in the top 10% of volume of code receive 40% of the bonus pool – a disproportionate share of the rewards available to employees.

Employee Ranking on Performance Curve	Percentage of Bonus Pool
90th–100th percentile	40%
70th–90th percentile	30%
40th–70th percentile	25%
20th–40th percentile	5%
0–20th percentile	0%

Bob evaluates an employee based on several key criteria: volume of completed work, ability to meet deadlines, and sales of the products he or she personally coded. Bob also considers how well each programmer complies with the stylistic preferences and unique formula that he developed for creating code when he founded the company. Although forcing programmers to stick to this protocol limits their creativity, Bob insists that the protocol is instrumental in producing successful programming games.

As Bob is thinking about the current climate at DG, his assistant interrupts to let him know that two more of his top programmers just submitted their letters of resignation. They are leaving to join a new startup firm that competes directly with DG.

DISCUSSION QUESTION

1. What do you think is the problem at DG?
2. Evaluate the DG's primary HR activities.
3. What changes to DG's HR activities would you advise Bob Menendez to make? Why?

CASE STUDY # 2 — PEOPLE'S HOME GADGETS

People's Home Gadgets (PHG) is a relatively young company that competes in the consumer electronics and appliances industry (TVs, computers, kitchen appliances, etc.). It has quite a large selection of items, and the range of the products PHG carries spans the price spectrum of very low cost to very high end. For example, some of the company's kitchen ovens cost just under $400, while others cost well over $4,000. The company also has low-end affordable televisions under $400 as well as very pricy large plasma televisions that cost over $6,000. Throughout the price range, PHG strives to be a low-cost leader for the quality of the product. Compared to its competition, PHG offers a very competitive, if not the lowest, price. In addition to the cost focus, PHG prides itself on providing exceptional one-on-one customer service. In fact, the name of the company—People's Home Gadgets—is intended to reflect both the strategy and the philosophy of the organization. With a focus on costs and customer service, the name reflects the company's concern with the financial burdens customers face as well as the vast amounts of information that customers must process when making purchasing decisions.

The name PHG also refers to the company's philosophy for managing customer service representatives: The company cares about its employees' long-term well-being and success. Most customer service representatives who work at PHG are typically hired through personal referrals of current employees, or occasionally an advertisement will be placed in the newspaper when more than one opening exists. Each month, customer service representatives receive product training to explore the new products they will be selling to ensure that they are knowledgeable and can respond to customer questions. To motivate them to sell, they are rewarded on a commission-based pay plan. What is interesting about this particular incentive plan is that the customer service representatives have some discretion regarding the final price of the products. Most products have a standard markup of 10% to 25%, of which the employee gets a portion. While many of the products sell for the list price, sophisticated buyers and repeat customers are often able to negotiate lower prices for their products. The challenge with this plan is that the company has a reputation for low costs, and customer service representatives who are not willing to negotiate the sales price are viewed as going against this objective. By lowering the prices, however, they are cutting into their own take-home pay.

Up to this point, the company has done fairly well, and it now has six stores on the East Coast between Philadelphia and New York. With a focus on low costs and customer service, the company has been able to sustain reasonable growth—it just opened two new stores—and a modest level of customer satisfaction among its consumers. At the same time, however, while the customer service representatives seem to be fairly happy and work hard, their turnover is around 70% per year. This turnover obviously involves costs associated with constantly hiring new employees, and it also has a negative impact on customer loyalty and the level of experience of the customer service representatives.

As the company has grown, Lukas Phillips, president of PHG, has realized that he doesn't have the time or expertise to attend to all the issues related to policies for managing people. Recognizing that it is time to hire a full-time director of HR, Lukas has decided to hire Paula Hillman. Paula has seven years of experience in HR in a manufacturing facility located nearby. Although Paula's experience is in manufacturing, Lukas was encouraged by her enthusiasm for creating a fun and effective workplace. During the course of their discussions, Lukas told Paula that his main goal for her in her new job is to design an HR system that reduces the turnover among customer service representatives, encourages them to work hard toward the company's competitive advantage of low costs and high customer service, and adheres to his principles of taking care of employees.

DISCUSSION QUESTIONS

1. Provide advice to Paula regarding the nature of the HR system she should recommend for the customer service representatives at the six stores.
2. Identify a key strategic performance driver for this organization.
3. How do the customer service representatives contribute to the strategic performance driver you identified?
4. Design an HR system to realize the strategic performance driver you identified. Be certain to explain how you would (a) design the work environment, (b) manage employee competencies, and (c) manage employee attitudes and behaviors.

Part V

PROSPERA EXERCISES

Now that you understand the importance of using metrics to gauge how well you are achieving your HR goals, it is time to develop the objectives that establish what you want to track relative to your goals. You will also have the opportunity to create a HR scorecard to use for tracking Visions Optical's progress in achieving those goals.

Section I: Establishing Objectives

Use the "Develop Objectives & Scorecard" feature in the "PLAN" area of the Prospera Web site (www.prospera.com) to identify the objectives for Visions Optical. Choose objectives that support the company's mission and goals. Discuss why you chose the objectives and indicate how they are important for monitoring progress toward lowering turnover and increasing productivity. What are some reasons the selected objectives might not be reached? What should you as a manager do to increase the likelihood that the objectives will be achieved?

Section II: Creating the Scorecard

The word *scorecard* brings to mind many imagines: a baseball scorecard, golf scorecard, keeping score. The HR scorecard provides ongoing information to management about how well the company is achieving its objectives. With that in mind, create an HR scorecard for Visions Optical, using the "Develop Objectives & Scorecard" feature at the Prospera Web site. Be prepared to justify the numbers you have selected as targets and indicate how they support the mission and objectives of the company.

Section III: Wrapping Up

Now that you have worked through many of the types of HR activities about which you have studied in this course, it is a good time to think back through the entire five sections associated with the Visions Optical case. Discuss what you have learned from participating in the activities. What were the most challenging aspects of the project? How might those challenges be real-world challenges? What advice would you give to someone about aligning their HR activities with the goals and objectives of the company? Why do you think this alignment does not happen all the time?

References

Chapter 1

1. America's most admired companies, 2007. *Fortune* online, http://money.cnn.com/magazines/fortune/mostadmired/2007/index.html.

2. Human Genome Sciences Web site, www.hgsi.com.

3. Pfeffer, J. *The human equation: Building profits by putting people first*. Boston: Harvard Business School Press, 1998.

4. Barney, J. B., & Hesterly, W. S. *Strategic management and competitive advantage*. Upper Saddle River, NJ: Prentice Hall, 2006.

5. Pfeffer, J. *Competitive advantage through people: Unleashing the power of the work force*. Boston: Harvard Business School Press, 1994.

6. Huselid, M. A. The impact of human resource management practices on turnover, productivity, and corporate financial performance. *Academy of Management Journal* 38:635–672, 1995; Guthrie, J. P. High-involvement work practices, turnover, and productivity: Evidence from New Zealand. *Academy of Management Journal* 44:180–192, 2001; and Eisenberger, R., Armeli, S., Rexwinkel, B., Lynch, P. D., Rhoades, L. Reciprocation of perceived organizational support. *Journal of Applied Psychology* 86:42–51, 2001.

7. Eisenberger, R., Armeli, S., Rexwinkel, B., Lynch, P. D., Rhoades, L. Reciprocation of perceived organizational support. *Journal of Applied Psychology* 86:42–51, 2001; Eisenberger, R., Huntington, R., Hutchison, S., & Sowa, D. Perceived organizational support. *Journal of Applied Psychology* 71:500–507, 1986; and Caudron, S. The myth of job happiness. *Workforce*, April 2001, pp. 32–36.

8. Schneider, B., White, S. S., & Paul, M. C. Linking service climate and customer perceptions of service quality: Test of a causal model. *Journal of Applied Psychology* 83:150–163, 1998.

9. For research findings regarding HR practices and turnover, see Guthrie, J. P. High-involvement work practices, turnover, and productivity: Evidence from New Zealand. *Academy of Management Journal* 44:180–192, 2001; and Huselid, M. A. The impact of human resource management practices on turnover, productivity, and corporate financial performance. *Academy of Management Journal* 38:635–672, 1995.

10. Laabs, J. Employee sabotage: Don't be a target! *Workforce*, July 1999, pp. 33–42.

11. See Arthur, J. B. Effects of human resource systems on manufacturing performance and turnover. *Academy of Management Journal* 37:670–687, 1994; Huselid, M. A. The impact of human resource management practices on turnover, productivity, and corporate financial performance. *Academy of Management Journal* 38:635–672, 1995; Guthrie, J. P. High-involvement work practices, turnover, and productivity: Evidence from New Zealand. *Academy of Management Journal* 44:180–192, 2001; Koys, D. J. The effects of employee satisfaction, organizational citizenship behavior, and turnover on organizational effectiveness: A unit-level, longitudinal study. *Personnel Psychology* 54:101–114, 2001; Hitt, M. A., Bierman, L., Shimizu, K., & Kochhar, R. Direct and moderating effects of human capital on strategy and performance in professional service firms: A resource-based perspective. *Academy of Management Journal* 44:13–28, 2001.

12. Delery, J. E., & Doty, D. H. Modes of theorizing in strategic human resource management: Tests of universalistic, contingency, and configurational performance predictions. *Academy of Management Journal* 39:802–835, 1996; Bailey, T., Berg, P., & Sandy, C. The effect of high-performance work practices on employee earnings in the steel, apparel, and medical electronics and imaging industries. *Industrial and Labor Relations* 54:525–543, 2001; and Youndt, M. A., Snell, S. A., Dean, J. W., Jr., & Lepak, D. P. Human resource management, manufacturing strategy, and firm performance. *Academy of Management Journal* 39:836–866, 1996.

13. Whitener, E. Do "high commitment" human resource practices affect employee commitment? A cross-level analysis using hierarchical linear modeling. *Journal of Management* 27:515–535, 2001.

14. Pfeffer, J. *The human equation: Building profits by putting people first*. Boston: Harvard Business School Press, 1998.

15. CIGNA. *What's it like to work here?* http://careers.cigna.com.

16. Hackman J. R., & Oldham, G. R. Motivation through the design of work: Test of a theory. *Organizational Behavior and Human Performance* 16:250–279, 1976; and Herzberg, F. One more time: How do you motivate employees? *Harvard Business Review* 65:109–120, 1987.

17. Houseman, S. N. Why employers use flexible staffing arrangements: Evidence from an establishment survey. *Industrial and Labor Relations Review* 55:149–170, 2001.

18. Bureau of Labor Statistics. *Contingent and alternative employment arrangements*, February 2005, www.stats.bls.gov/news.release/conemp.nr0.htm.

19. Chambers, E. G., Foulon, M., Handfield-Jones, H., Hankin, S. M., & Michaels III, E. G. The war for talent. *The McKinsey Quarterly* 1:, 1998.

20. For discussion of the influence of perceive equity and inequity, see Adams, J. S. Toward an understanding of inequity. *Journal of Abnormal and Social Psychology* 67:422–436, 1963. For discussion of social exchange, see also Tsui, A. S., Pearce, J. L., Porter, L. W., & Tripoli, A. M. 1997. Alternative approaches to the employee-organization relationship: Does investment in employees pay off? *Academy of Management Journal* 40:1089–1121, 1997; and Shore, L. M., & Barksdale, K. Examining degree of balance and level of obligation in the employment relationship: A social exchange approach. *Journal of Organizational Behavior* 19:731–744, 1998.

21. Lincoln Electric. *Working at Lincoln*. www.lincolnelectric.com/corporate/career/default.asp; and 3M. *A century of innovation*. www.3m.com/about3M/century/experiments.jhtml.

22. Miles, R., & Snow, C. C. Designing strategic human resource systems. *Organizational Dynamics* 13:36–52, 1984; Schuler, R. S., & Jackson, S. E. Linking competitive strategies with human resource management practices. *Academy of Management Executive* 1:207–219, 1987; Becker, B. E., & Huselid, M. A. High performance work systems and firm performance: A synthesis of research and managerial implications. In G. R. Ferris (ed.), *Research in personnel and human resources management*. Greenwich, CT: JAI Press, 1998, pp. 53–101; and MacDuffie, J. P. Human resource bundles and manufacturing performance: Organizational logic and flexible production systems in the world auto industry. *Industrial and Labor Relations Review* 48:197–221, 1995.

23. Miles, R., & Snow, C. C. Designing strategic human resource systems. *Organizational Dynamics* 13:36–52, 1984; Schuler, R. S., & Jackson, S. E. Linking competitive strategies with human

435

resource management practices. *Academy of Management Executive* 1:207–219, 1987; Becker, B. E., & Huselid, M. A. High performance work systems and firm performance: A synthesis of research and managerial implications. In G. R. Ferris (ed.), *Research in personnel and human resources management.* Greenwich, CT: JAI Press, 1998, pp. 53–101; and MacDuffie, J. P. Human resource bundles and manufacturing performance: Organizational logic and flexible production systems in the world auto industry. *Industrial and Labor Relations Review* 48:197–221, 1995.

24. Porter, M. E. What is strategy? *Harvard Business Review*, November 1:61–78, 1996.

25. Hitt, M. A., Ireland, R. D., & Hoskisson, R. E. *Strategic management: Competitiveness and globalization.* Cincinnati, OH: South-Western College Publishing, 2001.

26. Porter, M. E. *Competitive strategy.* New York: The Free Press, 1980; and M.E. Porter. *Competitive advantage.* New York: The Free Press, 1980.

27. Arthur, J. B. The link between business strategy and industrial relations systems in American steel minimills. *Industrial and Labor Relations Review* 45:488–506, 1992; Jackson, S. E., Schuler, R. S., & Rivero, J. C. Organizational characteristics as predictors of personnel practices. *Personnel Psychology* 42:727–786, 1989; and Schuler, R. S., & Jackson, S. E. Linking competitive strategies with human resource management practices. *Academy of Management Executive* 1:207–219, 1987.

28. Jackson, S. E., Schuler, R. S., & Rivero, J. C. 1989. Organizational characteristics as predictors of personnel practices. *Personnel Psychology* 42:727–786; Miles, R., & Snow, C. C. Designing strategic human resource systems. *Organizational Dynamics* 13:36–52, 1984; and Delery, J. E., & Doty, D. H. Modes of theorizing in strategic human resource management: Tests of universalistic, contingency, and configurational performance predictions. *Academy of Management Journal* 39:802–835, 1996.

29. Baird, L. & Meshoulam, I. Managing two fits of strategic human resource management. *Academy of Management Review* 13:116–128, 1988.

30. Schein, E. H. *Organizational culture and leadership.* San Francisco: Jossey-Bass, 1985.

31. Ostroff, C., & Bowen, D. E. Moving HR to a higher level: HR practices and organizational effectiveness. In K. J. Klein & S. W. Kozlowski (eds.), *Multilevel theory, research, and methods in organizations: Foundations, extensions, and new directions.* San Francisco: Jossey-Bass, 2000, pp. 211–266.

32. Southwest Airlines. *Southwest Airlines fact sheet.* www.southwest.com/about_swa/press/factsheet.html.

33. Cole, C. L. Sun Microsystems' solution to traffic that doesn't move? Satellite work centers. *Workforce*, January 2001, pp. 108–111.

34. Toosi, M. Labor force projections to 2012: The graying of the workforce. *Monthly Labor Review*, February 2004, pp. 37–57.

35. Charting the projections, 2006–2016. *Occupational Outlook Quarterly* online, Fall 2007, http://www.bls.gov/opub/ooq/2007/fall/contents.htm.

36. Bureau of Labor Statistics. *Employment projections: 2006-16 summary.* www.bls.gov/news.release/ecopro.nr0.htm; and Horrigan, M. W. Labor force. *Occupational Outlook Quarterly* online, Winter 2003–2004, http://stats.bls.gov/opub/ooq/2003/winter/art05.pdf.

37. Bureau of Labor Statistics. *Employment projections: 2006-16 summary.* www.bls.gov/news.release/ecopro.nr0.htm; and

Horrigan, M. W. Introduction to the projections. *Occupational Outlook Quarterly* online, Winter 2003–2004, http://www.newsok.com/ads/jobsok/freedom/freedom.pdf. See also Albrecht, D. G. Getting ready for older workers. *Workforce*, February 2001, p. 26; and Epstein, G. Tomorrow's jobs. *Barron's*, January 5, 2004, p. 84.

38. Albrecht, D. G. Getting ready for older workers. *Workforce*, February 2001, p. 26.

39. Kravitz, D. A. More women in the workplace: Is there a payoff in firm performance? *Academy of Management Executive* 17:148–149, 2003; and Richard, O., MacMillan, A. Chadwick, K., &. Dwyer, S. Employing an innovation strategy in racially diverse workforces: Effects on firm performance. *Group and Organization Management*, March 2003, pp. 107–127.

40. Mullich, J. Hiring without limits. *Workforce*, June 2004, pp. 53–58.

41. Greengard, S. Surviving Internet speed. *Workforce*, April 2001, pp. 38–43.

42. Mariani, M. Telecommuters. *Occupational Outlook Quarterly*, Fall 2000, pp. 10–17.

43. The push forward. *Workforce*, January 2000, p. 29.

44. Rottier, A. The skies are JetBlue. *Workforce*, September 2001, p. 22; and Salter, C. Calling JetBlue. *Fast Company* online, May 2004, http://www.fastcompany.com/magazine/82/jetblue_agents.html?page=0%2C1

45. Solomon, C. M. Don't forget your telecommuters. *Workforce*, May 2000, pp. 56–63.

46. Solomon, C. M. Moving jobs to offshore markets: Why it's done and how it works. *Workforce*, July 1999, pp. 51–55.

47. Greengard, S. What's in store for 2004. *Workforce*, December 2003, pp. 34-40.

48. Serwer, A. Factories shutting down? Good riddance. *Fortune online*, October, 13, 2003, http://money.cnn.com/magazines/fortune/fortune_archive/2003/10/13/350922/index.htm

49. Ricci, M. Outsourcing 3.0: It's a whole new world, this cost- and quality-control game. *Financial Week*, September 10, 2007.

50. Brewin, B. User complaints push Dell to return PC support to U.S. *Computerworld*, December 1, 2003, p. 6; and McDougall, P. L., & Claburn, T. Offshore "hiccups in an irreversible trend." *InformationWeek*, December 1, 2003, http://www.informationweek. com/story/showArticle.jhtml?articleID=16400977.

51. Fandray, D. The ethical company. *Workforce*, December 2000, pp. 75–77.

52. Meisler, A. Lockheed is doing right and doing well. *Workforce Management Online*, March 2004, http://www.workforce.com/archive/feature/23/65/12/index.php.

53. Mehta, S. N. Is being good good enough? *Fortune*, 148: 117-124, October 27, 2003.

54. Americans with Disabilities Act Web site, www.usdoj.gov/crt/ada/adahom1.htm.

55. Labich, K. No more crude at Texaco. *Fortune*, September 6, 1999, pp. 205–212.

56. Bland T. S., & Hall, R. D., Jr. Do the math. *HRMagazine* 46:121, 2001.

57. 22 tips for avoiding employee lawsuits. *HR Focus*, December 2003, p. 4. See also Buckman, R. The Microsoft settlement: Antitrust litigation takes toll on Microsoft—Fallout from suit includes low morale, executive departures. *Wall Street Journal*, November 5, 2001, p. A14.

Chapter 2

1. Porter, M. E., What is strategy? *Harvard Business Review* November 1:61–78, 1996; and Hitt, M. A., Ireland, R. D., & Hoskisson, R. E., *Strategic management: Competitiveness and globalization.* Cincinnati, OH: South-Western College Publishing, 2001.

2. Porter, M. E. *Competitive advantage: Creating and sustaining superior performance.* New York: The Free Press, 1985.

3. Montana State University, Center for Applied Economic Research. *The impact of big box retail chains on small businesses,* January 2000, www.msubillings.edu/caer/bix%20box%20r eport.htm; and Stone, K. E. Impact on the Wal-Mart phenomena on rural communities. *Proceedings of Increasing Understanding of Public Problems and Policies 1997.* Chicago: Farm Foundation, 1997.

4. Porter, M. E. *Competitive advantage: Creating and sustaining superior performance.* New York: The Free Press, 1985.

5. Arthur, J. B. The link between business strategy and industrial relations systems in American steel minimills. *Industrial and Labor Relations Review* 45:488–506, 1992; Jackson, S. E., Schuler, R. S., & Rivero, J. C. Organizational characteristics as predictors of personnel practices. *Personnel Psychology* 42:727–786, 1989; and Schuler, R. S., & Jackson, S. E. Linking competitive strategies with human resource management practices. *Academy of Management Executive* 1:207–219, 1987.

6. Arthur, J. B. Effects of human resource systems on manufacturing performance and turnover. *Academy of Management Journal* 37:670–687, 1994; and Youndt, M. A., Snell, S. A., Dean, J. W., Jr., & Lepak, D. P. Human resource management, manufacturing strategy, and firm performance. *Academy of Management Journal* 39:836–866, 1996.

7. U.S. Small Business Administration. *Newsrelease: Ten reasons to love small business,* February 9, 2006, www.sba.gov/advo/press/ 06-04. html.

8. Finegold, D., & Frenkel, S. Managing people where people really matter: The management of human resources in biotech companies. *International Journal of Human Resource Management* 17:1–24, 2006; and Heneman J. G., & Berkley, R. A., Applicant attraction practices and outcomes among small businesses. *Journal of Small Business Management,* 37:53–74, 1999.

9. Hornsby, J. S., & Kuratko, D. F. Human resource management in U.S. small businesses: A replication and extension. *Journal of Developmental Entrepreneurship,* 8:73–92, April 2003.

10. Shutan, B. What small business needs to know about pay and benefits. *Employee Benefit Plan Review,* 57:6–9, January 2003.

11. Hornsby, J. S., & Kuratko, D. F. Human resource management in U.S. small businesses: A replication and extension. *Journal of Developmental Entrepreneurship,* 8:73–92, April 2003.

12. Kok, J. D., & Uhlaner, L. M. Organization context and human resource management in the small firm. *Small Business Economics,* 17:273–291, December 2001.

13. Richard, O. C., Ford, D., & Ismail, K. Exploring the performance effects of visible attribute diversity: The moderating role of span of control and organizational life cycle. *International Journal of Human Resource Management* 17:2091–2109, 2006.

14. Baird, L., & Meshoulam, I. Managing two fits of strategic human resource management. *Academy of Management Review* 13:116–128, 1988.

15. Ibid.

16. Schein, E. H. *Organizational culture and leadership.* San Francisco: Jossey-Bass, 1985.

17. Southwest Airlines. *We weren't just airborne yesterday,* August 1, 2007, www.southwest.com/about_swa/airborne.html.

18. Harrison, J. R., & Carroll, G. R. Keeping the faith: A model of cultural transmission in formal organizations. *Administrative Science Quarterly,* 36, 552–582, 1991.

19. Guzzo, R. A., & Noonan, K. A. Human resource practices as communications and the psychological contract. *Human Resource Management,* 33:447–462, 1994. See also Rousseau, D. M. *Psychological contracts in organizations: Understanding written and unwritten agreements.* Thousand Oaks, CA: Sage, 1995.

20. Ostroff, C., & Bowen, D. E. Moving HR to a higher level: HR practices and organizational effectiveness. In K. J. Klein & S. W. Kozlowski (eds.). *Multilevel theory, research, and methods in organizations: Foundations, extensions, and new directions.* San Francisco: Jossey-Bass, 2000, pp. 211–266.

21. Bowen, D. E., & Ostroff, C. Understanding HRM–firm performance linkages: The role of the "strength" of the HRM system. *Academy of Management Review* 29:203–221, 2004.

22. Fister Gale, S. Memo to AOL Time Warner: Why mergers fail. *Workforce,* February 2003, p. 60.

23. Rousseau, D. M. *Psychological contracts in organizations: Understanding written and unwritten agreements.* Thousand Oaks, CA: Sage, 1995.

24. Hackman, J. R., & Oldham, G. R. *Work redesign.* Reading, MA: Addison-Wesley, 1980.

25. Murray, B., & Gerhart, B. An empirical analysis of a skill-based pay program and plant performance outcomes. *Academy of Management Journal* 41:68–78, 1998.

26. Robinson, S. L., Kraatz, M. S., & Rousseau, D. M. Changing obligations and the psychological contract: A longitudinal study. *Academy of Management Journal* 37:137–152, 1994.

27. Taylor, M. S., Tracy, K. B., Renard, M. K., Harrison, J. K., & Carroll, S. J. Due process in performance appraisals: A quasi-experiment in procedural justice. *Administrative Science Quarterly* 40:495–523, 1995.

28. Eisenberger, R., Huntington, R., Hutchison, S., & Sowa, D. Perceived organizational support. *Journal of Applied Psychology* 71: 500–507, 1986.

29. U.S. Bureau of Labor Statistics. *Table 6: Employment status of women by presence and age of youngest child, March 1975–2006,* www.bls. gov/cps/wlf-table7-2007.pdf; and U.S. Bureau of Labor Statistics. *Table 7: Employment status of women by presence and age of youngest child, 1975–2002,* www.bls.gov/cps/wlf-tables7.pdf.

30. U.S. Bureau of Labor Statistics. *Table 23: Married-couple families by number and relationship of earners, 1967–2005,* www.bls.gov/cps/wlf-table23-2007.pdf.

31. U.S. Bureau of Labor Statistics. *Table 30: Flexible schedules: Full-time wage and salary workers by selected characteristics, May 2004,* www.bls.gov/cps/wlf-table30-2007.pdf.

32. Kiger, P. J. A case for child care, *Workforce,* April 2004, pp. 34–40; Summer child care for working moms. ABC News online, March 28, 2008, http://abcnews.go.com/GMA/AmericanFamily/ story?id=2073583&page=2.

33. Ibid.

34. Hansen, F. Truth and myths of work/life balance. *Workforce,* December 2002, pp. 34–39.

35. Lester, S.W., Turnley, W. H., Bloodgood, J. M., & Bolino, M. C. Not seeing eye to eye: Differences in supervisor and subordinate perceptions of and attributions for psychological contract breach. *Journal of Organizational Behavior* 23:29–56, February 2002.

36. Rousseau, D. M. *Psychological contracts in organizations: Understanding written and unwritten agreements.* Thousand Oaks, CA: Sage, 1995, p. 128.

37. Ibid., p. 53.

38. Why loyalty is not enough. *HR Focus* 77:1–3, November 2000.

39. Coyle-Shapiro, J., & Kessler, I. Consequences of the psychological contract for the employment relationship: A large scale survey. *Journal of Management Studies* 37:39–52, 2002; Robinson, S. L. Trust and breach of the psychological contract. *Administrative Science Quarterly* 41:574–599, 1996; and Turnley, W. H., & Feldman, D. C. The impact of psychological contract violations on exit, loyalty and neglect. *Human Relations* 51:895–922, 1999.

40. Rousseau, D. M. *Psychological contracts in organizations: Understanding written and unwritten agreements.* Thousand Oaks, CA: Sage, 1995, p. 90.

41. Hansen, F. Weighing the truth of exit interviews. *Workforce*, December 2002, p. 37.

42. Toosi, M. Labor force projections to 2016: More workers in their golden years. *Monthly Labor Review*, November 2007, pp. 33–52.

43. Sommers, D. Charting the projections 2006–2016: Labor force. *Occupational Outlook Quarterly*, 51:42–48, Fall 2007, www.bls.gov/opub/ooq/2007/fall/art04.pdf. See also Albrecht, D. G. Getting ready for older workers. *Workforce*, February 2001, p 26; and Epstein, G. Tomorrow's jobs. *Barron's*, January 5, 2004, p. 84.

44. Sommers, D. Charting the projections 2006–2016: Labor force. *Occupational Outlook Quarterly*, 51:42–48, Fall 2007, www.bls.gov/opub/ooq/2007/fall/art04.pdf.

45. Velkoff, V., & Kinsella, K. World's older population growing by unprecedented 800,000 a month. *U.S. Census Bureau News*, December 13, 2001, www.census.gov/Press-Release/www/releases/archives/aging_population/000370.html. See also U.S. Census Bureau, *The world's 25 oldest countries: 2000*, www.census.gov/Press-Release/www/2001/cb01-198.pdf.

46. Associated Press. *More employers seek out seniors*, January 18, 2008, www.msnbc.msn.com/id/22731416/.

47. U.S. Bureau of Labor Statistics. *Table 10: Civilian labor force by age, sex, race, and Hispanic origin, 1996, 2006, and projected 2016*, www.bls.gov/news.release/ecopro.t10.htm. See also Sommers, D. Charting the projections 2006–2016: Labor force. *Occupational Outlook Quarterly* 51:43, Fall 2007.

48. Ibid.

49. Bergman, M. Foreign-born a majority in six U.S. cities; Growth fastest in south, Census Bureau reports. *U.S. Census Bureau News*, December 17, 2003, www.census.gov/Press-Release/www/releases/archives/census_2000/001623.html.

50. Toosi, M. A century of change: the U.S. labor force 1950–2050. *Monthly Labor Review*, May 2002, pp 15–28.

51. Kravitz, D. A. More women in the workplace: Is there a payoff in firm performance? *Academy of Management Executive*, 2003, pp. 148; and Richard, O., MacMillan, A., Chadwick, K., & Dwyer, S. Employing an innovation strategy in racially diverse workforces: Effects on firm performance. *Group and Organization Management*, March 2003, pp. 107–127.

52. Greengard, S. Surviving Internet speed. *Workforce*, April 2001, pp. 38–43.

53. Mariani, M. Telecommuters. *Occupational Outlook Quarterly*, Fall 2000, pp. 10–17.

54. The push forward. *Workforce*, January, 2000, p. 29.

55. Golden, T. Co-workers who telecommute and the impact on those in the office: Understanding the implications of virtual work for co-worker satisfaction and turnover intentions. *Human Relations* 60:1641–1667, 2007.

56. Cooper, C. & Kurland, N. B. Telecommuting, professional isolation, and employee development in public and private organizations. *Journal of Organizational Behavior* 23:511–532, 2002.

57. NAFTA: A ten year perspective and implications for the future, Hearing before the subcommittee on international economic policy, export, and trade promotion of the committee on Foreign Relations United States Senate, April 20, 2004. http://www.usembassy-mexico.gov/bbf/NAFTA10Yp.pdf

58. European Union Web site, www.eurunion.org.

59. Bartlett, C. A., & Ghoshal, S. *Managing across borders: The transnational solution.* Boston: Harvard Business School Press, 1998.

60. Ghoshal, S. Global strategy: An organizing framework. *Strategic Management Journal*, 8:425–440, 1987; and Hitt, M. A., Ireland, R. D., & Hoskisson, R. E. *Strategic management: competitiveness and globalization.* Cincinnati, OH: South-Western College Publishing, 2001.

61. Solomon, C. M. Moving jobs to offshore markets: Why it's done and how it works. *Workforce*, July 1999, pp. 51–55.

62. Hofstede, G. Cultural constraints in management theories. *Academy of Management Executive*, February 1993, pp. 81–90.

63. Dowling, P. J., Welch, D. E., & Schuler, R. S. *International human resource management: Managing people in a multinational context*, 3rd ed. Cincinnati, OH: South-Western College Publishing, 1999.

64. Carpenter, M. A., Sanders, W. G., & Gregersen, H. B. Bundling human capital with organizational context: The impact of international experience on multinational firm performance and CEO pay. *Academy of Management Journal* 44:493–511, 2001; and Daily, C. M., Certo, S. T., & Dalton, D. R. International experience in the executive suite: The path to prosperity? *Strategic Management Journal*, 21:515–523, 2000.

65. Daily, C. M., Certo, S. T., & Dalton, D. R. International experience in the executive suite: The path to prosperity? *Strategic Management Journal*, 221: 515-523, 2000.

66. Nakashima, E., & Noguchi, Y. Extensive spying found at HP. *Washington Post,* September 20, 2006, p. D01; and H.P. Names ethics officer. *New York Times* online, October 13, 2006, www.nytimes.com/2006/10/13/technology/13hewlett.html?scp=1&sq=H.P.+Names+ethics+officer&st=nyt.

67. Graves, S. P., Waddock, S., & Kelly, M. The methodology behind the corporate citizen rankings. Business *Ethics: Corporate Social Responsibility Report*, March/April 2002, and KLD Research. Frequently asked questions: Business Ethics' 100 Best Corporate Citizens List, 2006 http://www.kld.com/research/socrates/businessethics100/images/200604_BE100FAQ.pdf.

68. 100 Best corporate citizens. Business Ethics: The magazine of Corporate Responsibility, http://www.business-ethics.com/BE100_all.

69. Miller, M. 100 Best corporate citizens. Americans most responsible and profitable major public companies. *Business Ethics*, 2002, http://www.business-ethics.com/node/81.

70. How to help reinvigorate your organization's ethics program. *HR Focus*, June 2003, p. 80; and Schramm, J. A return to ethics? *HRMagazine*, 48:144, July, 2003.

71. Brown, D., HR feeling pressure to act unethically. *Canadian HR Reporter* 16:1, May 19, 2003.

72. How to help reinvigorate your organization's ethics program. *HR Focus* 80:7, June 2003.

73. Nike Web site, www.nikebiz.com; Survey: Sweating for fashion. *The Economist*, March 6, 2004, p. 14; and Locke, R., Kochan, T., Romis, M., & Qin, F. Beyond corporate codes of conduct: Work organization and labour standards at Nike's suppliers. *International Labour Review* 146:21–40, 2007.

74. Brown, D. HR feeling pressure to act unethically. *Canadian HR Reporter* 16:1, May 19, 2003.

75. Meisler, A. Lockheed is doing right and doing well. *Workforce*, March 2004, http://www.workforce.com/archive/feature/23/65/12/index.php

76. Mees, A. & Bonham, J. Corporate social responsibility belongs with HR. *Canadian HR Reporter* 17:11–12, April 5, 2004.

Chapter 3

1. Ledvinka, J., and Scarpello, V. G. *Federal regulation of personnel and human resources management*, 2nd ed. Boston: PWS-Kent, 1991, p. 215.

2. Sidel, R. Moving the market: Panel awards ex-Merrill broker $2.2 million in gender bias case. *Wall Street Journal*, April 21, 2004, p. C.3.

3. Anderson, J. After she sued Merrill, it's back to the job. *New York Times*, July 22, 2005, p. C2.

4. *Diaz v. Pan American World Airways, Inc.*, 442 F.2d 385 (5th Cir. 1971)

5. The Bona Fide Occupational Qualification Defense, *Diaz v. Pan American World Airways, Inc.*, 442 F.2d 385 (5th Cir. 1971), http://www.nsulaw.nova.edu/faculty/syllabi/Employment%20Discrimination%20Class%20Eight.pdf

6. The Bona Fide Occupational Qualification Defense, *Diaz v. Pan American World Airways, Inc.*, 442 F.2d 385 (5th Cir. 1971), http://www.nsulaw.nova.edu/faculty/syllabi/Employment%20Discrimination%20Class%20Eight.pdf.

7. U.S. Equal Employment Opportunity Commission. *EEOC resolves sex discrimination lawsuit against NBA's Phoenix Suns and Sports Magic for $104,500*, October 9, 2003, www.eeoc.gov/press/10-9-03b.html.

8. U.S. Equal Employment Opportunity Commission. *Discriminatory practices*, September 4, 2004, www.eeoc.gov/abouteeo/overview_practices.html.

9. *McDonnell Douglas v. Green*, 411 U.S. 793 (1973)

10. U.S. Equal Employment Opportunity Commission. *Selected Supreme Court decisions*, www.eeoc.gov/abouteeoc/35th/thelaw/supreme_court.html.

11. Holladay, A. Dinosaurs roamed Antarctic; American woman shoe size; First sidesaddles. http://www.wonderquest.com/dinosaur-shoe-sidesaddle.htm#shoe.

12. *Griggs v. Duke Power*, 401 U.S. 424 (1971)

13. Ibid.

14. U.S. Equal Employment Opportunity Commission. *Discriminatory practices*, September 4, 2004, www.eeoc.gov/abouteeo/overview_practices.html.

15. U.S. Equal Employment Opportunity Commission. *Relief for Afghan, Muslim workers harassed at Solano County car dealer chain*, April 6, 2004, www.eeoc.gov/press/4-6-04.html.

16. U.S. Equal Employment Opportunity Commission. EEOC directives transmittal number 915.003. *EEOC Compliance Manual*, May 20, 1998, www.eeoc.gov/policy/docs/retal.html.

17. U.S. Equal Employment Opportunity Commission. *Equal pay and compensation discrimination*, March 4, 2008, www.eeoc.gov/types/epa.html.

18. Simon, E. Study reveals male–female pay gap trend. *ABC News online*, April 23, 2007, http://abcnews.go.com/Business/wireStory?id=3066518.

19. Levy, P. B. *The civil rights movement*. Westport, CT: Greenwood Press, 1998.

20. U.S. Equal Employment Opportunity Commission. *Pre 1965: Events leading to the creation of EEOC*, www.eeoc.gov/abouteeoc/35th/pre1965/index.html.

21. U.S. Equal Employment Opportunity Commission. *Title VII of the Civil Rights Act of 1964*, January 15, 1997, www.eeoc.gov/policy/vii.html.

22. U.S. Equal Employment Opportunity Commission. *Shaping employment discrimination law*, www.eeoc.gov/abouteeoc/35th/1965-71/shaping.html.

23. U.S. Equal Employment Opportunity Commission. Henredon furniture industries to pay $465,000 for racial harassment, hangman's nooses, January 24, 2008, www.eeoc.gov/press/1-24-08.html; and U.S. Equal Employment Opportunity Commission. *Race/color discrimination*, March 4, 2008, www.eeoc.gov/types/race.html.

24. U.S. Equal Employment Opportunity Commission. *Race/color discrimination*, March 4, 2008, www.eeoc.gov/types/race.html.

25. U.S. Equal Employment Opportunity Commission. *Race/color discrimination*, March 4, 2008, www.eeoc.gov/types/race.html; The Look of Abercrombie & Fitch: Retail store accused of hiring attractive, mostly white salespeople. *CBS News online*, November 24, 2004, www.cbsnews.com/stories/2003/12/05/60minutes/main587099.shtml; U.S. Equal Employment Opportunity Commission. *EEOC sues two Indiana employers for race harassment*, May 23, 2001, www.eeoc.gov/press/5-22-01.html; and U.S. Equal Employment Opportunity Commission. *EEOC settles color harassment lawsuit with Applebee's Neighborhood Bar and Grill*, April 12, 2004, www.eeoc.gov/press/8-07-03.html.

26. U.S. Equal Employment Opportunity Commission. *Race/color discrimination*, March 4, 2008, www.eeoc.gov/types/race.html.

27. Society for Human Resource Management (SHRM). *Religion in the workplace survey*. Alexandria, VA: SHRM, 2001.

28. U.S. Equal Employment Opportunity Commission. *Religious discrimination*, March 4, 2008, www.eeoc.gov/types/religion.html.

29. U.S. Equal Employment Opportunity Commission. *Religious discrimination*, March 4, 2008, www.eeoc.gov/types/religion.html.

30. U.S. Supreme Court. *Price Waterhouse v. Hopkins*, 490 U.S. 228 (1989)

31. Ibid.

32. U.S. Equal Employment Opportunity Commission. *Facts about sexual harassment*, June 27, 2002, www.eeoc.gov/facts/fs-sex.html.

33. Cava, A. Sexual harassment claims: New framework for employers. *Business and Economic Review* 47:13–16, 2001.

34. Ibid.

35. U.S. Equal Employment Opportunity Commission. *National origin discrimination*, March 4, 2008, www.eeoc.gov/origin/index.html.

36. U.S. Equal Employment Opportunity Commission. *EEOC sues Plaza Hotel & Fairmont Hotels & Resorts for post-9/11 backlash discrimination*, September 30, 2003, www.eeoc.gov/press/9-30-03b.html.

37. U.S. Equal Employment Opportunity Commission. *The Plaza Hotel to pay $525,000 for post 9/11 backlash discrimination against employees*, June 8, 2005, www.eeoc.gov/press/6-8-05.html.

38. U.S. Equal Employment Opportunity Commission. *The Civil Rights Act of 1991*, January 15, 1997, www.eeoc.gov/policy/cra91.html.

39. Lorber, L. Z. The Civil Rights Act of 1991. *SHRM Legal Reports*, Spring 1992, www.shrm.org/hrresources/lrpt_published/CMS_000980.asp

40. U.S. Equal Employment Opportunity Commission. Directives Transmittal: Section 2: Threshold issues. *EEOC compliance manual*, www.eeoc.gov/policy/docs/threshold.html.

41. U.S. Equal Employment Opportunity Commission. *Older Workers Benefit Protection Act*, www.eeoc.gov/abouteeoc/35th/thelaw/owbpa.html.

42. Greene, K. AARP to recruit for Home Deport. *Wall Street Journal*, February 6, 2004, p. B2; and White, E. Some employers courting seniors. *The Arizona Republic*, January 15, 2008, www.azcentral.com/arizonarepublic/business/articles/0115biz-olderworkers0115.html.

43. U.S. Department of Labor, Employment Standards Administration, Office of Federal Contract Compliance. *Section 503 of the Rehabilitation Act of 1973, as amended*, www.dol.gov/esa/regs/compliance/ofccp/sec503.htm.

44. U.S. Census Bureau. United States: S1801: Disability characteristics. *2006 American Community Survey*, http://factfinder.census.gov/servlet/STTable?_bm=y&-geo_id=01000US&-qr_name=ACS_2006_EST_G00_S1801&-ds_name=ACS_2006_EST_G00_.

45. U.S. Equal Employment Opportunity Commission. *Disability discrimination*, February 28, 2008, www.eeoc.gov/types/ada.html.

46. Ibid.

47. Ibid.

48. Loy, B. A., & Gebremedhin, T. G. *Disability legislation: An empirical analysis of employer cost. Research paper 2001-3*. Morgantown, WV: West Virginia University Regional Research Institute, 2001.

49. U.S. Equal Employment Opportunity Commission. *Disability discrimination*, February 28, 2008, www.eeoc.gov/types/ada.html.

50. Ibid.

51. *Sutton v. United Air Lines, Inc.* (97-1943) 527 U.S. 471 (1999).

52. *Toyota Motor Manufacturing, Kentucky, Inc., v. Williams*, 534 U.S. 184 (2002).

53. *Toyota Motor Manufacturing, Kentucky, Inc., v. Williams*, 534 U.S. 184 (2002).

54. U.S. Equal Employment Opportunity Commission. *Sex-based discrimination*, March 4, 2008, www.eeoc.gov/types/sex.html.

55. U.S. Equal Employment Opportunity Commission. *The equal employment opportunity responsibilities of multinantional employers*, April 28, 2003, www.eeoc.gov/facts/multi-employers.html.

56. U.S. Equal Employment Opportunity Commission. *Facts about mediation*, November 1, 2004, www.eeoc.gov/mediate/facts.html.

57. U.S. Equal Employment Opportunity Commission. *Alternative dispute resolution policy statement*, March 25, 2002, www.eeoc.gov/policy/docs/adrstatement.html.

58. U.S. Equal Employment Opportunity Commission. *EEOC's charge processing procedures*, August 13, 2003, www.eeoc.gov/charge/overview_charge_processing.html.

59. U.S. Department of Labor, Employment Standards Administration, Office of Federal Contract Compliance Programs. *Facts on Executive Order 11246—Affirmative action*, January 4, 2002, www.dol.gov/esa/regs/compliance/ofccp/aa.htm.

60. Ibid.

61. Cox, T. *Creating the multicultural organization: A strategy for capturing the power of diversity*. San Francisco: Jossey-Bass, 2001; Brickson, S. The impact of identity orientation on individual and organizational outcomes in demographically diverse settings. *Academy of Management Review* 25(1):82–101, 2000; Harrison, D. A., Price, K. H., & Bell, M. P. Beyond relational demography: Time and the effects of surface- and deep-level diversity on work group cohesion. *Academy of Management Journal* 41:96–107, 1998.

62. U.S. Department of Agriculture, Office of the Chief Economist, Agricultural Labor Affairs. *IRCA antidiscrimination provisions*, May 16, 2006, www.usda.gov/oce/labor/ina.htm.

63. U.S. Department of Agriculture. *Immigration Reform and Control Act of 1986*, www.ers.usda.gov/publications/ah719/ah719f.pdf.

64. Collis, A. *Acceptable List A documents for I-9 forms*. Alexandria, VA: Society for Human Resource Management Knowledge Center, 2008.

65. Pivec, M. I-9 audits return. *SHRM Workplace Law Library—Selection and placement*. Alexandria, VA: Society for Human Resource Management, 2008.

66. Smith, A. Expanded FMLA will complicate coordination of leave. *SHRM Workforce Law Library—Employee benefits*. Alexandria, VA: Society for Human Resource Management, 2008.

67. U.S. Department of Labor, Employment Standards Administration, Wage and Hour Division. *Compliance assistance—Family and Medical Leave Act (FMLA)*, www.dol.gov/esa/whd/fmla/#press.

68. U.S. Department of Labor, Employment Standards Administration, Office of Federal Contract Compliance Programs. *Vietnam Era Veterans' Readjustment Assistance Act (VEVRAA) of 1974*, www.dol.gov/esa/regs/compliance/ofccp/fsvevraa.htm.

69. U.S. Department of Labor. *Overview of USERRA*, www.dol.gov/elaws/vets/userra/userra.asp.

70. Lewison, J. *Military call-up prompts focus on USERRA: The law that gives job and benefits protection to reservists returning from active duty*, January 2004, www.aicpa.org/pubs/jofa/jan2004/lewison.htm.

71. Thelen, J. Workplace rights for service members: The USERRA regulations deconstructed. *SHRM Legal Reports*. Alexandria, VA: Society for Human Resource Management, 2006.

72. Lewison, J. *Military call-up prompts focus on USERRA: The law that gives job and benefits protection to reservists returning from active duty*, January 2004, www.aicpa.org/pubs/jofa/jan2004/lewison.htm.

73. U.S. Department of Labor, Veterans' Employment and Training Service, Title 38, United States Code. *U.S. Department of Labor*, www.dol.gov/vets/usc/vpl/usc38.htm.

74. Bennett-Alexander, D. D., & Hartman, L. P. *Employment law for business*. Columbus, OH: McGraw-Hill, 2001.

75. Ibid.

76. Ibid., p. 20.

77. Roehling, M., & Wright, P. Organizationally sensible vs. legal-centric responses to the eroding employment at-will doctrine: The evolving nature of the employment relationship: Protecting workers from unjust dismissal versus safeguarding employer prerogatives. *Employee Responsibilities and Rights Journal* 16:89–103, 2004.

Chapter 4

1. Taylor, F. *Principles of scientific management*. New York: Harper, 1911; and Taylor, F. *Scientific management*. New York: Harper & Brothers, 1947.

2. Scott, W. R. *Organizations: Rational, natural, and open system*, 5th ed. Englewood Cliffs, NJ: Prentice Hall, 2003.

3. Witzel, M. A short history of efficiency. *Business Strategy Review* 13:38–47, 2002.

4. Krebs, M. The starting line. *Automotive News* 77:16, 2003.

5. Morgenson, F. P., & Campion, M. A. Minimizing trade-offs when redesigning work: Evidence from a longitudinal quasi-experiment. *Personnel Psychology* 55:589–612, 2002.

6. Hackman, J. R., Oldham, G., Janson, R., & Purdy, K. A new strategy for job enrichment. *California Management Review* 17(4):57–71, 1975.

7. Hackman, J. R., Oldham, G., Janson, R., & Purdy, K. A new strategy for job enrichment. *California Management Review* 17(4):57–71, 1975.

8. Renn, R. W., & Vandenberg, R. J. The critical psychological states: An underrepresented component in job characteristics model research. *Journal of Management* 21:279–303, 1995.

9. Hackman, J. Work design. In J. Hackman & J. Suttle (eds.), *Improving life at work*. Santa Monica, CA: Goodyear, 1976, pp. 96–162.

10. Gallagher, W. E., Jr., & Einhorn, H. J. Motivation theory and job design. *Journal of Business* 49(3):358–373, 1976.

11. Energize and enhance employee value with job rotation. *HR Focus*, January 2008, pp. 6–10.

12. Slack, N., Cooper, C. L., & Argyris, C. Empowerment. *Blackwell encyclopedic dictionary of operations management*. Boston: Blackwell Publishers, 1997, p. 44.

13. Leana, C. R. Predictors and consequences of delegation. *Academy of Management Journal* 29:754–774, 1986; and Chen, Z. X., & Aryee, S. Delegation and employee work outcomes: An examination of the cultural context of mediating processes in China, Academy of Management Journal, 50:226–238, 2007.

14. Hackman, J. R., Oldham, G., Janson, R., & Purdy, K. A new strategy for job enrichment. *California Management Review* 17(4)57–71, 1975.

15. Seibert, S. E., Silver, S. R., & Randolph. W. A. Taking empowerment to the next level: A multiple-level model of empowerment, performance, and satisfaction. *Academy of Management Journal* 47:332–349, 2004.

16. Cohen, S. G., & Bailey, D. E. What makes teams work: Group effectiveness research from the shop floor to the executive suite. *Journal of Management* 23:239–290, 1997; Kirkman, B. L., et al. Five challenges to virtual team success: Lessons from Sabre, Inc. *Academy of Management Executive* 16:67–79, 2002.

17. Zarraga, C., & Bonache, J. Assessing the team environment for knowledge sharing: An empirical analysis. *International Journal of Human Resource Management* 14:1227–1245, 2003.

18. Campion, M. A., Medsker, G. J., & Higgs, A. C. Relations between work group characteristics and effectiveness: Implications for designing effective work groups. *Personnel Psychology* 46:823–850, 1993.

19. Deci, E. L., Connel, J. P., & Ryan, P. M. Self-Determination in a work organization. *Journal of Applied Psychology* 74:580–590, 1989; E. E. Lawler, III. *High involvement management*. San Francisco: Jossey-Bass, 1986; Manz, C. C. Self-leading work teams: Moving beyond self-management myths. *Human Relations* 45:7–22, 1992; and Manz, C. C., & Sims, H. P., Jr. *Business without bosses: How self-managing teams are building high-performance companies*. New York: Wiley, 1993.

20. Tata, J., & Prasad, S. Team self-management, organizational structure, and judgments of team effectiveness. *Journal of Managerial Issues* 16(2):248–265, 2004; Wellins, R. S., et al. *Self-directed teams: A study of current practices.* Pittsburgh: DDI, 1990.

21. Kirkman, B. L., Rosen, B., Gibson, C. B., Tesluk, P. E., & McPherson, S. O. Five challenges to virtual team success: Lessons from Sabre, Inc. *Academy of Management Executive* 16:67–79, 2002.

22. Kirkman, B. L., Rosen, B., Gibson, C. B., Tesluk, P. E., & McPherson, S. O. The impact of team empowerment on virtual team performance: The moderating role of face-to-face interaction. *Academy of Management Journal* 47:175–192, 2004.

23. Campion, M. A. Ability requirement implications of job design: An interdisciplinary perspective. *Personnel Psychology* 42:1–24, 1989; and Gallagher, W. E., Jr., & Einhorn, H. J. Motivation theory and job design. *Journal of Business* 49(3):358–373, 1976.

24. Morgenson, F. P., & Campion, M. A. Minimizing trade-offs when redesigning work: Evidence from a longitudinal quasi-experiment. *Personnel Psychology* 55:589–612, 2002.

25. Ibid.

26. Campion, M. A. Interdisciplinary approaches to job design: A constructive replication with extensions. *Journal of Applied Psychology* 73:467–481, 1988; and Campion, M. A., & Thayer., P. W. Development and field evaluation of an interdisciplinary measure of job design. *Journal of Applied Psychology* 70:29–43, 1985.

27. Risher, H. Job evaluation: Validity and reliability. *Compensation and Benefits Review*, January—February 1989, p. 24.

28. Harvey, R. J. Book review, *Functional job analysis* by Sidney A. Fine and Steven F. Cronshaw. *Personnel Psychology* 55:202–204, 2002; Harvey, R. J. Job analysis. In M. D. Dunnette & L. Hough (eds.), *Handbook of industrial and organizational psychology*. Palo Alto, CA: Consulting Psychologists Press, 1991, pp. 2, 71–163.

29. Fine, S. A., & Wiley, W. W. *An introduction to functional job analysis*. Kalamazoo, MI: W.E. Upjohn Institute for Employment Research, 1971.

30. Jackson, S. E., Schuler, R. S., & Rivero, J. C. Organizational characteristics as predictors of personnel practices. *Personnel Psychology* 42:727–786, 1989; Miles, R., & Snow, C. C. Designing strategic human resource systems. *Organizational Dynamics* 13:36–52, 1984; and Delery, J. E., & Doty, D. H. Modes of theorizing in strategic human resource management: Tests of universalistic, contingency, and configurational performance predictions. *Academy of Management Journal* 39:802–835, 1996.

31. Hall, R. H. *Organizations: Structures, processes, and outcomes*, 8th ed. Upper Saddle River, NJ: Prentice Hall, 2002.

32. Brownfield, E. *2005 national study of employers reveals changes in work life assistance offered to America's employees*, October 13, 2005, www.familiesandwork.org/site/newsroom/releases/2005nse.html.

33. Small firms embrace flexible working. *Management Services* 48(11):4, November 2004.

34. Kok, J. D., & Uhlaner, L. M. Organization context and human resource management in the small firm. *Small Business Economics*, December 2001, pp 273–291.

35. Schein, E. H. *Organizational culture and leadership.* San Francisco: Jossey-Bass, 1985.

36. Harris, J. H., & Arendt, L. A. Stress reduction and the small business: Increasing employee and customer satisfaction. *SAM Advanced Management Journal*, Winter 1998, pp. 27–34.

37. Kacmar, K. M. Carlson, D. S., Bratton, V. K., & Andrews, M. C. *An integrated perspective of antecedents to ingratiatory behaviors.* Paper presented at the National Academy of Management Meetings, Seattle, WA, August 2003; and Kahn, R. L., et al. *Organizational stress.* New York: Wiley, 1964.

38. Kahn, R. L., et al. *Organizational stress.* New York: Wiley, 1964.. See also Walls, G. D., Capella, L. M., & Greene, W. E. Toward a source stressors model of conflict between work and family. *Review of Business* 22:86–91, 2001.

39. U.S. Bureau of Labor Statistics. *Table 30: Flexible schedules: Full-time wage and salary workers by selected characteristics*, May 2004, www.bls.gov/cps/wlf-table30-2007.pdf.

40. Huff, C. With flextime, less can be more. *Workforce Management*, May 2005, pp. 65–70.

41. Latack, J. C., & Foster, L. W. Implementation of compressed work schedules: Participation and job redesign as critical factors for employee acceptance. *Personnel Psychology* 38:75–93, 1985.

42. Ronen, S., & Primps, S. B. The compressed work week as organizational change: Behavioral and attitudinal outcomes. *Academy of Management Review* 6:61–74, 1981.

43. Smith, P. A., & Wedderburn, A. A. I. Flexibility and long shifts. *Employee Relations* 20:483–489, 1998.

44. Have you considered job sharing as a retention tool? *HR Focus*, September 2006, 83(9):10–11.

45. Nollen, S. Job-sharing. *Blackwell encyclopedic dictionary of human resource management.* Oxford, UK: Blackwell Publishing, 2005, pp. 213–213.

46. Bond, J. Galinsky, E., Kim, S. S., & Brownfield, E. *2005 National Study of Employers*, http://familiesandwork.org/site/research/summary/2005nsesumm.pdf.

47. Myths about job sharing. *T+D*, July 2007, 61(7):14.

48. Arthur, M. M. Share price reactions to work-family initiatives: An institutional perspective. *Academy of Management Journal* 46:497–505, 2003.

49. Mullich, J. They don't retire them, they hire them. *Workforce Magazine*, December 2003, pp. 49–54.

50. Ibid.

51. Ibid.

52. Ibid.

53. Mariani, M. Telecommuters. *Occupational Outlook Quarterly*, Fall 2000, pp. 10–17.

54. Stanford, P. Managing remote workers. *Executive Excellence*, June 2003, p. 6; and *Telework Statistics. Number of teleworkers in U.S.* http://www.suitecommute.com/Statistics.htm#Numberof Teleworkers

55. Bednarz, A. *Telework thrives at AT&T*, December 19, 2005, www.networkworld.com/net.worker/news/2005/121905-att-telework.html.

56. Solomon, C. M., Don't forget your telecommuters. *Workforce*, May 2000, pp. 56–63; and Richmond, R. It's 10:00 a.m. Do you know where your workers are? *Wall Street Journal,* January 12, 2004.

57. Kirkman, B. L., Rosen, B., Tesluk, P. E., & Gibson, C. B. The impact of team empowerment on virtual team performance: The moderating influence of face-to-face interaction. *Academy of Management Journal* 2:175–192, 2004; Lipnack, J., & Stamps, J. *Virtual teams: People working across boundaries with technology.* 2nd ed. New York: Wiley, 2000.

58. Ibid.

59. Townsend, A. M., DeMarie, S. M., & Hendrickson, A. R. Virtual teams: Technology and the workplace of the future. *Academy of Management Executive* 12:17–29, 1998.

60. Malhotra, A., Majchrzak, A., & Rosen, B. Leading virtual teams: Table 1: Practices of effective virtual teams. *Academy of Management Perspectives* 21:61–70, February 2007.

61. Next: Flexible upper lips. *Monthly Labor Review* 127(5):44, May 2004.

62. Harris, J. H., & Arendt, L. A. Stress reduction and the small business: Increasing employee and customer satisfaction. *SAM Advanced Management Journal*, Winter 1998, pp. 27–34.

63. Directors have best jobs and lowest stress. *Teachers Union College, Risk* 160, June 12, 2004, http://www.tuc.org.uk/h_and_s/tuc-8152-f0.cfm; and *Public contact adds job stress.* BBC News. June 8, 2004. http://news.bbc.co.uk/1/hi/uk/3789173.stm

64. National Institute for Occupational Safety and Health. et al. *Stress . . . at work*, www.cdc.gov/niosh/stresswk.html.

65. International Ergonomics Association. What is Ergonomics?, http://www.iea.cc/browse.php?contID=what_is_ergonomics/.

66. Heine, H. J. Ergonomics—A neglected science. *Foundry Management & Technology*, July 1999, pp. 28–30.

67. Croasmun, J. Office workers choose ergonomics over morale. *Ergonomics Today*, June 30, 2004, www.ergoweb.com/news/detail.cfm?id=950.

68. Paull, P., Kuijer, F. M., Visser, B., & Kemper, H. C. G. Job rotation as a factor in reducing physical workload at a refuse collecting department. *Ergonomics* 42:1167–1178, 1999.

69. U.S. Equal Employment Opportunity Commission. *Disability discrimination*, www.eeoc.gov/types/ada.html.

70. U.S. Equal Employment Opportunity Commission. *Question and answers: Policy guidance on Executive Order 13164: Establishing procedures to facilitate the provision of reasonable accommodation*, October 19, 2000, www.eeoc.gov/policy/docs/qanda-accommodation_procedures.html.

71. Occupational Safety and Health Administration. *OSHA's mission*, www.osha.gov/oshinfo/mission.html.

72. Fine, S. A., & Wiley, W. W. *An introduction to functional job analysis.* Kalamazoo, MI: W.E. Upjohn Institute for Employment Research, 1971.

73. U.S. Department of Labor. *United States Department of Labor Dictionary of Occupational Titles Fourth Edition, Revised 1991*, www.oalj.dol.gov/libdot.htm.

74. U.S. Department of Labor. *O*NET—Beyond information—Intelligence*, www.doleta.gov/programs/onet/

75. U.S. Department of Labor. *The O*NET Data Collection Program*, www.doleta.gov/programs/onet/datacollection.cfm

76. Friedman, L., & Harvey, R. J. Can raters with reduced job descriptive information provide accurate position analyses questionnaire (PAQ) ratings? *Personnel Psychology* 39:779–789, 1986.

77. Brannick, M. T., & Levine, E. L. *Job analysis: Methods, research, and applications for human resource management in the new millennium.* Thousand Oaks, CA: Sage Publications, 2002, p. 41.

78. McCormick, E. J., Jeanneret, P. J., & Mecham, R. C. A study of job characteristics and job dimensions as based on the position analysis questionnaire (PAQ). *Journal of Applied Psychology Monograph* 56:347–368, 1972; and Arvey, R. D., Salas, E., & Gialluca, K. A. Using task inventories to forecast skills and abilities. *Human Performance* 5(3):171–190, 1992.

79. Cornelius, E. T., III, DeNisi, A. S., & Blencoe, A. G. Expert and naive raters using the PAQ: Does it matter? *Personnel Psychology* 37: 453–464, 1984.

80. Bownas, D., & Bernardin, H. J. The critical incident method. In S. Gael (ed.), *The job analysis handbook for business, industry, and government*, Volume II. New York: Wiley, 1988, pp. 1120–1137.

81. Arvey, R. D., Salas, E., & Gialluca, K. A. Using task inventories to forecast skills and abilities. *Human Performance* 5(3):171–190, 1992.

82. Ibid.

83. Brannick, M. T., & Levine, E. L. *Job analysis: Methods, research, and applications for human resource management in the new millennium.* Thousand Oaks, CA: Sage Publications, 2002, p. 41.

84. Ibid.

Chapter 5

1. Pressman, A. Should the Dow ditch general motors? *BusinessWeek*, January 9, 2006, p. 34.

2. Krebs, M. The starting line. *Automotive News* 77:16, 2003; Putting America on wheels, December 23, 1999, www.economist.com/diversions/millennium/PrinterFriendly.cfm?story_id=347288; and Harrington, A. The big ideas. *Fortune* 140:98–103, November 22, 1999.

3. Welch, D. What my dad taught me about GM and the auto workers. *BusinessWeek*, November 7, 2005, p. 48; Pressman, A. Should the Dow ditch general motors? *BusinessWeek*, January 9, 2006, p. 34; and David, H. Can GM stop blowing cash? *BusinessWeek*, November 21, 2005, pp. 50–52.

4. Maurer, H. Downsizing in Detroit. *BusinessWeek*, December 5, 2005, p. 32.

5. Maynard, N. Ford eliminating up to 30,000 jobs and 14 factories. *New York Times,* January 24, 2006. http://www.nytimes.com/2006/01/24/automobiles/24ford.html?_r=1&pagewanted=2&oref=slogin

6. Haglund, R. GM offers early exit. *The Saginaw News* online, January 18, 2008, www.mlive.com/business/saginawnews/index.ssf?/base/business-2/1200669621115980.xml&coll=9.

7. Bates, S. Expert: Don't overlook employee burnout. *HR Magazine*, 48:14, August 2003; and Enterprises struggle to combat IT burnout. *Business Communications Review* 33:6, May 2003.

8. Shaw, J. D., Delery, J. E., Jenkins, G. D., Jr., & Gupta., N. An organization-level analysis of voluntary and involuntary turnover. *Academy of Management Journal* 41:511–525, 1998.

9. Henneman, T. Peer-coaching helps WFS financial curb turnover, *Workforce* online, February 2005, www.workforce.com/archive/article/23/93/77.php.

10. King, R. Turnover is the new enemy at one of America's oldest restaurant chains. *Workforce* online, April 2004, www.workforce.com/section/06/feature/23/68/40/.

11. Wendy's International chairman, CEO dies; successor isn't named. *Wall Street Journal*, December 20, 1999, p. 1.

12. Mahoney, H. A. Productivity defined: The relativity of efficiency, effectiveness, and change. In J. P. Campbell, et al. (eds.), *Productivity in organizations*. San Francisco, CA: Jossey-Bass, 1988, pp. 13–39.

13. Brockner, J., Greenberg, J., Brockner, A., Bortz, J., Davy, J, & Carter, C. Layoffs, equity theory, and work performance: Further evidence of the impact of survivor guilt. *Academy of Management Journal* 29:373–384, 1986.

14. Cascio, W. F. *Applied psychology in personnel management.* Englewood Cliffs, NJ: Prentice Hall, 1991.

15. Hitt, M. A., Ireland, R. D., & Hoskisson, R. E. *Strategic management: Competitiveness and globalization*, 6th ed. Cincinnati, OH: Thomson, South-Western, 2005.

16. German jobless rates at new record. *BBC News*, March 1, 2005, http://news.bbc.co.uk/1/hi/business/4307303.stm.

17. Apple. *iPod classic: Technical specifications*, www.apple.com/ipod/specs.html.

18. U.S. Department of Labor. *DOL's FairPay overtime initiative*, www.dol.gov/esa/regs/compliance/whd/fairpay/main.htm.

19. Robertson, S. Wheeling-Pitt outsourcing cuts logistics costs. *American Metal Market*, October 4, 2002; and Davis, C. Some steelmakers look for savings by outsourcing shipping operations. *Pittsburg Business Times*, January 10, 2003.

20. Houseman, S. N. Why employers use flexible staffing arrangements: Evidence from an establishment survey. *Industrial and Labor Relations Review* 55:149–170, 2001.

21. U.S. Department of Labor. *Contingent and alternative employment arrangements, February 2005*, July 25, 2005, www.bls.gov/news. release/conemp.nr0.htm; and Bureau of Labor Statistics. *Contingent and alternative employment arrangements, February 2005*, July 27, 2005, www.bls.gov/news.release/pdf/conemp.pdf.

22. David, J. The unexpected employee and organizational costs of skilled contingent workers. *Human Resource Planning*, June 2005, pp. 32–41; Lepak, D. P., & Snell, S. A. The human resource architecture: Toward a theory of human capital allocation and development. *Academy of Management Review* 24:31–48, 1999; and Zappe, J. Tracking the cost-benefit of using contingent employees. *Workforce* online, May 2005, www.workforce.com/archive/article/24/05/46.php.

23. Shuit, D. P. People problems on every aisle. *Workforce*, February 2004, pp. 27–34; and Wal-Mart. *Diversity is a way of life at Wal-Mart*. http://walmartfacts.com/FactSheets/Employment_and_Diversity.pdf.

24. Trevor, C. O. Interactions among actual ease of movement determinants and job satisfaction in the prediction of voluntary turnover. *Academy of Management Journal* 44:621–638, 2001.

25. Phone firm KPN to cut 8,000 jobs. *BBC News*, http://news.bbc.co.uk/2/hi/business/4307139.stm.

26. Michaels, D. British Airways puts focus back on service: passengers take precedence as competition intensifies, cost-cut options dry up. *Wall Street Journal*, March 2, 2005, p. A6.

27. Hitt, M. A., Ireland, R. D., & Hoskisson, R. E. *Strategic management: Competitiveness and globalization*, 6th ed. Cincinnati, OH: Thomson, South-Western, 2005.

28. Greenhalgh, L., Lawrence, L. T., & Sutton, R. I. Determinants of work force reduction strategies in declining organizations. *Academy of Management Review* 13:241–254, 1988; Brockner, J., Davy, J., & Carger, C. Layoffs, self-esteem, and survivor guilt.

Organizational Behavior and Human Decision Processes 36:229–244, 1985; Sutton, R. I. Managing organizational death. *Human Resource Management* 22:391–412, 1983; and Staw, B. M., Sandlelands, L. E., & Dutton, J. E. Threat-rigidity effects in organizational behavior: A multilevel analysis. *Administrative Science Quarterly* 26:501–524, 1981.

29. Ihrke, D. M., & Johnson, T. L. Regional variations in burnout rates in a natural resources agency. *Journal of Health & Human Services Administration*, Summer 2002, pp. 48–74; and Lindquist, C. A., & Whitehead, J. T. Burnout, job stress, and job satisfaction among southern correctional officers: Perceptions and causal factors. *Journal of Offender Counseling: Services and Rehabilitation* 10:5–26, 1986.

30. Haglund, R. GM offers early exit. *The Saginaw News* online, January 18, 2008, www.mlive.com/business/saginawnews/index.ssf?/base/business-2/1200669621115980.xml&coll=9.

31. Kiger, P. J. Early-retirement offers that work too well. *Workforce Management*, January 2004, pp. 66–68.

32. Lepak, D. P., & Snell, S. A. Examining the human resource architecture: The relationships among human capital, employment, and human resource configurations. *Journal of Management* 28:517–543, 2002.

33. Robb, D. Succeeding with succession. *HR Magazine*, January 2005, pp. 89–95.

34. Ibid.

35. Greenhalgh, L., Lawrence, A. T., & Sutton, R. I. Determinants of workforce reduction strategies in declining organizations. *Academy of Management Review* 13:241–254, 1988.

36. Conlin, M. Where layoffs are a last resort: Treating them as unthinkable can have big benefits. *BusinessWeek* online, October 8, 2001, www.businessweek.com/magazine/content/01_41/b3752712.htm.

37. Mishra, A. K., & Sprietzer, G. M. Explaining how survivors respond to downsizing: The roles of trust, empowerment, justice, and work redesign. *Academy of Management Review* 23:567–588, 1998.

38. Proctor, S. P., et al. Effect of overtime work on cognitive function in automotive workers. *Scandinavian Journal of Work, Environmental, and Health* 22:124–132, April 1996.

39. Brockner, J., Greenberg, J., Brockner, A., Bortz, J., Davy, J., and Carter, C. Interactive effects of procedural justice and outcome negativity on victims and survivors of job loss. *Academy of Management Journal* 37:397–409, 1994.

40. Greenhalgh, L., Lawrence, A. T., & Sutton, R. I. Determinants of work force reduction strategies in declining organizations. *Academy of Management Review* 13:241–254, 1988; and Brockner, J. Why it's so hard to be fair. *Harvard Business Review*, March, 2006, pp. 122–129.

41. Toosi, M. Labor force projections to 2012: The graying of the workforce. *Monthly Labor Review*, February 2004, pp. 37–57.

42. Lockwood, N. R. The aging workforce: The reality of the impact of older workers and eldercare in the workplace. *HRMagazine*, December 2003, http://findarticles.com/p/articles/mi_m3495/is_12_48/ai_n5989579.

43. Weintraub, A. Nursing: On the critical list. *BusinessWeek* online, May 28, 2002, www.businessweek.com/careers/content/may2002/ca20020528_7551.htm.

44. Ibid.

45. Canik, A., Crawford, C., & Longnecker, B. Combating the future "retirement gap" with tailored total rewards. *IHRIM Journal*, September/October 2004, pp. 32–37.

46. Mullich, J. They don't retire them, they hire them. *Workforce Management*, December 2003, pp. 49–54.

47. Cutler, D. M., & Madrain, B. C. Labor market responses to rising health insurance costs: Evidence on hours worked. *RAND Journal of Economics* 29:509–530, Autumn 1998.

48. Dean, J. W., Jr., & Snell, S. A. Integrated manufacturing and job design: Moderating effects of organizational inertia. *Academy of Management Journal* 34:776–804, 1991.

49. Aeppel, T. Firms' new grail: Skilled workers. U.S. Manufacturers report shortages are widespread; critics cite training cuts. *Wall Street Journal*, November 22, 2005, p. A2.

50. Snell, S. A., Lepak, D. P., Dean, J. W., Jr., & Youndt, M. A. Selection and training for integrated manufacturing: The moderating effects of job characteristics. *Journal of Management Studies* 37:445–466, 2000; MacDuffie, J. P. Human resource bundles and manufacturing performance: Organizational logic and flexible production systems in the world auto industry. *Industrial and Labor Relations Review* 48:197–221, 1995; Zuboff, S. *In the age of the smart machine: The future of work and power.* New York: Basic Books, 1988; and Walton, R. E., & Susman, R. I. People policies for the new machines. *Harvard Business Review* 65:98–106, 1987.

51. Lynch, L. M. Job loss: Bridging the research and policy discussion. *Economic Perspectives*, 2nd Quarter 2005, pp. 29–37.

52. Hendrickson, A. R. Human resource information systems: Backbone technology of contemporary human resources. *Journal of Labor Research* 24:381–394, 2003.

53. Byrnes, N. Star search: How to recruit, train, and hold on to great people. What works, what doesn't. *BusinessWeek*, October 10, 2005, pp. 68–78.

54. Patterson, B., & Lindsey, S. Weighing resources: Technology can streamline workforce planning and cost analysis. *HRMagazine*, October 2003, pp. 103–108.

55. Solomon, C. M. Managing virtual teams. *Workforce* 80:60–65, June 2001; Reich, R. B. Plenty of knowledge work to go around. *Harvard Business Review*, April 17, 2005.

56. Thibodeau, P. Offshoring fuels IT hiring boom in India. *Computerworld*, October 18, 2004, p. 8.

57. Kripalani, M. India's skills crunch: As the economy booms, companies scramble to find trained workers. *BusinessWeek*, November 7, 2005, pp. 54–55; and The perils of unskilled labor. *BusinessWeek*, November 7, 2005, p. 148.

58. International Labour Organization. *ILO projects global economic turbulence could generate five million more unemployed in 2008*, January 23, 2008, www.ilo.org/global/About_the_ILO/Media_and_public_information/Press_releases/lang—en/WCMS_090085/index.htm.

59. Patel, V. India, Inc. *Newsweek*, December 14, 2005.

60. Lakshman, N. Where the jobs are: Subcontinental drift. *BusinessWeek*, January 16, 2006, pp. 42–43.

61. Patel, V. India, Inc. *Newsweek*, December 14, 2005.

62. Thibodeau, P. Offshoring fuels IT hiring boom in India. *Computerworld*, October 18, 2004, p. 8; Thottam, J. Is your job going abroad? *Time*, February 23, 2004; Waldman, A. More "Can I help you" jobs migrate from U.S. to India. *New York Times*, May 11, 2003; and Porter, E. Not many jobs are sent abroad, U.S. report says. *The New York Times*, June 11, 2004.

63. Ewing, J. Based in New Jersey, thriving in Bulgaria. *BusinessWeek*, December 12, 2005, p. 54.

64. Solomon, J. India becomes collection hub: Low-cost workers help U.S. firms pursue debtors; local companies go abroad. *Wall Street Journal*, December 6, 2004, p. A13.

65. Aron, R., & Singh, J. V. Getting offshoring right. *Harvard Business Review*, December 2005, pp. 135–143; and Lepak, D. P., & Snell, S. A. Employment sub-systems and changing forms of employment. In P. Boxall, J. Purcell, & P. Wright (eds.), *Oxford handbook of human resource management*. Oxford, UK: Oxford University Press. Pp. 210–230.

66. Kripalani, M. Five offshore practices that pay off. *BusinessWeek*, January 30, 2006, pp. 60–61.

67. Lepak, D. P., & Snell, S. A. Employment sub-systems and changing forms of employment. In P. Boxall, J. Purcell, & P. Wright (eds.), *Oxford handbook of human resource management*. Oxford, UK: Oxford University Press. Pp. 210–230.

68. U.S. Department of Labor. *20 CFR 639.1—Purpose and scope*, April 20, 1989, www.dol.gov/dol/allcfr/ETA/Title_20/Part_639/20CFR639.1. htm.

69. DeGroff, C. J. Desperate measures: Invoking WARN's unforeseeable business circumstances. *Employee Relations Law Journal* 28:55–73, Winter 2002.

70. U.S. Department of Labor. *The Worker Adjustment and Retraining Notification Act: A guide to advance notice of closings and layoffs*, www.doleta.gov/programs/factsht/warn.htm; and DeMeuse, K. P., & Dobrovolsky, E. The worker adjustment and retraining notification act: A closer look. *Human Resource Planning*, 2004, pp. 19–22.

71. Internal Revenue Service. *Independent contractors vs. employees*, www.irs.gov/businesses/small/article/0,,id=99921,00.html; and Stumpj, M. L., & Sprohge, H. Independent contractor or not? *Journal of Accountancy*, May 2004, pp. 89–95.

72. Stumpj, M. L., & Sprohge, H. Independent contractor or not? *Journal of Accountancy*, May 2004, pp. 89–95.

73. Ibid.

Chapter 6

1. For more comprehensive discussion of the recruitment process, see Barber, A. E. (1998). *Recruiting employees: Individual and organizational perspectives*. Thousand Oaks, CA: Sage; and Breaugh, J. A., & Starke, M. Research on employee recruitment: So many studies, so many remaining questions. *Journal of Management* 26:405–434, 2000.

2. Morton, L. *Integrated and integrative talent management: A strategic HR framework*. New York: The Conference Board, 2004.

3. Breaugh, J. A., & Starke, M. Research on employee recruitment: So many studies, so many remaining questions. *Journal of Management* 26:405–434, 2000.

4. Harris, J., & Brannick, J. *Finding & keeping great employees.* New York: American Management Association, 1999.

5. Breaugh, J. A., & Starke, M. Research on employee recruitment: So many studies, so many remaining questions. *Journal of Management* 26:405–434, 2000.

6. Ibid.

7. Cintas. *Career paths*, www.cintas.com/careers/faqs/#12.

8. Frase-Blunt, M. Intranet fuels internal mobility. *Employment Management Today*, Spring 2004, www.shrm.org/ema/EMT/articles/2004/spring04cover.asp.

9. Ibid.

10. *Washington Post* Web site, February 3, 2008, www.washingtonpost.com.

11. CareerBuilder.com Web site, www.careerbuilder.com.

12. Maurer, S., & Liu, Y. Developing effective e-recruiting websites: Insights for managers from marketers. *Business Horizons* 50:305–314, 2007.

13. Williamson, I. O., Lepak, D., & King, J. The effect of company recruitment website orientation on individuals' perceptions of organizational attractiveness. *Journal of Vocational Behavior* 63:242–263, 2003.

14. Monster.com Web site, July 26, 2004, www.monster.com.

15. Frase-Blunt, M. Make a good first impression. *HRMagazine*, April 2004, www.shrm.org/hrmagazine/articles/0404/0404f-b.asp.

16. Floren, J. Constructing a campus recruiting network. *Employment Management Today*, Spring 2004, www.shrm.org/ema/EMT/articles/2004/spring04floren.asp.

17. Internship programs: What candidates find appealing. *Workforce*, April 2004, www.workforce.com/archive/article/23/68/53.php.

18. Business Owner's Toolkit. *Public employment services*, www.toolkit.cch.com/text/P05_0705.asp.

19. A recruiting spigot. *HRMagazine*, April 2003, www.shrm.org/hrmagazine/articles/0403/0403frase_defined.asp.

20. Ibid.

21. Overman, S. Searching for the top. *HRMagazine*, January 2008, p. 53.

22. Frase-Blunt, M. A recruiting spigot. *HRMagazine*, April 2003, www.shrm.org/hrmagazine/articles/0403/0403frase.asp.

23. SRI International. *Employee referral program*, www.sri.com/jobs/referral.html.

24. Breaugh, J. A. *Recruitment: Science and practice.* Boston: PWS-Kent, 1992.

25. Frase-Blunt, M. A recruiting spigot. *HRMagazine*, April 2003, www.shrm.org/hrmagazine/articles/0403/0403frase.asp.

26. Frauenheim, E. Company profile: Recruiters get LinkedIn in search of job candidates, *Workforce Management*, November 2006.

27. Casino careers online ensures confidentiality of candidate information. *BusinessWire*, August 27, 1999. For additional information on sourcing applicants online, see also Heritage, G., & Davidson, S. *Recruiter smarts—Part IX: Creative sourcing and networking—The Internet*, http://hr.monster.ca/articles/recruiter_smarts9/.

28. Align, perform, reward. *Personnel Today*, May 10,2005, p. 16.

29. Marriott, J. W., Jr. Our competitive strength: Human capital. *Executive Speeches* 15:18–21, 2001.

30. Chambers, E. G., et al. The war for talent. *The McKinsey Quarterly*, 1998, 3, p. 1.

31. Harris, J., & Brannick, J. *Finding & keeping great employees.* New York: American Management Association, 1999.

32. Barber, A. E. *Recruiting employees.* Thousand Oaks, CA: Sage Publications, 1998.

33. Michaels, E., Handfield-Jones, H., & Axelrod, B. *The war for talent.* Boston: Harvard Business School Press, 2001.

34. Cable, D. M., & Judge, T. A. Person–organization fit, job choice decisions, and organizational entry. *Organizational Behavior and Human Decision Processes* 67:294–311, 1996; and Turban, D. B., Eyring, A. R., & Campion, J. E. Job attributes: Preferences compared with reasons given for accepting and rejecting job offers. *Journal of Occupational and Organizational Psychology* 66:71–81, 1993.

35. Backhaus, K., & Tikoo, S. Conceptualizing and researching employer branding. *Career Development International* 9:501, 2004.

36. Align, perform, reward. *Personnel Today*, May 10, 2005, p. 16.

37. For a more complete discussion of what works and what doesn't in recruiting employees, see Breaugh, J. A., & Starke, M. Research on employee recruitment: So many studies, so many remaining questions. *Journal of Management* 26:405–434, 2000.

38. Barber, A. E. *Recruiting employees: Individual and organizational perspectives.* Thousand Oaks, CA: Sage Publications, 1998; and Breaugh, J. A., & Starke, M. Research on employee recruitment: So many studies, so many remaining questions. *Journal of Management* 26:405–434, 2000.

39. Michaels, E., Handfield-Jones, H., & Axelrod, B. *The war for talent.* Boston: Harvard Business School Press, 2001.

40. Barber, A. E., & Roehling, M. V. Job posting and the decision to interview: A verbal protocol analysis. *Journal of Applied Psychology* 78:845–856, 1993. See also Maurer, S. D., Howe, V., & Lee, T. W. Organizational recruiting as marketing management: An interdisciplinary study of engineering students. *Personnel Psychology* 45:807–833, 1992.

41. Rynes, S. L., Bretz, R. D., & Gerhart, B. The importance of recruitment in job choice: A different way of looking. *Personnel Psychology* 44:487–521, 1991.

42. Rynes, S. L. Recruitment, job choice, and post-hire consequences: A call for new research directions. In M. D. Dunnette (ed.), *Handbook of industrial and organizational psychology*, 2nd ed. Palo Alto, CA: Consulting Psychologists Press, 1991, pp. 399–444.

43. Sleeper, B. J., & Walter, R. J. Employee recruitment and retention: When company inducements trigger liability. *Review of Business*, 2002, 23, p. 17–22.

44. Saks, A. M., & Cronshaw, S. F. A process investigation of realistic job previews: Mediating variables and channels of communication. *Journal of Organizational Behavior* 11:221–236, 1990.

45. Wanous, J. P. *Organizational entry: Recruitment, selection, orientation, and socialization of newcomers*, 2nd ed. Reading, MA: Addison-Wesley, 1992.

46. Huff, C. Hospital aims for culture where employees "never want to leave." *Workforce Management* online, February 2005, www.workforce.com/section/06/feature/23/94/76/.

47. Shermont, H., & Murphy, J. Shadowing: A winning recruitment tool. *Nursing Management* 37:30–34, 40, 2006.

48. Porter, M. E. *Competitive advantage: Creating and sustaining superior performance.* New York: The Free Press, 1985.

49. Wanous, J. P. *Organizational entry: Recruitment, selection, orientation, and socialization of newcomers*, 2nd ed. Reading, MA: Addison-Wesley, 1992.

50. Time to start focusing on attracting older workers. *HR Focus* 81:13–14, 2004.

51. Lockwood, N. The reality of the impact of older workers and eldercare in the workplace. *HRMagazine* 48:A1, 2003.

52. Time to start focusing on attracting older workers. *HR Focus* 81:13–14, 2004.

53. Meet needs of older workers to avoid brain drain. *Inc.com*, April 2000, www.inc.com/articles/2000/04/18660.html.

54. Avon. *Awards & recognition for Avon*, www.avoncompany.com/responsibility/awards/index.html.

55. Williams, J. M. Cisco beats a path to disabled workers. *BusinessWeek* online, January 18, 2001, www.businessweek.com/bwdaily/dnflash/jan2001/nf20010118_432.htm.

56. Blind hope employers can see through misconceptions. *CNN.com*, August 3, 1999, www.cnn.com/US/9908/03/blind.unemployment/.

57. Ibid.

58. Perkins, L. A., Thomas, K. M., & Taylor, G. A. Advertising and recruitment: Marketing to minorities. *Psychology & Marketing* 17:235–255, 2000. See also Avery, D. R. Reactions to diversity in recruitment advertising—Are differences black and white? *Journal of Applied Psychology* 88:672–680, 2003.

59. Hoffman, T. 8 new ways to target top talent in '08. *Computerworld* 42:34–36, 2008.

60. Stern, L. Just don't ask if they're in their PJs. *Newsweek* 145:1,3, 2005.

61. Gowan, M. Development of the recruitment value proposition for geocentric staffing: Influence of cultural differences and previous international experience. *Thunderbird International Business Review* 46:678–708, 2004.

62. Overman, S. Recruiting in China. *HR Magazine*, 46, No. 3 March: 86, 2001.

63. Alenn, M. Recruiting in Baja California Tijuana is a qualified success. *Workforce Management Online,* May 22, 2007.

64. Antun, J., Strick, S., & Thomas, L. Exploring culture and diversity for Hispanics in restaurant online recruitment efforts. *Journal of Human Resources in Hospitality & Tourism* 6:85–107, 2007.

65. D'Agostino, D. Global recruiting: Star search. *CIO Insight*, March 26, 2006, www.cioinsight.com/article2/0,1540,1940172,00.asp.

66. 100 best companies to work for, 2008. *Fortune*, http://money.cnn.com/magazines/fortune/bestcompanies/2008/.

67. Sims, R. *Ethics and corporate social responsibility: Why giants fall.* Westport, CT: Praeger, 2003.

68. Walter, R., & Sleeper, B. Employee recruitment and retention: When company inducements trigger liability. *Review of Business* 23:17+, 2002.

69. Hansen, F. Avoiding truth-in-hiring lawsuits. *Workforce Management*, December 2007.

70. Myers, R. Ensuring ethical effectiveness: New rules mean virtually every company will need a code of ethics. *Journal of Accountancy* 195:28+, 2003.

71. Trofimov, Y., & Taylor, E. A tall order: As private banking booms in Singapore, demand for managers soars. *Wall Street Journal*, February 12, 2007, p. C2.

72. Joinson, C. Top-notch recruiting practices. *Employment Management Today*, Summer 2003, www.taleo.com/news/media/pdf/81En_20030701_EmployementMgt.pdf.

73. Joinson, C. Making a good match. *Employment Management Today*, Winter 2004, www.shrm.org/ema/EMT/articles/2004/winter04joinson.asp.

Chapter 7

1. Job applications for Southwest Airlines increase due to TV series. *Airline Industry Information*, June 18, 2004, p. 1.

2. Joinson, C. Capturing turnover costs. *HRMagazine* 45:107–118, 2000.

3. Kristof-Brown, A. L., Jansen, K. J., & Colbert, A. E. A policy-capturing study of the simultaneous effects of fit with jobs, groups, and organizations. *Journal of Applied Psychology* 87:985–983, 2002.

4. Caldwell, D. F., & O'Reilly, C. A., III. Measuring person–job fit with a profile comparison process. *Journal of Applied Psychology* 15:648–657, 1990.

5. U.S. Department of Labor. *Testing and assessment: An employer's guide to good practices.* Washington, DC: U.S. Department of Labor, Employment and Training Administration, 2000.

6. Gatewood, R. D., & Feild, H. S. *Human resource selection.* New York: Harcourt, 2001.

7. Posthuma, R. A., Morgeson, F. P., & Campion, M. A. Beyond employment interview validity: A comprehensive narrative review of recent research and trends over time. *Personnel Psychology* 55:1–81, 2002.

8. Arthur, W., Jr., Woehr, D. J., & Graziano, W. G. Personality testing in employment settings: Problems and issues in the application of typical selection practices. *Personnel Review* 30:657–676, 2001.

9. Gatewood, R. D., & Feild, H. S. *Human resource selection.* New York: Harcourt, 2001.

10. Woodward, N. H. The function of forms. *HR Magazine.* January 2000, pp. 67–73.

11. Klinvex, K. C., O'Connell, M. S., & Klinvex, C. P. *Hiring great people.* New York: McGraw-Hill, 1999.

12. Silverman, R. E. Career journal: The jungle. *Wall Street Journal*, December 5, 2000, p. B16.

13. Schmidt, F. L., & Hunter, J. E. The validity and utility of selection methods in personnel psychology: Practical and theoretical implications of 85 years of research findings. *Psychological Bulletin* 124:262–274, 1989; and Chun-Yan, G. A., & Cronshaw, S. F. A critical re-examination and analysis of cognitive ability tests using the Thorndike model of fairness. *Journal of Occupational and Organizational Psychology* 75:489–509, 2002.

14. Berry, C., Gruys, M., & Sackett, P. Educational attainment as a proxy for cognitive ability in selection: Effects on level of cognitive ability and adverse impact. *Journal of Applied Psychology* 91:696–705, 2006.

15. Hakel, M. D. *Beyond multiple choice: Evaluating alternatives to traditional testing for selection.* Hillsdale, NJ: Lawrence Erlbaum Associates, 1998.

16. Chun-Yan, G. A., & Cronshaw, S. F. A critical re-examination and analysis of cognitive ability tests using the Thorndike model of fairness. *Journal of Occupational and Organizational Psychology* 75:489–509, 2002.

17. U.S. Department of Labor. *Testing and assessment: An employer's guide to good practices.* Washington, DC: U.S. Department of Labor, Employment and Training Administration, 2000.

18. Ibid.

19. Schmidt, F. L., & Hunter, J. E. The validity and utility of selection methods in personnel psychology: Practical and theoretical implications of 85 years of research findings. *Psychological Bulletin* 124:262–274, 1998.

20. Hausknecht, J. P., Day, D. V., & Thomas, S. C. Applicant reactions to selection procedures: An updated model and meta-analysis. *Personnel Psychology* 57:639–683, 2004.

21. U.S. Department of Labor. *Testing and assessment: An employer's guide to good practices.* Washington, DC: U.S. Department of Labor, Employment and Training Administration, 2000.

22. Ibid.

23. Schmidt, F. L., & Hunter, J. E. The validity and utility of selection methods in personnel psychology: Practical and theoretical

implications of 85 years of research findings. *Psychological Bulletin* 124:262–274, 1998.

24. Gatewood, R. D., & Feild, H. S. *Human resource selection.* New York: Harcourt, 2001.

25. Ibid.

26. Furnham, A., & Fudge, C. The five factor model of personality and sales performance. *Journal of Individual Differences* 29:11–16, 2008.

27. U.S. Department of Labor. *Testing and assessment: An employer's guide to good practices.* Washington, DC: U.S. Department of Labor, Employment and Training Administration, 2000.

28. Emmett, A. Snake oil or science? *Workforce Management*, October 2004, pp. 90–92.

29. Gatewood, R. D., & Feild, H. S. *Human resource selection.* New York: Harcourt, 2001; and U.S. Department of Labor. *Testing and assessment: An employer's guide to good practices.* Washington, DC: U.S. Department of Labor, Employment and Training Administration, 2000.

30. U.S. Department of Labor. *Testing and assessment: An employer's guide to good practices.* Washington, DC: U.S. Department of Labor, Employment and Training Administration, 2000.

31. Weber, G. Preserving the Starbucks' counter culture. *Workforce Management*, February 2005, pp. 28–34.

32. Merritt, J. Improv at the interview. *BusinessWeek* 3818:63, 2003.

33. Maurer, S. D. A practitioner-based analysis of interview job expertise and scale format as contextual factors in situational interviews. *Personnel Psychology* 55:307–327, 2002; and DeGroot, T., & Kluemper, D. Evidence of predictive and incremental validity of personality factors, vocal attractiveness and the *situational interview. International Journal of Selection and Assessment* 15:30–39, 2007.

34. Maurer, S. D. A practitioner-based analysis of interview job expertise and scale format as contextual factors in situational interviews. *Personnel Psychology* 55:307–327, 2002; and Hough, L. M., & Oswald, F. L. Personnel selection: Looking toward the future—Remembering the past. *Annual Review of Psychology* 51:631–664, 2000.

35. Posthuma, R. A., Morgeson, F. P., & Campion, M. A. Beyond employment interview validity: A comprehensive narrative review of recent research and trends over time. *Personnel Psychology* 55:1–81, 2002; and Hough, L. M., & Oswald, F. L. Personnel selection: Looking toward the future—Remembering the past. *Annual Review of Psychology* 51:634–664, 2000.

36. Arnold, J. Getting facts fast. *HRMagazine* 53, 2008, article retrieved at http://www.shrm.org/hrmagazine/articles/0208/0208arnold.asp.

37. Klinvex, K. C., O'Connell, M. S., & Klinvex, C. P. *Hiring great people.* New York: McGraw Hill, 1999.

38. Burke, M. E. *2004 reference and background checking survey report.* Alexandria, VA: Society for Human Resource Management, 2004.

39. Ibid.

40. Capwell, R. Written policy is biggest tool in box for ensuring proper screening compliance. *SHRM Online Staffing Management Focus Area*, 2007, www.shrm.org/ema/library_published/nonIC/CMS_020120.asp.

41. Burke, M. E. *2004 reference and background checking survey report.* Alexandria, VA: Society for Human Resources Management, 2004.

42. Atkinson, W. Third-party screening: Weeding out the "bad apples." *Hotel and Motel Management* 219:36–37, 2004.

43. New FCRA rules change third-party investigations. *Accounting Office Management & Administration Report* 5:10, 2005.

44. U.S. Department of Labor. *Testing and assessment: An employer's guide to good practices.* Washington, DC: U.S. Department of Labor, Employment and Training Administration, 2000.

45. Shaffer, D., & Schmidt, R. Personality testing in employment. *SHRM Legal Report*, 2006, www.shrm.org/ema/library_published/IC/CMS_000991.asp.

46. U.S. Department of Labor. *Testing and assessment: An employer's guide to good practices.* Washington, DC: U.S. Department of Labor, Employment and Training Administration, 2000.

47. Gatewood, R. D., & Feild, H. S. *Human resource selection.* New York: Harcourt, 2001; and U.S. Department of Labor. *Testing and assessment: An employer's guide to good practices.* Washington, DC: U.S. Department of Labor, Employment and Training Administration, 2000.

48. Rafter, M. Candidates for jobs in high places sit for tests that size up their mettle. *Workforce Management*, May 2004, pp. 70–72; and U.S. Department of Labor. *Testing and assessment: An employer's guide to good practices.* Washington, DC: U.S. Department of Labor, Employment and Training Administration, 2000.

49. Procter & Gamble. *Recruiting blueprint: Recruiting philosophy*, http://www.pg.com/jobs/recruitblue/recphilosophy.jhtml.

50. Gatewood, R. D., & Feild, H. S. *Human resource selection.* New York: Harcourt, 2001; and U.S. Department of Labor. *Testing and assessment: An employer's guide to good practices.* Washington, DC: U.S. Department of Labor, Employment and Training Administration, 2000.

51. Overman, S. Debating drug test ROI. *Staffing*, October-December 2005, the article retrieved at: http://www.shrm.org/ema/sm/articles/2005/octdec05cover.asp.

52. U.S. Department of Labor. *Drug-free workplace advisor*, www.dol.gov/elaws/drugfree.htm.

53. U.S. Department of Labor. *Testing and assessment: An employer's guide to good practices.* Washington, DC: U.S. Department of Labor, Employment and Training Administration, 2000.

54. Ibid.

55. Ibid.

56. Robertson, I. T., & Smith, M. Personnel selection. *Journal of Occupational and Organizational Psychology* 74:441–472, 2001.

57. Wilk, S. L., & Cappelli, P. Understanding the determinants of employer use of selection methods. *Personnel Psychology* 56:103–124, 2003.

58. IBM. *Values*, www-03.ibm.com/employment/us/li_values.shtml.

59. Tahmincioglu, E. (2004). Keeping spirits aloft at JetBlue. *Workforce Management* online, December 2004, www.workforce.com/archive/article/23/90/36.php.

60. Kristof, A. L. Person–organization fit: An integrative review of its conceptualizations, measurements, and implications. *Personnel Psychology* 49:1–49, 1996.

61. Schein, E. H. *Organizational culture and leadership.* San Francisco: Jossey-Bass, 1985.

62. Weber, G. Preserving the Starbucks' counter culture. *Workforce Management*, February 2005, pp. 28–34.

63. Shah, T. Retailers sometimes turn to a different means of screening applicants. *Knight Ridder Tribune Business News*, June 21, 2004, p. 1.

64. Potosky, D., & Bobko, P. Selection testing via the Internet: Practical considerations and exploratory empirical findings. *Personnel Psychology*, 57:1003–1034, 2004.

65. Babcock, P. Spotting lies. *HR Magazine* 48:46–52, 2003; and Cullen, L. Getting wise to lies. *Time* 167:59, 2006.

66. Burke, M. E. *2004 reference and background checking survey report.* Alexandria, VA: Society for Human Resources Management, 2004.

67. Mason-Draffen, C. Lying on resume can cost workers their jobs. *Knight Ridder Tribune Business News*, June 10, 2004, p. 1.

68. Office of Communications. USCIS reaches FY 2008 H-1B Cap. *USCIS Update*, April 3, 2007.

69. Ladika, S. Unwelcome changes. *HR Magazine* 50:83–90, 2005.

70. U.S. Citizenship and Immigration Service. USCIS reaches FY 2009 H-1B Cap, http://uscis.gov/graphics/howdoi/h1b.htm.

71. Tung, R. L. Expatriate assignments: Enhancing success and minimizing failure. *Academy of Management Executive* 1:117–126, 1987. For a more detailed discussion of expatriate selection, see Dowling, P. J., & Welch, D. E. *International human resource management*, 4th ed. Cincinnati, Ohio: Thomson/South-Western, 2005; and Briscoe, D. R., & Schuler, R. S. *International human resource management*, 2nd ed. New York, New York: Routledge, 2004.

72. Katz, J. P., & Seifer, D. M. It's a different world out there: Planning for expatriate success through selection, pre-departure training and on-site socialization. *Human Resource Planning* 19:32–47, 1996.

73. Briscoe, D. R., & Schuler, R. S. *International human resource management*, 2nd ed. New York: Routledge, 2004; and Abdulla, F. Education and employment among women in the UAE. *International Higher Education*, Vol. 45 2006, p. 9–10.

74. Halley, J. Localization as an ethical response to internationalization. In C. Brewster & H. Harris (eds.). *International human resource management*. London: Routledge, 1999, pp. 89–101.

75. Ryan, A. M., McFarland, L., Baron, H., & Page, R. An international look at selection practices: Nation and culture as explanations for variability in practice. *Personnel Psychology* 52:359–391, 1999; and Levy-Leboyer, C. Selection and assessment in Europe. In H. C. Triandis, M. D. Dunnette, & L. M. Hough (eds.). *Handbook of industrial and organizational psychology*, Volume 4. Palo Alto, CA: Consulting Psychologists Press, 1994, pp. 173–190.

76. Briscoe, D. R., & Schuler, R. S. *International human resource management*, 2nd ed. New York: Routledge, 2004.

77. Stone-Romero, E. F., Stone, D. L., & Hyatt, D. Personnel selection procedures and invasion of privacy. *Journal of Social Issues* 59:343–368, 2003; and Buckley, M. R., et al. The ethical imperative to provide recruits realistic job previews. *Journal of Managerial Issues* 9:468–484, 1997.

78. Stone-Romero, E. F., Stone, D. L., & Hyatt, D. Personnel selection procedures and invasion of privacy. *Journal of Social Issues* 59:343–368, 2003.

79. Kegley, J. A. *Genetic knowledge: Human values and responsibility*. Lexington, KY: ICUS, 1998.

80. Buckley, M. R., et al. The ethical imperative to provide recruits realistic job previews. *Journal of Managerial Issues* 9:468–484, 1997.

81. U. S. Department of Labor. *Uniform guidelines on employee selection procedures*. http://www.dol.gov/dol/allcfr/Title_41/Part_60-3/toc.html

82. U.S. Department of Labor. *Testing and assessment: An employer's guide to good practices.* Washington, DC: U.S. Department of Labor, Employment and Training Administration, 2000.

83. U.S. Equal Employment Opportunity Commission. *Questions and answers: Definition of "job applicant" for Internet and related electronic technologies,* www.eeoc.gov/policy/docs/qanda-ugesp.html.

84. EEOC. *Questions and answers: Definition of "job applicant" for Internet and related electronic technologies* http://www.eeoc.gov/policy/docs/qanda-ugesp.html

85. Ibid.

86. U.S. Equal Employment Opportunity Commission. *EEOC Notice Number 915.002, May 22, 1996,* www.eeoc.gov/policy/docs/testers.html.

87. Gatewood, R. D., & Feild, H. S. *Human resource selection.* New York: Harcourt, 2001.

88. U.S. Department of Labor. *Testing and assessment: An employer's guide to good practices.* Washington, DC: U.S. Department of Labor, Employment and Training Administration, 2000.

89. Gatewood, R. D., & Feild, H. S. *Human resource selection.* New York: Harcourt, 2001.

Chapter 8

1. Pfau, B., & Kay, I. Playing the training game. *HRMagazine* 47(8): pp 49–54, 2002, www.shrm.org/hrmagazine/articles/0802/0802pfau.asp.

2. Starcke, A. M. Building a better orientation program. *HRMagazine* 41:107–112, 1996.

3. Joinson, C. Hit the floor running, start the cart . . . and other neat ways to train new employees. *Employment Management Today,* month 2001, p. 6; and O'Brien, J. The 100 best companies to work for 2008. *Fortune* 157:61–96, 2008. http://www.shrm.org/ema/emt/articles/01wintercov.asp

4. Moscato, D. Using technology to get employees on board. *HRMagazine* 50:107–109, 2005.

5. Ibid.

6. Wells, S. J. Diving in. *HRMagazine* 50:54–59, 2005.

7. Flynn, J. Linking human capital management and learning to business outcomes. *Learning & Training Innovations* 4:12–13, 2003.

8. ASTD Learning Circuit. *2008 corporate learning factbook values U. S. training market at $58.5 billion,* February 4, 2008, http://learning-circuits.org/news.html.

9 Salas, E., & Cannon-Bowers, J. The science of training: A decade of progress. *Annual Review of Psychology* 52:471–499, 2001.

10. Purington, C., & Butler, C. *Built to learn: The inside story of how Rockwell Collins became a true learning organization.* New York: AMACOM, 2003.

11. Donaldson, L., & Scannell, E. E. *Human resource development: The new trainer's guide.* Cambridge, MA: Perseus Publishing, 2000.

12. Sims, R., & Sims, S. J. *The importance of learning styles: Understanding the implications for learning, course design, and education.* Westport, CT: Greenwood Press, 1995.

13. Starcke, A. M. Building a better orientation program. *HRMagazine* 41:107–112, 1996.

14. Eichinger, R. W., & Lombardo, M. M. Learning agility as a prime indicator of potential. *Human Resource Planning* 27:12–15, 2004.

15. Salas, E., & Cannon-Bowers, J. The science of training: A decade of progress. *Annual Review of Psychology* 52:471–499, 2001.

16. Brown, K. G. Using computers to deliver training: Which employees learn and why? *Personnel Psychology* 54:271–296, 2001.

17. Salas, E., & Cannon-Bowers, J. The science of training: A decade of progress. *Annual Review of Psychology* 52:471–499, 2001.

18. Top 10: Booz Allen (#2). *Training,* May 1, 2005, www.trainingmag.com/training/search/article_display.jsp?vnu_content_id=1000791082.

19. Wentland, D. The strategic training of employees model: Balancing organizational constraints and training content. *SAM Advanced Management Journal* 68:56–63, 2003.

20. The National IT Apprenticeship System. *About NITAS,* www.nitas.us/about.aspx.

21. Speizer, I. State of the sector: Training. *Workforce Management,* July 2005, pp. 55–58.

22. Salas, E., & Cannon-Bowers, J. The science of training: A decade of progress. *Annual Review of Psychology* 52:471–499, 2001.

23. Speizer, I. State of the sector: Training. *Workforce Management,* July 2005, pp. 55–58.

24. Pont, J. Employee training on iPod playlist. *Workforce Management,* August 2005, p. 18.

25. Speizer, I. State of the sector: Training. *Workforce Management,* July 2005, pp. 55–58.

26. Brown, K. G. Using computers to deliver training: Which employees learn and why? *Personnel Psychology* 54:271–296, 2001.

27. Wilson, M. Some companies just aren't ready for CBT. *Workforce Management* 79:123–124, 2000.

28. Speizer, I. Simulation games score with trainees. *Workforce Management,* July 2005, p. 60.

29. Ibid.

30. Tyler, K. Train for smarter hiring. *HRMagazine* 50:89–93, 2005.

31. Stevens, G. H., & Frazer, G. W. Coaching: The missing ingredient in blended learning strategy. *Performance Improvement* 44:8–13, 2005.

32. O'Brien, J. The 100 best companies to work for 2008. *Fortune* 157: 61–96, 2008.

33. Shuit, D. P. Huddling with the coach. *Workforce Management,* February 2005, pp. 53–57.

34. Sparrow, S. A defining time for coaching. *Personnel Today,* September 6, 2005, p. 23.

35. Ibid.

36. Johnson, M. California requires sexual harassment training. *SHRM Legal Report,* 2005, www.shrm.org/hrresources/lrpt_published/CMS_010852.asp.

37. Ibid.

38. Hastings, R. Survey: People management training tops priorities for 2008. SHRM Online Workplace Diversity Library—Training, 2008. http://www.shrm.org/diversity/library_published/nonIC/CMS_024054.asp

39. Bendick, M., Egan, M., & Lofhjelm, S. Workforce diversity training: From anti-discrimination compliance to organizational development. *Human Resource Planning* 24:10–25, 2001.

40. National Institutes of Health Training Center Web site, http://learning- source.od.nih.gov/index.html.

41. Beugré, C. *Managing fairness in organizations.* Westport, CT: Quorum Books, 1998.

42. Thanks to Frances Lilly, SPHR, CEBS, of the Human Resource Development Committee, for contributing the information in this section. It is intended as information only and is not a substitute for legal or professional advice.

43. Davis, W., Fedor, D. B., Herold, D. M., & Parsons, C. K. Dispositional influences on transfer of learning in multistage training programs. *Personnel Psychology* 55:851–869, 2002.

44. Top 10: Booz Allen (#2). *Training*, May 1, 1005, www.trainingmag.com/training/search/article_display.jsp?vnu_content_id=1000791082[0].

45. Charney, C., & Conway, K. *The trainer's tool kit.* New York: AMACOM, 2005. and TOOL: Calculate the costs and benefits of training. *Workforce Management* online, www.workforce.com/section/11/article/23/95/44.html

46. National Institutes of Health. *Senior leadership program,* Spring 2008, http://learningsource.od.nih.gov/SLP-spring08.pdf.

47. Kranz, G. BAE Systems puts a spin on career growth. *Workforce Management* online. August 2007, http://www.workforce.com/archive/feature/25/07/02/index.php?ht=bae%20bae.

48. Minton-Eversole, T. Technology use transforming workplace learning. *SHRM staffing management library—Employee development,* January 2008, http://www.shrm.org/ema/library_published/nonIC/CMS_024368.asp.

49. Fred's Inc. Web site, www.fredsinc.com/index.htm.

50. Nordstrom. *About Nordstrom,* http://about.nordstrom.com/aboutus/.

51. Adams, S. Costs drive safety training needs. *HRMagazine* 48:63–66, 2003.

52. Hamburger University: Ensuring the future. *Nation's Restaurant News* 39:104–107, 2005.

53. Jossi, F. Lesson plans. *HRMagazine* 48:72–76, 2003.

54. Bendick, M., Egan, M., & Lofhjelm, S. Workforce diversity training: From anti-discrimination compliance to organizational development. *Human Resource Planning* 24:10–25, 2001.

55. Wexley, K. N., & Latham, G. P. *Developing and training human resources in organizations.* Englewood Cliffs, NJ: Prentice Hall, 2002.

56. Robinson, S., & Morrison, E. Psychological contracts and organizational citizenship behavior: The effect of unfulfilled obligations on civic virtue behavior. *Journal of Organizational Behavior* 16:289–298, 1995.

57. What to do now that training is becoming a major HR force. *HR Focus* 82:5–6, 2005.

58. Hammers, M. Wyndham looks to leap language gap. *Workforce Magazine,* July 2005, p. 17.

59. Greengard, S. Technology is changing expatriate training. *Workforce* 78:106–108, 1999.

60. Briscoe, D., & Schuler, R. *International human resource management.* London: Routledge, 2004, p. 271.

61. Digh, P. One style doesn't fit all. *HRMagazine* 47:79–31, 2002.

62. Perrin, S. Emphasis is on ethics education: Integrity is essential. *Financial Times,* September 13, 2004, p. 3.

63. Grossman, R. J. Demystifying Section 404. *HRMagazine* 5:46–53, 2005.

64. *City of Canton v. Harris,* 489 US. 378 (1989).

65. Garten, J. B-schools: Only a C+ in ethics. *BusinessWeek,* September 5, 2005, p. 110.

66. Myers, R. Ensuring ethical effectiveness: New rules mean virtually every company will need a code of ethics. *Journal of Accountancy* 195:28–33, 2003.

67. Johnson, M. California requires sexual harassment training. *SHRM Legal Report,* 2005, www.shrm.org/hrresources/lrpt_published/CMS_010852.asp.

68. Speizer, I. State of the sector: Training. *Workforce Management,* July 2005, pp. 55–58.

69. Cowart, C., & Blanchard, P. Dial "C" for compliance; Keeping Wachovia's on-call call center in compliance takes teamwork between center staff and corporate compliance experts. *ABA Banking Journal* 89:30–35, 1997.

Chapter 9

1. Beer, M. Performance appraisal. In J. W. Lorsch (ed.), *Handbook of organizational behavior.* Englewood Cliffs, NJ: Prentice Hall, 1987, pp. 286–300.

2. Ghiselli, E. E. Dimensional problems of criteria. *Journal of Applied Psychology,* 40:1–4, 1956; and Cascio, W. F. *Applied psychology in personnel management,* 4th ed. Englewood Cliffs, NJ: Prentice Hall, 1991.

3. Landy, F. J., & Farr, J. L., Performance rating. *Psychological Bulletin* 87(1):72–107,1980.

4. U.S. Department of Labor. *Testing and assessment: An employer's guide to good practices.* Washington, DC: U.S. Department of Labor, Employment and Training Administration, 2000.

5. Cascio, W. F. *Applied psychology in personnel management,* 4th ed. Englewood Cliffs, NJ: Prentice Hall, 1991.

6. Bernardin, H. J., & Beatty, R. W. *Performance appraisal: Assessing human behavior at work.* Boston: Kent-Wadsworth, 1984.

7. Bernardin, H. J., Hagan, C. M., Kane, J. S., & Villanova, P. Effective performance management: A focus on precision, customers, and situational constraints. In J. W. Smither (ed.), *Performance appraisal: State of the art in practice.* San Francisco: Jossey-Bass, 1998, pp. 3–48.

8. Ibid.

9. Bobko P., & Colella, A. Employee reactions to performance standards: A review and research propositions. *Personnel Psychology* 47:1–36, 1994.

10. Cascio, W. F. *Applied psychology in personnel management,* 4th ed. Englewood Cliffs, NJ: Prentice Hall, 1991.

11. Longnecker, B. M., Rank & yank: The problems with forced rankings. *Workforce Management* online, February 7, 2006, http://www.workforce.com/archive/feature/22/29/72/index.php.

12. Landy, F. J., & Farr, J. L. Performance rating. *Psychological Bulletin* 87(1):72–107, 1980.

13. Cascio, W. F. *Applied psychology in personnel management,* 4th ed. Englewood Cliffs, NJ: Prentice Hall, 1991.

14. Landy, F. J., & Farr, J. L. Performance rating. *Psychological Bulletin* 87(1):72–107, 1980.

15. Ibid.

16. Austin, J. T., & Villanova, P. The criterion problem: 1917–1992. *Journal of Applied Psychology* 77:836–874, 1992; Bernardin, H. J., & Smith, P. C. A clarification of some issues regarding the development and use of behaviorally anchored rating scales (BARS). *Journal of Applied Psychology* 66:458–463, 1981; and Jacobs, R., Kafry, D., & Zedeck, S. Expectations of behaviorally anchored rating scales. *Personnel Psychology* 33:595–640, 1980.

17. Austin, J. T., & Villanova, P. The criterion problem: 1917–1992. *Journal of Applied Psychology* 77:836–874, 1992; and Bernardin, H. J., & Smith, P. C. A clarification of some issues regarding the development and use of behaviorally anchored rating scales (BARS). *Journal of Applied Psychology* 66:458–463, 1981.

18. Bernardin, H. J., & Smith, P. C. A clarification of some issues regarding the development and use of behaviorally anchored rating scales (BARS). *Journal of Applied Psychology* 66:458–463, 1981.

19. Hoffman, C. C., Nathan, B. R., & Holden, L. M. A comparison of validation criteria: Objective versus subjective performance measures and self- versus supervisor ratings. *Personnel Psychology* 44:601–618, 1991.

20. Antonioni, D. The effects of feedback accountability on upward appraisal ratings. *Personnel Psychology* 47:349–356, 1994.

21. Borman, W. C. The rating of individuals in organizations: An alternate approach. *Organizational Behavior and Human Performance* 12:105–124, 1974.

22. Ghiselli, E. E. Dimensional problems of criteria. *Journal of Applied Psychology* 40:1–4, 1956.

23. Wherry, R. J., Sr., & Bartlett, C. J. The control of bias in ratings. *Personnel Psychology* 35(3):521–551, 1982.

24. Bingham, W. V. Halo, invalid and valid. *Journal of Applied Psychology* 23:221–228, 1939; Thorndike, E. L. A constant error in psychological ratings. *Journal of Applied Psychology* 4:25–29, 1920; and Bernardin, H. J., & Beatty, R. W. *Performance appraisal: Assessing human behavior at work.* Boston: Ken Publishing, 1984.

25. Kane, J. S., Bernardin, H. J., Villanova, P., & Peyrefitte, J. 1995. Stability of rater leniency: Three studies. *Academy of Management Journal* 38:1036–1051, 1995; and Builford, J. P. *Psychometric methods.* New York: McGraw-Hill, 1954.

26. Latham, G., Wexley, K., & Pursell, E. Training managers to minimize rating errors in the observation of behavior. *Journal of Applied Psychology* 60:550–555, 1975; and Bernardin, H. J., & Buckley, M. R. Strategies in rater error training. *Academy of Management Review* 6:205–212, 1981.

27. Woehr, D. J., & Huffcutt, A. I. Rater training for performance appraisal: A quantitative review. *Journal of Occupational and Organizational Psychology* 67:189–205, 1994; and Bernardin, H. J., & Buckley, M. R. Strategies in rater error training. *Academy of Management Review* 6:205–212, 1981.

28. Sulsky, L. M., & Day, D. V. Frame-of-reference training and cognitive categorization: An empirical investigation of rater memory loss. *Journal of Applied Psychology* 77:501–510, 1992.

29. Woehr, D. J., & Huffcutt, A. I. Rater training for performance appraisal: A quantitative review. *Journal of Occupational and Organizational Psychology* 67:189–205, 1994; and Bernardin, H. J., & Buckley, M. R. Strategies in rater error training. *Academy of Management Review* 6:205–212, 1981.

30. Beer, M. Performance appraisal. In J. W. Lorsch (ed.). *Handbook of Organizational behavior.* Englewood Cliffs, NJ: Prentice Hall, 1987, pp. 286–300.

31. Falcone, P. The fundamentals of progressive discipline. *HR Magazine* 42(2):90–93, February 1997.

32. Ghiselli, E. E. Dimensional problems of criteria. *Journal of Applied Psychology* 40:1–4, 1956.

33. Rousseau, D. M. *Psychological contracts in organizations: Understanding written and unwritten agreements.* Thousand Oaks, CA: Sage Publications, 1995.

34. Ibid.

35. Ibid.

36. Falcone, P. The fundamentals of progressive discipline. *HR Magazine* 42(2):90–93, February 1997.

37. Rousseau, D. M. *Psychological contracts in organizations: Understanding written and unwritten agreements.* Thousand Oaks, CA: Sage Publications, 1995.

38. Hirsch, P. M. *Pack your own parachute.* Reading, MA: Addison-Wesley, 1987; Rousseau, D. M. *Psychological contracts in organizations: Understanding written and unwritten agreements.* Thousand Oaks, CA: Sage Publications, 1995; and Robinson, S. L., & Rousseau, D. M. Violating the psychological contract: Not the exception but the norm. *Journal of Organizational Behavior* 15:245–259, 1994.

39. Austin, J. T., & Villanova, P. The criterion problem: 1917–1992. *Journal of Applied Psychology* 77:836–874, 1992.

40. Beer, M. Conducting a performance appraisal interview. *Harvard Business School Cases*, January 1997, pp. 1–16; and Black, J. S., Gregersen, H. B., Mendenhall, M. E., & Stroh, L. K. *Globalizing people through international assignments.* Reading, MA: Addison-Wesley, 1999.

41. Kraiger, K., & Ford, K. A meta-analysis of rate race effects in performance rating. *Journal of Applied Psychology* 70:56–65, 1985; and Landy, F. J., & Farr, J. L. Performance rating. *Psychological Bulletin* 87(1):72–107, 1980.

42. Geddes, D., & Konrad, A. M. Demographic differences and reactions to performance feedback. *Human Relations* 56(12):1485–1513, 2003.

43. Kraiger, K., & Ford, K. A meta-analysis of rate race effects in performance rating. *Journal of Applied Psychology* 70:56–65, 1985.

44. Latham, G. Wexley, K., & Pursell, E. Training managers to minimize rating errors in the observation of behavior. *Journal of Applied Psychology* 60:550–555, 1975; and Bernardin, H. J., & Buckley, M. R. Strategies in rater error training. *Academy of Management Review* 6:205–212, 1981.

45. Digh, P. The next challenge: Holding people accountable. *HR Magazine* 43(11):63–69, 1998.

46. Ibid.

47. Dutton, G. 'Round the clock performance management. *Workforce*, April 2001, pp. 76–78.

48. Murphy, K. R., & Cleveland, J. N. *Understanding performance appraisal: Social, organizational, and goal-based perspectives.* Thousand Oaks: Sage Publications, 1995.

49. Ibid.

50. Gordon, G. E., & Kelly, M. M. *Telecommuting: How to make it work for you and your company.* Englewood Cliffs, NJ: Prentice Hall, 1986.

51. Black, J. S., Gregersen, H. B., Mendenhall, M. E., & Stroh, L. K. *Globalizing people through international assignments.* Reading, MA: Addison-Wesley, 1999.

52. Gregersen, H. B., Hite, J. M., & Black, J. S. Expatriate performance appraisal in U.S. multinational firms. *Journal of International Business Studies*, Fall 1996, pp. 711–738.

53. O'Clock, P. The role of strategy and culture in the performance evaluation of international strategic business units. *Management Accounting Quarterly* 4(2):18–29, 2003.

54. Black, J. S., Gregersen, H. B., Mendenhall, M. E., & Stroh, L. K. *Globalizing people through international assignments.* Reading, MA: Addison-Wesley, 1999.

55. Ibid.

56. De Cieri, H., & Dowling, P. J. 1995. Cross-cultural issues in organizational behavior. In C. L. Cooper & D. M. Rousseau (eds.). *Trends in organizational behavior*, Volume 2. Chichester,

UK: Wiley, 1995, pp. 127–145; and Black, J. S., Gregersen, H. B., Mendenhall, M. E., & Stroh, L. K. *Globalizing people through international assignments*. Reading, MA: Addison-Wesley, 1999.

57. Suutari, V., & Tahvanainen, M. The antecedents of performance management among Finnish expatriates. *International Journal of Human Resource Management* 12(1):55–75, 2002.

58. Ibid.

59. Black, J. S., Gregersen, H. B., Mendenhall, M. E., & Stroh, L. K. *Globalizing people through international assignments*. Reading, MA: Addison-Wesley, 1999; Suutari, V., & Tahvanainen, M. The antecedents of performance management among Finnish expatriates. *International Journal of Human Resource Management* 12(1):55–75, 2002; and Gregersen, H. B., Hite, J. M., & Black, J. S. Expatriate performance appraisal in U.S. multinational firms. *Journal of International Business Studies*, Fall 1996, pp. 711–738.

60. Lachnit, C. A snoop in the machine. *Workforce Management* online, www.workforce.com/archive/feature/23/62/81/index.php.

61. Raphael, T. Think twice: Does HR want to be a digital snoop. *Workforce Management* online, www.workforce.com/archive/feature/22/30/06/index.php.

62. Meisler, A. Dead man's curve. *Workforce Management* online, July 2003, www.workforce.com/section/09/feature/23/47/39/index.html; Armour, S. Job reviews take on added significance in down times. *USA Today*, July 22, 2003, www.usatoday.com/money/workplace/2003-07-22-reviews_x.htm; and Meier, B. Ford is changing the way it rates work of managers. *New York Times*, July 12, 2001, http://query.nytimes.com.

63. Dawson, B. Failing grade: Goodyear faces lawsuit over evaluation system it will alter. *Rubber & Plastics News*, September 2002.

64. Osborne, T., & McCann, L. A. Forced rankings and age-related employment discrimination. *Human Rights Magazine*, www.abanet.org/irr/hr/spring04/forced.html.

Chapter 10

1. Watson, S. Building a better employment deal. *Workspan*, 46, 48-51, 2003, and WorldatWork. *What is total rewards?* http://www.worldatwork.org/waw/home/html/home.jsp.

2. CH2M HILL. *Total rewards*, www.careers.ch2m.com/total_rewards/default.asp

3. PMI, *Compensation philosophy* http://www.pmi-us.com/about_pmi/comp_philosophy.html.

4. Milkovich, G. T., & Newman, J. M. *Compensation*. New York: McGraw-Hill/Irwin, 2005.

5. Dornstein, M. The fairness judgments of received pay and their determinants. *Journal of Occupational Psychology* 62:287–299, 1989.

6. Office of Personnel Management. *Introduction to the position classification standards*. Washington, D.C.: U. S. Office of Personnel Management, 1995.

7. Caruth, D. L., & Handlogten, G. D. *Managing compensation (and understanding it too): A handbook for the perplexed*. Westport, CT: Quorum Books, 2001.

8. Ibid.

9. Milkovich, G. T., & Newman, J. M. *Compensation*. New York: McGraw-Hill/Irwin, 2005.

10. Ibid.

11. Risher, H. How much should federal employees be paid? The problems with using a market philosophy in a broadband system. *Public Personnel Management*, 34: 121-140, 2005.

12. Risher, H. Planning for the transition to pay for performance: What are the practical consequences of the federal government's increased emphasis on pay for performance and what can agencies do to prepare for this change in policy direction? *The Public Manager* 33:pp, 2004. *Questia*, 27 Apr. 2008 http://www.questia.com/PM.qst? a=o&d=5008790873.

13. Lawler, E. Pay strategy: New thinking for the new millennium. *Compensation & Benefits Review* 32:7–12, 2000.

14. Leanne H. Markus, Helena D. Cooper-Thomas, and Keith N. Allpress, "Confounded by Competencies? an Evaluation of the Evolution and Use of Competency Models," *New Zealand Journal of Psychology* 34.2 (2005), Questia, 27 Apr. 2008 http://www.questia.com/PM.qst?a=o&d=5012083525.

15. Hinchcliffe, B. The juggling act: Internal equity and market pricing. *Workspan* 46:46–48, 2003.

16. Heneman, R., LeBlanc, P., & Risher, H. Work valuation addresses shortcoming of both job evaluation and market pricing/response. *Compensation & Benefits Review* 35:7–11, 2003.

17. Yanadori, Y., & Marler, J. H. Compensation strategy: Does business strategy influence compensation in high technology firms? *Strategic Management Journal* 27:559–570, 2006.

18. Pfizer home page. *Working together for a healthier world*. www.pfizer. com/home/

19. Ibid.

20. U.S. Department of Labor, Bureau of Labor Statistics. *Overview: Consumer price index*, www.bls.gov/cpi/cpiovrvw.htm#itme1.

21. Milkovich, G. T., & Newman, J. M. *Compensation*. New York: McGraw- Hill/Irwin, 2005.

22. McDonald's Corporation. *Your pay and rewards*, www.mcdonalds.com/corp/career/employee_benefits/Pay_Rewards.html.

23. Zensar Technologies. *Zensar Technologies Ltd. annual report 2004–2005*, 2005, www.zensar.com/fileadmin/user_upload/LegalandSecretarial/Annual_Report_2005.pdf.

24. Schulz, E., & Tubbs, S. L. Stock options influence on manager's salaries and firm performance. *The Business Review* 5:14–19, 2006; Blasi, J., Kruse, D., & Bernstein, A. *In the company of owners: The truth about stock options (and why every employee should have them)*. New York: Basic Books, 2003.

25. Oi, W., & Idson, T. Firm size and wages. In O. Ashenfelter & D. Card (eds.). *Handbook of labor economics*. Amsterdam: North Holland, 1999, 3B, Ch 33.

26. Salas, E., Kosarzycki, M., Tannenbaum, S., & Carnegie, D. Aligning work teams and HR practices: Best practices. In R. J. Burke & C. L. Cooper (eds.). *Reinventing human resources management: Challenges and new directions*. New York: Routledge, 2004, 133-150.

27. Caruth, D. L., & Handlogten, G. D. *Managing compensation (and understanding it too): A handbook for the perplexed*. Westport, CT: Quorum Books, 2001.

28. VanVinnen, A. Person–organization fit: The match between newcomers' and recruiters' preferences for organization cultures. *Personnel Psychology* 53:115–125, 2000.

29. Sims, R. *Managing organizational behavior*. Westport, CT: Quorum Books, 2002.

30. Halstead-Acharya, L. Tight labor market fuels recruiting rivalry. *Knight Ridder Tribune Business News*, June 4, 2006, p. 1.

31. Caruth, D. L., & Handlogten, G. D. *Managing compensation (and understanding it too): A handbook for the perplexed.* Westport, CT: Quorum Books, 2001.

32. Cable, D., & Judge, T. Pay preferences and job search decisions: A person-organization fit perspective. *Personnel Psychology* 47:317–348, 1994.

33. Shermach, K. Tracking and invoicing billable hours without wasting time. *Workforce Management* online, September 2006, http://www. workforce.com/archive/feature/24/50/81/index. php?ht=shermach%20k%20tracking%20and%20invoicing%20 billable%20hours%20without%20wasting%20time%20.

34. Cherof, E. (2002). Legal issues in telecommuting. *Compensation & Benefits Library—Telecommuting,* 2002, www.shrm.org/ rewards/library_published/benefits/IC/CMS_000926.asp.

35. Marquez, J. McDonald's rewards program leaves room for some local flavor. *Workforce Management* 85:26, 2006.

36. Watson Wyatt. *Global compensation practices—Survey of WorldatWork members by WorldatWork and Watson Wyatt Worldwide,* 2006, www.watsonwyatt.com/research/resrender. asp?id=ONL014&page=1; and Hansen, F. Currents in compensation and benefits. *Compensation & Benefits Review* 37:6–17, 2005.

37. Reynes, R. Feelin' all right: Troubled times in foreign lands have not dislodged incentive plans. *CFO Magazine,* April 1, 1999, www.cfo.com/printable/article.cfm/2989385?f=options.

38. Hansen, F. Power to the line people. *Workforce,* June 2003, pp. 70–75.

39. Chiu, R., Wai-Mei Luk, V., & Tanp, T. Retaining and motivating employees: Compensation preferences in Hong Kong and China. *Personnel Review* 31:402–431, 2002.

40. Briscoe, D., & Schuler, R. *International human resource management.* London: Routledge, 2004.

41. HayGroup. *Managers in emerging economies winning on pay: HayGroup research finds U S managers lose out on disposable income,* July 16, 2007, www.haygroup.com/ww/media/headline. asp?PageID=9721.

42. U.S. Department of State. Vietnam, Country reports on human rights practices – 2007. http://www.state.gov/g/drl/rls/hrrpt/ 2007/100543.htm

43. China sets minimum wage rules. *People's Daily,* 2004, http://english.people.com.cn/200402/06/eng20040206_ 134134.shtml.

44. Reuters. China ups minimum age. *Houston Community News,* ChinatownConnection.com. pp.20 http://www.chinatown-connection.com/china-minimum-wage.htm; and Hilgers,L. Mounting labor costs pinching profits in China. *Business NewsBank.* April 7, 2008

45. LivingWage Resource Center. *Introduction to ACORN's Living Wage Web* site, www.livingwagecampaign.org/index.php?id=1961.

46. Minnesota Department of Employee Relations. *Minnesota local government pay equity compliance report,* January 2007, www.doer. state.mn.us/lr-peqty/payequity.pdf.

47. U.S. Department of Labor. *What are the Davis-Bacon and related acts?* www.dol.gov/esa/programs/dbra/whatdbra.htm.

48. Thieblot, A. J. A new evaluation of impacts of prevailing wage law repeal. *Journal of Labor Research* 17:297–322, 1996.

49. U.S. Department of Labor. *Employment law guide,* www.dol.gov/compliance/guide/walshh.htm

50. U.S. Department of Labor. *Fair Labor Standards Act advisor,* www.dol.gov/elaws/esa/flsa.

51. U.S. Department of Labor. *Minimum wage laws in the states— January 1, 2008,* www.dol.gov/esa/minwage/america.htm#content.

52. U.S. Department of Labor. *Questions and answers about the minimum wage,* www.dol.gov/esa/minwage/q-a.htm#full.

53. U.S. Department of Labor. *Fair Labor Standards Act advisor: Exemptions,* www.dol.gov/elaws/esa/flsa/screen75.asp.

54. U.S. Department of Labor. *DOL's FairPay overtime initiative,* www.dol. gov/esa/regs/compliance/whd/fairpay/main.htm.

55. U.S. Department of Labor. *Prohibited occupations for non-agricultural employees,* www.dol.gov/elaws/esa/flsa/docs/ haznonag.asp.

56. U.S. Department of Labor. *Fact sheet #21: Recordkeeping requirements under the Fair Labor Standards Act (FLSA),* www.dol.gov/ esa/regs/compliance/whd/whdfs21.htm.

Chapter 11

1. Steers, R. M., Mowday, R. M., & Shapiro, D. L. The future of work motivation theory. *Academy of Management Review* 29(3):379–387, 2004.

2. Gale, S. F. Incentives and the art of changing behaviour. *Workforce Management,* November 2002, pp. 80–82.

3. Seijts, G. H., & Latham, G. P. Learning versus performance goals: When should each be used? *Academy of Management Executive* 19(1):124–131, 2005; and Locke, E. A., & Latham, G. P. *A theory of goal setting and task performance.* Englewood Cliffs, NJ: Prentice Hall, 1990.

4. Latham, G. P. The motivational benefits of goal-setting. *Academy of Management Executive* 18(4):126–129, 2004.

5. Locke, E. A. Linking goals to monetary incentives. *Academy of Management Executive* 18:130–133, 2004.

6. Vroom, V. H. *Work and motivation.* New York: Wiley, 1964.

7. Steers, R. M., Mowday, R. M., & Shapiro, D. L. The future of work motivation theory. *Academy of Management Review* 29(3):379–387, 2004.

8. Campbell, J. P., Dunnette, M. D., Lawler, E. E., & Weick, K. E., Jr. *Managerial behavior, performance, and effectiveness.* New York, NY: McGraw-Hill, 1970.

9. Cascio, W. F. *Applied psychology in personnel management.* Englewood Cliffs, NJ: Prentice Hall, 1991.

10. Heneman, R. L., & Gresham, M. T. Performance based pay plans. In J. W. Smither (ed.). *Performance appraisal: State of the art in practice.* San Francisco: Jossey-Bass, 1998, pp. 496–536.

11. Milkovich, G. T., & Newman, J. M. *Compensation.* Boston: Irwin/McGraw-Hill, 1999.

12. Ibid.

13. Ibid.

14. Private firms recognize value of cash bonuses. *Workforce Management,* December 18, 2007, http://www.workforce.com/ section/00/article/25/27/40.html.

15. Cannon, L. Respect, rewards drive Golden Corral programs. *Nation's Restaurant News,* September 12, 2005, p. 58.

16. Mark, T. How BP aligns rewards and business strategy. *Strategic HR Review* 2(6):12–13, September/October 2003.

17. Huff, C. So plastic: Gift cards are most popular incentive. *Workforce Management,* September 11, 2006, pp. 30.

18. Gale, S. F. Small rewards can push productivity. *Workforce*, June 2002, pp. 86–90.

19. Clark, K. Circuit City drops commissions: Incentives and the economics of teamwork. *Chain Store Age*, April 2003, pp. 54–55.

20. Shenn, J. HomeBanc to pay base salary. *American Banker* 170(234):12, December 8, 2005.

21. White, J. K. The Scanlon plan: Causes and correlates of success. *Academy of Management Journal* 22(2):292–312, 1979.

22. Kaufman. R. T. The effects of Improshare on productivity. *Industrial and Labor Relations Review* 45(2):311–322, January 1992.

23. Ibid.

24. Arthur, J. B., & Aiman-Smith, L. Gainsharing and organizational learning: An analysis of employee suggestions over time. *Academy of Management Journal* 44(4):737–754, 2001.

25. Kim, D. The choice of gainsharing plans in North America: A congruence perspective. *Journal of Labor Research* 26(3):465–483, Summer 2005.

26. Blasi, J. Kruse, D., Sesil, J., & Kroumova, M. An assessment of employee ownership in the United States with implications for the EU. *International Journal of Human Resource Management* 14:893–919, September 2003.

27. Culpepper, R. A., Gamble, J. E., & Blubaugh, M. G. Employee stock ownership plans and three-component commitment. *Journal of Occupational and Organizational Psychology* 77:155–170, 2004; Case, J. The ultimate employee buy-in. *Inc. Magazine*, December 2005, pp. 107–116; and Shulman, C. C. Employee stock ownership plans: Part I. *Journal of Pension Planning and Compliance* 28(4):60–98, Winter 2003.

28. Case, J. The ultimate employee buy-in. *Inc. Magazine*, December 2005, pp. 107–116; and Blasi, J. Kruse, D., Sesil, J., & Kroumova, M. An assessment of employee ownership in the United States with implications for the EU. *International Journal of Human Resource Management* 14:893–919, September 2003.

29. Culpepper, R. A., Gamble, J. E., & Blubaugh, M. G. Employee stock ownership plans and three-component commitment. *Journal of Occupational and Organizational Psychology* 77:155–170, 2004; Long, R. J. The effects of employee ownership on organizational identification, employee job attitudes and organizational performance: A tentative framework and empirical findings. *Human Relations* 31:29–48, 1978; and Tannenbaum, A. S. Employee-owned companies. In L. L. Cummings & B. M. Staw (eds.). *Research in organizational behavior*, Volume 5. Greenwich CT: JAI Press, 1983, pp. 235–265.

30. Case, J. The ultimate employee buy-in. *Inc. Magazine*, December 2005, pp. 107–116; and Blasi, J. R., Kruse, D., & Berstein, A. *In the company of owners: The truth about stock options (and why every employee should have them)*. New York: Basic Books, 2003.

31. Barrionuevo, A., & Romero, S. Enron prosecutor attacks theory of 2001 collapse. *New York Times*, April 28, 2006, www.nytimes.com/2006/04/28/business/businessspecial3/28enron.html; and MSNBC. *Ex-Enron CEO indicted*, February 19, 2004, www.msnbc.msn.com/id/4311642/%5Benter%20URL%5D.

32. Berta, D. Bubba Gump nets low turnover with incentives. *Nation's Restaurant News*, September 12, 2005, p. 58.

33. Anderson, S., et al. Executive excess 2007: The staggering social cost of U.S. Business Leadership. *United for a Fair Economy*, October 2007, pp 1–32.

34. Mercer Human Resource Consulting. 2006 CEO compensation survey and trends. *Wall Street Journal*, www.mercer.com/summary.jhtml/dynamic/idContent/1089750.

35. Herbst, M. The elite circle of $1 CEOs. *BusinessWeek* online, September 17, 2007, http://www.businessweek.com/bwdaily/dnflash/content/may2007/db20070509_992600.htm?campaign_id=rss_tech.

36. Milkovich, G. T., & Newman, J. M. *Compensation*. Boston: Irwin/McGraw-Hill, 1999.

37. Cannon, L. Respect, rewards drive Golden Corral programs. *Nation's Restaurant News*, September 12, 2005, p. 58.

38. Heneman, R. L., Ledford, G. E., Jr., & Gresham, M. T. The changing nature of work and its effects on compensation design and delivery. In S. L. Rynes & B. Gerhart (eds.). *Compensation in organizations: Current research and practice*. San Francisco: Jossey Bass, 2000, pp. 195–240.

39. Lawler, E. E., III. *Motivation in work organizations*. San Francisco, CA: Jossey-Bass, 1994.

40. Heneman, R. L., Ledford, G. E., Jr., & Gresham, M. T. The changing nature of work and its effects on compensation design and delivery. In S. L. Rynes & B. Gerhart (eds.). *Compensation in organizations: Current research and practice*. San Francisco: Jossey Bass, 2000, pp. 195–240.

41. Tahmincioglu, E. Gifts that gall. *Workforce Management*, April 2004, pp. 43–46.

42. Bartol, K. M., & Locke, E. A. Incentives and motivation. In S. L. Rynes & B. Gerhart (eds.). *Compensation in organizations*. San Francisco: Jossey Bass, 2000, pp. 104–147.

43. Ittycheria, D. Developing a high performance organization. *Siliconindia Inc.*, June 2005, pp. 12–14.

44. Karau, S., & Williams, K. D. Social loafing: A meta-analytic review and theoretical integration. *Journal of Personality and Social Psychology* 65(4):681–706, 1993; and Heneman, R. L., & Von Hippel, C. Balancing group and individual rewards: Rewarding individual contributions to the team. *Compensation & Benefits Review* 27(4):63–68, 1995.

45. Vermeulen, P., & Benders, J. A reverse side of the team medal. *Team Performance Management: An International Journal* 9(5/6):107–114, 2003; and Latane, B., Williams, K. D., & Harkins, S. G. Many hands make light the work: The causes and consequences of social loafing. *Journal of Personality and Social Psychology* 37(6):822–832, 1979.

46. Digh, P. The next challenge: Holding people accountable. *HR Magazine* 43(11):63–69, October 1998.

47. McCloskey, F., & Barber, J. Georgia power turns a crisis into a diversity journey. *Diversity Factor* 13(4):16–22, Fall 2005.

48. Marquez, J. Happy returns. *Workforce Management* 86(7):20–25, April 9, 2007.

49. Canik, A., Crawford, C., & Longnecker, B. Combating the future "retirement gap" with tailored total rewards. *IHRIM Journal*, September/October 2004, pp. 32–37.

50. Interview with Paulette Gerkovich, catalyst. *Sloan Work and Family Research Network at Boston College*, February 2005.

51. Managing Generation Y as they change the workforce, January 8, 2008, www.reuters.com/article/pressRelease/idUS129795+08-Jan-2008+ BW20080108; and Business Wire 2008, http://www.pr-inside.com/managing-generation-y-as-they-change-r376306.htm.

52. Gilster, P. A. Online incentives sizzle—And you shine. *Workforce Management* 80(1):44–47, January 2001; and Poe, A. C. Online recognition. *HR Magazine* 47(6):pp 95-100. June 2002.

53. Gilster, P. A. January 2001. Online incentives sizzle—And you shine. *Workforce Management* 80(1):44–47, January 2001.

54. Speizer, I. Good intentions, lost in translation. *Workforce Management*, November 21, 2005, pp. 46–49.

55. Black, J. S., Gregersen, H. B., Mendenhall, M. E., & Stroh, L. K. *Globalizing people through international assignments*. Reading, MA: Addison-Wesley, 1999.

56. Eisenberg, J. How individualism–collectivism moderates the effects of rewards on creativity and innovation: A comparative review of practices in Japan and the U.S. *Creativity and Innovation Management* 8(4):251–261, December 1999.

57. Speizer, I. Good intentions, lost in translation. *Workforce Management*, November 21, 2005, pp. 46–49.

58. Marquez, J. McDonald's rewards program leaves room for some local flavor. *Workforce Management* 85:26, 2006.

59. Kerr, S. On the folly of reward A while hoping for B. *Academy of Management Executive* 9(1):7–14, 1995; Heneman, R. L., Ledford, G. E., Jr., & Gresham, M. T. The changing nature of work and its effects on compensation design and delivery. In. S. L. Rynes & B. Gerhart (eds.). *Compensation in organizations: Current research and practice*. San Francisco: Jossey-Bass, 2000, pp. 195–240.

60. Hymowitz, C. Sky-high payouts to top executives prove hard to curb. *Wall Street Journal*, June 26, 2006, p. B1.

61. Chauvin, K. W., & Ash, R. A. Gender earning differentials in total pay, base pay, and contingent pay. *Industrial and Labor Relations Review*, July 1994, pp. 634–649; and Milkovich, G. T., & Newman, J. M. *Compensation*. Boston: Irwin/McGraw-Hill, 1999.

62. Day, K. SEC to clarify rules on backdating of options. *Washington Post*, June 14, 2006, www.msnbc.msn.com/id/13306323/.

63. Ibid.

Chapter 12

1. Hudson. *Transforming pay plans: 2006 compensation and benefits report*, http://hudson-index.com/documents/us-hudson-index-execsummary-20060517.pdf.

2. Employee Benefits Research Institute (EBRI). *The basics of Social Security updated with the 2006 Board of Trustees Report. FACTS from EBRI*, May 2006, www.ebri.org/pdf/publications/facts/FS-195_May06_SocSecBasics.pdf; and Social Security Administration. *Historical background and development of Social Security*, March 2003, www.ssa.gov/history/briefhistory3.html.

3. Social Security Administration. *Historical background and development of Social Security*, March 2003, www.ssa.gov/history/briefhistory3.html.

4. Social Security Administration. *Social Security: A "snapshot,"* 2006, www.ssa.gov/pubs/10006.pdf.

5. Social Security Administration. *How you earn credits*. Social Security Administration Publication No. 05-10072, 2006.

6. Social Security Administration. *2006 Social Security changes*, October 2005, www.ssa.gov/pressoffice/factsheets/colafacts2006.htm.

7. Office of Workforce Security. *Unemployment compensation, federal-state partnership*. Washington, DC: U.S. Department of Labor, 2005; and U.S. Department of Labor. *State unemployment insurance benefits*, http://workforcesecurity.doleta.gov/unemploy/uifactsheet.asp.

8. U.S. Department of Labor. *Unemployment insurance data summary*, 2008, http://workforcesecurity.doleta.gov/unemploy/content/data_stats/datasum07/4thqtr/DataSum_2007_4.pdf.

9. Clayton, A. Workers' compensation; A background for social security professionals. *Social Security Bulletin*, 65:7–15, 2003/2004.

10. Ibid.

11. Kilgour, J. *A primer on workers' compensation laws and programs*. SHRM white paper, 2004, www.shrm.org/hrresources/whitepapers_published/CMS_000039.asp.

12. Sengupta, I., Reno, V., & Burton, J., Jr. *Workers' compensation: Benefits, coverage, and costs, 2004*. Washington, DC: National Academy of Social Insurance, 2006.

13. Ibid.

14. Ibid.

15. Lipold, A. Workers' compensation savings strategies. *Workforce*, February 2003, pp. 46–48.

16. Croft, B. Wiring up workers' comp claims. *Personnel Journal* 75:153–157, 1996.

17. Weatherly, L. Voluntary employee benefits and job satisfaction. *Briefly Stated, SHRM Research*, December 2005.

18. Conway, C. *J.C. Penney and J. B. Hunt win best of class benefits solution awards for retirement and health benefits best practices*, May 9, 2006, www.highbeam.com/doc/1G1-145516768.html.

19. More companies, workers adopt consumer-directed health plans. *Forbes*, March 13, 2008, www.forbes.com/prnewswire/feeds/prnewswire/2008/03/13/prnewswire200803131134PR_NEWS_USPR____NETH078.html; and Watson Wyatt. *The one percent strategy: Lessons learned from the best performers*, 2008, www.watsonwyatt.com/us/research/resrender.asp?id=2008-US-0037&page=1.

20. Hansen, F. Currents in compensation and benefits. *Compensation & Benefits Review* 37:6–17, 2005.

21. Milkovich, G., & Newman, J. *Compensation*. Boston: McGraw-Hill, 2005.

22. Wright, S., & Carrese, J. Ethical issues in the managed care setting: A new curriculum for primary care physicians. *Medical Teacher* 23:71–75, 2001; and Milkovich, G., & Newman, J. *Compensation*. Boston: McGraw-Hill, 2005.

23. Treadwell, K., & Cram, N. Managed health care and federal health programs. *Journal of Clinical Engineering* 29:36–42, 2004.

24. Milkovich, G., & Newman, J. *Compensation*. Boston: McGraw-Hill, 2005.

25. Ibid.

26. Hansen, F. Currents in compensation and benefits. *Compensation & Benefits Review* 37:6–17, 2005.

27. Aita, S. A rational approach to consumer-driven health care: Engaging consumers and providers in controlling health care costs. *Compensation & Benefits Review* 36:40–47, 2004.

28. More companies, workers adopt consumer-directed health plans. *Forbes*, March 13, 2008, www.forbes.com/prnewswire/feeds/prnewswire/2008/03/13/prnewswire200803131134PR_NEWS_USPR____NETH078.html; and Watson Wyatt. *The one percent strategy: Lessons learned from the best performers*, 2008, www.watsonwyatt.com/us/research/resrender.asp?id=2008-US-0037&page=1.

29. U.S. Department of the Treasury. *HSA frequently asked questions*, www.treas.gov/offices/public-affairs/hsa/faq_basics.shtml.

30. Saleem, H. T. *Health spending accounts*. U.S. Department of Labor, Bureau of Labor Statistics, December 19, 2003, www.bls.gov/opub/cwc/cm20031022ar01p1.htm.

31. Employer interest in consumer-directed health plans growing, Watson Wyatt/National Business Group survey finds, March 16,

2006, www.watsonwyatt.com/news/press.asp?ID=15826; and Crenshaw, A. Debating the impact of high-deductible health plans. *Washington Post*, April 30, 2006, p. F08.

32. Orin, R., & Healy, D. Ten traps to avoid when negotiating self-funded benefits plans. *Compensation & Benefits Review* 38:25–33, 2006; and Woodward, N. Is self-funded health a path for small firms? *HRMagazine* 51:85–86, 2006.

33. Cain, G. Benefit plan strategies to reduce health care and pre-scription drug cost increases. *Compensation & Benefits Review* 35:36–42, 2003.

34. Smerd, J. Firms try to wean employees from brand-name drugs. *Workforce Management*, June 26, 2006, p. 2.

35. Cain, G. Benefit plan strategies to reduce health care and pre-scription drug cost increases. *Compensation & Benefits Review* 35:36–42, 2003.

36. Frase-Blunt, M. Smile, you've got options. *HRMagazine* 49:101–105, 2004.

37. Ibid.

38. Woodward, N. I can see clearly now. *HRMagazine* 45:119–128, 2000.

39. Mitchell, K. Managing the corporate work-health culture. *Compensation & Benefits Review* 36:33–39, 2004; Crenshaw, A. Debating the impact of high-deductible health plans. *Washington Post*, April 30, 2006, p. F08.

40. Risk-assessment strategies: Fairview's wellness program cuts cost, number of high-risk employees. *IOMA's Report on Managing Benefits Plans* 6:1–5, 2006.

41. Miller, S. Developing a cutting-edge wellness program. *SHRM Compensation & Benefits Focus Area*, July 2005, www.shrm.org/rewards/library_published/benefits/nonIC/CMS_013248.asp; and Lincoln Industries Web site, www.lincolnindustries.com.

42. Incentives key to wellness programs. *Occupational Hazards* 67:16, 2005.

43. Marquez, J. Being healthy may be its own reward, but a little cash can also help keep workers fit. *Workforce Management*, September 2005, pp. 66–69.

44. Jamner, M., & Stokols, D. *Promoting human wellness: New fron-tiers for research, practice, and policy*. Berkeley, CA: University of California Press, 2000.

45. Shepherd, L. Mandatory health screenings reap huge rewards: Some employees, however, raised privacy concerns, question legal-ity of required tests. *Employee Benefit News*, April 1, 2006, p.1.

46. Langlieb, A., & Kahn, J. How much does quality mental health care profit employers? *Journal of Occupational and Environmental Medicine* 47:1099–1109, 2006; and Ruiz, G. Expanded EAPs lend a hand to employers' bottom lines. *Workforce Management* 20:46–47, 2006.

47. Ruiz, G. Expanded EAPs lend a hand to employers' bottom lines. *Workforce Management* 20:46–47, 2006.

48. *The basics of short term disability insurance*, 2005, http://info.insure. com/disability/shorttermdisablity.html.

49. Clark, M., & Bates, S. A torn safety net? *HRMagazine* 48:125–130: 2003.

50. Ahrens, A. Ahrens, A. Is a Return-to-work program right for your organization?. *SHRM Information Center White Paper*, 2003, www.shrm.org/hrresources/whitepapers_published/CMS_000188.asp.

51. Life beyond pay—Work–life balance. *Economist* 379:73–74, 2006.

52. Gurchiek, K. U.S. workers continue to leave vacation unused. *HRMgazine* 51:35, 2006; Liddick, B. More vacation time to be

left on the table in '06. *Workforce Management News in Brief*, August 20, 2006.

53. Halfond, J. Smarter tuition-assistance programs: Advice from academe. *SHRMOnline, Compensation & Benefits Library*, 2006, http://www.shrm.org/rewards/library_published/benefits/nonIC/CMS_010156.asp.

54. Pilzner, A. Educational assistance programs. *SHRMOnline, Compensation & Benefits Library*, 2006, www.shrm.org/rewards/library_published/benefits/IC/CMS_000020.asp.

55. Gordon, M. Adding long-term care benefits. *Compensation & Benefits Review* 36:47-52, 2004.

56. Storms, R. Benefits that save retirement. *Compensation & Benefits Review* 34:33, 2002.

57. Ibid.

58. Zimmerman, E. Personal debt can drive employees to distrac-tion. *Workforce Management* online, April 2006, www.workforce.com/archive/article/24/33/36.php.

59. Hira, T., & Loibl, C. Understanding the impact of employer-pro-vided financial education on workplace satisfaction. *Journal of Consumer Affairs* 39:173–194, 2005.

60. Kim, J., & Garman, E. Financial stress, pay satisfaction and work-place performance. *Compensation & Benefits Review* 36:69–76, 2004.

61. Robb, D. Portals offer gateway to financial education. *HRMagazine* 50:5–98, 2005.

62. Sammer, J. Call your attorney: Legal services as an employee benefit. *SHRMOnline, Compensation & Benefits Forum*, January 2005, www.shrm.org/rewards/library_published/benefits/nonIC/CMS_010947.asp; and Garvey, C. Access to the law. *HRMagazine* 47:83–92, 2002.

63. U.S. Department of Labor. *Health plans & benefits: Employee Retirement Income Security Act—ERISA*, www.dol.gov/dol/topic/health-plans/erisa.htm.

64. Parmenter, E. Employee benefit compliance checklist. *Compensation & Benefits Review* 34:29–39, 2002.

65. U.S. Department of Labor. *What you should know about your retirement plan*, 2006, www.dol.gov/ebsa/publications/wyskapr.html.

66. Colvin, G. The end of a dream. *Fortune* 153:85–92, 2006.

67. Ibid.

68. U.S. Department of Labor. *What you should know about your retirement plan*, 2006, www.dol.gov/ebsa/publications/wyskapr.html.

69. Colvin, G. How safe is your pension? *Fortune* 153:52–56, 2006.

70. Colvin, G. The end of a dream. *Fortune* 153:85–92, 2006.

71. Watson Wyatt. *Watson Wyatt urges Congress to seize opportunity to shore up nation's pension system*, June 27, 2006, http://benefitslink.com/pr/detail.php?id=39859.

72. Papke, L. E. Choice and other determinants of employee contri-butions to defined contribution plans. *Social Security Bulletin* 65:59–68, 2003.

73. Hewitt Associates. Trends and experiences in 401(k) plans. Lincolnshire, IL: Hewitt Associates, 2005.

74. IRS. 401(k) resource guide - plan participants - limitation on elec-tive deferrals, http://www.irs.gov/retirement/participant/article/0,,id= 151786,00.html.

75. U.S. Department of Labor. *Frequently asked questions about cash balance pension plans*, www.dol.gov/ebsa/FAQs/faq_consumer_cashbalanceplans.html.

76. The White House. *Fact sheet: The Pension Protection Act of 2006: Ensuring greater retirement security for American workers*, August 17, 2006, www.whitehouse.gov/news/releases/2006/08/20060817. html.

77. Employee Benefits Research Institute (EBRI). *Average couple today needs $295,000 for retiree health expenses*, July 21, 2006, www.ebri.org/pdf/PR_742_20July06.pdf.

78. Colvin, G., & Tkaczyk, C. The end of a dream. *Fortune* 153;85–92, 2006.

79. Sinclair, R., Leo, M., & Wright, C. Benefit system effects on employees' benefit knowledge, use, and organizational commitment. *Journal of Business and Psychology* 20:3–29, 2005.

80. Ads could show job perks. *Daily Post*, July 18, 2006.

81. *The 2005 what's working survey*. NewYork: Mercer Human Resource Consulting, 2005.

82. *Eighth annual Watson Wyatt/WBGH Survey*, www.watsonwyatt.com/research/resrender.asp?id=w-640&page=1.

83. Huff, C. The disappearing benefit. *Workforce Management*, November 21, 2005, pp. 34–38.

84. Babcock, P. SAFETY consciousness. *HRMagazine* 50:66–70, 2005.

85. U.S. Department of Labor. *OSHA 35-year milestones*, www.osha.gov/as/opa/osha35yearmilestones.html.

86. U.S. Department of Labor. *All about OSHA*. Washington, DC: U.S. Department of Labor, 2006.

87. U.S. Department of Labor. *OSHA facts—August 2007*, www.osha.gov/as/opa/oshafacts.html.

88. U.S. Department of Labor. *Job safety and health*. OSHA Fact Sheet No. OSHA 93-01, www.osha.gov/pls/oshaweb/owadisp.show_document?p_table=FACT_SHEETS&p_id=140.

89. Clark, R. A. *OSHA's system of inspection priorities*, September 22, 1993, www.osha.gov/pls/oshaweb/owadisp.show_document?p_table=INTERPRETATIONS&p_id=21280.

90. U.S. Department of Labor. *Partnership: An OSHA cooperative program*, www.osha.gov/dcsp/partnerships/index.html.

91. U.S. Department of Labor. *Voluntary Protection Programs: An OSHA cooperative program*, www.osha.gov/dcsp/vpp/index.html.

92. U.S. Department of Labor. *All about OSHA*. Washington, DC: U.S. Department of Labor, 2006.

93. U.S. Department of Labor. *Safety and health topics: Workplace violence*, www.osha.gov/SLTC/workplaceviolence/index.html.

94. National Institute for Occupational Safety and Health. *Violence in the workplace: Risk factors and prevention strategies*, www.cdc.gov/niosh/violrisk.html.

95. U.S. Department of Labor. *Safety and health topics: Ergonomics*, www.osha.gov/SLTC/ergonomics/index.html.

96. U.S. Department of Labor. *Ergonomics: Contributing conditions*, March 6, 2003, www.osha.gov/SLTC/ergonomics/review_of_ records.html.

97. Wal-Mart. *Benefits*, http://walmartstores.com/Careers/7750.aspx.

98. Perk place: The benefits offered by Google and others may be grand, but they're all business. *Financial Times Press*, April 27, 2007, www.ftpress.com/articles/article.aspx?p=715531.

99. Papke, L. E. Choice and other determinants of employee contributions to defined contribution plans. *Social Security Bulletin* 65:59–68, 2003.

100. Anatole, J. Long-term care insurance in the small business spotlight. *Employee Benefit Plan Review* 61:9–10, 2006.

101. Ruiz, G. Smaller firms in vanguard of flex practices. *Workforce Management* online, November 2005, www.workforce.com/archve/article/24/22/11.php.

102. Pfuntner, J. New benefits data from the National Compensation Survey. *Monthly Labor Review* 127: 6-20, 2004; and Hansen, F. Currents in compensation and benefits. *Compensation & Benefits Review* 38:7–19, 2006.

103. Seid, J. *Time for small businesses to get with 401(k)s*, August 15, 2006, http://money.cnn.com/2006/08/09/smbusiness/401kplans/index.htm.

104. Occupational Safety and Health Administration. *Penalty reductions for small business*, www.osha.gov/dcsp/smallbusiness/index.html.

105. SAS. *Working at SAS: An ideal environment for new ideas*, www.sas. com/jobs/corporate/index.html.

106. Training means zero accidents for FHm; Program exceeds all expectations. *Human Resource Management International Digest* 14:23, 2006.

107. Hoffman, M. Safety awareness is key. *Business Insurance* 40:4–5, 2006.

108. Babcock, P. SAFETY consciousness. *HRMagazine* 50:66–70, 2005.

109. Cole, N., & Flint, D. Opportunity knocks: Perceptions of fairness in employee benefits. *Compensation & Benefits Review*, March/April 2005, pp. 55–62.

110. Rappaport, A. Variation of employee benefit costs by age. *Social Security Bulletin* 63:47–56, 2000.

111. Equal Employment Opportunity Commission. *An act*, www.eeoc.gov/abouteeoc/35th/thelaw/owbpa.html.

112. Arnold, T., & Chester, S. The relationship between justice and benefits satisfaction. *Journal of Business & Psychology* 20:599–620, 2006.

113. Courtney, T., et al. Factors influencing restaurant worker perception of floor slipperiness. *Journal of Occupational & Environmental Hygiene* 3:593–599, 2006.

114. Roth, C. How to protect the aging work force. *Occupational Hazards*, January 20, 2005, www.occupationalhazards.com/Issue/Article/37390/How_to_Protect_the_Aging_Work_Force.aspx.

115. Koven, J. Streamlining benefit process with employee self-service applications: A case study. *Compensation & Benefits Management* 18:18–23, 2002; and Greengard, S. Building a self service culture that works. *Workforce* 77:60–64, 1998.

116. Carmbern, J. Online benefits management systems: An HR evolution. *Compensation & Benefits Review* 38:65–70, 2006.

117. Cherof, E. Legal issues in telecommuting. *Compensation & Benefits Library—Telecommuting*, 2002, www.shrm.org/rewards/library_ published/benefits/IC/CMS_000926.asp.

118. Ibid.; and Grensing-Pophal, L. OSHA, you and the home-based worker. *Compensation & Benefits Library—Telecommuting*, 2002, www.shrm.org/rewards/library_published/benefits/IC/CMS_000008.asp.

119. Society for Human Resource Management. Promoting productivity. *Workplace Visions: Exploring the Future of Work*, January 2006; and Kaiser Family Foundation. *Health care spending in the United States and OECD countries*, January 2007, www.kff.org/insurance/snapshot/chcm010307oth.cfm#back1.

120. Whitehouse, E. *Pensions panorama: Retirement-income systems in 53 OECD countries*. Washington, DC: The World Bank, pp. 43-45.

121. Cravens, K. S., & Oliver, E. Cultural influences on managerial choice: An empirical study of employee benefit plans in the United States. *Journal of International Business Studies* 30:745–762, 1999.

122. Curl, A., & Hokenstad, M. C. Reshaping retirement policies in post-industrial nations: The need for flexibility. *Journal of Sociology & Social Welfare* 33:5–106, 2006.

123. Liddick, B. More vacation time to be left on the table in '06. *Workforce Management* online, August 20, 2006, www.workforce.com/section/00/article/24/48/15.htm.

124. Leonard, B. Escalating health care costs pose new global HR challenges. *Global HR News: SHRMOnline,* July 2006, www.shrm.org/global/library_published/subject/nonIC/CMS_017709.asp.

125. Merkling, S., & Davis, E. Kidnap & ransom insurance: A rapidly growing benefit. *Compensation & Benefits Review* 33:40–45, 2001.

126. Pacific Bridge, Inc. Hong Kong: New anti-racism law affects expatriate benefits package. *SHRM Online: Global HR News—Asia,* 2006, www.shrm.org/global/library_published/subject/nonIC/CMS_016121.asp.

127. Whitehouse, E. New indicators of 30 OECD countries' pension systems. *Journal of Pension Economics and Finance,* 5: 275-298, 2006.

128. Wharton, L. Health & safety: Why safe is sound—Reducing workplace injuries in New Zealand. *New Zealand Management,* September 2003, p. 38.

129. Society for Human Resource Management. *Worldwatch: Health and safety,* http://shrm.org/global/worldwatch/BRsafety.asp.

130. Tyson, J. Tyson's "Bill of Rights." *Workforce Management* online, February 2005, www.workforce.com/archive/article/23/93/74.php.

131. U.S. Department of Labor. *Frequently asked questions about COBRA continuation health coverage,* www.dol.gov/ebsa/faqs/faq_consumer_cobra.html.

132. U.S. Department of Labor. *Fact sheet: Consolidated Omnibus Budget Reconciliation Act (COBRA),* www.dol.gov/ebsa/newsroom/fscobra. html.

133. Parmenter, E. Employee benefit compliance checklist. *Compensation & Benefits Review* 34:29–39, 2002.

134. U.S. Department of Health and Human Services. *Fact sheet: Protecting the privacy of patients' health information,* April 14, 2003, www.hhs. gov/news/facts/privacy.html.

Chapter 13

1. Lieberman, E. *Unions before the bar: Historic trials showing the evolution of labor rights in the United States.* New York: Harper Press, 1950.

2. Twarog, J. The benefits of union membership: Numerous and measurable. *Massachusetts Nurse* 76:6:9, 2005; and Belman, D., & Voos, P. Union wages and union decline: Evidence from the construction industry. *Industrial & Labor Relations Review* 60:67–87, 2006.

3. Reynolds, L. *Labor economics and labor relations.* Englewood Cliffs, NJ: Prentice Hall, 1978.

4. Ibid.

5. Ibid.

6. Ibid.

7. The Public Purpose. *US private sector trade union membership,* www.publicpurpose.com/lm-unn2003.htm.

8. Judis, J. Labor's love lost. *New Republic* 224:18–22, 2001.

9. Grossman, R. Unions follow suit. *HRMagazine,* 50: 46-51, 2005.

10. Dooley, F., & Thoms, W. *Airline labor law: The Railway Labor Act and aviation after deregulation.* Westport, CT: Quorum Books, 1990.

11. Reynolds, L. *Labor economics and labor relations.* Englewood Cliffs, NJ: Prentice Hall, 1978.

12. Lieberman, E. *Unions before the bar: Historic trials showing the evolution of labor rights in the United States.* New York: Harper Press, 1950.

13. Digital History. *The Wagner Act,* www.digitalhistory.uh.edu/database/article_display.cfm?HHID=475.

14. National Labor Relations Board. *National Labor Relations Act,* www.nlrb.gov/about_us/overview/national_labor_relations_act.aspx.

15. National Labor Relations Board. *Employee rights.* www.nlrb.gov/workplace_rights/employee_rights.aspx.

16. National Labor Relations Board. *NLRA violations,* www.nlrb.gov/Workplace_Rights/nlra_violations.aspx.

17. Beal, E., Wickersham, E., & Kienast, P. *The practice of collective bargaining.* Homewood, IL: Richard D. Irwin, 1976.

18. National Labor Relations Board. *Overview,* www.nlrb.gov/about_us/overview/index.aspx; and National Labor Relations Board. *Fact sheet,* www.nlrb.gov/about_us/overview/fact_sheet.aspx.

19. National Labor Relations Board. *Board,* www.nlrb.gov/about_us/overview/board/index.aspx; and National Labor Relations Board. *Fact sheet,* www.nlrb.gov/about_us/overview/fact_sheet.aspx.

20. Hartley, F., Jr. *Our new national labor policy: The Taft-Hartley Act and the next steps.* New York: Funk & Wagnalls, 1948.

21. Ibid.

22. Beal, E., Wickersham, E., & Kienast, P. *The practice of collective bargaining.* Homewood, IL: Richard D. Irwin, 1976.

23. National Right to Work Legal Defense Foundation, Inc. *Right to work frequently-asked questions,* www.nrtw.org/b/rtw_faq.htm.

24. Beal, E., Wickersham, E., & Kienast, P. *The practice of collective bargaining.* Homewood, IL: Richard D. Irwin, 1976.

25. Alston, R., & Taubman, G. Union discipline and employee rights. www.nrtw.org/RDA.htm; and National Right to Work Legal Defense Foundation, Inc. *About your legal rights: Private sector employees,* http://www.nrtw.org/about-your-legal-rights-private-sector-employee.

26. Beal, E., Wickersham, E., & Kienast, P. *The practice of collective bargaining.* Homewood, IL: Richard D. Irwin, 1976.

27. Ibid.

28. Federal Mediation & Conciliation Service Web site, www.fmcs.gov.

29. Beal, E., Wickersham, E., & Kienast, P. *The practice of collective bargaining.* Homewood, IL: Richard D. Irwin, 1976.;and The Association for Union Democracy. *The LMRDA and the union members' bill of rights,* www.uniondemocracy.com/pdfs/rights.PDF.

30. *Why join a labor union?* www.iuoe.org/organizing/whyjoin.htm.

31. Industrial Workers of the World. *IWW industrial unions and departments,* www.iww.org/en/unions.

32. AFL-CIO. *Union facts*, www.aflcio.org/aboutus/faq/.

33. Edsall, T. Two top unions split from AFL-CIO. *Washington Post*, July 26, 2005, p. A01

34. Masters, M., Gibney, R., & Zagenczyk, T. The AFL-CIO v. CTW: The competing visions, strategies, and structures. *Journal of Labor Research* 27:473–504, 2006.

35. Barnes, J. Is this divorce final? *National Journal* 38:41–44, 2006.

36. National Labor Relations Board. *Fact sheet*, www.nlrb. gov/about_us/overview/fact_sheet.aspx; and National Labor Relations Board. *Procedures guide*, www.nlrb.gov/publications/ Procedures_Guide. htm

37. Mayer, G. *Labor union recognition procedures: Use of secret ballots and card checks*, Congressional Research Service, 2005, assets.opencrs. com/rpts/RL32930_20070402.pdf.

38. *The George Washington University and Service Employees International Union, Local 500*, Case 5-CA-32568.

39. Mayer, G. *Labor union recognition procedures: Use of secret ballots and card checks*, Congressional Research Service, 2005, assets.opencrs. com/rpts/RL32930_20070402.pdf.

40. Manheim, J. *Trends in union corporate campaigns: A briefing book*. Washington, DC: U.S. Chamber of Commerce, 2005.

41. Ibid.; and Eaton, A., & Kriesky, J. *Organizing experiences under union-management neutrality and card check agreements*. Report to the Institute for the Study of Labor Organizations, George Meany Center for Labor Studies, February 1999.

42. Eaton, A., & Kriesky, J. Union organizing under neutrality and card check agreements. *Industrial and Labor Relations Review* 55:48+, 2001.

43. Gelinas, P. Flexibility framework for compensation and job security negotiations. *Compensation & Benefits Review* 38:24–29, 2006.

44. Woodhouse, S. A. P. (ed.). *The national employer*. Atlanta: Littler Mendelson, 2006.

45. Thomas, S., & Wisdom, B. Labor negotiations in the nineties: Five steps toward total preparation. *SAM Advanced Management Journal* 58: 32-37, 1993.

46. Walton, R., & McKersie, R. A behavioral theory of labor negotiations. New York: McGraw-Hill, 1965; and Society for Human Resource Management (SHRM). Module 5: Employee and labor relations. *The SHRM Learning System*. Alexandria, VA: SHRM, 2007.

47. Society for Human Resource Management (SHRM). Module 5: Employee and labor relations. *The SHRM Learning System*. Alexandria, VA: SHRM, 2007.

48. Woodhouse, S. A. P. (ed.). *The national employer*. Atlanta: Littler Mendelson, 2006.

49. Seeber, R. L., & Lipsky, D. B. The ascendancy of employment arbitrators in US employment relations: A new actor in the American system? *British Journal of Industrial Relations* 44:719–756, 2006.

50. Society for Human Resource Management (SHRM). Module 5: Employee and labor relations. *The SHRM Learning System*. Alexandria, VA: SHRM, 2007.

51. Ibid.

52. National Labor Relations Board. *Fact sheet*, www.nlrb. gov/about_us/overview/fact_sheet.aspx;.

53. National Labor Relations Board (NLRB). *N.L.R.B. election report, six months summary—April 2007 through September 2007 and cases closed September 2007*. Washington, DC: NLRB, 2007.

54. Manheim, J. *Trends in union corporate campaigns: A briefing book*. Washington, DC: U.S. Chamber of Commerce, 2005, pp. 17–18

55. Manheim, J. *Trends in union corporate campaigns: A briefing book*. Washington, DC: U.S. Chamber of Commerce, 2005.

56. Bentham, K. Employer resistance to union certification: A study of eight Canadian jurisdictions. *Industrial Relations*, 57: 159-185, 2002.

57. Wheeler, H. N. The future of the American labor movement. Cambridge, UK: Cambridge University Press, 2002.

58. AFL-CIO. *AFL-CIO rolls out solidarity charter program to reunite local labor movements*, August 26, 2005, www.aflcio.org/ aboutus/ns08262005.cfm.

59. Karimi, S., & Singh, G. Strategic compensation: An opportunity for union activism. *Compensation & Benefits Review* 36:62–67, 2004.

60. Lulli, L, & Hinson, M. Union organizing trends and tactics. *SHRMOnline*, 2006, www.shrm.org/hrresources/ WHITEPAPERS_Published/CMS_016762.asp.

61. Osterman, P. Community organizing and employee representation. *British Journal of Industrial Relations* 44:629–649, 2006.

62. Woodhouse, S. A. P. (ed.). *The national employer*. Atlanta: Littler Mendelson, 2006.

63. Participation in domestic labor unions drops to all-time low: Report. Seoul, Korea: *Yonhap News Agency of Korea*, November 9, 2006, http://www.accessmylibrary.com/coms2/summary_ 0286-25127062_ITM

64. Schifferes, S. The trade unions' long decline. *BBC News* online. March 8, 2004, http://news.bbc.co.uk/1/hi/business/ 3526917.stm.

65. Williams, P., & Bryson, A. Union organization in Great Britain. *Journal of Labor Research* 28:93, 2007.

66. Fairris, D. Union voice effects in Mexico. *British Journal of Industrial Relations* 44:781, 2006.

67. De La Cruz, J. Mexico's labor law and labor unions in the 1990s. *Memento Economico* 124:26–39, 2002.

68. Dongfang, H. Labor law strengthens Chinese union. *Asia Times* online, January 18, 2008, www.atimes.com/atimes/China_ Business/JA18Cb01.html.

Chapter 14

1. Baird, L., & Meshoulam, I. Managing two fits of strategic human resource management. *Academy of Management Review* 13:116–128, 1988; MacDuffie, J. P. Human resource bundles and manufacturing performance: Organizational logic and flexible production systems in the world auto industry. *Industrial and Labor Relations Review* 48:197–221, 1995; and Huselid, M. A. The impact of human resource management practices on turnover, productivity, and corporate financial performance. *Academy of Management Journal* 38:635–672, 1995.

2. Delery, J. E. Issues of fit in strategic human resource management: Implications for research. *Human Resource Management Review* 8:289–310, 1998; and Wright, P. M., & McMahan, G. C. Theoretical perspectives for strategic human resource management. *Journal of Management* 18:295–320, 1992.

3. Miles, R., & Snow, C. C. Designing strategic human resource systems. *Organizational Dynamics* 13:36–52, 1984; Schuler, R. S., & Jackson, S. E. Linking competitive strategies with human resource management practices. *Academy of Management Executive*

1:207–219, 1987; Becker, B. E., & Huselid, M. A. High performance work systems and firm performance: A synthesis of research and managerial implications. In G. R. Ferris (ed.), *Research in personnel and human resources management.* Greenwich, CT: JAI Press, 1998, pp. 53–101; and MacDuffie, J. P. Human resource bundles and manufacturing performance: Organizational logic and flexible production systems in the world auto industry. *Industrial and Labor Relations Review* 48:197–221, 1995.

4. Delery, J. E. Issues of fit in strategic human resource management: Implications for research. *Human Resource Management Review* 8:289–310, 1998; and Lepak, D. P., Liao, H., Chung, Y., & Harden, E. A conceptual review of HR systems in strategic HRM research. In J. Martocchio (ed.), *Research in personnel and human resource management*, Volume 25. Greenwich, CT: JAI Press, 2006, pp. 217–272.

5. Delery, J. E. Issues of fit in strategic human resource management: Implications for research. *Human Resource Management Review* 8:289–310, 1998; and Becker, B. E., Huselid, M. A., Pickus, P. S., & Spratt, M. F. HR as a source of shareholder value: Research and recommendations. *Human Resource Management* 36(1):39–47, Spring 1997.

6. Becker, B. E., Huselid, M. A., Pickus, P. S., & Spratt, M. F. HR as a source of shareholder value: Research and recommendations. *Human Resource Management* 36(1):39–47, Spring 1997.

7. Ibid.

8. 100 Best Companies to Work for 2008. *Fortune*, http://money. cnn.com/magazines/fortune/bestcompanies/2008/full_list/; America's Most Admired Companies for 2007. *Fortune*, http://money.cnn.com/magazines/fortune/mostadmired/2007/ ; Raphael, T. At Google, the proof is in the people. *Workforce*, March 2003, pp. 50–51; Withers, P. Retention strategies that respond to worker values. *Workforce*, July 2001, pp. 37–41; and Elgin, B. Google: Why the world's hottest tech company will struggle to keep its edge. *BusinessWeek*, May 3, 2004.

9. Barney, J. B., & Hesterly, W. S. *Strategic management and competitive advantage.* Upper Saddle River, NJ: Prentice Hall, 2006.

10. Zacharatos, A., Barling, J., & Iverson, R. D. High-performance work systems and occupational safety. *Journal of Applied Psychology* 90:77–84, 2005.

11. Liao, H., & Chuang, A. A multilevel investigation of factors influencing employee service performance and customer outcomes. *Academy of Management Journal* 47:41–58, 2004.

12. Speizer, I. Shopper's special. *Workforce Management*, September 2004, pp. 51–54; Trader Joe's. *Job descriptions*, www.traderjoes.com/job_ descriptions.html;McGregor, J. Leading listener: Trader Joe's. *FastCompany.com*, October 2004, www.fastcompany.com/magazine/87/customer-traderjoes.html; and Armstrong, L. Trader Joe's: The trendy American cousin. *BusinessWeek* online, April 26, 2004, www.businessweek. com/magazine/content/04_17/b3880016.htm.

13. Barney, J. Firm resources and sustained competitive advantage. *Journal of Management* 17:99–120, 1991; Porter, M. *Competitive advantage: Creating and sustaining superior performance.* New York: The Free Press, 1985; and Wright, P. M., & McMahan, G. C. Theoretical perspectives for strategic human resource management. *Journal of Management* 18:295–320, 1992.

14. Lopez-Cabrales, A., Vale, R., & Herrero, I. The contribution of core employees to organizational capabilities and efficiency. *Human Resource Management* 45(1):81–109, Spring 2006.

15. Robertson, S. Wheeling-Pitt outsourcing cuts logistics costs. *American Metal Market*, October 4, 2002; and Davis, C. Some steelmakers look for savings by outsourcing shipping operations. *Pittsburg Business Times*, January 10, 2003.

16. Houseman, S. N. Why employers use flexible staffing arrangements: Evidence from an establishment survey. *Industrial and Labor Relations Review* 55:149–170, 2001.

17. Temporary, contract worker hiring booming; So are entrepreneurs. *HR Focus*, August 2006, p. 8.

18. How organizations are managing contract workers now. *HR Focus*, November 2006. p. 5.

19. Snell, S. A., Lepak, D. P., & Youndt, M. A. Managing the architecture of intellectual capital: Implications for strategic human resource management. In P. M. Wright, L. D. Dyer, J. W. Boudreau, & G. T. Milkovich (eds.), *Research in personnel and human resource management.* Greenwich, CT: JAI Press, 1999, pp. 61–90; Purcell, J. High commitment management and the link with contingent workers: Implications for strategic human resource management. In P. M. Wright, L. D. Dyer, J. W. Boudreau, & G.T. Milkovich (eds.), *Research in personnel and human resource management.* Greenwich, CT: JAI Press, 1999, pp. 239–257; and Huselid, M. A., Becker, B. E., and Beatty, D. *The workforce scorecard: Managing and measuring human capital to drive strategy execution.* Boston: Harvard Business School Press, 2005.

20. Lepak, D. P., & Snell, S. A. Examining the human resource architecture: The relationships among human capital, employment, and human resource configurations. *Journal of Management* 28:517–543, 2002.

21. Lepak, D. P., & Snell, S. A. The human resource architecture: Toward a theory of human capital allocation and development. *Academy of Management Review* 24:31–48, 1999; and Lepak, D. P., & Snell, S. A. Managing the human resource architecture for knowledge-based competition. In S. Jackson, M. Hitt, & A. DeNisi (eds.), *Managing knowledge for sustained competitive advantage: Designing strategies for effective human resource management.* San Francisco: Jossey-Bass, 2003, pp. 127–154.

22. Perrow, C. B. A framework for the comparative analysis of organizations. *American Sociological Review* 32:194–208, 1967; and Coase, R. H. The nature of the firm. *Economica* 4:386–405, 1937; Williamson, O. E. *Markets and hierarchies: Analysis and antitrust implications.* New York: The Free Press, 1975.

23. Becker, G. S. *Human capital.* New York: Columbia University Press, 1964.

24. Rousseau, D. M. *Psychological contracts in organizations: Understanding written and unwritten agreements.* Thousand Oaks, CA: Sage Publications, 1995.

25. Lepak, D. P., & Snell, S. A. The human resource architecture: Toward a theory of human capital allocation and development. *Academy of Management Review* 24:31–48, 1999.

26. Snell, S. A., Lepak, D. P., & Youndt, M. A. Managing the architecture of intellectual capital: Implications for strategic human resource management. In P. M. Wright, L. D. Dyer, J. W. Boudreau, & G. T. Milkovich (eds.), *Research in personnel and human resource management.* Greenwich, CT: JAI Press, 1999, pp. 61–90; and Purcell, J. High commitment management and the link with contingent workers: Implications for strategic human resource management. In P. M. Wright, L. D. Dyer, J. W. Boudreau, & G. T. Milkovich (eds.), *Research in personnel and human resource management.* Greenwich, CT: JAI Press, 1999, pp. 239–257.

27. Snell, S. A., & Dean, J., Jr. Integrated manufacturing and human resource management: A human capital perspective. *Academy of Management Journal* 35:467–504, 1992; and Delaney, J. T., &

Huselid, M. A. The impact of human resource management practices on perceptions of organizational performance. *Academy of Management Journal* 39:949–969, 1996.

28. Becker, G. S. *Human capital.* New York: Columbia University Press, 1964; Lepak, D. P., & Snell, S. A. Managing the human resource architecture for knowledge-based competition. In S. Jackson, M. Hitt, & A. DeNisi (eds.), *Managing knowledge for sustained competitive advantage: Designing strategies for effective human resource management.* San Francisco: Jossey-Bass, 2003, pp. 127–154.

29. Koch, M. J., & McGrath, R. G. Improving labor productivity: Human resource management policies do matter. *Strategic Management Journal* 17:335–354, 1996; Snell, S. A., & Dean, J., Jr. Integrated manufacturing and human resource management: A human capital perspective. *Academy of Management Journal* 35:467–504, 1992; and Tsui, A. S., Pearce, J. L., Porter, L. W., & Hite, J. P. Choice of employee-organization relationship: Influence of external and internal organizational factors. In G. R. Ferris (ed.), *Research in personnel and human resources management*, Volume 13. Greenwich, CT: JAI Press, 1995, pp. 117–151.

30. Snell, S. A. Control theory in strategic human resource management: The mediating effects of administrative information. *Journal of Management* 35:292–328, 1992; and Snell, S. A., & Youndt, M. A. Human resource management and firm performance: testing a contingency model of executive controls. *Journal of Management* 21:711–737, 1995.

31. Lepak, D. P., & Snell, S. A. The human resource architecture: Toward a theory of human capital allocation and development. *Academy of Management Review* 24:31–48, 1999; and Lepak, D. P., & Snell, S. A. Examining the human resource architecture: The relationships among human capital, employment, and human resource configurations. *Journal of Management* 28:517–543, 2002.

32. Rousseau, D. M., & McLean-Parks, J. The contracts of individuals and organizations. In L. L. Cummings and B. M. Staw (eds.), *Research in organizational behavior*, Volume 15. Greenwich, CT: JAI Press, 1993, pp. 1–43.

33. Lepak, D. P., & Snell, S. A. Examining the human resource architecture: The relationships among human capital, employment, and human resource configurations. *Journal of Management* 28:517–543, 2002.

34. Mathieu, J. E, Tannenbaum, S. I, & Salas, E. Influences of individual and situational characteristics on measures of training effectiveness. *Academy of Management Journal* 35:828–847, 1992.

35. Dyer, J. H. Does governance matter? Keiretsu alliances and asset specificity as sources of Japanese competitive advantage. *Organization Science* 7:649–666, 1996.

36. Becker, B. E., Huselid, M. A., & Ulrich, D. *The HR Scorecard: Linking people, strategy, and performance.* Boston: Harvard Business School Press, 2001.

37. Ibid.

38. Ibid.

39. Schneider, C. The new human-capital metrics. *CFO*, February 15, 2006, pp. 24–27.

40. Ibid.

41. Bowen, D. E., & Ostroff, C. Understanding HRM–firm performance linkages: The role of the "strength" of the HRM system. *Academy of Management Review* 29:203–221, 2004.

42. Jackson, S. E., Schuler, R. S., & Rivero, J. C. Organizational characteristics as predictors of personnel practices. *Personnel Psychology* 42:727–786, 1989; and Schuler, R. S., & Jackson, S. E. Linking competitive strategies with human resource management practices. *Academy of Management Executive* 1:207–219, 1987.

43. FirstMerit Bank Web site, www.firstmerit.com/personal/index.aspx; and Dalton, A. *Pay-for-performance plan helps shrink bank's turnover*, www.workforce.com/archive/article/24/02/86.php.

44. Applebaum, E., Bailey, T., & Berg, P. *Manufacturing advantage: Why high performance work systems pay off.* Ithaca, NY: ILR Press, 2000.

45. Huselid, M. A., & Becker, B. E. Comment on "measurement error in research on human resources and firm performance: How much error is there and how does it influence effect size estimates?" by Gerhart, Wright, McMahan, and Snell. *Personnel Psychology* 53:835–854, 2000; Wright, P. M., & Snell, S. A. Toward an integrative view of strategic human resource management. *Human Resource Management Review* 1:203–225, 1991; and Wright, P. M., & Boswell, W. R. Desegregating HRM: A review and synthesis of micro and macro human resource management. *Journal of Management* 28:248–276, 2002.

Glossary

A

360-degree appraisals A comprehensive measurement approach that involves gathering performance data from as many sources as possible—supervisors, peers, subordinates, and customers.

401(k) plan A retirement plan that allows employees to defer receiving some of their compensation until retirement with contributions to the plan taken out of the employee's paycheck pretax and the funds accumulating tax free until retirement begins.

absolute approach The evaluation of employees' performance by comparing employees against certain "absolute" standards (rather than against each other) along a number of performance dimensions (rather than simply making a global assessment about them).

accidental death and dismemberment insurance (AD&D) An insurance plan designed to compensate employees for the loss of a body part or to compensate the employee's family if an employee suffers the loss of a limb or dies accidentally at work.

achievement test or **competency test** A test to measure an applicant's current knowledge or skill level in relation to the job requirements.

adverse impact, also **disparate impact** Discrimination that occurs when an employment practice results in members of a protected class being treated less favorably than members of a non-protected class even though the discrimination was not intentional.

affirmative action The process of actively seeking to identify, hire, and promote qualified members of underrepresented groups.

agency shop A labor union arrangement under which employees cannot be required to join a union but can be required to pay an agency fee for purposes such as initiation.

agency theory The theory that managers can motivate their employees to act in certain ways by aligning their interests with the interests of the firm's other stakeholders.

alignment The extent to which the three primary HR activities are designed to achieve the goals of the organization.

alliance partner External employee who makes unique contributions but whose contributions are limited in terms of strategic value.

alternative dispute resolution (ADR) A process for resolving disputes among employees and employers using a mediator or an arbitrator.

arbitration A method of resolving disputes in which a third party acts as an intermediary and actually makes the decision about how the issue should be resolved.

assessment center A selection process, often focused on internal promotions, in which candidates participate in a series of simulations designed to determine their ability to perform aspects of the jobs they are seeking.

attrition Not filling vacant positions that emerge as a result of turnover or other employee movements in a company.

audiovisual training Providing instruction to employees by having them watch a video presentation.

automation Using machines to perform tasks that could otherwise be performed by people.

B

backdating Choosing the date of a stock award based on when the stock price was low rather than the exact date the stock award was issued, thereby creating an immediate profit for the individual.

bad faith bargaining Entering into a collective bargaining situation with no intention of reaching an agreement or in some other way violating the protocol for appropriate collective bargaining, for instance bargaining with individual employees rather than with union representatives or refusing to meet at reasonable times to engage in bargaining.

bargaining unit The group of employees designated by the NLRB or identified by the union and employer together as eligible to participate in a union election.

behavioral interview An interview process based on the premise that past behavior is the best predictor of future behavior, therefore, having job candidates respond to questions about how they have handled job-related types of situations in the past will be the best predictor of their success at the job for which they are interviewing.

behavioral observation scales (BOS) A behavior-based approach that requires raters to evaluate how often an employee displays certain behaviors on the job.

behaviorally anchored rating scales (BARS) A behavior-based evaluation approach where raters must evaluate individuals along a number of performance dimensions with each performance rating standard anchored by a behavioral example.

benchmark job A job that represents the range of the types of jobs in the company and is used for comparison with jobs in other companies to establish salaries internally.

biodata (short for **biographical data**) A standardized questionnaire based on the premise that past behavior is the best predictor of future behavior and used with job applicants as part of a selection process to gather personal and biographical information to be compared with the same information for successful employees.

blended learning The use of multiple modes of training, often with one part being online, to accomplish a training goal.

bona fide occupational qualification (BFOQ) A protected classification that can legally be used to make an employment decision.

broadbanding An approach used to reduce the complexity of a compensation system by consolidating a large number of pay grades into a fewer number of broader grades (or bands).

broad-based stock option A stock purchase plan that applies widely to a firm's employees.

business necessity An employment practice that has some relationship to legitimate business goals and is essential to the company's survival.

C

card check A process whereby a company recognizes a union once the union has produced evidence that the majority of workers have signed authorization cards indicating that they want the union to represent them.

cash balance plan A type of retirement account in which the employer credits the participants' retirement account with a pay credit and an interest credit and the employer bears the risk because the employee, when fully vested, is entitled to receive the stated account balance upon leaving the company or retirement.

Civil Service Reform Act An act passed in 1978 that set up the Federal Labor Relations Authority (FLRA) as the oversight agency for labor-management issues at the federal level.

classroom training Traditional learning that includes lectures, role plays, discussions, and other experiential activities.

closed shop This type of union shop was outlawed under the Taft Hartley Act and is considered the most extreme form of union membership because it requires workers to join a union before they can be hired and requires employers to go to the union first to hire new employees.

coaching Short-term training provided one-on-one and primarily focused on performance improvement relative to a specific skill or ability.

cognitive ability test A test designed to measure general intelligence or level of specific aptitudes, such as numeric fluency and general reasoning.

collaborative-based HR system A system of managing external labor on a long-term basis through alliances or partnerships. The longer-term relationships help preserve continuity and ensure trust among partners, and they engender reciprocity and collaboration between external individuals and internal employees through the use of group incentives, cross-functional teams, and the like.

collective bargaining The process that labor unions and employers use to reach agreement about wages, benefits, hours worked, and other terms and conditions of employment.

commitment-based HR system A system of investing extensively in the development of core employees' competencies, empowering them to use their competencies in the performance of their jobs, and encouraging their full participation in decision making and discretion on the job.

comparable worth Eliminating inequity in wages by ensuring that jobs that require similar levels of education and experience and have other characteristics in common are paid at a similar wage regardless of gender.

compensable factor Aspects of jobs, such as skill, effort, responsibility, and working conditions, that exist across jobs in a company, are needed by employees for the firm to achieve its objectives, and for which the company is willing to pay.

compensation The monetary and nonmonetary rewards employees receive in exchange for the work they do for an organization.

compensatory approach A process for deriving a final score for each candidate in the selection process by weighting outcomes on multiple selection measures differentially so that some items are weighted more heavily than others and a high score on one part can offset a low score on another part.

competencies The knowledge, skills, abilities, and other talents that employees possess.

competency-based pay A highly structured pay system that identifies the competencies employees need to master to be eligible for pay raises.

competitive advantage A company's ability to create more economic value than its competitors.

compliance-based HR system A system that focuses on meeting preset rules, regulations, and/or procedures with an emphasis on short-term productivity and the efficient performance of tasks that are limited in scope, purpose, or duration.

compressed workweek The option to reduce the number of days employees work within a week.

conciliation A type of facilitation used when an impasse occurs in a collective bargaining session so that both parties keep working toward an agreement until they can resolve the issues at hand.

concurrent criterion-related validity The extent to which a selection measure accurately predicts job performance as determined by comparing the scores on the selection measure for current employees with information about their current job performance to see if there is a statistically significant relationship between the two sets of scores.

Consolidated Omnibus Reconciliation Act (COBRA) This act, passed in 1986, provides for employees and their families who participate in a group health plan sponsored by an employer with 20 or more employees to have the option to continue their group health, dental, and vision insurance coverage for up to 18 months when they are terminated for a qualifying reason as long as they pay the full cost of the premium.

construct validity The extent to which a selection method, such as a test, measures the job-related characteristic—the construct—that it claims to measure.

consumer-driven health plan (CDHP) An alternative type of health care plan that puts more of the decision making under the control of employees by letting them choose whether they prefer a plan with a higher deductible or other more expensive alternatives, how much to put into a savings plan for health care purposes, and which health care provider to use.

contaminated performance measure The reliance on information that is irrelevant to an individual's job performance.

content validity The extent to which a selection measure accurately and adequately represents the knowledge or other information it is designed to measure as determined by subject matter experts.

contingency recruiting agency A type of employment agency used by employers with payment made as a flat fee or percentage of the new hire's first-year salary and only paid if the search is successful.

contingent labor Employees hired on a temporary or contractual basis as opposed to a permanent basis.

contract worker External employee whose contributions are not unique and limited in strategic value.

contrast effect Bias that results when an evaluation of one or more persons is artificially inflated or deflated compared to the evaluation of another person.

contributory retirement plan A pension plan in which the employer and employee both put money into the retirement account.

copay The minimum amount employees must pay for health care as determined by their health insurance plan.

core employee Person who directly contributes to a firm's core competencies and competitiveness.

corporate campaign Tactical strategies designed to identify and exploit opportunities to interfere with the normal operation of a business and affect its reputation.

cost leadership strategy A strategy that focuses on outperforming competing firms within an industry by maintaining the ability to offer the lowest costs for products or services.

cost-of-living adjustment (COLA) A pay adjustment for employees to offset the increases in the prices of goods and services they purchase and to keep salaries from lagging behind the external market.

cost-per-hire The sum of all recruiting costs, including such items as advertising, travel, search-firm fees, and background checks, divided by the number of new hires.

craft union A union organized to represent the interests of members with specialized craft skills.

criterion-related validity (also empirical validity) The extent to which a statistically significant relationship exists between the selection test and some measure of job performance.

critical incident approach A behavior-based approach where the evaluation criteria consist of statements or examples of exceptionally good or poor performance employees display over the course of the evaluation period.

D

Davis-Bacon Act An act that requires contractors and subcontractors with contracts in excess of $2,000 with the federal government to pay their workers a minimum wage that is at least equal to the local prevailing wages and to provide them with the local prevailing benefits.

deadly combination HR practice that seems appropriate but presents problems when combined with other HR practices to manage employees.

decertification The process of terminating union representation in collective bargaining.

deferred profit sharing plan A group based incentive plan where the incentive money paid an employee is put into a retirement account for the person.

deficient performance measure An incomplete appraisal of an individual's performance when important aspects are not measured.

defined benefit pension plan A pension plan that provides an annuity to eligible employees upon their retirement with the amount paid per year based on a formula that usually includes a company determined percentage, the number of years worked, and either the last salary or some average of previous years' salaries.

defined contribution plan A pension plan in which the employer specifies where the money will be deposited and often gives the employee the power to decide how the money will be invested with the retirement income being a function of how well money put into the plan was invested.

demotion An employee's move to a lower-level position within the company.

desktop training A training approach in which employees access a software program housed on their computers or on a server.

development Learning experiences that are focused on the future and aimed at preparing employees to take on additional responsibilities in different jobs, usually at a higher level.

devil's horns effect The bias that occurs when a negative characteristic of a job candidate affects the evaluation of the candidate's other attributes.

diary Log of the tasks and activities that employees perform throughout the course of a day, week, or month.

Dictionary of Occupational Titles (DOT) A list of concise job definitions created by the Employment and Training Administration and published by the U.S. Department of Labor.

differential piecework plan An individual incentive plan in which the level of pay employees receive per unit produced or delivered changes at certain levels of output.

differentiation strategy A strategy that emphasizes achieving competitive advantage over competing firms by providing something unique for which customers are willing to pay.

direct market pricing Collecting salary information from the external labor market first rather than starting with the development of an internal structure based on the value of the jobs within the company.

direct measures approach A results-based evaluation in which managers gauge the outcomes of employees' work, such as their sales, productivity, absenteeism, and the like.

disability A physical or mental impairment that substantially limits one or more major life activities.

discrimination Treating people differently in employment situations because of characteristics, such as race, color, and gender, that have nothing to do with their ability to perform a particular job.

disparate impact, or **adverse impact** Discrimination that occurs when an employment practice results in members of a protected class being treated less favorably than members of a non-protected class even though the discrimination was not intentional.

disparate treatment Treating individuals differently in employment situations *because of* their membership in a protected class.

distributive bargaining strategy The negotiation strategy used when the goals of one party are in direct conflict with the goals of the other party and results in a winner and a loser.

distributive justice The fairness of what individuals receive from companies in return for their efforts.

diversity training A type of training designed to help reduce discrimination by making employees more aware of the value of differences in the workplace and the problems associated with stereotypes.

domestic strategy A strategy that focuses primarily on serving the market within a particular country.

E

e-learning Using the Internet, computers, and other electronic tools to deliver training programs.

employee assistance program (EAP) A resource for employees dealing with personal problems that provides services such as attorney consultation, child-care and elder-care options, budgeting information, and family counseling.

employee inventory A searchable database used to identify employees who meet specified job requirements.

employee orientation A process designed to ensure employees understand the policies and procedures of the company when they first begin work, as well as understand how their job fits with the goals of the company.

Employee Retirement Income and Security Act of 1974 (ERISA) A federal law that protects benefits for retirees in the private sector.

employee self-service (ESS) applications Web-based programs accessed via a company's intranet where employees can review their benefits information and make changes during open enrollment periods.

employee stock ownership plan (ESOP) A group based incentive plan where the company contributes shares of its stock to a trust set up for its employees.

employees The individuals who work for a company.

employer branding The development of a long-term strategy to manage how a firm's stakeholders—including its current and future employees—perceive the company.

employment-at-will Hiring provisions based on state laws that allow employers to terminate (or hire or transfer) employees at any time and that allow employees to quit at any time.

empowerment Providing employees with higher level tasks, responsibility, and decision making in the performance of their job.

environmental influences The pressures that exist outside companies that managers must consider to strategically manage their employees.

equal employment opportunity (EEO) The term used to describe laws, regulations, and processes related to fair treatment of employees.

Equal Employment Opportunity Commission (EEOC) Agency responsible for enforcing compliance with antidiscrimination laws such as the Civil Rights Act of 1964, the Age Discrimination in Employment Act, and the Americans with Disabilities Act.

equity theory The theory that employees compare their input (work effort) and outcome (wages) levels to those of other people in similar situations to determine if they are being treated the same in terms of pay and other outcomes.

ergonomics The science of understanding the capabilities of humans in terms of their work requirements.

error of central tendency A performance evaluation error that occurs when raters are unwilling to rate individuals as very high or very low on a performance evaluation scale.

essential functions Job tasks, duties, and responsibilities that must be done by the person in a particular job.

Excelsior list A list of names and addresses for employees who are eligible to vote in the representation election within seven days after the NLRB has indicated that an election will be held.

executive search firm See definition of **retained agency**.

exempt employee A worker whose job classification does not require the payment of overtime pay for time worked in excess of 40 hours a week.

expectancy The degree to which employees believe that, if they work toward a certain performance objective, they will be able to achieve that objective.

expectancy theory The theory that employees make decisions regarding how to act at work based on which behaviors they believe will lead to their most valued work-related rewards and outcomes.

external alignment The extent to which the three primary HR activities that a company uses help them meet its organizational demands, cope with environmental factors, and comply with regulatory issues.

external competitiveness Jobs in a company are valued appropriately relative to similar jobs in the company's external labor market.

external recruiting The process of seeking job applicants from outside the organization using activities such as advertisements, job fairs, and the Internet.

F

factor comparison A quantitative type of job evaluation that involves ranking benchmark jobs in relation to each other on each of several compensable factors, such as mental requirements and responsibility, and then assigning a portion of the hourly rate for the job to each factor.

fair employment practice laws State and local government employee management regulations.

Fair Labor Standards Act (FLSA) An act that governs what employers can and cannot do in regards to compensation, including regulating the use of child labor, defining the difference between exempt and non-exempt employees, setting a minimum wage, and stipulating the pay rate for overtime work.

Federal Labor Relations Authority (FLRA) The oversight agency for labor-management issues at the federal level.

final screening The in-depth look at the applicants who have made it through the initial screening prior to hiring by using techniques such as reviewing references, performing background checks, and conducting additional interviews.

flexible benefit plan (also called a **cafeteria plan**) This plan allows employees to choose which benefits they want to purchase from a menu of benefits.

flextime Work arrangement whereby employees may choose the starting and ending time of their workday as long as they work the appropriate number of hours per day or week.

forced distribution A form of individual comparisons whereby managers are forced to distribute employees into one of several predetermined performance categories.

forced-choice approach A behavior-based approach where managers must choose from a set of alternative statements regarding the person being rated.

four-fifths rule A guideline generally accepted by the courts and the EEOC for making a *prima facie* case of disparate impact by showing that an employment

practice results in members of a protected class being treated less favorably by an employment practice than members of a non-protected class.

frame-of-reference training Training that aims to help raters understand performance standards as well as performance dimensions.

free rider An individual who does not work as hard as the others on their teams.

functional flexibility A form of flexibility related to the ease of adjusting the types of skills a workforce possesses.

G

gain sharing plan A plan designed to help increase an organization's efficiency by increasing the productivity of the company's employees and/or lowering the firm's labor costs.

global performance measure The use of a single score to reflect an individual employee's overall performance.

global strategy A strategy whereby a company strives to achieve global efficiency.

globalization The blurring of country boundaries in business activities.

goal setting theory This theory suggests that goals serve as a motivator to focus the efforts of employees when the goals are specific, challenging, and attainable.

good faith bargaining The process that requires the parties to meet at a reasonable time and come to the bargaining table ready to reach a collective bargaining agreement.

graphic rating scale A method of evaluating employees based on various traits, or attributes, they possess relevant to their performance.

graphology A selection method that involves evaluating handwriting to infer personality attributes.

grievance A charge by one or more employees that management has violated their contractual rights.

grievance process The formal steps that must be followed to settle disputes between labor and management.

growth need strength The extent to which individuals feel a need to learn and be challenged, a need to develop their skills beyond where they currently are, and a strong need for accomplishment.

H

halo effect (also **halo error**) The bias that occurs when a positive characteristic of a person affects the evaluation of the person's other attributes.

harassment Subjecting employees to unwanted and unwelcome treatment because of their race, color, religion, sex, national origin, age, or disability.

headhunter See definition of **retained agency**.

Health Insurance Portability and Accountability Act (HIPAA) An act passed in 1996 that makes it easier for workers to maintain their health care coverage when they change employers because it specifies that coverage under a prior employer's health plan counts for meeting a preexisting condition requirement under a new plan.

health maintenance organization (HMO) A type of managed care health insurance program that requires employees to designate a primary care physician and have any visits to specialists referred by the primary care physician.

health reimbursement account (HRA) An account into which an employer puts money to reimburse employees for qualified medical expenses.

health savings account (HSAs) A special account established through employers, banks, credit unions, insurance companies, and other approved financial institutions into which an employee puts aside money pre-tax to help pay for his or her health care expenses.

high-deductible health plan (HDHPs) (also called a **catastrophic health plan**) A type of managed-care health insurance plan that costs the employer and employee less per month because they require the employee to pay the first few thousand dollars of medical costs each year and pays medical costs only when the employee has a major medical problem.

high-potential employees Employees with the greatest likelihood of being successful and making significant contributions to organizational goal achievement.

hiring freeze A temporary ban on the hiring of new employees for a specified period of time.

horn error A performance evaluation error that occurs when an overall negative view of an employee's performance that biases the ratings such that the individual receives lower ratings on specific performance dimensions than he or she really merits.

host-country national (HCN) Employees who are citizens of the host country in which the company is operating.

hostile work environment A situation that exists whenever an employee is the subject of unwelcome harassment because of his or her membership in a protected class and that harassment is severe and abusive.

HR challenges Challenges that managers must consider in the management of employees that relate to (1) organizational demands; (2) environmental influences; and (3) regulatory issues.

HR deliverable What is needed from a firm's HR activities, or the mechanism by which an HR system creates value for a company.

human resources department or **HR department** A support function within companies that serves a vital role in designing and implementing company policies for managing employees.

human resources practices, often **HR practices** The practices that a company has put in place to manage employees.

I

impasse The situation in which both parties have made their final offers and are not willing to make further concessions.

impression management The actions, such as ingratiation, self-promotion, and opinion conformity, used by applicants to present themselves in a positive light to the interviewer with the idea of biasing the outcome of the interview in their favor.

Improshare plan A group based incentive plan based on the number of hours a firm expects to take to reach a certain level of output.

independent contractor External worker who performs work for an organization but maintains substantial control over the means and methods of their services.

industrial union A union that has traditionally represented semi-skilled and unskilled workers in a particular industry.

initial screening The preliminary review of the information provided by job applicants and the collection of additional information to decide which applicants should be given more serious consideration for the job.

instructional objective Statements that describe what is to be accomplished in a training program and, therefore, drive the design of the program.

instrumentality The degree to which employees believe that achieving a performance objective will be rewarded.

integrative bargaining strategy The negotiation strategy used when each party cooperates and works to reach a win-win outcome.

interactional justice How employees feel they are treated by their managers and supervisors in everyday interactions.

interest-based bargaining (IBB) An extension of integrative bargaining in which each party looks for common goals in order to meet the interests of the other party.

internal alignment (for compensation) When each job in a company is valued appropriately relative to every other job in terms of its ability to help the firm achieve its goals.

internal recruiting The process of seeking job applicants within the company.

international strategy A strategy used by companies to expand the markets in which they compete to include multiple countries.

international unions Federations of local unions.

internship An employment situation in which students work during the summer or academic year in a job related to their chosen vocation to test out a vocation and to give the employer a chance to determine if the student is a good future employee.

J

job analysis The process of systematically identifying the tasks, duties, and responsibilities expected to be performed in a single job as well as the competencies—the knowledge, skills, and abilities (KSAs)—employees must possess to be successful in the job.

job-based employee Individual employed internally but does not contribute in a unique manner.

job characteristics model A motivational model of job design based on five job dimensions and three psychological states of employees that affect employees' internal motivation and satisfaction, as well as their absenteeism, turnover, and productivity.

job classification A type of job evaluation that involves the development of broad descriptions for grouping jobs that are similar in terms of their tasks, duties, responsibilities, and qualifications for the purpose of assigning wages.

job description A written summary of the specific tasks, responsibilities, and working conditions of a job.

job design Determining the tasks and responsibilities that employees in a particular job are expected to perform as well as how they need to interact with their coworkers to realize those contributions.

job enlargement The assignment of additional tasks to employees of a similar level of difficulty and responsibility.

job enrichment Increases in the level of responsibility or control employees have in performing the tasks of a job.

job evaluation The systematic process of determining the relative worth of jobs to a company.

job grade Grouping jobs with comparable points together to reflect the hierarchy of jobs within the company and establish pay rates.

job posting The most frequently used technique for notifying current employees about job openings within the company.

job pricing The systematic process of assigning monetary rates to jobs so that a firm's internal wages are aligned with the external wages in the marketplace.

job ranking A type of job evaluation that involves reviewing job descriptions and listing the jobs from highest to lowest in worth to the company.

job rotation Moving workers from one job to another job within the organization to provide exposure to different aspects of the company's operations.

job simplification Removing decision-making authority from the employee and placing it with a supervisor.

job specialization The process of breaking down jobs into their simple core elements.

job specification Description of the competencies—the knowledge, skills, abilities, or other talents—that a jobholder must have in order to perform the job successfully.

K

knowledge-based pay A pay system that requires employees to acquire certain skills or knowledge in order to receive a pay increase.

L

labor demand The number and types of employees the company needs to meet its current and future strategic objectives.

Labor Management Relations Act (also called the **Taft-Hartley Act**) This act protects the rights of employees and makes the NLRB a more impartial referee for industrial relations.

labor shortage The situation when demand for labor exceeds the available supply of it.

labor supply The availability of current or potential employees to perform a company's jobs.

labor surplus The situation when supply of labor is greater than the demand for it.

Landrum-Griffin Act This act protects union members from being abused by unions and outlines the responsibilities of union officers as well as the rights of union members via a bill of rights.

learning agility The willingness to seek new experiences and opportunities to learn new knowledge and skills.

learning style How people prefer to absorb and process new information.

legal compliance training Training that ensures that a firm's managers and employees know what they can and cannot do from a legal standpoint.

leniency error A performance evaluation error that occurs when employees are consistently rated on the higher end of a performance evaluation scale.

lesson plan A map of what should be done during each training session to achieve objectives.

leveraged ESOP A group based incentive plan that allows a trust to borrow funds against the company's future earnings, and as the debt is repaid, employees receive shares of the stock held by the ESOP in employee accounts.

line manager or **manager** The individuals who are responsible for supervising and directing the efforts of a group of employees to perform tasks that are directly related to the creation and delivery of a company's products or services.

living wage The concept that employees should be paid a wage that ensures that their basic costs of living are met.

long-term care insurance (LTCI) An insurance plan that provides assistance to aging, disabled, and ill persons who need daily help with tasks such as dressing, eating, or bathing for an extended time period.

long-term disability (LTD) An insurance plan that typically kicks in after 30 to 90 days from the time of a disability and pays a portion of the employee's salary until retirement age.

lump-sum merit bonus A one-time payment based on an employee's level of performance.

M

management by objectives (MBO) A results-based approach where managers meet with their employees and jointly set goals for them to accomplish during a particular time period.

mandatory bargaining topics Topics that must be negotiated, including compensation and benefits, hours of employment, and other conditions of employment.

McDonnell Douglas test A four-step test, named after the *McDonnell Douglas Corp. v. Greene* 1973 U.S. Supreme court case, used to make a case of disparate treatment.

mediation The arrangement whereby an outside party works with each side in a negotiation to reach an acceptable agreement.

Medicare The health insurance portion of Social Security for retirees age 65 or older and disabled workers.

mentoring A longer-term relationship that involves a more senior employee teaching a junior employee how the organization works and nurturing that person as she progresses in her career.

merit pay increase A compensation adjustment based on the results of an employee's performance evaluations.

minimum wage The lowest hourly wage rate an employer can pay.

mixed-level plan An incentive plan where employees are exposed to multiple incentive plans.

mixed motive A legitimate reason for an employment decision exists, but the decision was also motivated by an illegitimate reason.

mixed salary/commission plan A plan where employees receive a lower base salary, perhaps only 50% or 70% of what would be offered under a straight salary plan, with the remaining percentage commission-based.

multinational strategy A strategy used when companies establish autonomous or independent business units in multiple countries.

multiple-cutoff approach The final selection decision making approach that requires applicants to make a minimum score on each measure to remain under consideration for a particular job.

multiple-hurdle approach The final selection decision making approach that requires applicants to successfully pass each step (hurdle) to continue on in the selection process.

N

national emergency strike A strike or lockout prevented by the government because it affects an entire industry or a substantial part of it and/or national health and safety are imperiled.

National Labor Relations Act (NLRA) (also called the **Wagner Act**) This act protects the rights of employees and employers, encourages these parties to engage in collective bargaining, and controls their activities so that the economy won't be adversely affected by their actions.

National Labor Relations Board (NLRB) An agency of the U.S. government created by Congress to administer the NLRA.

needs assessment A means to identify where gaps exist between what employees should be doing and what they are actually doing.

negligent hiring The situation that occurs when an employer does not conduct a background check on an employee and that person commits a crime at work similar to a crime he or she committed in the past.

neutrality agreement An arrangement whereby a company will not express its views about unionization during the time when signatures are being collected.

noncontributory retirement plan A pension plan in which the employer puts funds into an employee's account without requiring the employee to make contributions.

nonexempt employee A worker who receives overtime pay for time worked in excess of 40 hours a week.

Norris-LaGuardia Act This act makes it easier for employees to engage in union-organizing activities.

numerical flexibility A form of organizational flexibility related to the ease of adjusting the number of individuals working for a company.

O

Occupational Information Network (O*NET) An online database created by the U.S. Department of Labor that serves as a comprehensive source of information for more than 800 occupations.

Occupational Safety and Health Act of 1971 (OSH Act) This act requires employers to provide a safe workplace for all employees, and provides a process for investigation of complaints of unfair practices as well as provides for worksite inspections.

Office of Federal Contract Compliance Programs (OFCCP) Agency responsible for developing guidelines and overseeing compliance with antidiscrimination laws relative to executive orders.

offshoring The practice of sending work that was once performed domestically to companies in other countries or opening facilities in other countries to do the work.

Older Workers Benefit Protection Act An amendment to the Age Discrimination in Employment Act prohibiting discrimination against older workers relative to their benefits except when reductions in employee benefit plans based on age are justified by significant cost issues.

onboarding The hiring and integration process used to ensure a smooth transition of new employees, especially mid- and upper-level executives, into their jobs and the company, including helping them acclimate to the culture and goals of the organization.

on-demand recruiting services A type of recruiting agency that charges based on the time spent recruiting rather than paying an amount per hire.

on-the-job training (OJT) Training that occurs when a manager or coworker teaches an employee how to perform some aspect of a job in the actual job location rather than in a separate training location.

organization analysis An assessment used to determine a firm's progress toward achieving its goals and objectives.

organizational culture The set of underlying values and beliefs that employees of a company share.

organizational demands The factors within a firm that affect decisions regarding how to manage employees.

outplacement assistance program A program to help employees who are being let go find new jobs.

outsourcing The practice of sending work to other companies.

overtime Work hours that exceed the number of hours established as the normal workweek.

P

paired comparisons An evaluation approach in which each employee in a business unit is compared to every other employee in the unit.

panel interview A type of interview process in which several people interview an applicant at the same time.

parent-country national (PCN) An employee who is a citizen of the country in which the company is headquartered but working for the company in another location.

participation The extent to which employees are permitted to contribute to decisions that may affect them in their jobs.

Pension Benefit Guaranty Corporation (PBGC) A not-for-profit organization created by the federal government that insures defined benefit pension plans.

Pension Protection Act (PPA) An act passed in 2006 and designed to strengthen the U.S. pension system by tightening rules relative to employer responsibilities for funding pension accounts and for administering and terminating pension funds.

performance dimension The specific tasks and activities for which employees are responsible.

performance management The process of (1) evaluating employee performance against the standards set for them and (2) helping them develop action plans to improve their performance.

performance standards The level of expected performance.

permissive topics Nonmandatory issues, such as employee rights, managerial control, and benefits for retired union members, that are often part of the collective bargaining negotiations and agreement.

person analysis An assessment of the gap between an individual's performance and desired job outcomes.

person–job fit The extent to which there is a good match between the characteristics of the potential employee, such as knowledge, skills, values, and the requirements of the job.

person–organization fit The extent to which the potential employee fits well within the broader organizational culture and values.

physical ability test A selection test that focuses on physical attributes of job candidates, such as a candidate's endurance, strength, or general fitness.

podcast A digital recording that can be downloaded and played back later.

point-of-service plan (POS) A hybrid of an HMO and a PPO where individuals can also receive treatment outside the network but must pay a higher deductible.

point method A quantitative method of job evaluation that involves assigning point values to jobs based on compensable factors to create the relative worth hierarchy for jobs in the company.

positive discipline The disciplinary process that is not punitive but rather focuses on constructive feedback and encourages employees to take responsibility for trying to improve their behaviors or performance at work.

powerful connection HR practices used in combinations that support and reinforce other practices that are in place.

prediction Making a determination about how likely it is that candidates selected will be successful in the job based on their current ability to do the job or the potential that they will be able to learn the job and do it well.

predictive criterion-related validity The extent to which a selection measure accurately predicts job performance as determined by comparing the scores on the selection measure used when the employee applied for the job with their current performance scores to determine if there is a statistically significant relationship between the two sets of scores.

preferred provider organization (PPO) A type of managed care program in which the employer negotiates with health care providers, usually in a network, for discounts and services for healthcare coverage for employees.

prima facie case Establishing the basis for a case of discrimination.

primacy error A performance evaluation error that occurs when a rater's earlier impressions of an individual bias his or her later evaluations of the person.

primary HR activities The strategic management of employees centers around three categories of HR activities (1) work design and workforce planning, (2) managing employee competencies, and (3) managing employee attitudes and behaviors.

private employment agency A business that provides job search assistance for a fee, and often to select professions only.

procedural justice Perceptions of whether the processes that are used to make decisions, allocate rewards, or resolve disputes or that otherwise affect employees are viewed as fair.

productivity The level of a firm's output (products or services) relative to the inputs (employees, equipment, materials, and so forth) used to produce the output.

productivity-based HR system A system that involves standardized jobs selection of people from the external labor market who can contribute immediately in these jobs, rewards based on efficiency and productivity improvements, and, results-oriented performance management system.

productivity ratio The number of employees (labor demand) needed to achieve a certain output level (level of sales, production, and so forth).

profit sharing plan A group based incentive plan where company profits are shared with employees.

progressive discipline A process by which an employee with disciplinary problems progresses through a series of disciplinary stages until the problem is corrected.

promotion An employee's move to a higher-level position, which often is associated with increased levels of responsibility and authority.

protected classification, or protected class Demographic characteristics that cannot be used for employment decisions.

psychological contract The *perceived* obligations that employees believe they owe their company and that their company owes them.

psychological states In the job characteristics model employees may experience three psychological states relating to (1) experienced meaningfulness of the work, (2) experienced responsibility for outcomes of the work, and (3) knowledge of the actual results of work activities.

public employment agency A not-for-profit job placement agency affiliated with a local or state government.

Q

quid pro quo harassment A type of harassment that is made explicitly or implicitly a condition of employment.

R

Railway Labor Act (RLA) The act that provides a peaceful way for railroads and their employees to resolve their disputes; also applies to common-carrier rail service and commercial airline employees.

ranking approach An evaluation approach in which employees are evaluated from best to worst along some performance dimension or by virtue of their overall performance.

realistic job preview Providing individuals with a balanced overview of a prospective job to encourage applicants who are not a good fit to screen themselves out of the hiring process and to ensure that applicants who are hired understand what the job will involve.

reasonable accommodation Making modifications in how the work is done or in the work environment so that someone who is qualified for the job and who has a disability can perform the job.

recency error A performance evaluation error that occurs when a rater narrowly focuses on an employee's performance that occurs near the time of the evaluation.

recruitment The process of identifying potential employees, communicating job and organizational attributes to them, and convincing them to apply for available jobs.

recruitment value proposition A marketing concept used in recruitment to design the advertising message in such a way that potential applicants can differentiate what one company offers to its employees versus what other companies offer.

reinforcement theory The theory that when people experience positive consequences after they do something, they are likely to repeat those actions.

relational relationship A relationship that involves a social or emotional commitment to the individual by the company and vice versa.

relevant labor market The location in which one can reasonably expect to find a sufficient supply of qualified applicants.

reliability The extent to which a selection measure yields consistent results over time or across raters.

replacement chart A method of tracking information about employees who can move into higher-level positions within the company in the future.

resume spidering A process of identifying passive job applicants by searching the Web for resumes on private Web pages, professional association sites, university and college alumni sites, and company Web sites.

retained agency (also **executive search firm** or **headhunter**) An employment firm used for recruiting high-level positions, such as CEOs and vice presidents, with the firm paid a retainer for the work it does.

retaliation Punishment that occurs when an employer takes an adverse action against an employee who has filed a discrimination complaint.

reverse discrimination A type of discrimination where members of a protected group are given preference in employment decisions, resulting in discrimination of nonprotected groups.

right-to-work laws Laws that prevent workers from having to join a union as a condition of employment, be prevented from joining a union as a condition of employment, or be forced to pay dues to a labor union or be fired for not paying such dues.

role ambiguity The uncertainty that employees may experience about the daily tasks expected of them and how to perform them.

role conflict Tension caused by incompatible or contradictory demands on a person.

role overload Too many expectations or demands placed on employees in the course of performing their jobs.

role underload Too few expectations or demands placed on employees in the course of performing their jobs.

S

salary compression (also **pay** or **wage compression**) A situation that occurs when the pay for jobs in the external marketplace rises faster than the pay for jobs inside the organization, resulting in new employees receiving higher salaries than existing employees.

salary survey A systematic way to collect information about wages in the external labor market.

Scanlon plan A group based incentive plan used to help reduce a firm's labor costs without corresponding decreases in productivity levels based on employee suggestions for increased efficiencies and productivity.

selection The systematic process of deciding which applicants to hire.

self-appraisal An evaluation done by an employee that rates his or her own performance.

self-efficacy The confidence that a person has that he can perform a particular task.

self-managed team Type of team in which team members, rather than a supervisor of the team, work collaboratively to make team decisions, including hiring, planning, and scheduling decisions.

short-term disability An insurance plan that will pay a portion of an employee's salary when the employee is out of work for a limited time due to a disability.

similar-to-me errors A performance evaluation error that occurs when managers give a higher rating to employees who resemble them in some way.

simulation A training activity that replicates the work employees will be doing without the safety and cost concerns often associated with various jobs.

situational interview A type of interview in which applicants are asked to respond to a series of hypothetical situations to determine how they would respond in a similar situation on the job.

skill-based pay A pay system that requires employees to acquire certain skills or knowledge in order to receive a pay increase.

social loafing A situation in which the motivation of individuals to exert effort diminishes when their outputs are combined with those of others.

Social Security Act A social insurance act put into effect in 1937 and funded by employer and employee contributions to provide old age, survivors, disability, and death benefits.

sourcing The process of identifying, attracting, and screening potential applicants who are not actively in the market for a new job.

specificity The clarity of performance standards.

spot award An incentive that companies use to encourage their employees to work toward specific outcomes.

standard hour plan An individual incentive plan in which employee's pay is based on how much time an employee is expected to need to complete some task.

stock option plan A group based incentive plan that provides employees with the right to purchase shares of their company's stock at some established price (often its market value) for a given period of time.

straight commission plan A plan that pays employees a percentage of the total sales they generate.

straight piecework plan An individual incentive plan in which employees receive a certain rate of pay for each unit produced.

straight salary plan A plan where employees receive a set compensation, regardless of their level of sales.

strategic performance driver Activities that enable a company to realize the potential of its source of competitive advantages.

strategic value The extent to which the contributions of employees are of value for organizational success.

strategy The company's plan for achieving a competitive advantage over its rivals.

strictness error A performance evaluation error that occurs when employees are consistently rated on the low end of a performance evaluation scale.

structured interview An interview process that uses a set of predetermined questions related to the job and usually includes a scoring system to track and compare applicant responses.

subject matter experts (SMEs) Individuals with skills, knowledge, and expertise related to a particular job or aspect of a job.

succession planning The process of planning for the future leadership of the company by identifying and developing employees to fill higher level jobs within the company as they become available.

T

task analysis An analysis used to identify gaps between the knowledge, skills, and abilities needed to perform work required to support an organization's objectives and the current KSAs of the employees.

telecommute Work away from the traditional office setting with the use of technology.

telecommuter An employee who uses technology such as the Internet, videoconferencing, and e-mail to connect to his or her job from remote locations.

temp to hire A person who is employed to work for the company for a short period of time but who may become a permanent employee.

third-country national (TCN) A foreign national who works in countries other than his or her home country or the parent company's home country.

time and motion studies A systematic evaluation of the most basic elements of the tasks that comprise a job.

time-to-fill A measure of the length of time it takes from the time a job opening is announced until someone begins to work in the job.

total rewards The sum of all the aspects of a compensation package (base pay, incentives, benefits, perks, and so forth) that signals to current and future employees that they are receiving more than just base pay in exchange for their work.

training The systematic process of providing employees with the competencies—knowledge, skills, and abilities—required to do their current jobs.

transactional relationship A relationship best described as *quid pro quo*, or "a fair day's work for a fair day's pay."

transfer An employee's move to another job with a similar level of responsibility.

transfer of training The degree to which the information covered in a training program actually results in job performance changes.

transition matrix A model for tracking the movement of employees throughout an organization over a certain period of time.

transnational strategy A strategy whereby a company strives to achieve the benefits of both a global strategy and a multinational strategy.

turnover The voluntary and involuntary termination of employees within an organization.

U

undue hardship Situation that exists when accommodating an employee would put the employer at a disadvantage financially or would otherwise make it difficult for the employer to remain in business and competitive.

Unemployment Insurance (UI) program Created by the Social Security Act of 1935 and administered by the states, this program provides temporary financial assistance to eligible workers who lose their jobs through no fault of their own.

unfair labor practices (ULPs) Violations of the NLRA that deny rights and benefits to employees.

union authorization card A document indicating that a worker is interested in being represented by a particular union.

union shop An arrangement under which all workers except managers in an organizational unit represented by a union have to become members of that union within a certain period of time after being hired or at least pay the equivalent of union dues.

union steward A union member elected to serve as a liaison between the rest of the employees and the leadership of the union.

uniqueness The extent to which the contributions employees make, and the necessary competencies to realize those contributions, are specialized or unique to a company and not readily available in the open labor market.

unstructured interview A general interview in which the interviewer has an idea of what a successful applicant should know and be able to do and uses that information to ask the candidate job-related questions but without a defined format and without asking the same questions of all applicants.

V

valence The degree of value employees place on different rewards.

validity The extent to which a selection method measures what it is supposed to measure and how well it does so.

vesting The time required before employees own part or all of their retirement funds.

voice A specific form of participation that gives employees access to channels within their company to complain or express concerns about their work situation.

voluntary benefits (also called **discretionary benefits**) Benefits that an employer voluntarily chooses to offer to its employees.

W

wage curve The market line that represents the relationship between the job evaluation points and the salaries paid for the jobs.

Walsh-Healey Act An act that applies to contractors with contracts over $10,000 who are involved in either manufacturing or providing goods and services to the U.S. government and requires these firms to pay their workers the federal minimum wage for the first 40 hours they work in a particular week and 1.5 times the minimum wage for any additional hours they work during the week.

Web-based training Learning experiences that are accessed through a secure Web site, such as online courses and Webcasts.

wellness program An employer provided program to keep employees healthy through a range of offerings, ranging from smoking cessation to weight loss management to membership in a fitness center.

work sample A test in which the person actually performs some or all aspects of the job.

Worker Adjustment and Retraining Notification (WARN) Act An act passed in 1989 that mandates the amount of notice workers, their families, and their communities must receive prior to a mass layoff.

workers' compensation A social insurance program that provides cash benefits and medical care to workers when they suffer injuries or illnesses related to their employment.

workforce planning The process of ensuring that individuals with the right skills are where they need to be, at the right time, to meet a firm's current and future needs.

work/life balance The balance between the demands of work and the demands of employees' personal lives.

Y

yield ratios A metric that shows the effectiveness of different recruiting sources by computing the ratio of number selected to number applied.

Photo Credits

Name Index

Company Index

Subject Index